DIAGNOSIS AND TREATMENT OF SKIN DISORDERS

DIAGNOSIS AND TREATMENT OF
SKIN DISORDERS

Dr. B. Haldar

M.D. [Derm.], Dip. B.M.S., D.T.M. & H., D. Dermat.

Director, Calcutta Skin Institute, Calcutta
Formerly, Head of the Department of Dermatology,
Calcutta National Medical College, Calcutta

To be had of

NEW CENTRAL BOOK AGENCY (P) LTD.

8/1 Chintamoni Das Lane, Calcutta 700 009
INDIA

DIAGNOSIS AND TREATMENT OF

SKIN DISORDERS

First Published : 1988
First Central Edition : 1999

Publisher : Mrs. Kanika Haldar
Calcutta Skin Institute
169 VI-M C.I.T. Scheme, Calcutta 700 054

Printer : Sreemudran
1 Khasmahal Road, Calcutta 700 006

Cover Designer : Swapan Debnath

Colour Photographs : Dr. B. Haldar

Price : Rs. 300·00 [Rupees Three Hundred] only
Dollars 15 [Fifteen] [Foreign]

To
MITHU
my dear, dearest daughter
who aspires to be a
dermatologist

DECLARATION

Profit out of sale proceeds of the book would be spent solely for the benefit of leprosy patients.

PREFACE

Dermatology is a relatively younger discipline of medicine and deals with the disorders of the skin. There are more than 1500 skin disorders, and text books describing them are naturally quite voluminous and shockingly costly. Besides, many of the disorders are rarely met with in actual practice. Hence there is always a need of a single volume consolidating the common and important skin diseases that are of interest and concern to the practising physicians, the general medical students at large and the students of dermatology in particular. This volume represents an attempt to cater to that long-felt need in the field with an optimum coverage, neither extensive nor reduced in scope.

Each disease entity has been described under three clear-cut sequential headings : diagnosis, treatment and discussion. As is well known, a correct diagnosis is a vital pre-requisite to any successful treatment. All the essential data in this context have therefore been provided under 'diagnosis'. Next come the treatment modalities that have been described rather in full detail and made up-to-date to the extent possible in a swiftly changing field like medicine. In a developing country as is ours, the limitations of both cost and availability of drugs and instruments can hardly be overlooked. An emphasis has thus been laid on the practical feasibility of the methods to be followed. Finally, under 'discussion', the author's personal experiences have also been embodied and, it is hoped, some of them might be instructive and illuminating to dermatologists practising in the tropical countries. With an eye to the practitioners' need, popular trade names of drugs have been liberally used, along with their pharmacological names.

Most of the dermatological disorders are essentially heterogeneous in character and this makes their classification extremely difficult. It would have been ideal to classify the diseases etiologically. But the task is an impossible one for the simple reason that in many diseases, the etiology is completely unknown. The alternative approach could have been a classification based on the morphological characters of the lesions. But, unfortunately, this would lead to groups of diseases of different etiology and pathology. In the circumstances, we were left with no other choice than to arrange the disorders in simple alphabetical order. In making a selection of the diseases, the guiding factor has been to include such diseases that are common and important in the Indian perspective or have special academic interest. This prompted us to elaborate the Hansen's disease and discuss, to a considerable length, the common venereal diseases. In a collection like this, a certain amount of repetition in some areas could not be avoided in spite of our intention to the contrary. As far as practicable, relevant charts and illustrations, including colour plates, have been given in the text so as to stimulate the visual memory for a lasting impression.

Apart from chapters dealing with specific diseases, several others such as 'Sexual inadequacy', 'Dermatopharmacology' and 'Dermatosurgery' have been incorporated for the sake of completeness of the work. No serious practitioner of to-day should rest satisfied without a knowlege in these three fields.

In preparing the manuscript, the standard book and journals in the field have been consulted liberally so much so that careful readers might trace similarities of thoughts and languages here and there. Most of these books and journals have been cited under 'Bibliography and General References' at the end. In spite of our best efforts, some minor spelling mistakes have unfortunately crept in, due mainly to oversight. Hopefully, they would be corrected in the next edition.

The spiralling price rise of every material related to publications—paper, printing, proof-reading, block-making, binding—compels the publishers to price their productions apparently prohibitive. In spite of this higher cost of production, particularly due to incorporation of numerous high resolution colour photograhs, the book has been priced reasonably with an idea to accommodate a wider cross-section of readers.

The labour and the time invested in bringing out such a publication, I believe, would be well appreciated. I shall deem my effort amply rewarded if it serves the purpose for which it is intended. Any criticism and suggestion for improving the content and quality of the work would be most thankfully acknowledged.

B Haldar

ACKNOWLEDGEMENT

In preparing the book I am indebted, directly or indirectly, to many persons—too many to exhaust. But I must acknowledge with a deep sense of gratitude the following, in particular.

1. The authors of the standard books which I have consulted freely and drawn from liberally.

2. The dermatologists of the Calcutta Skin Institute, Calcutta who have devoted much of their time in the production and refinement of the manuscript. Special mentions must be made of Drs. Subrata Malakar, Sanjoy Ghosh, Mridula Patra Paul and Susmit Haldar.

3. Prof. A. K. Dutta, formerly Head of the Department of Venereology, Calcutta Medical College, Calcutta for his lecture notes that have been consulted and incorporated, by and large, in the text.

4. Mr. M. N. Chakraborti for his immaculate typing of a large portion of the manuscript.

5. Mr. Arun Nandi, Messrs K. C. Taran and T. K. Majumdar of Book Home, Calcutta and the Sreemudran Press for their best efforts in quality printing and production.

6. Messrs Friends Graphic, Calcutta for the meticulous care in printing the colour photographs.

7. Prof. A. B. Gupta for his constructive criticism, matchless editing and proof reading, liason with the press and, above all, the overall supervision at every stage of the production.

CONTENTS

GENERAL PRINCIPLES OF MANAGEMENT

The **first and foremost** duty of a physician is to listen to the patient sincerely and question him systematically and persistently. This might yield valuble information about the previously used medications, pertinent family history, surrounding atmosphere, working conditions, hobbies etc. A doctor must impose his will on his patient and that can be best made with graciousness, diplomacy and reason. A good maxim is 'let it be apparent that something is being done'. Simple laying on of hands or seeing through a magnifying lens has a tremendous impact on the psyche of the patient. He feels that he is not having any infectious disease and the doctor is serious about his disorder. It has been said that the light touch with a cherry smile dispel gloom. The patient should be exposed to the bright day-light and seen completely from head to feet to minimise the diagnostic error.

It is better to know a **limited number of drugs** but to know them thoroughly and apply them with confidence. Frequent change of drugs is in most cases harmful. Remembering a large number of proprietary drugs by name only, without having any critical assessment of their components, is not a worth-while exercise. Most of the skin diseases can be cured by a limited number of drugs.

Vehicles are very important in topical applications. The type of vehicle to be used is decided primarily by the condition and site of the diseased skin. The traditional advice is that : if it's wet dry it, if it's dry wet it.

Acutely inflammed lesions with blistering and oozing should be treated with lotion (wet preparations). For example, soaks for lesions localised to extremities, wet dressings for localised lesions, or baths for generalised lesions. Sub-acute lesions which are less angry in look may be treated with lotion, emulsion or pastes. Chronic thickened and encrusted lesions of longer duration are to be treated with cream or ointment.

The effect of a drug can be **intensified** by covering the treated area by a sheet of impermeable polythene (occlusive dressing). By preventing evaporation of the sweat, this occlusive dressing causes hydration of stratum corneum and thus allows soluble drugs to penetrate more effectively. Occlusive dressing should not be placed over acutely inflammed or infected lesions. To start with, it is better to apply such dressings for about 4 hours. If no untoward effect arises, it may be kept overnight. Systemic absorption may occur from occlusive dressing.

The use of lotions or wet dressings over a very large area of skin may, by evaporation of the liquid, reduce the body temperature of an old or debilitated patient below the danger level.

Shake lotions (e.g. lotio calamine etc.) **should not** be used on oozing lesions because there would be much disturbing encrustation. Addition of oil to the shake lotion may reduce crust formation.

Application of keratolytics (e.g. salicylic acid) should be restricted to the actual lesion because these are **mild caustics** and may damage the normal skin. They are particularly useful in treating chronic scaling conditions.

Among the topical chemotherapeutic agents penicillin, sulphonamides, streptomycin and neomycin are highly allergenic to human skin. These should better be **avoided topically**. Neomycin has cross-reaction with soframycin.

Local anesthetics and topical antihistaminics also readily sensitize the skin. Proprietary drugs containing such preparations should not be used.

To avoid severe sensitization reaction, any topical application should be applied for the first time over a small area to see any adverse effect. In suspected cases, sensitive patch tests may be undertaken.

Use of systemic steroids should be restricted only to severe and otherwise unresponsive dermatoses. For trivial cases, the **unjustified use of steroids** may create problems in the long run. Before prescribing systemic steroids, their side reactions should always be critically weighed with their beneficial effects.

In chronic dermatoses, intralesional injection of steroid may be given instead of systemic steroids. This may provide high local concentrations without systemic effects.

Excessive use of highly potent topical steroids (fluorinated steroids) on delicate skin, particularly that of face, may lead to atrophy, striae, hypopigmentation, acneiform eruption etc.

The bases of the topical steroids may be allergenic. This may lead to confusion in diagnosis by aggravating the lesions instead of improving them.

Patient should be made cautious against exposure to the sun, as far as practicable, when he is being treated by any photosensitive drug either locally or systemically.

Patent drugs can do more harm than good in many occasions. This is particularly applicable in management of skin diseases. In fact, many skin lesions are induced by drugs — either systemic or topical. Treatment itself may precipitate further reactions in patients susceptible to allergens of the medicaments. Hence **minimum drugs** should be prescribed in dermatological practice.

Chemical cauterisation by agents such as trichloroacetic acid, podophylline, phenol etc. should always be made by a trained physician. It should never be allowed to be applied by the patients because this may create a disaster by damaging the normal tissue.

The treatment, as in all other branches of medicine, depends on a correct diagnosis. The general rule is to **diagnose before treating** and this be followed as far as practicable. If the diagnosis is not obvious, a bland local application may be prescribed. Indiscriminate use of proprietary preparations containing combined topical steroids, antifungal agents and antibiotics, in most cases, cannot cure the disease. On the contrary, it may change the morphology of the lesion leading to a difficulty in subsequent diagnosis.

The patients should be advised to gently massage a minimum quantity of ointment into the skin and then wipe away the excess. Too much application of even the correct ointment may paradoxically cause worsening of the lesion by maceration. Ointments should be applied liberally only on the hard lesions that are to be softened.

The majority of the skin lesions heal quickly if kept exposed. All sorts of heavy bandages and cotton wool should be avoided. To avoid staining of the clothing and friction, old cotton or linen cloth may be used as dressing.

Physical and mental rest and **change of environment** are sometimes just as important as actual medication in dermatological practice.

Caution ! The skin is a markedly resilient organ. Rough or inappropriate medication may cause it to rebel. One must therefore treat the skin diseases gently and courteously.

ACANTHOSIS NIGRICANS

DIAGNOSIS

1. This symmetrically distributed skin disorder is characterised by **hyperpigmentation** and **papillary hypertrophy**. The intertriginous areas such as axilla, neck, genital and submammary regions are commonly involved. Four types exist : malignant, inherited, endocrine and idiopathic.

2. The most pronounced and extensive lesions are found in the **malignant variety**. Commonly, it is associated with an abdominal malignant tumour, particularly a gastric adeno carcinoma. Rarely, it may be associated with lymphoma such as Hodgkin's disease or an osteogenic sarcoma. In this extensive variety even mucosal surface may as well be affected.

3. The **inherited type** may start during infancy, childhood or adulthood.

4. The **endocrine type** may be associated with pituitary tumour (manifesting clinically as acromegaly), diabetes, Addision's disease or the Stein-Leventhal syndrome. Obesity may or may not be present.

5. The **idiopathic type** is the commonest type. Obesity is frequently associated. This variety is not associated with malignancy, endocrinopathies or genetic predisposition.

6. A special variety of **pseudoacanthosis nigricans** has been described having similar features that are often found in obese brunettes. But in the tropics the condition may also occur in those who are not overweight.

7. Histopathologically, all four types show essentially the same picture. There are hyperkeratosis and papillomatosis but only slight, irregular acanthosis. Hyperpigmentation of the basal layer is only slight. Colour of the lesion is caused by hyperkeratosis.

TREATMENT

UREA CREAM	ISOTRETINOIN
TRETINOIN CREAM	CYPROHEPTADINE

1. Search for malignancy

In any acanthosis nigricans of recent onset, particularly in middle-aged and elderly people, all efforts should be made for finding any internal malignancy. Acanthosis nigricans may be the earliest sign of visceral malignancy and thus helps in an early detection of a serious underlying problem. Effective treatment of the accompanying malignancy may lead to regression of the skin lesion.

2. Detection of endocrinopathies

Investigations should be completed to detect any associated endocrinal abnormalities. If detected, associated endocrinal disorder should be corrected. Visual fields should be checked up in cases associated with endocrinopathies. Abnormality in visual testing should be followed up by a neurologist.

3. Reduction of weight

In the idiopathic variety, reduction of weight by dieting, exercise or medical treatment may help in clearing the skin lesion.

4. Topical applications

a. Topical applications of drying powders or wet dressings with potassium permanganate (1 in 8000) or Burow's solution may help in relieving discomfort and maceration.

b. Topical tretinoin 0.1% twice a day may reduce the thickening of the skin.

c. 20% urea in cream base is helpful as a desquamating agent.

DISCUSSION

There is no specific therapy for acanthosis nigricans. The most important aspect of the management is investigation and treatment of the underlying conditions. Symptomatic use of desquamating agents helps cosmetically to some extent. In some instances, isotretinoin and cyproheptadine have been used with success.

ACNE VULGARIS

DIAGNOSIS

1. It is characterised by the presence of various types of lesions such as **open comedones** (black head), **closed comedones** (white heads), **papules**, enlarged pores of hair follicles, **cysts, pustules** and occasionally **scars**.

2. The lesions are primarily distributed on the **face, upper back** and **chest** where there is dense population of large sebaceous glands. Other sites of distribution are arms, medial sides of thighs and rarely buttocks.

3. It occurs most commonly in **adolescents** though no age group is exempt. Sex variation has not been proved.

4. If a papule with a black head is compressed, the comedone is expressed out which is usually a minute egg shaped boiled rice-like material. Presence of comedone is the so-called **pathognomonic sign** of acne vulgaris. Cystic acne might show double comedones that result out of fistulous link between two neighbouring pilosebaceous units.

5. **Keloidal nodules** can be seen in long-standing patients.

6. **Pathophysiology** : Acne is a disease of complex genetic and hormonal factors. It often runs in families. Androgenic stimulation is necessary to increase sebaceous gland activity. Castrated men and oophorectomised women do not develop acne. Accumulation of comparted, dead, cornified cells within the duct of the sebaceous gland or at the outlet of the follicle causes blocking of the flow of sebum which dries up. Omnipresent propionibacterium acnes cause lipolysis of sebum to produce free fatty acids which are **inflammatogenic**. Comedone is the dried up sebum mixed with dead epithelial cells and bacteria. Exact sequence of events has yet to be settled.

TREATMENT

TETRACYCLINE	CLINDAMYCIN	DAPSONE	STEROIDS
ERYTHROMYCIN	ISOTRETINOIN	CIMETIDINE	TRETINOIN
	BENZOYL PEROXIDE		

Acne vulgaris often requires treatment over many months or years under medical supervision. On the very first day of treatment, the basic pathophysiology should be made clear to the patient in simple language so that he is convinced and can prepare his mind to undergo regular treatment for the required period.

1. Comedolytics

A. **Tretinoin** (trans-retinoic acid, Eudyna[R], Retino A[R]) is the most effective comedolytic agent. It acts by (i) increasing the epidermis cell turnover, (ii) decreasing the cohesiveness (stickyness) of horny cells, (iii) decreasing the number of normal cell layers of the stratum corneum (thus by decreasing the thickness of the barrier layer it increases the penetration of other topical agents). The time required to have the desired initial clinical effect is approximately 12 weeks. At the end of that period, maintenance therapy may be needed for several years. The duration and number of applications are to be so adjusted that the patient can achieve mild facial flush and slight peeling. Severe dryness is to be avoided. Fair-complexioned persons with easily irritable skin should begin with 0.05% cream or gel ; others may start with 0.1% cream. Excessive exposure to sun of tretinoin-treated skin is to be avoided, although the suspicion of increased incidence of skin cancer in tretinoin-treated skin on exposure to ultraviolet light has not been proved.

B. **Benzoyl Peroxide** (Benoxyl[R], Persol forte[R]) has potent bacteriostatic action against propionibacterium acnes, a normal inhabitant of the follicular duct (the enzyme associated with this anerobic diphtheroid releases, from the sebum, free fatty acid that acts as primary irritating substance in inflammatory acne). It is possibly decomposed by the cysteine present in the skin leading to a release of free radical oxygen which oxidises proteins in its vicinity including the bacterial one. In this way benzoyl peroxide decreases the number of P. acnes and consequently the amount of free fatty acids (FFA). Benzoyl peroxide also has some

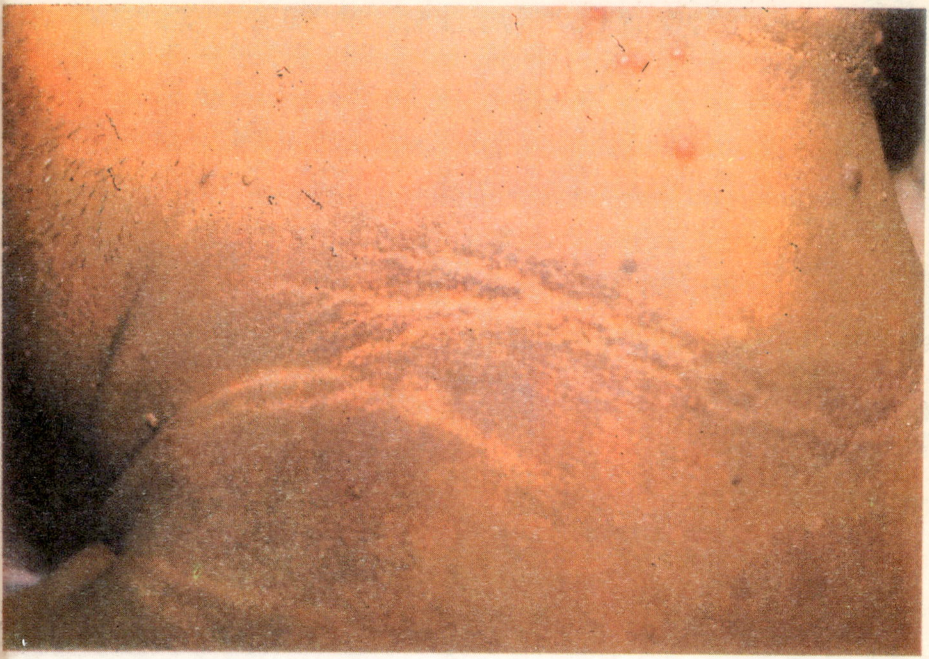

ig. A-1. **Acanthosis Nigricans** at neck, idiopathic type showing hyperpigmentation and papillary hypertrophy.

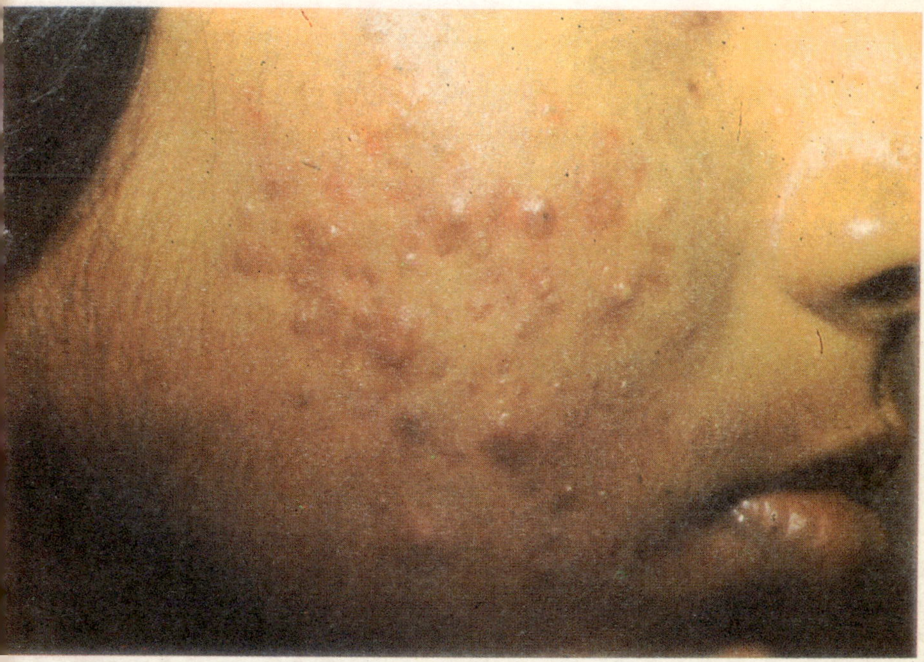

g. A-2. **Acne vulgaris** showing comedones, papules and pustules.

comedolytic action. It is used in concentration of 2·5 to 20%. Contact sensitivity may be found in 1-3% of patients with this medication.

C. **Combined tretinoin and benzoyl peroxide**—This combined regimen has shown excellent clinical results. Tretinoin helps in penetration of benzoyl peroxide. According to some, the two agents if used together are less irritating than tretinoin alone. The two agents however are to be applied at different times, and not simultaneously. The mixing of reactive oxidants such as benzoyl peroxide with highly unsaturated tretinoin would destroy both.

2. Chemotherapy

A. Topical agents

a. The most useful topical antibiotics are **clindamycin** (1%), **tertracyclin** (2%) and **erythromycin** (1·5-2%). Unfortunately they are not easily available in India for local use. All topical antibiotics are to be applied twice daily. Topical antibiotics do not have any role in clearing the existing lesions, but they prevent or reduce the formation of new inflammatory lesions. Clinical improvement is observed 3 to 4 weeks after the onset of the treatment. Papular and pustular lesions respond best. The comedonal and cystic acne may not improve to the desired level.

b. Aluminium chloride hexahydrate 6·25% in absolute ethyl alcohol is antibacterial and is also effective in reducing the sweat that contributes to bacterial colonization. It is specially helpful in inflammatory acne of the back.

B. Systemic chemotherapeutic agents — In acne where milder form of therapy fails or where there is severe involvement (inflammatory papules, pustules, cysts, abscesses or scarring) systemic antibiotics are indicated. They inhibit the growth of normal cutaneous flora and thus reduce the free fatty acid (FFA) level on the skin. Tetracycline, erythromycin and clindamycin also suppress leukocyte chemotaxis. They may also inhibit extracellular lipases which are agents responsible for production of inflammatory substances. With systemic antibiotic, clinical improvement is seen after a period of about 6-8 weeks. It may be continued for months to years to control the disease fully.

a. **Tetracycline** is the most widely used and safest antibiotic for long term management of more severe form of acne. A number of studies revealed that there is not much adverse effect of long-term systemic therapy. Vitamin B-complex should be supplemented along with it to avoid mild gastrointestinal disorder. Candidiasis of genital tract may rarely occur. Tetracycline should not be administered in children below the age of 12 and during pregnancy. It should not be taken along with antacids, dairy products or vegetables. To have the best absorption of the drug it should be taken rather in empty stomach or at least one hour before or after meals. To start with, 500 to 1000 mg of tetracycline is given for 4 weeks or until the desired result is obtained. Thereafter the dose is gradually reduced to the minimum level necessary for the maintenance of control.

b. **Erythromycin** is the second drug of choice. It is usually given in dose of 1000 mg per day. But many patients are unable to tolerate the drug for a prolonged period due mainly to gastrointestinal disorders.

c. **Doxycycline** is an alternative to tetracycline. It is an expensive drug with chances of phototoxicity.

d. **Minocycline** is not available in our country. It is highly lipid-soluble and enters the sebaceous follicles readily. Where other antibiotics fail, it may be effective. The initial dose is 50 mg in a day to be slowly increased to 100 mg twice a day. Occasional side effects are dizziness, nausea and vomiting.

e. **Clindamycin,** although very effective in recalcitrant acne, should only be applied when other regimens fail. The serious adverse effect is development of pseudomembranous colitis. The usual dose is 150-300 mg a day.

f. **Cotrimoxazole** (trimethoprim and sulphamethoxazole) is also lipid-soluble. It decreases FFA level and thus suppresses inflammatory acne. Usual dose is 2 tabs (single strength) twice a day. This may be increased up to 4 tabs b.i.d. But clinically the effect is much inferior to tetracycline.

g. **Dapsone** has been used as an adjuvant therapy in combination with oral antibiotic and topical therapy. It is claimed that 100 mg per day can suppress the severity of inflammation in some resistant cases. It is not indicated in comedonal acne. The dose is slowly tapered and the drug is withdrawm.

h. **Cimetidine** acts as antiandrogen by blocking peripheral conversion of testosterone to dihydrotestosterone. If used along with antibiotic, improvement occurs in inflammatory acne where the other modalities are unresponsive. The recommended dose is 300 mg 5 times a day. Theoretically, if it is administered along with tetracycline it interferes with the absorption of this antibiotic but, in practice, hardly any such problem is encountered.

3. Exfoliants

These agents produce irritation with consequent peeling and exfoliation. Usual exfoliants are elemental sulphur (2-8%), resorcinol (1-4%) and salicylic acid (1-2%). All of them are not comedolytics. They may irritate the already inflammed skin of the patients with acne. At present, they are of limited use as superior agents are easily available.

4. Comedone extraction

Gentle atraumatic removal of comedones by pressing over the lesions with comedone extractor or a fine dissecting forcep may prevent future inflammation or scarring. Occasionally, it may be required to incise the follicular opening by a fine neeele (27 or 30 gauge) or fine scalpel (No. 11). But the recurrence of comedone formation is not unusual.

5. Corticosterorids

A. **Intralesional corticosteroid injection**—Intralesional injection of corticosteroid (diluted with normal saline) may be given in nodular and cystic forms of acne. Recommended concentration is 2·5 mg/ml of triamcinolone acetonide or its equivalent. Atrophy may occur at the site of injection but it is usually reversible. Intralesional injection rapidly clears the nodulocystic acnes and thus prevent future scarring.

B. Systemic corticosteroid—Systemic corticosteroid itself produces papulo-pustular acneiform eruption. Hence the use of systemic steroid should be strictly reserved to nodulo-cystic acne with severe infimmation where all other standard regimens have failed.

6. Estrogens and antiandrogens

Estrogens (as birth control pill) may be given in young women with recalcitrant acne where the other therapy failed. Combined estrogen and non-androgenic **progesteron** such as norethynodrel and ethynodiol diacetate should be used. Pills containing androgenic progesterone norgestrel should be avoided (because they may aggravate acne). Results of this therapy have been found to be inconsistent and 3 to 6 months should be given to negate the effectivity. **Cyproterone acetate** 100 mg daily from day 5 to 14 of menstrual cycle and ethinyl estradiol 50 mg from day 5 to 25 of menstrual cycle are good regimens.

Antiandrogen drugs e.g. **Danazole** 200 mg q.i.d and Spironolactone 200 mg daily for three months are effective drugs in males.

7. Systemic retinoids (isotretinoin, accutane^{R})

Systemic retinoids are new agents very useful in reducing sebum formation and are thus remarkably effective in severe cystic acne lesions that are otherwise unresponsive. It is not available in India. It is teratogenic in animal and there are many dose-dependent side effects. One important side effect is hypertriglyceridemia. Usual dosage is 1-2 mg/kg given in two divided doses daily for 15-20 days. Some however advocate longer therapy.

8. Vitamin A

Vitamin A has been casually recommended in the dose of 50,000 to 500,000 units/day in divided doses in severe nodulo-cystic recalcitrant acne where othere regimens do not respond. Symptoms and signs of hypervitaminosis like headache, bone pain, scaliness of skin should be kept in mind during Vitamin A therapy. However, in most cases, the routine therapy with Vitamin A has not been found superior to mere placebo.

9. Non-steroidal anti-inflammatory agents

Benoxaprofen 600 mg per day for 1 month or Ibuprofen 600 mg q.i.d are helpful in nodulo-cystic acne.

10. Acne surgery

Cysts and abscesses may be carefully incised and drained. This may prevent severe scarring.

11. Cryotherapy

Cryotherapy is done with liquid nitrogen or solid carbon di-oxide. With a piece of gauge held in a clamp these are brushed lightly over the skin. To start with, they are kept over the skin only for few seconds. Duration of application is gradually increased. Consequent peeling helps the patients.

12. Ultraviolet light

Exposure to sunlight (in dry climate) may be effective in some acne patients. But in moist climate sunlight produces excessive sweating and this may aggravate acne lesions. Exposure to UVB sunlamps may sometimes be effective in reducing acne lesions.

13. Zinc

Recent studies show that oral zinc is not much effective in the treatment of acne. Patients receiving tetracycline should avoid oral zinc because zinc interferes with tetracycline absorption.

14. Diet

There is so far no reliable report to prove that a single dietary item or combination thereof is responsible for production or exacerbation of acne. But if, in practice, there is regular flare ups of acne on taking certain specific food items, they must be omitted from the diet.

15. Cosmetic surgery

Patients with residual ugly scars suffer, for cosmetic reason, severe mental depression and should be allowed to have various types of cosmetic surgery. However, unless done by experienced surgeons, the results are not likely to be satisfactory. Hypo- or hyperpigmentation after dermabrasion is often a serious problem in our country.

DISCUSSION

A close **co-operation of patient** is essential in obtaining good results in the treatment of acne. For this, the doctor should give a sympathetic hearing to the details of patient's suffering. Right at the ontset, the patient should be informed of **prolonged treatment** that would be required and convinced that the treatment is entirely harmless and to his or her own benefit.

In **mild involvement** (few to many comedones, no papule or pustule) it is better to start with combined tretinoin and benzoyl peroxide topical applications. The duration of application of each drug should initially be about four hours a week at night. The duration may be gradually increased according to the patient's response and tolerance. Comedone extraction may aid in quick healing. Patients with only few open comedones and without much inflammation may well be treated with application of Lotio sulphuris alba (Thiosol[R], Thiosol forte [R]) containing 2-5% zinc sulphate and 2-5% sulphuretted potash, 2-3 times daily after proper washing of the lesional area with lukewarm soap water. Some are of opinion that regular washing with sulphur soap is beneficial but the risk of sensitization should be borne in mind.

In **moderarte involvement** (few to many comedones, some papules and pastules) having a risk of permanent scarring, tetracycline alone with combined tretinoin-benzoyl peroxide topically may be given. The dose of systemic tetracycline should be gradually tapered to the minimum maintenance level. It should be continued at least three months even after the apparent cure.

In **severe involvement** (inflammatory papules, pustules, cysts, abscesses and/or scarring) the treatment should begin with systemic tetracycline in high dose (1-2 gm/day). Excepting washing with soap, local applications should better be avoided at this stage. When the inflammation and irritation subside, the dose of systemic tetratycline should be gradually reduced and topical tretinoin-benzoyl peroxide application introduced. On severely irritated and inflammed skin, topical tretinoin or benzoyl peroxide may exacerbate the lesions and the patient may be afraid of future treatment. Tetracycline, erythromycin or clindamycin lotion or gel topically applied often give good results.

Reassurance is extremely important and a good rapport between the patient and the doctor is a must. This would help to deal with the **psychic problems** inherent in this common disease developing in the prime of life—the **youth**. Depression due to sudden unexplained flare up should in particular be sympathetically handled. It should be explained to the patient that acne is unrelated to diet ; nothing to do with dirt ; choice of soap is not much important ; lesions should not be squeezed and greasy cosmetics and moisturizers should be avoided. Avoidance and indulgence in sex cannot alter the course of acne and patients of acne have sexuality within the normal limits.

Gram negative folliculitis sometime develop as a complication of long term high dose antibiotic therapy. It appears as superficial pustules about the nose in somewhat older patients. Ampicillin 250 mg q.i.d. for 7-14 days cures the condition.

It is to be remembered that the treatment modalities adopted should invariably be on individual basis.

ACTINOMYCOSIS

DIAGNOSIS

1. It is a chronic suppurative disease causing **hard, red, non-tender indurated area** having multiple sinuses discharging whitish or yellow granules often called **'sulphur granules'**. Regional lymphadenopathy is usually absent.

2. The cervicofacial region is affected in about 50% cases involving the face, neck, tongue or mandible (history of recent dental extraction may be present). Patient may present with trismus. Thorax is involved in about 20% cases showing abscesses or empyema. Similar number of cases show primary lesion in the cecum, appendix or pelvic organs developing multiple draining fistules. Abdominal actinomycosis causes pain in the ileocecal region, striking fever with chills, intestinal colic, vomiting and weight loss. Thoracic actinomycosis also begins with fever and cough with sputum expectoration. The patient may have night sweats, lose weight and become weak. Pleural pain may also be present.

3. Histopathologically, **characteristic grains** are seen inside extensive granulation tissues of non-specific nature. The centre of the granules shows basophilic gram positive branching filaments.

4. In the discharging pus **sulphur granules** may be found which should be washed and crushed to reveal a tangled mass of filaments that readily breaks up into coccoid or bacillary forms which are gram positive and non acid-fast showing characteristic V or Y branching.

5. In rare instances, pus may be inoculated and cultured into thioglycolate liquid medium, streaked into brain-heart infusion agar and incubated anerobically at 37°C to show fluffy balls (A. israelii) or general turbidity (A. bovis). Morphologically, the growth shows gram positive filaments.

6. X-ray reveals eventual involvement of the **bone** with rarefaction as well as some proliferation of the underlying bone. In lungs, X-ray might show massive consolidation frequently at the bases of the lungs.

7. Laboratory findings

(i) Anemia, (ii) Leucocytosis, (iii) High ESR

TREATMENT

PENICILLIN	CLINDAMYCIN	INH WITH RIFAMPICIN
AMPICILLIN	MINOCYCLINE	SURGERY

Treatment should be started as early as possible, for the response becomes poor after onset of bone involvement and sclerosis of soft tissues. Cervicofacial actinomycosis responds well to medical treatment.

1. Medical treatment

A. Penicillin G

It is the drug of choice. At the start, 10 to 20 million units IM or IV per day to be given for at least 6 weeks. Duration of treatment depends on the initial size of the lesion and the degree of sclerosis. If there is bone involvement and the disease is of long duration, treatment may be needed for even up to 18 months.

B. Tetracycline

Tetracycline, chlortetracycline or oxytetracycline may be prescribed in patients allergic to penicillin. The approved dose is 1 to 2 g daily in divided doses. Duration of treatment is the same as that of penicillin.

C. Other drugs

Among other drugs clindamycin (at present not easily available in India) may be used instead of tetracycline in patients hypersensitive to penicillin. Erythromycin, ampicillin, cephalosporin, lincomycin, minocycline, stilbamidine, vancomycin and chloramphenicol may be given to such patients. Streptomycin, sulfonamides and isoniazid were being used in the past. Rifampicin has also been found to be of benefit. Combination of isoniazid 300 mg and rifampicin 600 mg per day gives prompt improvement in the early stage, especially in thoracic actinomycosis.

2. Surgical treatment

Surgical intervention is not needed in most of the cases. If required, softened nodules or sclerosed fistula may be incised. Abscesses may be drained. Debridement of tissues, if necessary, should be made.

DISCUSSION

In actinomycosis hard, indurated, granulomatous suppurative lesions develop giving rise to sinus tracts. Most cases, in our country, show cervicofacial involvement. On an average, intramuscular injection of 3 to 6 million units of penicillin is required for 6 to 8 months for cure.

AIDS : ACQUIRED IMMUNE DEFICIENCY SYNDROME

AIDS has been defined as 'T-cell immunodeficiency in a previously healthy adult in association with opportunistic infection or Kaposi's sarcoma'.

DIAGNOSIS

1. **Etiologic agents**

   a. Human T-cell lymphotropic virus (HTLV-III)

   b. Lymphadenopathy associated virus (LAV)

   c. Aids related retrovirus (ARV)

It is probable that all these retroviruses are identical. Human immunodeficiency virus HIV has recently been a popular name. The virus has a prediliction for helper T-lymhphocytes and virtually converts them to HTLV-III virus factory reducing their number and interfering their function.

2. **High risk groups** include

   a. Homosexuals and bisexuals.

   b. Intravenous drug abusers.

   c. Hemophiliacs and transfusion recipients.

   d. Heterosexual partners of AIDS patients.

   e. Children of affected mothers.

   f. North American and Central African connections.

   g. Individuals of Haitian origin.

In the homosexual group, those who have multiple sexual partners and who are passive partners in rectal intercourse appear to be at the greatest risk.

3. **Epidemiological factors**

a. Male to female ratio is 10 : 1. Incubation period is 6 months to 5 years.

b. Transplacental transmission possible. Over 120 infants have been described who have clinical, laboratory and epidemiological features similar to those of AIDS in adults.

Most patients with pediatric AIDS are born to mothers who are intravenous drug abusers. This suggests vertical transmission of an infectious agent.

4. Racial and ethnic distribution

a. 60% Whites
b. 25% Blacks
c. 14% Hispanics
d. Asians < 1%

5. Clinical manifestations are protean in nature. Presentations are extremely varied e.g.

a. Non-specific : with fever, malaise, weight loss, lymphadenopathy, oropharyngeal candidasis and folliculitis

b. Opportunistic infections

i. Pneumocystis carinii pneumonia
ii. Cerebral toxoplasmosis
iii. Cryptococcal meningitis
iv. Herpes encephalitis
v. Intestinal cryptosporidiosis
vi. Burkitt like lymphomas

c. Miscellaneous associations

i. A history of hepatitis in intravenous drug abusers
ii. Chronic diarrhoea—Giardiasis, amebiasis
iii. Viral agents—herpes simplex, herpes-zoster, cytomegalovirus, adeno virus and Epstein Barr virus.
iv. Leukodystrophy
v. Lymphadenopathy syndrome characterised by fever, weight loss, chronic diarrhoea, spenomegaly and fluctuating lymphadenopthy.

Lymph node biopsy may show malignant cells but the usual histologic pattern is that of reactive hyperplasia.

vi. Squamous cell carcinoma of the oral cavity.
vii. Cloagenic carcinoma of the rectum.
viii. Abuse of amylnitrite.

d. Dermatalogic manifestations

i. Chronic candidal infection of skin and the mucous membrane. Other severe fungal infections.

ii. Kaposi's sarcoma (KS) : Probably early sign.

(1) May appear anywhere in the skin or the mucous membrane.

(2) Mainly observed on extremities.

(3) Lesions are dark blue or purple-brown plaques or nodules. Biopsy of these lesions shows atypical spindle cells, capillary like spaces, extra-vasated erythrocytes.

(4) Visceral lesions not uncommon

(5) Pulmonary KS aggressive

(6) Gastrointestinal KS is often silent.

iii. Miscellaneous

(1) Chronic pyoderma

(2) Seborrhoeic dermatitis

(3) Immune complex vasculitis

(4) Xeroderma

(5) Chronic acneiform folliculitis

(6) Florid beard and neck impetigo

6. Laboratory investigations

A documentation of immunodeficiency is essential to confirm a diagnosis for AIDS.

Average findings are :

a. Lymphopenia is marked ; less than 600/μl

b. Less total T-cells ; less than 30%

c. Low T-helper cell count

d. Functional studies of T-cell immunity are abnormal.

i. Lessened T-cell stimulation with mitogen and antigen.

ii. Reduced or absent delayed hypersensitivity skin test responses.

iii. Natural killer cell activity and lymphocyte cytotoxicity against virally infected cells is reduced.

e. Complement levels are normal or increased.

f. Lymphokinine production is reduced.

g. Immunoglobulin levels are usually elevated but most of the patients fail to form adequate antibody following immunization.

h. Positive serological tests against retrovirus. The screening test for HTLV-III antibody is an enzyme linked immunoassay (ELISA) test.

i. Isolation of virus, if possible. Absolute persistent decrease in OK T4 lymphocytes with relatively normal OK T8 lymphocytes is an important finding.

TREATMENT

PREVENTION	SYMPTOMATIC

1. A high index of suspicion should always be maintained to identify the high risk patient, if necessary, by **direct questioning**.

2. Many people who are positive for the HTLV-III antibody may be perfectly healthy but probably up to 50% of these individuals will subsequently develop AIDS. All those who are antibody positive should be regarded as **potential source** of infection and are capable of transmitting the disease through sexual contact and inoculation of blood or other body fluids.

3. Certain **precautions** are to be taken in handling the patients. These are

i. Gloves should always be worn when handling blood specimens and body fluids.

ii. Disposable aprons, face masks and goggles are necessary to avoid contact with splashed material.

iii. Needles and scalpel blades should not be used bare handed.

iv. Laboratory specimens should be marked **'risk of infection'**. There should be a second polythene bag.

4. Drug therapy

Currently there is no treatment for combating the immunodeficiency of AIDS.

Following measures are generally tried.

i. For **mycobacterial infections**—multiple agents ; usually ineffective.

ii. Pneumocystis carinii infection—Cotrimoxazole

iii. Virus infection—Acyclovir, Zidovudine

iv. Candida infection—Amphotericin B, Ketoconazole

v. For **minimal KS**—Interferon, Interleukin

vi. **Aggressive KS**—Vincristine and vinblastine in alternate weeks ; Etoposide daily for 3 days each month.

vii. Attempts at immunologic reconstitution have not yet been successful but encouraging results have been obtained in experimental studies.

viii. As yet no vaccine is available.

DISCUSSION

Diagnosis of AIDS is established by **epidemiological, clinical** and **laboratory** observations.

It is a recently described entity but has gained global importance due to high mortality and dramatically rapid increase in the number of patients.

The most important features of the disease are profound cellular immunodeficiency, serious opportunistic infections, especially Pn. carinii pneumonia and Kaposi's sarcoma.

Management depends upon supportive measures and the treatment of secondary infection.

The adage 'Prevention is better than cure' aptly applies to this disease. Transmission can be reduced by

(1) Avoidance of **sexual promiscuity** and **anal intercourse.**

(2) **Screening** of **donated blood** or **blood products** of HIV antibody and, if found, to discard them.

(3) Counselling of persons found to be antibody positive ; they should be properly inspected and guarded.

About 80% of patients with AIDS succumb to the disease within 2 years of diagnosis.

ALOPECIA AREATA

DIAGNOSIS

1. Lesions are well-defined–single or multiple, round or oval–**areas of complete hair loss.** Most commonly it involves the scalp ; but eyebrow, beard region and any hair-bearing area may also be the site of involvement. Three varieties are seen : **alopecia areata** where there are localised patches ; **alopecia totalis** where there is the total loss of scalp hair and **alopecia universalis** where there is complete loss of both scalp hair and body hair.

2. Usually the alopecia is **asymptomatic, non-inflammatory** and **non-scarring.** In the early stage, there may be erythema with edema and slight tenderness and in later stage the bald area may sometimes become palpably depressed.

3. At the periphery of active lesions, the **'exclamation mark hair'**—the **pathognomonic sign** of alopecia areata—is seen. These hairs are 3-10 mm in length and have a dark, rough, brushlike tip, a narrower less pigmented shaft and an atrophic root. Probably premature entryof follicles into telogen is the cause of production of 'exclamation mark hairs'.

4. The disease may start at any age, but usually occurs before the fourth decade. One fourth of the patients are children.

5. Nail changes are found in 10-20% cases. There may be pitting, longitudinal ridging or thickening of nail plates.

6. In 10-25% cases there is a positive **family history.** An **atopic background** is often found in recurrent alopecia areata, and vitiligo is present in about 4% of patients.

7. Indication of regrowth is development of fine, downy, often white, hairs in a previously bald area which are gradually replaced by normal terminal hair.

8. **Ophiasis** is a variety of alopecia areata usually found in children in which the primary patch develops in the occipital region that extends in a band along the scalp margins.

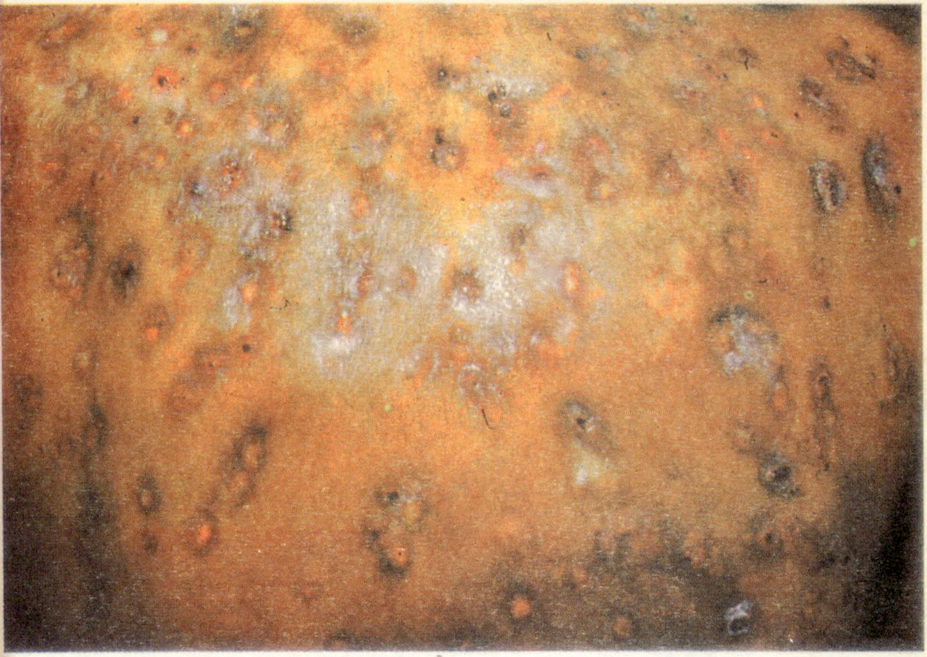

Fig. A-3. **Actinomycosis** of thorax, showing multiple draining sinuses and granulation tissue.

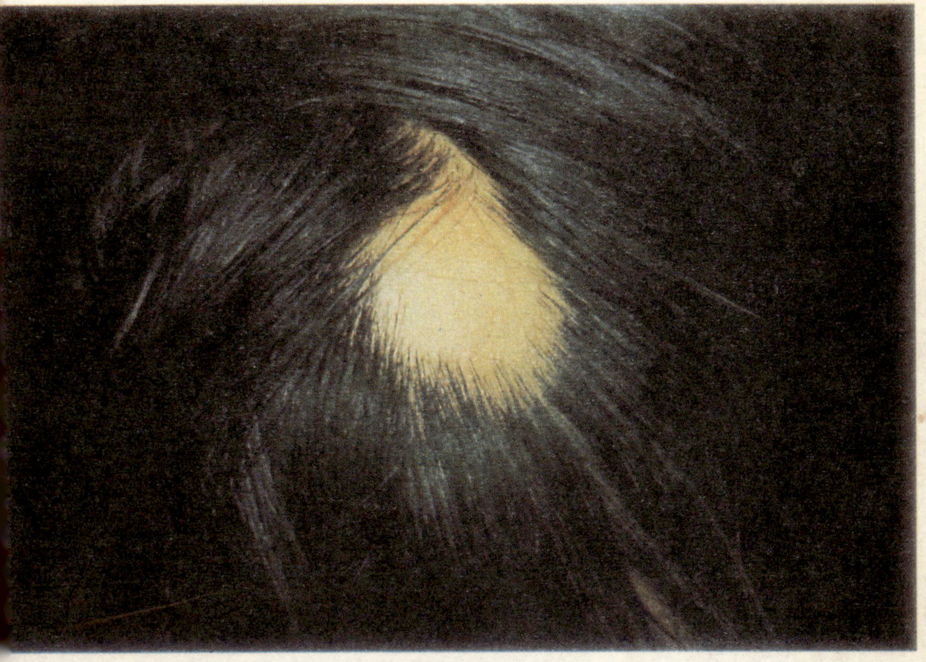

Fig. A-4. **Alopecia Areata** showing localised total loss of hairs.

9. Posterior subcapsular cataracts occur as a rare complication of alopecia universalis.

TREATMENT

TOPICAL CORTICOSTEROIDS	CONTACT ALLERGENS
INTRALESIONAL STEROIDS	COUNTER IRRITANTS
MINOXIDIL : INTERNAL AND LOCAL	

1. Corticosteroids

A. Topical corticosteroids

A high potency topical steroid e.g. clobetasol, if used a number of times daily, may help in regrowth of hairs. If after a regular trial of 1 month there is no regrowth, topical application should be discontinued. Occlusive dressing is in some cases found to be beneficial.

B. Intralesional corticosteroid

This may be useful in small persistent cosmetically disturbing areas, particularly on scalp or eyebrows. The recommended concentration is 2.5 -10 mg/ml of triamcinolone acetonide at 3 to 4 weeks interval. 0.1 ml/site is to be injected deep into dermo-subcutaneous junction and one injection is to be given for each sq. cm. of affected skin. Some prefer triamcinolone hexa-acetonide rather than triamcinolone acetonide. Regrowth is expected within a month.

C. Systemic steroid

It may stimulate hair growth but recurrence is frequent after withdrawal. Serious side effects of systemic steroids have made its use limited only to very exceptional cases.

2. Contact allergens

Topical sensitizers such as di-nitro-chloro-benzene (DNCB) and squaric acid di-butyl ester (SADBE) may stimulate hair growth in 70-90% cases. They may (i) enhance the T-lymphocyte pool, or (ii) induce 'antigenic competition' that inhibits autoimmune reactions. At first, a sensitizing dose of 2 mg DNCB is placed over the skin of inner aspect of arm and covered with tape for 24 hours. A dermatitis is seen in 90% of patients within 3 weeks. If sensitization is not detected, it may be induced by repeated application of DNCB or by intake of cimetidine. Mechanism is as yet not known. After sensitization has set in, 0.1% DNCB in acetone is applied to the affected bald area once a week to have a mild degree of dermatitis without blistering. Even a subclinical reaction may induce hair growth. It is to be applied till the desired result is achieved. DNCB, added to aquaphor, can be used at home daily. Side effects of DNCB therapy are mild rash, pruritus and adenopathy (possibly due to autosensitization). DNCB has also potent mutagenicity in bacteria.

3. Topical irritants

These are non-antigenic. The mode of action thus differs from DNCB and other contact sensitizers. Irritants are sometimes useful in inducing regrowth of hairs. Commonly applied agents are anthralin, phenol, trichloroacetic acid and resorcin. A 0.2 – 0.8% anthralin ointment applied daily may stimulate regrowth of hair in 5 to 8 weeks.

4. PUVA

Oral methoxsalen or topical 0.1% oxsoralen ointment along with UVA radiation should be given twice a week. PUVA decreases a subset of T-lympocytes and is thus effective in alopecia areata by altering immune mechanism. The results are satisfactory and recurrences are relatively uncommon.

5. Minoxidil

This antihypertensive agent is an interesting newly suggested drug in the treatment of alopecia areata. But it is not a standard therapy. Thirty 10 mg tablets of minoxidil are to be powdered and added to 3 ml of propylene glycol in 6 ml of water. The resultant mixture is to be diluted to 30 ml with 95% ethanol. The lotion should be applied twice daily at night and should be covered with white petrolatum. A 2 % minoxidil (Mintop®) solution has recently been marketed.

DISCUSSION

On the day of the first visit, the natural course of the disease is to be explained clearly to the patient. He or she should be reassured that the disease heals spontaneously in most cases. Treatment may help in quicker healing. Recurrent nature of the disease is also to be discussed.

Prognosis should be guarded in alopecia totalis, universalis, ophiasis, in severe nail changes or atopy and patients with repeated attacks.

In recalcitrant patients, wig is of much help to avoid the psychological trauma from social embarrassment. Intralesional injections of triamcinolone 2.5 to 10 mg per c.c. at three week interval have been found to be most effective. However, prognosis is still not predictable in many patients. Topical medications could not show more than a placebo effect. More elaborate study is needed for routine therapy with DNCB.

Application of **minoxidil lotion twice daily** has shown encouraging results in about 50% patients. Minoxidil, 20 mg orally b.i.d, for several months is effective but has many side effects.

ANGIOKERATOMA SCROTI

DIAGNOSIS

1. Among all varieties of localised cutaneous angiokeratomas, those of the scrotum are the commonest.

2. Prevalence and intensity of the disease increase with age and about 15% of mid-adult men have the disease.

3. Multiple vascular **erythematous papules**, 2 to 4 mm in diameter, are seen on the scrotum. To start with, the lesions are red, soft and compressible. Later, they become bluish, keratotic and incompressible.

4. Usually the lesions are **scattered** on the scrotal skin. They may assume a **linear** arrangement that corresponds to the underlying venous pattern.

5. Similar lesions may also be found on the vulva but much less frequent and fewer in number.

6. Angiokeratomas are believed to be due to increased pressure in the underlying venules.

7. If traumatised, they may cause bleeding which generally stops spontaneously.

TREATMENT

ELECTRODESICCATION PLASTIC SURGERY

Very small asymptomatic angiokeratomas require no treatment. Occasionally, on minor trauma surprisingly profuse bleeding may occur from such small lesions. In these cases, angiokeratomas may be destroyed individually by electrosurgical operation. They may as well be excised surgically.

DISCUSSION

In 5-10% of patients, recurrence is observed in electrosurgically destroyed or excised angiokeratomas even when the normal skin is included in the treated margin. The fear of patients about severe bleeding should be removed and they be assured that pressure with a piece of gauze is sufficient to control the bleeding. This has **nothing to do with cancer** and is mostly a **harmless** cosmetic problem.

ANGULAR STOMATITIS

DIAGNOSIS

1. It is a **non-specific maceration** and **fissuring** with **inflammation** at the **angles of the mouth** and on adjacent cutaneous surface and contiguous labial mucous membrane. Perleche is often used as a synonym, especially in cases of children where some infective agent is the causative factor.

2. It may be due to a variety of causes. **Riboflavine deficiency** and general **protein malnutrition** are the most important. Deficiency of niacin, pyridoxine, pantothenic acid, ascorbic acid, folic acid, Vitamin B_{12} or iron may also contribute to its pathogenesis. If it is due to deficiency, it would most often affect both angles of the mouth.

3. The actual inflammation is usually due to candida, staphylococcus aureus and occasionally beta-hemolytic streptococcus. Contact allergy e.g. lollipops or toothpaste sensitivity, is rarely found.

4. In elderly edentulous patients, loss of vertical dimension of intermaxillary space and consequent **overclosure of the bite** is the most important cause of angular stomatitis. The upper lip overhangs the lower causing a small area of skin constantly to macerate. Prognathism may be the cause in young due to similar mechanical defect. Atopic and seborrheic dermatitis, excessive salivation and wearing of faulty denture are other etiological factors.

5. A few patients have leukoplakia of the adjacent mucosal surface. Biopsy is to be done of this leukoplakia.

6. In KOH preparation from the angles of mouth reveals yeast whereas, on culture, candida and bacteria may be found.

7. Candida may be found on the mucosal aspect of upper plate of denture in majority of denture wearers.

8. In mongoloids, it is often due to the **large tongue** and constant dribbling. Very rarely, fistulae of developmental origin at the angles of mouth are the cause.

TREATMENT

NYSTATIN	CLOTRIMAZOLE
ECONAZOLE	MICONAZOLE
KETOCONAZOLE	

1. The underlying **dental defect** and **denture problem** if any, should be corrected first. A dentist should be consulted, if necessary.

2. A combination of triamcinolone, neomycin and **nystatin** or **miconazole, clotrimazole, econazole** cream is to be applied thrice daily to the corners of the mouth. In chronic debilitated cases with lack of resistance, nystatin suspension (or tab) 100,000 IU four times daily is to be taken orally along with the topical medication.

3. 1% vioform hydrocortisone lotion, 3% ammoniated mercury ointment, 10% balsam of Peru in petrolatum at night, silicone cream and 10% silver nitrate solution have been used having various rates of success.

4. Deficiencies of protein, riboflavine, niacin, pyridoxine, pantothenic acid, ascorbic acid, folic acid, Vitamin B_{12} or iron, if any, should be corrected.

5. All denture wearers should remove their dentures at night. In the morning, after the denture has been brushed, clean nystatin ointment is to be applied to the mucosal surface of upper denture.

6. In candidal angular stomatitis, 200 mg tablet of **ketoconazole**, one daily after dinner, for two weeks is extremely beneficial.

DISCUSSION

Each individual case must carefully be assessed. The successful management of this condition depends basically on the **removal of the underlying causes** e.g. avitaminosis, contact allergy, lip licking, thumb sucking, poor denture hygiene, trapping of saliva in commisural folds and malnutrition.

Where infection is the cause, the application of steroid with antibacterial and anticandidal agents (Kenacomb[R], Becloform G[R], Eclospan[R]) is the method of choice.

If an eczematous dermatitis extends some distance over the cheek as infective eczematoid reaction which sometimes occur, steroid with antibiotic solution is the drug of choice (Pyrimon eye drop[R]).

Applications are to be prolonged 1-2 weeks even after the apparent cure.

In severe outbreaks of acute pustular and fissured cheilitis in malnourished children, systemic antibiotics e.g. erythromycin, oleandomycin should be advised along with the topical therapy.

In all cases, an **improvement of general health** helps in the recovery.

APHTHOUS ULCERS

DIAGNOSIS

1. Recurrent aphthous stomatitis (RAS), also termed **canker sores,** appears as **single** or **multiple,** small (1-10 mm in diameter), **painful, recurrent shallow erosions** at the mouth with clearly defined borders covered by a grey membrane and surrounded by an erythematous halo.

2. The movable part of the oral mucosa is primarily involved. The **lips, buccal mucosa, tongue** (mucobuccal folds) and the **floor of the mouth** are the commonly involved sites. The disease rarely affects the keratinized mucosa of gingiva and hard palate (**Cf.** in recurrent intraoral herpes, keratinized areas of oral mucosa are usually involved). Genital mucosa may sometimes be concomitantly affected.

3. After a brief prodrome of tingling or burning sensation, the lesions start as **erythematous macules** followed rapidly by **superficial ulceration.** For the first 2-3 days, the lesions may be extremely painful leading to difficulty during eating or speaking.

4. 15-50% of the population is affected with RAS. The number of lesions may vary from 1-100 but, on an average, it is less than 10. Time required for healing is usually 5-10 days. Incidence is slightly commoner in women than in men and is low above the age of 50.

5. Clinically, RAS may be divided into 3 types : **minor aphthae** are the most common form (80%), **major aphthae** are less common and herpetiform lesions are least common. Minor aphthae (crops of about 10 ulcers) are less than 10 mm in diameter and usually heal spontaneously without scarring within 1-2 weeks. Major aphthae are more than 10 mm in diameter and heal with scar formation after a month or slightly more. In **herpetiform lesions,** there are crops of about 100 small lesions which may heal after 2 weeks and may coalesce before healing.

Fig. A-5. **Angular Stomatitis** showing non-specific maceration and fissuring with inflammation.

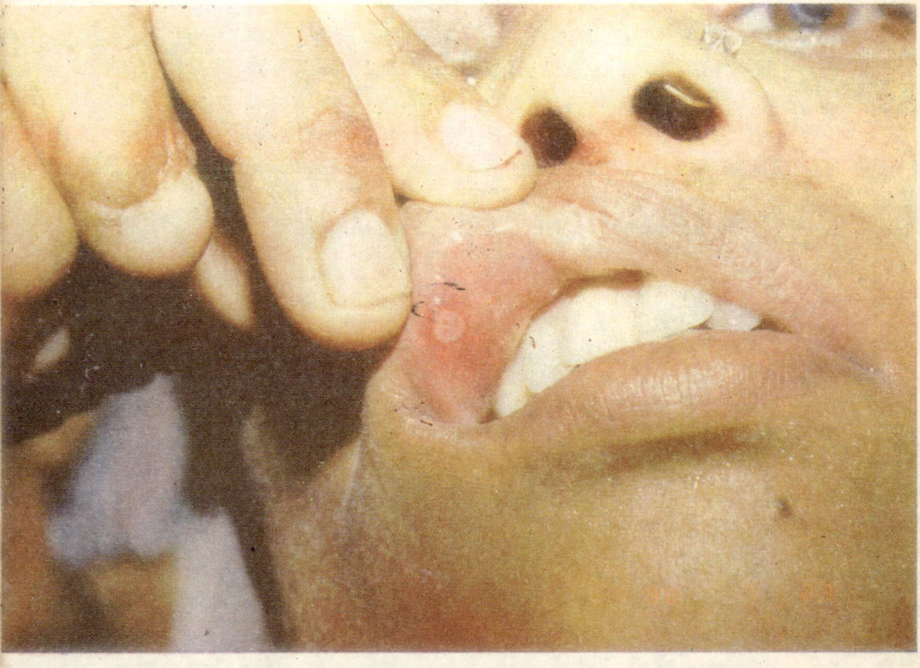

Fig. A-6. **Aphthous Ulcer** inside the upper lip showing single painful erosion with erythematous border.

6. The lesions are not related to herpes simplex virus. In 20% of patients deficiencies in iron, folic acid and Vitamin B_{12} are noted. About 50% of the patients show jejunal villous atrophy. Some patient may have gluten-sensitive enteropathy. Alpha-hemolytic streptococcus and streptococcus sanguis have been regularly isolated from the base of aphthous lesions. RAS is significantly associated with HLA types A2 and B12. Behcet's syndrome (oral and genital lesions associated with iritis) is probably the severe form of aphthous stomatitis.

7. Pre-menstrual flare up of lesions is common in women. There is remission during pregnancy. Food allergy has been found to be associated. The incidence is decreased among the cigarette smokers. Autoimmune mechanism has recently been considered as the most important etiological factor in causing aphthous ulcers. In practice, psychological trauma has often been seen as a precipitating factor for an acute attack.

TREATMENT

TETRACYCLINE	COLCICHINE	STEROIDS
ERYTHROMYCIN	DAPSONE	ZINC
VITAMIN B_{12}	FOLIC ACID	IRON

1. Hematinics

The patients of aphthous ulcer having deficiencies of iron, folic acid and Vitamin B_{12} should be treated with replacement therapy. This may induce complete remission or marked improvement.

2. Diet

Suspected allergenic food should be omitted from the diet. This may cause clinical improvement. A gluten-free diet might be helpful. Zinc supplements help some patients, the dose being 220 mg t.i.d with food.

3. Topical antibiotics

These cause suppression of oral streptococci. Topical tetracycline is the drug of choice. 250 mg of tetracycline is to be dissolved in 30 ml of water and to apply it for 10-20 min,

4-6 times daily. The patient should not take anything orally within half an hour. The treatment is to be given for 5-7 days. In many cases, this treatment reduces pain and shortens the duration of the lesions. Some patients may be resistant to tetracycline, in which case 250 mg of cephalexin is to be dissolved in 30 ml of water and applied similarly. After the application, the antibiotic solution may be swallowed for extra benefit of internal therapy. Antibiotic anesthetic lozenges, 4 tablets taken 4 times daily, in milk help some patients. Erythromycin elixir gargle helps equally well as tetracycline.

4. Topical steroids

These are beneficial if used in the initial stage. Triamcinolone acetonide 0.1% in orabase (a base which adheres to mucous membrane for long) is to be applied 4 times daily. If orabase is not available, steroid in ordinary base is to be applied 8-10 times daily. 2.5 mg tablets of hydrocortisone sodium succinate or 0·1 mg tablets of betamethasone 17-valerate may be allowed to dissolve slowly near the lesion, 3-4 times in a day. Intra-mucous membrane injection of steroids has been tried by some in severe patients and benefits have been claimed.

5. Systemic steroids

If administered during prodromal phase, it can abort the attacks. But its use should be restricted to patients with severe erosive and otherwise unresponsive lesions only.

6. Topical anesthetics

Topically applied dyclonine HCl solution may reduce the severe pain by producing anesthesia rapidly. The numbness may persist for about an hour. Lignocaine (5% ointment or viscous) may be used instead of dyclonine. Some recommend gargling with diphenhydramine HCl (Benadryl elixir[R]) for 5-10 minutes 4 times a day. After gargling, the remaining solution in the mouth may be swallowed or expectorated. Topical anesthetics should not be applied over an extensive area because this may lead to a disturbing **"cotton-mouth"** feeling or total loss of taste. An effective mixture is decadron elixir 10 c.c, benadryl elixir 20 c.c, tetracycline elixir 300 c.c in 60 c.c viscous lidocaine. A tea-spoonful of this, if held in mouth 5-6 times daily, helps in rapid recession of symptoms.

7. Silver nitrate, trichloroacetic acid and phenol cautery

Cauterisation of the lesions by silver nitrate stick may reduce pain by destroying local nerves. But it should better be avoided because of its toxicity on mucosa. By its application, ulcer may enlarge in size and healing may be delayed. 25% trichloroacetic acid coagulates the sensitive raw area and gives some comfort. Phenol cautery has relieved pain in many cases but delayed the healing.

8. Levamisole

This commonly used antihelminthic is also a stimulator of cell-mediated immunity. It is effective in some patients with recurrent aphthae. According to some, however, it is no better than mere placebo.

9. Oral contraceptives

In women with pre-menstrual flare up of lesions, oral contraceptives (with high estrogen contents) are said to be effective.

10. Avoidance of trauma

Dental trauma, irritation from tooth brushing, trauma from rough foods are the precipitating factors for flare up. These should therefore be avoided as far as possible. A soft nylon tooth brush should be used.

11. **Flagyl** taken orally has been said to have some effect. But currently it is not at all popular.

12. **Intramuscular injection of gamma-globulin** has been tried with dubious results.

13. Repeated **cowpox vaccination** was at one time thought to be beneficial. But it is now proved to be no better than mere placebo.

14. **Sedatives** occasionally have been used to allay the stress factor.

15. **Dapsone** has been found to be effective in treatment of severe recurrent oral aphthae.

16. **Colcichine** 0.6 to 1.2 mg per day helps in clearing the condition.

17. **Thallidomide** 200 mg b.i.d with or without colcichine has been used in recalcitrant cases.

18. **Phenelzine sulphate** (Nardil[R]) 15 mg t.i.d has been found to be helpful.

DISCUSSION

The exact cause of recurrent aphthae is still unknown. Too many therapeutic procedures have therefore been suggested without any definite proof of cure. As yet there is no specific treatment.

The most effective treatment is to keep the suspension of 250 mg tetracycline in 5 to 10 ml of water for 2 to 5 minutes 4 times daily in the mouth and then swallowed. About 70% of patients get benefit with this treatment.

Prognosis of any particular patient is mostly unpredictable. Patient may often suffer throughout the life. However, a thorough search for the precipitating factors e.g. emotional stress, microbial infection, alteration of immune mechanism, menstruation, fatigue etc. should be made and, if detected, such factors should be scrupulously avoided.

In most cases, recurrence ceases at the fourth decade.

In severe gangrenous aphthosis destroying the uvula and other parts of oral organs, systemic steroid with internal antibiotic might save necrosis and permanent damage.

Lotions containing steroid and antibiotic (Pyrimon eye drop[R]) applied at 2-4 hourly intervals in early erosions help to ameliorate many discomforts.

BALANOPOSTHITIS

Balanitis means 'inflammation of the glans penis' and posthitis denotes 'inflammation of the prepuce'. They occur frequently concurrently and is hence called **balanoposthitis.** Balanitis may also occur alone in the circumcised penis but it is relatively uncommon.

DIAGNOSIS

A. Etiology (including secondary to ulcerative lesions)

1. **Infective**

a. Venereal—Syphilis, chancroid, gonorrhoea, LGV, herpes progenitalis, donovanosis, trichomoniasis, fusospirochetosis (gangrenous, circinate, erosive and pustulo-erosive types).

b. Pyogenic—Staphylococcus aureus and streptococcus hemolyticus.

c. Fungal (i) **Superficial** : candidiasis.

(ii) **Deep mycosis** : blastomycosis, histoplasmosis, coccidioidomycosis.

d. Miscellaneous bacterial—Tuberculosis, diphtheria, pseudodiphtheria, Hansen's disease, anthrax, actinomycosis.

e. Parasitic—Scabies, pediculosis, schistosomiasis, enterobius vermicularis, guinea worms.

2. **Traumatic**

a. Physical trauma—Sexual, cold, radium burn.

b. Chemical trauma—Dettol, tinct. iodine, alkalies, nitric acid, podopyllum.

3. **Allergic**

a. Dermatitis medica mentosa—Fixed drug rash, erythema multiforme.

b. Allergic contact dermatitis — Contraceptive gels, condome, vaginal secretion, mercury, sulfonamides and hydrarg ammon.

4. **Irritation**

Poor hygiene, smegma, soap, glycosuria, nonspecific urethritis, pyelonephritis.

5. **Specific diseases**

Balanitis circinata, plasma cell balanitis of Zoon, balanitis xerotica obliterans, Bowen's disease, malignant conditions, Paget's disease.

6. **Associated** with other dermatoses

Vesiculobullous diseases, psoriasis, lichen planus, seborrheic dermatitis, exfoliative dermatitis, Behcet syndrome.

B. Clinical features

These depend upon the etiological factors. Features differ in acute, subacute and chronic inflammation.

1. **Symptoms**

Itching, burning, pain, secretion, foul smell, urinary symptoms, painful coitus.

2. **Signs**

Erythema, edema, papules, vesicles, erosion, ulcer, plaques, discolouration, longitudinal cracks in prepuce, lymphadenopathy.

C. Common investigations

i. **Swab for smear** (a) Candida albicans
(b) Trichomonas vaginalis
(c) Bacteria

ii. **Swab for culture** (a) Bacterial culture
(b) Fungal culture

iii. **Blood** for post prandial blood sugar

iv. **Dark field illumination test** for spirochetes

v. **Biopsy** for histological studies.

TREATMENT

TOPICAL ANTIBIOTIC	CLOTRIMAZOLE	KETOCONAZOLE
SYSTEMIC ANTIBIOTIC	NYSTATIN	METRONIDAZOLE
	CIRCUMCISION	

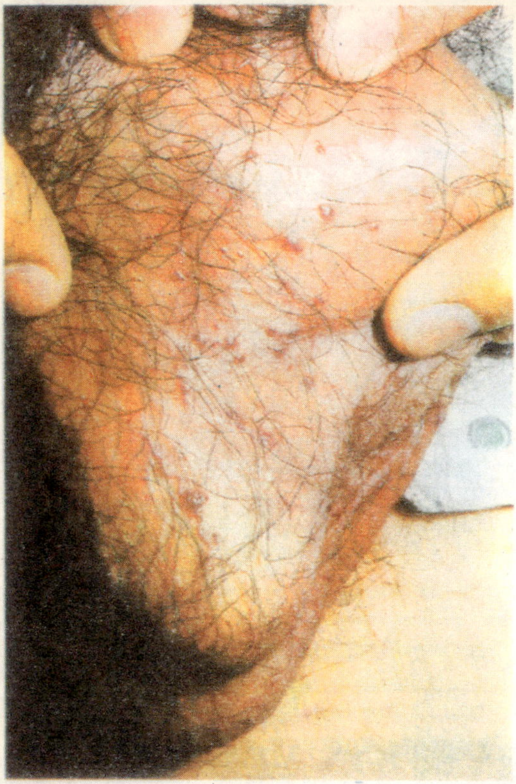

Fig. A-7. **Angiokeratoma Scroti** showing erythematous papules.

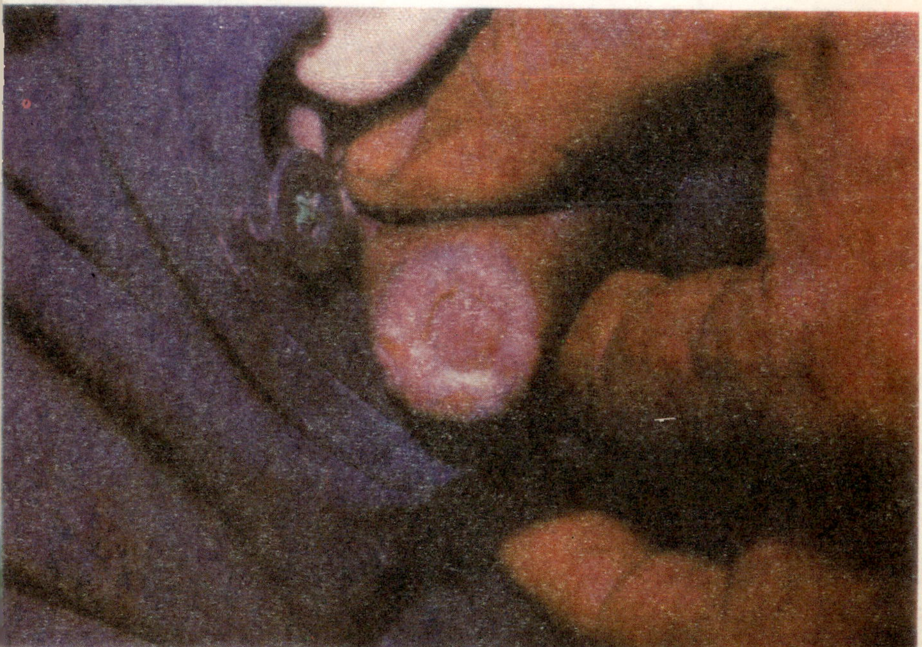

Fig. B-1. **Balanoposthitis** showing cracks and erosions of the prepucial margin and inflammation of the glans.

1. **Preventive**—Proper hygiene, control of diabetes and etiological factors.

2. **Symptomatic** : (a) **Local**—Condy's wash, antibacterial lotion or cream, antifungal lotion or cream, steroid lotion or cream—alone or with the above.

(b) **Internal**—Specific according to etiology. Antibiotics, antifungal drugs, antihistaminics.

3. **Specific** — According to the etiological factor.

DISCUSSION

Balanoposthitis is very frequent. More often it is secondary to other conditions. Only balanitis is seen in fusospirochetosis, chancroid, syphilis, herpes progenitalis, trichomoniasis, pyococcal infections and plasma cell balanitis of Zoon. Non-specific balanoposthitis is usually mild but, although rarely, may as well be severe. Many cases are due to inadequate hygiene especially when there is phimosis. Mild cases show patchy or diffuse erythema with scanty exudate. Severe cases show erosions, ulcers and profuse exudate. Painful inguinal lymphadenopathy may also be found.

Plasma cell balanitis of Zoon, characterised by red moist shiny plaques, occurs in middle aged or elderly people. Biopsy shows characteristic plasma cell infiltration.

Balanitis diabetica is very common. It is caused by candida albicans. It begins generally with severe itching. Minute vesicles, erosions, longitudinal cracks of prepuce and plaques due to chronic inflammatory infiltrate are seen later.

Balanitis erosiva circinata is diagnosed if there is a polycyclic form of balanitis often in the area of coronary sulcus. Lymphadenopathy is frequently present. It is generally caused by fusospirochetosis. In very rare cases of necrotic ulceration vibrio-like necrotic bacilli are found.

Follmann's balanitis is an erosive circinate balanoposthitis occuring in primary syphilis.

Zoon's plasmacellular balanoposthitis is a rare disease showing shiny, smooth, infiltrated, erythematous plaques.

Erythroplasia of Queyrat shows finely granular, velvety, persistent plaques.

Balanitis circinate parakeratotica is due to Reiter's disease which consists of arthritis, conjunctivitis and urethritis. It is like psoriatic balanitis.

Most cases of balanoposthitis are not specific infections by one agent. It is rather a result of mixed bacterial growth with toxin and irritant production.

The most important therapeutic approach to balanoposthitis is the daily **post coital** and **post urination cleansing** with water alone. If soap is used, adequate rinsing is necessary.

Diagnosis and proper treatment of balanitis demand both serious attention and skill of the physician.

BASAL CELL EPITHELIOMA

DIAGNOSIS

1. This is the most frequent **locally invasive tumour** in dermatology and is very common in fair-skinned individuals exposed to sunlight for a prolonged period. Genetic predisposition has probably a role. Arsenic and X-rays may also act as causative factors.

2. It arises from the **basal layer** of the epidermis or its appendages, almost exclusively from **hair bearing skin**, especially on face.

3. **Clinically**, it is characterised by various types of lesions e.g. nodules which may be pigmented, nonpigmented or ulcerated, morphea-like plaques, erosive ulcers and the superficial, erythematous, slightly indurated, scaly patches. **Pearly** or **translucent borders** and **telangiectasia** are important diagnostic features. It is very slow-growing and draining lymphnodes are not generally enlarged.

4. **Histologic diagnosis** which is most important varies enormously according to the type of lesions. The lesions are as follows.

a. **Solid basal cell epithelioma** contains tumour masses of various sizes and shapes in the dermis. Tumour cells are called **'basalioma'** cells and have large oval or elongated nucleus and less cytoplasm. Very often a connection between the tumour mass and the epidermis exists.

b. **Keratotic basal cell epithelioma** shows parakeratotic cells, horn cysts and undifferentiated cells which have deeply basophilic cytoplasm.

c. **Cystic basal cell epithelioma** has many cystic spaces within the tumour masses which occur due to necrobiotic changes in central cells.

d. **Adenoid basal cell epithelioma** is characterised by tubular gland like structures. The cells are arranged in a lace like pattern and the stroma has mucoid appearance.

TREATMENT

DINITROCHLOROBENZENE	ELECTROSURGERY
MOH'S CHEMOSURGERY	CRYOSURGERY
5 FLUOROURACIL	LASER

Various modalities of treatment are now available and they are as follows.

1. Excision

Wherever possible total excision is the best treatment. As the tumour underlies much beyond the clinically visible lesion, it is always better to excise at least 2 to 5 mm more of the surrounding tissue. If facilities are available, microscopically controlled excision should be undertaken.

2. Curettage and electrodesiccation

It is possible only in small tumours and is both easy and rapid. But the confirmation of adequacy of the destroyed tissue is not available. Healing is prolonged and scar is inevitable.

3. Cryosurgery

This is done with liquid nitrogen. It is both safe and painless. It should better be done with cryoprobes.

4. Superficial radiation

It should be done in elderly patients aged 60 to 65 years. Good cosmetic results are not assured. Aluminium sheet of thickness 0·9 mm is interposed. Total dose is about 3500 rad. It is best for morphea-form basal cell epithelioma. Some suggest that radiotherapy should not be used second time if there is a recurrence. Morpheic lesions are relatively radio-resistant.

5. Topical 5-fluorouracil

It is used only in superficial basal cell epithelioma. Nodular tumours should never be treated by this because it enhances the chance of developing deeper viable tumour cells.

6. Moh's chemosurgery

This method is extremely helpful in recurrence. Microscopically controlled excision is done. Serial excisions are made in the case of chemically fixed tissue with microscopic control study. It is highly effective in poorly defined tumours.

7. Laser

Multiple basal cell epitheliomas which may be difficult to treat in other ways are often treated by laser beam with greater success.

8. Immunologic therapy

It is a treatment of great interest in tumour destruction by the induction of a specific immunological response in the area of skin neoplasia. This is done easily by contact sensitization to a hapten e.g. dinitrochlorobenzene and then challenging the affected area with a concentration of the sensitizer just sufficient to produce a response in normal skin. Tumour generally regresses by this way.

9. Prevention

It is done by using PABA having sunblocking properties. This would be useful to those who are over exposed to solar radiation.

DISCUSSION

In our country, basal cell epithelioma is generally treated by surgical specialists. However, with the advent of electro- and cryosurgery, experienced dermatologists can also cure and are in fact curing this common malady well and with ease.

BULLOUS PEMPHIGOID

DIAGNOSIS

1. Pemphigoid means '**pemphigus-like**' and pemphigoid was differentiated from pemphigus vulgaris in 1953 by clinical, histological and immunological criteria.

2. **Age, sex and race** : It occurs most commonly in elderly persons usually in the seventh decade, though occasionally childern and young adults may become the victims. There is no sex, ethnic or racial predilection.

3. Commonly, it starts with a non-specific rash on the limbs which may be

A. **Urticarial**—Where bulla formation occurs after about 1-3 weeks, or

B. **Eczematous**—Where bulla formation occurs after several months.

4. The **characteristic lesions** are **large, tense bullae** having the following features.

A. Though the bullae occur over wide areas, the **groins, axillae, flexor** surfaces of **forearms** and central **abdomen** show the largest number of bullae.

B. Contents of the bullae are usually **clear serum,** but occasionally may be blood-stained.

C. When the bullae break, the resulting denuded areas show a tendency to heal.

D. The bullae arise both on the erythematous and the normal skin.

E. Bullae are **generally symmetric** in distribution.

5. Another clinical feature, in addition to bullae, is the area of erythema with an **irregular outline** and a **central clearing.** Annular lesions may also be seen.

6. Involvement of oral mucosa is much less than pemphigus vulgaris and is **characterised by** the following.

A. It occurs in about one third of the cases.

B. Usually it is confined to mouth.

C. Bullae are small, may remain intact and, if rupture, heal rapidly.

7. Fresh crops of bullae may arise after variable periods of remission.

8. Patient's general condition remains good.

9. If untreated, the disease will run a chronic course over a period of years and does not carry a high mortality like pemphigus vulgaris.

10. An association with malignant neoplasms is controversial. It has been suggested that concurrent malignant disease is prevalent only in patients without circulating antibodies, and occur in about 25% of these cases.

11. **Etiology** : It is an auto-immune disorder. The antibodies can be detected by both direct and indirect immunofluorescent studies which are IgG, IgA, IgM and/or C_3. The antibodies are active against lamina lucida of the basement membrane zone.

12. The illness usually is accompanied by leukocytosis.

13. Rarely, the disease has been induced by the treatment of renal failure with frusemide.

14. **Histopathology** : The specimens for biopsy should be taken from early bullae arising on an erythematous base. Following are the histopathological features.

A. Bulla is present **sub-epidermally** in most cases.

B. In older lesions, bulla may be **intra-epidermal** or even **sub-corneal** in location due to regeneration of the epidermis at the floor of bulla.

C. There is **no acantholysis.**

D. The bulla may contain a **few eosinophils** within a net of fibrin.

E. In the upper dermis and around upper dermal blood vessels, chronic inflammatory infiltrates containing usually eosinophils are seen ; some mononuclear cells and neutrophils are also present.

F. Microabscesses may be present at the periphery of some bullae or at the tips of papillae and are composed largely of eosinophils.

TREATMENT

CORTICOSTEROIDS AZATHIOPRINE DAPSONE
CYCLOPHOSPHAMIDE ERYTHROMYCIN

A. Systemic therapy

1. Internal steroid

a. Systemic corticosteriod is the main treatment, though it may sometimes be self-limited.

b. Old age should not be a contraindication.

c. Prednisolone should be started as 40-60 mg daily orally as a single dose in the morning. Once new lesions cease to appear, the dose should be gradually reduced. A maintenance dose of 10-15 mg may be required for sometime until spontaneous remission occurs.

d. Sometimes it may be difficult to control the blisters with prednisolone alone.

2. Immuno-suppressive drugs : In relatively prednisolone resistant cases, immuno-suppressives such as azathioprine and cyclophosphamide are helpful. These drugs are not given alone, but along with prednisolone.

The immuno-suppressives used are as follows.

a. Azathioprine–2 mg/kg of body weight orally in three equally divided doses is preferred to cyclophosphamide. Average dose is 100 to 150 mg per day.

b. Cyclophosphamide is given in a dose of 2-3 mg/kg of body weight in three equally divided doses. Average dose is 50-100 mg per day.

3. DDS (Dapsone) and sulfapyridine : They have been used as in dermatitis herpetiformis but not uniformly successfully.

4. Erythromycin, cyclosporine and **plasma exchange** are sometimes found helpful.

B. Local therapy

1. Soaks with

a. Burow's solution **b.** Oat meal suspension **c.** Saline

These will gently debride crusts and serous exudate.

2. Bandaging the skin with an antibiotic ointment or vaseline and gauze allows freedom of movement.

3. Oral mucosal therapy with triamcinolone in orabase is usually sufficient for oral disease.

4. In mild limited disease, when it is first diagnosed, injection of triamcinolone 2.5 mg/c.c just beneath the bullae often brings about resolution.

5. On erythematous plaques potent topical corticosteroids may be of benefit either with or without antibiotics.

DISCUSSION

Commonly, the elderly patients are affected by bullous pemphigoid which is characterised by stable blisters often on an erythematous base. Mucosal involvement is less common. Histopathologically, there is sub-epidermal blister occasionally with eosinophils in the fluid. By immunofluorescent studies, band of immuno-globulin and complement are found present at dermo-epidermal junction. Systemic corticosteroid in a dose of 60 mg orally with gradual tapering is the mainstay of treatment. Recurrences are not uncommon. Cytotoxic drugs are required rarely. General condition of the patient remains good throughout the course of the disease excepting some other conditions which may be associated with old age. Some prefer combination of low doses of steroids with an immunosuppressive agent. Symptomatic local therapy is an additional help.

CANDIDIASIS

DIAGNOSIS

It is a fungal disease caused by candida albicans. Extremely varied lesions of the skin, nails, mucous membranes and viscera are the clinical manifestations. They are summarised briefly as follows.

1. Candidiasis of the scalp

Clinically, it is manifested as erythematous, mildly scaly, inflammed, moist lesions. It is found either in babies or elderly people. Severe **immunodeficiency** caused by the damage of reticulo-endothelial system is often the cause of infestation in adults. It may be localised or generalised or even be a part of the whole body involvement. Mild itching is often a symptom.

2. Candidal conjunctivitis and keratitis

It is characterised by chronic erosive ulcers with discharge.

3. Oral candidiasis

Candidiasis often involves tongue and buccal mucous membrane. The most frequent lesion is a **greyish white plaque** which, when removed, shows raw bleeding surface. Vesicles, pustules and erosions are the other lesions. Due to friction, vesicles and pustules burst out easily and leave erosive ulcers. Papillae of the tongue are denuded and smooth reddish surface is often obvious. Chronic erosions are often found at the middle of the tongue, buccal mucous membrane and on hard palate. Rarely, there may be **grannlomatous** lesions.

4. Perleche (Angular stomatitis)

Those who have ill-fitted dentures are often the victims. More often only one side is affected first, but later both the sides may get involved. There is painful fissuring surrounding which a raw inflammed area is seen. At the periphery, **collarette fringe of epithelium** whose free margin is towards the fissure may be visible.

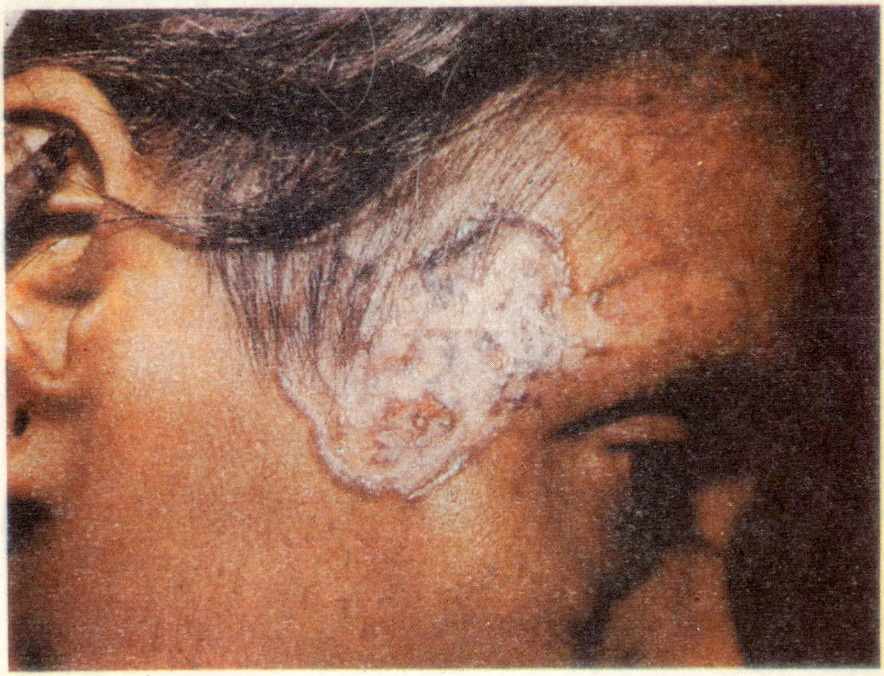

Fig. B-2. **Basal Cell Epithelioma** showing morphea-like plaque with translucent border.

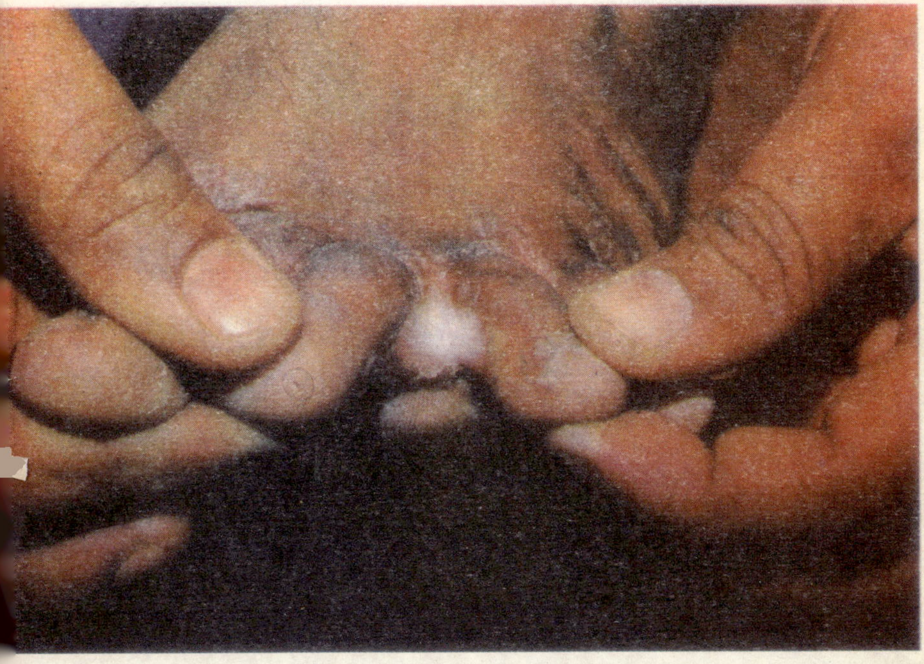

Fig. C-1. **Candidal Intertrigo** of the intertoe-space showing soddening.

5. Candidal intertrigo

Intertrigo means 'inflammation of the folds'. It may involve neck, rear side of the ears, axillae, areas under pendulous breasts, umbilicus, groin, folds of abdominal wall, areas between penis and scrotum, and between labia minora and majora, the natal cleft, perianal region and the region between toes and fingers. Third web space between the middle and ring finger and fourth intertoe space between the fourth and little toe are most often affected. This is caused by the narrowness of these places which are the constant seats of moisture.

The basic feature is erosion having burning sensation. Cracks are very common. **Collarette epithelium** at the margin is a diagnostic feature. Rarely, vesicles and pustules may be seen. **Satellite lessions** are not uncommon.

In children the diaper area, neck and axillae are the common sites of involvement. In housemaids, the webs of fingers and toes are frequently affected.

6. Candida of palms and soles

Those who work in wet condition are the worst sufferers e.g. bar tenders, sweatmeat sellers and cooks.

Main lesion is erosion with collarette fringe. Burning is more prominent than itching. Pustules may be seen. Satellite lesions are frequent. In chronic cases, there are hyperkeratosis, scalings and cracks. In extreme cases, **clawing deformity** may also be seen.

7. Candidal paronychia

In this case, the posterior and lateral nail folds are swollen, edematous and mildly painful. Cuticle and eponychium are destroyed resulting in **a gross gap between the nailfold and nail** where moisture remains for prolonged period. Creamy pus may be expressed by pressure. Ingrowing nails make the condition chronic. Manicuring or habit of traumatising the nailfolds often precipitates the condition. Bacterial paronychia may be superimposed when the pain is severe. Nails are discoloured and transverse clefts are often seen. Pitting and ridging may also be found.

8. Candidal onychia

This is extremely rare. However, from some dystrophic and discoloured nails candida albicans have been isolated.

9. Candidal balanoposthitis

The condition is most prevalent in middle aged persons having diabetes mellitus. It is characterised by eruptions of **vesicles, pustules, erosions and granuloma** formation. Itching along with burning may be present.

10. Candidal vulvovaginitis

Rawness, irritation, burning, severe itching and mucopurulent discharge are important features. Clinically, it is often difficult to differentiate with trichomonal and bacterial vulvovaginitis. Per vaginal examination may show pustules, erosion and white flakes.

11. Disseminated candidiasis

It is mostly seen in hematologic malignancies or when the patient is under immunosuppresive therapy. Besides cutaneous manifestations of papular rash, patient may have fever and diffuse muscle tenderness. The characteristic skin lesions are multiple red or **purpuric papulo-nodules** of 0·5 to 1 cm diameter at the trunk and proximal portion of the extremities. Blood culture shows positivity in about 25% cases.

12. Candidal cervicitis

Erosion is the main feature. Rarely, minute pustules may also be seen.

13. Candidal granuloma

It can occur in any site where candidiasis is persistent for prolonged period. It is characterised by granulomatous growth which often shows pus points.

Predisposing factors : Predisposing factors are as follows.

1. Obesity 2. Hot humid atmosphere 3. Diabetes mellitus 4. Hypoplasia of thymus 5. Endocrinopathies e.g. hypoadrenalism, cushing syndrome, hypothyroidism 6. Agammaglobulinemia 7. Impaired function of lymphocytes and of neutrophils 8. Hereditary susceptibility 9. Severe malnutrition 10. Severe anemia.

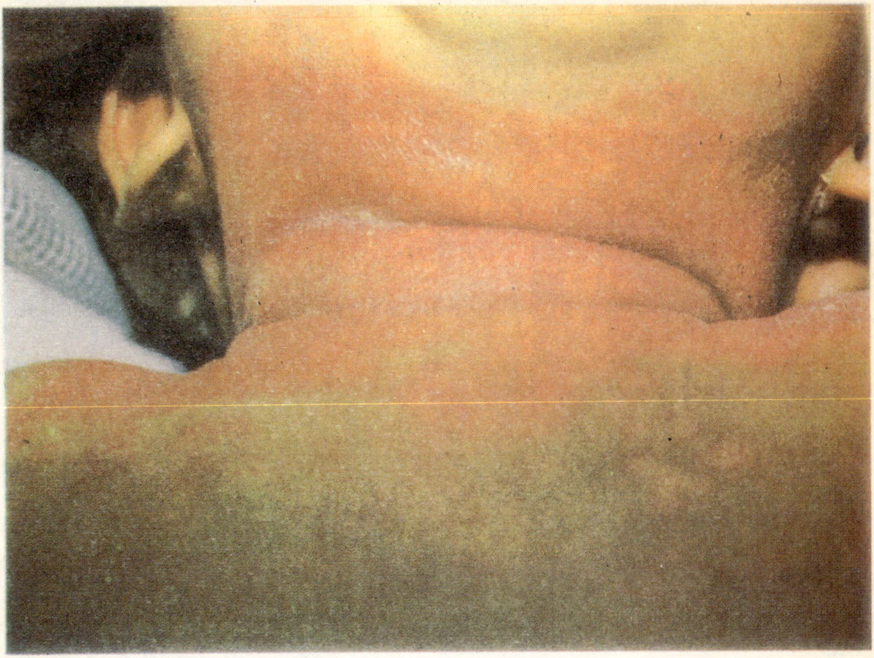

Fig. C-2. **Candidal Intertrigo** at the neck of a child showing inflammation and satellite lesions.

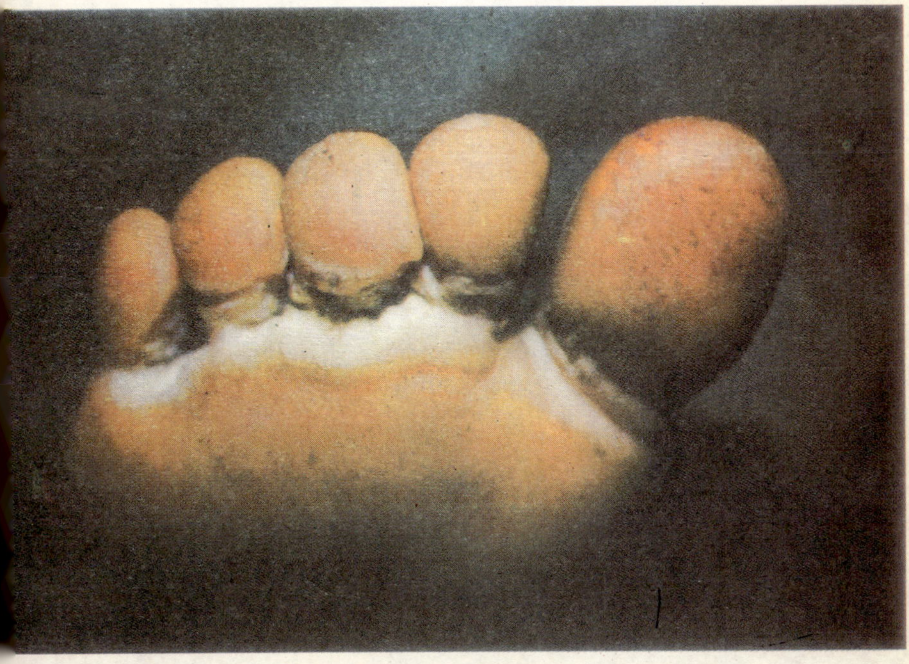

g, C-3. **Candidiasis** showing severe erosion of the under surface of the toes.

Laboratory diagnosis

1. Skin and mucous membrane scraping shows budding yeast cells and pseudomycelia. They are gram positive.

2. Culture in Sabauraud's dextrose agar media shows creamy moist colonies which on smear show terminal clamydospore.

3. Biochemical studies should be done to identify species of candida albicans which would differentiate it from krusei, parakrusei, stellatoidea etc.

4. Rabbit animal inoculation shows pathognomonically confirmative features.

TREATMENT

CLOTRIMAZOLE	MICONAZOLE	ECONAZOLE
KETOCONAZOLE	HALOPROGIN	NYSTAIN

A. **General measures**

1. Avoid the predisposing factors e.g.

   a. Treat diabetes, obesity and hyperhidrosis.

   b. Keep the parts dry and airy.

   c. Combine prolonged broad spectrum antibiotic therapy with oral nystatin tablets 1·5 million units t.i.d.

   d. Discontinue oral contraceptives.

   e. Change poorly fitting dentures.

   f. If found low, compensate serum iron, folic acid and Vitamin B_{12} level.

   g. Administer immunosuppresive agents cautiously.

2. Increase the body resistance.

   a. Increase local resistance by keeping the part dry with antifungal powder e.g. nystatin powder, tineafax[R] powder and such other commercial preparations.

   b. Increase internal resistance by thymosin, transfer factor, levamisole and cimetidine in proper dose.

   c. Correct malnutrition and anemia.

3. Avoid the reinfection. Treat conjugal partners at the same time.

B. Local

Choice of a particular drug depends upon the place of involvement, extent, state of inflammation, chronicity and it varies naturally from patient to patient.

1. 1-2% Gentian violet (aqueous or alcoholic solution) to be applied thrice daily.

2. 4% thymol in chloroform to apply thrice daily.

3. 20% sulfacetamide lotion controls candidiasis as well as secondary bacterial infection and should be applied thrice daily along with other drugs. It is specially effective in chronic paronychia.

4. 30% aluminium chloride lotion, applied thrice daily, between the toes cures intertrigo.

5. Castellani's paint, applied twice daily, is effective in intertriginous lesions.

6. 5% resorcinol in tinct. benzoin co, b.i.d. application in between toes.

7. Soaking with 0·25% acetic acid or 1 : 20 Burow's solution.

8. Miconazole 2% lotion or cream—apply b.i.d.

9. Clotrimazole 1% solution or cream—apply b.i.d.

10. Econazole 1% solution or cream—apply b.i.d.

11. Haloprogin 1% solution or cream—apply b.i.d.

12. Canicidin tablets or chlordantion cream to apply b.i.d. in vulvovaginitis.

13. Amphotericin B 3% lotion, cream or ointment—to apply b.i.d.

14. Nystatin tablets, oral suspension (100,000 units/c.c.), ointment or vaginal tablets/suppositories (500,000 per tablet).

15. Whitfield ointment in palms and soles—apply b.i.d.

16. 4-8% Iodohydroxyquinoline cream—apply b.i.d.

17. Hamycin suspension—t.i.d. application, especially in oral cavity.

C. Internal drug

1. Ketoconazole—200 mg tablet daily for 3-4 weeks.

2. Intravenous Amphotericin B—total dose 500-700 mg with 5% glucose solution.

These are required in candidal granuloma, systemic candidiasis or recalcitrant disseminated mucocutaneous candidiasis.

DISCUSSION

Correction of predisposing factors is of utmost importance. To increase the general immunity is helpful.

Treatment modality varies according to the situation, acuteness or chronicity and naturally also from individual to individual.

Keeping the part dry and application of 20% sulphacetamide lotion added with either clotrimazole, miconazole, econazole or mycostatin solution, cream or ointment are helpful in paronychia.

Intertriginous lesions are better treated with acetic acid or Burow's solution soak followed by application of imidazole preparations mentioned above (e.g. clotrimazole, econazole or miconazole). Their mode of action is probably inhibition of ergosterol synthesis, an essential cell wall sterol of yeast and fungi. Dusting of antifungal powders is a good preventive measure.

Oral candidiasis is best treated by nystatin suspension. Amphoteric B, Hamycin and Gentian violet are the good alternatives.

For vulvovaginitis imidazole creams, tablets, suppositories or troches give good results. Both the partners should be treated at the same time if balanoposthitis is present.

For chronic intertrigo of fourth intertoe space, 30% aluminium chloride solution, 5% resorcin in tinct. benzoin co, imidazole creams or solutions are helpful. Antifungal dusting powders should be added.

Treatment should be continued for **2-4 weeks more,** even after the apparent cure. Prevention is imperative to get a permanent success.

CHANCROID

Chancroid is an acute genito-infectious disease caused by Hemophilus ducreyi.

DIAGNOSIS

1. Epidemiology

a. It is very common in some parts of the world, especially the tropical belt of Africa, South America and Far East.

b. It is comparatively rare in rich and developed countries.

c. Its incidence differs widely. In Calcutta, it is about 30% of STD, in contrast to syphilis which is about 20%.

d. It is invariably transmitted through sex, but women suffer less.

e. It is more common in uncircumcised males.

f. The age group that is most commonly affected is 20-30 years.

g. Infection offers no immunity to the patient.

2. Infective agent

a. Hemophilus ducreyi is a fine, short, non-spore forming, non-acid fast gm negative bacillus with rounded ends.

b. In smears from primary lesions, it is seen most commonly in single and rarely in clusters along the strands of mucous threads.

c. In bubo aspirate, the organism shows no pattern.

d. In culture, they form straight or tangled chains occasionally looking like 'School of fish' (fish in stream) appearance.

3. Pathology

a. Pre-existing abrasions facilitate the entry of the organism.

b. The earliest lesion is an erythematous macule which changes to a painful papule and then to a vesicle or a pustule.

c. Pustule ruptures to form a sharply circumscribed non-indurated ulcer with a granulating base.

d. Multiple lesions may develop rapidly by auto-inoculation.

e. This is followed by suppurating lymphadenitis.

f. Systemic spread does not occur.

g. Superadded fusospirochetal infection produces very rapidly evolved destructive lesions.

4. Histology

In histopathology generally 3 layers can be distinguished.

a. Shallow surface layer which contains fibrin, polymorphs, RBCs and debris.

b. Wide mid-zone which is edematous with epithelial proliferation of blood vessels and neutrophilic infiltration indicating vasculitis. There is leakage of RBCs and degeneration at places.

c. Zone of dense infiltration of plasma cells and lymphocytes where H. ducreyi bacillus can be seen.

5. Clinical features

a. Incubation period varies from 1 to 14 days. Average is 3 to 5 days.

b. Primary lesions are ulcers having the following characterstics.

i. Have irregular margin.

ii. Show undermined edge.

iii. Floor is covered with pus which, if removed, shows fine granular sieve-like base surrounded by a sharp erythematous margin.

iv. Floor bleeds very easily.

v. Lesions are tender and soft (in contrast to the induration of primary chancre).

vi. Usually multiple ulcers of varying shapes and sizes are seen.

vii. Individual lesion varies from 1-2 cm.

viii. Lesions may become confluent and serpiginous along coronal sulcus.

ix. Sites are

(a) **In male**–prepucial margin and its inner aspect, frenum, coronal sulcus, glans penis.

(b) **In female**–labia minora, clitoris, fourchette, vestibule.

x. Lesions may develop from autoinoculation on inner thighs, perineum and on scrotum.

xi. In some cases pain and tenderness may be either absent or insignificant.

xii. Clinical varieties of the primary lesions are the following.

(1) Single–may look like herpetic ulcer.
(2) Necrotic–commonly involves coronal sulcus.
(3) Erosive–mostly on glans or shaft of penis.
(4) Miscellaneous

(a) Transient (b) Follicular (c) Hypertrophic (d) Dwarf (e) Giant (f) Extragenital–very uncommon on fingers, tongue, lips, breasts and eyes.

c. Lymphadenopathy shows the following features.

(1) Appears 7-10 days after primary lesion.
(2) Seen in 25-60% of cases.
(3) Usually unilateral, painful and tender.
(4) Spherical with marked redness on overlying skin.
(5) Unilocular abscess may form and it may burst.
(6) After bursting, abscess collapses and chancroidal lesion develops at the point of bursting.

d. Laboratory investigations

i. Smear of pus from undermined edge or intact bubo aspirate.

ii. Gram stain shows the organisms.

iii. Culture

(a) Old media — contain human or defibrinated rabbit blood.

(b) New media — **Borchardt-Hoke method.** In 10 c.c. of patients' serum inactivated at 56°C for 30 minutes pus is incubated for 48 hours at 35° C. Smear from this culture, organisms are seen in **'school of fish'** appearance.

iv. Intradermal skin test : Ito-Reenstierna test

a. Antigen—suspension of killed organisms. Commercially antigen is not available.

b. Amount—0.1 c.c. of standard antigen.

c. Injected into flexure surface of one forearm.

d. Control—0.1 c.c. of normal saline in other forearm.

e. Results : (1) usually becomes positive after 1-2 weeks of initial lesion. (2) Forms, after 48 hours, an inflammatory papule having diameter more than 5 mm. (3) It is a hypersensitivity immune-reaction and hence once positive, it persists for life.

v. Immunofluorescent test—preferably from direct smear.

vi. Biopsy

vii. Autoinoculation.

viii. It is obligatory to do dark-field examination for 3 consecutive days to exclude syphilis.

e. Differential diagnosis should be done from

1. Syphilis 2. Genital herpes 3. LGV 4. Traumatic ulcer 5. Granuloma inguinale 6. Various types of lymphadenitis.

f. Complications are

i. Phimosis

ii. Secondary infection with fusospirochetal organism having foul smell discharge.

iii. Phagedenic ulcer with destruction.

iv. Extension to pubis, scrotum and penis.

TREATMENT

CO-TRIMOXAZOLE	TETRACYCLINE	ERYTHROMYCIN
DOXYCYCLINE	MINOCYCLINE	CEPHALOTHIN
KANAMYCIN	STREPTOMYCIN	

A. Local

a. Saline compress or Condy's compress.

b. Cleaning the ulcer with soap and water.

c. Icepacks may be applied to painful inguinal buboes.

B. Specific

a. Cotrimoxazole : 2 tabs b.i.d. for 10 to 14 days.

b. Tetracycline : 500 mg q.i.d. for 7 to 14 days.

c. Injection of Streptomycin : 1 g I.M. daily for 7-10 days.

d. Injection of Kanamycin : 0.5 g I.M. b.i.d. for 10 days.

e. Cephalothin : I.V. 1 g q.i.d. for 7 days.

f. Erythromycin : 500 mg q.i.d. for 10 days.

g. In associated fusospirochetosis specific treatment should be added with a course of metronidazole.

h. Amoxycillin/clavulanic acid : 500 mg/200 mg t.i.d. for 7 days.

i. Doxycycline : 100 mg daily for 15 days.

j. Minocycline : 100 mg daily for 15 days.

C. Other measures

a. Bubo to be aspirated (not to be incised).

b. Phimosis with severe edema—Dorsal or lateral slit should be undertaken.

c. For surveillance, clinical and serological check up should be done monthly for 3 months.

d. Sexual partners should be treated.

DISCUSSION

Chancroid is probably more common than it is realised. It affects most commonly uncircumcised men living in unhygienic condition in underdeveloped countries. It is caused by H. ducreyi — a gram negative bacilli. It is transmitted mostly through sexual exposure.

Infection is mostly limited to genital organs. Non-genital disease is extremely rare. Systemic dissemination is never seen. After an incubation period of 3-5 days, a vesicle or a papule is formed and rapidly becomes a pustule followed by an ulcer. Multiple lesions are common at prepucial margin. The ulcers are **painful, undermined, bleeds easily, non-indurated** and **autoinoculable**. Tender unilateral regional adenopathy is present in about 50% cases. They suppurate spontaneously and may drain. Fever, chills and malaise may accompany the bubo. Dignosis is confirmed by finding organisms from the ulcer or from bubo material, either in smear or by culture.

External signs are less evident in women although they can serve as sources for infection from contacts. They should be traced and properly treated.

Prognosis is good and relapse is uncommon. However, no immunity develops and reinfection that may occur should be treated again.

CHILBLAINS

DIAGNOSIS

1. It is characterised by **recurrent, localised, erythema** and **swelling** caused by exposure to cold. Blistering and ulceration may occur in severe cases. It involves mainly acral parts e.g. hands and feet, tip of the ear and ear lobules. Onset is favoured by dampness. Females are affected more than males.

2. **Redness**, **itching** and **burning** are the usual complaints, especially by children. On examination, the local part is found to be bluish red, cold, cyanotic and wet with **excessive sweating.** Colour disappears on pressure. In severe cases, pain may be complained of.

3. In elderly patients, there may be arterial diseases. **Acrocyanosis** and **erythrocyanosis** are often associated and so also cryoglobinemia and discoid systemic lupus erythematosus.

4. In rare cases of lupus erythematosus, the lesions may be hyperkeratotic and fissures are more often present. In such cases, direct immunofluorescence shows the presence of IgG and IgM and complement at the dermo-epidermal junction. Hypothyroidism may have a role.

5. Though recurrent, it tends to improve gradually and **spontaneously** over the years.

TREATMENT

ULTRAVIOLET RADIATION	STEROID APPLICATION

General measures

Patients should avoid exposure to cold. Warm clothing in cold environment would prevent the disease. Regular exercise is helpful in that it increases circulation. Overweight should be reduced. Daily massage of warm oil increases the circulation.

Drugs : A. Local

a. Application of steroid lotions or creams reduces the inflammation.

b. Luke warm soaks with Condy's solution reduces itching.

c. Application of erythema-producing dose of ultra-violet light, 2-3 times per week, at the onset of winter sometimes helps to abort the disease.

d. Wollen socks and electric pads to warm the parts should be used.

e. Smoking is strictly prohibited.

B. Internal

1. Vasodilators

a. Nicotinamide 100 mg t.i.d.

b. Inositol micotinate hydrochloride 500-1000 mg t.i.d.

c. Phenol benzamine hydrochloride 10 mg b.i.d.

d. Etophyline 100-200 mg t.i.d.

All these have inconsistent results.

2. Various calcium preparations orally, I. M. on I. V. have been tried with dubious results.

3. Thyroxine may help in hypothyroid patients.

4. Chlorquin 200 mg b.i.d. is prescribed in lupus erythematosus.

5. Corticosteroids 40–60 mg daily in severe cases help to ameliorate inflammatory symptoms.

6. Antihistaminics usually do not help except in reducing itching and causing mild sedation.

C. Surgery

In severe cases of chilblains sympathectomy may be required.

Respones to treatment in chilblain is poor. Preventive measures should invariably be advocated.

CORNS AND CALLUSES

DIAGNOSIS

1. **Corns** (Clavus) are circumscribed, **horny, cone-shaped thickening** over bony prominences, particularly in the **foot.** They are usually **painful.** The spike of hard translucent horny tissue presses inward on sensory nerves with each step. They are not present on normal foot and hence signify abnormal pressure or friction.

Two types of corns are usually seen and they are :

a. **Hard corns**—usually present over lateral aspect of the fifth toe. They indicate ill-fitted shoes giving pressure to the part. Often they are present at pressure points of soles avoiding the medial hollows. Corns can also occur on the tip of the second or third toe, particularly if hammer toe is present or if the shoes are pointed.

b. **Soft corns**—commonly present about the fourth inter-digital web space of the foot ; the usual cause is **pressure** from head of the proximal phalanx of the fifth toe to the base of the proximal phalanx of the forth toe. Occasionally, an underlying bony spur is at fault. Soft corns may be misdiagnosed as macerated fungal infections. On paring away the hyperkeratosis the central area of keratosis, usually in concentric layers, and perhaps a small sinus tract are revealed. Bleeding does not occur commonly. The formation of the centre (nucleus, radix) of a corn is secondary to vascular changes and fibrosis underlying the maximum stress.

2. **Calluses,** like corns, also result from **abnormal pressure** due to anatomical abnormality (bony spur), improperly fitted shoes or abnormality of gait. They are **diffuse areas** of hyperkeratosis having normal surface skin markings but are without a central core. Most frequently they are seen on the sole particularly at the metatarsal heads or on the heels. They are also seen on hands at the sites of repeated friction or trauma.

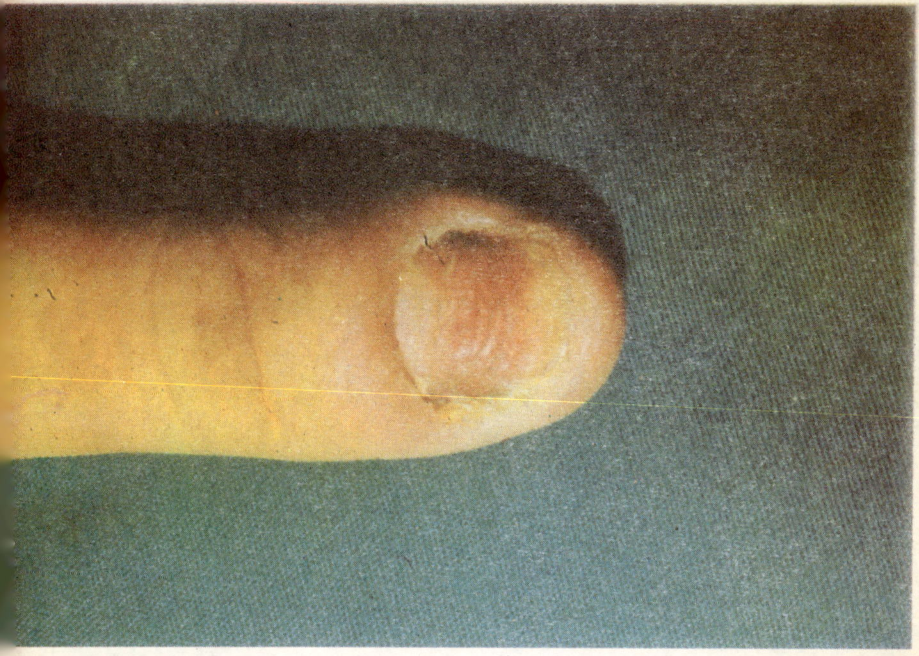

. C-4. **Candidal Paronychia** having swollen, edematous and mildly painful posterior and lateral nail folds. ticle and eponychium are destroyed.

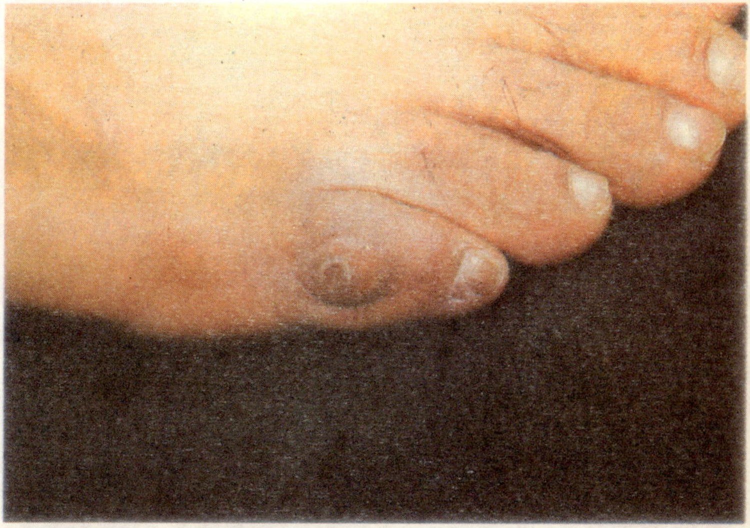

Fig. c-5. **Hard Corn** over lateral aspect of the fifth toe. It is painful.

Calluses may be mistaken as plantar warts but the following points are of help in differentiation :

(i) Calluses are invariably present at pressure points whereas warts may or may not be present at pressure points.

(ii) On shaving, superficial bleeding points appear in the warts but not on the calluses.

(iii) Calluses may be painful on ventral pressure whereas inflammed warts are painful on both lateral and ventral pressures. However, infected calluses may be painful like inflammed warts.

TREATMENT

CRYOTHERAPY WITH LIQUID NITROGEN
IONTOPHORESIS WITH SODIUM SALICYLATE
SALICYLIC ACID

1. Appropriately fitted footwear should be worn.

2. Abnormal gait, if present, should be corrected. An orthopedic surgeon may be consulted for the purpose.

3. Paring the lesion with a No. 15 blade may give symptomatic relief.

4. Application of one of the following **keratolytic/caustic** preparations may be helpful.

a.	Salicylic acid	2 g
	Lactic acid	1 g
	Flexible collodion ad	10 ml
	Mft pig	
b.	Salicylic acid	1 g
	Lactic acid	1 g
	Glacial acetic acid	1 g
	Flexible collodion ad	10 ml
	Mft pig	
c.	Salicylic acid	4 g
	Acetone	4 ml
	Flexible collodion ad	15 ml
	Mft pig	

d.	Salicylic acid	20 g
	Soft paraffin ad	50 g
	Mft ointment	
e.	Silver nitrate	1 g
	Distilled water ad	10 ml
	Mft lotion	

The concerned part should be soaked in warm water for 10 minutes and after paring the lesion with a new blade, one of the above preparations should be applied and then covered with adhesive plasters in criss-cross manner. After 2-3 days, the plaster should be removed and the lesion re-pared by a new blade. The adhesive plaster with the keratolytic agent should then be reapplied. The method is to be repeated until the central crore of the hyperkeratosis is totally removed. As the corn thins out, protective felt padding is all that is necessary.

5. Injection of small amount of **corticosteroid** (inj. Kenacort[R] 10 mg/ml) beneath a painful corn often results in dramatic relief of symptoms.

6. For marked hyperkeratosis of heal, superficial abrasion with dermabradar is often helpful, especially for removal of cracks and fissures.

7. X-ray therapy : Shielding the area with lead, a dose of 300-600 rad at 100 kV unfiltered 20 cm 'tube-skin distance' at intervals of 2 weeks for a maximum of three treatments may be successful for long periods.

8. Cryotherapy with liquid nitrogen for about 15 seconds to 2 minutes often produces resolution. The dose of course varies enormously. A painful blister may have to be pared later.

9. Tincture of Merthiolate with 5% salicylic acid applied three times a day and on soft corns of the toe web clears many cases.

10. Injection of a cushion of fluid silicone between the corn and the bone give a high rate of cure.

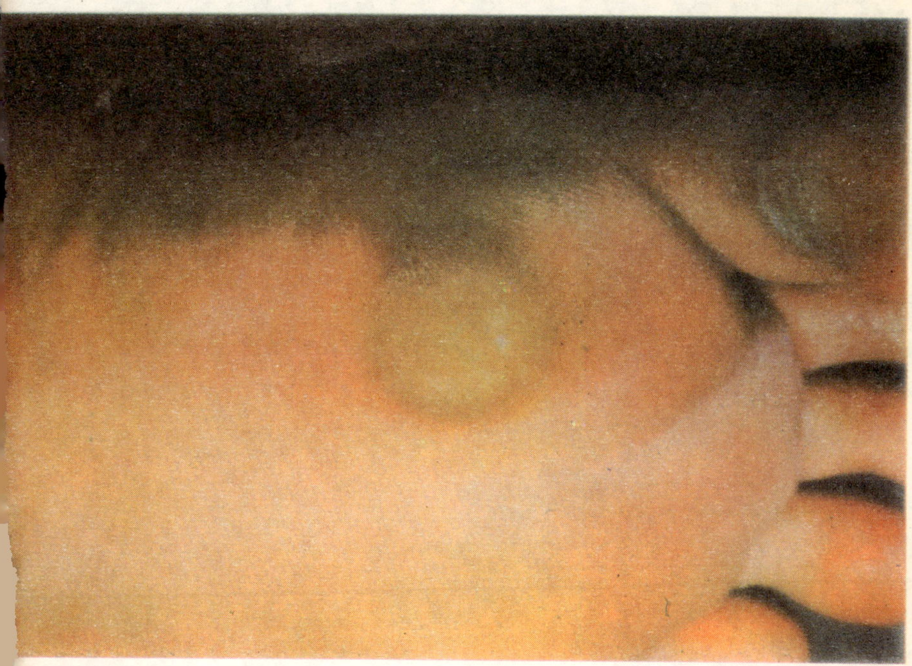

C-6. **Callus** at the sole showing diffuse area of hyperkeratosis.

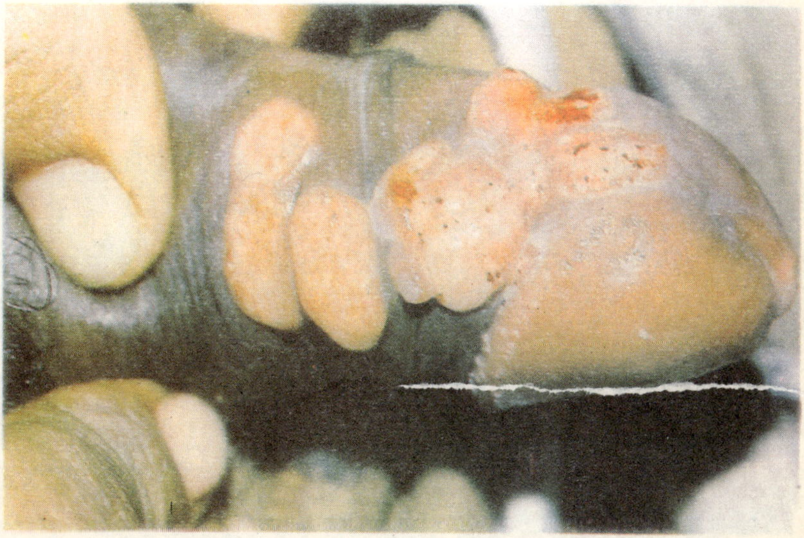

Fig. C-7. **Chancroid** showing multiple ulcers having fine granular sieve-like bases which bleed easily.

11. **Iontophoretic application** of 10% aqueous solution of **sodium salicylate** twice a week for about 5 weeks is found effective in many corns or calluses.

DISCUSSION

For permanent cure of corns and calluses, removal of lesions is not the only aim of management. The cause of the lesions should be traced. The underlying factors such as ill-fitted footwear, anatomic abnormalities, faulty weight distribution should be carefully corrected. Otherwise, the recurrence is prompt.

However, applications of salicylic acid and silver nitrate alternately for a prolonged period are often effective. Foam padding under the sole and inside shoes is a practical approach to lessen the pressure. 100% silver nitrate, applied every 3 weeks after pairing, will sometime cure, if the protection is continued.

Electrosurgery usually produces scars which are no better than cure.

Orthopedic appliances and accurate plastering to avoid pressure are to be thought of in certain recalcitrant cases.

Small sponge rubber pads used to keep the toes separated help curing soft corns of toes. If soft corns continue to persist, the surgical removal of condyles or even of the toe, usually provides a cure.

DERMATITIS HERPETIFORMIS

DIAGNOSIS

1. It is characterised by eruptions of **symmetrical,** highly **itchy** groups of **papules** and **tense vesicles** surrounded by erythema on urticarial wheals or edematous plaques. Vesicles coalesce to form **bullae.** Burning sensation may occasionally be present. Rarely, hemorrhage may be found in some bullae. Spontaneous resolution of the lesions may occur leaving pigmentation and sometimes scars. **New crop** of lesions may **abruptly erupt**. This is a **highly characteristic feature** of the disease. The lesions are usually polymorphous. In rare cases, vesicles may be absent. Only pigmentation and group of scars over sites of predilection **might indicate the diagnosis.**

2. It is found in the age group of 30-50 years. Extensors of extremities, elbows, shoulders, buttocks, thighs and knees are mostly affected. Oral mucosa is involved only in about 10% cases. Some patients have enteropathy indistinguishable from celiac disease.

3. The general health is not usually affected.

4. There is a **children variety** in which boys under five are affected more than girls of the same age. The ratio is about 2 : 1. The lesions are generally asymptomatic inspite of extensive papular, papulo-vesicular, vesicular or bullous eruptions and are highly **recalcitrant.**

5. Dermatitis herpetiformis is said to be associated with various types of internal malignancies. About 70% patients show microspcopic abnormalities in the jejunal mucosa. They often show gluten enteropathy. Prolonged gluten-free diet improves the condition in some cases.

6. 77 to 87% of patients with IgA deposition in the skin show that HLA-B8, HLA-D, HLA-DW3 are positive. These indicate probable immunologic mechanism behind its pathophysiology.

7. Bulla fluid shows 20 to 90% eosinophils. Blood eosinophils may rise up to 40%.

8. Direct **immunofluorescence test** invariably shows the deposits of IgA at the dermal-epidermal junction in uninvolved skin. In vesicular lesions, the test is negative. Probably in involved skin the IgA deposits are destroyed through phagocytosis. In 80% cases the deposits are granular and located at the tips of the dermal papillae.

9. On indirect immunofluorescence test, circulating anti-basement-zone antibodies of the IgA class are found in 2% of the cases with granular deposit.

10. **Histopathology** : Histopathological features vary according to the stage of lesions and they are as follows.

a. In **early** erythematous and edematous **lesions**

i. Accumulation of neutrophils and some eosinophils at the tips of papillae.

ii. The accumulations may form micro-abscessses separating the epidermis from the papillae leading to formation of multilocular bulla.

iii. Due to the presence of fibrin the papillae have necrotic appearance.

b. In **late lesions**

i. The rete ridges loose their coherence with the dermis forming an unilocular bulla.

ii. At the periphery papillary microabscess may still be found present.

iii. The sub-papillary dermis shows large number of neutrophils and eosinophils. Many neutrophils disintegrate showing nuclear dusts.

iv. Sub-papillary vessels show a perivascular infiltrate of mononuclear cells, neutrophils and eosinophils.

TREATMENT

DAPSONE	COLCHICINE	SULPHAPYRIDINE
HEPARIN	PREDNISOLONE	CHOLESTERAMINE
	GLUTEN-FREE DIET	

1. Spontaneous remission occurs in 10 to 15% of cases.

2. **Dapsone**—This is the drug of choice. Initial dose should be 100 mg daily. If the lesions do not subside within 1-2 weeks, the dose should be increased to 200 or 300 mg per day. In extremely rare cases, 400 mg per day may be needed.

After the complete control of the disease, maintained for about two weeks, the dose should be **very gradually** reduced to the lowest level which is about 25-50 mg daily.

Patient should be followed closely with pre-therapy G6PD determination. In deficiency, dapsone **cannot** be prescribed. Discontinuation of therapy may sometimes lead to a relapse within 1 to 4 days.

3. **Sulphapyridine**—Usually given to patients who cannot tolerate dapsone. It is a toxic drug. Dose is 2 g per day. In rare cases, 4 g per day may be needed. Patient should be watched every two weeks to reduce the dose after the control.

4. **Sulphamethoxypyridazine**—Initial dose is 1 g daily ; if necessary, may be increased to 1.5 g daily. Fortnightly check-up is to be carried out to reduce the dose to the lowest level.

5. **Combination of drugs**—If side effects are found to occur with higher dose of dapsone, a lower dose of dapsone combined with sulfapyridine or sulfamethoxypyridazine may control the eruption.

In some patients, 10 to 30 mg internal corticosteroid along with dapsone help in quicker healing.

6. **Gluten-free diet**—Patients with IgA in the dermal papillae show improvement with gluten-free diet. But the diet must be strictly gluten-free and lesions subside only after 6 to 12 months of having such a diet. Drug-treatment can be completely withdrawn only after 6 to 48 months. In general, this is too severe a task for both the patient and the physician. However, with the introduction of gluten-free diet, drug therapy should be withdrawn very gradually. Compliance of the patient is imperative to get good result in a gluten-free diet.

7. **Fowler's solution**—Patients with G6PD deficiency who cannot tolerate dapsone and who are aged 60 or more can be treated by Fowler's solution, 3-7 drops daily.

8. **Antihistaminics**—Help in controlling pruritus.

9. If secondary bacterial infection occurs in burst-out bullous sites, proper antibiotic therapy should be taken recourse to. Steroid and antibiotic lotion or cream can be applied locally if the area involved is not too wide. Application of calamine lotion makes the skin dry up quickly. Bath or soak with Condy's lotion helps in cleansing and it acts both as antiseptic and deodorant.

10. Iodides and bromides are contraindicated in dermatitis herpetiformis.

11. **Colchicine**—0.6 mg t.i.d. or q.i.d. shows beneficial effect if prescribed to some patients who cannot tolerate dapsone. They might however have to tolerate diarrhoea due to this drug.

12. **Oral cholesteramine**—4 mg t.i.d. has been found to be effective. It perhaps binds the gluten or iodine in the intestine.

13. **Miscellaneous drugs**—Pyribenzamine, indomethacin, nicotinic acid and heparin have been tried in limited number of patients and are found to be minimally effective.

DISCUSSION

By far the most effective drug is **dapsone**. It should be started with 50 mg dose, gradually increasing to the level of about 200-300 mg daily. After a complete control of the disease and maintenance for at least a month, the dose is to be gradually decreased to 50 mg at 2 weeks interval until the lowest level for control is reached, which should be continued indefinitely. It can be withdrawn only if the patient remains symptom-free continuously for several months. Patient should be regularly examined for hemolytic anemia, leucopenia, meth-hemo globinemia, agranulocytosis and peripheral neuropathy. In patients who have G6PD deficiencies, **sulphapyridine** is the drug of choice. Red or brown urine or blue nail beds or lips are the signals for **immediate stoppage** of dapsone.

DERMATOMYOSITIS

DIAGNOSIS

1. It is polymyositis involving the proximal muscles e.g. limb-girdle muscles, neck flexors, pharyrgeal, esophagial and respiratory muscles, along with cutaneous changes. Women are more affected.

2. **Skin lesions**—The cutaneous lesions consist of **erythematous** or **dusky-red, edematous rashes** involving butterfly area of the face, neck, shoulders, upper chest and back. Peri-orbital edema with purplish tinge over the upper eye lids is a **classical sign**. In hands, the **characteristic lesions** are sub-ungual erythema, cuticular telangiectasis and flat-topped violaceous papules over the knuckles (**Gottron's sign**). In later stage, subcutaneous calcified nodules may be found, especially at elbows and knees. These are more in childhood dermatomyositis, but by far the peak incidence is in the fifth and sixth decades of life. Alopecia of the scalp, hypertrichosis of the body and Raynaud's phenomenon are the other signs. Urticaria, erythema multiformi and photosensitivity may be found. Eventually, **poikiloderma** develops on many parts of the skin. Minute telangiectasis may be seen on eyelids. Ulceration of the fingertips might also occur.

3. **Muscle lesions**—Muscle changes consist of severe muscular weakness with acute swelling and pain. Eyelid muscles, orbicularis occuli, may be the first to get involved. Paralysis of the extra-occular muscles may occur. Neck flexor muscles are involved in two-third of the cases. Myocarditis is not uncommon. Leg weakness with awkward gait is often present. Dyspnea and respiratory failure are due to involvement of diaphragmatic and intercostal muscles.

Myopathic electromyographic changes show polyphasic potentials, fibrillations and high frequency action potential. Dysphagia, dysphonia, weakness of the proximal limb muscles and respiratory muscles are frequently complained of by the patients. Anorexia, malaise, intermittent fever and marked weight loss are the other common complaints.

Steriod induced myopathy should not be confused with it.

4. Associations

a. Respiratory illness in children.

b. Malignancy in 20 to 40% cases.

c. Cell mediated hypersensitivity.

d. SLE, scleroderma, rheumatoid arthritis and also rheumatic fever.

5. Laboratory findings

a. Elevation in the serum of the skeletal muscle enzymes.

(1) Creatine phosphokinase, (2) Transaminases, (3) LDH, (4) Aldolase, (5) Glutamic acetic transaminase.

b. Urine

(1) Creatine is more but creatinine is decreased. (2) May contain myoglobin. (3) Albuminuria (4) Hematuria.

c. Serum gamma-globulin increases.

d. Rheumatoid factor may be present.

e. E.S.R. may be raised.

f. Leucopenia or leucocytosis may be found. Anemia and low serum iron may be present.

g. Positive antinuclear factor is present in few cases.

h. Positive L.E. cells may be found.

i. SGOT is raised.

j. Direct immunofluorescent tests are positive in 30-40% cases. Speckled pattern is usually seen with deposition of IgG.

6. X-ray studies — Barium swallow may show weak pharyngeal muscles and collection of barium in the pyriform sinuses and valleculae.

7. Histopathology—The findings depend upon the stage of the disease and also the place of biopsy.

A. Skin

a. Erythemato-edematous skin may show nonspecific inflammatory changes.

b. Later, one may find changes like SLE e.g. (1) Flattening of epidermis, (2) Hydropic degeneration of the basal layer, (3) Edema of upper dermis with scattered inflammatory infiltrates, (4) PAS positive fibrinoid deposits at the dermal-epidermal junction and around the capillaries.

c. Old lesions show changes like poikiloderma atrophicans vasculare e.g. (1) Atrophy of the epidermis, (2) Band like infiltrate in upper dermis, (3) Focal accumulation of mucin that can be stained with alcian blue, (4) Focal areas of panniculitis with mucoid degeneration of fat cells, and (5) Calcification in subcutis.

B. Muscle

Biopsy of tender proximal muscle should be made to get the following changes.

a. Degenerative changes

(1) Loss of transverse striation, (2) Hyalinization of sarcoplasm, (3) Fragmentation of muscle fibre, (4) Granular degeneration, (5) Vacuolar degeneration, (6) Phagocytosis of degenerated muscle fragments by macrophages.

b. Regenerative changes

(1) Regenerating muscle fibres show basophilia, (2) Reduction in diameter of fibre.

c. Fibrosis—Diffuse with atrophy of muscle fibres and little inflammation.

d. Necrotising vasculitis leading to occlusion of small perimysial and endomysial vessels by intimal hyperplasia and fibrin thrombi.

e. Interstitial inflammation

(1) Patchy lymphocytic infiltrate around the vessels. Plasma cells may be present. (2) Edema separates the muscle fibres.

TREATMENT

PREDNISOLONE	METHOTREXATE
CYCLOSPORINE	AZATHIOPRINE
HYDROXYCHLOROQUIN	CYCLOPHOSPHAMIDE

1. **Corticosteroids**–Prednisolone 50-100 mg daily is the usual dose for clinical improvement. Thereafter, 5 mg should be reduced every fortnightly. At 10-20 mg level, the reduction should be more gradual e.g. 2.5 mg reduction fortnightly. Maintenance therapy should be done by alternate day therapy. In relapse, dose should immediately be increased. Treatment may have to be continued for 2-3 years.

2. **Immunosuppresive agents**

a. **Methotrexate**—2.5 mg 12 hourly for 3 doses a week orally. 10-15 mg I.V. is a risky alternative. It may help sharing the higher dose of steroid.

b. **Azathioprine**—100 to 150 mg daily may be tried to decrease the dose of steroid.

c. **Cyclophosphamide**—50-100 mg daily.

d. **6-mercaptopurine**—100 mg daily for 3 weeks, followed by azathioprine 200 mg daily, has been found to be beneficial.

e. **Cyclosporine**—3 mg/kg/day I.V. may temporarily reverse the progressive myositis.

3. **Miscellaneous drugs**

a. Testesterone propionate : 50 mg once a week is given in convalescence.

b. Potassium para-amino-benzoic acid : 8-12 g daily has been used with doubtful benefit.

c. Hydroxychloroquin : 200-400 mg/day has been used as a supplementary drug for improving the skin lesions.

4. **Supportive therapy**

(a) Physiotherapy to prevent contracture and rebuild the muscles (b) Better nutrition (c) Breathing exercises and (d) Occupational therapy.

5. **Therapy for skin condition**

(a) Sun protection (b) Non-specific emollients (c) Topical steroids have limited value.

6. **Treatment of calcinosis**

(a) Low calcium diet (b) Chelating agents e.g. diphosphonates and aluminium hydroxide (c) Painful calcium deposits may have to be excised.

DISCUSSION

Corticosteroids are the **mainstay** of treatment. However, they do not appear to shorten the course of the disease. Only the complications are lessened and the remissions facilitated in the long run. Prolonged treatment for about 1-2 years may be needed.

Those who are unresponsive to steroids or require high level of maintenance dose should be treated with azathioprine or methotrexate. The two drugs may also be combined with steroids when lower dose of steroid may bear fruit.

When the inflammation subsides, physiotherapy should be started to improve the muscle performance and prevent contracture. Measure for the rehabilitation of the patient is extremely important.

Malignancy should be **critically searched for** and immediate operative measures should be undertaken.

Modern therapy has increased the remission expectancy. While spontaneous remission has been reported, preventive measures are not known.

DERMATOPHYTOSIS

DIAGNOSIS

1. **Pathophysiology**—Dermatophytes are fungi. A fungus is a saprophytic or parasitic plant having cells lacking in true chlorophil. Dermatophytes have three species (1) **Microsporum,** (2) **Epidermophyton** and (3) **Trichophyton.** They attack different sites of the body and manifestations are also different. They may be transmitted to man from infected animals (**zoophilic** fungus), from one person to another (**anthropophilic** fungus) or from soil (**geophilic** fungus). Children are commonly infected by zoophilic fungi. The first response to fungal colonies on the skin is a cell mediated immune response with **erythema, spongiosis, vesicle formation, oozing, weeping** etc. This disrupts the epidermis, producing symptoms and, if violent, seems to shorten the course of the infection. Without cell mediated immunity, the skin is only slightly inflammed with scaling, erythema and pruritus. Unsaturated transferrin has been identified as a part of the defence against fungal invasion. Moisture, immune deficiencies due to disorders of reticulo-endothelial system (e.g. lymphomas, leukemias), atopy, gluco-corticosteroid therapy, immune suppressive drugs and diabetes help in acquiring superficial dermatophytosis. Acute inflammatory reactions with polymorphonuclear leucocytes, mononuclear cells and tissue destruction occur with zoophilic fungi such as microsporum canis and trichophyton verrucosum. These are self-limited infections because inflammation itself probably destroys the fungus; but the artificially induced inflammation cannot hasten the cure. Non-inflammatory infections are generally chronic e.g. in trichophyton rubrum and microsporum audouini. Patients of chronic or recurrent superficial fungal infections develop reduction in delayed hypersensitivity. They may even be anergic to various extracts of fungal elements as measured by lymphocyte transformation. About 40% of these patients are atopic. Sometimes a local antagonism of immune

process seems to develop. If immediate type I hypersensitivity is high, cell mediated immunity seems likely to be defective and a dermatophyte infection may become chronic. On the whole, the factors determining the resistance to fungal infections are complex and are not completely understood. We know, however, that atopic patients are unduly susceptible and some factor of local resistance may prevent the spread. Attempts at immunization have resulted in increased inflammation but in no lasting protective immunity.

As with any other disease, etiological diagnosis according to causative organism is ideal even in fungal diseases. But except in good mycological laboratories, identification is not always possible. So the approach to the subject remains mostly clinical and regional diagnosis appears rational and pragmatic.

2. **Regional classification**
   - **i.** Tinea capitis affecting scalp.
   - **ii.** Tinea barbae affecting beard region.
   - **iii.** Tinea corporis affecting body.
   - **iv.** Tinea axillaris affecting axilla.
   - **v.** Tinea cruris affecting groin.
   - **vi.** Tinea manum affecting hands.
   - **vii.** Tinea pedis affecting feet.
   - **viii.** Tinea unguium affecting nails.

Short diagnostic features of each of the above is given below.

Tinea Capitis

1. This is common among children and rare in adults. Sometime epidemics are found in hostels. It is expressed in four different forms and they are as follows.

a. **Black dot ring worm**–In it, hairs are fallen at skin level showing the remaining stumps as black dots.

b. **Scaly dermatitis**–Diffuse alopecia is accompanied with mild dermatitis mimicking seborrheic dermatitis.

c. **Kerion**–It looks like carbuncle with less acute inflammation and having absence of systemic symptoms.

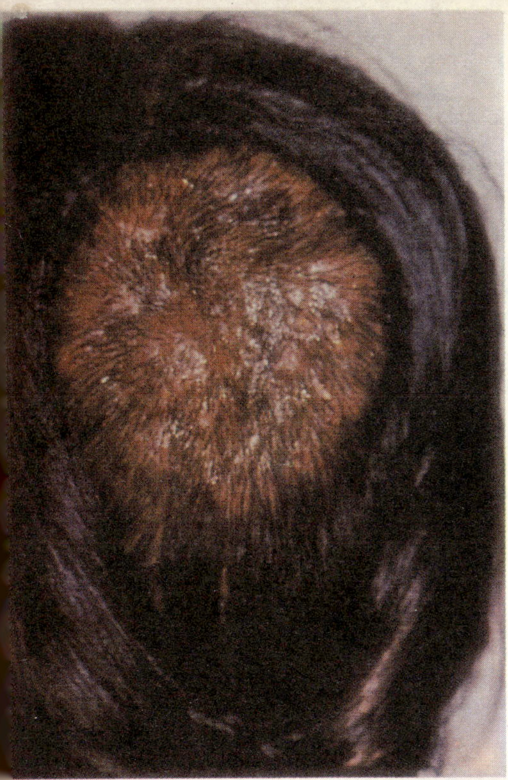

Fig. D-2. **Kerion** showing a big inflammed lesion with pustules.

Fig. D-3. **Tinea Faciei** showing erythematous patch with well defined margin, central clearing and satellite lesion.

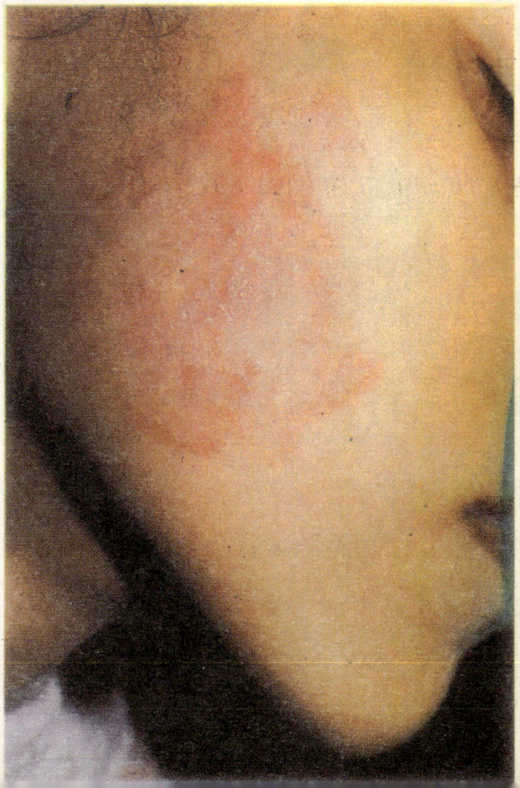

d. **Favus**—It is formed by conglomeration of cup-shaped depression called **scutula,** each cup representing a fungal colony, often pierced by hairs. Mousy odour is generally found to be present.

2. Whenever an inflammatory episode in a child persists for long, even after proper antibiotic therapy, and gives abnormal smell and some amount of hair loss, one should think of fungal infection. The diagnosis however should be confirmed by seeing the scales and hairs with KOH preparation under a microscope. It would often show spores and hyphae.

Tinea Barbae

1. It is generally found in male adults, especially those in agricultural pursuits, coming in contact with farm animals. Clinically, there are two types.

a. **Deep, nodular, suppurative lesions**—Characterised by chronic granulomatous lesions. There is not much pain. Squeezing may show pus. Acute inflammatory signs are not present unless secondary bacterial infection is there. Hair roots are destroyed and hairs fall out.

b. **Superficial, crusted, partially bald patches with chronic folliculitis**—Hairs are often loose or absent and pus may be expressed through the follicular openings. The lesions are asymmetrical and the upper lip is rarely involved, whereas in sycosis barbae (staphylococcal folliculitis) the reverse is true. This is a **good differentiating point**. Hairs easily come out from fungal folliculitis without any pain. Pustules have not much of surrounding erythema. They are very irregularly scattered. Fungal elements are found in KOH preparation and response to antifungal antibiotic is good.

Tinea Corporis

(Syn : Tinea Circinata)

It can express itself in various forms according to different causative fungi and host responses.

1. **Commonest type**—This shows the following clinical characteristics.

a. A ring like patch with prominent border.

b. Border is studded with scales, papules, vesicles and rarely pustules (fungus can produce pus in itself and it is not due to secondary strepto-staphylo infection).

c. Central clearing is there but mild scaling or lichenification may be present.

d. Border may be indented with rather healthy non-infected regions.

e. There may be satellite lesions near a big patch.

f. There may be post-inflammatory hypo- or hyperpigmentation on the patch.

g. There may be secondary bacterial invasions giving rise to impetiginous lesions and furuncles.

h. There may be secondary microbic eczema.

i. Itching is very often a prominent symptom.

j. Patches may be few to multiple or may conglomerate to form big sized patches or may show various gyrate forms.

k. The lesions spread centrifugally.

There is, of course, wide variations in the above classical form. For instance, there may be only superficial scaliness without central clearing, itching may be absent, lichenification may be prominent (causing difficulty in differentiating from lichen simplex) and the whole patch may be very eczematous. It is also not always true that all the features would be present in a single patch.

2. **Verrucous tinea**—It shows widespread verrucous lesions which are very often resistant to local therapy.

3. **Granulomatous tinea**—Lesions resemble carbuncle or kerion. It is often seen to be circumscribed, annular, raised, crusty and boggy granuloma in which the follicles are distended with purulent material.

4. **Tinea imbricata**—It shows concentric rings of scales forming extensive patches with polycyclic borders simulating the appearance of ripples in a pond when the water of it is disturbed by a stone.

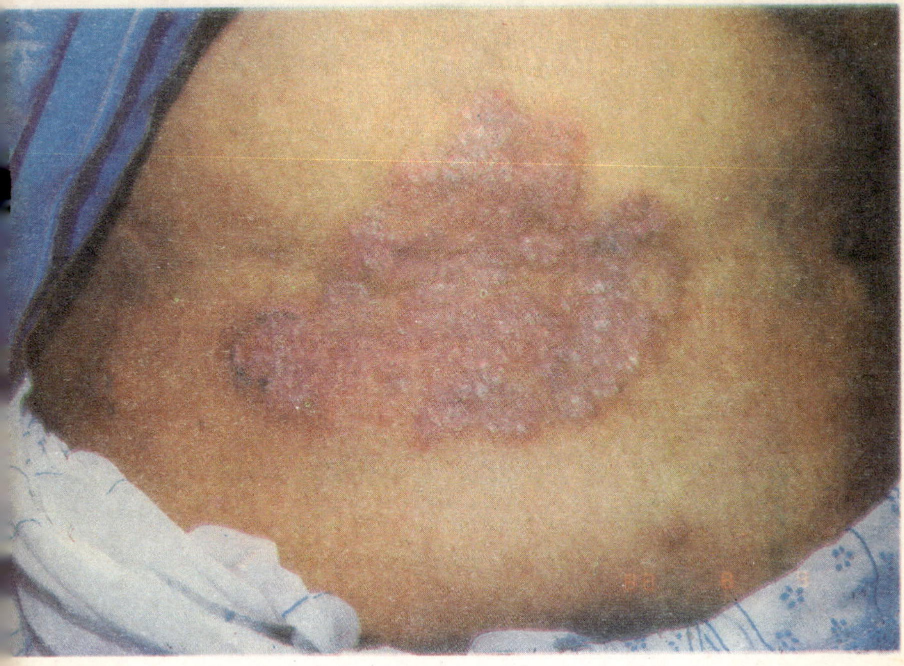

■. D-4. **Tinea Corporis** showing a scaly patch on abdomen. The border is well defined and indented with
althy non-infected region.

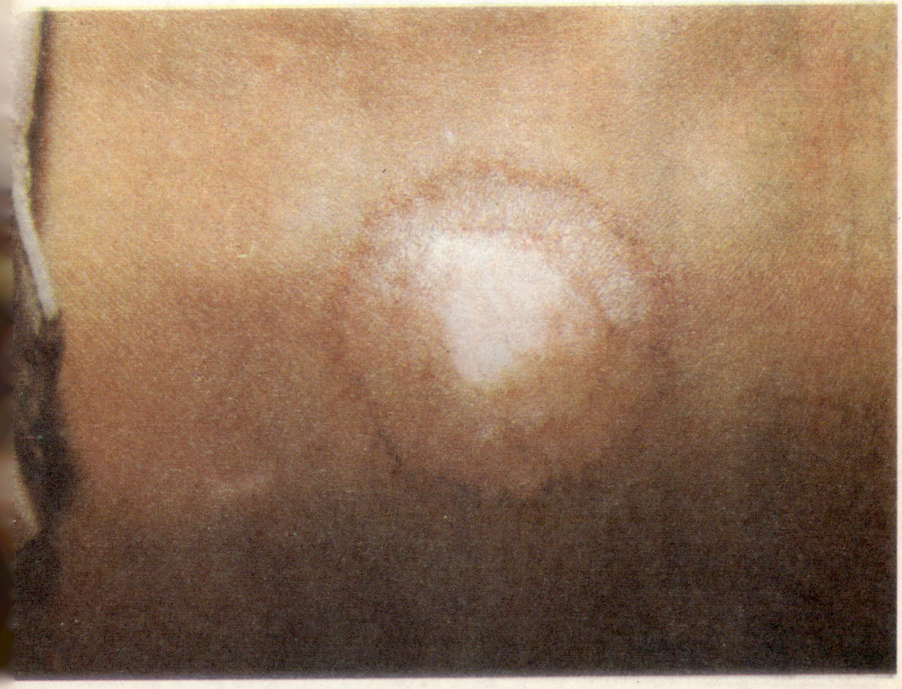

D-5. **Tinea Lmbricata** showing concentric rings.

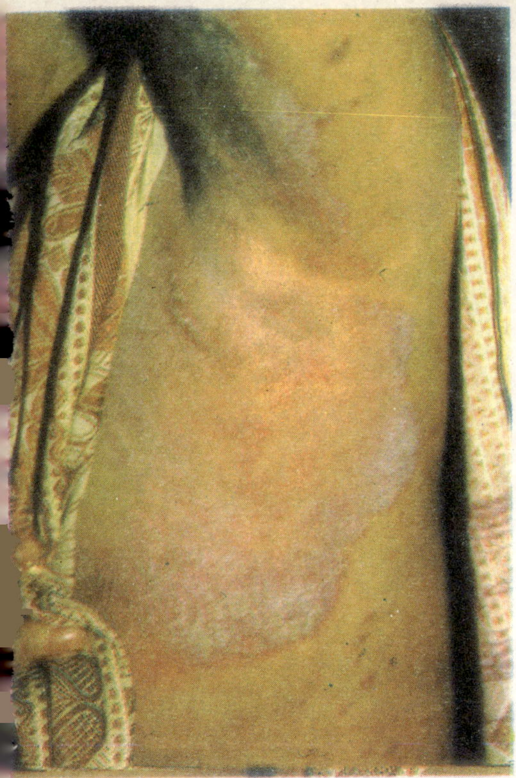

Fig. D-6. **Tinea Axillaris** showing and extensive patch with well-defined scaly border, minute pustules, central clearing, healthy indentation and satellite lesions.

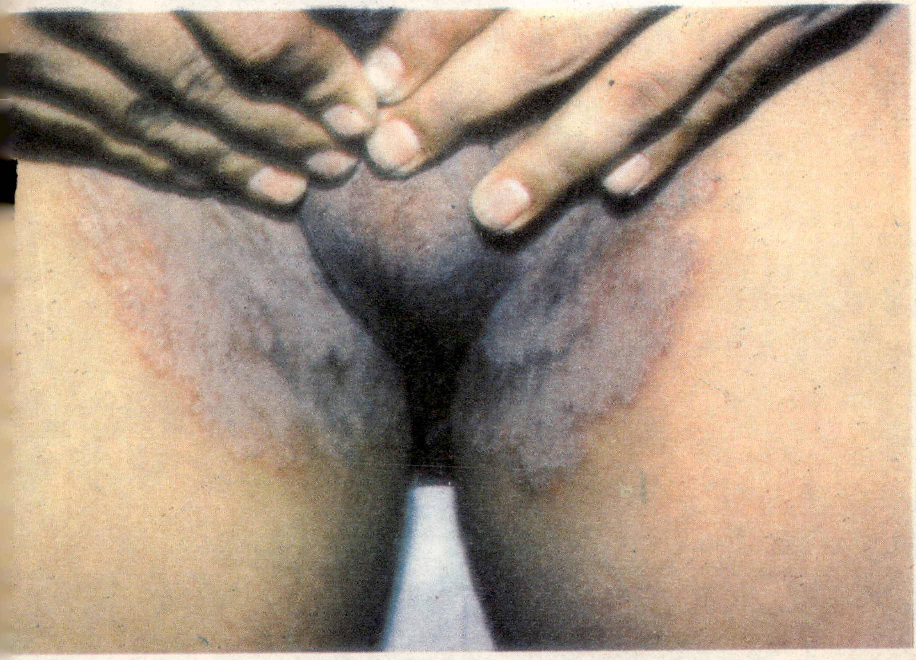

ɟ. D-7. **Tinea Cruris** showing itchy well defined margin. The patch is lichenified and scaly. Satellite lesions ɘ present.

8. Various types of dystrophic changes of nail plate may be seen according to structural changes made by the fungus.

9. Often tinea manum and tinea pedis or even tinea corporis are associated with tinea unguium which becomes the primary source of infection to other sites.

10. Usually few nails escape infection and remain healthy.

Laboratory diagnosis

1. **Microscopic examination** of skin scrapings, hair and nail for the presence of fungal elements in 10-15% KOH solution shows the following.

    a. Branching mycelia crossing the epithelial cells.

    b. Ectothrix or endothrix spores in hair.

2. **Wood's light examination**

This is a UV lamp with a nickel oxide filter that cuts out all but those wavelengths (about 360 nm) that are responsible for a type of fluorescence. When the beam of light strikes the infected hairs, the fungus alters the wavelength of the beam producing fluorescence.

3. **Culture of fungus and its biochemical behaviour**

Culture is done generally in Sabourand's dextrose agar media. Corn meal agar or blood agar are often used. Biochemical study helps in identification of species. Culture mount is a special method in which direct microscopical vision is possible.

4. **Animal pathogenicity tests**

5. **Biopsy**—**a.** PAS stain shows red hyphae.

    b. Methenamine silver stain shows black hyphae.

6. **Cell surface cytology**—Microscopic examination with cellotape adhesive method.

7. **Skin tests**—Trichophytin test shows specific allergy to the fungus by the host and indicates immunological status of the patient.

TREATMENT

TOLNAFTATE	TOPICAL KETOCONAZOLE
CLOTRIMAZOLE	ORAL GRISEOFULVIN
MICONAZOLE	ORAL KETOCONAZOLE
ECONAZOLE	WHITFIELD OINTMENT

A. **Prophylactic measures**

1. Avoidance of heat, moisture and maceration.
2. Intertriginous areas be dried thoroughly after bath.
3. Regular use of talcum or antifungal powder.
4. Footwear should fit well and be non-occlusive.
5. Hyperhidrotic patients should wear cotton socks and avoid wool or synthetic fibres.
6. Clothings and towels should be changed frequently.

B. **Local therapy**—Many topical antidermatophytic agents are available today. They differ widely in their potency and side effects. They are to be selected according to different clinical situations. Infections of the body and groin, and superficial involvement of the beard area, palms and soles usually can be treated by topical measures alone applied twice or thrice daily. Treatment should be continued for 10-15 days more even after the apparent cure. Important drugs are as follows.

1. **Tolnaftate solution, cream or ointment 1% and powder**

This synthetic antifungal agent is highly effective against dermatophytes but with no effect on candida.

2. **Miconazole 2% lotion, cream or powder**

Effective in 75%- 95% of the cases. Acts against both dermatophytes and yeasts.

3. **Clotrimazole 1% lotion, cream/powder** : Similarly effective.
4. **Econazole 1% lotion, cream/ointment** : Equally effective.
5. **Haloprogin 1% cream and solution**

Similarly effective but tends to produce burning.

6. **Sodium omadine 1% cream**

Highly effective and has prolonged action.

7. **Ciclopirox 1% lotion, cream or ointment** : Not much used.
8. **Undecyclenic acid preparations**

a. Ointment containing 5% undecyclenic acid, 20% Zinc undecyclenate.

Favus

As already described in Tinea Capitis, favus may occur also on the other areas of the body.

Tinea Cruris et axillaris

1. Tinea cruris is very common in adult males and rare in females. Tinea axillaris is probably common in adult females.

2. The clinical features are basically the same as in tinea corporis.

3. The lesions generally exaggerate during the rains and summer and remain dormant in winter.

4. Itching is a very prominent symptom.

5. Lichenification is not uncommon.

6. Tinea cruris often involves adjoining parts of scrotum and buttock. Half of the circular border may be on the scrotum and other half may be on the medial side of thigh. Vault of the groin may remain free, contrary to moniliasis.

7. Penile skin may be affected but glans penis is not generally affected in uncircumcised patients.

8. It is very chronic in some susceptible persons and they suffer for years together.

9. It is very common in tropical, hot and humid climate.

Tinea Manum (or manus) and Tinea Pedis

1. The lesions may be of four different types affecting palms and soles. These are

   a. Dry, scaly and erythematous type.
   b. Moist, vesicular and eczematous type.
   c. Verrucous type.
   d. Intertriginous type.

Intertrigo of the fourth intertoe space showing soddening, mild inflammation, cracking and having bad smell is often referred to as Athlete's foot. This is extremely chronic in nature and is owing to closeness of the toes and soddening due to moisture by the constant wearing of boots. Bare footed persons rarely, if at all, get it.

2. Special characteristics of tinea manum or tinea pedis may be summarised as under.

a. Central clearing may not be present. Since fungi constantly get a good amount of keratin as food due to thickened keratin layer, they are not required to move from centre towards the periphery for fresh food.

b. Asymmetrical lesions are usually the rule in fungal infection. But absolutely symmetrical, scaly-erythematous, itchy lesions may be found both in hand and feet. This is because of constant exchange of fungus by direct contact due to mutual itching by one hand with the other or due to exchange of socks.

c. Tinea unguium is often present along with chronic tinea manum or pedis which might be the primary source of infection.

d. Hyperkeratosis and fissuring are more common. But on the dorsum of hands and feet, classical features of tinea corporis may often be present. **Hyperhidrosis** of palms and soles is an **important predisposing factor**.

e. Dermatophytid characterised by groups of minute, vesicles with intense itching and with absolute symmetrical distribution may occur frequently. This is an immunological reaction due to fungal antigen.

Tinea Unguium (Onychomycosis)

Cardinal **clinical features** are as follows.

1. Distal erosion of the nail plate.
2. Subungual hyperkeratosis.
3. Discolouration of the nail plate (yellow, yellowish brown and black)
4. Brittleness of the nail plate.
5. Separation of nail plate from its bed (onycholysis).
6. Generally, there is no paronychial inflammation which is more a feature of monilial infection.
7. Leukonychia trichophitica is a type of superficial nail infection in which small chalky white spot appears on or in the nail plate.

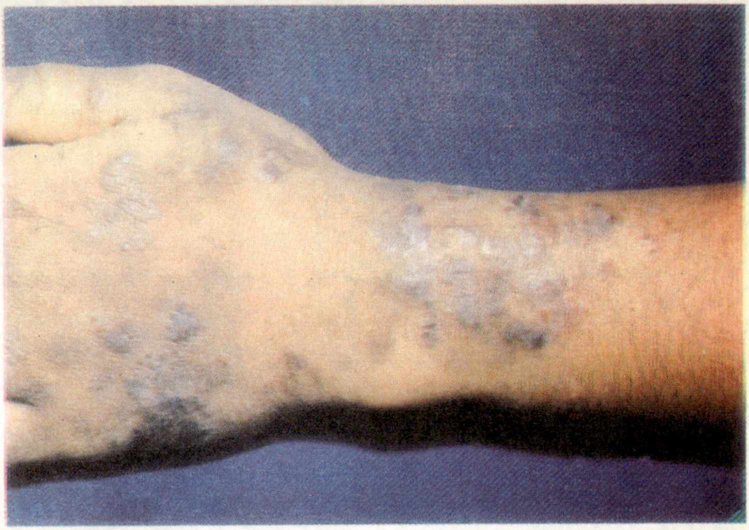

Fig. D-8. **Tinea Manum** on the dorsum of the hand showing lichenified scaly well defined patch with healthy indentation.

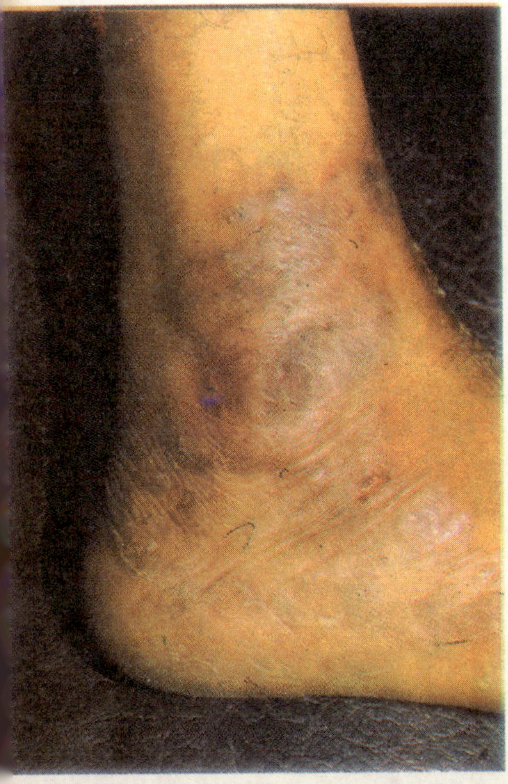

Fig. D-9. **Tinea Pedis** showing well defined lichenified patch.

b. Powder containing 2% undecyclenic acid, 20% Zinc undecyclenate.

These are reasonably effective against tinea pedis.

9. Preparations containing **sodium propionate** and **sodium caprylate** in solution, ointment and powder (5-15%).

10. Occlusive dressing with 40% urea cream to infected nail and to keep it for 7-10 days. Thereafter the diseased portion of the nail is avulsed.

11. **Whitfield lotion and ointment** (3% salicylic acid and 5% benzoic acid). Time honoured drug. Causes stinging sensation in soft skin.

12. **Miscellaneous drugs**

a. 10% glutaraldehyde solutions buffered to a pH 7.5 are used in onychomycosis.

b. 20-30% Aluminium chloride solution in athlete's foot.

c. 1-2% Gentian violet solution in intertrigo.

d. Castellani's paint in intertrigo.

e. 4-8% vioform cream.

f. Various dusting powders containing combination of antifungal agents.

g. 10-20% urea cream or lotion as keratolytic agent.

h. Local steroids are often mixed with antifungal drugs to reduce inflammation. In extensive inflammatory lesions, systemic steroids have been used.

i. Local antibiotics have often been mixed with antifungal agents to have action against secondary bacterial infection.

j. **Selenium sulphide shampoo 2-5%** – Used in black dot ringworm. It is sporicidal.

k. **Burow's solution**–Soaks in eczematoid lesions and intertrigo.

l. **Vinegar solution**–Similarly used.

m. **Thiabendazole**–10% suspension b.i.d application for a period of 2-4 weeks.

n. Topical ketoconazole cream.

o. Ointment containing 10% Buclosomide and 2% Salicylic acid (Jadit[R]).

p. 5% thymol in absolute ethyl alcohol.

C. **Systemic Antifungal Agents**

1. **Griseofulvin**

It is an antifungal antibiotic effective only against dermatophytes. It probably acts by inhibiting cell wall growth of the growing tip of the mycelial thread. It is fungistatic.

Dose : 500 mg micronised form once or twice daily after fatty meals (this causes better absorption). To be continued for 2 weeks more even after the apparent cure.

Indications

a. Extensive lesion.

b. Tinea unguium.

c. Kerion, favus and other tinea of scalp.

d. Tinea barbae.

e. Verrucous type of Tinea barbae and Tinea corporis.

f. Highly eczematoid lesions where local antifungal therapy should be postponed.

Contraindication

a. Liver disease

b. Porphyria

c. Pregnancy

d. Patients using anticoagulants, barbiturates and penicillin.

e. DLE and SLE

Side effects

Headache, nausea, gastrointestinal intolerance, phototoxicity, urticaria, skin rashes, temporary leucopenia and agranulocytocis.

2. **Ketoconazole**

It is a new oral agent used generally in griseofulvin resistant cases. It is given during breakfast as gastric acidity helps absorption.

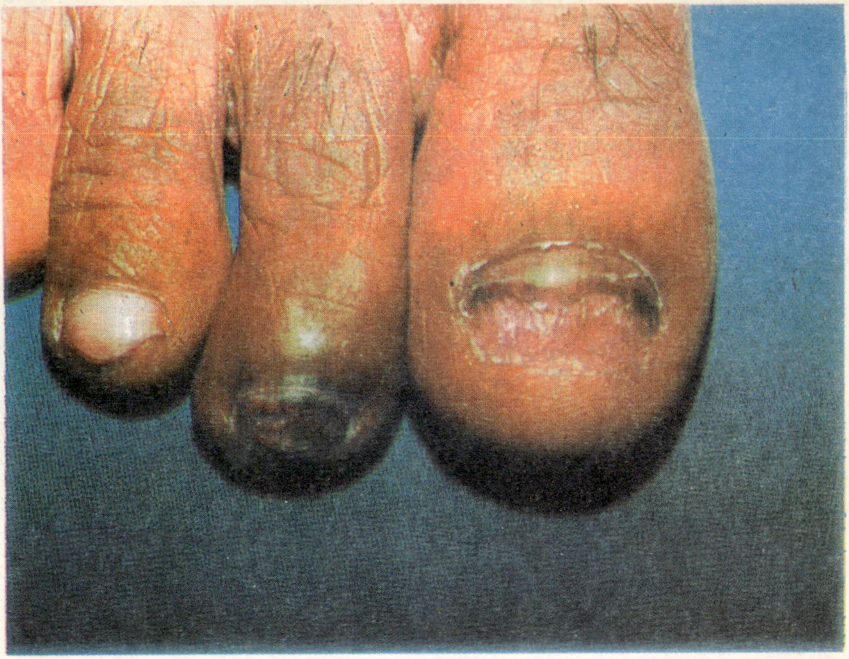

Fig. D-10. **Tinea Unguium** of the great and second toe nails showing distal erosion and brownish discolouration.

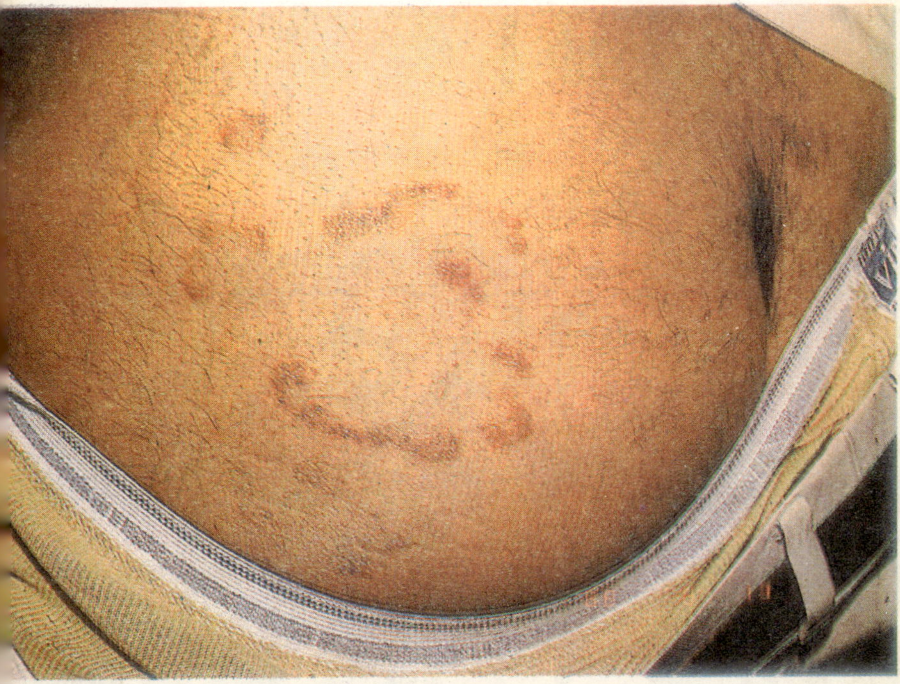

ig. D-11. **Tinea Incognito** due to application of topical steroids.

Dose : 200 mg daily for weeks to a month. It is also effective against moniliasis. It is fungicidal.

DISCUSSION

Preventive measures are of enormous practical value. Clinical diagnosis and, if possible, mycological diagnosis should be precisely made before embarking on therapy.

Therapy depends upon acuteness, areas involved, secondary eczematisation and bacterial infection.

In average patient, where involvement is limited to skin and not wide spread, application of tolnaftate, miconazole, clotrimazole or econazole for 4-5 weeks is sufficient in most cases. Application should include a few cm healthy area surrounding the patches, for dermatophytes are also present in those apparently healthy areas.

In secondarily infected and eczematoid cases, combination of local steroid and antibacterial agents is effective.

In tinea capitis, sycosis barbae, tinea manum, tinea pedis, tinea unguium and wide spread tinea corporis or verrucous tinea, prolonged therapy with griseofulvin or ketoconazole is needed.

Failure rate is rather high in tinea unguium. Some people are immunodeficient against dermatophytes and recurrence is a common feature. Diabetic patients and those having internal steroid therapy should be specially taken care of.

In recurrent cases, 400 mg of ketoconazole every 2 weeks interval sometimes prevent re-infection.

In immunodepressed patients the treatment should be continued for a longer period.

DIFFUSE HAIR LOSS

Physiology of hair growth

Undoubtedly, human hair still retains a significant social and protective importance. Pilosebaceous unit comprises the hair, hair sheath or follicles, attached sebaceous glands, dermal papilla and the associated blood vessels and nerves. Hair growth is a cyclic phenomenon and the hair production a repeatitive process. The pilosebaceous apparatus at any time is either proliferating actively (**anagen stage**) or regressing or resting (**telogen stage**). A transition from the end of anagen to the beginning of telogen is the short, actively involuting **catagen stage.** In a normal scalp, total number of hairs ranges from 100,000 to 150,000. Of these, the active growing hair constitutes more than 85% in women and 80% in men. The most actively growing hair is in the vertex. The normal hair loss in adults ranges from 20 to 100 per day, a fact we often ignore and thereby succumb to mental upset at the sight of our falling hairs. Montagna set up the criterion that unless the hair fall per day exceeds 100, it is not a case of diffuse alopecia. The metabolic activity of the hair matrix is unique in the body. It produces 30 m of protein-rich hair every day. Hair growth reflects to a great extent the state of health. The formation of hair is the result of rapid cellular activity that ceases or slows down in febrile illness, severe anemia, iron deficiency, inadequate dietary protein and generally debilitating disorders. Androgens, glucocorticoids, thyroid and estrogens have a profound effect on hair growth and its control, and the most vital role is played by the genes.

A. Diffuse Alopecia

Also called physiological alopecia, diffuse alopecia of women, male pattern alopecia and common baldness.

DIAGNOSIS

Hair regression over the anterior portion of the scalp, followed by similar changes over the vertex, may become apparent in normal males in the late teens or early twenties. The presence of androgenic hormone and a genetic predisposition are the causative factors. Such alopecia is therefore also termed **'androgenetic'**. Hair, in fact, is not lost ; it only regresses to vellus form. Its presence in fine non-pigmented form in follicles can be easily demonstrated microscopically.

This condition also occurs in women, particularly in mild forms. The process in the female begins with thinning of hair over the vertex. Unlike the pattern in male, there are well-preserved fringes in the hair line. There may be early fronto-temporal recession in females as well. The thinning at vertex may be severe leading eventually to baldness by menopause.

Hereditary patterns must be differentiated from early virilising syndromes. Castrated men do not develop this type of baldness ; castration rather prevents extension of the process. Administration of testesterone, however, does not produce extension.

To confirm or reject a hereditary etiology, it is imperative to have family histories. The degree of baldness of parents, grand parents, siblings, uncles and aunts should be carefully studied. The disorder is inherited but the mode of inheritance is not certain. Both the hair follicles and sebaceous glands are found to decrease and pigmented coarse hairs replaced by nonpigmented finer ones. Excessive shedding is not a feature, although the concerned individual may feel depressed at each shedding.

TREATMENT

IMPROVEMENT OF NUTRITION	IRON
PLACEBO	MINOXIDIL

1. A young man in his late teens or early twenties would naturally be concerned at gradual hair loss, particularly if there is a positive family history. To prevent any psychological upset, the patient is to be taken sympathetically into confidence and frankly apprised of the situation. **Hair restorers** flood the market and he may fall a prey to their tempting claims to regrow his hair. To save his hair and money he is to be timely informed and cautioned.

2. For patients who are virtually disabled by their baldness, transplantation of hair may result in a cosmetically acceptable appearance.

3. In young women with severe baldness, who do not have amenorrhea or clitoral hypertrophy, it is very likely that antiandrogens such as cyproterene acetate would be of some help. Unfortunately, it is not easily available in India. Amenorrhea and clitoral enlargement might indicate virilising syndromes.

4. Application of **2% minoxidil solution** or taking the drug internally has been advocated in recent years.

B. Telogen effluvium
(Hair loss occurring after high fever)

A diffuse form of hair loss may become apparent up to several weeks after the febrile episodes. Usually hair regrows subsequently. But sometimes it may take even four to six months for the regrowth. In such cases, nails may form ridges. Other types of stress such as accidents, surgical shock, hemorrhage and other traumatic episodes may also produce similar effects.

Treatment — In most cases, normal regrowth is usual. Reassurance is what is most important in handling such patients.

C. Hair loss from endocrine causes

1. **Post partum hair loss** : During pregnancy, less than one third of the usual number of hairs is resting and, after pregnancy, more than twice the usual number are in that stage ready for being shed. Diffuse alopecia may occur from the 1st to the 12th week after delivery and last for few months.

Regrowth however is complete. It may be a glucocorticoid-produced phenomenon. Some women, in the habit of taking contraceptive pills, report hair loss on discontinuation of the drug. The mechanism however is not understood and the period required for regrowth is also that what is needed in post partum.

2. **Hypothyroidism, hypoparathyroidism, diabetes mellitus, and hypopituitarism :** These disorders may result in reversible thinning of the scalp hair.

D. Hair loss caused by malnutrition

'Crash' diets have been demonstrated to cause hair loss by slowing down growth rates in anagen, or by turning hair into resting or telogen phase. Protein deficiency results in dry, brittle, fine, sparse hairs that are easily shed but to have such changes a severe and continued malnutrition must exist. Iron deficiency results in a diffuse thinning of scalp hair and is the most common causative factor in developing countries. Serum iron determination is by far the most valuable index to assess this problem.

Treatment

1. Proper nutritive diet with adequate amount of protein.
2. Iron.

E. Hair loss caused by drugs

The anticoagulant drugs such as heparin, folic acid, antagonists and thalium are often responsible for diffuse hair loss. Coumarins, anti-metabolites, quinacrine, arsenic, dextran, boric acid, clofibrate, triparanol, Vitamin A excess, thiouracil, carbimazole, potassium thiocyanate, bismuth, amphetamines, androgens and trimethadione all have been acused of initiating a temporary alopecia. Salicylates may also cause hair loss.

Treatment—Stoppage of the drug, if possible.

F. Hair loss caused by genetic defect

1. There are as many as 48 syndromes in which hair loss is a common feature. Sparsity of hair is often accompanied

by hypopigmentation, thinness and brittleness. Abnormal dentition, nail defects and sweat gland aplasia may also present as congenital ectodermal defect.

2. Genetic structural defects of hair : Monilethrix (beaded hair), trichorrhexis invaginata (telescoped hairs), trichorrhexis nodosa (fractured, frayed hair), pili torte (twisted hair) may cause diffuse alopecia. Microscopic examination distinguishes the disorders.

Treatment—No treatment is available.

G. Seborrhea capiti

Mild amount of dandruff is physiological and does not cause alopecia, but severe seborrheic dermatitis may produce alopecia due to inflammatory changes and concomitant secondary infection.

Treatment

1. **Shampooing** with cetavlon once a week.
2. In **dermatitis**—Steroid lotion and cream with or without the antibiotic.
3. In **secondary infection**—Oral antibiotic.

H. Shampooing

Too frequent and severe alkaline shampooing causes alopecia, especially in dry scalp. However, patients suffering from seborrhea oleosa do require this type of treatment and it must therefore be optimum.

I. Trauma

Too much combing of hair causes trauma to hair roots and may therefore cause diffuse alopecia.

DISCUSSION

Malnutrition involving iron deficiency is, in most cases, the causative factor, particularly in developing countries. Often the complaint of diffuse alopecia appears to be psychic in origin with no pathological basis.

However, one should be critical in analysing the anxiety and mental depression of the patients, especially the youth. Hair-consciousness is universal and reassurance is the basis of therapy. As placebo, a multivitamin tablet is helpful. Non-irritant local applications may be prescribed to allay the depression.

In most cases of telogen effluvium, regrowth is the rule. But if a patient suffers from severe repeated hair-loss due to telogen effluvium, permanent thinning may result.

In nagging recalcitrant patients, cosmetically acceptable wig is a good alternative.

Good **nutrition, vitamins, iron** and **reassurance** are still the basic treatment of diffuse hair-loss.

Minoxidil is still a debatable drug.

DISCOID LUPUS ERYTHEMATOSUS (DLE)

DIAGNOSIS

1. It is characterised by discoid plaques having the following characteristics.

a. Well-defined **b.** Infiltrated **c.** Erythematous

d. Have adherent scales which, when removed, show follicular plugging.

e. Atrophy and scarring **f.** Telangiectasis

g. Hyperkeratosis, often verrucous

h. Pigmentation and hypopigmentation

i. Inflammatory border surrounding the margin

j. Rarely vesicles may be present.

2. **Sites of the lesions**

a. Malar areas, **b.** Nose, **c.** Ears and behind the ears, **d.** Scalp, **e.** Front and back of chest, **f.** Upper limbs, **g.** Dorsum of hands, **h.** Front of the knees and toes, **i.** Heals.

3. **Female to male** ratio is 4 : 1

4. **Histology**

A. Epidermis

a. Hyperkeratosis and keratotic plugging.

b. Atrophy or hypertrophy of the stratum malpighii.

c. Focal hydropic degeneration of basal layer.

B. Dermis

a. Edema of the upper dermis.

b. Thickening of the basement membrane zone and around the hair follicles.

c. Extravasation of erythrocytes.

d. Clumps of melanin in melanophages.

e. Dilatation of capillaries and larger vessels.

f. Fibrinoid deposits.

g. Patchy inflammatory infiltrate, mainly in the vicinity of hair follicles and sebaceous glands. May extend

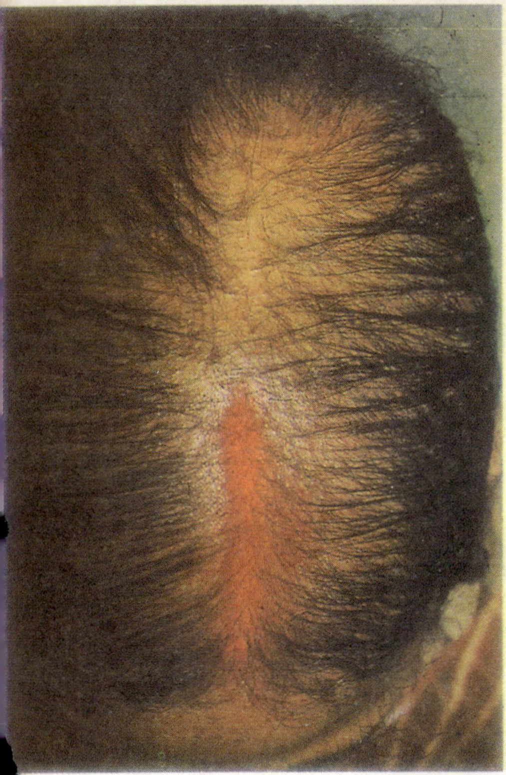

Fig. D-12. **Diffuse Alopecia** of a woman

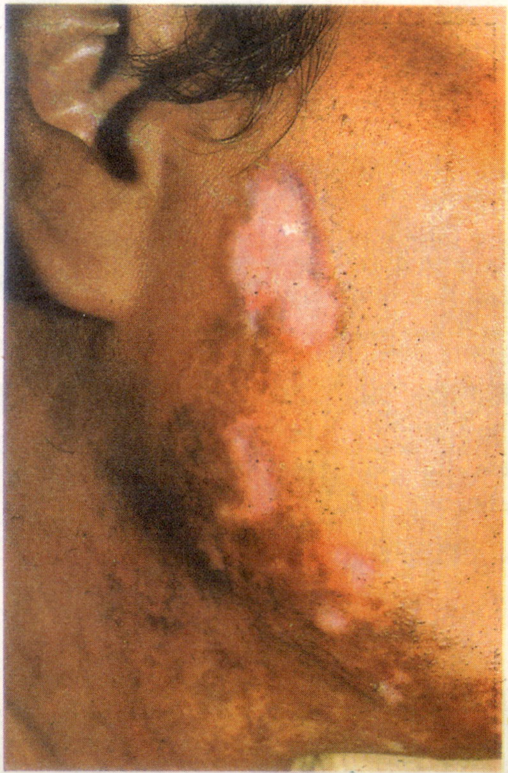

Fig. D-13. **DLE** showing well defined infiltated erythematous patch with adherent scales

into subcutaneous fat. Infiltrate consists mainly of lymphocytes, histiocytes and small number of plasma cells.

h. Colloid or civatte bodies which are round or ovoid, eosinophilic, homogeneous, aproximately 10 μm in diameter, are present in the upper dermis or lower epidermis. They represent nonspecific dyskeratosis of individual epidermal cells.

i. In the dermis, they are PAS-positive and diastase resistant and the direct immunofluorescence staining shows IgG, IgM, IgA, complement and fibrin.

j. Capillary walls show thickening, homogenization and an increase in the intensity of the PAS reaction.

k. Follicle inside the dermis may contain concentric layers of keratin instead of hairs.

5. Laboratory findings

About 50% patients show the following abnormalities.

a. Anemia **b.** Leucopenia **c.** Thrombocytopenia

d. Raised gamma-globulin.

e. Presence of rhematoid factor.

f. Positive Coombs' test.

g. Positive Wassermann reaction.

h. Presence of cryoglobulins and cold agglutinins.

i. Antinuclear antibodies.

j. Increased incidence of $HLAB_7$ and $HLAB_8$.

TREATMENT

STEROID OINTMENT	DAPSONE
INTRALESIONAL STEROIDS	QUININE
CRYOTHERAPY	BETA-CAROTENE
CHLOROQUINE	AZATHIOPRINE
HYDROXY CHLOROQUINE	CLOFAZIMINE
ATABRINE	THALIDOMIDE

1. Avoidance of exposure to sun or, if exposed, use of proper sun-screening agent e.g..

a. 5% para-aminobenzoic acid in 70% alcohol

b. Benzophenone compounds such as

(1) cream containing 4% ethyl hexylparacinnamate, 3% 2-hydroxy 4-methoxy benzophenone and 2% phenyl benzimidazole sulphonic acid,

(2) cream containing 3% oxybenzone and 3% dioxybenzone, and

(3) cream containing 10% sulisobenzone.

c. Red veterinary petrolatum

d. Titanium dioxide 5%

e. Combinations

(1) 5% titanium dioxide and 5% methyl anthranilate

(2) 5% titanium dioxide and 20% Zinc oxide.

(3) 5% titanium dioxide and 4% PABA

2. **Topical steroid** to be applied twice daily

a. 0.1% betamethasone cream/ointment

b. 0.025% fluocinolone cream/ointment

c. 0.1% triamcinolone cream/ointment

d. 0.05% clobestol propionate ointment

e. 0.1% halcinonide cream/ointment

f. Tape impregnated with steroid (Haelan tape[R])

3. **Intralesional steroids**

a. 2.5 mg triamcinolone suspension at 2-3 weeks interval.

b. 1% hydrocortisone acetate.

4. **Oral antimalarials**

a. Hydroxychloroquine (Plaquenil) 200-400 mg daily

b. Chloroquine sulphate or phosphate 200-500 mg daily

c. Atabrine 100 mg tab daily.

d. Camoquin 200 mg tab daily.

e. Quinine bisulphate 300 mg b.i.d.

f. Combinations of the above e.g. Triquin (Chloroquine 65 mg, Atabrine 25 mg and Plaquenil 50 mg) for 6-8 weeks and then the dose gradually reduced to the lowest level.

5. **Oral steroid**

Prednisolone 40-60 mg daily for 6 weeks and then gradually tapered.

6. **Oral antimalarial and oral steroid combination**—To be used in resistant cases.

7. **Clofazimine**—100 mg thrice weekly to 200 mg per day. Improvement occurs in about 60% of patients.

8. **Vitamin E**—1600 mg per day has been claimed to be beneficial.

9. **Beta carotene**—50 mg t.i.d. might help some patients.

10. **Cyclophosphamide**—100 mg to 200 mg per day in resistant cases.

11. Azathioprine—100 mg per day

12. Dapsone—50-100 mg daily has been found to be effective in some patients.

13. **Physical measures**

   a. Freezing small lesions with CO_2 snow or liquid N_2.

   b. Cauterising with 10% trichloroacetic acid.

   c. Painting with pure phenol.

14. Thalidomide—200 mg b.i.d.

15. **Surgical excision** : With or without grafting in the case of scarred lesions.

DISCUSSION

Chloroquine is the drug of choice. If the patient does not have G6PD deficiency, chlorouine phosphate – one tab t.d.p.c should be started and continued until clinical lesions improve. In some patients, whose tolerance is less, the dose has to be gradually built up starting with 1/2 to 1 tab daily. On having complete clinical improvement, which requires few months, the dose is to be reduced gradually to minimum maintenance level. This may be even 1/2 tab twice a week. A 3-6 monthly routine check-up of the patient is essential for few years. About 6% patients may turn to systemic lupus.

Initially, application of local steroid is helpful and later cosmetic cover mark may have to be used.

Patients should be advised to avoid exposure to sun and consult ophthalmologists for any sign of chloroquin kerato-retinopathy.

DRUG ERUPTIONS

Diversities of drug eruptions appear, to a great extent, puzzling. Etiological agents are numerous and the lesions are extremely variable. Allergic drug reactions are most common. They occur due to mediators released after exposure to sensitising drug molecules. Clinically, drug reactions can be divided into two main groups : (1) **Fixed drug rashes** and (2) **Generalised drug eruptions.**

Fixed drug rashes (FDR)

DIAGNOSIS

1. Clinically, it is characterised by a typical sequence of events. A localised area starts itching followed by erythema, edema and even vesiculation or central necrosis. The area heals up with slaty-dark pigmentation that persists for long—3 months to 1 year.

2. History of exposure to the following common drugs are often found.

- **a.** Salicylates, aspirin, phenacetin.
- **b.** Sulphonamides, sulphones.
- **c.** Butazolidin group.
- **d.** Barbiturates.
- **e.** Belladonna group.
- **f.** Phenolphthalein.

The reactional sites are often fixed having certain areas of predilictions e.g. (1) mucocutaneous junctions, (2) oral and genital mucosa, (3) flexors of extremities, (4) webs of fingers and toes, (5) palms and soles. However, any site may be affected.

Repeat exposure to the offending drug initiates inflammation in the originally affected sites and newer areas may also be involved.

3. Histologically, the lesion shows non-specific inflammatory changes of various degrees and stages. Melanin pigment is increased and vasculitis may occur. Exact pathogenesis is not yet known.

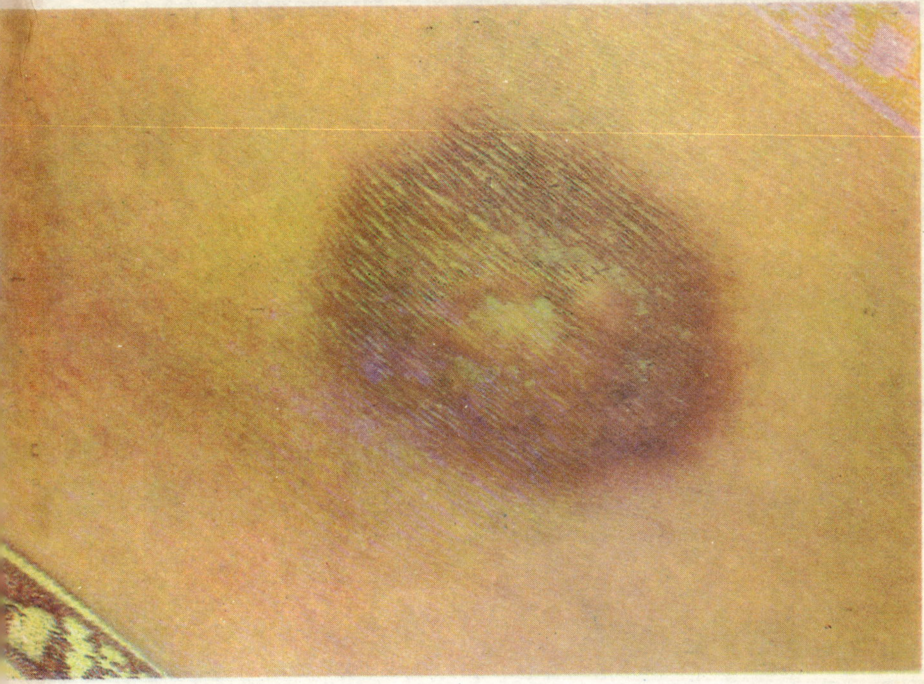

Fig. D-14. **Fixed Drug Rash** showing inflammation and pigmentation.

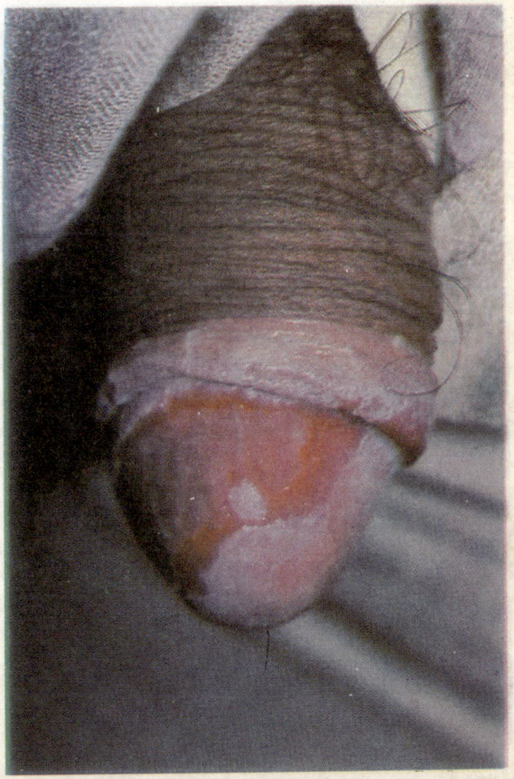

Fig. D-15. **Fixed Drug Rash** at the genitalia due to sulphonamide.

1. Prompt withdrawal of the offending drug.

2. In acute stage, steroid lotion with or without antibiotic should be applied thrice daily.

3. If secondary infection is apprehended, internal antibiotic is prescribed for 7 days.

4. In severe cases involving wide-spread mucocutaneous lesions, a course of internal steroids should be prescribed to prevent the sequel of scarring or other permanent damage.

5. Antihistaminics have doubtful role.

6. Prolonged intake of Vitamin C for quicker removal of black spots is a sheer wastage of money.

DISCUSSION

Correlation of drug intake and the development of FDR should be patiently tried. Diagnosis can be confirmed by another exposure to the drug in quiescent stage when there would be reappearance of inflammation in old spots.

Prevention of exposure to the offending drug is the best way to get rid of FDR lesions.

Generalised drug eruptions (GDR)

DIAGNOSIS

A. **History** of taking an offending drug that developed various types of morphological lesions.

More than 1% people develop drug eruptions with the following drugs.

1. Trimethoprim—Sulphamethoxazole **2.** Ampicillin
3. Semisynthetic penicillins **4.** Erythromycin
5. Sulphisoxazole **6.** Penicillin G
7. Gentamycin sulphate. **8.** Cephalosporins
9. Quinidine **10.** Barbiturates
11. Butazolidines **12.** Antituberculous drugs
13. Halogens—bromides, iodides

B. **Characteristics of GDR**—These are as follows.

1. Wide-spread bilaterally symmetrical lesions of various morphology.

2. History of taking an offending drug and time interval in the development of lesions.

3. Progress in acuteness and involvement of new areas if the offending drug is continued with gradual deterioration of general condition.

4. Gradual improvement of the patients' condition if the offending drug is identified and totally withdrawn.

6. Lesions mostly start and get cleared first from the head and upper extremities to the trunk and lower legs.

7. Palms, soles and mucous membranes are often involved.

8. There may be cross-reaction of locally applied drugs with the internally administered ones.

9. Reactions are basically allergic in nature and are described below.

a. Immediate allergic reactions within 1 hour.

b. Accelerated reactions within 1-72 hours.

c. Late reactions start generally after 3 days.

d. Exanthematous eruptions appear within 1 week.

C. Types of rashes

Various types of rashes are seen. They are as under.

a. Erythema and edema b. Papular c. Vesicular

d. Bullous e. Ulcerative f. Granulomatous

g. Iris or target type of lesions

h. Purpura and petechiae i. Exfoliative dermatitis

j Stevens-Johnson syndrome

k. Toxic epidermal necrolysis

l. Polymorphous lesions having a mixture of various types of lesions.

Size, severity and the acuteness of the lesions are found to vary enormously.

Many types of drugs can produce identical eruption and the morphology of the lesions should not be relied upon as to the clue of the causative agent.

For ready reference various clinical types of drug eruptions with common etiologic agents are given below.

1. **Acnelike or pustular lesions**—Bromides, iodides, trimethadione, testosterone, methandrostenolone and ACTH.

2. **Alopecia**—Methotrexate and other antineoplastic agents, colchicine, clofibrate, testosterone, heparin, dicumarol and coumarin derivatives.

3. **Eczematous eruptions**—Quinine, procaine, antihistamines, gold, mercury, sulphonamides, penicillin and organic arsenic.

4. **Erythema multiforme-like eruptions**—Penicillin and other antibiotics, sulphonamides, phenolphthalein, barbiturates, phenytoin and meprobamate.

5. **Erythema nodosum-like eruptions** — Sulphonamides, iodides, bromides, salicylates, contraceptive drugs, dapsone.

6. **Exfoliative dermatitis** — In course of any generalised drug eruption, particularly due to arsenic, penicillin, sulphonamides and barbiturates.

7. **Keratoses and epitheliomas** — Arsenic, mercury and PUVA therapy.

8. **Lichen planus-like eruptions**—Atabrine, arsenic, naproxen and gold.

9. **Measles-like eruptions**—Barbiturates, arsenic, sulphonamides and quinine.

10. **Mucous membrane lesions**—Bismuth, phenytoin, sulphonamides and antineoplastic agents.

11. **Nail changes**— Dimethylchlortetracycline and tetracyclines.

12. **Nummular eczema-like eruptions**—Combination of isoniazid and para-amino-salicylic acid.

13. **Pemphigus-like eruptions**—Rifampicin, phenylbutazone, penicillamine and captopril.

14. **Photosensitivity reactions** — (a) Sulphonamides, (b) Sulphonyl urea hypoglycemics—Tolbutamide, chlorpropamide, acetohexamide, (c) Antibiotics — Dimethylchlortetracycline, Griseofulvin and tetracycline, (d) Benzofurans—Amiodarone,

(e) Chlorothiazide Diuretics—Chlorothiazide, hydrochlorothiazide and methyclothiazide, (f) Phenothiazines – chlorpromazine, promazine, prochlorperazine, promethazine and trimeprazine, (g) Psoralens—8 Methoxypsoralen.

15. Pityriasis rosea-like eruptions—Bismuth, gold, barbiturates and antihistamines.

16. Pigmentary changes—Contraceptive drugs, atabrine, chloroquin, chlorpromazine and silver salts.

17. Purpuric eruptions—Barbiturates, salicylates, meprobamate, organic arsenic, sulphonamides, chlorothiazide diuretics, dicumarol and long term use of corticosteroids.

18. Scarlet fever like eruptions or toxic erythema—Arsenic, barbiturates, codeine, morphine, mercury, quinidine, salicylates, sulphonamides and others.

19. Seborrheic dermatitis-like eruptions—Gold and ACTH.

20. Urticaria—Penicillin, salicylates, serums, sulphonamides, barbiturates, opium group, contraceptive drugs and Rauwolfia alkaloids.

21. Vesicular eruptions—Sulphonamides, penicillin, phenylbutazone and mephenytoin.

22. Whitening of hair—Chloroquin and hydroxychloroquin.

TREATMENT

STOPPAGE OF THE DRUG ANTIHISTAMINES
STEROIDS : LOCAL AND INTERNAL
LOCAL SOOTHING AGENTS

Immediate withdrawal of the drug is the first duty.

1. Local

a. Soothing tepid water bath along with corn-starch or Condy's lotion.

b. Lotio calamine with or without either 0.25% menthol or 1% phenol.

c. Steroid lotion.

2. **Internal**

a. Antihistamines. b. Steroids in severe cases.

c. Antibiotics, if secondary infection exists.

3. **Supportive measures**

a. Nutrition—Nourishing diet, electrolyte balance, extra protein and vitamins.

b. Avoidance of air-borne molecules of drugs.

c. Rest.

DISCUSSION

Correct suspicion of the offending drug is what is most needed and once that is made, the drug should be immediately stopped.

Treatment is mainly symptomatic and depends on the stage and extent of the lesions.

In most cases, after the withdrawal of the drug, the patient improves gradually. Severe damage of the vital organs should always be prevented.

ECZEMA

Eczema is inflammation of the skin due to a variety of causes. It is thus synonymous with dermatitis. However, according to some, only those dermatitis which have allergy at the background should be called **eczema** and the others should be termed **dermatitis.** Here we would take eczema as equivalent to dermatitis.

DIAGNOSIS

1. **Clinically,** eczema is characterised by a patterned reaction of skin having an evolution of the lesions in the following order.

A. **Erythema**→edema→papulation→vesiculation→bursting →oozing→ ± secondary infection→**pustulation** (**Acute eczema**)

B. **Erythema**→edema→papulation ± vesiculation→**Lichenification** consisting of

(i) thickening of skin

(ii) increased criss-cross marking of skin surface

(iii) hypo-or hyperpigmentation

(iv) itching (**Subacute eczema**)

C. **Lichenification**→severe thickening of skin with

(i) hyperkeratosis

(ii) cracking and fissures

(iii) hypo and hyperpigmentation ±

(iv) **scaling** (**Chronic eczema**)

In a given patient, a particular pattern of reaction may be seen or there could be a combination of various patterns or stages in one and different patches. There is thus an enormous variation of clinical expressions.

2. **Etiology** of eczema is varied and, for convenience, eczema is classified as :

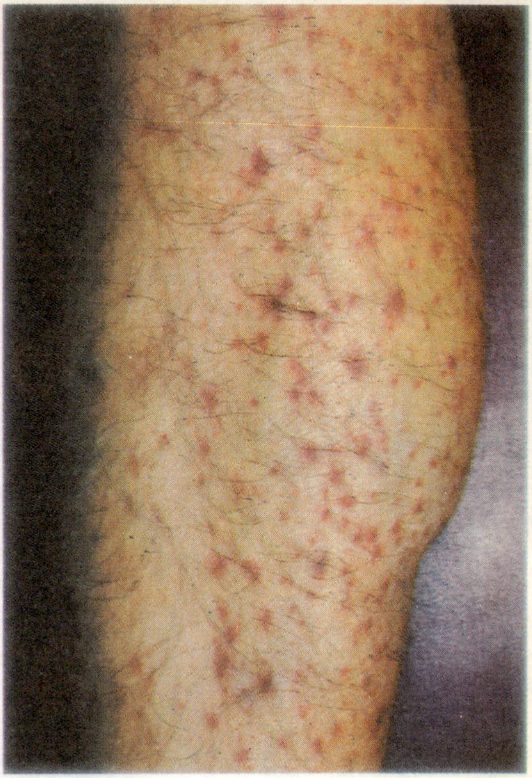

Fig. D-16. **Purpuric Drug Eruption** due to barbiturate

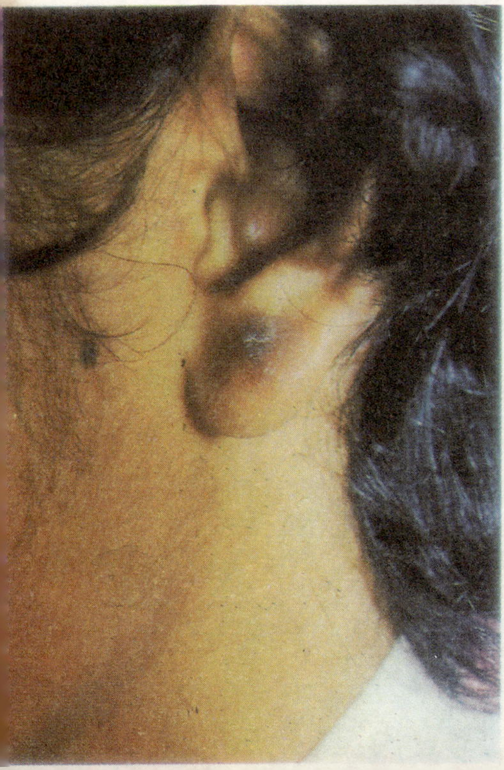

Fig. E-1. **Contact Dermatitis** of the ear lobule due to ornament

Exogeneous (Cause is outside the body)	Endogeneous (Cause is mainly in the body)
1. **Contact dermatitis**	1. **Atopic** dermatitis
a. **Primary irritant** dermatitis	2. **Seborrheic** dermatitis
b. **Allergic contact** dermatitis	3. **Lichen simplex**
2. **Microbic** eczema	4. **Pompholyx**
3. **Scabious** eczema	a. **Cheiro** pompholyx
	b. **Podo** pompholyx
4. **Photosensitive** dermatitis	5. **Pityriasis alba**
5. **Plant** dermatitis	6. **Varicose** eczema
6. **Phytophoto** dermatitis	7. **Nummular** eczema
7. **Winter** eczema	8. **Lichen striatus**
8. **Dermatitis venenata** or **topical drug** dermatitis	9. **Id eruption**
	10. **Autoimmune progesterone** dermatitis
	11. **Stress** eczema
	12. **Exfoliative** dermatitis

Each of the above eczema has its own characteristics. But often they show in general some clinical signs of eczema.

3. Pathogenesis of eczema is complex. But basically it is an immunological reaction with liberation of many lymphokinins. About 25 lymphokinins have so far been identified. All of them are to some extent inflammatogenic. Prostaglandins are also liberated at the site of eczema and add to inflammation. Histamine, serotonin and SRS-A also take part in the formation of eczema. The origin of these are mast cells and basophils.

Certain important facts having clinical relevance are known about eczema. They are the following.

A. There is a predisposition to eczema that often runs in family. This susceptibility is inherent and may be traced to genetic factors.

B. Internal metabolic disturbances may also precipitate eczema.

C. Hundreds of contactants (allergens) may cause eczema.

D. Expression of eczema is extremely varied.

E. Exogenous eczemas are cured if the patient remains free from contactants or allergens.

F. Endogenous eczema can be treated well to keep the patient symptom-free.

G. Facts about the exact pathogenesis of eczema are not yet fully known.

H. Dermatitis venenata or allergic contact dermatitis due to local application of drugs is often caused by

1. Sulphonamides
2. Penicillin
3. Antihistamines
4. Neomycin
5. Streptomycin
6. Formaldehyde
7. Caine group of drugs e. g. benzocaine, lignocaine, novocaine etc.

I. Allergic contact dermatitis are generally caused by

Sites	Causing Agents
a. Face	Cosmetics, Hair dyes
b. Ear and Ear lobule	Ornaments
c. Ear canal	Locally appiled drugs
d. Eyelids	Cosmetics, Nail polish
e. Nose	Spectacles
f Lips	Lipsticks, Toothpaste
g. Neck	Perfumes (scents), Woollen clothes
h. Axilla	Deodorants, Cosmetics, Clothes
i. Back	Nickle straps
j. Breast	Elastic and synthetic materials of brassier
k. Waist	Elastic material
l. Perianal area	Drugs used for anal fissure and piles, Toilet paper
m. Genitalia	Topical contraceptives, Condomes
n. Arms and thigh	Plants (perthenium)
o. Wrist	Watch bands, Ornaments
p. Hands	Soaps, Detergents, Plants, Gloves
q. Feet	Drugs, Shoes

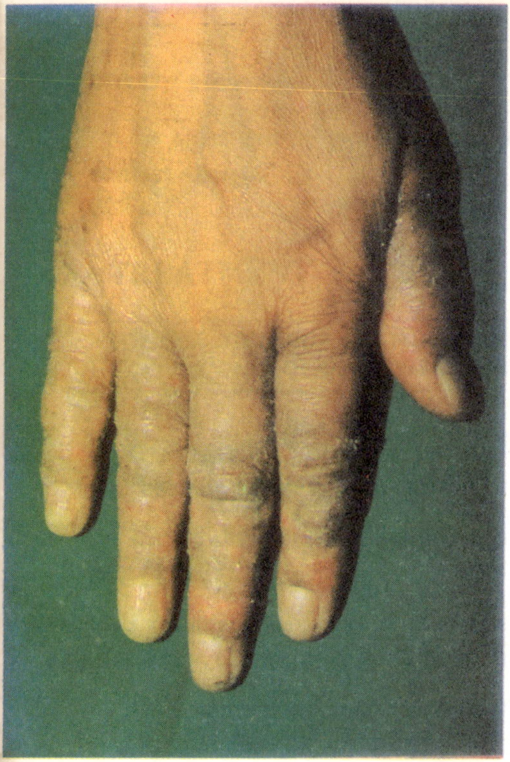

Fig. E-2. **Contact Dermatitis** of the dorsum of hand showing chronically inflammed patch with erosion scaling and cracks.

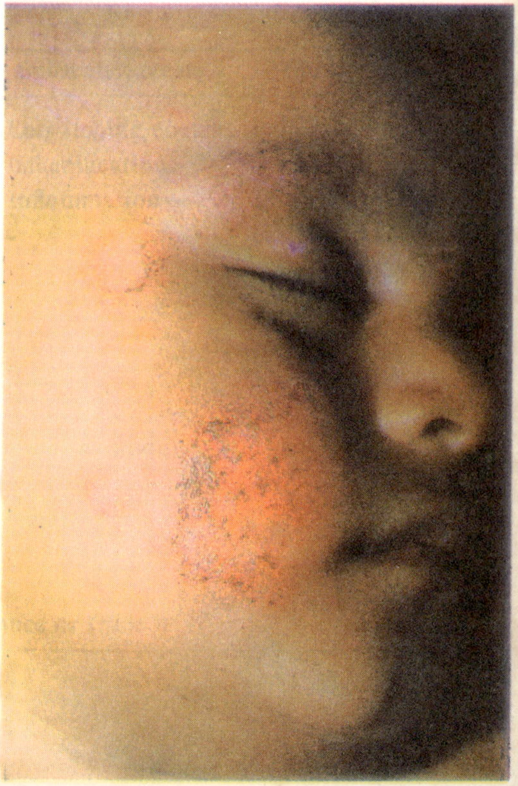

Fig. E-3. **Atopic Dermatitis** (infantile eczema) showing mildly inflammed patches on face.

Acute eczema	Subacute eczema	Chronic
2. Local application of a. Steroid lotion ± antibiotic b. Calamine lotion	Steroid cream	2a. Steroid ointment 2b. Do + polythene occlusion at night 2c. Injection of steroid intralesionally i. 25 mg per cc. of hydrocortizone ii. 10 mg per cc. of kenacort^{R}. 3. Grenz ray 4. Thorium X
B. Internal drugs 1. Antihistamines 2. Antibiotics 3. Tranquilisers 4. Sedatives 5. Oral or injection of calcium 6. Internal steroid in fulminating case or acute urgency.	May be continued according to necessity.	1. Antihistamines 2. Sedatives 3. Tranquilisers

DISCUSSION

Etiology and pathogenesis of eczema are complex. Diagnosis is made if itching, erythema, edema, vesiculation and lichenification are observed.

Treatment according to etiological factor is ideal. However, in many patients, exact etiology cannot be determined. Symptomatic management is then necessary and many do respond well with this approach.

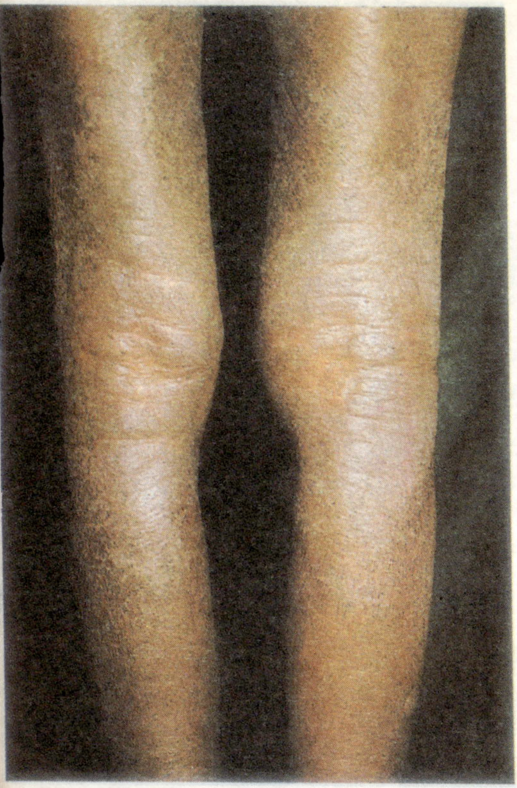

Fig. E-4. **Atopic Dermatitis** showing flexual lichenified eczema at the popliteal fossae.

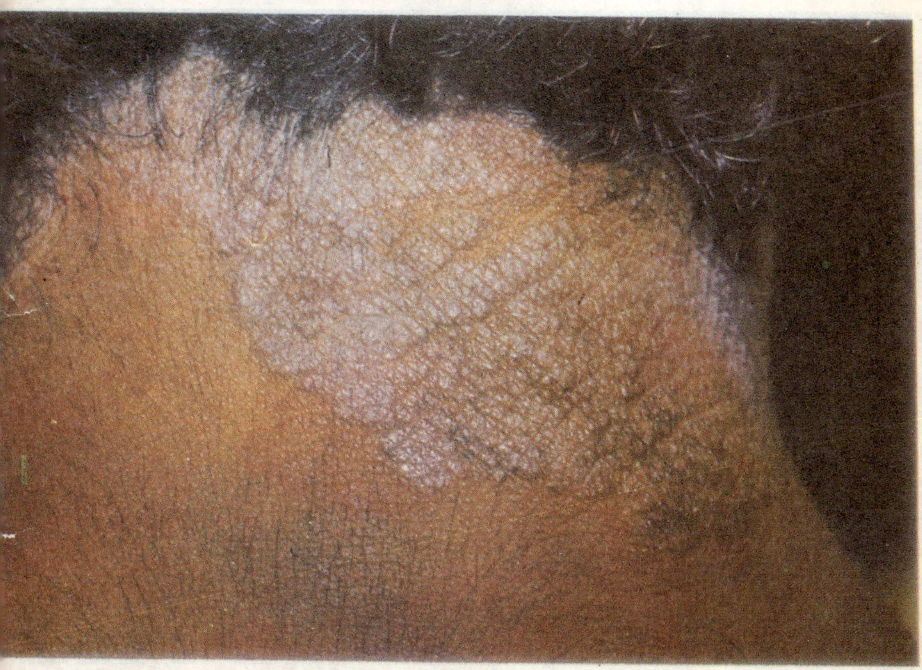

Fig. E-5. **Lichen Simplex** of the neck showing gross lichenification

Rest, cold compress with Condy's lotion 10-15 minutes before bath, local application of steroid lotion with or without antibiotic, internal antibiotic and antihistamines can control most of the acute eczema cases. Rarely in wide spread cases or in exfoliative dermatitis 30-60 mg of prednisolone internally may be needed.

In subacute cases, steroid cream, antihistamines and rarely mild antibiotics are necessary.

In chronic patients, application of steroid ointment under occlusion at night for 6-8 hours and intralesional injection of steroid by multiple puncture technique with intradermal needle weekly or fortnightly under cover of antibiotic and antihistamines are extremely helpful.

Recurrence, which is not uncommon, should be re-treated with more attention to avoid precipitating factors.

Sympathy and reassurance are extremely helpful.

ERYTHEMA MULTIFORME

It is an uncommon disease of unknown etiology and is characterised by red iris-shaped macules, papules and bullae confined primarily to the extremities, the face and the lips. Some believe that it is rather a symptom complex than a well defined disease.

DIAGNOSIS

1. **The characteristics of lesions** are as under.

a. **Pathognomonic lesion** is called 'target' (iris-shaped) lesion. It is a plaque, 1-2 cm diameter, with an elevated circular border and a depressed inner ring with a central erythema. Hence the name 'target'. Instead of erythema, there may be a small vesicle or even bulla.

b. The lesions **at the onset** are papules on the dorsa of hands and feet. They grow larger, become numerous, extend proximally and often become vesicular. They are bilaterally symmetrical.

c. Onset may be sudden with **constitutional symptoms** of malaise, fever, cough, muscular aches and pains, joint pains and general weakness. A mild amount of pruritus and urticaria are often observed. Rarely, there may be severe toxicity.

d. **Mucous membrane lesions** are not uncommon. They are vesicles or bullae on lips and white patches or erosions of buccal cavity, tongue or other mucous membranes. Condition with plentiful of bullae is termed **'Erythema multiforme bullosum'.**

e. **Stevens-Johnson syndrome** is a severe and often fatal variant of erythema multiforme. It is characterised by high fever, extensive purpura, bullae, ulcers of skin and mucous membrane. It affects buccal cavity, nasal passage, eyes and genitalia. Conjunctival and corneal lesions are present in 90% of cases. Serious complication is blindness. A patchy pneumonia is often present. General prostration is severe. Arthritis may be present. Acute tubular necrosis has been

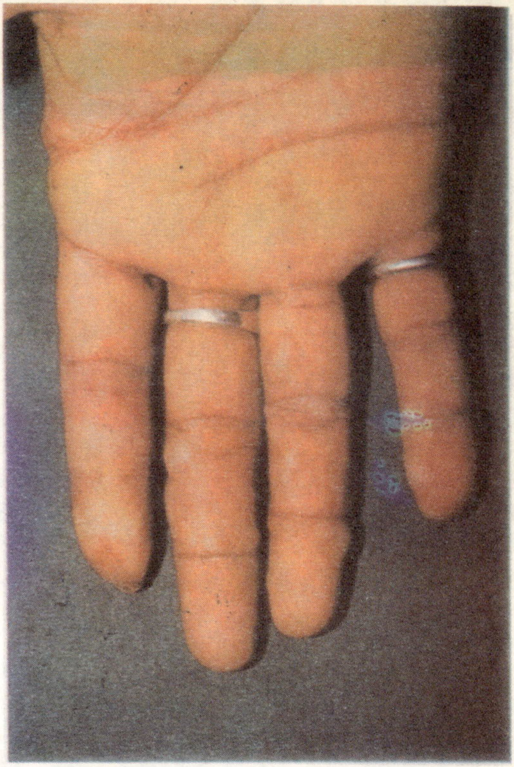

Fig. E-6. **Cheiropompholyx** showing vesicles of the fingers.

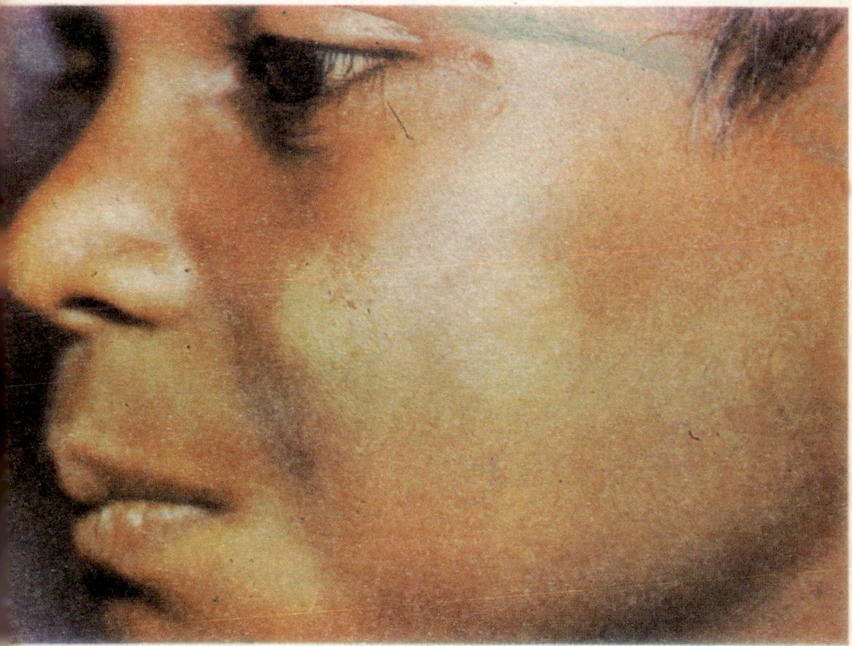

g. E-7. **Pityriasis Alba** showing white patches on the face of a child.

reported. This is called **'major form'** of E. multiforme. Large bullae may be painful. There may be photophobia and inability to ingest food or fluids due to erosion of mucosa.

f. Some believe that **toxic epidermal necrolysis of the Lyell type** is a variant of erythema multiforme. Blister formation is so extensive that sheets of skin lift off.

2. Etiological factors

a. Affects mainly young adults, male and female equally. Children are sometimes affected.

b. Causes are many and difficult to trace. They are grouped as under.

i. Drugs—Sulphonamides, penicillin, trimethadione, phenolphthalein, phenytoin, phenacetin, hydralazine, quinine, barbiturates, phenyl butazone, nitrogen mustard, antitoxins, gold, birth control pills, mercury.

ii. Virus—Herpes simplex (commonest cause), coxsackie B5, ECHO 9 virus, infectious mononucleosis, hepatitis B, viral pneumonia, milkers nodules, orf, mumps, Influenza A, lymphogranuloma venereum, ornithosis, adenovirus, small pox vaccination.

iii. Bacterial — Gonorrhea, streptococcus hemolyticus, staphylococcus, tuberculosis, vibrio para-hemolyticus, dental infection.

iv. Mycoplasma—M. pneumoniae (PPLO agent, walking pneumonia, Eaton agent pneumonia).

v. Fungus—Histoplasmosis, coccidioidomycosis and dermatophytosis.

vi. Neoplasia—Leukemia.

vii. Collagen disease—SLE, dermatomyositis.

viii. X-ray therapy. **ix.** Pregnancy. **x. Idiopathic.**

xi. Miscellaneous—Trichomoniasis, inhalants, eye drops, cold, sunlight, pollens, syphilis, exposure to trichloroethylene and formaldehyde.

Many etiologic agents are common to E. multiforme and E. nodosum and they are often found together.

Careful examination reveals the potential cause only in 50-60% cases.

3. **Pathophysiology** : It is a reaction pattern of skin. Etiological agents are varied and diverse. Probably, it is an immunological disorder. The initial characteristic histologic change is the endothelial cell swelling followed by dermal papillary edema and perivascular lymphohistiocytic infiltrate. Later, epidermal necrosis, dermal-epidermal interface alteration and subepidermal or, less frequently, intraepidermal separation and bulla formation occur. Complement and immunoglobulin are present in the superficial cutaneous microvasculature in early lesions and also circulating immune complex in serum. Immune complex deposition in vessel walls probably plays the main role in pathophysiology. In severe oozing from the bullous lesions, there may be electrolyte imbalance and protein loss.

4. **Histology**

a. Necrotic keratinocytes.

b. Sometimes spongiosis, rarely intraepidermal vesicles.

c. Basal layer liquefaction, sometimes there may be subepidermal blisters.

d. Edema of the papillary dermis.

e. Perivasuclar lymphohistiocytic infiltrate, often at dermal-epidermal junction, rarely with eosinophils.

f. Sometimes red blood cell extravasation.

5. **Laboratory investigations**

a. Leucocytosis **b.** Raised ESR **c.** Albuminuria **d.** Hematuria e. Raised ASO titer **f.** Immunofluorescence studies g. X-ray chest **h.** Cold agglutinin estimation.

6. **Course and prognosis**

a. Most cases of E. multiforme continue for 10 to 15 days followed by slow, spontaneous resolution.

b. Post inflammatory pigmentation may be left at some lesional sites.

c. Recurrent episodes are common in herpes simplex infection (10-15% of cases).

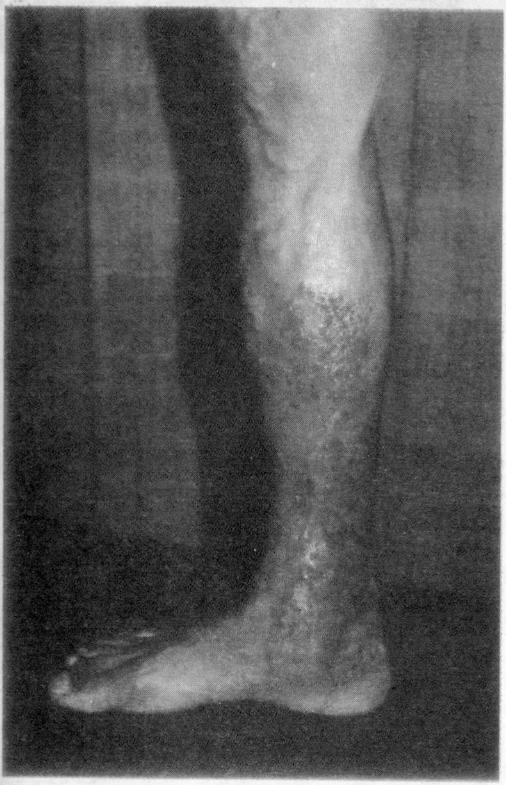

Fig. E-8. **Acute Varicose Eczema** with visible varicose veins.

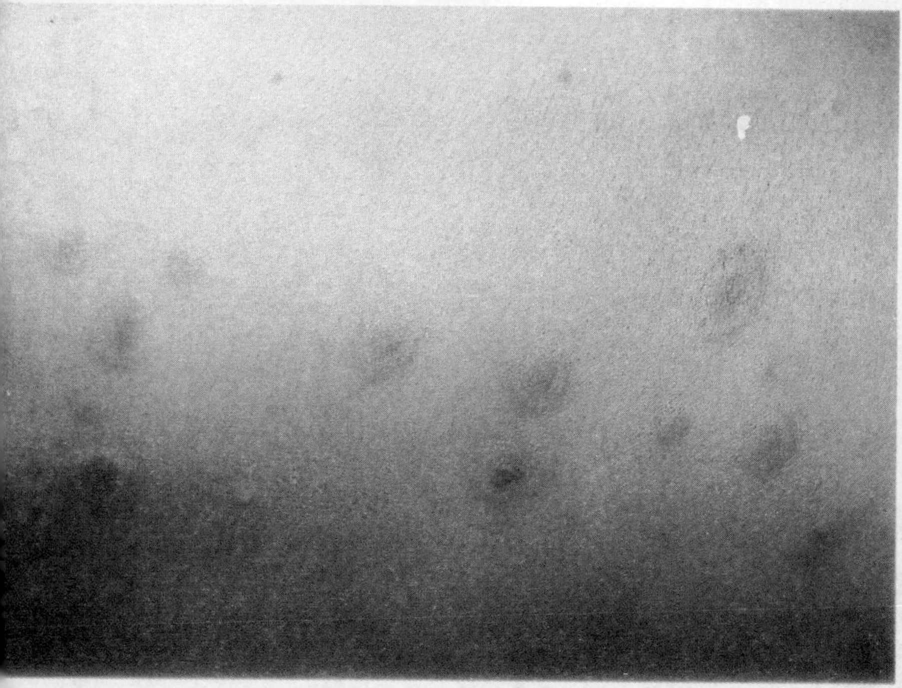

. E-9. **Erythema Multiforme** showing characteristic 'target' lesions.

d. Prognosis of Stevens-Johnson syndrome is often uncertain and may be serious and life threatening.

e. Keratitis sicca with corneal pannus is a serious sequel. Symblepheron, entropion and stricture of lacrimal puncta may occur.

TREATMENT

CORTICOSTEROIDS ANTIBIOTICS	ACYLOVIR AZATHIOPRINE

A. General measures

a. Potential etiologic agent should be eliminated.

b. Maintenance of nutrition with bland foods. **c.** Rest

B. Local measures

a. Wet compress with Condy's lotion or Burow's solution for bullous and erosive lesions.

b. Povidone iodine mouth washes for asepsis.

c. Benadryl[R] elixir mouth washes for lessening pain and facilitating intake of food.

d. In severe cases, viscous xylocaine may be kept in mouth for relief of pain.

e. If eye is involved, ophthalmologist should invariably be consulted.

f. Genital involvment should be tenderly cared. Sitz bath relieves symptoms. Catheterisation may be required.

g. For painful erosions, vaseline, polysporin or bacitracin ointment application might be helpful.

C. Internal

a. Mild form of erythema multiforme requires no treatment and heals spontaneously in 2-3 weeks.

b. Antihistaminics, as needed, for the relief of itching.

c. Aspirin 600 mg q.i.d.

d. In Stevens-Johnson syndrome **prednisolone** 80-120 mg orally or equivalent in I. M. or I. V., gradually to be tapered within 3 to 6 weeks. Some, however, do not believe in its efficacy.

e. Antibiotics as needed e.g. erythromycin, tetracylines, cephalosporins etc.

f. Proper fluid and electrolyte balance.

g. Symptomatic treatment of pneumonia and urinary tract infection, if any.

h. Acyclovir locally or orally and idoxyuridine locally in viral infection.

i. **Azathioprine** 100 mg/day for three months in idiopathic persistent cases.

j. Aqueous zinc sulphate (0.05%) as a compress or mouth wash is helpful in patients with active herpes simplex. Zinc ion inhibits replication of herpes simplex virus type 1.

k. **Dapsone** 100 mg/day for 3-5 months is effective in recalcitrant cases.

l. **Hydroxychloroquin** 200 mg/day in photoallergic cases.

m. **Thalidomide** 200 mg/day is sometimes helpful in recurrent E. multiforme.

n. Potassium iodide 300 mg t.i.d. for 2 weeks might prove useful.

DISCUSSION

E. multiforme is an acute skin eruption having an immunologically determined reaction pattern of the skin to a number of infections and drugs. The commonest etiology is a reaction to recurrent herpes simplex virus infection, both type 1 and type 2.

Target lesions are said to be pathognomonic but multiform lesions e.g. erythema, papules, plaques, urticaria, vesicles or bullae are also present in the same patient with more or less bilateral symmetry. The lesions appear in crops for 2 to 3 weeks and finally, in most cases, heal without scarring.

Stevens-Johnson syndrome represents the severest form of E. multiforme having serious complications threatening the life.

Treatment is mostly symptomatic. However, search for etiologic agents should be made seriously and, if found, should be rectified urgently.

Electrolyte balance, maintenance of nutrition and internal steriods are the tripods on which the successful therapy rests in severe cases. If infection is suspected as the cause, antibiotics are the rational and necessary weapon. In the totally idiopathic case, a short course of erythromycin may abort the lesions of E. multiforme.

It is a disease to be fought with all our weapons at the armoury and skill of the trade. We must aim at detecting its cause, treating the disease, eliminating its source and preventing the recurrence.

ERYTHEMA NODOSUM

DIAGNOSIS

1. It is an acute **hypersensitivity** reaction characterised by **painful nodules** seen usually on anterior and lateral aspects of lower legs or trunk.

2. The etiological agents responsible are :

 a. **Microbial agents** : Tuberculosis, Streptococcus, Lympho-granuloma venereum, Leprosy, Cat-scratch disease, Yersinia enterocolitica, Coccidioidomycosis, Histoplasmosis, Dermatophytosis etc.

 b. **Drugs** : Oral contraceptives, Sulphonamides, Penicillin, Chlorothiazides, Dilantin, Bromides, Iodides, Arsphenamine, Phenacetin, certain metal salts.

 c. **Colitis** : Ulcerative colitis, regional enteritis.

 d. **Miscellaneous** : Sarcoidosis, Behcet's syndrome.

 e. **Idiopathic**

3. **Malaise** and **joint pain,** with or without fever, may last for 2 weeks before the onset. Lesions are painful, red, rounded or oval, tense, shiny nodules reaching full size of 2 to 5 cm diameter in 24 hours. Nodules appear in crops and are usually symmetrical in distribution. Pre-tibial area is the commonest site of involvement. But sometimes arms, and rarely, face are involved. Nodules usually subside in 2-3 weeks without sequel. Mild hyperpigmentation might however in some cases persist.

4. Cause must be sought from complete history, physical examination and laboratory study. Chest X-ray, Mantoux test, throat culture, ASO titre, erythrocyte sedimentation rate, slit skin smear for acid-fast bacilli are some of the procedures that might help.

5. **Histopathologically,** there is **septal inflammation** together with inflammation of septal blood vessels in subcutaneous

tissue. Usually the inflammation is **lymphohistiocytic** with only a slight admixture of neutrophils. The dermis may show a moderate amount of a perivascular, chronic, inflammatory infiltrate.

TREATMENT

REST UNDERLYING CAUSE ANTIBIOTICS
NON-STEROIDAL ANTIINFLAMMATORY DRUGS
IODIDES STEROIDS

1. No specific therapy is needed for majority of patients.

2. Pain may be reduced by **bed rest.** During sitting, legs should be kept elevated. **Salicylates** in routine dosage are adequate to relieve pain.

3. Potassium iodide 360 to 900 mg or saturated solution of potassium iodide (SSKI) 0.36 to 0.90 ml (6-15 drops) in **fruit juice** daily in two divided doses for 3 to 4 weeks is often helpful. The dose should be gradually tapered for otherwise recurrence is likely.

4. If any etiological agent could be traced, treatment for the same should be carried out.

5. In chronic or recurrent, but otherwise unresponsive, case where cause remains obscure **injection of** litle **corticosteroid intra-lesionally** may cause involution of the lesion within 48-72 hours. A short term course (1 to 2 weeks) of **oral corticosteroid** may also prove beneficial. In this case, underlying turberculosis (if any) must be excluded cautiously.

6. **Chloroquine** 250 mg daily with gradual tapering has also been suggested in unresponsive cases.

7. **Analgesics**—Aspirin, Indomethacin, Colchicine, Phenylbutazone.

8. **Miscellaneous drugs**—Dapsone, chloroquine.

DISCUSSION

In a developing country like India, turberculosis, streptococcal infection and leprosy are the common associates of erythema nodosum. No stone should thus be left unturned to seek for the underlying problem of which erythema nodosum is only an external expression. Treatment of the underlying disorder is very important, more than that of erythema nodosum alone.

However, the nodular vasculitis giving rise to erythema nodosum might overlap with figurate erythemas, erythema multiforme, necrotising vasculitis group and even urticaria. A thorough search for the precipitating agent e.g. drugs, infection, infestation, stings, bites, damaged tissue acting for autoimmune process, sarcoidosis, dysproteinemias, collagen diseases and even the food or inhalants, must therefore be made at all cost.

ERYTHRASMA

DIAGNOSIS

1. It is a common superficial **bacterial infection** of **intertriginous areas** caused by corynebacterium minutissimum.

2. Clinically, it is characterised by **fine scaling, pink to brown-coloured patches.** Most often it is symptomless, but **mild itching** may be present.

3. Sites involved

a. Axillae and groin. **b.** Intramammary folds.

c. Umbilicus. **d.** Gluteal cleft.

e. Toe webs—involved in 30% of cases but clinical detection of involvement of this site is often overlooked. It is characterised by (1) Maceration, (2) Fissuring and (3) Scaling.

f. Wide spread involvement of trunk and proximal extremities is seen occasionally in obese diabetic adults.

Differentiation from fungal infection is difficult. C. minutissimum may be cultured. However, there may be combined infection. There may be infection with dermatophytes or candida albicans.

4. Laboratory investigation

a. Wood's light—All forms show coral red fluorescence due to porphyrin.

b. Gram stain—(1) Scales and (2) histologic materials show gram positive rods.

c. Electron microscopy—Shows organisms within cells of stratum corneum.

d. Culture—In special media containing 20% fetal bovine serum shows colonies which produce pigment and fluoresce coral-red under Wood's light.

TREATMENT

TOPICAL	INTERNAL
CLOTRIMAZOLE	ERYTHROMYCIN
ECONAZOLE	TETRACYCLINE
MICONAZOLE	CHLORAMPHENICOL
ERYTHROMYCIN	
TETRACYCLINE	

1. **Topical**

a. **Whitfield ointment**—Twice application for 2-3 weeks.

b. **3-6% Sulphur salicylic ointment.**

c. **1% Clotrimazole, econazole** and **1-2% miconazole cream**—Twice application for 4 weeks.

d. **2% Sodium fucidate ointment**— Applied similarly is found to be equally effective.

e. **Topical erythromycin** or **tetracycline ointment.**

f. **Antibacterial soap** is found to help in the clearance of lesions in some patients.

2. **Internal**

a. **Erythromycin** is the drug of choice ; 250 mg tab taken q.i.d. clears the lesions within 10-21 days.

b. **Tetracycline** is proved equally effective.

c. **Chloramphenicol** might have side effects but is found to be rather effective.

DISCUSSION

Erythrasma is too often misdiagnosed as fungal infection and treated with tolnaftate solution, mycostatin[R] ointment and internal griseofulvin. They are simply uselsss. Absence of central clearing and satellite lesions should be borne in mind.

Erythromycin is the **drug of choice** but any keratolytic ointment clears the condition in 3-4 weeks. However, recurrence is very common, especially in moist and humid weather or in obese diabetic patients.

Reduction of **obesity,** control of **diabetes,** regular application of **antiseptic soaps** and **keeping** the part **dry** by antibacterial powder would mostly prevent the relapse.

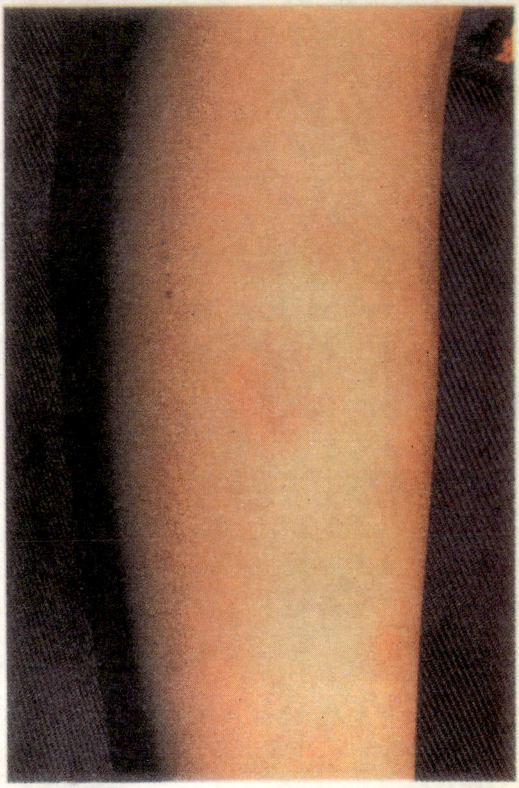

Fig. E-10. **Erythema Nodosum** showing nodular eruptions.

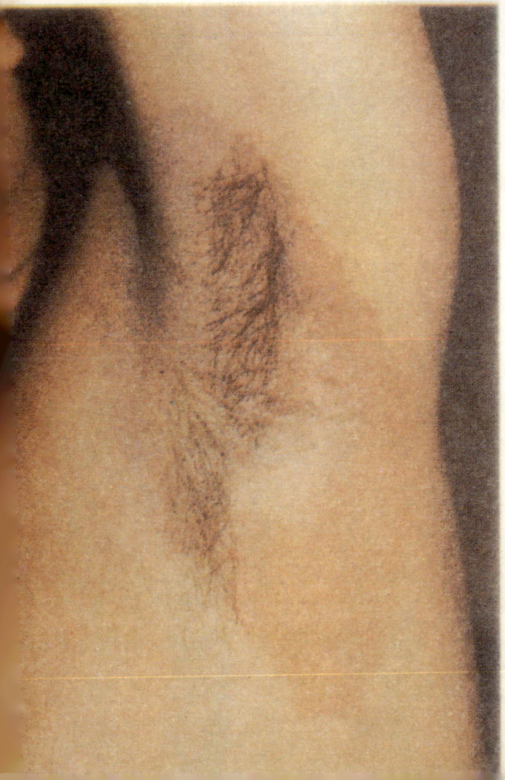

Fig. E-11. **Erythrasma** showing brown coloured patch at the axilla.

EXFOLIATIVE DERMATITIS

It is an **inflammatory disorder** of the skin with **generalised erythema** associated with small scale desquamation.

DIAGNOSIS

1. Etiology

In 50% patients exact etiology cannot be determined. Hence it is called **'idiopathic erythroderma'**. The rest is caused by (1) pre-existing skin disease (30%), (2) systemic disease (10%) and (3) drugs (10%). These are mentioned below in a tabular form alphabetically arranged.

Pre-existing skin disease	Systemic disease	Drugs
Atopic dermatitis	Acute leukemia	Allupurinol Amithiosone Antimalarials
Contact dermatitis	Carcinoma of lungs	Antimonials Arsenic Aspirin Atabrine
Dermatophytosis	Carcinoma of rectum Chronic leukemia	BAL
Eczema	Hodgkin's disease	Barbiturates
Leiner's disease	Lymphoma	Captopril Cephalosporins Codeine Chloroquine Chlorpropa- mide
Lichen planus	Multiple myeloma	
Mycosis fungoides	Mycosis fungoides	Dapsone Dactinomycin Diethylstilbesterol Dilantin
Norwegian scabies		Dimercaprol

Pre-existing skin disease	Systemic disease	Drugs
Pemphigus foliaceous	Reticulum cell sarcoma	Ethylene-diamine
		Gold
		Iodides
Pityriasis rubra pilaris		Iodine
Psoriasis		Isoniazid
		Lidocaine-hydrochloride
Reiter's syndrome		Lithium-carbonate
		Mephentoin
		Mercury
		Mercurials
Seborrheic dermatitis		Para-amino-salicylic acid
		Penicillin
		Phenacemide
		Pheneturide
Stasis dermatitis		Phenindione
		Phenobarbital
		Phenothiazines
		Phenylbutazone
		Potassium-thiocyanide
		Practolol
		Quinine
		Quinacrine
		Quinidine
		Sulphonamides
		Streptomycin
		Tetracyclines
		Trimethadione
		Vitamin-A

2. Pathology

a. There is an increase in the rate of epidermal turn over. This leads to a continuous exfoliation. The number of germinative cells and their absolute mitotic rate are increased. Transit time of the cells through the epidermis is shortened. About 20-30 g of exfoliated material is lost every day.

b. Many of the epidermal constituents are re-absorbed by the tissue after enzymatic hydrolysis. Nucleic acids and their degradation products are lost considerably. Soluble proteins are also similarly lost but free amino acids are retained.

c. There is generalised cutaneous vasodilatation and continuous heat loss along with evaporative water loss.

d. Lymphadenopathy occurs in 60% of patients.

e. Hepatomegaly is found in 20-35% of patients.

f. Spenomegaly is present in 3% patients, mostly those who suffer from lymphoma.

g. Abnormalities in vasculature and temperature control

i. About 40-80% patients show rise of temperature above 38° C.

ii. There may be marked hypothermia ; it may be as low as 28 to 30°C.

iii. Skin responds less to vasoconstrictive stimuli.

iv. Tachycardia and elevated cardiac output are present in most of the cases.

v. Cardiac failure may also occur.

h. Metabolic changes

(a) Basal metabolic rate is +50 to +100.

(b) Metabolic changes are similar to burns e.g. negative nitrogen balance causes **hypoalbuminemia, edema** and **loss of muscle mass**; negative potassium balance; large amount of extra-renal water loss due to defect in barrier function.

i. Changes in blood

(a) Anemia (b) Eosinophilia (c) Serum electrolyte abnormalities (d) Elevated ESR (e) Leucocytosis (f) Peripheral blood lymphocytosis (g) Pathologic serum electrophoresis (h) Elevated serum IgE.

j. **Histopathology**

(a) Hyperkeratosis and parakeratosis

(b) Acanthosis

(c) Variable degree of spongiosis along with micro-abscess formation.

(d) Dermal papillae are elongated and widened.

(e) Dilated blood vessels with perivascular infiltrate containing lymphocytes, histiocytes, plasma cells, eosinophils and rarely mast cells.

(f) Features of original skin disease may be found e.g. psoriasis, mycosis fungoides, seborrheic dermatitis, leukemia and such others.

(g) Lymphnode biopsy is necessary for finding the etiologic factors.

3. **Clinical features**

a. **Complaints** : Malaise, severe weakness, fever, chillness, low body temperature, itching, burning, exfoliation, loss of hairs, nail deformities, loss of weight.

b. **Average of patients** : About 70% patients are males, mean age is 50 years, mean duration of illness is 5 years.

c. **General survey** : Erythema, exfoliation, anemia, tachycardia, pedal edema, hair loss, nail deformity or nail loss, ectropion, high or low body temperature, congested eyes, wasting of muscles, cracks in palms and soles, dryness of skin or moist and exudative skin with superficial yellow crust due to dried serum protein or secondary infection, generalised lymphadenopathy—also called **'dermatopathic lymphadenopathy'**.

4. **Prognosis and complications**

a. Sometimes fatal even after proper treatment

b. Septicemia c. Severe debility

d. Pneumonia e. High output cardiac failure

f. Undiminished erythroderma for indefinite period

g. Many recover completely or improve greatly over time.

TREATMENT

ETIOLOGIC APPROACH	SALINE COMPRESS
HOMEOSTATIC MEASURES	BLAND APPLICATIONS
STEROIDS : TOPICAL, SYSTEMIC	ERYTHROMYCIN

1. A thorough search to determine the etiology is essential. If it is found to be drug related, withdrawal of the drug cures the condition.

2. General measures

a. Balanced diet to compensate protein and mineral loss.

b. Sufficient fluid intake to compensate for the increased cutaneous loss.

c. Patient should be kept in warm environment in order to prevent heat loss.

d. Bland emollients may often relieve pruritus and also lessens the heat loss.

e. Oral antihistaminics to lessen pruritus.

f. Observation of skin hygiene.

g. Treatment of local infection.

h. Physiological saline compress is ideal.

3. Internal steroids

Exfoliative dermatitis is a serious emergency medical problem due to (1) the loss of protein and electrolyte balance, (2) change in circulatory status and (3) severe imbalance of body temperature. Large oral dose of prednisolone can help in emergent situation. Most patients would require 60 mg daily dose to control the exfoliation. This should be continued as long as necessary and on achieving normality of the skin, the dose should be gradually tapered to the lowest minimal dose. Necessary precaution for long term steroid therapy e.g. supplementation with anabolic steroids, calcium, vitamins, minerals and potassium should always be taken.

4. Miscellaneous therapy

a. Corticosteroid ointments are effective in relieving the inflammatory component, although there is a high possibility of percutaneous absorption.

b. Photochemotherapy i.e. PUVA is of value in the case of mycosis fungoides.

c. Internal antibiotics are necessary in controlling secondary infection or pneumonia.

d. Daily warm bath followed by application of bland oily lotion of equal parts of arachis oil and lime water gives relief to some patients.

DISCUSSION

Exfoliative dermatitis is the ultimate inflammatory response of the skin. About 90% of the skin is involved with erythema and various grades of exfoliation. Massive vasodilatation causes a circulatory shunt which strains the heart. Vascular bed of the skin and sweat glands can no longer provide the normal themoregulatory control. Patient becomes poikilothermic. Critical loss of water, proteins and electrolytes occur through the skin. Pathologic permeability of the skin causes intolerance to many local applications and homeostatic crisis develops.

Patient should be kept at rest in warm and moist atmosphere. Blandest compresses and lubricants should be used and all possible nutritional supplements be given.

For secondary infection in damaged skin and for extra bacterial growth, a course of antibiotic, especially erythromycin, is needed.

Specific therapy for the cause is always advisable e.g. methotrexate in psoriasis, chemotherapy in lymphoma, correction of vascular problem in stasis ulcer.

The patient needs gentle care and support during the lengthy period of treatment.

The common causes of death are pneumonia, heart failure and septicemia.

Prolonged **internal steroid** therapy is still the **mainstay** in idiopathic exfoliative dermatitis. Fortunately, however, many patients improve automatically and get rid of the malady.

GONORRHOEA

DIAGNOSIS

1. It is the most common sexually transmitted disease (STD) and is caused by Neisseria Gonorrhoea, a gram negative diplococci typically found inside polymorphonuclear cells.

Clinical manifestations are a bit different in men and women. Asymptomatic patients are not uncommon.

Usual Age : 15-30 years and Incubation period : 2-8 days.

2. Symptoms and signs

Men

i. Initially–Burning on urination, serous or milky discharge.

ii. 24 to 72 hours after–Urethral pain is pronounced, discharge is yellow, creamy, profuse and sometimes blood tinged and fever.

iii. Without treatment–There may be regression, or it may progress to involve prostrate, epididymis and periurethral glands with acute painful inflammation. Later, these lead to chronic prostratitis and urethral strictures. Rectal infection is common in homosexual men. In anogenital coitus pharynx may be infected.

iv. Systemic complications via blood stream—Bacteremia characterised by intermittent fever, arthralgia, maculopapular, pustuler and hemorrhagic rashes. Endocarditis, arthritis of knees, ankles and wrists, tenosynovitis, iritis, conjunctivitis and ophthalmia neonatorum, panophthalmitis.

Women

i. Dysuria, frequency and urgency of micturition

ii. Purulent urethral discharge

iii. Vaginitis with discharge

iv. Cervicitis : acute or chronic (main reservoir of infection in the society)

v. Bartholinitis **vi.** Infection of the uterus

vii. Acute or chronic salpingitis

viii. Scarring of tubes and sterility

ix. Proctitis in anal coitus x. Pelvic inflammation

xi. Systemic complications as in men

4. **Laboratory findings**

a. Urethral smear shows typical gram negative diplococci in polymorphs. Less positive in women.

b. **Culture**

In selective media such as

i. Thayer–Martin media

ii. Transgrow media (it is suitable for transport if laboratory is not easily available)–incubated at 37°C in 10% CO_2 atmosphere.

c. **Specimens are**

i. urethral pus ii. material from prostratic massage iii. cervical pus or material iv. rectal material v. pharyngeal secretion vi. specimen from joint vii. material from skin lesions.

Colonies are identified by (1) Gram stain, (2) Oxidase test and (3) Immunofluorescence.

d. **Serologic tests**

In infected individuals, antibodies to gonococcal pili and outer membrane proteins can be detected by several serologic methods, including radioimmunoassay and enzyme-linked immunosorbent assay (ELISA) test.

TREATMENT

PROCAINE PENICILLIN	DOXYCYCLINE
PROBENECID	SPECTINOMYCIN
AMPICILLIN	ROSAXACIN
AMOXICILLIN	NORFLOXACIN

1. **Prevention**

a. Proper **social education** is most important.

b. **Mechanical prophylaxis**—Condome can reduce the risk of infection.

c. **Chemical prophylaxis**

i. Penicillin prophylaxis contributes to the selection of penicillinase producing gonococci.

ii. Some believe in abortion of the disease by effective drug taken within 24 hours in adequate therapeutic dose.

iii. Intensive search for sex contacts by public health agencies should be made.

iv. Full treatment of contacts are sometimes necessary to assure reduction of reservoir of infection.

v. Ophthalmia neonatorum is prevented by applying (1) 1% silver nitrate solution, (2) 1% tetracycline ointment and (3) 1% erythromycin ointment immediately after birth.

2. **Uncomplicated gonorrhoea** (urethral, cervical, pharyngeal, rectal) : For both men and women the following are the effective regimens.

a. 1 g of probenecid orally followed by

b. 4.8 million units of **procaine penicillin** injected I.M. in 2 sites (buttocks).

c. **Amoxicillin** or **ampicillin** : 3.5 g orally in one dose followed by 500 mg of tetracycline 4 times daily for 7 days.

d. **Spectinomycin hydrochloride** : 2 g I.M., especially in penicillin failure cases.

e. 1 g of probenecid by mouth + cefoxitin 2 g I.M.

f. Trimethoprim-sulphamethoxazole 2 tab t.i.d. for a period of 1 week.

g. **Doxycycline** : 200 mg daily orally for 1 week.

h. **Erythromycin** : 500 mg orally, q.i.d. for 10 days.

i. **Rosaxacin** : 300 mg 1 cap stat.

j. **Norfloxacin** : 800 mg 1 tab stat.

k. **Cephalosporin** in usual dose.

3. **Acute epididymitis**

a. **Tetracycline** : 500 mg q.i.d. for 10 days.

b. **Doxycycline** : 100 mg b.i.d. for 10 days.

c. **Amoxicillin** : 500 mg t.i.d. for 10 days.

4. Arthritis and Gonococcemia—**Aqueous crystalline penicillin** 10 million units I.V. daily until there is improvement, followed by ampicillin or amoxicillin 500 mg q.i.d. for 10 days.

5. Meningitis and endocarditis and disseminated gonorrhoea. Same as above but

a. In meningitis : 10-14 days.

b. In endocarditis : 4 to 6 weeks.

6. Pelvic inflammatory disease

a. Indication for hospitalisation

i. Uncertain diagnosis

ii. Suspicion of pelvic abscess formation

iii. Severely ill patient. iv. Pregnancy

v. Inability to follow up

vi. Failure of response to average therapy

b. Treatment in hospital

i. **Doxycycline** : 100 mg I.V. b.i.d.+cefoxitin 2 g I.V. q.i.d. for 96 hours followed by doxycycline orally 100 mg b.i.d. for 10-14 days.

ii. **Clindamycin** : 600 mg I.V. q.i.d.+Gentamycin or Tobramycin 2 mg/kg I.V. followed by 1.5 mg/kg. t.i.d. for at least 96 hours. This is followed by oral clindamycin 450 mg q.i.d. for 14 days.

iii. **Doxycyline** : 100 mg I.V. b.i.d+metronidazole, 1 g I.V. b.i.d. for at least 96 hours followed by oral clindamycin 450 mg q.i.d. for 14 days.

c. Treatment as out-patient

i. **Cefoxitin** : 2 g I.M. with 1 g probenecid orally

ii. **Ampicillin/Amoxicillin** : 3.5 g orally + 1 g probenecid.

iii. **Aqueous procaine penicillin G** : 4.8 million units I.M.+1 g probenecid.

Any of the above is to be followed by doxycyline 100 mg b.i.d orally for 10-14 days.

7. **Prostatitis**

a. Usual drugs + **b.** sitz baths + **c.** diathermy.

8. **Symptomatic and supportive treatment**

a. Bed rest in acute stage.

b. Analgesics for pain.

c. Physical therapy in chronic cases.

8. Prognosis

a. 95% cure rate with proper therapy

b. Relapses require re-treatment.

c. Irreversible damage

i. Urethral stricture **ii.** Sterility

iii. Persistent tubo-ovarian abscess

iv. Valve destruction in endocarditis

v. Peritoneal adhesion with intestinal obstruction.

Proper surgical measure might help in these conditions.

d. Gonorrhoea may very often be combined with non-specific urethritis, syphilis, genital herpes or chlamydial infection. Proper follow up is thus necessary.

DISCUSSION

Essentials of diagnosis are : purulent discharge from urethra and cervix having positive smear and culture, dysuria, cervicitis, epididimytis, prostatitis, proctitis, vaginitis, salpingitis, periurethral inflammation, bartholinitis, fever, arthritis, skin lesions, conjunctivitis and pharyngitis.

The **best treatment** is injection of 4.8 million units of **aqueous procaine penicillin** with previous administration of 1 g probenecid. But most patients are treated now-a-days with second line of drugs e.g. ampicillin, amoxicillin, doxycyline, tetracycline, erythromycin and clindamycin. Eradicil and norfloxacin are new effective drugs.

Adequate dose is a must to get higher cure rate. Asymptomatic carriers deserve special attention.

GRANULOMA INGUINALE

This skin disorder is also known as Granuloma Venereum and Donovanosis.

DIAGNOSIS

1. It is a mildly contagious, **sexually transmitted auto-inoculable granulomatous infectious** disease involving **genitalia** and surrounding skin. It is caused by calymatobacterium granulomatis. It is prevalent more in tropics and subtropics and affects all races.

2. The incubation period is uncertain but probably in the range of 1 to 12 weeks. Male to female ratio is 3 : 1. Highest incidence occurs in the age range 20-45 years.

3. The initial lesions are **painless papules** on genitals. They ulcerate and slowly develop into granulation tissue and spreads in contiguity.

4. Inguinal adenitis does not occur, but subcutaneous granulation in the inguinal region can give rise to pseudobubos. The pseudobubos may burst and give rise to sinus formation.

5. Granulating lesions confined to anus may be the initial lesions in anoreceptive homosexuals. Ultimately, however, they get extended outside the anus.

6. **Characteristics** of the lesions are as follow.

a. Relatively painless **infiltrated nodules** which soon slough out.

b. A shallow, sharply demarcated, **ulcer** is formed with beefy-red friable base of granulation tissue.

c. Large ulcerations may advance onto the lower abdomen and thighs.

d. Scar formation and healing may occur in one border while the other border may be advancing.

e. The process may become indolent and stationary for years together.

f. Satellite lesions are common. They coalesce with one another to form **plaques.**

g. **Usual sites** of involvement—**1.** Prepuce **2.** Coronal sulcus **3.** Glans **4.** Penile shaft **5.** Anus **6.** Perianal area **7.** Labia majora **8.** Labia minora **9.** Inguinal region and groin **10.** Fourchette **11.** Cervix **12.** Perineum.

h. **Extragenital sites–1.** Oral cavity **2.** Lips **3.** Cheeks **4.** Neck **5.** Hands **6.** Gastrointestinal tract **7.** Periorbital area **8.** Bones.

i. **Different forms** of presentations are :

i. **Nodular form**—Nodules are **reddish** and **soft** which eventually **ulcerate.**

ii. **Ulcerovegetative form**—This is the most frequent type. It starts as nodular type but soon there is **excoriation** and **maceration** with friable surface. The surface is initially clean and pinkish but soon becomes **seropurulent** with greyish and dirty hue. The border is sharply demarcated, indurated and raised and spreads along inguinal creases. Spontaneous healing might take place with atrophic depigmented scars.

iii. **Hypertrophic type**—This consists of vegetating masses with a fetid odour.

iv. **Esthiomene type** – Similar to lymphogranuloma venereum, it is clinically manifested as mild hypertrophic ulceration to true elephantiasis having deep ulceration.

v. **Cicatrical type**—This leads to **keloidal lesions** which are progressive and characterised histologically by dense collagenous fibrous tissue.

j. Lymphatic obstruction may result in marked swelling in labia, clitoris, penis and scrotum.

k. During pregnancy the disease progresses rapidly.

7. Systemic **symptoms** and **signs**

a. Are generally slight.

b. But do have in secondary infection, **deep ulceration, rectal stricture,** or if there is extension to the fallopian tubes and ovaries. These may be

i. Excrutiating **pain** on walking.

ii. Symptoms of involvement of rectum, urinary tract and the vagina.

iii. Symptoms of concurrent venereal diseases.

iv. Symptoms of concomitant fusospirochetal infection giving rise to severe local mutilation.

8. **Squamous cell carcinoma** may occur in long-standing non-healing ulcers. Urethral stricture and rectal stenosis may also develop.

9. **Laboratory diagnosis**

a. **Specimen**—1. Aspiration material from pseudobubo 2. Material from papule, ulcer or granulation tissue and 3. Biopsy specimen.

b. **Grams stain**

1. Gram negative rods measuring 1.5 by 0.5 microns are present as encapsulated inclusions in large histiocytes.

2. In Wright-Giemsa or Worthin-Starry stains (argentaffin), polar staining causes a 'closed safety pin' configuration.

c. **Culture**

1. In artificial media
2. In chicken embryo } Difficult to get growth.

d. **Histopathology**

1. Central portion of the lesion shows absence of epidermis. 2. Lateral portion shows acanthosis and pseudo-epitheliomatous hyperplasia. 3. Dermal infiltrate consists of

a. predominantly histiocytes

b. plasma cells

c. neutrophilic abscess

d. parasitized histiocytes appear as vacuolated and multicystic. They contain intracytoplasmic inclusion bodies within each vacuole measuring 1-2 microns in diameter. Less seen with H & E stain but better with bipolar staining with Geimsa. Silver stain shows distinct bodies without capsules.

e. Ultra-thin sections, specially prepared for electron microscopy and stained with toluidine blue, show clear bodies.

TREATMENT

TETRACYCLINE	COTRIMAZOLE
STREPTOMYCIN	MINOCYCLINE

An early diagnosis and treatment give better therapeutic results. The following modes of treatment are available.

1. **Internal**

a. **Tetracycline :** 500 mg cap q.i.d. for 3 to 5 weeks.

b. **Ampicillin** : 500 mg cap q.i.d. for 12 weeks.

c. **Inj. Gentamycin** : 80 mg I.M. b.i.d for 3 weeks.

d. **Chloromycetin** : 500 mg q.i.d. for 2-3 weeks.

e. **Lincomycin** : Orally or by injection 500 mg t.d.s. for a period of 2-3 weeks.

f. **Sulphamethoxazole and trimethoprim tab** : 2 tab b.i.d. for 4-6 weeks.

g. **Inj. Streptomycin :** 1 g I.M. b.i.d. for 10 days.

h. **Erythromycin** : 500 mg q.i.d. for 2-3 weeks.

i. **Erythromycin** and **Lincomycin** combined in severe cases, especially in pregnancy.

j. **Minocycline** : 100 mg b.i.d. for 2 weeks.

k. **Triacetyl oleandomycin** : 1-2 g daily for 3 weeks.

2. **Local**

a. Cleansing with Condy's lotion.

b. Electrodesiccation of resistant lesions.

c. Plastic surgical repair of large lesions.

DISCUSSION

Earliest lesion may be a minute vesicle and may often be missed. Resistant granulomatous ulcer without much pain and lymphadenopathy should be investigated for laboratory diagnosis.

Early treatment resolves the lesions without any sequel. To prevent relapse, treatment is to be continued for 1 to 2 weeks more, even after the apparent cure. If the lesions are not improved by ten days, it should be inferred that either there is antibiotic resistance or the diagnosis is at fault. Reports of **tetracycline** resistance is not uncommon although it is still the **drug of choice**. Cotrimazole is quite good. Due to intolerance, earlier therapy of 4 g of streptomycin I. M. daily for five days has been modified to 1 g b.i.d. for a period of 10 days.

Gastrointestinal dysfunctions due to prolonged antibiotic therapy should be compensated by adequate administration of Vitamin B-complex, digestive enzymes and yeast cells.

Plastic surgery helps in the reorganisation of severely damaged tissues.

Injection of even high doses of penicillin is found to be totally ineffective.

Follow up for other sexually transmitted diseases e.g. syphilis, non-specific urethritis and herpes progenitalis should always be made.

HANSEN'S DISEASE (H. D.)

It is a chronic infectious disease caused by mycobacterium leprae. It affects primarily the nerve tissue at all levels from peripheral nerve twigs to the dorsal root ganglia. Skin is involved only secondarily. Mucous membrane of the upper respiratory tract, eyes, liver, muscles and bones are also affected. Spinal cord and brain are spared.

DIAGNOSIS

Clinical features and histopathology have a wide spectrum of manifestations. They depend on the degree and extent of host-parasite interaction. Only salient features are mentioned here in brief.

1. Incubation period

It is not yet exactly known. It ranges from 3 months to 40 years, the average being 5 ± 2 years.

2. Prevalence

It prevails mostly in tropics e.g. Central Africa, South America, South-East Asia and especially India. Total number of patients in the world is about 11.5 millions. In India, it is about 4 millions, roughly 1 in 200.

3. Important epidemiological factors

a. Conjugally affected patients are only about 5% and attempts to infect volunteers have failed.

b. Multibacillary patients, who constitute the main source of infection, are 4 to 11 times more infective than the paucibacillary cases.

c. Transplacental infection is unknwon but the bacillary antigen can cross the placenta.

d. Mode of transmission is uncertain but the following facts are worth mentioning.

i. Infection via skin—It is suspected that skin contact and transmission by flies and other arthopods can infect a person. M. leprae can remain viable in desiccated nasal secretion for 1-7 days. Scratched, abraded or insect-bitten skin may facilitate the passage of the organisms in droplets deposited on skin surface.

ii. Droplet infection—Nasal droplets of multibacillary patients carry the living bacilli and enter through the respiratory tract by inhalation. The organisms are carried therefrom to sites suitable for multiplication.

iii. Infection through gastrointestinal tract could not be substantiated.

4. Age, sex, racial and environmental factors

a. Peak incidence occurs between 10-20 years.

b. Male to female ratio in adult is 2 : 1.

c. Susceptibility to infection might have some genetic role partly by HLA-linked genes (recessive) in the tuberculoid form of HD.

d. Americans, Europeans, Anglo-Indians, Parsees, Burmese, Chinese and Japanese are more susceptible than Africans and Indians.

e. Exact role of climatic factors is yet to be settled.

f. Domestic overcrowding, under-nourishment and the reduced cell-mediated immunity probably have roles as predisposing factors.

5. Hansen's bacillus

It was discovered in 1873 by Dr. Armauer Hansen in Norway. The **characteristics** of the bacillus are :

a. It is an **obligate, intracellular, acid fast, gram positive** bacillus. Length is 3-8 microns. It is comparatively less acid fast than M. tuberculosis.

b. It multiplies mainly inside the macrophages of skin (**histiocytes**) and of the nerves (**Schwann cells**).

c. In properly stained smear, the bacilli appear as **bright red.** But the red colour is lost when treated with pyridine. This is known as **pyridine extractibility.**

d. They are pleomorphic—straight or curved—rod like ; solid, fragmented or granular. Solid and uniformly staining bacteria are considered living whereas irregularly stained granular bacteria are taken as dead.

e. They lie **singly,** in **clumps** or in compact masses known as **globi.** A globi is surrounded by a limiting membrane and may contain 50 or more bacilli.

f. Bacterial index (BI)

The density of bacilli in smears is known as **bacterial index.** This can be measured by **Ridley's logarithmic scale** based on the number of bacilli seen in an average microscopic field under an oil-immersion objective. Readings of the BI are as follow.

1+ = 1 to 10 bacilli in 100 fields.

2+ = 1 to 10 bacilli in 10 fields.

3+ = 1 to 10 bacilli in an average field.

4+ = 10 to 100 bacilli in an average field.

5+ = 100 to 1000 bacilli in an average field.

6+ = Many clumps ($>$1000) of bacilli in average field.

g. Morphological index (MI)

It indicates the **percentage** of living bacilli (solid) calculated after examining 200 red staining elements lying singly. MI of lepromatous patients is generally between 25-75 at the start, but there is a steady fall to zero in 4-6 months of Dapsone monotherapy, but much quicker with multidrug therapy.

h. Number of M. leprae may reach up to 10^9 per gramme of tissue in multibacillary patients.

i. The **generation time** of M. leprae in the mouse foot pad is 12-13 days.

j. Habitat of the bacilli

i. Schwann cells and axons of nerves

ii. Smooth and striated muscles

iii. Arrectores pilorum of the skin

iv. Hair follicles **v.** Sweat glands

vi. Muscular media of arterioles

vii. Endothelial lining of small blood vessels

viii. Dartos muscle ix. Smooth muscle of iris

x. Nasal mucosa and secretions

xi. Posterior root ganglia and sympathetic ganglia. Nerves invaded by Hansen's bacilli are either dermal cutaneous nerves or nerve trunks. The most vulnerable regions are where the nerves are (a) **most cool** and (b) **subject to trauma.**

The spinal cord and the brain are devoid of bacteria.

6. Histopathology

Histopathological examination is necessary for accurate classification of HD. Skin biopsies should include full depth of dermis and should be taken from the most active edge of the lesions. To show the bacilli in sections, Fite-Faraco's method of staining is used. Formalin should not be used as a fixative as it causes distortion of the granuloma. Choice lies between Zenker's fluid or FMA fixative (formaldehyde, mercuric chloride and glacial acetic acid).

a. **Tuberculoid HD** (TT)—Bacilli entering the Schwann cells multiply within and slowly destroy them. The bacilli emerge out from the destroyed Schwann cells to re-enter the neighbouring Schwann cells. The intraneural infection thus gets spread.

Later, the nerve is invaded by lymphocytes and histiocytes (macrophages) which become fixed epithelioid cells. Groups of these unite to become giant cells and a tuberculoid granuloma is formed. It leads to nerve destruction which in turn results in anesthesia or muscle weakness depending on the type of nerves involved—sensory or motor. **Pain is present in the early stages of destructive process. About 30% of sensory fibres must be destroyed to detect sensory impairment.** When the infection is limited to one or more nerves without any skin lesion, it is known as **pure neural** tuberculoid HD. In skin biopsy, tuberculoid granuloma collect in foci surrounding neuromuscular elements. Some of these foci invade the papillary zone (the zone which is always free in lepromatous and boderline HD) immediately beneath the epidermis. They may even erode the basal layer of the epidermis. Bacilli are not present. Dermal nerves within the tuberculoid foci are either completely destroyed or appear greatly swollen by epithelioid cell granuloma and lymphocytes. Occasionally, tubercles may caseate with the formation of a sterile abscess in the nerve.

b. **Borderline HD (BT, BB, BL)**—In this case, bacilli are found within the affected nerves : smaller in number at the tuberculoid end and larger at the lepromatous end. Clinical evidence of nerve damage often precedes skin lesion by some months or even years. In BT, there is epithelioid cell granuloma more diffuse than TT, free but narrow papillary zone and foreign body type of giant cells. Dermal nerves are moderately swollen by cellullar infiltrate or show Schwann cell proliferation. Bacilli are absent in the dermis ; few may however be present within the dermal nerves.

In BB, there is diffuse epithelioid cell granuloma, few lymphocytes, no giant cell and clear papillary zone. Dermal nerves show slight swelling and cellular infiltrate. Bacilli are present both in the dermis and dermal nerves.

BL shows macrophage granuloma and foamy change in some cells. Lymphocytes are present in dense clumps. Few epithelioid cells may be seen. Dermal nerves contain some cellular infiltrate and perineurium show onion-skin appearance. Papillary zone is clear. Leprosy bacilli are plentiful—singly or in clumps or in globi.

c. **Lepromatous HD**—In this case, there is thinning of the epidermis and flattening of the rete-ridges with clear papillary zone. Deep in the dermis lies diffuse leproma consisting of histiocytes and/or macrophages, few lymphocytes and plasma cells. Foamy appearance of the macrophages is due to the presence of fragmented and granular bacilli within it and their cytoplasm undergoing fatty change. Dermal appendages are intact until late in the disease. Large numbers of bacilli are found in Schwann cells of cutaneous nerve fibres, in perineural and vascular endothelial cells. Schwann cells reduplicate in an attempt to repair the damage and form concentric rings around the nerve fibres creating an onion skin appearance on histologic sections. Fibrosis of nerves is the inevitable end result of LL causing bilateral 'glove and stocking' anesthesia.

d. Nerve biopsy—It is helpful in primary polyneuritic HD showing a typical tuberculoid or borderline histology. Cutaneous sensory nerves suitable for biopsy are

i. Radial cutaneous nerve above the wrist.

ii. Any nerve twig in the region of elbow or knee.

iii. Sural nerve at the back of the leg or the lateral border of the foot.

iv. Superficial peroneal nerve on the dorsum of foot.

There is no risk of motor damage as these nerves do not contain any motor fibres.

7. Hematology and serology

In LL and BL, there may be normocytic, normochromic anemia, raised ESR, impaired platelet adhesiveness and platelet aggregation to collagen, increased prothrombin time due to a circulating anticoagulant (an IgM immunoglobulin). There are certain tests for syphilis which give a biological false positive reaction in 60% cases e.g. (i) Wassermann reaction (ii) rapid plasma reagin test (Flocculation test) and (iii) the automated reagin test.

Certain tests for diagnosis of autoimmune diseases may also be positive in some cases e.g. (i) Thyroglobulin antibodies (ii) Antinuclear factor (iii) Rheumatoid factor (iv) LE cells (v) Cold precipitable protein (vi) Anti-spermatozoa antibodies (vii) Immunoglobulins IgG, IgA and IgE are significantly raised in LL and BL and IgM is raised in TT.

8. Other diagnostic tests

a. Histamine test : Wheal and flare responses to histamine depend on the integrity of sympathetic nerve fibres. If a hypopigmented patch is due to HD, the response of the skin to histamine will be delayed, diminished or absent. It thus measures the degree of damage to the sympathetic nerves. A drop of 0.001% histamine acid phosphate is placed on the hypopigmented lesion and another drop to the normal skin. Skin is pricked with a needle through each drop. Intensity and extent of the flare during the next ten minutes are recorded. In a HD macule, the flare is delayed and feeble in indeterminate and borderline leprosy, and absent in TT. In lucio leprosy, there is depression or absence of flare all over the skin. However, since there is a depression of histamine flare in all types of peripheral neuropathy, this cannot help in differential diagnosis with neuralgia paraesthetica (Bernhardt's syndrome).

b. Sweating test : Sweating is dependent on the integrity of parasympathetic nerve fibres. If a hypopigmented patch is due to HD, the response of the sweat glands to a cholinergic drug will be diminished. 0.1 ml of 0.06% pilocarpine nitrate is injected intradermally into the patch and into a normal control site. Sweat response is assessed visually or more accurately by the conversion of colur of quinizarine powder from white to blue, or in case of non-availability of quinizarine, tinc. of iodine can be painted and allowed to dry before injecting pilocarpine and then dusted with starch powder. Sweating turns the powder blue.

c. Lepromin test : This test is not of diagnostic help in leprosy. It is simply (i) a guide to the resistance of the patient against leprosy and (ii) a test to confirm the precise immunological classification and (iii) of value in indicating the prognosis.

It is strongly positive in TT, weakly positive in BT and negative in BB, BL and LL. 0.1 ml of lepromin is injected intradermally and the reaction is read at 72 hours or after 3-4 weeks depending on whether Dharmendra antigen or Mitsuda antigen is used. Dharmendra antigen is a purified chloroform ether extracted suspension of M. leprae and Mitsuda antigen is an autoclaved suspension of human tissue naturally infected with M. leprae, containing variable amounts of soluble tissues and bacillary extract. It contains 160 million bacilli per ml. Reaction to Dharmendra antigen is known as **Fernandez reaction** whereas response to Mitsuda antigen is known as **Mitsuda reaction** which takes the form of erythematous papulo-nodule. Both are delayed hypersensitivity reactions and probably are manifestations of cell mediated immunity. Interpretation of the two reactions are as follows.

Fernandez reaction (After 72 hours)	**Mitsuda reaction** (After 3-4 weeks)
Negative: Nothing visible, or erythema without induration, or erythema and induration less than 5 mm in diameter.	**Negative**: Nothing visible **Doubtful** (±): A papule 3 mm or less in diameter.
Weakly positive (+): Erythema and induration 5-10 mm in diameter.	+ : Erythematous papule 4-6 mm in diameter.
Moderately positive (++): Erythema and induration 11-15 mm in diameter.	++ : Erythematous papule 7-10 mm in diameter.
Strongly positive (+++): Erythema and induration 16 mm or more in diameter.	+++ : Erythematous nodule larger than 10 mm in diameter or of any size which ulcerates.

d. Serological assays : Specific serological tests can detect subclinical infection. Major serological assays include

i. FLA-ABS : Fluorescent leprosy antibody absorption test for detection of M. leprae specific antibodies.

ii. RIA : Radioimmuno-assay for antibodies to the cell wall antigen 7 of M. leprae.

iii. ELISA : Enzyme-linked immuno-sorbent assay for antibodies against the phenolic glycolipid derived from the cell wall of M. leprae.

9. Evolution of the disease : Most individuals exposed to multibacillary leprosy patients develop a subclinical infection. In about 95% of such persons, the infection fails to establish itself and they never develop any manifestation of the disease. In the remaining 5%, a single or few **ill-defined hypopigmented** or **faintly erythematous patches** of indeterminate leprosy may develop. Indeterminate leprosy is often the clinical beginning of the disease. Lesions of indeterminate leprosy may heal spontaneously or persist as indeterminate leprosy or enter into the clinical spectrum of the disease.

The increasing definition, hypo-pigmentation, hyperesthesia, anesthesia or **elevation of margin** indicate movement towards the **tuberculoid pole**, while **increase in the number of lesions, erythema** and **vagueness of border** or **central elevation** indicate movement towards the **lepromatous pole**. Progression of the disease or development of reaction may give way to infiltrated lesions.

10. Clinical spectrum of the disease

Lepromatous leprosy can be subdivided into LLp and LLs. In LLp, the patient has been lepromatous throughout ; LLs patients have undergone an earlier borderline phase or, in other words, they have downgraded due to lack of treatment. Main clinical reason for this subdivision of lepromatous leprosy into LLp and LLs is that LLs patients are capable of rapidly ragaining their lost CMI during an upgrading reaction. Although controversial, it is believed that at the opposite end of the spectrum TT, there are subdivisions into TTs and TTp. The TTs has evolved from borderline as a result of upgrading and, because of immunological instability, is capable of downgrading to BT and further along the borderline spectrum (Fig. 1).

11. Clinical features

a. Indeterminate leprosy : Main types of leprosy usually develop from indeterminate leprosy. Patient is usually a child presenting with a single or multiple, asymmetrical, slightly hypo-pigmented or faintly erythematous, ill-defined, macules on the skin, usually on the covered areas. Sensation of the affected area varies from normal to slight impairment. Sweating and hair growth usually remain unaffected. Peripheral

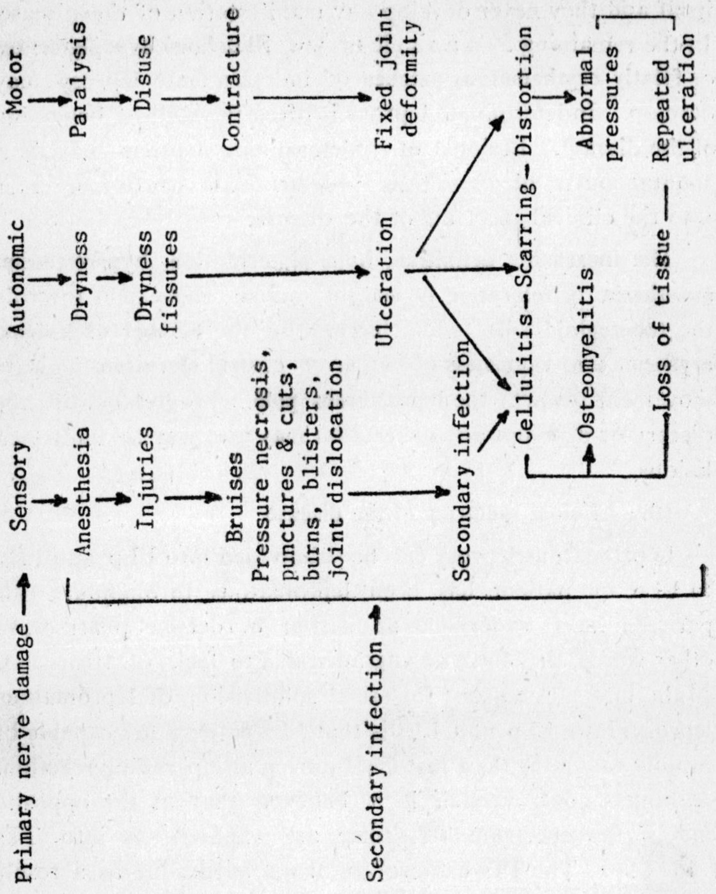

Fig. 1. Clinical spectrum of HD

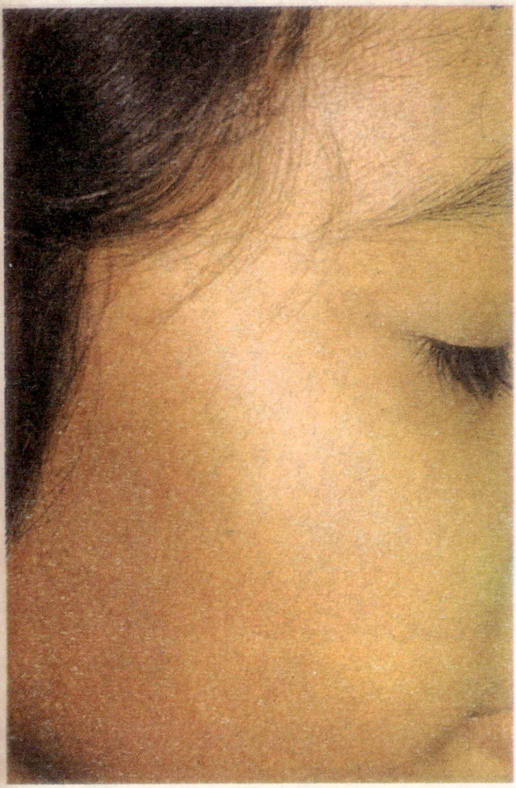

Fig. H-1. **Hansen's Disease** indeterminate lesion at the face.

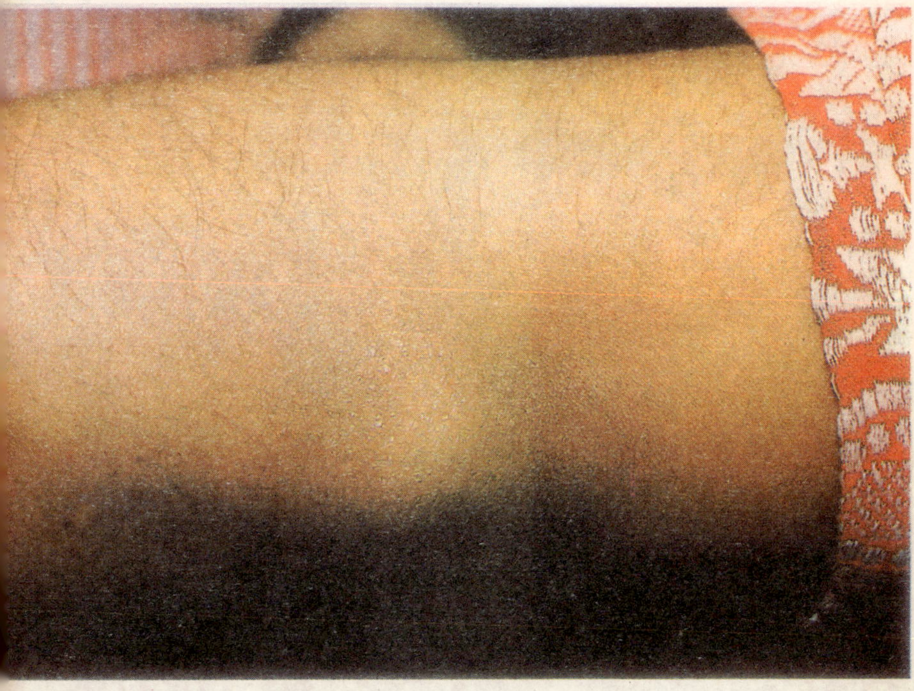

ig. H-2. **Hansen's Disease** tuberculoid lesion showing hypopigmented anaesthetic patch.

nerves are normal. Slit skin smears are mostly negative. Howevcr, AFB may be present in dermal nerve fibres infiltrated with lymphocytes in well-stained serial sections. Lepromin test is either negative or positive. Indeterminate leprosy is usually self-limiting, but may progress to other forms of leprosy and hence three or six monthly check up is necessary to assess the progress of the lesions.

b. **Tuberculoid leprosy :** In TT, lepromin test is positive indicating effective cell-mediated immunity. M. leprae are phagocytosed and digested by macrophages forming epithelioid cells. Symptoms of TT may be neural or dermal or both.

i. **Primary polyneuritic leprosy** : Only the nerves are involved without any evidence of skin lesions. Symptoms consist of pain, loss of feeling, tingling, muscle weakness or paralysis. Male to female ratio is 3 : 1 in contrast to 2 : 1 in other forms of leprosy. There is asymmetrical leprous involvement of one or several peripheral nerve trunks. Nerves may be affected by infection through blood. Commonly affected nerves are greater auricular, ulnar, median, lateral popliteal, posterior tibial, fifth and seventh cranial; ulnar nerve being most commonly affected. Affected nerve may be tender and uniformly enlarged. Sometimes liquefaction degeneration may give rise to a nerve abscess. Sensation of touch and temperature is lost earlier than that of pain and pressure. Heaviness, tingling and numbness can be present, acute inflammation of the affected nerve may lead to severe neuralgic pain. Polyneuritic leprosy may lead to paresis, hypotonia and atrophy, particularly of the muscles of hands and feet. Paralysis of muscles leads to deformities like claw hands, claw toes, wrist drop, foot drop etc.

ii. **Skin lesions of TT** are few in number, often single, seldom exceeding 10 cm in diameter. They are asymmetrical ; may cross the midline, hypopigmented in dark skin and copper coloured in pale skin. The margin is well defined. Lesions are anesthetic, hairless and dry. Anesthesia of the lesions may be absent or slight in face because of rich overlapping nerve supply.

iii. Minor tuberculoid : Lesions are small, markedly hypopigmented ; there is rapid central healing and severe nerve involvement is infrequent.

iv. Major tuberculoid : These are large lesions, more numerous, more markedly and uniformly raised and often associated with severe nerve involvement. These lesions may invade even the generally spared areas, especially scalp, axillae, groins, palms and soles.

c. Borderline (BB) : This is the immunologically most unstable form of leprosy having a tendency to move in either direction along the borderline spectrum. With treatment, it moves towards the tuberculoid pole (**reversal reaction** or **upgrading**) and without treatment towards lepromatous pole (**downgrading**).

It may be subdivided into BT (Borderline Tuberculoid), BB (Borderline) and BL (Borderline Lepromatous).

Depending on the patient's position in the borderline spectrum the macules vary greatly in number, size and shape. The nearer the patient is to the lepromatous end, the more numerous, more shiny, less well-defined, less anesthetic they are. Skin lesions are more asymmetrical in distribution than LL. Hypoesthesia and impairment of the hair growth are characteristics of borderline leprosy, being more marked in BT than in BL. Damage to the nerves is wide-spread and frequently leading to crippling deformities. Tendency to lepra reaction is also high. AFB is present, fewer in number near the tuberculoid pole and larger near the lepromatous pole. Lepromin test is generally negative. Of the various types of skin lesions found in borderline leprosy, the following are characteristic.

i. Macules : Erythematous in light-skin and hypopigmented in dark skin.

ii. Plaques : Hypopigmentation and central flattening are less obvious.

ig. H-3. **Hansen's Disease** borderline tuberculoid type.

Fig. H-4. **Hansen's Disease** tuberculoid type showing thickening of the greater auricular nerve.

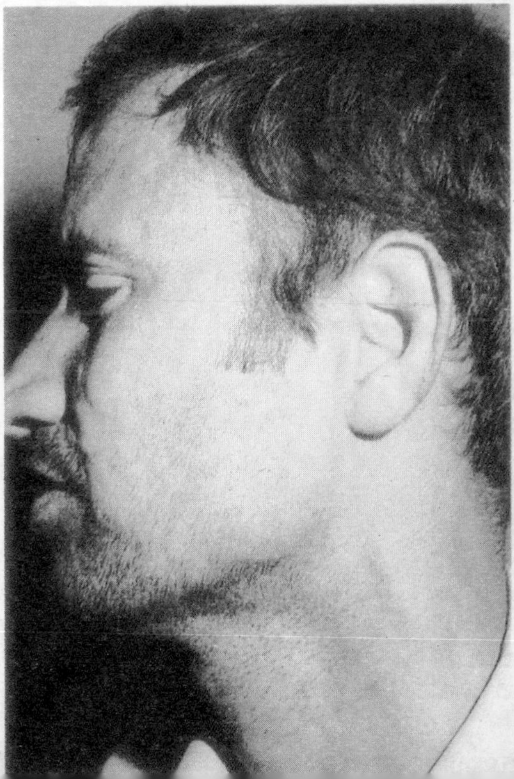

iii. Annular lesions : May assume various sizes and shapes but are predominantly circular or oval.

iv. Punched out lesions : Erythematous plaque, vague outer edges and a punched out central portion. The edge is palpable. Their look is inverted saucer-shaped.

v. Bizarre lesions : Take the form of raised bands or the contour of a map.

vi. Nodules : Occur rarely in BL, scanty, small and asymmetrically distributed.

In borderline leprosy, bacilli are found in lymphnodes, liver and skeletal muscles, but there is no clinical indication of such tissue invasion.

d. Lepromatous leprosy (LL) : Although the first clinical manifestations are likely to be dermal, these may go unnoticed by the patient and (s)he may complain of nasal symptoms such as stuffiness, discharge and epistaxis and edema of legs and ankles due to increased capillary permeability. Skin signs consist of macules, papules, nodules or small plaques or all the four. Nodules and plaques may breakdown to form ulcerations.

i. Macules are small, multiple, erythematous or faintly hypopigmented with vague edges ; shiny surfaces are not anesthetic.

ii. Papules, nodules and small plaques are usually of normal skin colour but are sometimes erythematous, having bilaterally symmetrical distribution favouring face, arms, legs and buttocks or any part of the body apart from hairy scalp, axillae, groins and perineum—regions with higher temperature.

Hair growth and sensation are not impaired over the lesion. Papulo-nodules are often seen on the lips, mucosa of the mouth and nose, where they tend to ulcerate. If the patient remains untreated, the lines of forehead become deeper due to thickening of the skin. The eyebrows and eyelashes become sparse or lost (**supercilliary** or **cilliary madarosis**). The nose becomes mis-shapen and may collapse due to septal perforation and loss of anterior nasal spine. The earlobes are thickened, voice becomes hoarse, upper incisor teeth loosen or fall out. The skin of the legs becomes ichthyotic and thickened, ulcers may form on the legs when nodules break down. Slow fibrosis of peripheral nerves results in nerve-thickening and bilateral 'glove and stocking' anesthesia which in turn leads to shortening of fingers and toes due to painless repeated trauma. Nerve damage is bilateral and symmetrical, but one side may precede the other. Anesthetic skin is particularly liable to blister when exposed to heat. Three cranial nerves e.g. olfactory, trigeminal and facial are affected. Damage to motor nerves is shown by muscle weakness. Affected muscles later become wasted and paralysed. If the affected muscles are those supplied by facial nerves, it causes facial palsy; ulnar nerve causes claw hand or main-en-griffe, median nerve causes ape hand deformity, lateral popliteal nerve the dropped foot, posterior tibial nerve the claw toes or hammer toes. Enormous number of leprosy bacilli may be found in skin smears and nasal scrapings. In addition to skin and nerves, following tissues may be involved in LL.

iii. **Nails, fingers and toes :** Nails are dry, lustreless, longitudinally ridged. The digits become distally narrowed because of bone atrophy.

iv. **Nose :** Nasal stuffiness, nasal discharge, epistaxis are the prominent symptoms. Patients rarely complain of anosmia. Mucosa may be insensitive. Nose blow are full of AFB. Later, perforation of nasal septum develops and destruction of nasal cartilage causes nasal collapse.

v. **Mouth, pharynx and larynx :** Papules may appear on mucosal surface of lips and nodules on tongue, palate and uvula. Palatal nodules often ulcerate and hard palate may become perforated. Upper incisor teeth may be loose or missing (**facies leprosa**). Larynx is involved in two ways : (i) In fibrotic form, vocal cords become immobile causing hoarseness of voice and (ii) Ulcerative form causing pain and hoarseness of voice. Later glottis becomes increasingly narrowed and stridor is to be relieved by tracheotomy.

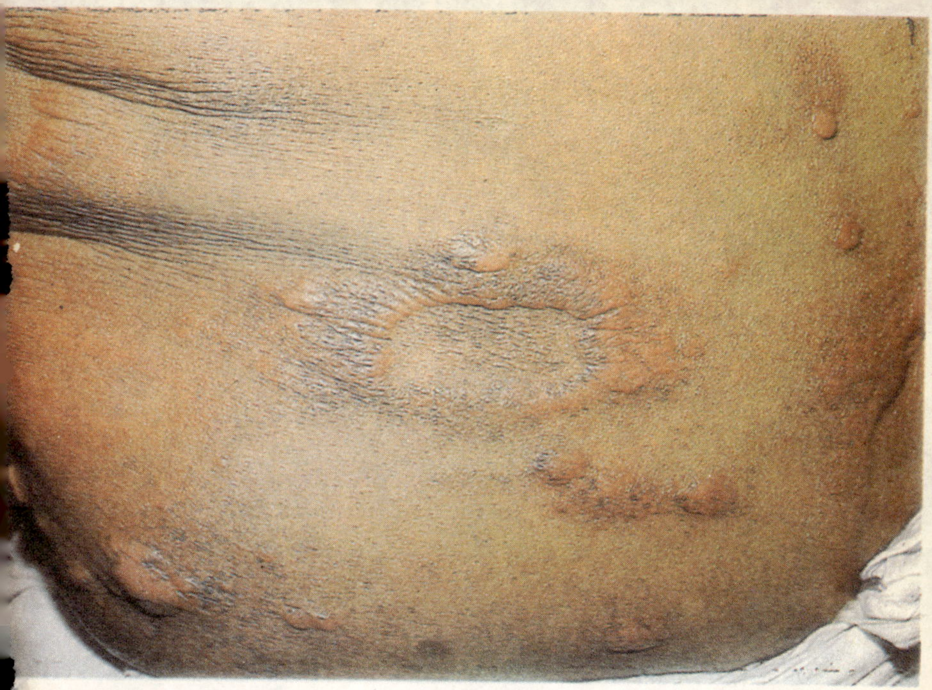

ig. H-5. **Hansen's Disease** borderline type showing inverted saucer-shaped lesion.

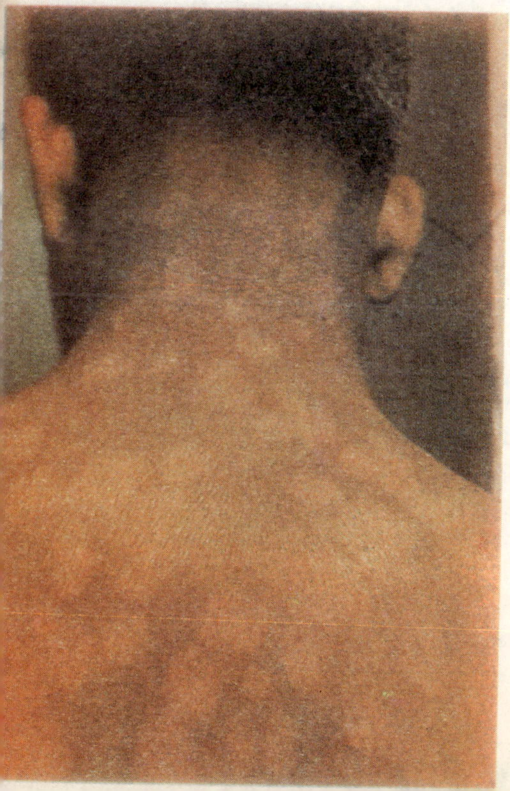

Fig. H-6. **Hansen's Disease** borderline lepromatous type.

vi. Eyes : Eye manifestations include iritis, iridocyclitis, superficial punctate keratitis, characterised by milky haze in upper cornea and punctated by white spots (that resemble grains of chalk) representing aggregations of leprosy bacilli (**miliary lepromata**) ; pannus formation commencing at the superior limbus and spreading all round the cornea leads to sclerosing keratitis. Yellowish gelatinous nodules may also appear at the sclero-corneal junction and at 3 and 9 O'clock positions.

All these eye changes are painless and do not affect vision. Anterior segment of the eye is cooler than the posterior and hence the nerves of cornea and iris are involved. In the iris, miliary lepromata or iris pearls may be seen using corneal microscope. Iris pearls are deposits of tightly packed bacilli within swollen macrophages and are situated in the autonomic nerve-plexuses in the iris. Iris shows progressive signs of atrophy and disintegration leading to miosis, unresponsive to atropine. Acute iritis may occur also as one of the manifestations of lepra reaction. Other ophthalmic complications are secondary cataract, glaucoma, ciliary staphyloma. Lesions in the posterior segment is rare consisting of yellowish retinal nodules. Damage to the fifth cranial nerve leads to corneal anesthesia, repeated injury and thus produces corneal ulceration. Involvement of seventh nerve leads to facial palsy, lagophthalmos and these, together with corneal anesthesia, produce exposure keratitis. If neglected, this may lead to blindness.

vii. Bones : The bone changes occur in neglected, untreated cases and once started, cannot be checked by treatment. Bone damage is confined to hands, feet and the skull.

In hands, distal phalanges undergo atrophy, absorption and shortening of the fingers. Middle and proximal phalanges may undergo similar atrophy but metacarpal and carpal bones are spared. In the feet, similar atrophic changes occur in the phalanges, metatarsal and tarsal bones. Distal phalanges show rarefying osteitis known as **concentric bone atrophy**. In the metatarsals, first and most pronounced change commences in the fifth metatarsal, affected bones becoming thin and pointed (pencilling or sucked candy appearence). In the skull, two pathognomonic changes occur e.g. atrophy of the anterior nasal spine and maxillary alveolar process causing nasal collapse and loss of upper central incisors respectively. These two skull changes cause **'facies leprosa'**.

viii. Testes : Testicular atrophy occurs in neglected patients or patients undergoing repeated attacks of epididymo-orchitis during lepra reaction. Sexual potency is retained in the earlier stage but later sterility, impotency and gynecomastia develop. **Female reproductive organs are not affected in leprosy.**

ix. Kidneys : It is an important cause of morbidity and mortality in leprosy. Kidney changs are non-specific i.e. not related to the disease and include renal amyloidosis, glomerulonephritis, interstitial nephritis, pyelonephritis and renal tuberculosis.

x. Muscles : There may be few palpable nodules within the muscles, biopsy revealing interstitial myositis with granular bacilli between the muscle bundles.

xi. Lymph glands : Specially femoral and inguinal groups are enlarged and become tender during lepra reaction.

The commonest **cause of death in leprosy** may be due to chronic glomerulonephritis, proliferative glomerulonephritis, interstitial nephritis or renal amyloidosis. Death may occur also from a severe reactional state either from necrotizing reaction or from edema of the glottis.

e. Special forms of leprosy

i. Histoid leprosy : It is charactersied by the formation of firm, erythematous or coppery glistening nodules and/or plaques in the skin and subcutis of multibacillary patients who either discontinued the treatment or for whom

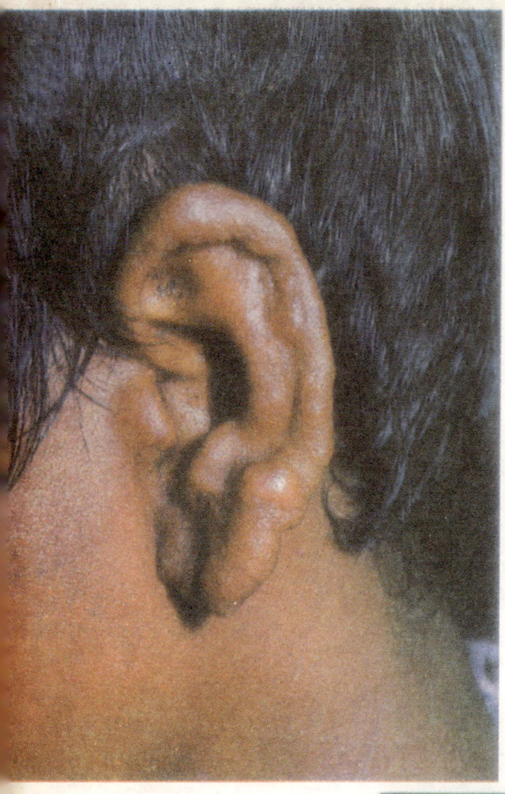

Fig. H-7. **Hansen's Disease** lepromatous type showing nodules at the ear.

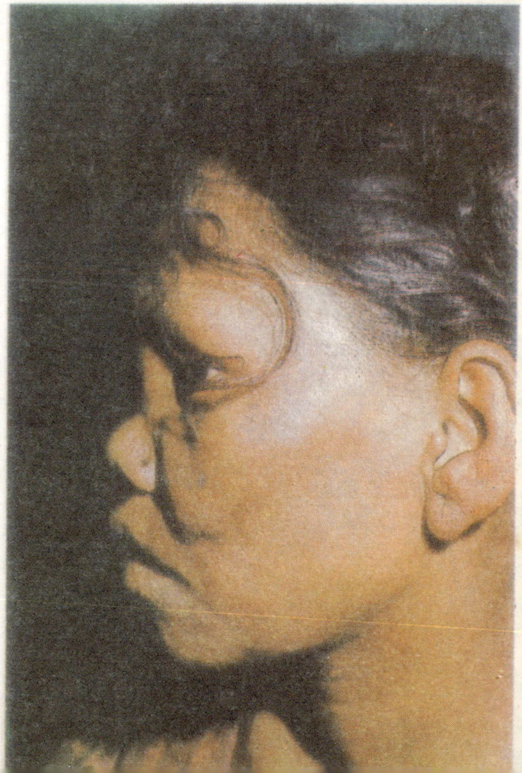

ig. H-8. **Hansen's Disease** promatous type showing depressed nose ue to atrophy of the anterior nesal pine causing **'facies leprosa'**

M. leprae became drug resistant. Less commonly, few such nodules may be seen in non-relapsing cases of lepromatous leprosy when first examined. It is called histoid because the biopsy shows elongated or spindle-shaped histiocytes and the bacilli within them are longer than normal. It was first described by Wade in 1963.

ii. **Lucio-leprosy** : It is a special form of lepromatous leprosy, first described by Lucio and Alvarado in 1852. It is characterised by diffuse, wide spread infiltration of the skin without formation of nodules. There is loss of body hair, eyebrows and eyelashes and wide spread sensory loss, skin containing numerous leprosy bacilli. In older patients, dermal infiltration may smooth out the wrinkles of the face resulting in a youthful appearance called **lepra bonita** (pretty leprosy). Lucio leprosy is due to total lack of host resistance. Chronic edema and chronic ulceration of both legs may occur. Patients develop a peculiar form of lepra reaction known as **Lucio's phenomenon** seen only in untreated patients. Painful and tender red patches appear on the skin, particularly on the extremities ; they become purpuric, the centre of the purpuric lesion becomes necrotic and ulcerated and finally a brown or black crust is developed. The crust falls off after a few days to leave a superficial atrophic scar. Lesions are most common on the legs and less on thighs, forearms and buttocks ; trunk and face are spared. Good results are obtained by treatment with dapsone and rifampicin. This form of leprosy may be misdiagnosed as myxedema.

iii. **Pregnancy and leprosy** : In a pregnant woman with leprosy the following may happen.

1. **Worsening of leprosy** : Possibly due to depressed CMI and the increased circulating thyroxine (T4) during pregnancy, an exacerbation of the disease is caused.

2. **Intercurrent infections** : Specially viral infections and falciparum malaria.

3. **Increased incidence of lepra reactions** : Both type I and type-II reactions.

iv. Effects on infants : (1) Babies of mothers with leprosy weigh less than those of healthy mothers. They also grow up slowly. (2) Infants run a high risk of contracting leprosy. Untreated lepromatous HD ultimately succumbs to renal failure or concomitant tuberculosis.

f. Reactions in leprosy : The term reaction is described as the appearance of a sudden inflammatory phase of exacerbation in lesions of a patient with leprosy. Reactions occur in all types of leprosy except in early indeterminate form. There are two types of lepra reactions : (1) **Type-I** lepra reaction and (2) **Type-II** lepra reaction (Erythema Nodosum Leprosum =ENL reaction)

i. Type-I lepra reaction

1. Cause : It is a delayed hypersensitivity reaction (Type-IV hypersensitivity reaction of Combs and Gell). Antigens from effete leprosy bacilli react with T-lymphocytes and are associated with a rapid change in CMI.

2. Type of leprosy : It is mostly seen in borderline patients because of their immunological instability. It may also occur in LLs (upgrading). When the reaction is associated with rapid increase in CMI, as in patients under treatment, it is known as **upgrading** or **reversal reaction**. If the reaction is associated with a reduction in immunity, it is called **downgrading reaction**. The various shifts across the leprosy spectrum are as follows.

Upgrading : **LLs→BL→BB→BT→TTs**
Downgrading : **TTs→BT→BB→BL→LLs**

3. Onset : In BT and BB patients, the most likely time for upgrading reaction to occur is during the first six months of treatment. Longer intervals have been recorded in BL. Downgrading reaction occurs spontaneously or in patients whose treatment has been interrupted.

4. Clinical features : Some or all the existing leprosy lesions show signs of acute inflammation e.g. pain, tenderness, erythema and edema looking like erysipelas. Necrosis and

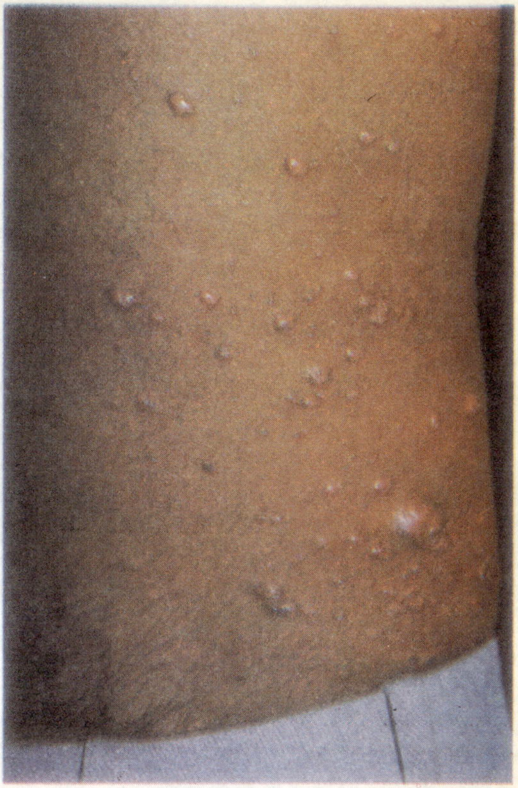

Fig. H-9. **Hansen's Disease** histoid variety.

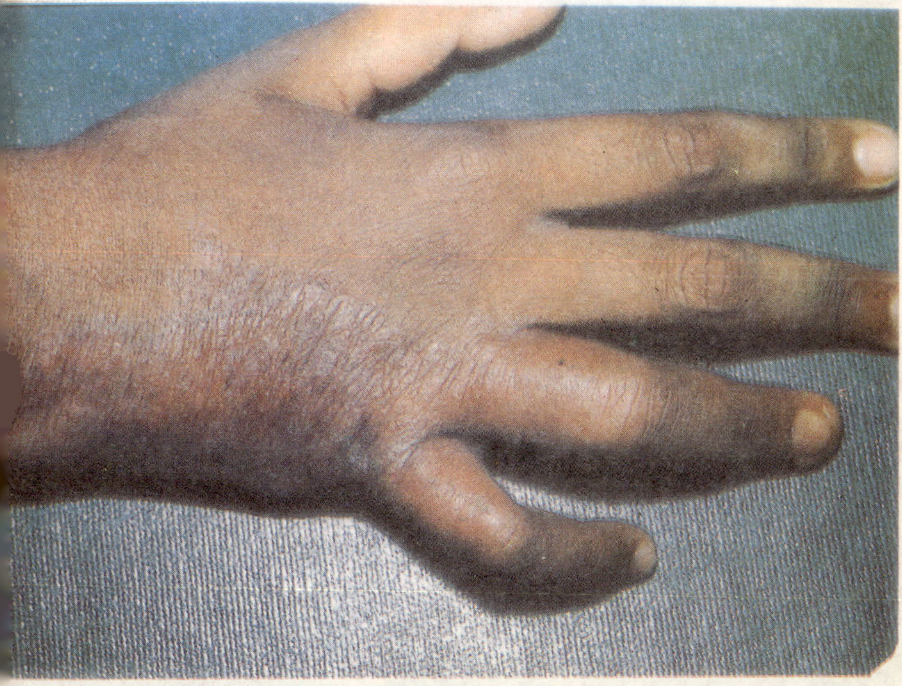

ig. H-10. **Hansen's Disease** showing tuberculoid patch and early ulnar clawing.

ulceration occur in severe cases. Lesions desquamate as reaction subsides. New lesions may appear in upgrading reactions. In downgrading reactions lesions worsen and progress towards the lepromatous pole and new lesions may as well appear. Systemic disturbances such as malaise, fever etc. are unusual.

Nerve-involvement : There occurs rapid swelling of one or more nerves with pain and tenderness at the site of swelling, usually where it is most superficial. Nerve pain is due to increased intraneural pressure from edema and cellular reaction (Granuloma formation) aggravated at sites where swollen nerve trunks are entrapped in bony or fascial tunnel. Rarely, a nerve abscess may form producing a fluctuant swelling attached to the affected nerve. Mostly, the ulnar nerve is involved.

Motor disturbance : The nerves most at risk are the ulnar causing claw hand, lateral popliteal causing dropped foot, facial causing facial palsy. These paralyses are likely to be permanent if neglected or incorrectly treated but will recover with correct and prompt treatment.

Associated features are edema of hands, feet or face.

5. **Histology** : In upgrading reaction there is increased defensive cells such as lymphocytes, epithelioid cells and giant cells. The number of bacilli decreases. In downgrading reactions defensive cells are replaced by macrophages. The number of bacilli increases.

6. **Hematological change** : None.

7. **Lepromin test** : Becomes positive in upgrading reactions and negative in downgrading reactions.

8. **Course** : Seldom persists for more than a few months.

ii. Type-II lepra reaction

1. **Cause** : It is an immune complex syndrome—an antigen-antibody reaction that involves complement–an

example of type-III hypersensitivity reaction of Combs and Gells.

2. Types of leprosy : Occurs almost exclusively in lepromatous leprosy, both LLs and LLp. Only occasionally it appears in BL.

3. Onset : When it occurs in relation to therapy, it tends to occur later during the course of treatment when skin lesions appear quiescent and all or most of the bacilli in the skin are granular. It may occur in untreated cases of very long duration.

4. Clinical features : Existing leprosy lesions do not show clinical aggravation. Crops of evanescent (lasting for a few days), pink coloured tender nodules or plaques, which may become vesicular, pustular, bullous or gangrenous suddenly appear and break-down (Erythema nodosum necroticans). ENL may be the first manifestation of leprosy. Systemic disturbances such as fever, malaise etc. are common and the patient is toxic. Associated features include edema of hands, feet and face. Paralysis may occur but nerve damage does not threaten so quickly as in type-I reaction. Other associated features are iritis, iridocyclitis, epistaxis, muscle pain, bone-pain (confined to tibiae), nerve pain, joint pain, lymphadenitis, epididymo-orchitis and proteinuria.

5. Histology : Contains large number of polymorphs. Bacilli may be numerous and mostly fragmented and granular. **ENL may show features of vasculitis.**

6. Hematology : Polymorphonuclear leucocytosis, increased gamma-globulins : IgG, IgM and C_2 and C_3 are found.

7. Course : Mild reactions disappear rapidly but severe ENL may persist for years resulting in death.

8. Precipitating factors : Factors known to precipitate type-II reactions are the intercurrent infection, injury, surgical operation, physical stress, mental stress, protective immunizations (vaccination against small pox), strongly

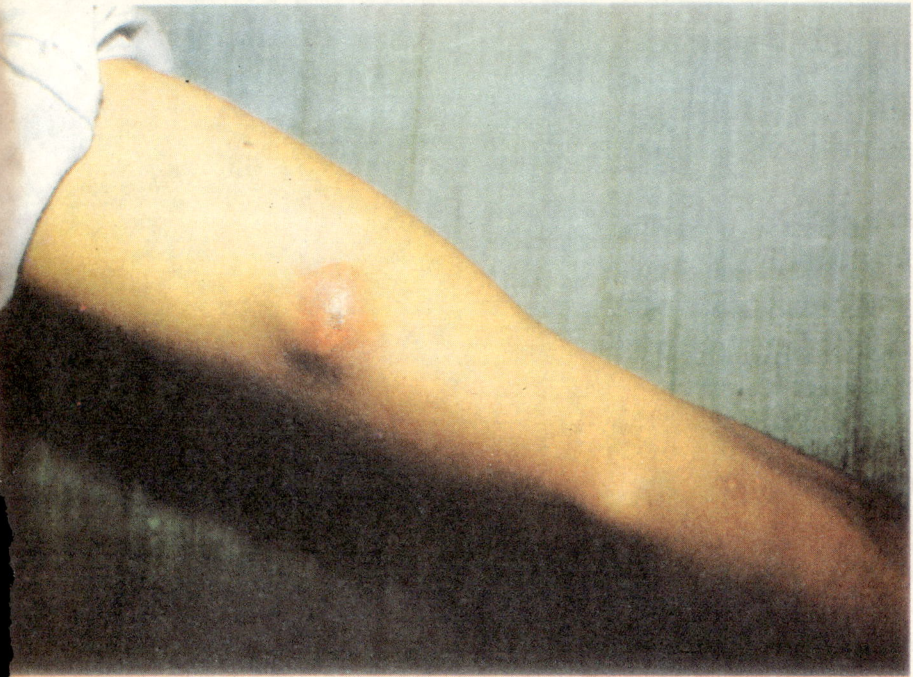

Fig. H-11. **Hansen's Disease** showing a nerve abscess.

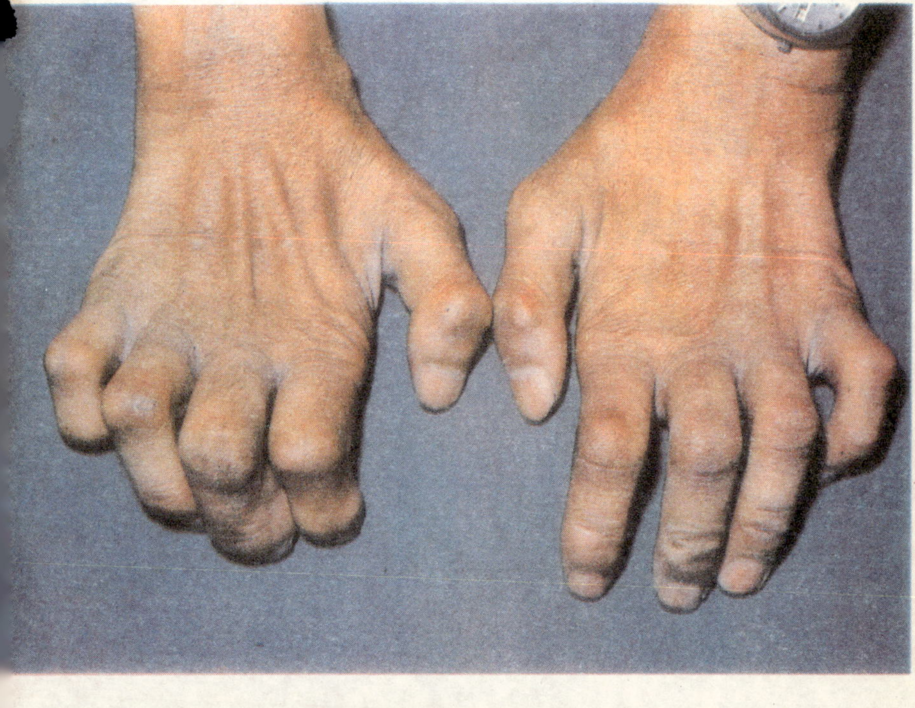

Fig. H-12. **Hansen's Disease** showing typical **'claw-hand'**.

positive Mantoux test, pregnancy and parturition, ingestion of potassium iodide and antileprosy drugs.

iii. Treatment of lepra reactions : Four principles in the management of reactions are :

1. Control the acute neuritis in order to prevent anesthesia, paralysis and contracture.
2. Halt eye damage and prevent blindness.
3. Kill the bacilli and prevent extension of disease.
4. Control the pain.

Early diagnosis and treatment and energetic management of reactional state should prevent the development of all disabilities. A practical approach to management involves **four measures : I. Anti-inflammatory therapy II. Analgesic therapy III. Splinting and Exercise IV. Antibacterial therapy.**

I. Anti-inflammatory therapy

a. Mild reactions : These may be either type-I reaction with absence of pain and tenderness in nerves and no severe skin inflammation or type-II reactions confined to minor skin lesions with little systemic disturbances.

Drugs used are

i. **Aspirin :** Still the best and cheapest drug for controlling moderate degrees of pain and inflammation. 600 to 1200 mg are given 4 hourly 4-6 times daily. Aspirin may cause gastric erosion. Prolonged and heavy doses of salicylates may cause hypo-prothombinemia which also causes blood loss due to delayed clotting of blood.

ii. **Chloroquine :** Antimalarial drugs, especially chloroquine, have an anti-inflammatory action and are effective in controlling mild reactions. 150 mg chloroquine base is given up to 3 times daily. Prolonged administration of chloroquine may cause photosensitization, pruritus, gastrointestinal disturbances, visual disturbances and tinnitus.

iii. **Antimonials :** Antimony is of some benefit in controlling mild reactions. It is particularly useful in relieving pains in bones and joints in type-II reaction. Toxic effects of antimonials include rashes, joint pains, bradycardia, hypotension and electrocardiographic changes. Organic trivalent antimonials are less toxic than inorganic ones. Stibophen contains 8.5 mg antimony per ml. On alternate days, 2-3 ml are given intramuscularly ; total dose should not exceed 30 ml.

iv. **Thalidomide** : This drug is used only in controlling the manifestations of Type II reactions, including neuritis and iritis and is often helpful in weaning patients of corticosteroids. It is given in a dose of 400 mg daily until the reaction is controlled and then reduced to a maintenance dose of 50 mg daily. The drug must never be used in pre-menopausal women because of its teratogenic effect. It seems that thalidomide requires a functioning adrenal cortex or concurrent small doses of steroid when the adrenal cortex is not functioning. Side effects include constipation, drowsiness, dryness of oral and nasal mucosa, peripheral edema, dizziness, erythema of face and chest, skin rashes and irreversible peripheral neuritis.

b. **Severe reactions** : A reaction is considered severe if

i. Paralysis and anesthesia threaten to follow neuritis. This occurs commonly in type-I reaction in BT and BB and also in type-II reaction.

ii. Skin ulceration is threatened. This occurs in severe type-I reaction but is commonest in ENL. It is often accompanied by iritis, orchitis, arthritis, dactylitis, fever and prostration.

iii. Iritis or orchitis develops independently.

Drugs considered are :

1. **Corticosteroids** : Prednisone or prednisolone is given in a single daily dose of 40-80 mg. This daily dose should be halved after three to four days and then reduced by further 10 mg each week, finishing with 10 mg on alternate days for 10-14 days. Dose may vary according to the need of the individual. Corticosteroids are given as long as there

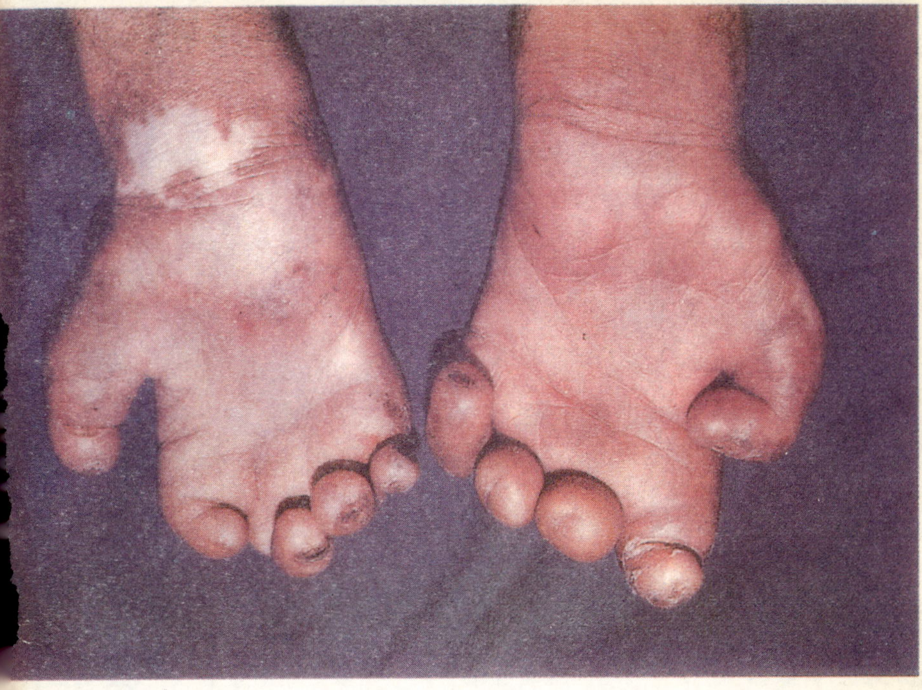

Fig. H-13. **Hansen's Disease** showing atrophy, absorption and shortening of the fingers.

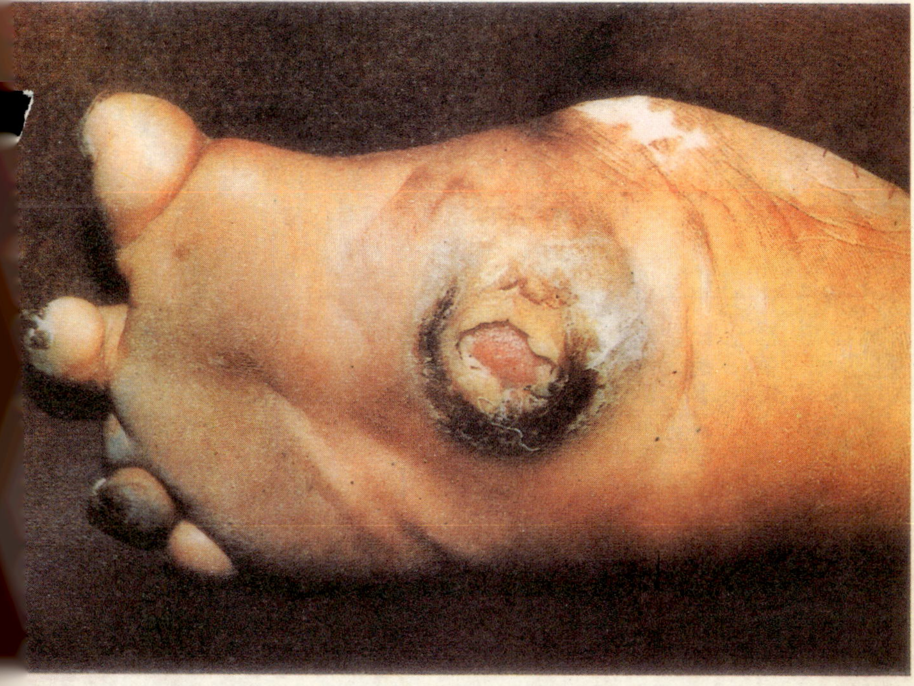

H-14. **Hansen's Disease** showing absorption of toes and trophic ulcer.

is active neuritis. Patient should be provided with a corticosteroid treatment card and should be instructed to prodcue it to any doctor in case of injury or illness, because corticosteroid causes atrophy of adrenal cortex and demands and extra supply of exogenous steroid.

Corticosteroids suppress immune-responses and thereby encourage bacillary multiplication. It is thus necessary to continue antileprosy therapy while corticosteroids are given. Other side effects include hematemesis, peptic ulcer, edema due to sodium retention, hypokalemia, hypertension, diabetes, spinal osteoporosis, striae, moon face and steroid purpura.

2. **Clofazimine** : It is used for reactions in patients who cannot be weaned off corticosteroids or who suffer from persistent ENL and where thalidomide cannot be used. As it is also an antileprotic drug, dapsone may be stopped. Clofazimine may temporarily aggravate reactions and is started under cover of an increased dose of steroids which are then gradually withdrawn. Initially, 300-400 mg is given daily in divided doses for 2 weeks, reducing to 200 mg daily for a month and then to 100 mg daily. When the reaction subsides, clofazimine is stopped and dapsone re-started.

3. **Adjuvant therapy** : Zinc sulphate 220 mg daily given orally after meals was found to restore the initial low serum zinc levels of patients with multibacillary leprosy and has been reported to be effective in recurrent ENL requiring high dosage of clofazimine and corticosteroids for prolonged period. After instituting oral zinc treatment, the dose of clofazimine could be reduced to 100 mg twice a week and corticosteroids withdrawn completely.

II. Analgesic therapy

i. In mild reactions, analgesics are synonymous with anti-inflammatory drugs. These are aspirin, clofazimine etc. Opiates should not be used because of danger of addiction.

ii. Intraneural injections of lignocaine and triamcinolone can relieve pain of acute neuritis. But this damages the nerves and increases scarring and should better be avoided.

iii. **Surgery**—If a nerve abscess develops, it may be aspirated through a wide bored needle. If this fails, the nerves may be exposed and abscess incised along the axis of the nerve. Small abscesses usually resolve spontaneously. A nerve that has become totally functionless for many months, may be slit down its length or completely excised for the relief of intractable pain.

III. **Splinting and exercise** : In cases of severe reactions, immobilization of affected limbs is helpful to relieve pain. Joints should be splinted in the position of function. Splints are most conveniently made of plaster slabs padded with plenty of cotton wool and secured with bandages. The splint should be left in position for a day until the inflammation begins to subside being removed only for exercises. To start with, gentle passive exercises are carried out daily. Active exercises are introduced gradually until the complete function is restored.

IV. **Antibacterial therapy** : It must be continued so long the infection is present. It is particularly important in the management of patients on corticosteroid therapy for it is an immuno-suppressive drug and may lead to increased bacillary multiplication. Dapsone therapy does not affect the incidence, may marginally affect the severity of type-II reaction. For a patient presenting for the first time with tender nerves, dapsone should better be avoided and treatment started with clofazimine. If patients with borderline disease go into severe reaction within few weeks after starting dapsone, dapsone should be stopped and clofazimine should be given. However, if dapsone is continued as antileprotic drug during reaction, it must be maintained in full dose. Daily dose of dapsone is less likely to precipitate reaction than the weekly dose.

TREATMENT

DAPSONE	ETHIONAMIDE	ASPIRIN
CLOFAZIMINE	THIACETAZONE	CHLOROQUINE
RIFAMPICIN	THALIDOMIDE	STEROIDS

A. General consideration : Segregation of HD patients is not necessary. This is because only about one fifth of the sufferers are infectious prior to treatment and these open cases can be rendered closed by chemotherapy relatively rapidly. Further, segregation causes groundless fears to the general public regarding the infectivity of leprosy and thus leading to a tendency to hide the disease and thus the spread of infection. Leprosy bacilli can remain viable outside the body in desiccated nasal secretions for 1-7 days ; hence the possible danger to others arises not from the leprosy patient under treatment but from undiagnosed cases. The major problem in out patient management is defaulting and the doctor must therefore convince the patient that he should take the treatment completely and regularly.

Balanced diet and general health must be maintained. If patient's hemoglobin is below 10 gm/100 ml, the cause should be investigated and anemia treated before starting antileprosy treatment.

B. Drug resistance and bacterial persistence

Drug resistance : It is a type of resistance which develops as a result of long term monotherapy. It is a secondary resistance and is largely confined to LL, because of the absence of CMI and the very long treatment. Drug resistant mutants develop in a step-wise manner with a **multistep type mutation** occurring **in dapsone resistance,** whereas **a single step mutation occurs in rifampicin resistance.**

Primary resistance occurs in persons who are infected by dapsone resistant M. leprae. In contrast to secondary resistance, primary resitance occurs in any type of leprosy.

Bacterial persistence : This is a phenomenon defined as the capability of micro-organisms to survive in the host irrespective of adequate antimicrobial treatment. The sites favoured by persisters are the peripheral nerves, the smooth muscle (dartos) and the striated muscle (tricep)

C. Chemotherapy : Until 1941, there was no effective antileprosy drug. Hydnocarpus (chaulmoogra) oil which had been used in India and China for centuries, was of little value. At present, dapsone, rifampicin, clofazimine, ethionamide and thiacetazone are the main antileprosy drugs.

i. Dapsone : This is the most important, and cheapest drug in the treatment of leprosy. It is 4 : 4 diaminodiphenylsulphone (DDS) and was first synthesised in Germany in 1908. Dapsone acts as a synthetase inhibitor in the folate synthesizing enzyme system of M. leprae. It thus works bacteriostatically in leprosy. Minimal inhibitory concentration of dapsone in mice infected with M. leprae is 0.015 μg/ml. Its half life in man is about 24 hours (range 13 to 40 hours). A single dose of 100 mg in man gives a blood level of about 1.5 μg/ml which falls to the minimal inhibitory concentration in 4-12 days. Morphological index of bacilli from smears of lepromatous leprosy treated with dapsone falls to zero in 5-8 months. Dapsone is commonly made up in 10, 25, 50 and 100 mg tablets. Dapsone should be given as a single daily oral dose of 50-100 mg for an adult and 2 mg/kg body wt/day for a child. In order to prevent secondary dapsone resistance, treatment should be based upon the following **three improtant principles.**

1. Dapsone should be started and maintained in full dosage from the very beginning.

2. Treatment should be continued regularly without interruption and, if possible, daily.

3. Combination therapy should be given to patients with multibacillary disease.

Side-effects of dapsone include hemolytic anemia, reduced life span of RBC, methemoglobinemia, hepatitis, dermatitis, psychoses. Few cases of agranulocytosis have been reported when used in high dose (200-300 mg/day as in D.H.). Insomnia, irritability, delusions and disordered thought and speech may occur. A few cases of peripheral neuropathy have been recorded. F. D. R. is a known complication of this drug. Erythema nodosum leprosum and other manifestation of type II lepra reaction may be precipitated by dapsone.

ii. **Clofazimine** : It is an iminophenazine, bright red dye synthesized in 1954 in Dublin. The drug is mainly bacteriostatic and weakly bactericidal. It interacts with mycobacterial DNA. It does not show cross-resistance with dapsone or rifampicin. It is highly lipophilic and tends to be deposited predominantly in the fatty tissue and in cells of reticulo-endothelial system. Mean half life of elimination of plasma clofazimine following a dose of 50-100 mg is 10 days. It is not posssible to determine the minimum inhibitory concentration of clofazimine against leprosy bacilli since the drug is not homogeneously distributed in the tissues.

It is the only antileprosy drug possessing an anti-inflammatory effect which is clinically usable in controlling the ENL reaction. The dose is 300-350 mg per week, preferably administered as a daily capsule of 50 mg or 100 mg on every alternate day.

Side-effects include red brown pigmentation of skin and cojunctivae with darkening of skin lesion to slate grey or black ; red colouration of urine, stool, sputum, sweat and tears ; dryness of skin that may progress to typical ichthyosis. Irritation or burning discomfort in skin lesions may occur. Gastro-intestinal disturbance is insignificant in low dose, especially if taken after food. High dose of clofazimine may cause severe abdominal pain.

iii. **Rifampicin** : It is a semi-synthetic derivative of a fermentation product of Streptomyces mediterranei. Minimum inhibitory concentration is 0.3 μg/ml. Rifampicin acts by inhibiting bacterial RNA synthesis. It is the most potent bactericidal antileprosy drug. It should be given at least half an hour before food. Morphological index of bacilli in skin reaches to zero in 5 weeks. Choice lies between daily or monthly treatment. Second alternative is preferred because it is well tolerated, less expensive and can be supervised.

Monthly dosage of 1500 mg is ideal but 600 mg is a satisfactory alternative ; side effects include red colouration of urine, skin rash, gastro-intestinal symptoms, drowsiness, weakness and dizziness.

Serious side effects can be divided into (1) those having **daily doses**: psychosis, osteomalacia, porphyria cutanea tarda, pemphigus vulgaris, Stevens-Johnson syndrome and (2) those confined to **intermittent administration** e.g. flu syndrome, which may also include shock, hemolytic anemia and renal failure. Effectiveness of steriods and oral contraceptives is impaired in patients receiving rifampicin.

iv. **Ethionamide**: It acts bacteriostatically. Available in tablets of 125 mg. The dose in leprosy is 5 mg/kg/day.

Side-effects include gastro-intestinal symptoms, ptyalism, metallic taste, stomatitis, skin rash, acne, headache and dizziness, peripheral neuropathy, hepatitis, hypothyroidism, hypoglycemia, psychosis, alopecia and gynecomastia.

v. **Thiacetazone**: It is an established antileprosy drug acting bacteriostatically. Optimum dosage is 150 mg/day. For children, it is 2 mg/kg/day. Side effects include nausea, anorexia, headache and drowsiness. In skin, exfoliative dermatitis, toxic epidermal necrolysis and Stevens-Johnson syndrome may occur. In blood, hemolytic anemia, agranulocytosis, thrombocytopenia may occur. Abnormality in liver function tests, with or without jaundice, may also occur. Ethionamide and thiacetazone have cross-resistance.

vi. **Diuciphon**: It is a pyrimidine derivative and is effective against dapsone resistant leprosy. Along with its antileprosy properties, it has an immuno-stimulating effect nearly three times stronger than that of levamisole. Dose is 0.1 g six times a day or 0.2-0.3 g 2-3 times a day.

vii. **Immunotherapy**: The main objective of immunotherapy is to increase CMI in LL. Five methods are under investigations.

1. B.C.G. vaccination every 2 weeks for a year or more + chemotherapy.

2. Intravenous injections of peripheral blood lymphocytes from donors suffering from TT or healthy donor giving a strong positive Mitsuda reaction.

3. Intravenous injections of transfer factor (extract of human lymphocyte from donor).

4. Heat killed M. leprae and living BCG.

5. Levamisole.

viii. Multidrug therapy as recommended by WHO

1. **Multibacillary leprosy (LL, BL and BB)**—It consists of rifampicin 600 mg once monthly, supervised; dapsone 100 mg daily self-administered, clofazimine 300 mg once monthly, supervised; and 50 mg daily self-administered. Treatment should be continued at least for 2 years and then continued up to smear negativity.

2. **Paucibacillary leprosy (TT and BT)**

Rifampicin 600 mg/month and dapsone 100 mg/day. To be continued for a period of six months.

ix. Treatment of acute iritis: Daily inspection of eyes during type-II lepra reaction. Acute iridocyclitis is a medical emergency. Treatment comprises hourly instillation of corticosteroid eye drop (1% hydrocortisone) by day and/or subconjunctival injections of hydrocortisone and the application of corticosteroid eye ointment at night. Eye drops containing 1% homatropine must be instilled twice a day for keeping the pupil as dilated as possible and to prevent adhesions. Complete iridectomy may be advisable in neglected cases.

x. Treatment of acute epididymo-orchitis: Patient needs bed rest, analgesics, oral corticosteroids. Scrotum should be supported by suspensory bandage.

13. **Deformities and management**: Damage to the three physiological components of nerves is followed by anesthesia, dryness of the skin and muscular paralysis. These three primary factors underlie deformities and disability of the hands and feet, for they predispose the affected limb to misuse,

ulceration, scar formation and secondary infection. A further cause of damage in LL is the direct invasion of tissues by M. leprae.

Pathogenesis of disability following nerve damage (After Bryceson and Pfaltzgraff, 1984)—See Fig. 1. page 144.

A. **Primary deformities due to paralysis of nerves**

a. **Ulnar nerve** : Claw hand with hyper-extended metacarpophalangeal joints and flexion of interphalangeal joints of ring finger and little finger. Motor changes are wasting of hypothenar eminence and hollowing of interosseous spaces.

b. **Median nerve** : Clawing of index and middle finger, wasting of hand and radial side of thenar eminence.

c. **Radial nerve** : Wrist drop, inability or difficulty in extending the wrist and fingers. Paralysis of thumb, fingers and wrist extensors.

d. **Lateral popliteal** : Foot drop. Patient drags the foot while walking and has a high stepping gait due to inability or difficulty in dorsiflexing the foot.

Paralysis of peroneal muscles and dorsiflexors of the foot.

e. **Posterior tibial** : Clawing of toes and collapse of foot arches, paralysis of almost all the intrinsic muscles of foot.

f. **Facial** : Lagophthalmos due to zygomatic branch, mask face, paralysis of orbicularis oculi, paresis of orbicularis oris.

B. **Management of primary deformities** : Reconstructive surgery.

C. **Management of secondary deformities**

a. Due to **anesthesia**—Prevention of injury by regular and daily examination of hands and feet is a must. Prompt treatment should be started if there is any. Protective foot wear to be used to avoid injury to anesthetic feet.

b. Due to **paralysis**—Passive exercises and education of the family members are needed.

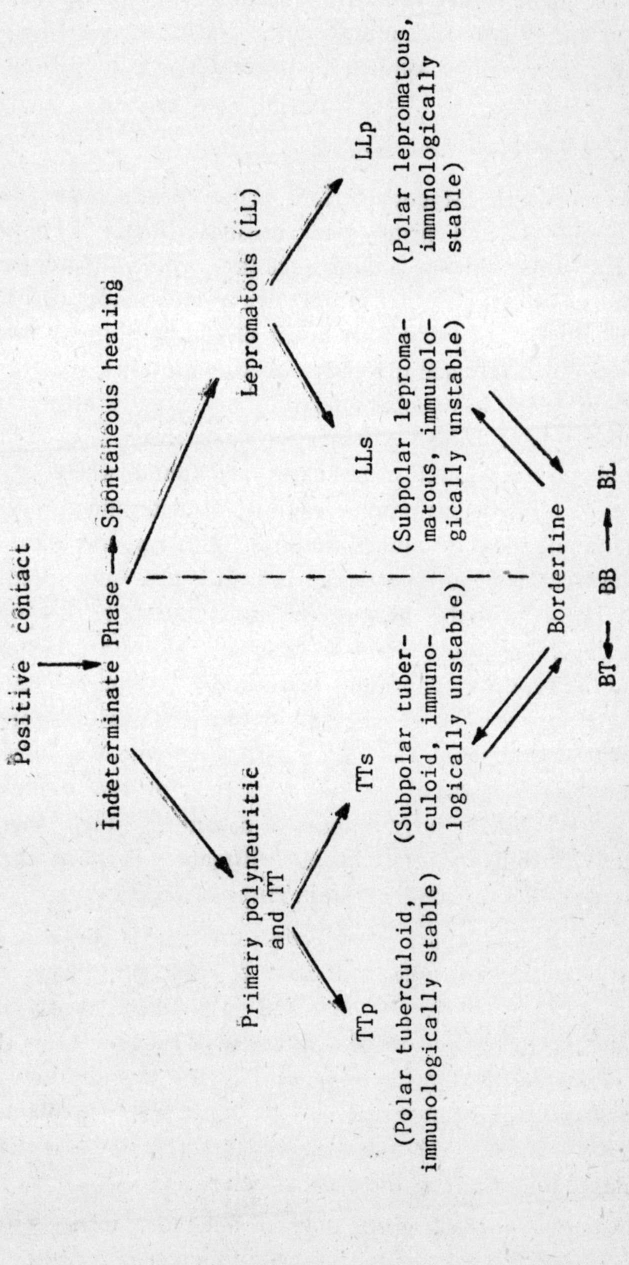

Fig. 2 Evolution of the disease

c. Due to **dry skin**—Hands and feet should be soaked in water for about 30 minutes daily and then vaseline or vegetable oil is to be applied to prevent the evaporation of water.

DISCUSSION

Infection with Mycobacterium leprae produces a wide range of clinical and histological manifestations. TTp and LLp are polar forms having definite clinico-histological features. The classification of HD are usually made as TTp, TTs, BT, BB, BL, LLs and LLp but it should be borne in mind that these constitute definite parts of a continuous spectrum. A patient may have characteristics not exactly fitting any particular class. This classification has been based on immunologic facts, but often cases are found where exact location of a particular patient cannot be determined either with immunological or clinical findings. Further, the effect of the drug treatment on a particular patient is not fully predictable. This is probably because the contribution of his own immunological response might be variable. However, keeping in mind the aspect of enormous variations, it can be stated that the polar varieties of tuberculoid and lepromatous forms have certain stability. The TTp is associated with low infectivity and high degree of natural resistance to the organism whereas LL is having large number of organisms, high degree of infectivity and very little natural resistance. Between these two extremes lies a widely variable range of presentations.

The mode and route of infection are yet to be exactly known. Probably, droplet infection is most prevalent. As the M. leprae could not be cultured in artificial media, incubation period remains to be a rather wide range. After the entry of organisms into the body, correct and exact follow up studies have not been made to get a definitely explained pathogenic pathway. Knowledge in this regard is sketchy and unable to explain all the clinical details.

In TT, well-formed granuloma invade the dermis from within the nerve trunks and in LL, granulomata lies deeper in the dermis and contain large number of foamy histiocytes. M. leprae are present in large number. As the spectrum starts from TT and proceeds to LL, the number of lesions gradually increases and symmetrical features come in. Number of bacteria increases, epithelioid cells decrease, foamy histiocytes increase and lepromin negativity increases. Bacteriological status is judged by BI and MI. Immunological status can be assessed by the results of lepromin test, estimations of immunoglobulins, DNCB skin sensitization test, lymphocyte blast transformation test etc. Modern sophisticated tests may also help.

Early diagnosis and treatment are essential. Cardinal signs of HD e.g. finding of skin patch with sensory anomaly, thickening of nerves and finding of AFB by slit-skin smear are still the most important diagnostic signs.

Modern therapy is highly effective. WHO has put forward standard regimens. These are the minimum but may not always be the optimum for all patients in our country where it is better to overtreat a patient having endemicity. We should be conscious of the resistant strains of bacilli as well as the persisters.

Multidrug therepy is definitely a boon at least in reducing the reservoir of infection quickly.

We are looking forward to have an effective vaccine.

All qualified doctors should be confident and capable of treating HD without hesitation and the disease should be treated even in remote clinics. A fruitful treatment of all patients is probably the best way of eradicating the disease from our country.

HERPES SIMPLEX (HS)

Two viruses showing no cross-immunity can cause herpes simplex. Such two viruses are

(i) Herpes simplex virus type-1 **(HSV 1),** also called the **orofacial type,** and (2) HSV type-2, **(HSV 2)** also called the **genital type.**

DIAGNOSIS

1. Age of onset : Primary type-1 herpes infections occur mainly in infancy and early childhood. Maternal antibody protects most infants for the first few months, but neonatal infections may occur if the protective mechanism is not adequate.

2. Predisposing factors : The newborn, especially the prematures, the malnourished persons and infants e.g. those with kwashiorkor, associated infections like measles, in compromised hosts being treated with immuno-suppressive drugs, Hodgkin's and other related diseases, Wiskott-Aldrich syndrome, dysplasia of the thymus, lymphoma or leukemia, severe burns and underlying skin diseases such as atopic eczema.

3. Recurrence : It is one of the most important characteristics of HSV infection. This is due to persistence of virus in human trigeminal and sacral ganglia. Some mechanism is believed to trigger the reactivation. The precipitating factors may be sunlight exposure, menses, physical trauma, emotional stress, fever, sexual intercourse in case of genital herpes simplex. Recurrent infections differ from primary one in the smaller size of the vesicles, close grouping and absence of constitutional symptoms. Prostaglandins possibly play a major role in the recurrence. Rarely, recurrence may occur from newly acquired viral strain. With increasing age, the recurrence becomes less frequent.

4. Accompaniment : Herpes simplex regularly accompanies some febrile diseases such as pneumonia, influenza, malaria, meningococcal meningitis. But it is not usually associated with any constitutional disorder.

5. **Mode of infection** : It spreads by (i) droplet infection and (ii) direct contact. After the primary infection, it persists throughout the life of over half the population. Antibody does not fully protect against further infection by inoculation. In such cases, trauma is often a contributory factor. Multiple lesions develop from the combined effect of exposure to infected saliva and to trauma.

6. **Sites of involvement** : **Lips** are the most frequent site. But it may appear in any location. The **nose**—both inside and outside—is the next most common location. **Cheeks**, other parts of the face and ears are also involved. **Genital regions** are involved in HSV 2 infection. Rarely, lesions appear within the mouth, tongue or within the pharynx, larynx and the esophagus.

7. **Description of the lesion** : The lesions are self-limiting eruption of grouped vesicles on an erythematous base. They may occur singly or in multiple, at or near the mucocutaneous junction, and are preceded by itching, burning and erythema of several minutes to hours duration. Neuralgic pain may precede in very rare cases. Fully developed eruption consists of cluster of pinhead-sized vesicles. In a few days, they rupture and dried serum forms a crust beneath which epithelialization occurs. Neighbouring lymphnodes sometimes become enlarged and tender. Lesions tend to heal without scarring except in case of unusual suppuration.

8. **Types of herpes simplex lesion**

a. **Herpetic gingivostomatitis** : It occurs in children between 1-5 years. Family epidemics have been reported. It begins with fever, malaise, restlessness and excessive dribbling. Vesicles are present on the tongue, pharynx, palate and buccal mucous membranes. Breath is foul. Gums are swollen and bleed easily. Vesicles are followed by ulcers with a yellowish pseudomembrane. Regional lymphnodes get enlarged. Complete recovery occurs within 2 weeks.

b. Herpes genitalis : It is generally caused by HSV 2. Lesions are similar to thoses caused by HSV 1. Sites of involvement are prepuce, glans penis and shaft of the penis. Anal lesions and proctitis may occur in homosexuals. There may be evidence of urethritis. In females, labia majora, labia minora, clitoris, perineum, introitus and sometimes the perianal area, thighs, buttocks and mons pubis, cervix uteri are involved. Occasionally, throat or fingers are affected. Inguinal lymphnodes may become enlarged and tender. They heal within 2-4 weeks. There is evidence that suggests probable association of infection with HSV 2 and the later development of malignancy in the cervix uteri.

c. Keratoconjunctivitis : Primary infection may cause severe and purulent conjunctivitis with opacity and superficial ulceration of cornea. Preauricular gland is enlarged and tender.

d. Inoculation herpes simplex : Direct inoculation of virus into an abrasion or normal skin gives rise to indurated papules, large bullae or scattered vesicles after an incubation period of 5 days to a week. Regional lymphnodes get enlarged. Inoculation of the fingertip results in the so-called **herpetic whitlow.**

e. Eczema herpeticum : Patients, especially the children, with atopic dermatitis sometimes develop, when infected with herpes simplex, severe varicelliform eruptions in eczematous patches (Kaposi's varicelliform eruption). In addition, eczema herpeticum may be a complication of severe seborrheic dermatitis, impetigo, scabies, Darier's disease, pemphigus vulgaris and pemphigus folliaceous. Herpes virus hominis may be isolated from such cases by human amnion cell tissue culture.

f. Disseminated herpes : It is a disease of children of six months to three years. It also occurs in pregnancy. It starts with severe herpetic gingivostomatitis. Dissemination to the viscera, especially liver, lungs and a massive viremia may follow to produce gastroenteritis, encephalitis, hepatic and adrenal dysfunction. Death occurs during the stage of severe viremia. Disseminated H. S. is found in malnourished child e.g. kwashiorkor, infections like measles, in compromised hosts treated with immuno-suppressive drugs, Hodgkin's and other related lymphomas, Wiskott-Aldrich syndrome, severe burns and atopic eczema due to their predisposition as stated earlier.

g. **Intrauterine and neonatal herpes simplex** : Herpes virus contracted in utero may result in anomalies of the new born. Anomalies include microcephaly, microphthalmia, encephalitis, intracerebral calcification and the vesicular skin lesions. Association of maternal genital herpetic infection with abortions, still births and premature delivery has been reported. Most cases of intrauterine herpes simplex are the result of ascending infections from the cervix (caused by HSV 2) and transplacental route of infection seems likely. Most cases of neonatal infection are also caused by HSV 2 contracted from birth passage during parturition. Perinatally acquired herpes simplex ranges from localized skin infection to severe disseminated disease with encephalitis, hepatitis, pneumonia and coagulopathy. Caesarian section is therefore recommended as a prophylactic measure in parturient women with lesions of genital herpes simplex.

9. **Histopathology** : Histologic features are

i. Ballooning degeneration of epidermal cells, seen mainly at the base of the viral vesicle, and reticular degeneration of epidermal cells seen mainly in the upper portion and periphery of viral vesicles.

ii. Acantholysis. **iii.** Intraepidermal vesicle.

iv. Inflammatory infiltrate in the upper dermis. In severe reactions, dermis shows severe vasculitis charactersied by fibrinoid deposits and a dense inflammatory infiltrate with many neutrophils both within and around the capillary walls. There may be extravasation of erythrocytes, fragmentation of the nuclei of neutrophils and occasionally necrosis of the vascular walls.

v. Inclusion bodies are seen in the centre of enlarged round nuclei of balloon cells. They are eosinophilic and are usually surrounded by clear space or halo measuring from 3 μm to 8 μm in diameter.

10. Tzanck smear : It is a rapid method of diagnosis carried out on a smear taken from the floor of an early freshly open vesicle, where ballooning degeneration is prominent, and stained with Giemsa's stain. Many acantholytic balloon cells with one or several nuclei are seen.

11. Viral identification

a. Culture—Material from the floor of a blister is inoculated on cell cultures consisting of Hela cells or human amnion cells or fibroblasts.

b. Direct **immunofluorescence** for the presence of viral antigen— It is carried out by preparation of smears of such cells to which is first added rabbit serum containing herpes simplex antibody and then fluorescein conjugated anti-rabbit serum globulin of mice.

c. Determination of **antibody titre** in patient's serum : Complement fixation reaction is usually used.

TREATMENT

PREVENTION — SILVER SULPHADIAZINE — ACYCLOVIR

Concepts and goals for the therapy of herpes simplex include (i) Prevention of infection and/or (ii) shortening the clinical course of the disease including the frequency of complications of primary infection, (iii) preventing the development of latency and subsequent clinicial recurrences, (iv) preventing subsequent recurrences of disease in established latency, (v) decreasing the transmission of the disease (vi) eradicating established latent infection.

Chemotherupeutic approaches to the treatment of HSV can be categorised into 5 headings. (1) Antiviral compounds

(2) Topical surfactants or detergents (3) Photodynamic dyes (4) Immune modulators and (5) Vaccines.

1. Antiviral compounds

i. **Acyclovir**—Has potent inhibitor activity against both HSV 1 and HSV 2 and, if administered within 96 hours of inoculation of virus, can prevent ganglionic latency. It is a potent inhibitor of viral DNA polymerase. Acyclovir cream 5% in propylene glycol applied 5 times daily for 5 days or longer is effective. Oral acyclovir 200 mg is given 5 times a day for 10 days.

ii. **Vidarabine** (Adenine arabinoside, ARA-A)—It is also an antiviral compound selectively inhibiting DNA polymerase of HSV. It is used in a dose of 10-15 mg/kg for 10 days, particularly in encephalitis and visceral dissemination.

iii. Topical applications of **idoxuridine in dimethylsulphoxide** would promote healing of the lesions.

iv. **Phosphonoformate** and its related compound phosphonoacetic acid (PAA) are potent inhibitors of DNA polymerase of HSV. Topical preparations of phosphonoformate appear to speed up the rate of healing.

2. Topical surfactants or detergents

HSV is a lipid enveloped virus and dissolution of the envelope reduces infectivity. A double-blind placebo controlled investigations of topical surfactants such as ether and chloroform have shown these medications to be ineffective.

3. **Photodynamic inactivation :** Certain heterocyclic dyes such as neutral red and proflavine can be bound irreverisbly to herpes virus which becomes inactivated by a subsequent brief exposure of the dye to fluorescent light. But this form of treatment was found hardly beneficial. The lack of clinical benefit and potential toxicity have made these medications totally unusable in muco-cutaneous HSV infection.

4. **Nonspecific immune modulators :** The stimulation of cellular immunity by levamisole and transfer factor was tried to prevent recurrence. But the result is not encouraging. Vaccination with BCG is also equally disappointing.

5. **Heterologous vaccines :** Heterologous vaccines such as smallpox, BCG, influenza and polio vaccines have been used as therapies for HSV infection. There have been reported deaths from disseminated vaccinia infection and this potentially dangerous form of therapy should be actively discouraged.

6. If there is any secondary infection, patients might require a local antibiotic and/or occasionally a systemic antibiotic.

7. **Other ancillary measures :** (1) For pain or fever, analgesics and antipyretics. (2) For relief of the cutaneous symptoms, cool soaks with Burow's solution, saline or dilute acetic acid or aluminium chloride hexahydrate 20% in anhydrous ethyl alcohol for 10-20 minutes several times a day. (3) For a relief of pain of oral lesions, antihistamine mouth washes e.g. Benadryl[R] or Atarax[R] elixir or viscous lidocaine. (4) For disuria, urinating while soaking in a tub of lukewarm water is helpful. (5) 0.01 to 4% zinc sulphate solution applied 4 times daily for about an hour helps drying of the lesions and probably reduces recurrence. (6) Since prostaglandins seem to be responsible for flare up of herpes, it is reasonable to take 2 aspirin tablets before potentially inciting event. (7) Avoidance of foods high in arginine (chocolate, nuts, seeds and grains) helps some patients. (8) Application of silver sulphadiazine cream heals the lesions more quickly.

8. **Miscellaneous drugs**

(a) Oral lysine—1000 to 3000 mg/day during attack and for preventing recurrences.

(b) Chlorpheniramine—12 mg t.i.d. for 2 weeks before each period.

(c) Propranolol—20 mg t.i.d. before and during significant stress.

(d) Superficial epidermal subsection if the recurrences are at the same site.

(e) 4% thymol in chloroform applied b.i.d. for first 3 days of attack.

(f) 2% glutaraldehyde buffered to pH 7.5 with sodium bicarbonate application b.i.d.

(g) 0.5% sodium hypochlorite to apply b.i.d. or 0.1% solution mouth wash b.i.d.

(h) Lithium–900 mg/day for about 8 months reportedly prevented recurrent labial herpes.

(i) Cotrimoxazole–2 tabs b.i.d. give symptomatic relief.

(j) Amantadine—100 mg b.i.d helps the patients who do not respond to cotrimoxazole.

(k) Local use of povidone iodine probably helps in killing the secondary infection.

DISCUSSION

Recurrent herpes simplex, particularly H. progenitalis, is a great therapeutic challenge. At the earliest sensory warning immediate acyclovir therapy shows some positive result, but if used late, it is much less effective. It cannot kill the virus in the neural ganglia but it can prevent its harmful growth in the skin.

The known precipitating factors should always be avoided. Herpetic keratitis should be properly treated by ophthalmologists. Herpes present in the birth canal during delivery will affect about half of the babies ; death or severe retardation is more often the outcome. Hence, in such cases, caesarian section should be done.

Lesions in the early stage is highly contagious. Caution against social encounters until lesions are healed is very important.

Although there is a significant cofactor in the process of cancer by HSV, the newspaper propaganda about development of cervical cancer appears disproportional.

The only redeeming feature is that with increasing age there is more and more spontaneous healing.

HERPES ZOSTER

H. Zoster is a localised vesicular eruption. It is caused by the virus H. varicellae and is the result of reaction of residual latent infection, usually of sensory neurones infected by the viremia of chicken-pox.

DIAGNOSIS

1. **Age and sex incidence** : Both sexes are equally affected. Patients are over 45, with an increased incidence between 60 and 70. It is uncommon in children and very rare in infancy. This is the result of intrauterine exposure to the virus, inparting immunity.

2. **Mode of infection** : Most people contract the infection in the form of chicken-pox in childhood. The virus is believed to remain latent in the dorsal root or cranial nerve ganglion. Immunity against reinfection is generally the rule. But later the virus becomes reactivated causing an attack of zoster. The stimuli for reactivation are unknown, but anything that usually lowers the individual's immunological mechanism may precipitate an attack.

3. **Precipitating factors** : Hodgkin's disease, leukemias, malignancies including lymphomas and antimitotic therapy are important precipitating factors. In many cases, local pressure of neoplastic deposits on nerve roots may both provoke the development of zoster and determine its site. Reports of the onset of zoster at the site of external trauma are many. It may also follow radiotherapy, usually at the level of irradiation.

Herpes zoster occurring in immuno-compromised patients assumes a disseminated form which may prove fatal.

4. **Immunity** : Second attacks of zoster are unusual, but have been reported.

5. **Sites involved** : Thoracic, cervical, trigeminal, including ophthalmic and lumbosacral dermatomes are most commonly

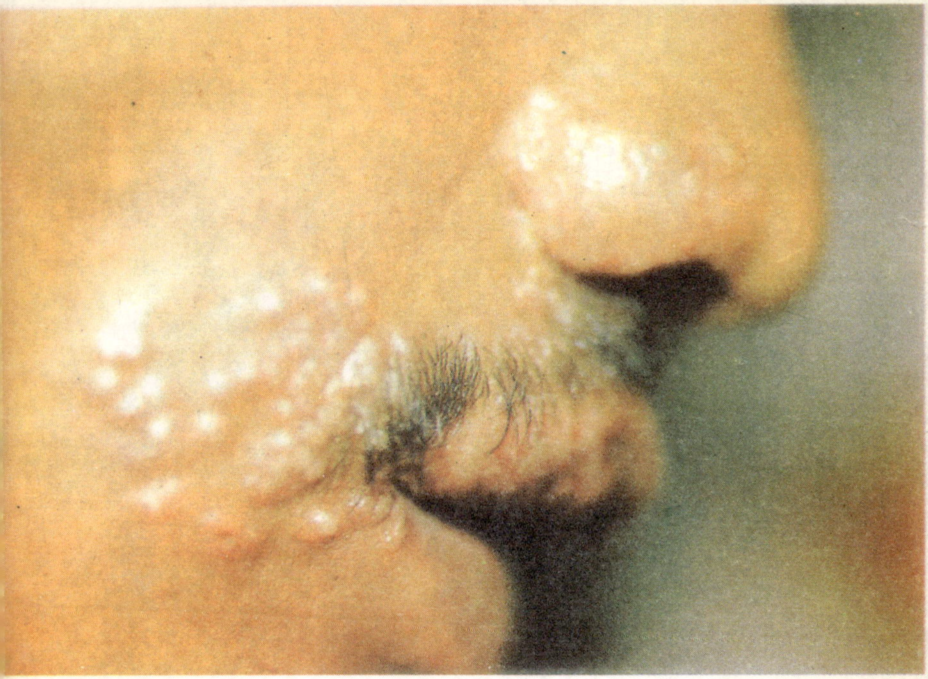

Fig. H-15. **Herpes Simplex** showing grouped vesicular lesions.

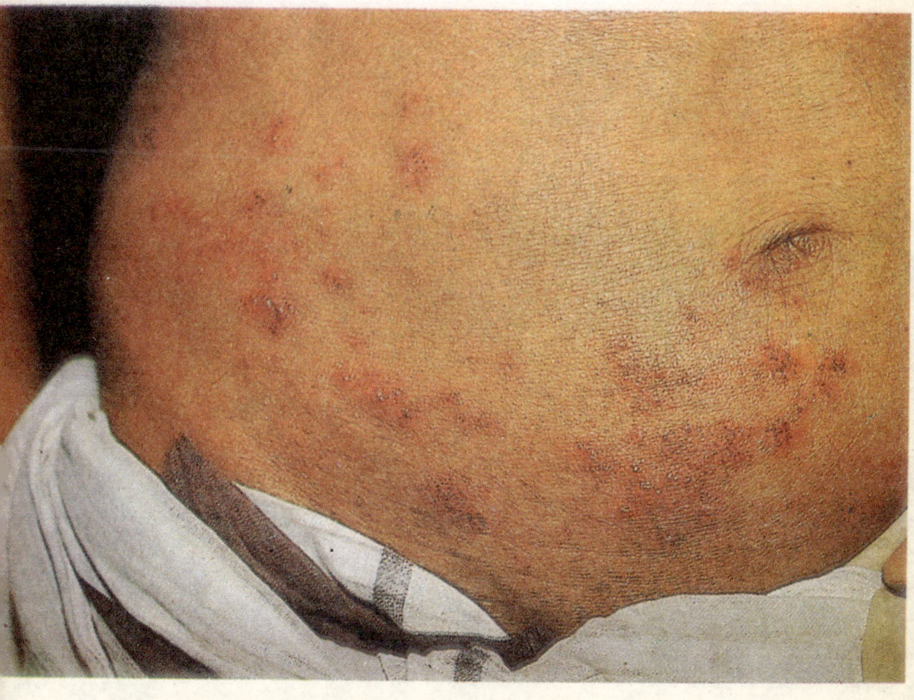

Fig. H-16. **Herpes Zoster** showing grouped papulo-vesicular eruptions affecting one half of the body (front).

involved at all ages but the relative frequency of ophthalmic zoster increases in old age. Rarely, the eruption may be bitateral. Bilateral herpes and disseminated form should arise the suspicion of internal malignancy.

6. **Description of the lesions** : The first manifestation of zoster is usually pain, accompanied by fever, headache, malaise and tenderness localised to areas of one or more dorsal roots. Pain may be localised or diffuse. After 3 or 4 days, closely grouped red papules rapidly become vesicular and then pustular, developing in a continuous or interrupted band in the area of usually one, seldom two or hardly more dermatomes. Mucous membranes within the affected dermatomes are also involved. New vesicles continue to appear for several days. Lymph nodes draining the affected area are enlarged and tender. Recovery is complete in 2-3 weeks in children and young adults. In older patients, it is about 3-4 weeks.

7. **Sequelae and complications** : In elderly and undernourished patient, the local eruption often becomes necrotic when healing requires many weeks and may be followed by severe scarring. In children, complications such as encephalomyelitis and persistent facial palsy may occur. Visceral involvement may be responsible for abdominal pain, pleural pain or temporary electrocardiographic abnormalities with or without precordial pain. Ocular palsies and facial palsies have been reported in cases of ophthalmic zoster. Zoster of the anogenital area may be associated with disturbances of defecation and urination. The commonest and most intractable sequel of zoster is neuralgia. It is unusual in childhood, but increases both in incidence and severity with age.

8. **Ramsey-Hunt syndrome** : It was formerly attributed to involvement of the geniculate ganglion. Pain in the ear is associated with vesicles on the pinna and in the external auditory canal. The facial palsy, sometimes permanent, is a frequent complication.

9. **Histopathology** : (1) Ballooning degeneration of keratinocytes (2) acantholysis and (3) intraepidermal vesicle

and/or ulceration (4) intranuclear eosinophilic inclusion bodies (5) multinucleated keratinocyte formation (6) perivascular infiltrate of lymphocytes, histiocytes or many neutrophils and (7) sometimes changes of leucocytoclastic vasculitis. Degree of leukocytoclastic vasculitis and hemorrhage are often more pronounced. Eosinophilic inclusion bodies are seen in the dermis within the nuclei of capillary endothelial cells and of fibroblasts bordering the affected vessels. Inclusion bodies have been demonstrated within neurilemmal cells of the small nerves in the dermis underlying the vesicles.

10. **Tzanck smear** : Same as that of herpes simplex.

11. **Viral identification** : Varicella zoster virus does not grow in ordinary tissue culture. But it does grow in tissue cultures containing human fetal diploid kidney cells or monkey kidney cells. Varicella-zoster virus is not pathogenic to any animal whereas herpes simplex virus is a pathogen for many laboratory animals.

TREATMENT

ACYCLOVIR	CARBAMAZINE
STEROID	CHLORPROMAZINE
ANTIBIOTICS	ZOSTER IMMUNE GLOBULIN

1. **Drying** of vesicles hastens healing which can be done with soaks with Burow's solution, dilute vinegar, saline, Condy's lotion etc. Ointments should never be applied, for they occlude the skin and allow to prolong the viral presence and even super-infection. Topical steroids are best avoided during vesicular stage. Lotio calamine helps drying but may occlude the skin. A 2% glutaraldehyde with sodium bicarbonate (pH 7.5) applied b.i.d for 2 weeks is a good remedy. Painting of lesions with equal parts of tincture of benzoin and flexible collodion, twice daily, helps in both drying and protecting the lesions from extraneous injuries.

2. **Itching** can be controlled by antihistaminics.

3. **Pain** is relieved by aspirin or nonsteroidal analgesics. Codeine or stronger narcotic may be needed.

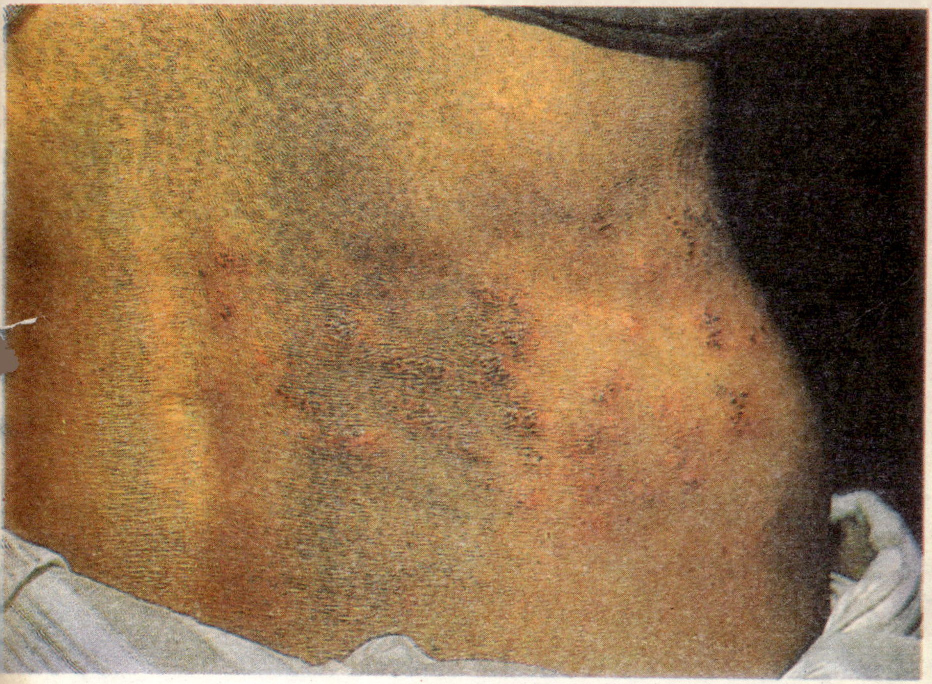

Fig. H-17. **Herpes Zoster** showing grouped papulo-vesicular eruptions affecting one half of the body (back).

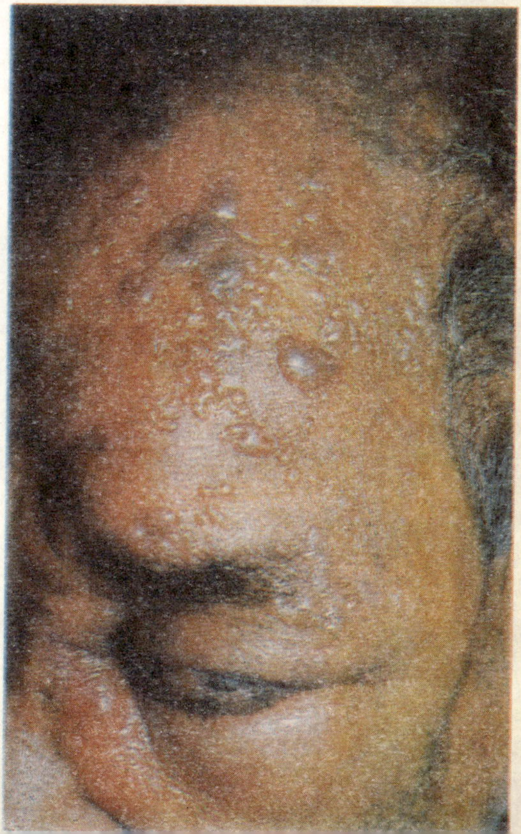

Fig. H-18. **Herpes Zoster Ophthalmicus** showing vesicular lesions of forehead. There is edema of the eyelids.

4. **In mild attacks,** rest and analgesics are sufficient. In severe painful attacks, corticosteriods may be prescribed to otherwise fit patients who have not received immunosuppressive therapy, for suppressing the inflammatory changes. Treatment should start with 40-60 mg of prednisolone daily for a week, and smaller doses for the next two weeks. It is believed that steriod therapy, if started within one week, prevents post-herpetic neuralgia, especially in the elderly people. ACTH is probably capable of blocking the pain by way of attacking the endorphin receptors.

5. **Antiviral agents**

Effective antiviral agents should be used within hours of the vesicle formation.

a. High does of acyclovir—800 mg (4 capsules) 5 times daily for 10 days is claimed to give the best result.

b. **Idoxuridine** (5%) in dimethyl sulphoxide applied b.i.d and acyclovir topically have some effect. Most patients show rapid relief of pain and healing of the skin lesions.

c. **Bromo-venyl-deoxyuridine** is a new antiviral drug of good promise.

d. **Vidarabine** (Ara-A) 10 mg/kg/day I.V over 12 hours for five days can accelerate healing and reduce the chance of post-herpetic neuralgia.

6. **Post-herpetic neuralgia**

a. **Chlorpromazine** may sometime bring relief when the analgesics have proved ineffective. If it is combined with tricyclic antidepressant, probably it is more effective. If severe pain persists, a neurosurgical opinion should be taken.

b. **Paravertebral x-ray therapy** to affected nerve ganglia may be extremely beneficial and is clearly indicated where the systemic corticosteriods are contraindicated.

c. **Intralesional injection of triamcinolone** (0.2%)

d. **Various tranquillizers**

e. **Chlorprothixene** : 10 to 100 mg. q.i.d.

f. **Alpha-tocopherol acetate** (Vitamin-E) : 400 I.U once to thrice daily.

g. **Carbamazine** (Tegretol)—100 mg q.i.d is said to have effect in reducing the pain of post-herpetic neuralgia.

h. **Stellate ganglion block or epidural block**—Has been tried by 0.25 to 0.5% bupivacaine.

i. **Pimozide** (Orap)—2 mg t.i.d may give dramatic relief of neuralgic pain.

j. **Cimetidine**—600 mg t.i.d plus zinc sulphate 200 mg t.i.d can relieve pain.

k. **Adenosine monophosphate**—100 mg in aqueous gel I.M. three times a week can give good relief to pain.

7. **In immunosuppressed patients** : Zoster immune globulin injections may be life-saving.

8. **In disseminated zoster** : I. V. therapy with vidarabine is indicated.

9. **Controlling of secondary bacterial infection** is best done by erythromycin 250 mg q.i.d for 7 days.

10. **Cryocautery of sensitized skin** areas have relieved pain in post-herpetic neuralgia.

11. **Phenytoin sodium** (Dilatin) : 300-400 mg/day with 50-100 mg of **nortriptylene** and **carbamazine** 100 mg/day have shown beneficial results.

12. **Transcutaneous electrical stimulation** : A very high percentage of patients got relief to pain by this therapy.

DISCUSSION

Diagnosis of herpes zoster is made whenever grouped papulo-vesicular eruptions are seen involving one or more dermatomes. Prominent symptoms are burning, pain and sometimes itching. The disease is acute and self-limiting. More than 50% of cases clear within 2 weeks. Post-herpetic neuralgia might occur in about 2% of cases. One in five of these patients may suffer for more than six months. Zoster is more severe and prolonged in older patients.

Acylovir is non-toxic, non-mutagenic compound that selectively inhibits specific, critical polymerases found in viruses but not in the host cells. Hence high doses of this drug is being used now-a-days.

Drying of lesions by astringent antiseptic lotions helps in quicker healing. Secondary infection should he treated by antibiotics. It is believed that early relief to pain probably lessens the chance of post-herpetic neuralgia. In elderly patients, a course of steriod is worth giving a trial.

In our country, carbamazine and chlorpromazine with or without tricyclic antidepressant may be used for post-herpetic neuralgia. But the results are often unpredictable. Neurosurgical intervention is the last resort.

ICHTHYOSES

DIAGNOSIS

1. Ichthyoses form a group of diseases having disorder of keratinization characterized clinically by dry and scaly skin. The term ichthyosis means **'resembling fish skin'**. All ichthyosis scales show: (a) thickened stratum corneum (b) enhanced corneocyte adhesion and (c) low water binding capacity.

2. The **ichthyoses group** includes a number of different forms. Four of them are major and three minor.

a. Four **major forms**

i. Ichthyosis vulgaris ii. X-linked ichthyosis iii. Epidermolytic hyperkeratosis iv. Lamellar ichthyosis.

b. Three **minor forms include**

i. Harlequin ichthyosis **ii.** Erythrokeratoderma variabilis and **iii.** Ichthyosis linearis circumflexa.

c. **Associated syndromes** are

i. Sjogren-Larsson syndrome **ii.** Rud's syndrome **iii.** Conradi's syndrome **iv.** Netherton's syndrome and **v.** Refsum's syndrome.

d. **Secondary ichthyosis** may occur in

i. Lymphoma, particularly Hodgkin's disease

ii. Carcinoma, reticulum cell sarcoma **iii.** Sarcoidosis

iv. Myxedema, panhypopituitarism

v. Lepromatous leprosy

vi. Taking oral contraceptives

vii. Having anti-cholesterol agents e.g. clofibrate

viii. Drugs—clofazimine, nicotinic acid

ix. Malnutrition

Ichthyosis vulgaris

Ichthyosis vulgaris is an autosomal dominantly inherited disease **characterised** by the following features.

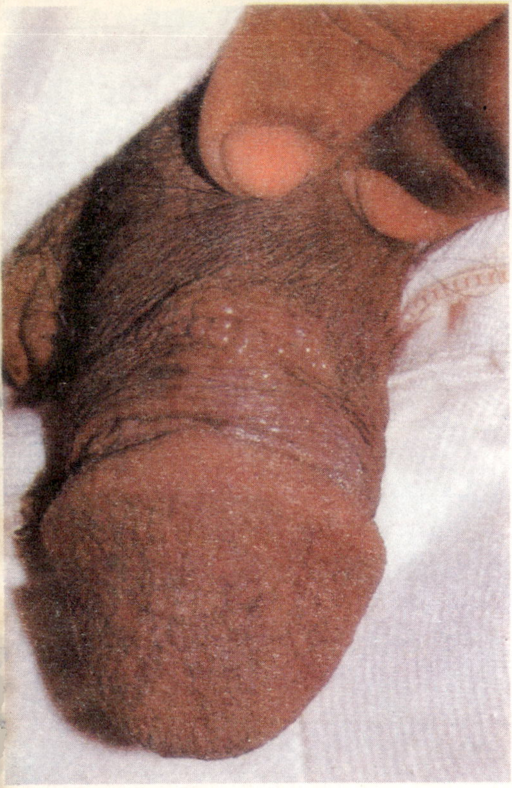

Fig. H-19. **Herpes Genitalis** showing grouped vesicles.

I-1. **Ichthyosis Vulgaris** showing dry and scaly skin.

A. It develops few months after birth.

B. Large adherent scales are present mainly on the extensor surfaces of the extremities. Occasionally, trunk may be involved. Flexural areas remain free.

C. It exacerbates during the winter but remission is seen to occur during summer.

D. Often keratosis pilaris is present.

E. Palmoplantar hyperkeratosis may also be present.

F. **Histological examination** shows

i. Moderate hyperkeratosis

ii. Thin or absent granular layer

iii. Normal dermis

G. **Pathogenesis**

i. Hyperkeratosis is regarded as retention keratosis.

ii. The retention keratosis results from increased adhesiveness of the stratum corneum.

iii. The increased adhesiveness is due to delay in dissolution of the desmosomal disks in the horny layer.

X-linked ichthyosis

X-linked ichthyosis is inherited autosomal recessively. The **characteristic features** are

A. It is rarely present at birth.

B. In contrast to ichthyosis vulgaris, the flexural creases are found to be involved.

C. The thickness of the large adherent scales increases during childhood.

D. **Histological examination** shows

i. Hyperkeratosis

ii. Granular layer is normal or slightly thickened but, unlike ichthyosis vulgaris, not thinned.

E. **Pathogenesis**

i. It is due to retention hyperkeratosis, being the result of delay in dissolution of desmosomal disks.

ii. The cause of the retention hyperkeratosis is the virtual absence of steriod sulphatase activity.

Epidermolytic hyperkeratosis

It is inherited autosomal dominantly and is **characterised** by the following features.

A. Generalized erythema from the time of birth.

B. Thick, brown, verrucous scaling follows the erythema after a few days.

C. There is marked involvement of flexural areas.

D. In the first few years, vesicles and bullae may usually be encountered.

E. **Histological examination** shows

i. Compact hyperkeratosis

ii. Markedly thickened granular layer

iii. Clear spaces of different sizes around the nuclei in the cells of upper stratum malpighii.

iv. Indistinct cellular boundaries—peripheral to the clear spaces.

F. **Pathogenesis**—Keratinization is both execessive and abnormal.

Lamellar ichthyosis

It is inherited antosomal recessively. The **characteristic** features arc

A. The newborn at birth is encased in a tight shiny membrane which resembles collodion.

B. This membrane detaches itself after a few days.

C. After its detachment, the skin of the whole body appears red and scaly. It also involves the flexural surfaces.

D. It may persist thoughout the life, but in milder cases found to gradually subside.

E. Histologic findings are non-specific.

F. **Pathogenesis**

i. Excessive keratogenesis

ii. Increased amount of intercellular substance in the horny layer. This is responsible for the increased adherence of the horny cells.

TREATMENT

HYDRATION	LACTIC ACID
EMOLLIENTS	PROPYLENE GLYCOL
RETINOIC ACID	ISOTRETINOIN
SALICYLIC ACID	TIGASON

Skin is dry because it lacks water. The treatment should thus be aimed at replacing the water in the skin.

1. **Preventive measures** which help are

a. Bathing should not be excessive and bath water should be warm but not hot. Oatmeal or bath oil may be added which probably increases hydration of the skin.

b. Too much use of soap is to be eschewed.

c. Emollients are helpful. Vaseline, glycerine, coconut oil etc. are best applied when the skin is moist.

2. **Treatment of pre-existing dryness and scaling**

a. Bath for 5-10 min. and immediate application of vaseline. This may be done twice daily.

b. Symptomatic xerosis with eczematous changes may be treated effectively by applying topical corticosteriod e.g. betamethasone valerate cream twice or thirce daily.

c. Maximum hydration can be done by the use of 40-60% propylene glycol in water under occlusion by polythene.

An extremely effective keratolytic and hydrating gel can be prepared by adding 6-10% salicylic acid to propylene glycol. This is to be used initially once or twice weekly, and there-after whenever needed. Salicylic acid ointment may also be combined with lactic acid.

d. Creams containing urea and those containing lactic acid may be used to produce prolonged hydration.

e. Vitamin A orally, in toxic doses, is effective.

f. Oral isotretinoin—an oral retinoid—is effective in the doses of 1-2 mg/kg of body weight daily, in major types of ichthyoses e.g. lamellar ichthyosis, x-linked ichthyosis.

g. Alpha-hydroxy acids and related compounds—They alter the keratinization process.

i. A 5% lactic acid in hydrophilic ointment.

ii. About 40-60% propylene glycol in water has been mentioned earlier.

iii. Most patients are benefitted by the use of propylene glycol at night with daily use of lactic acid.

h. Many patients improve with Retin A cream (Retinoic acid 0.1%) applied twice daily. Turnover of the skin is increased and cohesiveness of cells is reduced. It has been used under occlusion in lamellar ichthyosis and epidermolytic hyperkeratosis.

i. Mechanical removal of scales by (1) baths with rubbing (2) compresses and (3) pumice stone : after skin is hydrated, gentle circular friction should be applied to the scaly surface.

j. Methotrexate has been shown to improve lamellar ichthyosis and epidermolytic hyperkeratosis but it can produce blisters in the latter case.

k. Temperature controlled incubator in which air saturated with water is circulated—It is used in case of collodion baby. The humidity will allow the membrane to remain pliable and prevent respiratory difficulty.

3. Miscellaneous agents

a. A 6% salicylic acid in 60% propylene glycol gel.

b. Tretinoin 0.05% in 70% isopropyl alcohol to apply thrice daily.

c. A 10% cholesterol cream to apply twice daily.

d. Tigason 1 mg/kg/day is found to be much helpful in lamellar ichthyosis.

e. Low dose cyclophosphamide e.g. 50 mg tab every three days.

f. PUVA therapy in ichthyosis linearis circumflexa.

For ready reference, salient features of congenital ichthyotic disorders are charted below.

Congenital ichthyotic disorders (Landow, 1983)

Type	Incidence	Inheritance	Onset	Collodion baby possible	Age related	Clinical	Associated diseases	Cell adhesiveness
Ichthyosis vulgaris	1 : 300	AD	Childhood	—	Lifelong	Fine, light scales ; spares the flexures; involves palms and soles.	Atopy, keratosis pilaris.	Increased
X-linked ichthyosis	1 : 600	X-linked	Less than 1 year	+	Lifelong	Large, dark scales; involves flexures ; spares palms and soles.	Corneal opacities	Increased
Lamellar ichthyosis	Rare	AR	Birth	+ +	Same or worse with age	Large thick scales, especially about joints; generalised.	Ectropion	—
Epidermolytic hyperkeratosis	Rare	AD	Birth	+ + +	Improves with age	Coarse, dark scales, especially in creases, not palms and soles.	Infection	—

DISCUSSION

A number of diseases have been included in the ichthyoses group which is characterised by dry and scaly skin. While winter season worsens the disease, the patients get some relief during summer.

The commonest and the mildest form of the disease is ichthyosis vulgaris. The various syndromes associated with ichthyosis often show severest manifestations and may even terminate the patient's life.

Histopathology, in most of these diseases, is nonspecific with hyperkeratosis, hypergranulosis and acanthosis except in ichthyosis vulgaris where it is characterised by hyperkeratosis without any granular layer.

All these genodermatoses have basically a disorder in keratinization.

The aim of treatment is to hydrate the skin by emollients. Dry and scaly condition of skin may also be improved by keratolytics e.g. urea 10% cream or 6-10% salicylic acid. Salicylism should be prevented by using ointment less than 30 g per day. Oral retinoids have been tried with good results in severest form of the disease but the result is nominal in milder forms e.g. ichthyosis vulgaris. Retinoids are toxic drugs.

Maintenance of an aqueous micro-environnent for ichthyotic skin is ideal.

IMPETIGO

It is a very common superficial bacterial infection of the skin caused by group A B-hemolytic streptococci or coagulase positive staphylococcus aureus, either alone or more commonly in combination.

DIAGNOSIS

1. It occurs mainly in the **summer** among those living in crowded situation in poor **hygienic** condition.

2. It affects mainly **children** and **young** adults.

3. Causative organisms

a. Pathogenic streptococci : Group A

i. Several M types (2, 49, 55, 56, 57)

ii. Several T types (25/imp, T-12, 19, 3/B 3264, 14/19)

These may produce **glomerulonephritis** after impetigo.

A small break in epidermis helps penetration by direct physical contact or through fomites. Most lesions are on the exposed parts of the body. Scabies and insect bites frequently cause break in the epidermis. Nasopharynx is often contaminated with streptococci from impetigo. About 60 to 90% lesions are **non-bullous.** Pure culture is found in about 30% of cases.

b. Coagulase positive staphylococci : Phage group II S. aureus.

They probably spread from nasopharynx to normal skin. They also produce a toxin **epidermolysin** which produces **bullae.** Pure culture is found only in 10% of cases. But the culture is positive in 60-80% of lesions which contain streptococci. So **mixed infection** is very common.

4. Clinical manifestations

a. Non-bullous impetigo starts with **minute vesicle** which turns quickly into **pustule** and becomes **crusted.** The margins remain mildly inflammatory. The lesions gradually expand in size and number and produce **yellow brown crusts** of 1-3 cm in diameter. They occur mostly in **face**, **arms** and **legs**. Regional lymphadenopathy is present in streptococcal impetigo but systemic symptoms are absent.

b. Bullous impetigo, mostly caused by staphylococcus, also start with **vesicle** which quickly evolves into a **bulla** of 2-5 cm in diameter. The bulla may turn into **pustule** having **clear serum** in the upper half and **cellular deposits** in the lower half with a distinct line of separation. They may **rupture** leaving a raw, red base. In infants and children, they may spread very rapidly and is called **pemphigus neonatorum.** Sometimes vesicles remain at the spreading periphery having a depressed scaling centre. Spreading may continue to produce big bizzare and serpiginous lesions.

c. In India, the lesions are often itchy and, in severe cases, malaise and weakness may be complained of.

5. Histopathology is characterised by

a. Subcorneal bulla or separation with **polymorphs.** Organisms may also be found.

b. Moderate **spongiosis** is present.

c. Old lesions contain heavy **cellular infiltrate** of neutrophils and few lymphocytes.

d. Crusts contain **bacteria, exudate, epidermal cells** and also **neutrophils.**

e. In bullous impetigo, there is **subgranular split** with few inflammatory cells.

6. Laboratory findings

a. Leucocytosis. **b.** Anti DNase level is high.

c. Hematuria in certain patients.

d. Low serum complement level in some.

e. In **culture** : (i) S. aureus phage group II are often isolated **(ii)** Group A hemolytic streptococci in other cases, either alone or with S. aureus **(iii)** Sensitivity tests against antibiotics often show penicillin resistance to S. aureus.

TREATMENT

ERYTHROMYCIN	CLINDAMYCIN
CEPHALOSPORIN	LINCOMYCIN

1. **Cleansing** : It is very important and is done with antibacterial soap containing **chlorhexidine** or **povidone iodine.**

2. **Commpresses** help to debride the crusts with

   a. Condy's solution b. Burow's solution
   c. 1 : 10,000 solution of acriflavin
   d. 0.5% silver nitrate solution
   e. 5% boric acid solution.

3. **Topical therapy**

   a. **Antibiotic** ointments/creams

   i. Neosporin® ii. Terramycin,® Ledermycin®, iii. Soframycin® iv. Fucidine v. Povidone iodine vi. Chloromycetin vii. Savlon cream viii. Silver sulphadiazine.

   b. **Steroids**—The steroids are combined with antibiotics in eczematoid lesions.

4. **Oral antibiotics**

   a. Penicillin V 250 mg q.i.d. for 10 days.
   b. Erythromycin 250 mg q.i.d. for 10 days.
   c. Cephalosporin 250 gm q.i.d. for 10 days.
   d. Tetracyline in the same dose.
   e. Cloxacillin in the some dose.
   f. Clindamycin 15 mg/kg daily for 10 days.
   g. Cefaclor 30 mg/kg daily for 10 days.
   k. Lincomycin 250 mg cap q.i.d. for 10 days.

5. **Injection of antibiotics**

   a. Crystalline penicillin 5-10 lac units I.M. b.i.d for 10 days in streptococcal impetigo to prevent nephritis.

   b. Gentamycin. c. Broad spectrum antibiotics.

DISCUSSION

Impetigo is a common disorder in our country, especially among children during summer. In most cases, the lesions start in face and then spread to other parts. **Pustule** having **lower half full of dense pus** is a **good diagnostic sign. Honey coloured crusting** is also clinically important. Peripheral spreading is often obvious. Mild erosion with crusting and the peripheral spread may be the **only sign** in some patients.

Cleansing is important to get a good contact with antibiotic ointment and causative organisms. Application should be continued for few days more, even after apparent cure.

Internal antibiotic therapy should be instituted to prevent chances of nephritis.

In recurrent cases, suitable antibiotic or antiseptic ointment or creams should be applied at carrier sites twice daily at least for one month. Infectivity should be controlled by proper hygienic measures.

In secondary impetigo, as in scabies, tinea or eczema the original disease should be treated adequately.

INSECT BITES OR LICKS

Numerous insects surround us and often they come in contact with our skin. They might bite or lick or their bodies may be crushed on the skin due to pressure. This often leads to various grades of skin inflammation. It is not always possible to identify the insect since different types of insects may cause similar type of inflammation. The inflammation may be acute, subacute or chronic ; it may be localised or wide spread and with or without the general symptoms. The biomediators of insects can give rise to primary irritant dermatits or allergic dermatitis.

DIAGNOSIS

There are some **common features** of insect bites or licks. These might help in diagnosis. They are briefly mentioned below.

1. Onset

Symptoms usually appear within a very short period of time. All on a sudden the patient may discover an acutely inflammed area on the skin in the early morning, the contact with insect being at night during sleep. The patient might as well see the insect biting or crawling on the skin.

2. Evolution and development of lesions

At first there is erythema followed by edema. There might be burning or severe itching. A puncta, indicating the biting site, may be seen surrounding which there is erythema and edema. Later, there may be a minute blister at the centre of the lesion. The inflammatory areas may be (a) **scattered,** generally at the face or other open areas of the body, (b) **localised** and **circumscribed** or (c) **wide spread**, depending on the number of insects and the response of the patients.

Sometimes the lesions are **linearly distributed**. This indicates the crawling or scratching of the insect causing contact with the poisonous material in a linear way.

There may be aseptic pustules at the periphery of the lesion or gross necrosis and ulcer at the centre.

The lesion might be secondarily infected with bacteria giving rise to **impetigo, lymphangitis** and **cellulitis.** Draining **lymphnodes** may be enlarged and tender.

Furuncle-like lesions may be caused by several arthropods.

Migrating tender **erythematous patches** might be the presenting sign.

Generalised urticaria or **erythema multiforme-like** lesions are seen not infrequently. Severe attacks may be accompanied by insomnia, restlessness, fever and faint or even collapse.

Frequently, lesions are seen **in clusters.**

3. Sequale

Unless there is complication, the lesions gradually subside within about a week. There is scaling hyper- or hypopigmentation persisting for few more weeks or even months. In rare cases, there might be scarring.

Common insects are :

1. Mosquitos 2. Biting flies 3. Body lice (described in other chapter) 4. Fleas 5. Bed bugs 6. Venomous stinged-wasps, hornets, bees, ants, scorpions 7. Fly maggots 8. Migrating larva 9. Ticks 10. Chiggers or red bugs 11. Bird mites, mites in stored products 12. Caterpillar of moths 13. Tungiasis 14. Spiders :

a. Brown (Loxosceles laeta, L. reclusa)
b. Black widow (Latrodectus mactans)

Important Arthropods

1. **Bed bugs** (Cimex lectularius)

(a) They live in beds or furniture.

(b) Bites often tend to occur in lines or clusters.

(c) Pustular urticaria is a characteristic lesion.

(d) Probably, they have a role in the transmission of hepatitis B. Virus.

2. **Fleas**

(a) They are blood-sucking ectoparasites that feed on dogs, cats and humans.

Fig. I-2. **Insect Bites** showing central puncta.

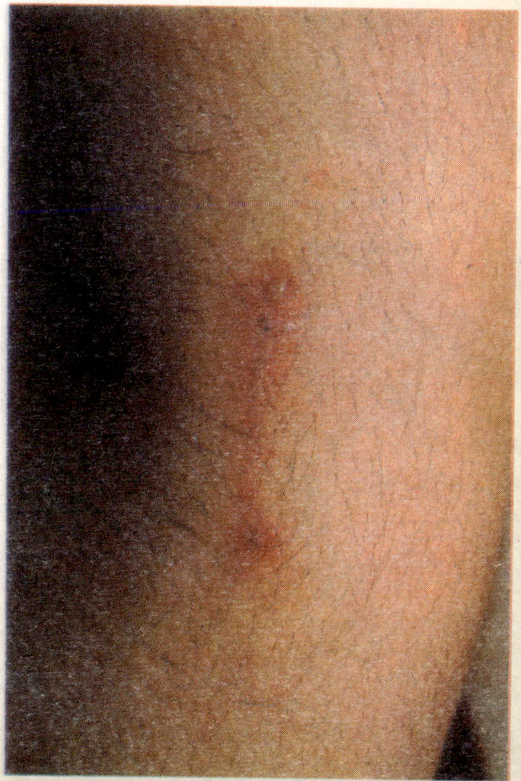

Fig. I-3. **Insect Lick** showing linear lesion with aseptic pustules.

(b) Flea saliva produces papular urticaria in susceptible individuals.

(c) Species found on cats (C. tenocephalides felis) and dogs (C. canis) often attack humans.

(d) The human fleas (pulex irritans) are relatively rare.

(e) Disinfection of the house by Baygon[R] spray is needed.

3. Ticks

(a) Larval tick may attack the human being in large number and may cause severe distress.

(b) Ascending paralysis may occasionally be traced by tick bite and removal of tick is essential.

(c) Ticks may transmit Rocky Mountain spotted fever and Lyme disease.

4. Chiggers or red bugs

(a) They are larvae of trombiculid mites.

(b) They often attack around the waist, on the ankles, or in flexures.

(c) Lesions are intensely itchy, erythematous, papules developing after few hours.

(d) The red chiggers may sometimes be seen at the centre of papules not yet scratched.

5. Bird mites

(a) They are larger than chiggers.

(b) They live in chicken houses, pigeon lifts or nests.

(c) Poultry handlers are most often attacked on the hands and the forearms.

(d) Bites may be anywhere and multiple.

(e) Air-conditioning units may suck the mites inside.

(f) Mites from mice or rats or carpet mites may also cause similar lesions.

(g) Suspicion of mites is necessary for diagnosis.

6. Mites in stored products

(a) These mites are white and often invisible.

(b) They infest copra, vanilla pods, sugar, straw, cotton seeds and cereals.

(c) Persons who handle these products are attacked on the hands, feet and forearms.

(d) Infested beddding may cause generalised dermatitis.

7. **Caterpillars of moths with urticating hairs**

The hairs are blown from cocoons or carried by emergent moths to cause severe, often recurrent, outbreaks.

8. **Tungiasis**

(a) This is caused by burrowing flea : Tunga penetrans.

(b) The female burrows under the skin, sucks blood, swells to 0.5 cm and then ejects her legs into the ground.

(c) Ulceration, lymphangitis, gangrene and septicemia may result in fatality.

(d) Ethyl chloride spray will kill the insect.

(e) Disinfection should be done with insecticide.

TREATMENT

LOCAL STEROIDS	ANALGESICS
ANTIBIOTICS	INTERNAL STEROIDS
ANTIHISTAMINICS	DISINFECTION

1. **Prevention** by

a. Avoidance of contaminated area.

b. Personal cleanliness.

c. Disinfection of clothings, bed clothes and furnitures, e.g. by Gammexane®, Baygon® etc.

2. **Local**

a. Living arthropods should be removed carefully with tweezers after application of alcohol. The arthropods can be preserved in alcohol for future identification.

b. Scratching the area may cause secondary infection. Hence this tendency should be checked.

c. Application of topical steroid lotion or cream with or without antibiotic.

d. Application of calamine lotion (but never with antihistaminic, since that is potentially allergenic).

e. Intralesional steroids in recalcitrant cases.

f. Local anesthetics should not be applied as they are sensitizing.

g. Stings produced by many arthropods may be alleviated by papain powder mixed with water.

3. **Internal**

a. **Antihistaminics** b. **Analgesics** c. **Antibiotics** and d. **Steroids in** extremely severe cases.

4. **Immunotherapy**

Extracts from venom sacs of bees, wasps, yellow jackets and hornets are now available in developed countries.

DISCUSSION

Suspicion of insect bites should always be borne in mind. Sudden onset of an inflammatory area with itching or pain, central puncta, grouping of lesions, linear lesions, central necrosis, peripheral aseptic pustules, recurrence, and finding of insects are all helpful in diagnosis.

Prevention by disinfection is the best policy. Application of local steroid solution, with or withont antibiotic (Pyrimon eye drop[R]), applied q.i.d. helps relieving symptoms and quicker healing in acute phase. Later, cream can be supplemented.

Internal antibiotics are necessary in cases of secondary infection. Antihistaminics relieve itching ; analgesics relieve pain and internal steroids help resolving inflammation.

Rare sequel of ugly scars should be treated by cosmetic surgeons.

INTERTRIGO

It is an inflammatory dermatosis affecting the body-folds. It is extremely common in our country.

DIAGNOSIS

1. Etiological factors

a. Hot **humid** weather. **b.** Diabetes mellitus.

c. Increased **moisture** and **maceration** of opposing skin surfaces.

i. Urinary incontinence. **ii.** Faecal incontinence. **iii.** Vaginal discharge. **iv.** Rubbing and friction of body-folds due to obesity. **v.** Physical activity causing injury to folds. **vi.** Application of thick ointments and occlusive dressing.

d. It is not really a specific entity from the etiologic point of view. Multiple complex mechanisms are at play in its causation.

e. A **variety of organisms** have been isolated which may not have the primary role. They are

i. Bacterial—Streptococcus, staphylococcus, pseudomonas, E. coli. **ii. Fungal**—Candida albicans and other yeast cells.

f. Other diseases that often manifest as intertrigo are

i. Seborrheic dermatitis. **ii.** Flexural eczema. **iii.** Candidiasis. **iv.** Flexural psoriasis. **v.** Dermatophytosis. **vi.** Erythrasma.

However, these should be taken as entities distinct from non-specific intertrigo. Often intertrigo is qualified as **monilial, seborrheic** etc.

g. Blood dyscrasia. **h.** Dysproteinaemia.

2. Clinical features

a. The lesions are **characterised** by

i. Maceration. **ii.** Redness. **iii.** Erosions. **iv.** Weeping and occasional crusting. **v.** Vesicle and pustule formation. **vi.** Vegetative changes in chronic cases.

b. Symptoms are

i. Itching. **ii.** Burning. **iii.** Pain.

c. Sites involved are usually the

1. Genitocrural region. 2. Peno-scrotal fold. 3. Folds of neck. 4. Inframammary region. 5. Naval region. 6. Abdominal folds. 7. Axillae. 8. Natal cleft and perianal region. 9. Antecubital fossae. 10. Popliteal fossae. 11. Between fingers and toes. 12. Retroauricular areas. 13. Vulval folds.

d. Intertrigo may rarely lead to cellulitis.

3. **Histology** : Non-specific inflammatory changes.

4. **Laboratory findings** : Isolation of bacteria and fungi helps in adopting specific therapeutic measures.

TREATMENT

LOCAL STEROIDS	ANTIBIOTICS	POWDERS
IMIDAZOLES	KETOCONAZOLE	

1. **Avoidance of etiological factors** such as

a. Keeping the involved area dry and cool e.g. by air-conditioning and using fans.

b. Avoid local irritation, friction and maceration. Use light clothing and avoid prolonged sitting.

c. Separation of opposing surfaces with dry, finest linen. Liberal use of talc.

d. Exposure of folds to electric bulb helps keeping the part dry.

2. **Cold compress** with

a. Condy's lotion (1 : 8000 potassium permanganate lotion). **b.** Burow's solution.

3. **Local applications** (twice or thrice daily)

a. Steroid lotion or creams, with or without antibiotics, for optimum period. Ointments **should not** be used.

b. Appropriate topical therapy to kill bacterial or fungal invaders e.g. imidazoles, antibiotics.

c. Lotio calamine. **d.** Castellani's paint.

e. 0.5 to 1% Gentian violet lotion.

f. Iodochlorhydroxyquin 3%, with and without steroid.

4. **Systemic**

a. Antibiotics in bacterial infection.

b. Ketoconazole in fungal infection.

c. Antihistaminics to relieve itching.

5. **In recalcitrant cases**

Grenz ray, 200 R weekly to a total of 800 R.

DISCUSSION

Intertrigo is a non-specific superficial inflammatory process. It involves directly the opposing skin surfaces. Itching, burning and pain are the prominent symptoms. Prevention is better than cure. If predisposing factors are not controlled, relapses are common even after adequate therapy. Treatment consists in keeping the parts dry, application of astringent antiseptic lotions, steroid creams and lotions with or without antibiotics, and antifungal agents. Systemic antibiotics are necessary if severe secondary bacterial infection or cellulitis occur. Antihistaminics help allaying the severe pruritus. Anticandidal application may be needed in some cases.

Prolonged use of fluorinated steroid may lead to intertriginous striae and cutaneous atrophy.

KELOID

It is a dermal mass of fibrous tissue and an headache to the dermatologists.

DIAGNOSIS

1. Orientals and Negroes have a predisposition to keloid formation after even slight or insignificant injuries. Polynesians are most susceptible.

2. There is a marked **familial tendency**.

3. Keloids are often precipitated by some sort of injury e.g. burns, wounds, foreign bodies, and tension along a flexor surface of a joint.

4. Site of involvement has a great influence on its size and persistence.

5. It may occur anywhere but **trunk** seems to be specially susceptible. Keloids after surgery are seen more on exposed areas e.g. face, neck, ears, hands, and extremities. This is because those areas are more susceptible to injury.

6. Keloid grows rapidly at first in a few weeks and then becomes stationary for years. There may be **itching** initially.

7. The size, shape and the configuration of keloid vary enormously. They may present as papules, nodules, plaques or great masses. They may cause disabling contracture across joints. There are often pseudopoda. They are firm, smooth, hairless and shiny.

8. Keloid may occur **without a history of trauma.**

9. Pathology

a. Keloids are composed of dense, firm, gray white connective tissue overgrowths. They are the products of excessive formation of dense, broad, hyalinized, glossy bundles of collagen which interwine.

b. Reticulin fibres are also present but there is no elastic fibre.

c. Mucoid degeneration of connective tissue may also be seen.

d. Fibrous proliferation destroys or pushes the skin appendages and stretches the overlying epidermis to the point of atrophy.

e. To distinguish **keloid** from **hypertrophic scar** may be difficult. Both represent excessive growth of fibrous tissue. But in hypertrophic scar the growth is limited to the area of trauma and it does not contain dense hyaline collagen bundles so characteristic of a mature keloid. **Keloids do not regress spontaneously** but **hypertrophic scars generally do by 6-12 months.** In contrast to hypertrophic scar, mucinous ground substance may be abundant in keloid. Foreign body reaction is present more in hypertrophic scar.

10. The deformity that keloids cause is a distressing cosmetic problem and may interfere with motion of body parts. Keloids are sometimes tender and painful and may ulcerate at the middle. Very rarely, neoplasia may occur after 20 to 30 years.

TREATMENT

TRIAMCINOLONE	PRESSURE
CRYOTHERAPY	SURGERY

1. Intralesional injection of 10 to 40 mg/c.c. of triamcinolone, with or without hyaluronidase, at 15 days interval. To be used as long as necessary.

2. Irradiation with x-ray.

3. Application of thorium-X.

4. Surgical excision combined with local x-ray and followed by intralesional injection of triamcinolone.

5. Oral administration of tetrahydroxyquinone.

6. Cryotherapy has doubtful success. It has been supplemented with intralesional triamcinolone therapy.

7. Constant mechanical pressure by elastic bandage or tape has proved to be beneficial if applied for 4-9 months. It probably produces anoxia of the tissue.

8. Topical retinoic acid 0.05% solution sometime decreases the size and lessens the pruritus. It should be applied twice daily for 3-12 months.

9. Laser surgery is often successful.

10. Penicillamine has been shown to inhibit the collagen synthesis.

11. Colchicine inhibits procollagen molecules.

12. Lathyrogen is a recent drug which has been used with colchicine following surgical removal. It is a toxic drug.

13. Post-operative administration of systemic methotrexate has been tried with limited success.

14. Electron beam therapy has been used.

15. Interstitial radiation therapy inserting radioactive wires inside the keloids has been proved successful.

16. Combination of various modalities of therapy.

DISCUSSION

Keloid is frustrating to treat. Relapse is too often the problem. The pathogenesis is yet to be clearly delineated. A genetic predisposition is well accepted but no definite biochemical abnormality has been identified.

There is a wide variation in symptomatology and clinical appearance. Itching, burning, tenderness and pain may be of varying extent. Size, shape and configuration show bizarre patterns.

Treatment modalities are too many. Intralesional injection of high concentrate (40 mg/c.c) triamcinolone is the most popular. Complications of hypopigmentation and atrophy are to be anticipated. Frequent follow-up and assurance are essential to remove the anxiety of patient.

Judicious combination of surgery, radiotherapy, laser and electron beams, pressure therapy and intralesional injection of triamcinolone have been found beneficial to a great extent. With increased knowledge of pathophysiology, a reliable therapeutic modality would hopefully be developed.

LICHEN PLANUS (LP)

DIAGNOSIS

1. It is an inflammatory dermatosis of unknown etiology. It produces a characteristic eruption having the following features.

a. Basic lesions are **itchy, polygonal, violaceous, flat-topped** papules. They may be scattered or grouped ; some may be umbilicated.

b. May have **slightly scaly** surface with **'Wickham's striae'** which are fine white lines (best seen by a magnifying glass) on the surface of the papules. Application of oil helps in better visualisation due to keratin layer becoming more transparent.

c. Usually lesions are **pruritic** and often there is eruption of new lesions on the **linear scratch** marks. This is called **Koebner's phenomenon** or **isomorphic reaction.**

2. Types : LP may be divided into

a. Acute LP—characterised by **sudden profuse eruption** of typical LP papules throughout the whole body surface, mainly the extremities. It usually resolves within 6 to 18 months. After resolution, hyperpigmentation is usually left and it takes nonths to clear.

b. Chronic LP—develops insiduously or from acute LP. It may persist for **more than a decade**. Oral LP, hypertrophic LP and lichen planopilaris tend to be chronic. LP might involve only nails giving rise to various types of **dystrophic changes.**

3. Age and sex : Both sexes are **equally** affected, commonest age group is 30-60 years.

4. Incidence is 0.14% to 1.2%.

5. Sites involved

a. The disease classically involves the **flexor surfaces of wrists and forearms.**

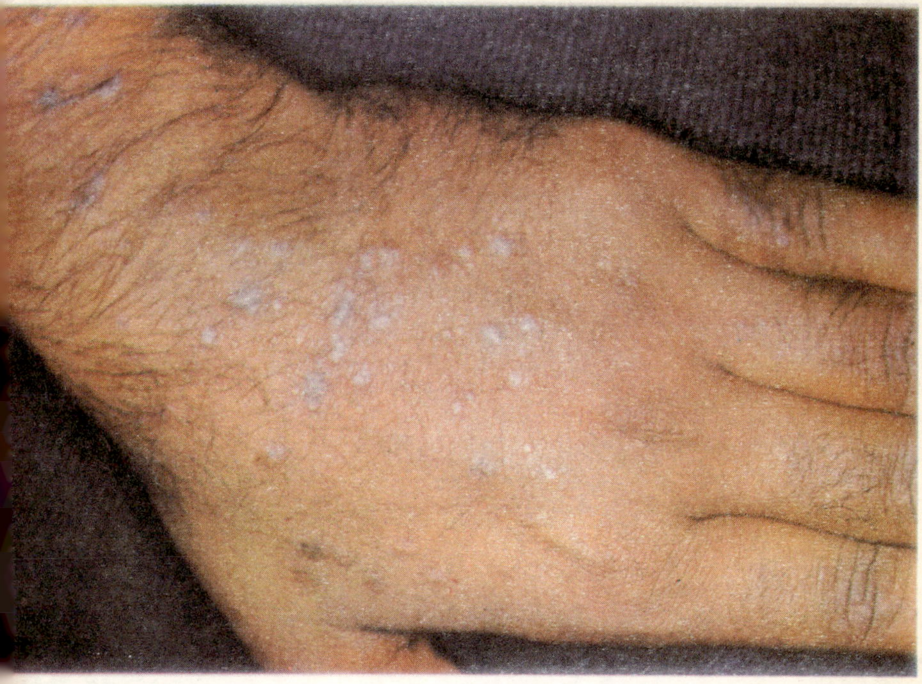

ig. L-1. **Lichen Planus** showing characteristic flat-topped violaceous polygonal itchy papules.

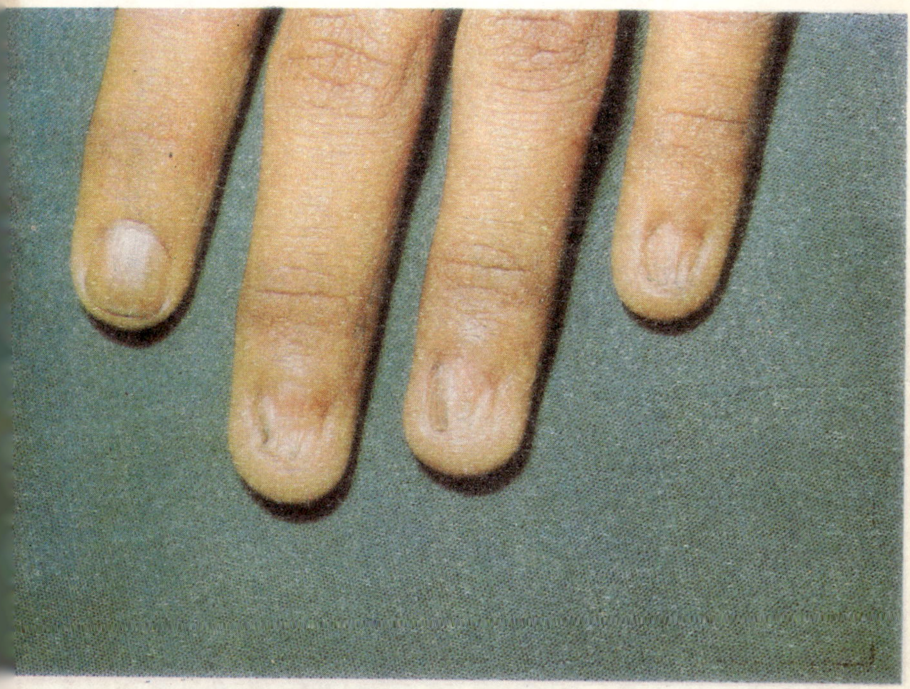

L-2. **Lichen Planus** showing 'pterygium unguis'.

b. Other common areas of involvement are **lumbar area, ankles, glans penis, anterior aspect of lower legs** and **dorsa of hands.**

c. Mucosal surfaces are affected in more than 50% of cases. LP lesions are often found in **buccal mucosa, tongue, lips, gums, palate, conjunctivae, larynx, anus, genitalia** and rarely in gastrointestinal mucosa, urinary bladdar and the tympanic membrane.

The **mucosal lesions** consist of : **i.** lacy, reticulated white streaks, **ii.** white papules and plaques, **iii.** atrophic and ulcerated patches and **iv.** granlomatous lesions.

Chronic erosive or atrophic oral LP may predispose to **oral squamous cell carcinoma.**

About 15-25% of patients who present oral LP never have skin lesions. 25% of male patients with LP have the genital involvement, most commonly, the glans penis. Characteristically, the typical papules takes **annular configuration** with violaceous hue.

Grinspan's syndrome–It consists of an interesting triad : **i.** oral LP, **ii.** diabetes mellitus, and **iii.** hypertension.

So the patients with oral LP should be screened for diabetes mellitus and hypertension.

d. Nails are affected in about 10% of cases and the **changes** include.

i. thinning of nail plate **ii.** longitudinal spliting and ridging **iii.** subungual hyperkeratosis **iv.** onycholysis **v.** red or brown discolouration **vi.** pterygium formation **vii.** complete loss of nail plate.

Pterygium formation is fairly **distinctive for LP** but may also result from trauma, infection or peripheral vascular disease.

e. Palms and soles may also be affected by LP producing **hyperkeratotic, yellowish papules** which usually lack the characteristic morphology of typical LP. In these areas LP is often **non-pruritic.**

6. Variants of LP

Special mention to these variants is useful, because lack of characteristics of typical LP in these variants often makes the diagnosis difficult. The variants include

a. Annular LP—Usually forms a ring of typical LP papules that spread peripherally often with central clearing. Commonly occur on glans penis.

b. Linear LP—Linear group of typical LP papules. Commonly seen in children.

c. Hypertrophic LP — Are highly pruritic, lichenified, scaly, violaceous, hypo- or hyperpigmented plaques, usually symmetric, commonly occur on shins and ankles. Malignant degeneration may occur in this variant.

d. Atrophic LP—It is characterised by atrophy of the skin. This variety may have to be distinguished from LSA and guttate morphea.

e. Vesiculobullous LP—May occur on pre-existing LP or on previously normal skin. It has been termed **LP pemphigoides** by some authors. Bulla may contain blood.

f. LP actinicus (LP tropicus, LP pigmentosus)—Commonly occurs in tropical countries, involves sun-exposed surfaces of children and young adults. It is mildly pruritic. Pigmentation is characteristic. Typical papules are generally absent.

g. LP erythematosus—Non-pruritic, soft, red papules, especially on the forearms. Observed in older patients. Although histologically typical features of LP are found, it is doubted if it represents a true variant of LP or not.

h. Lichen planopilaris—The features of this variant are

i. accuminate, keratotic, follicular papules, primarily on the scalp.

ii. atrophy, alopecia and scaling.

iii. sometimes scarring and permanent alopecia. A variant of lichen planopilaris is Graham-Little-Piccardi-Lassueur syndrome which consists of

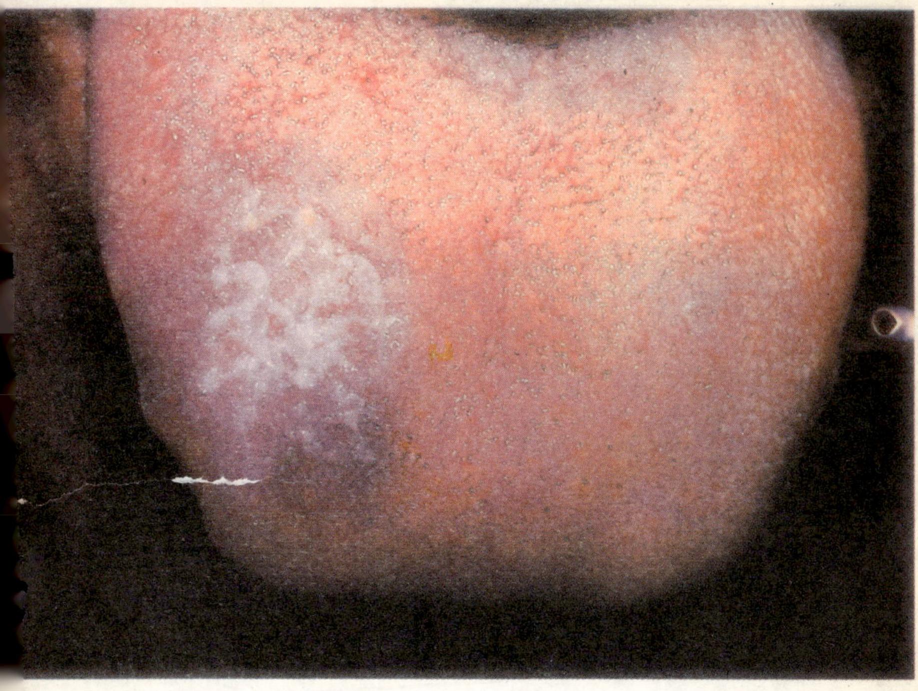

. L-3. **Lichen Planus** of tongue showing a plaque with lacy, reticulated white streaks.

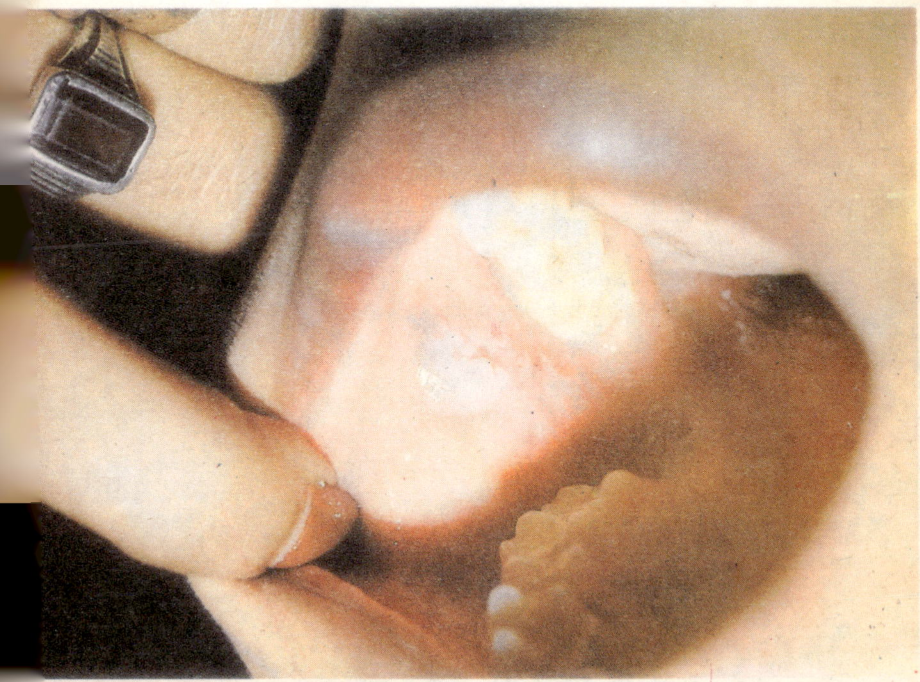

_-4. **Lichen Planus** of buccal mucous membrane showing white plaque.

1. cicatrical alopecia of scalp.
2. non-cicatrical alopecia of axillae and groins.
3. follicular keratotic lesions of glabrous skin.

i. Ulcerative LP—Consists of chronic bullae and ulcerations of soles and sometimes of the mouth and other mucosae. Definite risk of development of squamous cell carcinoma is there.

j. Twenty nail dystrophy—Usually seen in children. All nails are thin, ridged, roughened and often also split. Other manifestaions of LP are absent.

k. LP-LE overlap syndrome—This variant shows features of both the diseases. Chronic, bluish red, atrophic patches are seen most commonly on the acral portions of the extremities.

7. **Histopathology** of LP is fairly diagnostic and consists of

i. Hyperkeratosis without parakeratosis.
ii. Focal hypergranulosis.
iii. Irregular acanthosis producing a saw-toothed appearance of rete ridges.
iv. Liquefaction degeneration of basal cell layer.
v. Band-like upper dermal lympho-histiocytic infiltrate.
vi. Considerable incontinence of pigment.
vii. Colloid bodies in deep epidermis and upper dermis.
viii. **Max-Joseph spaces,** which are small separations between the epidermis and dermis, may lead to sub-epidermal vesicle formation.

Hypertrophic LP lesions show hyperkeratosis, acanthosis and paillomatosis. Oral lesions often show parakeratosis rather than hyperkeratosis and frequently have an atrophic epidermis.

8. **Etiology** is unknown. Some suggestive points are

a. Infective : Either a viral or a bacterial agent, based mainly on identification of a morphologic structure on microscopy. Urinary tract infection is often a cause of LP.

b. Immunologic : This is suggested by

i. Direct immunofluorescence showing numerous ovoid globular structures (representing colloid bodies) of IgM,

IgG, IgA and/or complement just below the dermo-epidermal junction.

ii. LP-like eruption is seen as a chronic form in graft-versus-host reaction, following the bone-marrow transplantation.

c. **Emotional stress** : may account for its onset or the relapse but to establish a causative relationship is difficult.

d. **Genetic** : Familial cases, though not common, do occur and these patients may have a common HLA type. An increased incidence of HLA-A3, HLA-B5 and HLA-B7 have been found.

e. **Several neurological conditions** : though not common, have been found in association with LP.

f. **Drugs** : LP-like eruptions have been caused by several drugs e.g. Amiphenazone, Chloroquine, Chlorothiazide, Chlorpropamide, Demeclocycline, Hydrochlorothiazide, Heavy metals e.g. Antimony, Arsenic, Bismuth, Mercury, Gold etc., Iodides, Methyldopa, Para-amino-salicylic acid, Paraphenylene-diamine salts, Penicillamine, Phenothiazines, Quinacrine, Quinine, Quinidine, Streptomycin, Tetracycline.

9. **Associated diseases :** Two diseases are said to be associated : bullous pemphigoid and lichen nitidus.

10. **Development of squamous cell carcinoma** is rare but may occur on lesions of oral mucosa and ulcerative LP.

TREATMENT

STEROIDS ANTIHISTAMINICS	RETINOIDS	GRISEOFULVIN PUVA

1. LP is a **self-limiting disease** and in most cases **resolves spontaneously** after a varying period of time (average 18 months).

2. The treatment is mainly **symptomatic.**

3. **Rest** and **relaxation** in emotionally labile persons are essential.

4. **Oral antihistamines** e.g. chlorpheniramine maleate as 4 mg tablets or as long-acting 8 mg tablets are used twice daily after food to alleviate the itching. They have also sedative effect which is particularly useful to emotionally stressed persons.

5. **Corticosteroids**

a. **Topical corticosteroids**

i. In long-standing and severe cases, potent corticosteroids e.g. betamethasone valerate 0.12% cream or ointment may be used.

ii. In mild cases, less potent corticosteroid e.g. hydrocortisone acetate 1% ointment is usually sufficient.

iii. In tropical countries like India, corticosteroid lotion, instead of cream or ointment, is better accepted by the patients in summer.

b. **Topical corticosteroid under polythene occlusive dressing overnight** is suitable for LP hypertrophicus and in long standing LP that does not respond well to topical corticosteroid without occlusive dressing.

c. **Corticosteroids intralesionally** e. g. hydrocortisone acetate 25 mg/ml or triamcinolone acetonide 10 mg/ml, once in a week or every fortnightly, are of great advantage in LP hypertrophicus and oral LP.

d. **Systemic corticosteroids :** May be used in acute LP.

i. Oral prednisolone 30 to 40 mg as a single morning dose and is tapered according to the response.

ii. Intramuscular triamcinolone acetonide 40 mg/ml as depot at the interval of 2-6 weeks.

6. **Oral LP** is treated by

a. Corticosteroids in carboxymethylcellulose, gelatin and pectin (Orabase[R]) applied twice daily.

b. Corticosteroids intralesionally.

c. Vitamin A acid (tretinoin) 0.01% once or twice daily.

7. **LP affecting nails :** Intralesional triamcinolone acetonide 10 mg/ml at the base of nail root may be tried. However,

it is a very painful procedure and the benefit is obtained rather slowly.

8. **Oral retinoids**: Tried recently with good results. Among the oral retinoids, etretinate 1 mg/kg of body wt. is effective in LP. Because of its teratogenic effect, it is to be given cautiously to women of child-bearing age.

9. Metronidazole : 400 mg t.i.d for 2 weeks.

10. Cotrimoxazole : 2 tab b.i.d for 1 week.

11. **Photochemotherapy,** with psoralen and UVA, has been tried with good results.

12. Good results have also been reportedly claimed following oral **griseofulvin.**

13. In malignant changes, patient needs
    i. Surgery ii. Radiotherapy

DISCUSSION

Diagnosis is made mainly by the clinical features—violaceous, flat-topped, polygonal, itchy papules.

In very mild asymptomatic patients only reassurance and placebo are all that is needed. But the most other cases require treatment.

In mild cases, application of steroid lotion, cream or ointment and antihistamine orally are sufficient, but with highly itchy, wide spread lesions, patients are to be treated with oral prednisolone 30-60 mg per day. It is to be tapered within 6-12 weeks period.

In hypertrophic lesions, occlusive topical steroid therapy or intralesional mode is advocated.

Application of kenalog orabase[R] ointment is the treatment of choice for oral LP.

Suspected lesions are to be biopsied for detection of malignant changes and, if found, wide excision should be done.

A good rapport between patient and doctor is essential.

LICHEN SIMPLEX (LS)

It is a common disorder in our country and is a type of **chronic eczema** characterised by **highly itchy, lichenified, plaque** or **hypertrophic nodules.** Generally, the nape of the neck ankles, genitalia, wrists, external surfaces of forearms, inner thighs, post-popliteal and antecubital areas are involved.

DIAGNOSIS

1. Clinical features

A. Evolution of lesions

It starts with **itchiness** that leads to **erythema, edema** and **papulation.** The papules are scattered, to start with, but soon coalesce to form a **plaque.** In chronic cases, there is **lichenification** and hypo- or hyperpigmentation. In a classic case, three distinct zones may be seen : (1) **central mildly lichenified** or normal area, (2) surrounding the above area there are **conglomerated papules** with erythema and edema and (3) there is a zone at the periphery containing **itchy papules,** the density of which gradually diminishes. There might also be scaling.

B. Variations

a. Itchy pigmented lichenified plaque : there may be **scaling, crusting** and **fissuring.**

b. Exaggerated skin lines overlying a thickened well circumscribed scaly plaque.

c. Highly **thickened hyperkeratotic itchy** patches with linear, oval or irregular configuration.

d. Hypertrophic nodular lesions : highly itchy, mostly on shin or ankle.

e. Extremely itchy **lichenified skin of scrotum or vulva.**

f. Some patches show **sharp borders** where the lines of the skin are well exaggerated and divide the lesion into rectangular areas.

g. Single or multiple sites are found to be involved with equal frequency.

C. Sites

a. There are predilection of sites, as has already been mentioned. Other favoured sites are perineum, perianal region, scalp, behind the ears, natal cleft. Any site, however, may be affected.

b. It is usually rare at areas outside the range of itching by hand.

D. Etiology and Pathogenesis

a. The most common explanation for lichen simplex is that it represents a **self-perpetuating scratch-itch cycle.** In long standing lesions, hypertrophic nerve fibres have been found. Itching is precipitated by some external or internal factors that cause lichenification and more the lichenification, more is the itching. A **vicious cycle** is thus generated leading to chronicity.

b. Definite personality patterns seem to be associated with the disorder. Some are highly emotional and unable to be aggressive. Some are high-stung and are really aggressive. In some, the disease may be a compensation equivalent of a psychosis.

c. Atopic patients suffer more from LS.

d. Intermittent episodes of severe itching incite the patient to manipulate the lesions.

Itching may be so intense as to interfere with sleep.

e. Probably there is a predisposition to develop LS. Not all individuals are capable of developing lichenification. LS patients are readily conditioned to a scratch response to an itch stimulus.

f. Emotional tension probably plays a vital role in favouring the development and perpetuation of lichenification.

g. Histopathology

i. Hyperkeratosis with focal parakeratosis.

ii. Hypergranulosis.

iii. Impressive irregular acanthosis, and occasional spongiosis.

iv. Perpendicular orientation of collagen fibers in the dermal papillae.

v. Perivascular lympho-histiocytic infiltrate.

vi. Occasional prominent fibroblasts.

E. Age, sex and race

a. It is uncommon in childhood. The peak incidence is found between 30 and 50 years of age.

b. Women are affected more than the men.

c. Orientals and blacks are said to be more prone to develop lichenification. **Prurigo nodularis** is said to be **a variant of LS, especially in blacks.**

F. Complications

a. Secondary infection.

b. Rare development of malignancy in hypertrophic LS.

c. Koebner's phenomenon may also occur.

TREATMENT

TOPICAL STEROID	SEDATIVES
ANTIHISTAMINICS	ANTIBIOTICS
TRANQUILLISERS	INTRALESIONAL STEROID

1. Those who are prone to develop lichenification should **avoid tension** and **anxiety**. If required, **tranquillisers** may be prescribed. Atopic patients should avoid all sorts of precipitating factors including mental and physical irritation.

2. In an average case, a **fluorinated steroid cream** may be applied t.i.d. until cure and a few weeks more. Recent steroid, **clobetasol propionate** 0.05%, is very effective.

3. In thicker lesions, **occlusive dressing** under polythene at night helps in quicker resolution.

4. In a very thick lesion or LS hypertrophicus, **intralesional triamcinolone** 2-5 mg/ml, if injected fortnightly, has been found to be curative.

5. If secondary infections occur, a course of **internal antibiotic** should be prescribed.

6. Itching can be controlled by potent **antihistaminics.**

7. In hyperkeratotic lesions, **tar-salicylic ointment** or **urea cream** may help in reducing the barrier of thick keratin layer and thus in the penetration of local steroids. Tar is probably directly helpful.

8. Adhesive tape impregnated with potent steroid, if applied on the lesion and kept for 24 to 72 hours or longer, may cure the condition quicker.

DISCUSSION

LS is a common recalcitrant skin disease and its diagnosis is not difficult. Secondary lichenification could complicate the persistent skin lesions of chronic dermatophytosis, stasis dermatitis, asteatotic eczema, atopic eczema and low grade chronic contact dermatitis and should be ruled out.

Local steroids, tar ointments, antihistaminics, tranquillisers, sedatives and antibiotics are the standard drugs. Psychotherapy is rarely needed. **Internal steroid** should always be **avoided.** Chronicity of the disease should be explained to the patient to obtain his or her co-operation and patience. The belief that the cure of LS lesion would precipitate bronchial asthma is probably a myth. Grenz rays and x-ray therapy are now obsolete.

LS is still an enigma as it often recurs even after the most careful treatment.

Limitation of therapeutic success is due to atrophy, telangiectasia and hypopigmentation that are often caused by local steroid.

LICHEN STRIATUS

DIAGNOSIS

1. It is an uncommon, **self-limited, unilateral, linear dermatosis** of unknown etiology. Usually, it is seen in children from 5 to 15 years of age. However, it can occur at any age. Girls are affected two to three times more frequently than boys.

2. It **erupts suddenly**, develops fully over days to weeks, and then undergoes **spontaneous involution** in several months to a year or more. It first appears as **discrete, pink, red** or flesh coloured, **flat-topped papules,** often with a **fine silvery scale.** The papules coalesce into a continuous or interrupted **linear band,** 1 to 3 cm in width ; in some areas it may extend to the entire length of an extremity and onto the trunk.

3. Multiple lesions and bilateral involvement are rare.

4. Lichen striatus is usually **asymptomatic,** but may be occasionally **pruritic.**

5. After involution, a temporary post-inflammatory **hypopigmentation** may occur.

6. Nail changes are rare and consist of longitudinal ridging, splitting, fraying, onycholysis and total nail loss.

7. The etiology of lichen striatus is unknown. The factors involved in determining the linearity of the disease are also not known. Peripheral nerve or vessel distribution, or embryologic cleavage lines cannot account for the linearity of all the cases.

8. Histopathology is **non-specific.** Basically, it shows a **lichenoid reaction** in the dermis with sccondary epidermal changes. There is a **chronic perivascular** or **bandlike infiltrate of lymphocytes** and **histiocytes** in the papillary dermis. The epidermis may exhibit intercellular and intracellular edema, exocytosis and parakeratosis.

TREATMENT

TOPICAL STEROID

Usually unnecessry, unless pruritus is significant or the location is of cosmetic concern. In such cases, application of topical corticosteroids, under occlusion or intralesionally, usually resolves the lesion.

DISCUSSION

Idiopathic, usually asymptomatic, lichenoid papules arranged in a linear pattern down one extremity in children typify lichen striatus. The only other diagnostic consideration is a linear epidermal nevus ; the latter condition is present from birth, whereas lichen striatus is an acquired disorder.

The clinical course of lichen striatus is perhaps its most distinctive feature. It erupts suddenly, develops fully over days to weeks, and then undergoes spontaneous involution in several months to a year or more.

In India, parents often take the condition as vitiligo and become psychologically depressed. They should be convinced of the fact that this is not to be identified with vitiligo and reassured by showing some raised lesions which are not at all found in vitiligo.

Fig. L-5. **Lichen Simplex** of scrotum.

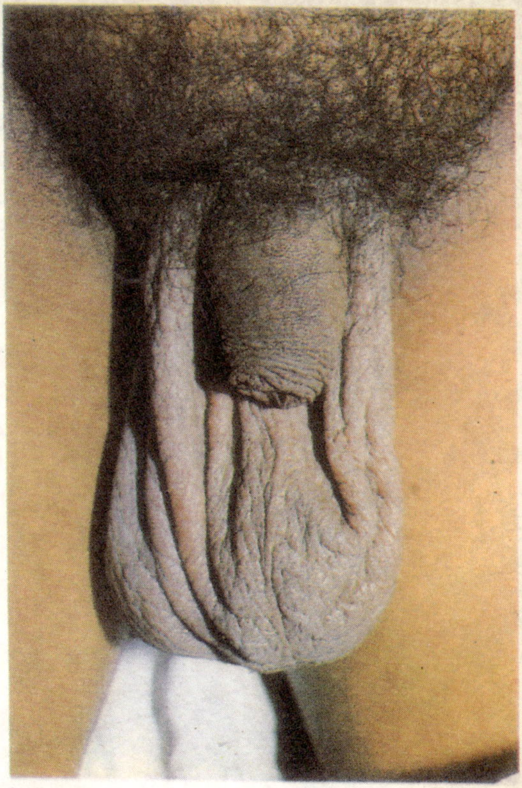

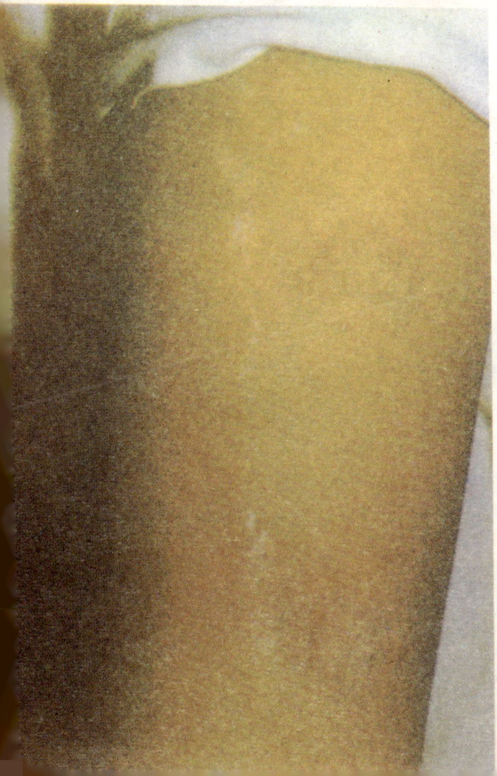

Fig.L-6. **Lichen Striatus** showing coalescing papules forming interrupted linear band.

LYMPHO-GRANULOMA VENEREUM (LGV)

This is a sexually transmitted systemic contagious disease. It is caused by a number of chlamydia having a transitory primary lesion and is followed by suppurative lymphadenitis, constitutional symptoms in early stage and later by severe manifestations, such as chronic discharging sinuses, fistulae, elephantiasis, destructive ulceration of the genitalia and stricture.

DIAGNOSIS

1. Epidemiology

a. **Distribution**— It is distributed **world wide** but is more common in the **tropics** : southern part of North and South America, Arab, West Africa, India, South East Asia (most common), South China, some inland areas of Europe.

b. Homo sapiens are the victims without any distinction of race, colour and religion. Common age group is 15-30 years. Male to female ratio is 9 : 1. Children may be infected by sexual or non-sexual contact.

c. It is most common in urban population, in industrial belts and sea coasts. Incidence is very high in sexually promiscuous persons and among the prostitutes.

d. In India, **Calcutta** : About 5% of STD. **Madras** : Also similar.

2. Etiology

a. The agents (Miyagawanella lympho-granulomatosis) are a number of related chlamydial organisms of immunotypes L_1, L_2 and L_3.

b. They form basophilic inclusion bodies (Halberstaedter-Prowazek inclusion body) in polymorphs and the histiocytes.

c. They are larger than virus containing both DNA and RNA.

d. Some are obligate intracellular parasites.

e. They have cell wall like the bacteria and divide by binary fission.

f. Size is 250-300 μm.

g. They can be grown in tissue culture in (i) irradiated McCoy's media, (ii) Hela media and (iii) BKH 21 media.

h. Organisms are unaffected by freezing and killed in 10 minutes at 56°C.

i. They have two types of antigens : (1) Specific, but heat labile and (2) Group antigen which is stable and resistant to physical and chemical agents.

3. Immunity

Host response varies greatly. Some have mild lymphadenopathy which subsides spontaneously, whereas the others develop chronic draining fistula that may be present for years. Relapse after treatment is quite common.

4. Pathology

a. Entry of the organisms occurs through the break of mucous membrane, which may be produced due to friction of sexual act or even by accident.

b. Organisms enter the subcorneal loose areolar tissue and pick up the lymph radicle and go up to the regional lymph node.

c. From lymphnode via lymphatics they go to cisterna chyle, then to thoracic duct and finally to subclavian vein and become a systemic infection within 18 to 24 hours.

d. It may cross the blood-brain barrier and may enter the central nervous system very early.

e. Lesions produced are

i. At the point of entry—Non-specific erosion or ulcer.

ii. In the pathway to gland-lymphangitis having tiny abscesses called bubonules.

iii. At the lymphnode and around—(1) Acute adenitis and (2) Periadenitis. These produce lump.

(3) Inflammation of the periglandular tissue extends to the surface of the skin producing erythema, edema, rugosity and adherence. The **groove sign** is produced due to the inflammatory swelling above and below inguinal ligament.

(4) Lymphnode may suppurate to form abscess which bursts giving rise to discharging sinuses. Discharge is gluey, blood-stained material.

(5) Because the abscess wall is thick, it does not collapse and persisting discharge continues simulating scrofuloderma.

(6) The structure of the lymphnode is lost and flow from the drainage area is retarded to form elephantiasis.

(7) In the rectum, the inflammation may be direct or it may have the organisms from the pelvic or sacral group. Rectum is directly involved in homosexuals or in most females as retrograde extension from pre-sacral or internal iliac lymphnodes.

In majority of females, the organisms enter through the posterior vaginal fornix and cervix which drain into internal iliac and pre-sacral group of lymphnodes.

Submucosal rectal glands and pararectal glands may also be involved. Highly inflammed rectum shows features very **similar to ulcerative colitis.**

All these glands may suppurate and tract down to ischio-rectal fossoe, vagina, urethra and urinary bladder producing ischio-rectal fistula, recto-vaginal, recto-urethral and recto-vesical fistulae. In very chronic stage, rectal wall is thickened giving rise to stricture.

The **keywords** to describe the **pathology of LGV** are **acute, suppurative, lymphadenitis** with **periadenitis, endolymphangitis** and **perilymphangitis.**

5. Histopathology

a. Primary lesion—non-specific.

b. Lymph gland

i. Acute stage—Appearance of foci of neutrophils which conglomerate to form an abscess. The abscess has very often angular extension. Hence it is called **stellate abscess** which is a **diagnostic sign** in the early stage. The abscess is surrounded by lymphocytes, plasma cells, epithelioid cells and give rise to a picture of pallisading granuloma.

ii. Chronic stage—Histology is like that of Koch's and is very difficult to diagnose.

6. Clinical features

a. Incubation period : 5-21 days. Average is 10 days.

b. Early signs

i. Primary lesion

In about 60% of patients, primary lesion cannot be detected. Rash of the cases might show the following.

(1) Single herpetiform lesion which heals spontaneously. This is the commonest form of primary lesion. Other types of lesions are (2) Papule or nodule (3) Non-specific ulcer (4) Balanoposthitis and (5) Sub-acute urethritis.

ii. Sites of the lesions

In male : (1) Inner aspect of the prepuce (2) Coronal sulcus (3) Frenum and (4) Glans penis.

In female : (1) Labia minora (2) Fourchette (3) Vestibule (4) Clitoris (5) Wall of the vagina, especially posterior fornix and (6) Cervix.

iii. Extragenital primary lesions—They are found at the following regions : (1) Anal (2) Perianal (3) Rectal wall (4) Lips and fingers (in doctors and nurses)

c. Regional lymphadenopathy

The **characteristics** are as follow.

i. Develops within 7-10 days of the appearance of primary lesion.

ii. Inguinal lymphnodes are involved unilaterally, mostly on the left side.

iii. Swelling is associated with pains and aches.

iv. Skin overlying is red or bluish-red in colour rugosed with increased and prominent skin creases.

v. Dumbell-shaped swelling occurs with a groove at the middle (a **diagnostic sign**). The groove is produced by inguinal ligament.

vi. Lymphnodes are firm and tender.

vii. At first discrete, followed by matting and then fluctuations are found at different points.

viii. Skin is adherent to underlying lump which again adheres to the underlying tissue.

ix. In about 60% cases, external iliac lymphnodes become tender and palpable. This is said to be a **pathognomonic sign.**

x. As the portal of entry in female is the posterial vaginal fornix or cervix, the inguinal lymph glands are spared.

xi. If pelvirectal (internal iliac or presacral group) lymphnodes are enlarged, there may be backache.

xii. In case of homosexuals, the portals of entry are anus, perianal region and rectal wall.

If the infection is below pectinate line, it would involve inguinal lympnodes but, if above, rectal group of lymph nodes would be involved.

All these clinical features taken together constitute what is called **inguinal syndrome.**

The **fate of this lesion,** if **untreated,** may be as follows.

(1) Suppuration→ Bursting→ Formation of multiple discharging sinus.

(2) In about 25% cases, the lesion remains indolent, having neither suppuration nor resolution. It then produces elephantiasis of genitalia.

(3) In some cases, spontaneous involution is found to occur which might reappear again after 5-6 weeks.

d. Constitutional symptoms and signs

The disease is systemic from the beginning, having fever, anorexia and arthralgia.

A. Late signs include

i. Anorectal syndrome

(1) There is inflammation of the anorectal tissue giving rise to clinical features similar to ulcerative colitis.

(2) In neglected cases, there is suppuration of lymph glands which may cause ischiorectal abscess that may burst inside or outside producing various types of fistulae.

While in **female** there may be rectovaginal fistula, in **male** there is commonly rectovesical or, less commonly, recto-urethral fistula.

(3) If untreated, chronic inflammation gives rise to fibrosis, and anorectal stricture is produced.

(4) Hypertrophic skin tags, which contain dilated lymph vesicles, may be produced around the anus.

ii. Genital syndrome

(1) Esthiomene is produced giving rise to elephantiasis of female genitalia with prominent skin folds.

(2) There may be chronic ulceration which are generally quite painful.

iii. Urethral syndrome

Inflammation of the urethra gives rise to stricture or urethral fistula.

B. Skin and mucous membrane lesions

i. In early stage, there are (1) Primary lesions as already described, (2) Papulo-pustulo-eczematous lesions, (3) Erythema nodosum, (4) Erythema multiforme, and (5) Eye lesions consisting of conjunctivitis and episcleritis.

ii. In late stage, there is cutaneous LGV, producing features of scrofuloderma.

C. Miscellaneous lesions

(1) In joint Arthralgia (2) Meningitis rarely (3) Encephalomyelitis (4) Pneumonitis.

7. Laboratory diagnosis

a. Smear examination

Materials — Bubo aspirates, pus. Stain — Giemsa. Findings—Intracytoplasmic inclusion bodies inside monocytes and polymorphs.

b. Culture

Material–Bubo aspirate

Media–(1) Yolk sac of chick embryo, (2) Tissue culture.

c. **Direct immunofluorescent** test with bubo aspirate.

d. Frei's skin test

i. It is a hypersensitivity test and usually becomes positive 10 days after the appearance of bubo.

ii. Antigen is made from dead LGV organisms cultured in yolk sac of chick embryo (Lygranum). Antigen can also be acquired from untreated human bubo aspirate with control done by normal saline.

iii. Control is done with protein material of yolk sac.

iv. 0.1 c.c of antigen is injected intracutaneously into forearm. Induration more than 6 mm indicates positivity.

v. An initial negative Frei's test followed by a positive test is of more diagnostic value.

vi. Once positive, it generally remains positive throughout the life except during severe anergy.

D. LGV-CFT test

a. It is the earliest test to be positive.

b. Antigen is obtained from another chlamydial disease, namely 'enzootic abortion in ewes'.

c. If the test titre is 16 or above, it is **diagnostic**.

E. Indirect immunofluorescent test.

F. Radioisotopic precipitation test—It is most diagnostic and highly sensitive.

G. Hematological findings

a. There is a slight increase in leucocytes with moderate lymphocytosis.

b. Total serum protein is increased with alteration of albumin and globulin ratio.

c. Aldehyde test may be positive.

d. Immunoglobulin A is increased during the active period of the disease and level goes down to normal as the treatment proceeds.

In a treated case, if the immunoglobulin A rises again, it indicates a relapse.

e. E.S.R. is high to the level of 40-70 mm per hour.

f. Cryoglobulins and rheumatoid factor may also be found in some patients.

Lesions of lympho-granuloma venereum

(After Holmes, K. K., Mardh, P. A. et al, 1984)

Early	Late
Inguinal syndrome	
Primary genital lesion(s)	Genital elephantiasis
Inguinal bubos	Genital ulcers and fistulas
Bubonulus	
Anorectal syndrome	
Proctitis	Rectal stricture
	Lymphorrhoids
	Perirectal abscesses
	Anal fistula
Others	
Urethritis	Frozen pelvis
Cervicitis	Infertility
Salphingitis	
Parametritis	
Conjunctivitis	Scarring
Regional lymphadenitis	
Meningitis	

TREATMENT

TETRACYCLINE	SULFISOXAZOLE	MINOCYCLINE

A. Supportive measures

1. Adequate rest 2. Good nutrition 3. Warm compresses to buboes 4. Analgesics as and when necessary.

B. Specific : The treatment should be started as early as possible to get the best result.

1. Sulphonamides

a. Short acting—Sulphadiazine : 4 g daily for 15 days or even more.

b. Semi-long acting

i. Sulfisoxazole : 4 g stat and 1 g q.i.d. for 3 weeks.

ii. Sulfamethoxazole : 2 g stat and 1 g b.i.d. for a period of 3 weeks.

c. Long acting—e. g. sulphamethoxypyridiazine 2 g stat and 1 g daily for 3 weeks.

d. Cotrimoxazole : 2 tab b.i.d. for 15 days.

2. Tetracycline : 500 mg q.i.d. for 3 weeks or more.

3. Both sulphonamides and tetracyclines can be used together or alternatively.

4. Erythromycin—500 mg q.i.d. for 3 to 4 weeks.

5. Minocycline—2 g q.i.d. for 10 to 20 days.

6. In proctitis and severe urethral inflammation, specific drug may be combined with internal steroid.

C. Buboes that have softened and obviously contain pus should be drained by aspiration through a wide-bore needle inserted through healthy skin.

If they are incised or allowed to burst, the resulting sinuses heal very slowly or there may be local extension to form cutaneous LGV.

D. Surgical procedures

Before, during or after any surgical intervention, specific therapy must be given.

1. Urethral reconstruction.

2. Surgical repair of rectal stricture and fistula.

3. Rectovaginal fistula, the stenosis of vagina and fenestration of the external genitalia are difficult to cure even by the best possible surgery.

4. If any stricture is short, periodic gentle dilatation at 1-2 weeks interval may prevent further narrowing of lumen.

5. Colostomy may be needed in extensive rectal stricture with or without abdominoperitoneal resection.

6. Colpoperineorrhaphy for rectal stricture has been tried with partial success.

DISCUSSION

Clinical manifestations of LGV vary widely. Evanescent primary genital lesion, lymphnode enlargement, softening and suppuration with draining sinuses, proctitis and rectal stricture in women and homosexual men, involvement of joint, eye and CNS, positive CFT and skin test, and elevated serum globulin are the **essential features for diagnosis**. Non-apparent infections and the latent disease are not very uncommon in promiscous individuals.

Blocking of the lymphatic channels gives rise to elephantiasis and disfiguration of external genitalia with extensive scarring, urethral, rectal and vaginal scarring. Various types of fistulae are the complications of the disease.

Tetracycline is the **drug of choice** but should be given in adequate dose and for full length of time which is usually 3 to 4 weeks. Relapses are not uncommon and repeat courses of therapy should be instituted whenever the situation demands.

Prompt early treatment often cures the condition without any complication. But if the treatment is delayed, it is difficult to eradicate the infection and also to reverse the pathologic changes. There are reports of higher incidence of anorectal carcinoma if chronic involvement of the areas persists for a long period. In critically demanding cases, surgery may be done after proper evaluation.

MELASMA

DIAGNOSIS

1. It is characterised by **brown patches** on **face** usually occurring on the malar prominences, forehead, temples, nose, upper lip and neck.

2. The patches have the following **characteristics.**

a. They are sharply **demarcated**, but often small satellite lesions are found round the main patch. Usually, they are **symmetrically distributed.** Initially they start as mottling which coalesce to form large patches. They may have irregular borders.

b. They are generally **symptomless.**

c. They may occur

i. in pregnancy due probably to potentiating effect of combined estrogen and progesterone.

ii. in those who are taking contraceptive pills.

iii. in menopause. iv. sometimes in males.

v. more in sun-exposed people.

vi. in those who are taking mesantoin, diphenylhydantoin or other oral photosensitive drugs.

vii. in ovarian tumor or disorders and sometimes in other endocrinological disfunctions.

viii. with certain cosmetics.

3. Etiology is not fully known but there is an **increased epidermal melanization** without any melanocytic proliferation. Melanocytes, in affected area, are more efficient in producing melanin granules. The role of genetic predisposition is still debated.

4. **Histological findings** are

a. increased melanization in basal cells.

b. perivascular and also perifollicular lymphocytic infiltration.

TREATMENT

HYDROQUINONE
COMBINATION OF TRETINOIN, HYDROQUINONE AND DEXAMETHASONE
CHEMICAL PEELING WITH PHENOL

1. **Causative factors** e.g. contraceptive pills, photosensitive drugs, cosmetics and exposure to sun should **be avoided.**

2. **Sun screens**

Regular use of **sun screens** is necessary for those who are exposed to the sun.

a. Para-amino-benzoic acid (**PABA**) 15% cream.

b. Paba ester with benzophenone, and

c. A proper hat to avoid sun exposure.

3. **Bleaching agents**

a. 2-4% hydroquinone in 60% alcohol or in stabilized cream to be applied b.i.d.

b. Stabilized hydrophilic ointment or equal parts of ethanol and propylene glycol containing

i. 5% hydroquinone

ii. 0.1% retinoic acid

iii. 0.1% triamcinolone or dexamethasone to be applied b.i.d for 6-8 weeks.

c. 5% hydroquinone in 0.025% tretinoin gel or in 0.1% cream to be rubbed b.i.d.

d. Cream containing

i. 5% hydroquinone

ii. 2-3% salicylic acid

iii. 0.025% fluocinolone acetonide ; to apply b.i.d.

e. Application of 95% phenol until whitening occurs and neutralised by isopropyl alcohol. The area at first turns red, then black and forms eschars to peel off in a week.

f. 5-10% ammoniated mercury to apply b.i.d.

g. 0.1-1% hydrarg perchlor to apply b.i.d.

4. Dermabrasion is temporarily useful.

5. **Chemical peeling agents**

a. Phenol 100% b. 50% Trichloroacetic acid.

DISCUSSION

Melasma is a common cosmetic disorder in our country.

To prevent it, sun-exposure, contraceptive pills and photosensitive cosmetics or drugs are to be avoided.

2-4% hydroquinone in lotion or cream (Depig[R], Melalite[R]) is very safe but takes a long time, even up to one year, to show effect. Recurrence, after the withdrawal, however is not uncommon. A combination of hydroquinone, tretinoin and triamcinolone or dexamethasone in equal parts of ethanol and propylene glycol is said to be the best. However, this might cause allergic sensitization in susceptible persons.

Application of monobenzyl ether of hydroquinone is abandoned due to frequent allergic sensitization. Local application of lemon, oral vitamin C and vitamin A have doubtful values.

A sincere rapport of the doctor with the patient is a must to continue prolonged and effective treatment.

MILIA

DIAGNOSIS

1. Milia are generally **asymptomatic, tiny, pearly white, keratinous cysts** appearing chiefly on **face.**

2. Their **characteristics** are as follow.

a. They are globoid and of 1 to 4 mm in diameter.

b. They are discrete but sometimes grouped.

c. The sites of predilection are

(1) On the eyelids. (2) Under the eyebrows. (3) Around the eyes (4) The temples (5) The cheeks (6) The forehead (7) The genitalia (8) Whole face.

d. They may be of various colours : White, Yellow white.

e. Their surface is smooth.

f. They resemble rice grain embedded in the skin.

g. They may occur spontaneously at any age and in both the sexes.

h. They may occur in the newborn as congenital lesions.

i. They may be primary where they arise *de novo* or they may be secondary to some skin disease.

3. Etiological factors implicated are the following.

a. They are thought to be retension cysts developing from plugged hair follicles.

b. They very often arise after trauma e.g. after dermabrasion.

c. They occur during the healing process of bullous disorders such as

(1) Epidermolysis bullosa (2) Pemphigus (3) Porphyria cutanea tarda (4) In congenital ectodermal defect (5) After x-ray therapy (6) In acne (7) In herpes zoster (8) In lichen sclerosus et atrophicus (9) After burn and (10) In seborrheic dermatitis.

d. Naturally occurring facial milia arise from undifferentiated epithelial pedicles derived from the external root sheath of vellus hair follicles.

e. After trauma they may arise from isolated nests of undifferentiated epithelium of sebaceous gland origin.

f. A heritable factor has been implicated since familial occurrence has been seen. Some patients seem to be predisposed to develop it.

4. Histology and histogenesis

a. They are, in fact, small **epithelial inclusion cysts** within the dermis.

b. Attachment to hair follicle by a cord of undifferentiated epithelium can often be traced.

c. Post-traumatic milia may contain a nest of **sebaceous cells** within their walls.

d. They are lined by a **stratified epithelium,** a few cell layers thick, and contain **concentric lamellae of keratin.**

e. Secondary milia that follow blistering may arise from (1) the eccrine sweat duct, (2) the hair follicles and (3) aberrant epidermis.

f. Primary milia represent probably keratinizing type of **benign tumours** and secondary milia are the **retension cysts** caused by the proliferative tendency of the epithelium after some injury.

TREATMENT

INCISION AND EXPRESSION	ELECTRODESICCATION

1. They may easily be shelled out with a hypodermic needle or a cataract knife.

2. Alternatively, they may be pricked by fine needle and squeezed to get rid of the keratinous mass. After removal, the cyst wall may be touched with liquid phenol.

DISCUSSION

Primary milia probably represent true benign tumours but those arising secondarily are retension cysts.

Treatment consists in lightly incising the top of the lesions and expressing the contents. Electrodesiccation can be done with fine needle and low current.

MILIARIA

DIAGNOSIS

Miliaria are the eruptions due to eccrine sweat retention in the skin caused by impeded free flow. They are of four types. (1) **Miliaria crystallina** (2) **Miliaria rubra** (3) **Miliaria profunda** and (4) **Miliaria pustulosa**. The depth of skin at which the sweat escapes determines the type of lesions.

A. **Clinical features** of these are as follow.

Miliaria crystallina

1. It occurs in males and females of any age and is most often seen **after sunburn** or in association with acute febrile illness.

2. The lesions appear as **asymptomatic, superficial, non-inflammatory, crystal-clear, fragile vesicles** which resemble **dew drops** on the skin.

3. Anhidrosis is not generally present since the number of lesions are not plenty.

Miliaria rubra (Prickly heat)

1. It appears as **small, discrete, erythematous, papules, vesicles** or **papulovesicles** at the **sweat pores** in hot, humid atmosphere. **Humidity** is more important than temperature.

2. The lesions are never associated with hair follicles.

3. Sites of predilection are : (1) covered parts—trunk, abdomen, (2) parts where friction with clothing occurs, (3) folds—elbows, knees and axillae.

4. Palms and soles are never involved. Face is rarely seen to be affected.

5. The lesions **burn, itch** or **sting.**

6. Clinical anhidrosis may occasionally be present in extensive involvement.

7. Miliaria rubra predisposes to intertrigo from fungus or coccal infection of the macerated skin, and pyoderma.

8. Living in air-conditioned room makes the lesions disappear in a few days.

Miliaria profunda

1. In it, the skin is uniformly studded with **asymptomatic discrete, flesh-coloured** and **non-inflammatory papules** strictly **localised to sweat pores.**

2. **Anhidrosis** of the involved area is **a constant feature.** It may lead to heat exhaustion with fatigue, anorexia, drowsiness, headache and vertigo.

3. The papules increase in size during exercise or in hot environment and lessen in cool place.

Miliaria pustulosa

1. It can be taken as **a variant** or complication of miliaria rubra consisting of **discrete, distinct, superficial, pustules** not associated with hair follicles.

2. Lesions tend to appear in previously inflammed skin. Flexures are sites of election.

3. Miliaria pustulosa and rubra frequently coexist.

4. In most cases, pustules are either sterile or contain non-pathogenic organisms.

B. Etiology and pathogenesis

The issue is highly controversial. However, the following factors are considered to be important.

1. Diverse methods and agents can cause miliaria e.g.

a. Iontophoresis. **b.** Application of irritating substances. **c.** Maceration in hot and humid environment. **d.** Ultraviolet irradiation. **e.** Electrodesiccation of sweat pores. **f.** Presence of staphylococcus aureus in plenty in the epidermis. **g.** Over-hydration of stratum corneum. **h.** De-fatting of the stratum corneum. **i.** Excessive sodium chloride on the skin.

2. It is probably a three stage process.

a. Initially, some changes in the distal portion of the sweat duct occur e.g. change of normal electronegative charge would impede the egress of sweat. Experimental miliaria can be induced in normal individuals with electropositive agents.

b. **Secondly** : i. The accumulation of Schiff-positive, diastase-resistant, material in the distal pore, which is excreted by small dark cells of eccrine secretory coil.

ii. This accumulation produces a plug so that the flow of sweat to the surface is blocked.

iii. With further sweating, there is rupture of the sweat duct at different levels.

(1) In M. crystallina, rupture occurs within or just beneath the stratum corneum.

(2) In M. rubra, rupture is at a greater depth within the epidermis. Ductal rupture causes damage to the surrounding cells.

c. **Thirdly**, the injured epidermal sweat duct unit degenerates and forms a hyperkeratotic or parakeratotic 'keratin plug' which then obstructs the pore of the newly regenerated epidermal sweat duct unit.

3. In some individuals, repetitive episodes of miliaria lead to a progressively deeper obstruction of sweat duct at the upper dermis causing miliaria profunda.

4. Any injury to sweat pore can lead to obstruction and consequent miliaria as is often observed in inflammatory dermatoses.

5. In M. rubra, there is a variable degree of spongiosis within the epidermal sweat duct unit and the adjacent epidermis. A hyperkeratotic or parakeratotic 'keratin plug' may overlie the spongiosis. The blood vessels of the upper dermis are dilated and surrounded by lymphocytes. Lymphocytes are also present in spongiotic epidermis.

6. In M. pustulosa, numerous polymorphs are present within the involved epidermis.

7. Inhibitory effect of antibiotic on miliaria emphasises the role of bacteria. Cocci might secrete a toxin that causes inflammation, ductal and periductal spongiosis and precipitates intraluminal cast secondary to injury of luminal cells.

C. Complications

a. Secondary bacterial or fungal infections in M. rubra giving rise to (1) Bullous impetigo, (2) Furunculosis, (3) Hidradenitis, (4) Periporitis, (5) Multiple sweat gland abscesses, (6) Microbic eczema, (7) Syringadenitis suppurativa tropicalis.

b. Impediment of sweat flow may cause

(1) Thermal asteatosis consisting of superficial circinate, erythematous and scaling areas.

(2) Tropical anhidrosis with asthenia.

(3) Primary appearance of psoriasis on the eruptions of miliaria in predisposed persons.

TREATMENT

LIVING IN AIR-CONDITIONED ROOM	ANTIBIOTIC
LOOSE LIGHT GARMENTS	ANTIHISTAMINIC

A. Preventive

a. Living in less humid and cooler atmosphere e.g. in air-conditioned room.

b. Loose clothing having ventilation.

c. Too much bathing with soap is harmful.

d. High salt intake may cause aggravation.

B. Curative

a. Miliaria crystallina is self-limiting and therefore needs no treatment.

b. Adequate ventilation, light weight clothing and leisure are much helpful.

c. Air-conditioning is ideal.

d. Local application of neomycin lotion may help.

e. Possible benefit of oral ascorbic acid and vitamin A is questionable.

f. Oral antibiotic, especially tetracyclines, might help some patients of M. rubra, profunda and pustulosa.

g. Application of calamine lotion and steroid lotion symptomatically help in some patients.

h. Dusting of powders produce drying of macerated skin.

DISCUSSION

Miliaria is one of the most common disorders in our country during summer. Poor standard of living in crowded, non-hygienic, humid atmosphere is the important contributing factor. Besides the various lesions, secondary complications of impetigo, microbic eczema, furunculosis and abscesses are frequent.

Light clothing and dusting of powders are helpful. Bath for too long a time would cause more wetting of keratin and poral occlusion of the sweat ducts. Living in air-conditioned room for at least eight hours a day improves the condition within a few days.

High dose of Vitamin C does not help in any way. It can rather precipitate kidney stones, especially the oxalate variety, in predisposed persons.

The best objective should be the prevention by avoiding the etiologic factors as far as practicable.

Complications should be treated promptly. Role of bacteria in the pathogenosis of miliaria is being gradually recognised. A course of antibiotic is probably not unreasonable especially in M. rubra, profunda and pustulosa.

If there is associated itching, proper antihistaminic should be prescribed.

MOLLUSCUM CONTAGIOSUM

It is a viral disease that usually occurs in children and manifests clinically as waxy umbilicated papules. The virus is a DNA containing poxvirus of large size (300×200×100 c. nm).

DIAGNOSIS

1. **Description of the lesion** : Single or multiple, round, dome-shaped, waxy, pink or flesh-coloured papules, 2-5 mm in diameter (rarely up to 1 cm) with a central depression (umbilication), and containing caseous-plug.

2. **Sites of involvement** : Neck and trunk, face and hands, eyelids, scalp, mucous membranes of the lips, tongue, buccal mucosa, any part of the body-surface including the soles. In sexual transmission, the lower abdomen, anogenital regions and genitals get involved.

3. **Susceptible persons** : Atopic subjects, patients receiving corticosteroids and cytotoxic drugs.

4. **Associated features** : Perilesional dermatitis and conjunctivitis attributed to toxic substances produced by the virus or to a hypersensitivity reaction to the virus.

5. **Mode of infection** : Close personal contact probably helps in getting infected. Lesions also spread by autoinoculation. Incubation period varies from one to several weeks. Lesions are contagious ; children acquiring them at schools and swimming pools are common. Genital lesions are transmitted sexually. Lesions may develop along linear scratch marks showing Koebner's phenomenon.

6. **Fate of the lesion** : Most are self-healing within 6-9 months ; may persist for 3-4 years. Inflammatory changes might occur after trauma, or spontaneously after several months resulting in suppuration, crusting and eventual destruction of the lesions.

7. Histopathology

a. Growth of the epidermis into the dermis as closely packed lobules.

b. Intracytoplasmic inclusion bodies (molluscum-bodies) in the epidermal cells.

c. Slight inflammatory changes in the dermis induced by the discharge of contents of a papule into the dermis. Infiltrate is mainly composed of lymphoid cells, neutrophils, macrophages and also a few F. B. giant cells. During the period of spontaneous involution, a mononuclear infiltrate may be seen.

Molluscum-bodies

a. Single, minute, ovoid, eosinophilic structures in the lower cells of the stratum malpighii (one or two layers above the basal cells)

b. Basal cells do not contain molluscum bodies.

c. In the mid-epidermis, the size of molluscum bodies exceeds the original size of the invaded cells. The nucleus of each invaded cell is displaced and compressed to appear as a thin crescent at the periphery of the cell.

d. In the granular layer, staining reaction of molluscum body changes from eosinophilic to basophilic.

e. In the horny layers, they appear as basophilic molluscum bodies, measuring 35 μm in diameter, enmeshed in a network of eosinophilic horny fibres.

8. Tissue culture

Virus of molluscum contagiosum has not been grown in tissue culture. This is explained by the fact that the virus of molluscum contagiosum fails to induce the synthesis of uncoating protein in the host cells.

TREATMENT

CHEMICAL CAUTERY ELECTRODESICCATION
CRYOTHERAPY

1. Choice of treatment is determined by the age of the patient, the number and distribution of the lesions and the presence or absence of inflammatory changes.

2. Solitary or a small number of lesions can be treated by **spiking** the lesion with a sharpened orange stick or hypodermic needle dipped in liquid phenol or 40% trichloroacetic acid.

3. When many lesions are present, they may be treated with a sharpened wooden probe dipped in liquid iodine or painted twice weekly with 20% podophyllin in 95% ethanol.

4. **Electrocautery** may also be done. When the lesions are on the eyelids, electrodesiccation under procaine or intradermally injected normal saline anesthesia may be needed.

5. **Cryosurgery**—Application of liquid nitrogen (10-15 s) destroys the lesions.

6. Application of **cantharidin,** 0.9% in equal parts of acetone and flexible collodion, causes vesiculation and destroys the lesions.

7. In children, **duofilm**[B] (containing salicylic acid and lactic acid) applied as drops over the lesions and kept overnight for 1-2 weeks may resolve the disease.

8. **Pricking** of the lesions and application of **silver nitrate** may destroy the lesions.

9. **Benzoyl peroxide** application may dissolve the lesions.

10. Application of **retinoic acid,** 0.1% alcoholic tincture, t.i.d., can clear the lesions.

11. **Oral retinoid** can clear multiple molluscum lesions in immunosuppressed children.

12. **Hypnotherapy** has claimed to cure the disease.

DISCUSSION

DNA poxvirus causes molluscum contagiosum. Clinically, it is characterised by asymptomatic, flesh-coloured, waxy **umbilicated** papules of 2-6 mm in diameter. They are transferred from person to person by direct contact, occasionally through fomites, and are autoinoculable. They may occur in groups or linear arrays.

They usually **resolve spontaneously** over a period of several months to 2 years.

Expressing the molluscum bodies after pricking the top and thereafter an application of phenol or trichloroacetic acid cures most of the lesions.

Punctate cryosurgery with liquid nitrogen or **electrodesiccation,** if carefully done, gives excellent results. However, there is a risk of scar formation and post-inflammatory hypo- or hyperpigmentation.

Infected children **should not be permitted** to swim in public swimming pools.

Application of topical steroids depresses local immune defences. Secondary infection in lesions sometimes destroys them. Rigorous application of ointments may spread the disease by autoinoculation.

MORPHEA (LOCALISED SCLERODERMA)

Morphea is a skin condition characterised by **localised hardening** and **tightening of skin** occurring in variety of patterns and locations.

DIAGNOSIS

1. **Age and sex**—Primarily in children and young adults. More in females.

2. **Etiological factors**

a. Histologically **morphea** and **systemic sclerosis** are **indistinguishable** but they are probably **separate entities** because transition from morphea to systemic sclerosis is extremely rare.

b. However the following associations have been fonnd with morphea which deserve special mention.

i. Edema of the extremities often precedes the development of linear morphea.

ii. Myositis may be present beneath the area involved.

iii. Calcinosis cutis may be seen at the site.

iv. Atrophy of the underlying bone has been found.

v. Polyarthritis and arthralgia have been found to be associated.

vi. Migraine is often present.

vii. Raynaud's phenomenon has been present in many patients.

viii. Unexplained abdominal pain is another association.

ix. Abnormal electroencephalogram is present in high percentage of cases.

x. In certain patients, trauma precipitates morphea specially in **'coup de sabre'** variety.

xi. Bullous lesions are seen in patients of generalised morphea.

3. **Clinical manifestations**

a. Morphea starts as flesh coloured or erythematous and edematous **plaques** that evolve into waxy ivory-to-yellow-white lesions. The skin becomes **tough** and **tight.**

b. There is often a **violaceous** or lilac-tinged **inflammatory border** around each lesion. There may be hypo-or hyperpigmention at the patches.

c. Sub-varieties of morphea are

i. Guttate—few mm diameter lesions at neck and chest resembling lichen sclerosus et atrophicus without follicular plugging.

ii. Plaque—Indurated solitary or multiple lesions of few cm diameter.

iii. Linear—Affects the limbs of children often unilaterally with adherent sclerodermatous bands in the fascia. Hemiatrophy may be present. 'Coap de sabre' affect lateral to midline at the forehead.

iv. Generalised—The entire face, scalp and trunk may be involved. If scalp is involved alopecia is the result.

v. Segmental—It occurs in one side of face resulting in hemiatrophy.

4. Pathology

Early inflammatory and late sclerotic stage exist in morphea.

a. In early inflammatory stage

i. at the violaceous border of enlarging lesions moderately severe inflammatory infiltrate specially of lymphocytes is present between collagen bundles and around blood vessels.

ii. pronounced inflammatory infiltrate is present in dermis and subcutaneous fat.

iii. deposits of new collagen is marked. They are fine wavy fibres.

iv. vascular changes are mild having endothelial swelling and edema of the walls of vessels.

b. In late sclerotic stage, specially at the center of old lesions, it is observed that

i. Epedermis is normal.

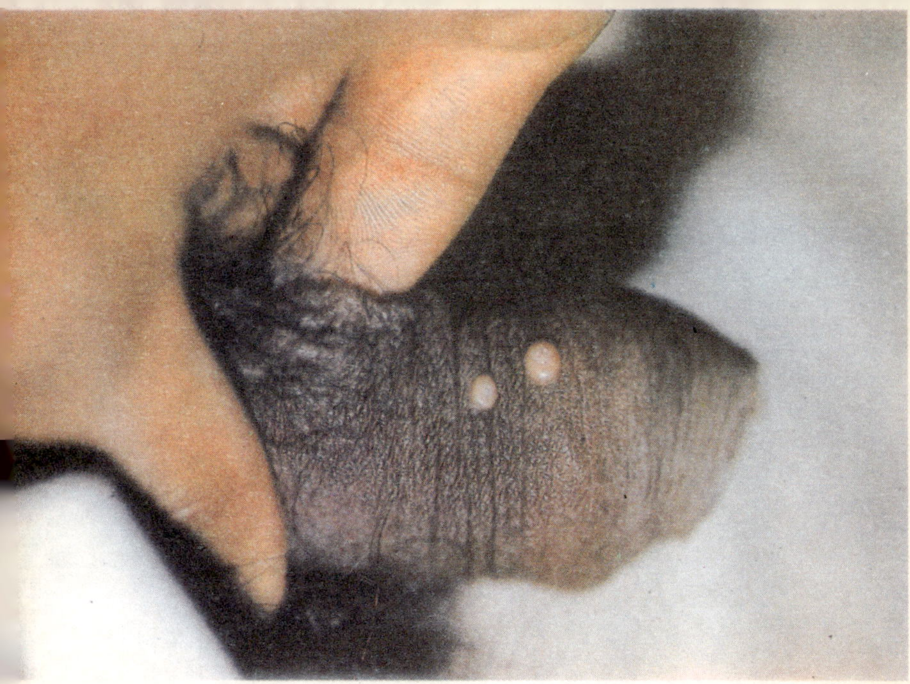

M-4. **Molluscum Contagiosum** showing two umbilicated papules over penis; sexually acquired.

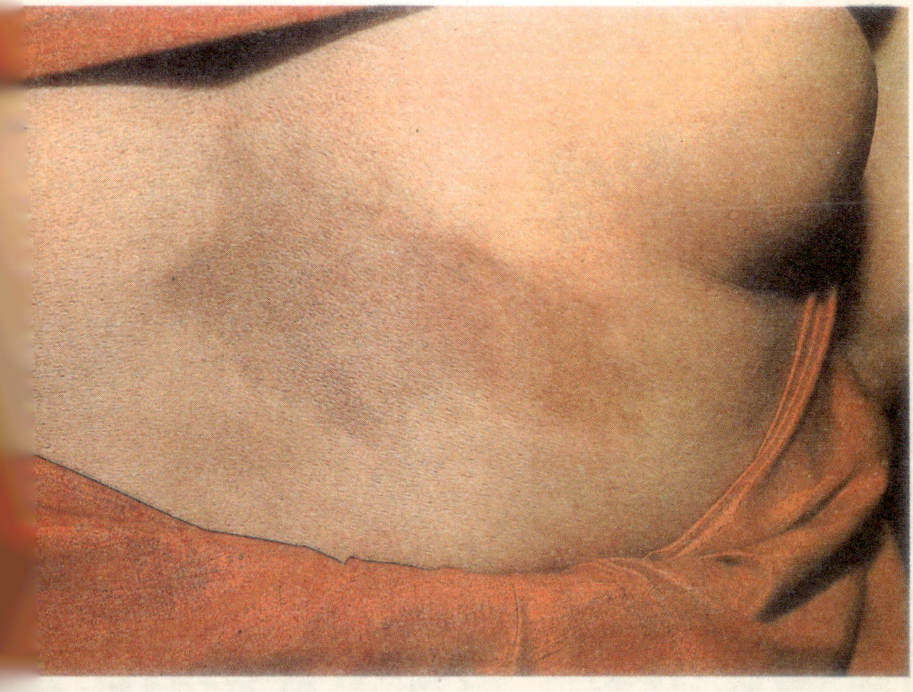

M-5. **Morphea** showing localised hyperpigmented plaque.

ii. There is no inflammatory infiltrate.

iii. Collagen bundles are thick, closely packed and stains more deeply eosinophilic. In papillary dermis, collagen seems homogeneous.

iv. Eccrine glands are atrophic with surrounding tightly bound newly formed collagen. They lie well inside the dermis due to the replacement of most of the subcutaneous fat by newly formed collagen. There are fibroblasts in the collagen.

v. Very few blood vessels are seen within the sclerotic collagen which very often have fibrotic wall and narrowed lumen.

c. Fascia underlying linear or segmental morphea shows fibrosis and sclerosis.

d. The muscle fibres appear vacuolated and separated from one another by edema and focal collection of inflammatory cells.

e. Bullae of generalised morphea are subepidermal being caused by edema due to lymphatic obstruction.

TREATMENT

TRIAMCINOLONE	SULPHASALAZINE
PHENYTOIN	ANTIMETABOLITES
PENICILLAMINE	

1. Physiotherapy

a. Improves contractures and increases the function of the affected limbs.

b. Warm paraffin bath to increase circulation.

c. Lubrication and massage, exercise.

d. Diathermy.

e. Trauma should be avoided.

2. Drugs

a. Local : (1) Intralesional injection of 5 mg/c.c. of triamcinolone acetonide in early lesions. (2) Occlusive application of fluorinated steroid preparations.

b. Internal : (1) Azathioprine—50-100 mg daily orally (2) Phenytoin, 100-400 mg daily has marked interference in fibroblast properties. (3) Penicillamine (4) Alpha-methyl dopa (5) Potassium para-aminobenzoate (6) DMSO (7) Prednisolone (8) Antimalarials (9) Antihistaminics (10) Vitamin A, D and E. (11) Testosterone (12) Bismuth (13) Vasodilators (14) Sulphasalazine 1 g b.i.d. for 5 to 9 months (15) Cyclophosphamide (16) Colchicine (17) Cyclofenil, 300 mg per day for 21 days each month. (18) Chlorumbucil.

All these in normal doses have controversial results.

DISCUSSION

Localised scleroderma characterised by skin induration has protracted course but there are reports of spontaneous healing. Intralesional and topical steroids should judiciously be used and closely monitored to prevent atrophy. Phenytoin has been shown to give good results but has got many toxic effects. Physiotherapy in selected cases seems to be beneficial. Surgery may be needed to correct dysfunction.

MYCETOMA

It is a localised disease usually affecting foot causing **swelling** and **draining sinuses** caused by a variety of fungi and actinomycetes (filamentous bacteria).

DIAGNOSIS

1. Organisms, generally from soil, are implanted by trauma into subcutaneous tissue. Hence it is primarily a disease of people who do not wear shoes. It is world-wide in distribution but is mostly prevalent in the tropical countries especially Africa.

'Maduromycosis' is the term used when the infective agents are fungi but clinically it resembles actinomycotic mycetoma.

2. Pathology

a. Causative agents are various filamentous fungi such as (1) Petriellidium boydii, the commonest organism; others are of the species of (2) Phialophora (3) Madurella (4) Acremonium.

b. Actinomycotic : (1) Nocardia brasiliensis (acid fast) (2) Actinomadura madurae.

2. Entry—mostly by trauma into the subcutaneous tissue usually of foot, hand or back.

3. Results in the formation of abscesses that may extend through muscles to bone and drain through chronic sinuses. They may drain white, yellow, red or black granules. The granules due to fungi consist of interwingled, septate hyphae and, depending on the species, they may have larger thick walled periphery. The actinomycotic granules consist only of filamentous hyphae.

The untreated lesions persist for years and extend deeper and peripherally causing deformity and loss of function.

4. **Histology**

The lesions resemble actinomycosis e.g.

a. Abscess formation. **b.** Granulation tissue. **c.** Necrotic foci. **d.** Fibrosis. **e.** Granule formation within abscess : granule is surrounded by an eosinophilic matrix representing host materials and perhaps antigen-antibody complexes.

5. Some granules have a characteristic morphology as well as colour that aids in identification when cultures cannot be made. Diagnosis should be made after seeing granules.

6. **Clinical features**

a. Usually swollen foot studded with granulomatous nodules and fistulae oozing viscid serum that contains the characteristic granules of various colours.

b. In chronic cases, gross hard swelling and deformity of the foot are produced with deep abscesses and fibrosis in the tissues. There are destructive and proliferative changes in the small bones.

c. There is generally no pain.

d. Secondary infection is a danger.

7. **Loboratory diagnosis**

a. Smear of the pus and granules.

b. Culture on Sabouraud's dextrose agar or Lowenstein Jensen media.

c. Biochemical tests of culture.

d. Serological tests.

e. Chromatographic analysis of cell wall components.

f. X-ray changes of bone destruction.

g. Eumycetomas : (1) Dark grain e.g. Madurella myctomii. (2) Pale grain e.g. P. boydii.

h. Actinomycetomas : (1) Pale grain e.g. Streptomyces somaliensis. (2) Red grain e.g. A. pelletierii (3) Small grain e.g. N. brasiliensis.

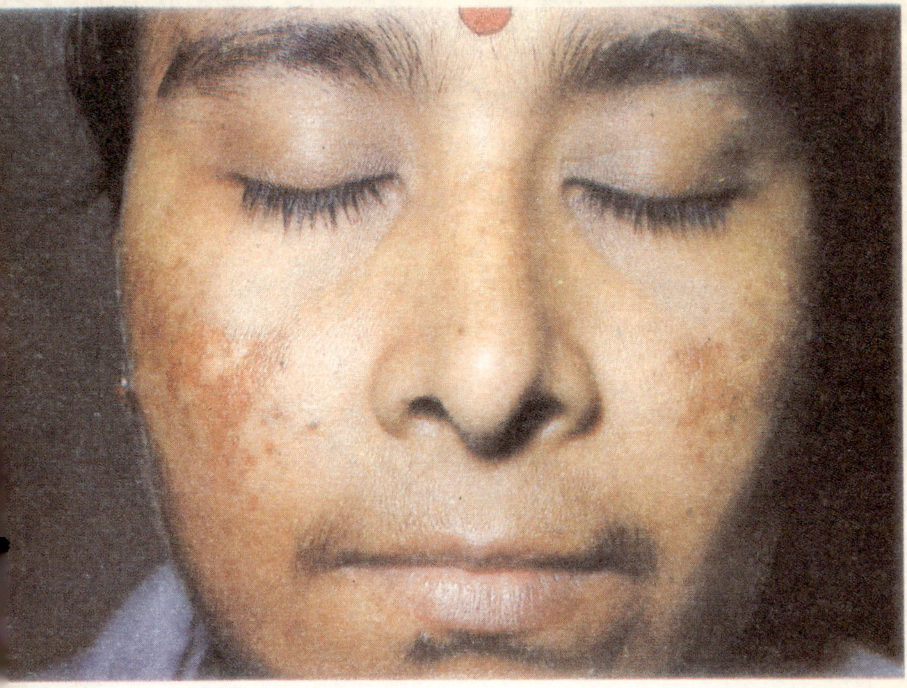

g. M-6. **Melasma** showing brown patches on face.

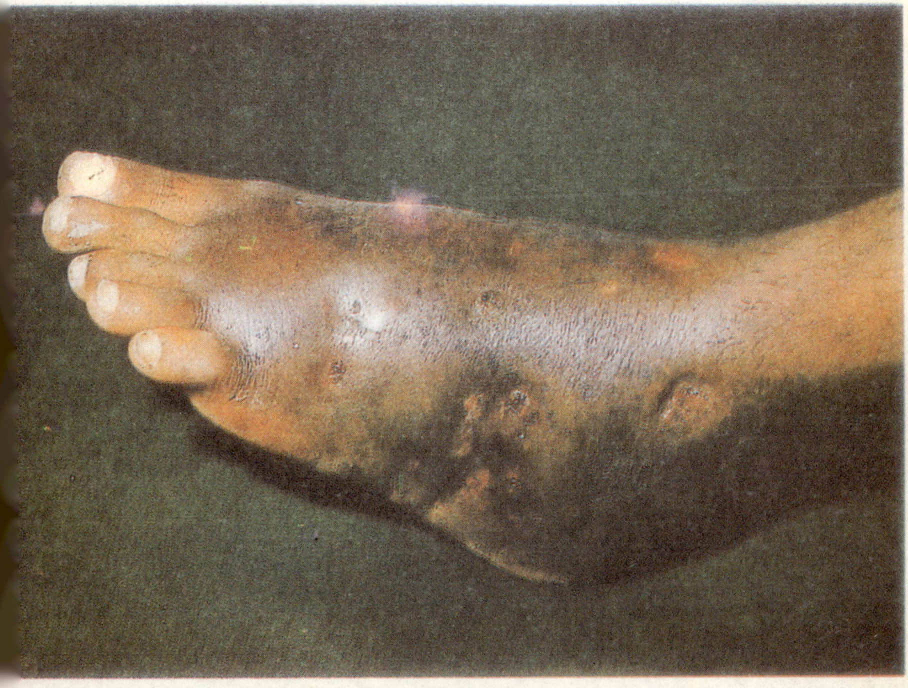

M-7. **Mycetoma** showing the affected foot with swelling and draining sinuses.

TREATMENT

DAPSONE	COTRIMOXAZOLE	KETOCONAZOLE

1. **Dapsone**—100-200 mg daily.

2. **Sulphonamides**—(a) Cotrimoxazole, 2 tabs b.i.d. for 3 to 9 months. (b) Short and long acting sulphonamides e.g. sulphamerazine, sulphadiazine 5 g daily ; sulphadimethoxin, sulfisoxazole and sulphamethoxy pyridiazine.

3. **Streptomycin** : 1 g I.M. daily or on alternate days. May be added with sulphonamides.

4. **Tetracycline**—2000 mg daily for months.

5. **Rifampicin**—600 mg daily for months.

6. Amphotericin B. **7.** 5-fluorocytosine. **8.** Griseofulvin.

9. Ketoconazole—200 mg daily. **10.** Isoniazid.

11 Large doses of penicillin in cases caused by N. asteroides.

12. Carbomycin. **13.** Surgical intervention.

DISCUSSION

Maduromycosis is the term to denote mycetoma caused by true fungi whereas actinomycotic mycetoma is caused either by nocardia or actinomadura species.

Starting with papule, nodule or abscess, the disease slowly grows to granulomatous swelling with draining sinuses, deformity and bone destruction. Area is indurated and the skin becomes discoloured. Atrophic scars are seen. Secondary infection causes large ulcers. Extensive fibrosis may cause elephantiasis.

Actinomycotic mycetoma responds well to treatment but there is no specific treatment for maduromycosis. Amputation is necessary for advanced cases.

NEWBORN DERMATOSES

Neonatal or newborn period refers to the first four weeks of life. As it ends, the infanthood begins to last upto one year.

Neonatal period is particularly important because of **recognition of non-diseases** or **transient lesions.** They require no intervention but a masterly inactivity. The transient lesions are normal phenomena, relatively common and benign and lasts only a few days to weeks. Appreciation of these non-diseases and their differentiation from the actual diseases require both experience and skill. Some of the important ones are as under.

1. Desquamation
2. Milia
3. Epstein and Bohn's pearls
4. Sucking blisters
5. Harlequin colour change
6. Acrocyanosis
7. Sebaceous gland hyperplasis
8. Cutis marmorata
9. Salmon patch
10. Mongolian spots
11. Erythema toxicum neonatorum
12. Transient neonatal pustular melanosis
13. Acne neonatorum

A brief discussion of these follow.

Desquamation

1. It is not normally present at birth but occurs within 24 to 36 hours after delivery and may not be complete until the third week of life.

2. If desquamation is seen at birth, it is an abnormal phenomenon and is indicative of

a. Postmaturity **b.** intrauterine anoxia **c.** congenital ichthyosis.

Milia

1. Milia are of two types–**primary** and **secondary.**

2. Primary milia represent a **keratinizing type** of **benign tumour.**

3. Secondary milia represent **retention cysts** caused by proliferative tendencies of the epithelium occurring either after injury e.g. dermabrasion or in diseases associated with subepidermal bullae e.g. bullous pemphigoid, epidermolysis bullosa dystrophica, porphyria cutanea tarda and lichen sclerosus et atrophicus.

4. Milia occurring in neonate represents a primary type. These are minute superficial inclusion cysts resulting from the **retention of keratin and sebaceous material** within the pilosebaceous apparatus of the newborn. The milium is a firm yellowish white papule, 1 to 2 mm in diameter, usually appearing over cheeks, nose, nasolabial furrow, chin and occasionally over the upper trunk and limbs.

5. About 40% to 50% of normal neonate may have milia at birth.

6. Usually they disappear spontaneously within the fourth week of life.

7. Wide spread and persistent milia, particularly in an unsuual distribution, may be a clinical marker of hereditary trichodysplasia or oral-facial-digital syndrome type I.

8. **Histologically,** milia appear as superficial epithelial cysts in the upper dermis. The cyst cavity is lined by a few layers thick stratified epithelium and filled with concentric lamellae of keratin.

9. **Treatment :** It is not necessary. The cystic spheres rupture, exfoliate their contents onto the skin surface and are thereby spontaneously cured.

Epstein's and Bohn's pearls

1. Clinico-histologically they are same as milia.

2. Yellowish white firm papules, 2-3 mm-diameter, are termed **Bohn's pearls** when present at gum margins and are called **Epstein's pearls** on the midline of palate.

3. They disappear spontaneously within few weeks of life.

Sucking blisters

1. These are solitary or scattered intact oval blisters on non-inflammed skin of the newborn.

2. They usually occur on the radial aspect of forearm, wrist, thumb, index finger and the central portion of the upper lip.

3. They are supposed to be the result of vigorous sucking of the affected part of the fetus in utero.

4. The bullae resolve rapidly within a few days without any sequelae.

Harlequin colour change

1. This is a dramatic vascular phenomenon occurring in a newborn lying on one side. It consists of erythematous flush on the dependent side with a clear line of demarcation along the midline of the body. The upper half of the body becomes pale.

2. This condition usually occurs in prematures and is seen in about 10% of newborns.

3. It develops suddenly and lasts only for a brief while of 30 seconds to 20 minutes.

4. The change of colour may be reversed by changing the baby's position. Within a few seconds of placing the baby in supine position, the colour change gets rectified.

5. The first attack is usually seen between the second and fifth day of life. The attacks may be few or multiple.

6. The other systems of the body show not abnormality during the attacks.

7. The exact mechanism of the phenomenon is not known. Probably, it reflects an immaturity of the hypothalamic centers that control the tone of peripheral blood vessels.

8. The condition is self-limiting, requiring no therapy.

Acrocyanosis

1. Most of the newborns develop purplish discolouration of hands. feet and lips during the period of breath-holding,

crying or chilling. This is a normal transient phenomenon called acrocyanosis.

2. It is suggested that the acrocyanosis is due to pooling of blood in the venous plexus as a result of increased tone of peripheral arterioles. This greater pooling of blood in venous plexuses is responsible for the cyanotic appearance of the acral areas.

3. Reassurance to the parents is the only logical answer to this complaint.

Sebaceous gland hyperplasia

1. Minute profuse yellowish papules, representing sebaceous gland hyperplasia, are seen on the cheeks, nose, upper lip and forehead of newborns.

2. Milia, which are white and cystic in appearance, can be easily differentiated from sebaceous gland hyperplasia.

3. This normal phenomenon is a manifestation of maternal androgenic stimulation which is responsible for the increased number and size of sebaceous glands.

4. It resolves spontaneously within the first few weeks of life.

Cutis marmorata

1. It is a normal physiologic response of a newborn characterized by lacelike red or blue vascular pattern on the trunk and extremities.

2. It appears when the newborn is exposed to low environmental temperatures and disappears on rewarming.

3. Immaturity of autonomic nervous system controlling the cutaneous vascular plexus is considered responsible for this phenomenon. The mottling is due to constriction of the deeper plexus and opening of the superficial one.

4. It disappears spontaneously within a few months. It has no medical significance and treatment is unnecessary.

5. The cutis marmorata that persists beyond six months of life may be a sign of congenital hypothyroidism. Persis-

tent and pronounced cutis marmorata may be seen in patients with Down's syndrome, trisomy 18 and Cornelia de Lange syndrome.

6. **Congenital phlebectasia of Bockenheimer** may mimic this phenomenon but rewarming does not change the mottling pattern in this disorder.

7. Similarly, **livedo reticularis** also persists on rewarming. Livedo reticularis is seen in certain collagen diseases such as neonatal lupus erythematosus.

8. In some neonates, a white negative pattern of this phenomenon called **cutis marmorata alba** may be created by a transient hypertonia of deep vasculature. This is also a short-span disorder and has no medical importance.

Salmon patch (Nevus simplex)

1. The salmon patch, which occurs in about 30 to 50% of newborn infants, is the most common vascular lesion in this age group.

2. It appears as a pale, pink, macular lesion, often with telangiectasia, and occurs on the glabella, eyelids, upper lip, nasolabial regions and on the nape of the neck ; 20% have the lesions on both the glabella and the eyelids, and only 5% on the other sites.

3. Histology shows distended dermal capillaries which represent the presistence of fetal circulation rather than newly formed capillaries.

4. The lesions on the face eventually fade and disappear completely, but for some infants the lesions over nuchal area persist. However, they do not possess any cosmetic problem as they are covered eventually with hairs. In the nuchal region, salmon patch persists in abont 50% of individuals.

5. The treatment is not necessary. It should be noted that a mild erythematous colour may be more persistent or may reappear in salmon patches during episodes of crying, breath holding or physical exertion. Except in the nuchal area, the lesion usually fades within the first year of life.

6. Salmon patches should not be confused with nevus flammeus which is a permanent lesion.

Mongolian spots

1. These are poorly circumscribed blue or slate-gray macular lesions resembling a bruise.

2. They occur most commonly on the lumbo-sacral region. Occasionally, they occur as aberrant mongolian spots over the middle or upper part of back, shoulder, buttocks and lower limbs.

3. Extensive and persistent mongolian spots are commonly seen in patients with bilateral nevus of Ota.

4. It is frequently found in mongoloid and negroid infants and occasionally in caucasoids.

5. It is present at birth and usually disappears within a few years. It may however persist up to adult life in about 3-4% of cases among the Japanese.

6. **Histologically,** the melanocytes are present in the dermis in its lower half or two-thirds.

7. This typical spot is due to delayed disappearance of the dermal melanocytes. The melanocytes migrate from neural crest through dermis into the epidermis. Normally, they start migrating from dermis to epidermis between the 11th and 14th week. They gradually disappear from the dermis after the 20th week.

8. The peculiar hue of the mongolian spot is due to the Tyndall phenomenon (scattering of light).

9. The diagnosis is based on clinical morphology and can be confirmed by histopathologic examinations.

10. Treatment is unnecessary as this is a benign disorder.

Erythema toxicum neonatorum

1. This is a bengin, self-limiting, asymptomatic eruption of skin of unknown etiology seen only in the neonatal period.

2. **Clinically,** it presents as 1-3 mm yellow-white papules or pustules, either alone or in combination, in a patch of

erythema. Sometimes, erythematous patches are the only presenting feature. The diameter of the patches varies from a few milimeters to several centimeters.

3. It appears most frequently during the first 3 to 4 days of life. It may be seen at birth or as late as the 10th day of life. The duration of individual lesions varies from a few hours to sixteen days. Exacerbations and remissions may occur during the first two weeks of life.

4. A small or a large area of skin may be involved. The chest is more involved than the back, the proximal parts of limbs more than the distal ones.

The lesion may occur anywhere in the body except palms and soles. The sparing of palm and soles is due to the absence of pilosebaceous follicles in these sites.

5. The etiology is unknown. Perhaps, it represents a transient reaction of newborn skin to normal mechanical or thermal stimuli.

6. There are plenty of disparity among its reported incidence.

7. No sexual or racial predisposition has been noted.

8. **Histopathology** of a papule of erythema toxicum neonatorum shows an accumulation of eosinophils about the pilosebaceous apparatus just below the dermo-epidermal junction of the skin. A pustule of this disorder reveals perifollicular accumulation of eosinophils in a subcorneal or intradermal location.

9. Therapy is unnecessary as this is self-limiting.

Transient neonatal pustular melanosis

1. First described in 1976, it is a transient, self-limiting, benign dermatosis of newborn characterized by three types of lesions :

i. Superficial small vesicles and pustules.

ii. The vesicles and pustules soon rupture leaving a a collarette of fine scale surmounting a central hyperpigmented macule.

iii. Hyperpigmented macules without any collarette of scale.

2. The lesions are usually present at birth. During the first bathing, the superficial small vesiculo-pustules rupture leaving a collarette of fine white scales with a central pinhead sized hyperpigmented macule. One or all the types of lesions may be found in an extensive or localized distribution.

3. They are most often seen in clusters under the chin, on the forehead, nape of the neck, lower back and shin. Scalp, trunk, limbs, palms and soles may also be affected.

4. The hyperpigmented macules generally fade away within a period of several weeks to months.

5. The etiology is unknown. **Incidence** : It affects about 2% of all newborns.

6. Histopathology of the vesiculo-pustules reveal intra-corneal or subcorneal aggregates of neutrophils with a small admixture of eosinophils. The dermis may not be involved or may show an infiltrate of neutrophils or eosinophils.

The histophathology of hyperpigmented **macules** show focal hyperpigmentation of basal layer.

7. Culture of pustules is always sterile. Stained smears of pus can be used to distinguish the lesions from those of erythema toxicum and pyoderma, for they do not contain bacteria by gram stain or dense aggregates of eosinophils by Wright stain.

8. It has no associated systemic manifestions and requires **no therapy**.

Acne neonatorum

1. Neonates may develop comedones and papulo-pustules that resemble acne vulgaris.

2. The etiology is obscure but it is suggested that it develops in response to increased androgens and progesterones in the maternal circulation. Their hormones stimulate sebaceous glands that have not yet involuted to their childhood state of immaturity.

3. It occurs mainly in male neonates and often with a history of severe acne in one or both the parents.

4. Papules, pustules, open and closed comedones are usual but rarely nodulocystic lesions may develop.

5. The course is usually brief.

6. It is self-limited and therapy is not usually required. Daily cleansing with soap and water may be needed in mild cases. Occasionally, mild keratolytic agents and/or a benzoyl peroxide gel may help.

DISCUSSION

Neonatal dermatoses are not uncommon. Most of them are self-limiting and do not require any active treatment. Reassurance to the parents is all that is necessary. However, there is no reason why the dermatologists should not be conversant with these entities.

NON-GONOCOCCAL URETHRITIS (NGU)

Urethritis is caused by Neisseria gonorrhoeae and other diverse etiological agents. Non-gonococcal urethritis (NGU) is that urethritis where gonococcal infection has been excluded. Often non-specific urethritis (NSU) and NGU are considered synonymous but all cases of NGU are not NSU, whereas all cases of NSU are non-gonococcal. NGU is probably the commonest sexually transmitted human disease, and the most frequent cause of urethritis in heterosexual men. Homosexual and bisexual men also suffer from NGU but in far less number. NGU persisting after 2 weeks, when on successful treatment all symptoms and signs of gonococcal urethritis subside, is called **post-gonococcal urethritis** (PGU). Although it can occur both in men and women, NGU is usually diagnosed in men.

DIAGNOSIS

1. **Epidemiology** : **a**. Accurate data of incidence of NGU in India are not available.

b. Standard diagnostic criteria of NGU are still unfortunately lacking.

c. Two-thrids of reported urethritis cases in England and Wales are non-gonococcal.

d. The global incidence of NGU, and also in our country, is probably on the increase.

e. NGU has been known since the beginning of this century, but the epidemiological studies have started only in 1960 after the development of simplified cell culture methods. These have made possible the isolation of chlamydia trachomatis, one of the most important causes of NGU.

f. Epidemiologic studies are still severely hampered due to unknown etiology in majority of NGU cases.

g. **Incubation period** : The range of incubation period is 1-5 weeks. But usually the symptoms appear within 2-3 weeks. However, it is often difficult to accurately determine the incubation period. This is due to (1) high frequency of asymptomatic disease, (2) tendency for symptoms to be missed or ignored, (3) difficulty in knowing if a sex partner had had other recent sex partners, (4) probability of numerous causes of urethritis having different incubation periods.

h. In contrast to patients with gonorrhoea, NGU patients are (1) more often white, (2) better educated, (3) of higher socio-economic status, (4) less likely to be unemployed, (5) older at the age of first intercourse and (6) having fewer number of sexual partners.

i. Incidence of NGU in homosexual males is lower than in heterosexuals. Possibly, it indicates more efficient vaginal transmission than rectal intercourse.

j. The risk factors of NGU are similar to gonorrhoea. The age distribution also is almost identical. The largest number of cases is seen in males aged 20-24, followed by 15-19. The less frequent group is between 25-29.

2. Etiology : The etiological factors are many and vary enormously : (1) from country to country, (2) with different sexual behaviour patterns and (3) with different self-medication, e.g. if a patient is under treatment with tetracycline or erythromycin, ureaplasma urealyticum becomes the most evident etiologic agent.

The **important causes** of NGU are as follow.

a. Bacterial : **Chlamydia trachomatis,** especially the immune type D, E, F, G, H, I, J and K. It is the most frequent cause. Ureaplasma urealyticum, Staphylococcus : S. saprophyticus, Streptococcus : S. agalactiae, Enterococcus, E. coli, Proteus, Klebsiella, Clostridium difficile, Corynebacterium genitalium type 1, Hemophilus group e.g. H. vaginalis, Dorderlein's bacillus crassus, Tuberculosis, Anerobic gram negative bacteria.

b. Protozoal : Trichomonas vaginalis.

c. Viral : Herpes simplex, wart virus e.g. Condyloma accuminata, Herpes Zoster, Foot-and-mouth disease.

d. **Mycotic** : Candida albicans.

e. **Chemical** : Dettol, phenol, iodine and other self-or iatrogenic medications.

f. **Traumatic** : Thermal, mechanical (catheter urethritis, habitual squeezing).

g. **Spirochaetal** : Intrameatal syphilitic chancre, mucous patches.

h. **Foreign bodies**

i. **Neoplasms** : Carcinoma.

j. **Structural abnormalities** : Urethral stricture, urethral varicosities during cirrhosis of liver.

k. **Crystalluria**

l. **Hypersensitivity** : Fixed drug eruption, Stevens-Johnson syndrome, with allergic cystitis after excessive consumption of asparagus or celery.

m. **Non-specific causes** : Even with scrupulous search, exact etilogical agent cannot be found in many cases.

Among the varied etiological agents, chlamydia trachomatis is one of the major causes of NGU. This infection persists for a long time, manifests often in subtle way and may be completely asymptomatic. These asymptomatic individuals constitute the major reservoir of infection in the community, contributing significantly to the spread of the disease. Chlamydial infection is often associated with gonococcal urethritis. In such cases, N. gonorrhoeae can be diagnosed more rapidly than concurrent chlamydial infection which is still incubating.

Ureaplasma urealyticum, also known as T-mycoplasma, is found both in the urethra of men having NGU and healthy individuals. Whether it causes NGU or is a commensal or non-pathogenic organism, changing into pathogenic under certain conditions, has not been definitely determined. But it causes urethritis in a small proportion of men. That it is a pathogen causing NGU has been supported by inoculation experiments recently conducted in human volunteers.

3. Clinical features

In male, symptoms are

a. The usual presentation is with low-grade urethritis with **scanty** or **moderate mucoid** or **mucopurulent urethral discharge.** In minority, the appearance of discharge and the severity of the condition often make it indistinguishable from gonorrhoea.

b. Urinary symptoms include variable degree of **dysuria.** Sometimes, it is associated with **frequency** but rarely **nocturia.**

c. In a small number of cases, urethral discharge is accompanied by **hematuria** and symptoms of cystitis (hemorrhagic cystitis).

d. At times, there is no urethral discharge, but often the patient complains of **vague penile discomfort** and **tenderness** which may or may not be associated with urination. This is often described as **tingling** or **itching in the pipe.**

e. Wetness and dribbling, after urination, are often complained of. Non-caucasians often feel **burning pain on ejaculation** and difficulty in maintaining an erection.

f. At the other end, the condition may remain **completely asymptomatic.** The patient is not aware of it and it may be found in course of routine examination or if the datient presents with a complication.

In male, signs are

a. Signs of urethritis e.g. **meatitis** and **urethral discharge.**

b. The **discharge varies in colour.** It may be clear mucoid, white when appeared speckled, grey or yellow like gonococcus.

c. Occasionally, no obvious discharge is seen.

d. The terminal urethra may be damp with the lips of meatus and may stick together.

In female, symptoms are

a. The patient is often asymptomatic.

b. If symptoms are present, they are often of minor degree and may be disregarded.

c. Symptoms of acute or recurrent cystitis for which no causative agent is demonstrated by intense search suggest the possibility of NGU.

d. There may be **vaginal discharge** if cervix is seriously affected.

In female, signs are

a. Signs of cervicitis with purulent or muco-purulent cervical exudate.

b. Cervix is sometimes seen with edematous and congested erosion.

c. With colposcopy, microfollicles are found in the marginal area. These follicles are considered pathognomonic sign of chlamydial infection.

d. In a minority of cases, the condition presents with inflammatory signs and symptoms of pelvic organs.

4. Investigations

Laboratory investigations are required in any case of suspected NGU to

a. identify if there is actual urethritis by demonstrating increased number of polymorphonuclear leucocytes in urethral material.

b. exclude Neisseria gonorrhoeae infection by gram staining of urethral smear and culture and to prove the case to be NGU, and

c. find out the causative agent of NGU.

To identify the presence of urethritis

1. Demonstration of increased number of polymorphonuclear leucocytes.

a. Urethral smears obtained from meatal exudate or endo-urethral swab and first voided urine are the specimens for examination. For both the specimens, the patient should be examined as long an interval as possible without voiding.

b. The swab of exudate taken from urethra is rolled back and forth over the slide to cover an area of 1 cm^2.

c. Slide is gram-stained or stained with methylene blue.

d. It is then scanned at a magnification of ×100 and areas having the largest number of polymorphonuclear leucocytes under oil (×1000).

e. The number of polymorphs in each of the five fields is then counted.

f. The presence of a mean of polymorphs more than 4 per field appears to be significant.

g. To detect **polymorphs in urine sediments,** the first 10-15 ml of voided urine is collected.

h. It is then centrifuged at 400×G for 5-10 minutes.

i. 0·5 ml of the supernatant is discarded and the sediment is resuspended in residual urine.

j. Sufficient sediment is placed over slide and cover slip is placed over it.

k. The number of polymorphonuclear leucocytes in each of 5 ml×400 power field is counted.

l. The 15 or more polymorphs in one or more of the five fields appear to be suggestive.

2. Two-glass urine test

a. The foreskin is fully retracted and the patient is asked to urinate in two clean specimen of glasses.

b. If the urine is hazy, sufficient 5% acetic acid is added to dissolve haze-producing phosphates, if any.

c. If there is anterior urethritis, the haze will persist (owing to pus cells) as threads or sheds (casts of Littre's glands) in the first glass of urine, but the second one will be clear.

d. If both the glasses are hazy, the infection has involved posterior urethra, bladder and kidneys.

This **simple test** may thus **provide supportive evidence of urethritis.**

Detection of Nesseria gonorrhoeae

a. Gram stain of the urethral smear or of material obtained with an endo-urethral swab in case of no clear urethral discharge will elicit typical gram-negative intracellular diplococci.

b. Culture is obtained (i) when the gram stain is interpreted as being equivocal, (ii) when the person reading the gram stain is not experienced, (iii) for test of cure, (iv) for treatment failures and (iv) when penicillinase producing N. gonorrhoeae infection is suspected.

To find out the causative agent of NGU

a. Chlamydia trachomatis : Various methods are there to detect and diagnose this infection in laboratory. They are -

(i) Microscopy : Demonstration of inclusion bodies within the infected columner epithelial cells by staining. Of the various techniques of staining, Giemsa is the most popular. Direct microscopy however is often insensitive and unnecessarily time-consuming.

(ii) Culture : (a) Chlamydiae cannot grow outside a living cell. So a special tissue culture technique is needed. The previous method of using yolk sacs of developing hen's egg as tissue culture is time-consuming and unsuitable for large scale use and gives cross-infection between eggs.

(b) McCoy cells (mouse fibroblasts) culture simplified the problem. These cells are first pretreated. The method may be either by irradiation or with idoxyuridine or cytochalasin B. This would prevent replication when inclusions are difficult to see. Various modifications of methodology such as HeLa cells for McCoy cells, addition of cyclohexamide to cell line during processing to curtail pretreatment of cells have also been made.

(c) A suspension of pretreated cells is taken with growth medium in a flat-bottomed test tube with a sterile cover slip on it. It is incubated at 37°C for 48 hours. This would facilitate the growth of a monolayer of McCoy cells on the cover slip. The growth medium is then replaced by the transport medium containing basic cell growth medium with fungizone and gentamycin. This would reduce contamination. The swab of the clinical specimen is next inserted and broken off into the transport medium stored at 4°C until inoculated into the cell monolayer. For a higher yield of isolation, it must be completed within 48 hours. 'Snap' freezing to $-70°$ C helps the specimen to be stored for longer periods. To help penetration of organism to McCoy cells, high speed centrifugation is performed. The tubes are next incubated for 48 hours and finally fixed with methanol, stained and mounted for microscopic examination, for inculsions. C. trachomatis, with its glycogen-rich cell wall, stains dark brown with iodine. Yellow inclusions are seen in Giemsa stain.

(d) LGV subtype and C. psitacci usually penetrate into the cell without any centrifugation. C. psitacci does not stain as dark brown in iodine. *In vitro* sulphonamide and D. cycloserine sensitivity testing, C. trachomatis is sensitive, whereas C. psitacci is not.

(e) Specimens are collected by a sterile cotton wool swab from the endocervix and junctional area in female patients. In male patients, urethral smears are obtained by special calcium alginate swabs on flexible aluminium shafts passed at least 5 cm into the urethra.

Specimens should be transported to the laboratory in special transport media as early as possible.

iii. Serological tests

a. Measurement of group antibody : Antichlamydial group antibody (common to all chlamydial infections) can be measured by **complement fixation test** (**CFT**) and **radio-immune precipitation** (**RIP**) **test**. RIP is more sensitive than CFT. But these tests are of little value in diagnosis as they lack specificity.

b. Micro-immunofluorescence (**MIF**) **test** : This test, as sensitive as RIP, helps to detect type specific antibodies to chlamydial infection. In spite of this advantage over RIP, MIF is also of limited value in diagnosis for (i) antibodies detected remain long in the blood after the agent disappears from the tissues and (ii) high prevalence of antibody among populations, especially in populations of clinics of sexually transmitted diseases.

b. Ureaplasma urealyticum : **i.** In patients with obvious urethritis, culture of the first voided urine and an endo-urethral swab give similar diagnostic results.

ii. In men, with no or minimal urethritis, an endo-urethral swab is preferable.

iii. Ureaplasma urealyticum can be cultured both in broth and agar media. In broth, a pH shift indicates presence of the organism. On agar, it produces typical colonies which are identified directly on differential agar or by addition of a reagent making use of the urease production.

iv. Serology is of no help in diagnosing ureaplasma urealyticum.

v. Detection of U. urealyticum from a man suffering from acute urethritis does not necessarily mean that it is the cause of urethritis. Detection is only significant when isolated at the end of a course of treatment from a male with persistent urethritis.

c. The remaining **other bacterial causes** of NGU can be identified in the laboratory by different staining techniques, particularly by gram stain and also by different cultural methods employed for isolation.

d. Trichomonas vaginalis : **i.** It can be identified by direct microscopy using freshly obtained secretion on a slide with cover slip.

ii. It can also be identified by hanging drop preparation. It is usually recognised with 4 mm or 2 mm objective by its characteristic jerky movements.

iii. It can also be grown in various artificial media e.g. modified Diamond's media, cysteine-peptone-liver maltose (CPLM) media etc. The combination of both smear and culture tests is more reliable in diagnosis than either test alone.

e. Viral causes

i. For **Herpes simplex virus (HSV)** infection, tissue culture method, using animal cells or cells from human embryos, is the best. Alternatively, the Tzanck and the Papanicolaou smear test could be done to find out multinucleated giant cells, and both multinucleated giant cells and intranuclear eosinophilic inclusions respectively. These smear tests are easily available than cultures but are less sensitive. Electron microscopy is of value in rapid diagnosis. Serologic diagnosis is useful in confirming a primary infection. Monoconal antibodies to HSV-1 and HSV-2 are now being tested and will soon become a powerful tool for rapid diagnosis and typing of HSV.

ii. For **genital wart virus** infection e.g. condyloma accuminata, diagnosis is usually clinical. Histology and examination of Papanicolaou stained smears of cervical lesions may help in diagnosis.

f. **Candida albicans** : i. It is commonly identified by stained smears and culture. They are more sensitive diagnostic methods. Yeast-forms or mycelia can be seen in the moist saline preparations.

ii. Yeast spores, with or without buds, and the mycelium are found to be gram positive.

iii. Culture is taken usually onto a maltose peptone agar (Sabouraud's medium) plate which is then incubated at 36°C for 2-5 days.

g. Spirochaetal cause of NGU can be investigated by dark ground illumination microscopy and by various serological and immunological tests.

h. NGU by chemical and traumatic causes are investigated according to specific history and clinical findings.

i. NGU by neoplasm is established by biopsy.

j. Foreign bodies and urethral structural abnormalities can be investigated with the help of straight x-ray of the lower abdomen, urethroscopy, urethrogram and other relevant radiological procedures.

k. In **fixed drug eruptions** such as Stevens-Johnson syndrome and other hypersensitive reactions, diagnosis is based on the patient's history and the characteristic appearance of the lesions.

5. Complications

A. Local

a. In male : These are similar to those which follow gonorrhoea such as tysonitis, paraurethral duct infection, littritis, periurethral abscess, cowperitis, prostatitis, and prostatovesiculitis. But these are hardly seen now-a-days and are usually less severe.

b. In female : Skenitis, salpingitis, pelvic infection, and tubal occlusion are seen. Tubal occlusion is found to be more common after non-gonococcal salpingitis than the gonococcal, and it is likely to be after multiple attacks.

B. General : Reiter's disease in both sexes, but it is much less common in females. This is a rare complication.

C. Psychological complications : Confusion and psychological distress are common, especially when a couple has a monogamous relationship and urethritis persists after treatment. The problems are mistrust of the partner, fear of infertility, of spreading STD, of impotence and of physical sequelae.

TREATMENT

TETRACYCLIN	DOXYCYCLINE
ERYTHROMYCIN	MINOCYCLINE
COTRIMOXAZOLE	STREPTOMYCIN

The innumerable therapeutic regimes for NGU are in account. But unfortunately there is still a lack of standardisation of criteria used to diagnose and assess the cure of NGU. This makes the successful treatment problematic. It is still therefore empirical.

A. Treatment in male : (I) Certain advice are to be given to the patients with the first attack of NGU and also to those with recurrent and/or resistant NGU. These are

a. Total abstinence from sexual intercourse during treatment and until the possible cure.

b. Abstinence from alcohol intake. There is however no scientific rationality worth the name behind it.

c. Holding of urine for at least 4 hours before the next visit. It helps in assessing the two-glass urine test.

d. Avoidance of squeezing or milking urethra as it is often done for self-examination.

e. Avoidance of milk or milk products, particularly of the patients with resistant NGU on oral tetracycline, as it often hampers absorption of the drug.

f. Ensuring partner(s) to attend clinics for examination and treatment.

II. Commonly used therapeutic regimes

a. **Tetracyclines** : Oxytetracycline or tetracycline hydrochloride 250-500 mg q.d.s × 7-14 days. Long acting tetracyclines 1 tab b.i.d. × 7-21 days.

Tetracycline is the drug of choice. It is effective against all isolates of C. trachomatis *in vitro* and *in vivo* and about 90% of isolates of U. urealyticum.

b. **Doxycycline** or **Minocycline**—100 mg b.i.d × 7 days.

c. **Erythromycin**—Erythromycin tablets 250-500 mg q.i.d × 7-14 days. Erythromycin stearate 500 mg b.i.d × 7-21 days. Erythromycin is used as the first alternative to tetracycline. Although less active than tetracycline, erythromycin is effective against C. trachomatis *in vitro* but not always *in vivo.* It is also effective against U. urealyticum in men, but it can never eradicate it from vagina. **Erythromycin estolate should be avoided** due to chance of hepatotoxicity.

d. **Cotrimoxazole**—2 tab b.i.d × 7-14 days.

a. **Streptomycin**—1 g I. M + single dose of long acting sulphonamide 1 g × 7-14 days.

III. Duration of treatment : There are differences in opinion regrding duration of treatment. Treatment will be inadequate or excessive if continued for less than 1 week or more than 2 weeks respectively. Long continued treatment helps patient's partner to have time for treatment before intercourse is resumed. It also delays the time of recurrence as defined by time after treatment is initiated.

IV. **Follow-up treatment** : **a.** Usually review of the patient is done 1 week after the onset of treatment in initial stage. The patient, either asymptomatic or with no sign of urethritis, is considered probably cured at the end of 1 week of treatment.

b. Patients with persisting signs of urethritis at the end of 1 week are treated for further 1 week. If the urethritis still persists, an alternative drug is to be used.

c. Some patients complain of symptoms at the end of 1 week, though smear and two-glass urine tests are negative. Reassurance with potassium citrate mixture 10 ml t.d.s × 1 week is to be made. If it fails, antibiotics are to be prescribed again for 1 week for such patients.

d. Patients who are asymptomatic after 2-3 weeks treatment but still have signs of urethritis create problem. If few pus cells on smear and/or slight abnormal first glass urine are found, no treatment is required ; but re-exposure must be confidently prohibited. These patients usually develop prostatitis and follow up must, therefore, include prostatitic bead examination.

B. Treatment in female : **a. Tetracyclines** as prescribed in male are also given in females. Tetracycline is contra-indicated during pregnancy.

b. Erythromycin stearate can probably be prescribed after the first trimester.

c. The risk of pelvic sepsis following termination of pregnancy in NGU should be well-guarded.

d. Other advice as given to males are also equally applicable to females with NGU.

DISCUSSION

NGU is probably the commonest sexually transmitted disease throughout the world. The etiologic agent however might vary in different countries. Among the diverse etiologic agents, **ureaplasma urealyticum** and **chlamydia trachomatis** are the most important and common. Even after intensive search for all the causal agents, some cases remain unexplained and are termed as NSU which, of course, is always sexually transmitted.

In men, symptoms of urethritis appear between 1 and 4 weeks of the intercourse. **Discomfort in the urethra, mild dysuria** and **a clear to muco-purulent discharge** are the common complaints. Symptoms are more marked early in the morning when the lips of the meatus are stuck together with dried secretions. **Meatus is red** and **dried secretions may be found on underclothes.** Rarely, a patient may complain of severe dysuria, intense frequency of micturition and copious purulent discharge. Following rectal and orogenital contact, proctitis and pharyngitis may also develop.

In women, there may be no symptom. However, occasionally **vaginal discharge**, **dysuria, frequency,** pelvic pain, dyspareunia, symptoms of proctitis, pharyngitis and cervicitis may be present.

Diagnosis requires **intensive investigation.** Gonorrhoea should be excluded. Obvious causes of vaginal discharge should be ruled out. In most cases, **urethral smear** would show many polymorphs, epithelial cells, but no pathogenic organisms.

Microscopic examination of urine will show 5 or more polymorphs per 1000 oil immersion fields. The first voided morning urine is ideal for examination. Tissue culture of urethral swab might show C. trachomatis. In the modern laboratories, fluorescent staining would identify chlamydia in urethral secretions. Specific monoclonal antibodies may also be detected. In women, gram stain of purulent cervical discharge often shows neutrophils but no gonococci. NGU is a **serious disorder** because, if not adequately treated, complications may develop. In men, urethral stricture and chronic epididymitis are serious handicaps. In women, bartholinitis, cysts of Bartholin's glands, salpingitis and perihepatitis may create problems. Reiter's syndrome is another important complication. Chlamydial ophthalmia neonatorum is a potential danger to infants born to women with clamydial cervicitis.

Tetracycline, erythromycin, minocycline and **doxycycline** are the drugs used for treating NGU. In pregnant women, instead of tetracycline, erythromycin should be the drug of choice. About 20% of patients have one or more relapses on follow-up. They should be re-treated. Even if no treatment is given, the symptoms would subside in 60-70% of patients, but in women chronic pelvic infection may develop.

Patients should abstain from sexual intercourse until treatment is completed. Sexual partners should thoroughly be investigated and, if needed, treatment must be given. All patients should be followed for six months by regular monthly check up. **Serological tests for syphilis** should be done before and three months after the trcatment.

PAPULAR URTICARIA (PU)

It is a chronic and recurrent eruption of itchy papules, often grouped in irregular clusters, that generally affect children between 2 to 7 years. The attacks are seasonal and coincide with the species of insect that cause it. In India, the mosquito is found to be the commonest cause. It is basically an allergic reaction to various insects occurring in susceptible children.

1. Etiology

a. Insects like **mosquitoes, dog and cat flea, bird flea, bed bugs, rat mites** are the common offending agents. The pattern of eruption closely corresponds to the bites. The seasonal incidence coincides with the peak prevalence of the insects.

b. It has no relation with poverty or malnutrition, but the prevention of insect bites by repellants or insecticides often cures the condition.

c. In most cases, **atopic background** has been detected.

2. Clinical features

a. It first appears as **irregular, inflammed, wheals** or **firm papules** on the top of wheals. This inflammation subsides in a day or two leaving only small elevated itchy papules. There may be **vesicles,** especially on the legs. Wheals, papules and vesicles are accompanied by intense itching. Sometimes, **puncta** of insect bite at the centre of the papule may be palpably visible.

b. The distribution of the lesions is mainly on **extensor aspects of extremities** and **buttocks**; the lesions develop in **crops** at irregular intervals. They persist for 2 to 8 days and leave **hyperpigmented spots**. These spots may again be inflammed during a repeat attack. **Face** is generally **spared.**

c. Both sexes are equally affected.

d. The patients may present with complications such as secondary infections causing recurrent **impetigo** and also **eczematisations.**

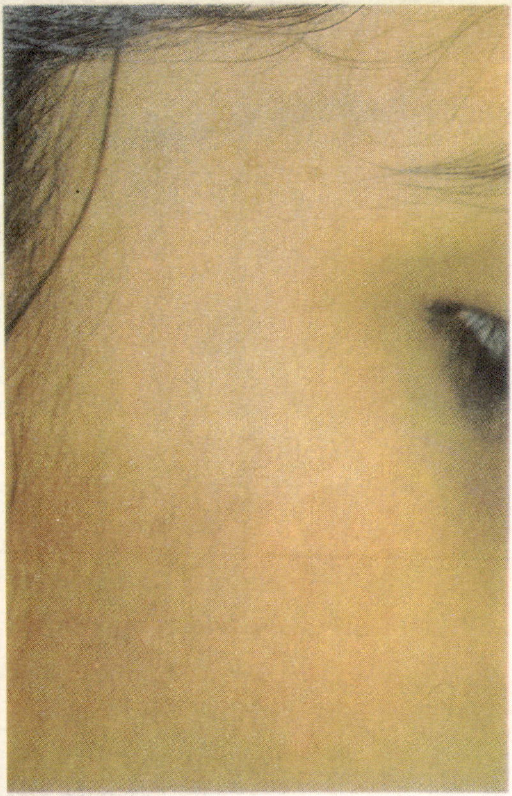

Fig. M-8. **Milia** showing asymptomatic, tiny, pearly white, keratinous cysts on face.

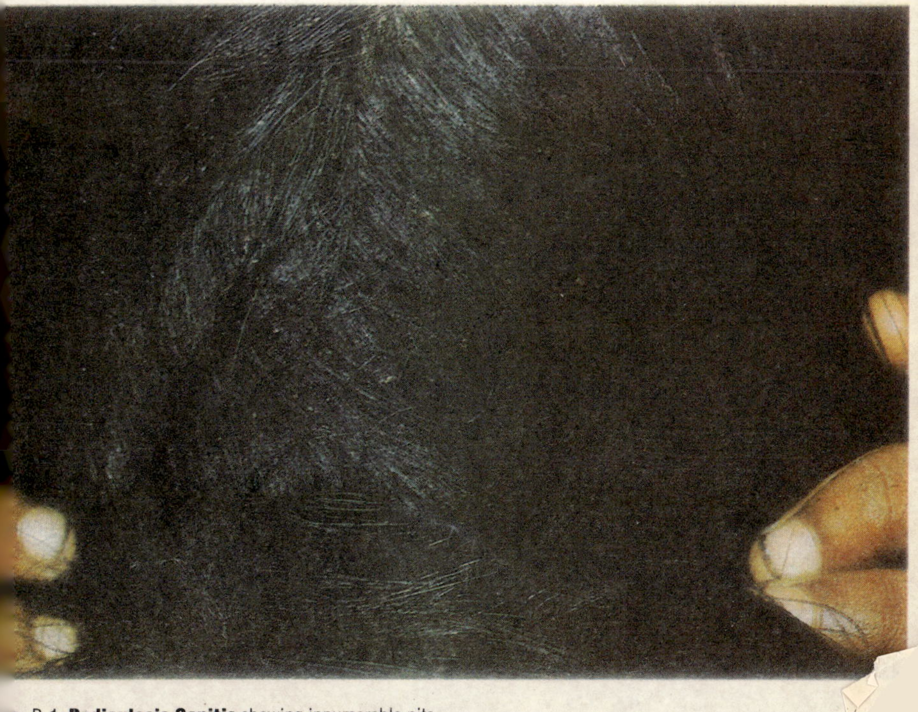

g. P-1. **Pediculosis Capitis** showing innumerable nits.

4. Pediculosis pubis should be treated by applying GBH (1%) to infested and adjacent hairy areas with particular attention to pubic mons and perianal region for 8-12 hours. Sexual contacts should be simultaneously treated. Clothings, towels and bed linens should be washed in boiling water, followed by ironing.

5. Eyelash involvement should be treated by application of (1) Petrolatum applied thickly twice in a day for 8 days with mechanical removal of nits or (2) 0·25% **physostigmine** ophthalmic ointment with cotton-tipped applicator or (3) 1% **yellow oxide of mercury** ointment. 4. **Fluorescein** eye drops applied to the lashes produce instantaneous death of lice.

6. **Complications** should be treated as follow.

a. Secondary impetigo and folliculitis by systemic or local antibiotic.

b. Eczematous change by local steroid lotion or cream and systemic antibiotics.

c. Urticaria with systemic antihistaminics and anti-serotonin drugs.

7. In Pediculosis pubis, other venereal diseases should also be investigated and necessary treatment instituted.

8. **Cotrimoxazole** in full dose **internally** for 7 days destroys the bacteria present in the intestine of lice and thereby disturbs the metabolism of the meal of lice and they are killed.

DISCUSSION

The possibility of having pediculosis even among cultured patients should not be ruled out. The disease is undoubtedly common in people with unhygienic habit but the author has the experience of seeing it even in highly hygiene-conscious ladies. To convince them of the disease is often a problem. However, demonstration of a nit through lens makes them dumb-founded. In pubic and axillary pediculosis, shaving helps proper contact of the topical agent. Reassurance is necessary about persistent lymphadenopathy and maculae caerulea. Source of infection must also be treated.

PEMPHIGUS

Pemphigus is the most serious autoimmune bullous disorder of the skin. It has been subdivided into four types (1) **Pemphigus vulgaris** (2) **Pemphigus vegetans** (3) **Pemphigus foliaceus** with its variant **Brazilian pemphigus** and (4) **Pemphigus erythematosus.** This subdivision is primarily based on the level of blister formation at the epidermis. There is also a variety of drug induced pemphigus. It is not a common disease but is important for it may endanger life. Full cure is yet not attainable.

General Etiological Consideration

It is essentially an **autoimmune disorder.**

1. All patients have IgG antibodies in the intercellular areas of epidermis or mucosa which can be demonstrated on direct immunofluorescence. Further, 70-95% of the patients have IgG antibody in their sera which reacts with normal skin by indirect immunofluoresence.

2. Pemphigus antigen

a. It is apparently a normal epidermal substance.

b. Most pemphigus antibodies react with 130 kilodalton glycoprotein antigen synthesized and expressed by keratinocytes on their surfaces.

c. It is not a viral antigen, nor an HLA antigen, nor even a blood group substance.

3. Pemphigus antibody

a. The antibodies belong to all subclasses of IgG.

b. They can fix the complement which however is not necessary for the induction of the disease.

4. Pemphigus complements

a. They are C 3, C 3 proactivator, properdin, C 1q, and C 4.

b. They all have been found in the intercellular areas of the lesional skin and imply local activation by both classical and alternative pathways or by proteolytic enzymes.

c. Complement level of blister fluids is low probably because they are consumed in the lesional skin.

5. **Evidence of autoimmunity in pemphigus**

a. Antibodies can be detected in skin and in sera.

b. The titer of these antibodies correlates with the disease activity. In wide-spread active patients, the titer is high and as the patients improve the titer falls.

c. Removal of pemphigus antibodies by plasmapharesis induces remission of the disease.

d. When pemphigus serum is added to immune primary cell cultures, epidermal cells detach from the culture dish.

e. When sera of patients with pemphigus are incubated *in vitro* with normal skin organ cultures, antibodies bind to the intercellular spaces of the epidermis of the tissue explant. This binding causes acantholysis as seen in histological studies in pemphigus.

f. By injecting the IgG fraction of pemphigus serum intraperitonially in neonatal mice, the lesions of pemphigus can be produced.

g. Children of pemphigus mothers show pemphigus which disappears when maternal pemphigus antibodies are catabolised.

h. Pemphigus has been found to be associated with other autoimmune disorders e.g. lupus erythematosus, myasthenia gravis, pernicious anemia and thyroiditis.

i. Pemphigus antibodies are bound to antigenic sites within the surface coat of keratinocytes (ultramicroscopic study)

6. **Mechanism of autoimmune action**

a. IgG antibody in pemphigus stimulate epidermal cells to dissolve the intercellular cement.

b. Acantholysis does not occur if inhibitors of proteases are added to epithelial cell cultures along with the pemphigus antibody. This suggests that the epithelial cells activate a protease due to binding of pemphigus antibody which can alter the adhesion of one keratinocyte to the other causing acantholysis. The protease, however, has yet to be identified from amongst plasminogen activators that create plasmin and complement protease.

c. Heat inactivated pemphigus sera, devoid of complement-fixing ability, can induce acantholysis in models for induction of pemphigus in tissue explants. F $(ab)_2$ fragment of human pemphigus antibodies can produce pemphigus in model systems even if they lack the complement-fixing Fc fraction. In the intercellular areas of lesional skin, C 3 is present and complement activation is probably associated with cytotoxicity to keratinocytes.

d. Complement can alter the integrity of cell membrane and promote acantholysis induced by other mediators. In acantholytic skin, C 3 is probably generated secondarily rather than primarily, mediating the antibody damage to cells.

e. Pemphigus antibodies when bound to cell surfaces cluster together and fuse with lysosomes. This fusion coincides with spongiosis leading to acantholysis.

7. **Genetic basis**

HLA-A10 and specially Dw4 have been associated with Jewish pemphigus patients.

The exact **nature of true pemphigus antigen needs** further **clarification.** It is, however, established that the **antigen reactive with pemphigus antibody** is produced by **stratified squamous epithelial cells.**

Diagnostic features of each type of pemphigus are briefly described below.

Pemphigus Vulgaris (P. Vulgaris)

1. **Cutaneous manifestations** are characterised by

a. Presence of flaccid bullae which burst easily leaving large denuded areas of skin often with crusting.

b. Lesions generally arise on normal skin but may appear on erythematous bases.

c. **Nikolsky's sign,** i. e. dislodging of the epidermis with lateral finger pressure in the close vicinity of the bullae, is present.

d. **Sites** commonly affected are : trunk, arm, forearm, thigh, scalp, axillae and groin. Wide-spread lesions involving almost the whole body is not uncommon.

e. Rawness, burning and itching may be the complaints.

2. Mucous membrane lesions

a. Oral lesions frequently precede the cutaneous lesions by several months. They involve oral mucosa, pharynx and larynx. Bullae are not seen ; instead, erosions are found.

b. Conjunctival lesions may precede oral lesions by several weeks.

c. Nasal, vaginal and anal mucosa may be involved.

d. Vermilion border of the lips is commonly affected.

e. Lesions may be confined only to mucous membrane.

f. Bleeding may occur from erosions of mucous membrane.

Both skin and mucous membrane lesions heal very slowly leaving hyperpigmentation. Scarring generally does not occur.

3. General features

a. **Age** : 40-60 years ; but may occur at any age.

b. Both **sexes** are **equally** affected.

c. **Race** and **ethnic groups** : All races are affected but the people of Jewish or Mediterranean origin are found to be specially susceptible.

d. **Genetic link** : Familial incidence has been reported. Frequency of leucocyte antigen HLA-A13, HLA-A 10 and HLA-Dw4 in Jewish patients has been found.

4. Histopathology

a. Suprabasal intraepidermal bulla with acantholytic cells is the most **important diagnostic feature.**

b. In the early stage, eosinophilic spongiosis i.e. invasion of epidermis by cluster of eosinophils may be seen.

c. Dyskeratotic keratinocytes are not present.

d. In the dermis there might be mild perivascular lymphohistiocytic infiltrate with eosinophils and, sometimes, neutrophils.

5. Acantholysis : It is the loss of cohesion between keratinocytes as a result of dissolution of desmosomes or intercellular connections. The acantholytic keratinocytes tend to be rounded and the desmosomal spines are destroyed. According to the stage of acantholysis, the size of the nucleus varies. The depth of the stain also varies accordingly. In most instances, deeply stained nucleus with very little surrounding cytoplasm is seen. The cell is generally well defined and may be present either in clump or in singles being attached to the base or roof of the bulla or lying loose inside the vesicle. The cell is much bigger than lymphocytes.

6. Tzanck test : It is a very useful procedure. Scrapings from base of the bulla are smeared on a slide and stained with Giemsa's stain. If the acantholytic cells are found, pemphigus is highly suggested.

7. Immunofluorescence

a. Indirect : Immunofluorescence staining of monkey esophageal mucosa with pemphigus serum shows fluorescence of intercellular substance.

b. Direct : Immunofluorescent staining of the lesion demonstrates deposition of C 3 in the intercellular substance.

8. Electron microscopy : The earliest change seen is the dissolution of intercellular cement. There is destruction of desmosomes and tonofilaments as well.

9. Course and prognosis

a. If untreated, death occurs within about 14 months from the onset.

b. The mortality rate has been lowered to a considerable extent by moden treatment and patients have lived even up to 20 years after the diagnosis.

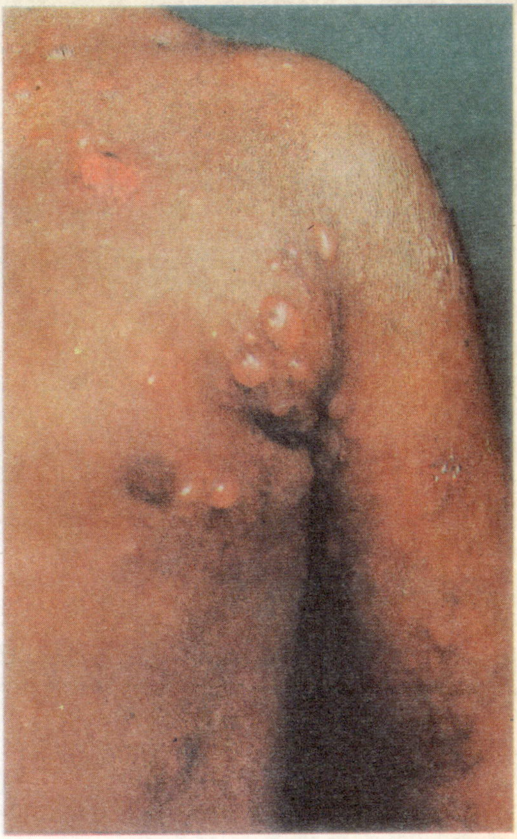

Fig. P-2. **Pemphigus Vulgaris** showing multiple vesicles and bullae.

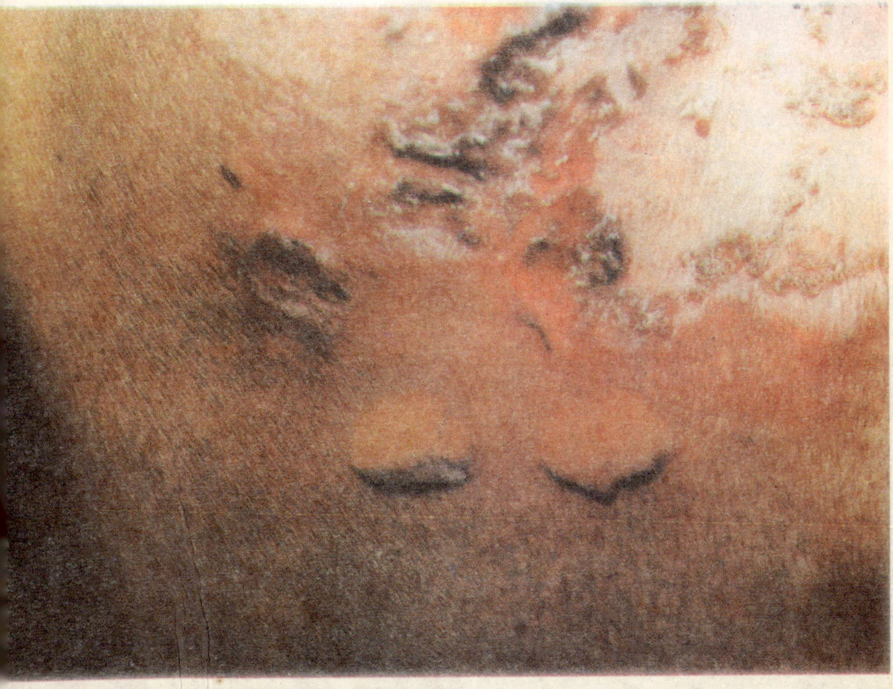

P-3. **Pemphigus Vulgaris** showing positive 'Nikolsky's sign'.

c. Death is mostly due to biochemical abnormalities and secondary infection due to immunosuppression.

d. In extremely rare case, spontaneous remission is possible but the course is prolonged.

Pemphigus Vegetans (P. Vegetans)

It actually represents a variant of pemphigus vulgaris. There are two types (1) Neumann type in which the course and prognosis are almost like pemphigus vulgaris and (2) Hallopeau type which is much less severe. Many feel that the subclassification is unnecessary and is of historical interest only.

1. Cutaneous manifestations

a. In the early stage, the lesions are like P. Vulgaris ; flaccid, weeping bullae are seen.

b. In the healing stage, **hypertrophic, verrucoid, granulations** are seen to develop. They arise from the denuded areas of ruptured bullae.

c. **Pustular lesions** are often seen at the periphery of the vegetating lesions.

d. Later, the lesions are mainly hypertrophic and papillomatous, and are particularly found in intertriginous areas of groin and axillae.

e. Oral lesions are not infrequent and may be the earliest sign. Vermilion border of the lips is often affected.

2. Histopathology

a. In early lesion, there is suprabasal acantholytic bulla.

b. Later, there are (i) hyperkeratosis (ii) pseudoepitheliomatous hyperplasia and (iii) papillomatosis.

c. There are often intraepidermal abscesses of the eosinophils.

d. Intraepidermal vesicle may contain neutrophils.

e. Dermis contains perivascular diffuse infiltrate of lymphocytes, histiocytes and eosinophils.

3. Course and prognosis

It is probably a milder variety of P. Vulgaris where the resistance of the patient to the disease is quite high.

Pemphigus Foliaceus (P. Foliaceus)

It is less common than P. vulgaris and represents a superficial and less severe form of the disease.

1. Cutaneous manifestations

a. Except in very early stage, the bullous lesions may be entirely absent.

b. They often arise on erythematous base.

c. Small bullae may be seen.

d. Eczematoid patch may be an early sign.

e. **Shallow erosions, scales** and **crusting** are the predominant features.

f. Onset may be abrupt or slow and insidious.

g. Common sites are scalp, face, upper chest, abdomen and the back.

h. It may spread to the entire body-surface leading to exfoliative dermatitis.

i. Oral lesions are relatively rare.

j. Nikolsky's sign is present.

k. Severe pruritus and burning are the main symptoms.

l. Sun-exposure aggravates the lesion.

2. Age, sex and race

a. **Age** : 40-60 years, but it can occur at any age.

b. **Sex** : Equal in both sexes.

c. **Jewish** people probably suffer more.

3. Histopathology

a. Intraepidermal bulla, usually in or near granular layer, with acantholytic cells. Sometimes, cleft may be present at subcorneal position.

b. Hyperkeratosis, especially follicular, is seen.

c. In the dermis, there is moderate cellular infiltrate. Eosinophils often predominate.

Brazilian Pemphigus

It is often termed **'fogo selvagem'** and is identical with P. foliaceus in all respects. It is endemic in South-central Brazil,

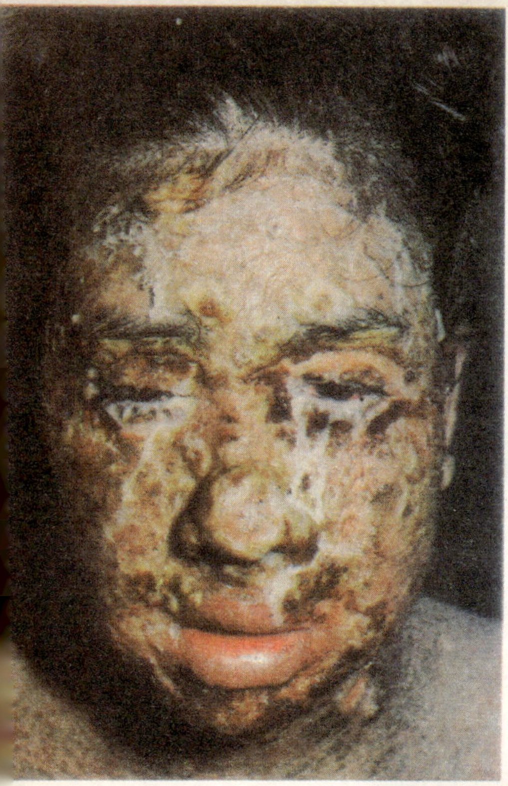

Fig. P-4. **Pemphigus Vulgaris** showing severe crusted lesions on the whole of face.

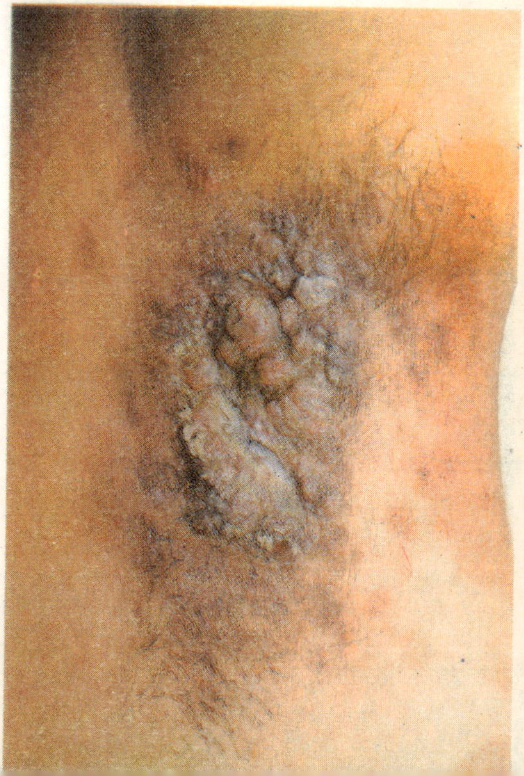

Fig. P-5. **Pemphigus Vegetans** showing hypertrophic, verrucoid granulations at the axilla.

particularly in Sao Paulo where about 1000 new cases occur every year. People suffering from the disease improve when they change their living in urban area but on return to the endemic area they get it again. This suggets that it might be an arthropod-borne disease. But it is yet to be proved. Children and young adults are commonly affected and male to female ratio is 1 : 2.

Pemphigus Erythematosus (P. Erythematosus)

It is considered to be localised and a less severe superficial variety of P. foliaceus.

1. Cutaneous manifestations

a. The lesions develop as erythematous rashes at the butterfly area of face as in **lupus erythematosus.**

b. There are superficial bullae and scaling lesions elsewhere as well, often having a look exactly like **seborrheic dermatitis**. It has often been called 'seborrheic pemphigus'.

2. Histopathology and immunology

a. Histology is identical with P. foliaceus.

b. Antinuclear antibodies are often present.

c. There is the deposition of immunoglobulins at the dermal-epidermal junction along with typical immunofluorescence of pemphigus.

d. Patients suffering simultaneously from systemic lupus erythematosus and P. erythematosus have been reported.

e. P. erythematosus has been associated with thymoma, myasthenia gravis and rheumatoid arthritis. Thymectomy cures the condition.

Drug induced pemphigus

Drug induced pemphigus looks like P. foliaceus and has been reported with D-penicillamine. Lesions similar to P. vulgaris and P. erythematosus have also been seen. Clinically and histologically, drug induced pemphigus cannot be distinguished from real pemphigus. However, it disappears completely on withdrawal of the offending drug. Other drugs that

Approach to Patient : Diagnostic Features of the Pemphigus Group of Bullous Diseases (Lebwohl, M : 1988)

	Clinical Features	Histology	Immunopathology
Pemphigus vulgaris	Oral lesions often precede cutaneous bullae Nikolsky sign	Suprabasalar clefts extending along adnexa Acantholytic keratinocytes	Normal or perilesional skin : IgG and C 3 at intercellular spaces of epidermis Serum anti-intercellular substance antibodies correlate with disease activity
Pemphigus vegetans	Bullae are followed by hypertophic, papillomatous lesions in intertriginous sites	Suprabasalar clefts Acantholytic cells Eosinophilic abscesses Epidermal hyperplasia	Resembles pemphigus vulgaris
Pemphigus foliaceus	Oral lesions rare Rapid crusting of bullae	Subcorneal or granular layer cleft Acantholytic cells Dyskeratotic cells in granular layer Eosinophilic pustules	Resembles pemphigus vulgaris, immune deposits more superficial
Pemphigus erythematosus	Bullae, crusts and impetiginous lesions Prominent facial involvement	Identical to pemphigus foliaceus	Immunoglobulins and complement at dermal-epidermal junction, intercellular IgG and C 3 Positive antinuclear antibody
Penicillamine-induced pemphigus	Often resembles pemphigus foliaceus	Identical to pemphigus foliaceus or pemphigus vulgaris	IgG and C 3 at intercellular spaces

Approach to the Patient : Diagnostic Features of the Pemphigoid Group of Bullous Diseases (Lebwohl, M : 1988)

	Clinical Features	Histology	Immunopathology
Bullous pemphigoid	Large tense bullae Oral lesions rarely the initial manifestation	Subepidermal bullae Infiltrate with eosinophils can be present	Perilesional skin : C 3, IgG, and other immunoglobulins in linear pattern at basement membrane zone (BMZ) (lamina lucida) Serum anti-BMZ antibodies
Herpes gestationis	Urticarial, vesicular and bullous lesions in pregnancy	Subepidermal blisters Spongiosis Papillary edema Infiltrate with eosinophils	Perilesional skin : C 3 and occasionally IgG in linear patterns at BMZ Serum HG factor
Cicatricial pemphigoid	Scarring blisters of mucous membranes	Subepithelial blisters	Linear deposition of immnuoglobulins and complement in BMZ
Localized scarring pemphigoid (Brunsting-Perry)	Localized patches of recurrent scarring blisters on head and neck	Subepidermal blisters	Resembles cicatricial pemphigoid

might induce pemphigus are rifampicin, INH, ethambutol, phenylbutazone, ibuprofen, heroin, practolol, penicillin and ampicillin.

TREATMENT

CORTICOSTEROIDS	CYCLOPHOSPHAMIDE	AZATHIOPRINE
DAPSONE	PLASMAPHARESIS	CYCLOSPORINE
METHOTREXATE	GOLD	LEVAMISOLE

1. Corticosteroids

To start with 100-200 mg of prednisolone per day should be the dose. It should be continued at this dose until any new blister formation stops.

Alternatively, 40-80 mg units of ACTH in I.V. drip have been used with success.

In patients with only oral lesions or in P. foliaceus, lower dose e.g. 60 to 100 mg is enough to control the disease.

After the control of bullous lesions, the dose should be reduced to 60 mg of prednisolone. Thereafter, the reduction should be very gradual. Maintenance dose should be individualised by seeing the absence of any active lesion. Some inactive and mildly keratotic lesions may persist. When the patient is absolutely stable, the maintenance dose may be given on alternate days to minimise steroid induced hazards.

If facilities are available, the dose schedule can be monitored along with the level of antibody titer.

2. Immunosuppressive therapy

In acute stage, immunosuppressive drugs are of little value; but on control of the disease by high dose steroids, these drugs could be extremely beneficial to the patient. The immunosuppressive agents should be started at the dose level of 40-60 mg of prednisolone. It takes 3-4 weeks to feel their effect. Regular intake of these modern drugs could lessen the dose of prednisolone to an appreciable extent. In some cases, steroids can even be completely withdrawn.

a. Methotrexate—Dose : 25 to 35 mg orally or I. M. weekly.

b. Cyclophosphamide—Dose : The starting dose should be 100 to 200 mg daily. After 2-3 weeks, the maintenance dose may be 100 mg daily.

c. Azathioprine—Dose : 50-100 mg daily. Long term follow up study has shown that it can help reducing the dose of prednisolone after 3-4 weeks and can be continued for as long as 9 years. Mortality could be reduced to 5%.

3. **Gold therapy** : Can be used with or without steroid.

Dose : Test dose is 10 mg of gold-sodium thiomalate I.M.; 7 days later, 25 mg is given and thereafter 50 mg weekly until stable clinical improvement is achieved. Maintenance dose is 50 mg every 2 to 4 weeks.

New oral gold preparation is **auranofin.** It can be used 3 mg b.i.d.

4. **Plasmapharesis**

The method can be used with or without steroid therapy. Often an immunosuppressive drug is also used along with it and steroid.

Dose : Weekly removal of 400 to 1200 ml of plasma for six weeks followed by replacement with 200 to 400 ml of 5% albumin solution+500 ml of saline.

5. **Miscellaneous measures and drugs**

a. Topical fluorinated corticosteroids, with or without wet dressing, are valuable in superficial wide-spread pemphigus.

b. Cleansing baths, cool compresses and wet dressings are beneficial to almost all patients.

c. In secondary infection, a course of proper internal antibiotic is helpful and essential.

d. In oral lesions, keeping xylocaine viscous or Benadryl[R] elixir in mouth facilitates the intake of food.

e. Attention should be given to electrolyte balance, proper nutrition and I.V. hyperalimentation.

f. **Concurrent immunosuppressants** have been used.

i. Azathioprine, 150 mg per day. **ii.** Gold-sodium thiomalate, 50 mg I.M. every 2 weeks. **iii.** Cyclophosphamide, 100 mg per day. **iv.** Methotrexate, 20 mg per week and **v.** Dapsone, 100 mg per day.

g. For **oral complications**

i. **Halitosis** for Vincent's infection, penicillin or metronidazole. **ii. Candidiasis,** Amphotericin B lozenges to suck 4 times daily.

iii. Triamcinolone in adhesive base e.g. kenalog orabase[R] in non-healing oral ulcers, to apply 3-4 times daily.

h. Levamisole : 50 mg every other day or 50 mg daily for 3 consecutive days in a week has been used as an immunopotentiating drug. It has probably the steroid sparing effect.

i. **Cyclosporine,** 6 mg/kg/day orally, has recently been used with success. The drug could suppress T-cell immune rejection of transplants.

DISCUSSION

Pemphigus is a disease where every cell of the epidermis is a target for immune rejection. The intensity and extent of this however vary with the type of pemphigus. Hence, each patient has his/her own clinical and immunological status.

Clinical diagnosis should always better be supplemented, where such facilities are available, with histology, Tzanck test, antibody titer and immunofluorescence.

Treatment varies according to the type and extent of the disease. Usual practice is to start the treatment with high dose of prednisolone or equivalent steroid and continue till eruptions of bullae or other active manifestations stop. It takes about 4 weeks. An immunosuppressive drug, either cyclophosphamide or azathioprine, is next started and continued along with gradual withdrawal of steroids. Thereafter, only a maintenance level is continued. In rare cases, the drugs may be completely withdrawn. Superficial forms of pemphigus are less life-threatening than the deeper varieties. Topical therapy probably helps in such cases.

One should be aware of the hazards of continued high dose steroid therapy. They are mainly : infection by bacteria, superficial and deep fungus, tuberculosis ; precipitation of pulmonary embolism, hypertension, diabetes mellitus, peptic ulceration ; negative nitrogen balance ; osteoporosis ; steroid psycosis ; cushingoid syndrome with striae and thinning of skin. To some extent, these can be prevented by concomitant use of anabolic hormones, calcium, maintenance of eletrolyte balance, high protein diet, diuretics with potassium supplementation and prompt treatment of any infection. In our country, x-ray of the lung is advised to exclude tuberculosis that may flare up with steroid therapy.

Use of immunosuppressive drugs should be closely monitored by close hematologic investigations. Methotrexate is a hepatotoxic drug. Increased incidence of malignancy has also been reported due to long continuous use of azathioprine.

The advent of immunosupressive drugs holds a promise to these patients to live with a skin that has strangely become foreign to them.

PITYRIASIS ALBA

DIAGNOSIS

1. It is a common condition found in **children** and is characterised by **asymptomatic, superficial, hypopigmented, scaly, numular patches** of the face, upper trunk and proximal extremities. Rarely, young adults may be affected.

2. Various characteristics of the patches are as follow.

a. Most often **well defined.**

b. There are **fine scalings** which are loosely attached.

c. Patches are **hypopigmented** or **erythematous** or **skin coloured.** Hypopigmentation is said to be due to less melanogenesis caused probably by parakeratosis. It is a prominent feature in black skin.

d. Patches are of 5 mm to 5 cm in diameter.

e. Margin may be slightly elevated.

f. The lesions may be slightly **pruritic.**

g. The patches are round or oval in shape.

h. Inflammation is very mild.

i. Sites involved, in order of frequency, are

i. Cheeks ii. About the mouth iii. Neck iv. Upper arms v. Trunk vi. Legs vii. Thighs.

3. Etiology is not definitely known. It is accepted as a non-specific dermatitis of unknown cause.

4. Some believe that it represents a mild form of atopic eczema ; often present in atopic family.

5. The lesions become prominent in winter and dry season. Soap, wind and sunshine also make them more obvious.

6. **Histologic characteristics** are

a. Hyperkeratosis b. Parakeratosis c. Mild acanthosis d. Reduced melanins in basal layer e. Edema of upper dermis f. Dilatation of superficial vessels g. Chronic inflammatory infiltrate around vessels.

TREATMENT

MOISTURISER	WEAK STEROID CREAM
EMOLLIENTS	TOPICAL TARS

1. In most cases, the disease disappears even without any treatment. So reassurance of its benignity and its natural resolution without any sequale should be the message to be communicated to the patient or guardian.

2. Bland lubricants or **emollient creams** are helpful in dry lesions.

3. **Corticosteroid creams** might diminish the mild inflammation.

4. Vitamins act as good placebos.
5. Antimicrobial therapy has got no value.
6. Malnutrition, if any, should always be taken care of.
7. Excessive soap application should be avoided.
8. Modern **moisturiser** creams sometime help.
9. **Topical tars,** applied thrice daily, may be helpful.

DISCUSSION

Although the exact etiology of this mild form of dermatitis is not known, a personal or family history of atopy has been found in about 50% patients.

It should be stressed that it has nothing to do with liver dysfunction. The patients are otherwise absolutely healthy. The spots disappear in natural course.

However, recurrence is very common only to disappear again. Most patients get rid of the disease permanently in the adult life.

In our country, differential diagnosis with pityriasis versicolor, seborrheic dermatitis, vitiligo and Hansen's disease is rather important.

Placebos play the most important role in treatment.

PITYRIASIS ROSEA (PR)

It is a very common erythematous, scaly, pruritic disease found generally in young adults.

DIAGNOSIS

1. Etiology is unknown. The following theories are only suggestive.

A. An infectious etiology, particularly viral, has been thought of. Bacteria and mycoplasma have also been considered.

Points in **favour** are

(1) Seasonal occurrence : in spring and late autumn.

(2) Young are mostly affected : 10-30 years of age.

(3) Presence in family members or contacts.

(4) Shortened duration of the disease if treated with convalescent serum.

(5) Prodromal symptoms of fever, malaise, headaches, arthralgias, anorexia, nausea and sore throats.

(6) Lymphadenopathy. (7) Tonsilitis.

(8) Occurrence of PR after vaccination.

(9) Cytopathic changes in tissue culture have been observed.

Points **against** are

(1) Infective agent as yet could not be isolated.

(2) Compared to the matched control, there is no increased throat infections.

(3) No elevation of antistreptolysin O titers.

(4) Not much of constitutional symptoms.

B. Stress and **mental illness** were previously considered to provoke the illness.

C. Immunologic theory

Increase in total number of B-lymphocytes containing IgD and IgM markers and reduction in T-lymphocytes. However, serum and immunoglobulin levels are found to be normal.

D. Drugs—Arsenic, Bismuth, Gold and Metronidazole have produced lesions like PR.

2. Clinical features

a. Incidence is **universal**. All races are affected. Atopics may be more susceptible.

b. History of **sore throat** is often present.

c. **Herald patch,** the characteristics of which are

(1) Usually solitary, rarely multiple (2) circular or oval (3) slightly scaling (4) often asymptomatic (5) usually less than 5 cm in diameter (6) rarely, may be gigantic (7) mostly seen on the trunk (30-45%) (8) may be absent (9) develops 1-2 weeks after sore throat (10) finely scaly border (11) inner edges of scales are free (**collarette scales**).

d. Secondary lesions

(1) Start developing after 7-14 days of herald patch. (2) Salmon-pink or fawn coloured but in black skin whitish. (3) Macular or minimally elevated. (4) 1-2 cm in diameter. (5) Round or oval. (6) Collarette scales at the margin. (7) Central clearing. (8) Long axis of the oval lesions coincide with the long axis of ribs giving rise to 'christmas tree' distribution. (9) Lesions may be hundreds in number. (10) **Variations of lesions** : May be papular, plaques, urticarial wheals, vesicles or bullae (especially in palms and soles) and eczematous. (11) Mostly in trunk, but face, groin, arms and legs may also be involved. (12) Generally bilateral, but may be unilateral. (13) Rarely, asymptomatic oral lesions may be seen. There may be petechiae, red macules or red annular, eroded plaques with areas of greyish desquamation. (14) There may be nail pitting. (15) Pruritus may be moderate to severe. (16) Post-inflammatory hypo- or hyper-pigmentation may occur. (17) The eruptions become worse by heat (hot showers and exercise) and probably with soap.

e. Pathology and histology

i. Focal parakeratosis. **ii.** Mild irregular acanthosis.

iii. Focal spongiosis or vesicle formation.

iv. Extravasated erythrocytes and edema within the papillary dermis.

v. Superficial dermal perivascular infiltrate, mainly with lymphohistiocytic cells. Rarely, there may as well be eosinophils.

vi. KOH preparation for fungal elements is negative.

vii. VDRL is also negative.

TREATMENT

CALAMINE LOTION	ANTIHISTAMINICS

There is no specific treatment as yet available. It is a self-limiting disease that resolves within 3-10 weeks. Following measures often give beneficial results.

1. For **pruritus** : A. **Internally**

(1) **Antihistaminics** (2) Rarely, in extensive cases, a short course of **steroid.**

B. **Locally**

(1) **Lotio calamine** with phenol or menthol (2) **Steroid lotion** or cream (3) 3-5 erythematagenic doses of UV-light.

2. **Dapsone** in vesicular PR.

3. **Photochemotherapy,** with **psoralens,** helps in early period.

DISCUSSION

It is a disease common among the teenagers and young adults with a history of sore throat and development of herald patch usually on abdomen or trunk. The patches are characterised by oval, erythematous, finely scaly, lesions. This is followed by similar lesions having their long axis parallel to the ribs. In the early stage, they simulate tinea corporis and later imitate drug eruptions or syphilis. Spontaneous resolution is usually the rule. But in India, the period varies from 3 weeks to 6 months. Recurrences are uncommon. Symptomatic treatment and reassurance only are necessary. Rarely, it involves children below 10 years of age and may lead to exfoliative dermatitis.

POST-KALA-AZAR DERMAL LEISHMANIASIS (PKDL)

This is a type of cutaneous lesion sporadically seen often as a sequele to kala-azar in West Bengal, Bihar, Madras and Assam.

DIAGNOSIS

1. It develops in about 10% of kala-azar patients, generally 1-2 years after completion of antimonial treatment of kala-azar. Visceral infection disappears but the skin lesions develop. Cases with history of kala-azar type fever 3-4 years ago but having no previous treatment have been recorded.

2. The causative organism is Leishmania donovani which appears to change its viscerotropic character biologically to dermatropism.

3. **Clinical manifestations** are divided mainly into the following three groups.

a. **Depigmented macules** : These are the earliest lesions that start as minute hypopigmented macules gradually enlarging to form lesions of 1 cm diameter. They may further coalesce to form irregular patches extending over considerable areas. They appear all at a time in various parts of the body, especially trunk and extremities. Face and neck may also be affected. In certain cases, whole body may be affected leaving only a portion of waist line. Except hypopigmentation, the skin is otherwise normal. There is no loss of sensation, hairs or sweating.

b. **Erythematous patches** : These are also early lesions which affect butterfly area of face including the nose and cheeks and are often called 'butterfly erythema'. Chin may also be affected. The affected areas are highly photosensitive, become more prominent at the middle of the day or after exposure to sun. Along with this erythematous flush, depigmented macules are often present in trunk and extremities.

c. **Yellowish pink nodules** : The nodules may appear from the very beginning or on other earlier lesions. They generally express themselves on the skin but mucous membrane may also be affected, especially of tongue and the eyes. They are mostly found on face. Waxy papules of chin are highly characteristic. The nodules are soft, painless, granulomatous growths of various sizes.

Ulceration does not occur. If the nodules are injured they heal up quickly.

Appearance of nodules on lips, buccal mucous membrane and hard palate are not uncommon. According to the clinical feature of the nodules, some rare varieties have been described as : (1) Xanthomatous type (2) Hypertrophic type (3) Verrucous type (4) Papulomatous type and (5) Punctate hemorrhagic type.

There may be combinations of many types. Cases have been seen with extensive granulomatous lesions spread widely over the whole body.

4. General symptoms and signs

Generally, there is no fever, weakness or other signs of visceral leishmaniasis. Very rarely, cases have been reported having at the same time features of both PKDL and kala-azar. Keratitis of both eyes as a complication of PKDL has been reported. Nodules have also been found in sclera and adjoining cornea.

5. Parasitology of PKDL

a. Inside the vertebrate host, Leishmania donovani (LD bodies) is always intracellular, occurring in the leishmanial form. It is essentially a parasite of reticulo-endothelial system. In certain sandfly, leishmanial form develops into the leptomonad one. Similar forms are also seen in artificial culture.

b. The parasite in leishmanial stage is aflagellar and it multiplies by binary fission. The infected cell becomes enlarged and packed with these parasites. In blood, the parasites are carried by neutrophils and monocytes.

c. In shape, the **leishmanial forms** are round or oval bodies measuring 2 to 4 microns along the longitudinal axis. The nucleus is oval or round and is situated usually in the middle or placed along the side of the cell-wall. Lying tangentially or at right angles to the nucleus is the kinetoplast which is either rod-shaped or dot like. Basically, this organism, often called LD body, looks like a biconvex lens, the nucleus lying close to the more convex ventral border and the kinetoplast along the less convex dorsal border. With Leishman's stain the cytoplasm appears blue, the nucleus pink or violet and the kinetoplast bright red.

d. **Leptomonad form** (flagellar stage) is found in its arthropod host i.e. insect vectors or in the culture. It is a long slender spindle-shaped body measuring 15 to 20 microns in length by 1-2 microns in breadth. The nucleus is situated centrally and the kinetoplast lies transversely near the anterior end. A light staining area, called the eosinophilic vacuole, lies in front of the kinetoplast over which runs the root of the flagellum. The flagellum is delicate, of the same length of the body or even longer, and project from the anterior extremity. There is no undulating membrane.

e. **Life cycle :** In man, leishmanial form exists. A sandfly (Phlebotomus argentipes) draws this leishmanial form during its blood meal. Inside the midgut of sandfly, the leishmanial forms develop into leptomonad forms and multiply by binary fission to an enormus number of flagellates. Then they proceed to the anterior part of the alimentary canal e.g. in the pharynx and buccal cavity. A good number of flagellates accumulate between the 6th to 9th day after taking the blood meal. This type of development is called **anterior station development.**

This sandfly again bites a human being and injects the flagellates into the skin. But in the intervening period, it takes suitable plant and fruit juice as meal before the second blood-meal on human body. At the second bite, the flagellates are ejected into the wound caused by its proboscis. Some of the flagellates enter the circulation of the body directly and are either destroyed or take refuge inside the cells of the reticulo-endothelial system. They are changed there into leishmanial forms and undergo a slow multiplication. In PKDL, it is likely that the LD bodies remain mostly at the cutaneous or mucocutaneous places.

6. Laboratory findings

a. Smear from skin lesions : Leishmania parasites can be demonstrated easily from nodular lesions and rarely from depigmented and erythematous lesions.

b. Culture in NNN blood agar media or Noguchi's medium : A portion of the lesional skin may be cultured to get a positive growth.

c. Histopathology

i. Nodular lesions often show specific granuloma and intra- or extracellular parasites.

ii. Depigmented macules show less amount of melanin in the basal layer.

iii. Erythematous lesions show dilatation of dermal blood vessels and there are non-specific infiltrate. Macrophages containing the parasites may rarely be seen.

d. Serological tests are usually negative.

i. Complement fixation test with WKK antigen is usually negative.

ii. Aldehyde test of Napier is usually negative. Formol antimony test and Brahmachari's serum globulin tests are also negative.

e. Skin test : The test is conducted by injecting 0.1 ml of antigen containing 100,000 parasites in a phenolised saline emulsion intradermally into the skin. A reddish papule is formed at the end of 24 hours. This grows to a larger size within 2 to 3 days.

TREATMENT

PENTAVALENT SODIUM ANTIMONY	RIFAMPICIN
KETOCONAZOLE	AMPHOTERICIN B

1. Prophylactic measures

a. Eradicating the sandflies by proper insecticides. Spraying of DDT and gammabenzene hexachloride is probably helpful.

b. Reservoir of infection e.g. rodents, dogs and cats should not come in contact with susceptible persons.

c. A vaccine made from leishmanial culture would probably be of some prophylactic value in the endemic area.

2. Curative

It is one of the most difficult task to cure PKDL patients. Following drugs are used.

a. For few small nodular lesions, infiltration with 1% mepacrine or emetine hydrochloride solution, or berberine solution (Orisol[R]) is used. It causes inflammatory reaction for 2-3 days ; repeated for 3-12 infiltrations until complete disappearance. They may be destroyed by liquid nitrogen cryotherapy or by electrodesiccation. Glucantimine (N methyl glucamine antimonate) has also been used with success. Local x-ray, 600 r to 800 r, of 2 doses resolves these local lesions.

b. **Antimony** : Both trivalent and pentavalent antimony preparations are used.

Neo-antimosan or **Fuadin**[R] containing 13.5% antimony in trivalent form and **anthiomaline**[R] containing lithium antimony thiomalate 10 mg/c.c are used, I.M., 2-3 ml bi-weekly, total dose 25 ml.

Potassium or sodium antimony tartarate : 10-50 mg, I.V., is also employed but these have doubtful values.

Pentavalent compounds e.g. Stibanyl[R] or Stibacetin[R], Urea stibamine[R], Stibosan[R], Neostibosan[R] and Solustibosan[R] are now difficult to find in the market. Only Stibanate[R] is available.

Sodium antimony gluconate, i.e. **Stibanate**[R] 800 mg I.M. daily or in alternate days for 20-30 injections are helpful. **Sodium stilbogluconate** is excreted in the urine within few hours in contrast to slow excretion of trivalent compounds.

Repeated low dose courses may permit renewed proliferation of surviving parasites. There is therefore a tendency now toward chemotherapy at higher dosage over longer periods of time. Dose : 20 mg/kg/I.V./b.i.d for 30 days.

N-methyl glucamine antimonate, Glucantin[R] : 60 mg/kg/I.V/day/12 days ; to repeat after 15 days.

Dose required to cure PKDL is about 10 times the dose for kala-azar.

c. **Other miscellaneous drugs or agents**

i. **Ketoconazole**

ii. **Amphotericin B** : A polyene antibiotic ; it has been found to be effective.

iii. **Pentamidine isethionate** is an aromatic diamine compound and is found effective both in Kala-azar and PKDL. It is however a toxic drug.

iv. **Cotrimoxazole** probably is valuable in controlling the secondary infections that might complicate the disease.

v. **Rifampicin**, alone or with INH, shows limited antileishmanial activity. It is better used as adjunct therapy with antimonials. **Mononycin is equally effective.**

vi. **Metronidazole** has been used probably empirically considering its effect in trichomona.

vii. **Nifurtimox** has some antileishmanial activity. It is still in the investigational stage.

viii. **Allupurinol** is converted to a toxic metabolite by the parasite. In combination with antimonials, it acts as an adjunct therapy.

ix. **Cyclogunil** is a nitroimidazole, and has been given clinical trials. But it has not been found curative.

x. **Pyrimethamine** has not been very promising.

xi. **Thermo-therapy** : By raising the temperature of lesions to 40°- 42°C for 12 hours the lesions, in some patients, could be healed.

xii. **Grenz rays therapy** has also been tried with partial benefit.

All these drugs require further critical assessment for a final say in the matter.

DISCUSSION

In most cases, PKDL is diagnosed clinically by seeing **hypopigmented macules, butterfly erythema, nodular or granulomatous lesions** in various parts of the body. **History of kala-azar** or prolonged fever 2-5 years ago helps in diagnosis. **Demonstration of LD bodies** in smear or biopsy specimen is the **surest sign**. It is mostly found in waxy papules or nodules. Biochemical tests are not much helpful in the diagnosis. Although sporadic, kala-azar cases are still seen throughout India. PKDL is limited mostly to **West Bengal, Bihar** and Assam.

Stibanate[R] containing 100 mg of pentavalent sodium antimony gluconate per ml in 30 ml vial is the usually available drug. After a test dose of 0.5 to 1 ml I.M., it is given in 3 to 5 ml I.M. daily or alternate days even up to 30 injections. With a gap of about 1 month thereafter, the course is repeated once or twice. Results however are more often not satisfactory. After the initial improvement, lesions reappear. Relapses are frequent. Three to 9 times the dose for Kala-azar (total of 4 to 8 g) is needed in PKDL. It is usually painless and well tolerated. It is however contraindicated in liver disease, lung tuberculosis and nephritis.

Rifampicin, metronidazole, ketoconazole, cotrimoxazole, amphotericin B (I.V) and **dapsone** are other important drugs. However, **none of them is cent per cent effective.** Sometimes they are combined or given alternately with antimony.

Although not common, PKDL continues to be a problem disease. **Indolent PKDL patients are still seen.**

PSORIASIS

Psoriasis is one of the commonest non-infectious, chronic, relapsing, papulo-squamous skin diseases.

DIAGNOSIS

1. Clinical features

a. The lesions

i. Classically, psoriasis presents as **erythematous, scaly** lesions. They are **elevated,** palpable and topped by **grayish-white** or **micalike scales.** The scales may be easily removed by scratching, when minute bleeding points are seen from dilated superficial capillaries (**Auspitz sign**).

These plaque type psoriasis is often called **psoriasis vulgaris.**

ii. Minute **papules,** topped with **silvery scales,** are the presentations of **guttate psoriasis.** They often develop after an attack of streptococcal sore throat and may be wide spread, especially on trunk. Children are usually affected.

iii. Sometimes central clearing is seen and various **gyrate patterns** develop with **raised, red, scaly margin.**

iv. Koebner phenomenon : Development of scaly papular lesions in **linear orientation** at scratch points are often seen and is called **isomorphic phenomenon.** This is probably due to triggering off an immune response. This can explain why lesions develop in sites of trauma such as mechanical friction, sunburn or at the sites of varicella.

v. Lesions vary enromously from tiny papules through various sized plaques, giant patches to gyrate lesions of varied patterns. The area affected may range from a few tiny lesions to almost all over the entire body surface.

vi. It occurs in all races, in both sexes and is particularly common in second and third decades of life.

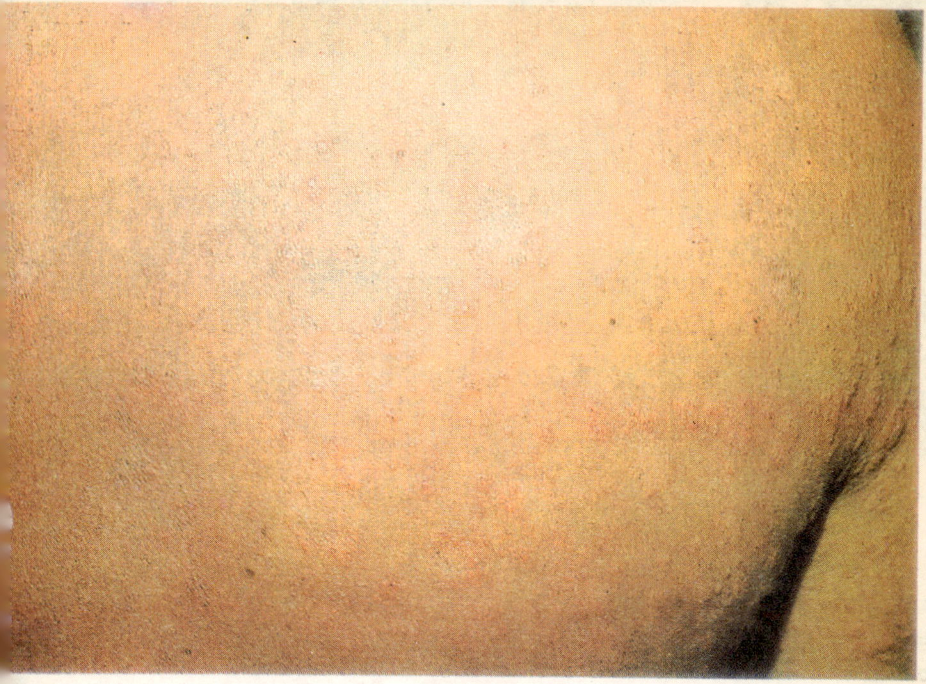

ig. P-6. **Pityriasis Rosea** showing scaly, round or oval patches with collarette scales at the back.

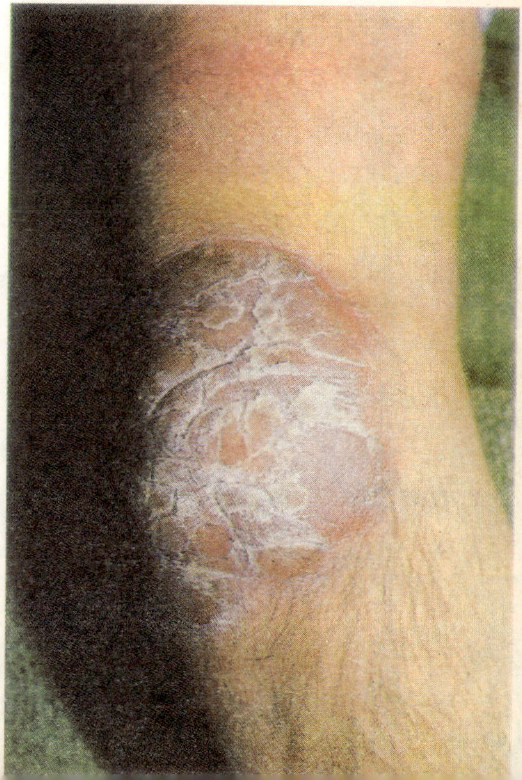

Fig. P-7. **Psoriasis**
showing scaly plaque at the knee.

2. **Sites**

a. The commonly involved sites are **extensor aspects** of the **knees** and **elbows** and the **scalp**. Hands, feet, sacral areas and post auricular areas are also often affected.

b. Nails also are often affected. **Small pittings** are the **classical signs**. These are due to quicker fall of minute conglomerated loosely bound parakeratotic cells of nail plate. Subungual hyperkeratosis, discolouration of the nail and separation of the part of nail from the nail bed (**onycholysis**) are the other features. Nail plate may be thickened and rarely there may be onychogryphosis showing an **abnormal overgrowth of nails** with inward curvature. In certain patients, only nails may be affected. Nail changes are found more in cases of distal interphalangeal arthropathy.

3. **Variants of psoriasis**

a. Guttate or **'raindrop'** psoriasis mentioned above.

b. Psoriasis inversus or **flexural psoriasis.** In this erythematous, finely scaling lesions affect the body-folds, especially the groins, axillae and inframammary region.

c. Erythrodermic psoriasis presents with wide-spread erythema having fine scaling. Few classical psoriatic lesions may be found. Grossly increased blood flow through the skin may lead to loss of thermoregulation and to high output **cardiac failure**. The patient feels cold and shivers. There are dehydration, hypoproteinemia and anemia.

d. Pustular psoriasis shows sterile pustules.

i. Localised : Most often they are seen on thenar and hypothenar eminences in the palms and central and medial aspects of soles.

ii. Generalised : This is often called von Zumbusch type. Along with it, there may be erythroderma. This is a **serious condition** and at times life-threatening. Crops of sterile pustules erupt on the whole body. There is **toxemia, high fever** and leucocytosis. It often occurs due to maltreatment with steroids.

e. Psoriatic arthropathy

This is a distinctive seronegative arthropathy usually seen in patients with chronic cutaneous psoriasis. But this may occur much before the cutaneous lesions, or arthropathy may develop much later in cutaneous psoriasis.

Arthropathy may be of various types.

i. Small joint arthropathy : classically distal interphalangeal joints are mostly affected.

ii. Sacroiliac joints are very often affected.

iii. Intervertebral joints might be affected.

iv. Knees and elbows are not exceptions.

v. Rarely, there may even be mutilating generalised arthropathy.

f. Involvement of scalp hairs

Alopecia due to psoriasis is unusual, because the normal growth rate of cells at hair root is higher than even the highly accelerated cell turn over of psoriatic skin. It is likely that the application of local medication might be responsible in certain cases of alopecia in scalp psoriasis.

g. Mucous membrane psoriasis—Although rare, psoriatic lesions may be seen in buccal mucosa and genitalia.

h. Itching—It is said that psoriatic lesions are generally non-itchy, but many patients complain of severe pruritus and the consequent scratching elicits fresh lesions due to Koebner's phenomenon.

4. Etiological factors

Exact etiology is not known. Altered gross pathology, ultrastructure and biochemical hehaviour of skin have been reported, but whether they are primary or secondary is yet to be settled. The **important factors** are enumerated below.

a. Incidence is about 1-2% and the genetic factors probably have a role as it often runs in family members, approximately in one-third of the patients.

Fig. P-8. **Psoriasis** showing typical plaques at the elbow.

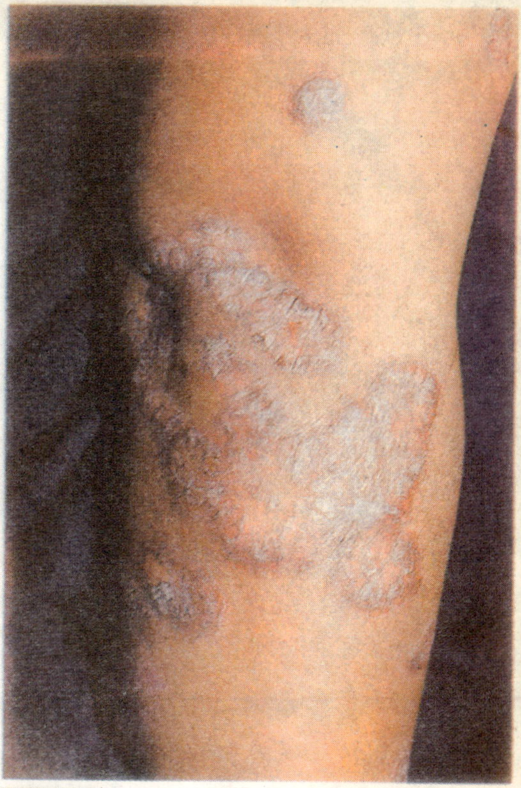

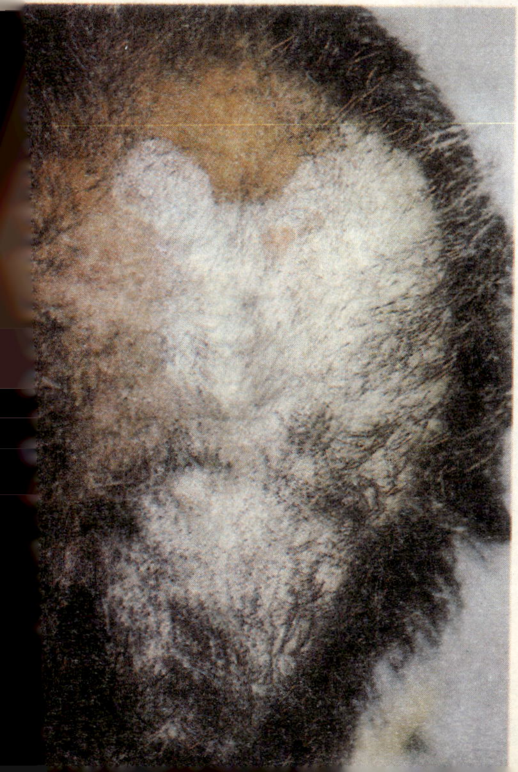

Fig. P-9. **Psoriasis** of the scalp showing well demarcated scaly plaque.

A comparative chart of clinical features and laboratory findings of several arthropathies is given below (Fitzpatrick et al, 1979)

	Psoriatic arthritis	Rheumatoid arthritis	S.L.E.	Gout	Reiter's syndrome
1. Associated cutaneous lesions	Yes	No	Yes	No	Yes
2. Subcutaneous nodules	No	Occasional	No	No (except tophi)	No
3. Mucous membrane lesions	No	No	Occasional	No	Occasional
4. Associated urethritis	No	No	No	No	Yes
5. Distribution of joint involvement					
a. Distal inter phalangeal	Yes	Rare	No	No	No
b. Sacroiliac	Yes	Rare	No	No	Occasional
c. Symmetry	Occasional	Yes	Occasional	No	No
6. Serologic test	No	Rheumatoid factor	LE	No	No
7. Elevated uric acid level	Occasional	No	No	Yes	No
8. Improvement after colchicine	No	No	No	Yes	No

About the **genetic implications** again the following factors are worth mentioning.

i. Twin studies suggest that the pattern of inheritance is multifactorial and the environmental factors are required for the expression of clinical manifestations of latent disease.

ii. Association of human leucocyte antigen (HLA)

a. In caucasians HLA-B13 and HLA-BL-17 are associated.

b. Pustular psoriasis has been associated with HLA-B27 antigen.

c. HLA-D and HLA-Dr locus antigens are probably related to the expression of the disease.

iii. It is remarkable how lesions occurring on one side of the body are reduplicated on the other.

b. The most important and consistent abnormality observed in psoriasis is **increased epidermal cell proliferation rate.** Radiolabelling techniques have measured the turnover time to be 4 days instead of normal 27 days. There is increased mitotic activity and DNA synthesis. Recent observations, however, have shown that speeding up of **epidermal transit time** in psoriasis, in comparison with normal, is only **two to three-fold.**

c. Germinative component in normal skin lies only in the basal layer but in psoriatic skin it comprises the three lower layers of epidermal cells.

d. Immunological aspect has been studied and it has been revealed :

i. Psoriatic keratinocytes have an abnormal surface antigen exposed to the immune system. When immune response is triggered off, antibodies against abnormal keratin are produced, immune complexes are formed and the damage starts. Koebner's phenomenon is probably explainable by the fact that unstable keratinocyte surface antigens or the abnormal keratin formed due to genetic predisposition are exposed to immune system by trauma which then reacts triggering a hyperproliferative response in the epidermis.

ii. Lithium, beta-blockers and chloroquin often increase psoriasis. They might have an immunological role.

5. **Miscellaneous abnormalities** found in psoriatic skin are:

(1) The increased levels of phospholipid A activity leading to availability of free arachidonic acid.

(2) Presence of keratin proteins of molecular weights different from normal skin. It might be a primary disorder or a consequence of rapid turnover time.

(3) Elevated levels of polyamine synthesis. May well be due to rapid cell proliferation.

(4) There is increased level of plasminogen activator.

6. **Histopathology**

a. **Epidermis**

(1) Confluent parakeratosis, and some areas of orthokeratosis.

(2) Neutrophils in stratum corneum (Munro micro-abscess) and in malpighian layer (spongiform pustule of Kogoj).

(3) Hypogranulosis.

(4) Suprapapillary thinning of epidermis.

(5) Regular acanthosis, often with clubbed rete ridges.

b. **Dermis**

(1) Dilated and tortuous thin walled capillaries in dermal papillae.

(2) Perivascular lymphohistiocytic infiltrate. In guttate psoriasis, parakeratosis is focal and there is less acanthosis.

In pustular psoriasis, neutrophils accumulation is more in stratum corneum and form pustules. There is less hyperkeratosis and less acanthosis.

7. **Laboratory abnormalities**

(1) Elevated uric acid (2) Mild anemia (3) Negative nitrogen balance (4) Increased sedimentation rate (5) Increased alpha-2 macroglobulins (6) Immunoglobulin abberations, increased IgA levels, and increased quantities of immune complexes.

8. **Course and prognosis**

The course of psoriasis is influenced by a varitety of factors.

(1) It waxes and wanes in intensity throughout life but prolonged, and occasionally permanent, remission does occur in natural course.

(2) Physical illness and emotional stress worsen it.

(3) Moderate sunshine and rest can improve it.

(4) Trauma, lithium, beta-blockers and chloroquin can exacerbate it as already indicated.

(5) Guttate psoriasis usually resolves spontaneously within 3 months, often permanently. However, in some cases a few chronic plaques may develop and stay.

TREATMENT

SUNLIGHT	STEROIDS	RETINOIDS	CALCIUM
TAR	PUVA	HYDROXYUREA	VITAMIN-D
ANTHRALIN	MTX	DAPSONE	ANTIBIOTICS
ANTIHISTAMINICS		TRANQUILISERS	

Proper treatment of psoriasis is an art. Each individual patient needs a different form of treatment. A good rapport between the patient and the doctor is a must. Patient should know that although complete cure is unattainable, he may remain symptom-free and live an active long life with modern management. Judicious use of modern therapies helps a lot to psoriatic patients.

The following local and systemic drugs are used in psoriasis. It is absolutely the discretion of physicians to decide which one to use, when and where.

A. Topical agents

1. Anthralin (1, 8, 9-dihydroxy-anthracene, dithranol, cignoline)—It is applied topically in either vaseline, zinc paste or chloroform. It is rapidly oxidised in air. So salicylic acid (0.5 to 1.0%) is added as an antioxidant. Treatment should start with weaker concentration e.g. 0.05%. Gradually the strength is to be increased according to tolerance ; may be up to 2% and continued until plaques are completely resolved.

A short-term contact therapy has recently been developed in which high strength anthralin (1-2%) is applied for 20-30 minutes and thereafter removed with olive oil and soap.

In Ingram method patients take bath in coal tar and are irradiated with UVA near erythema dose. Then anthralin 0.2 to 0.8% in stiff **Lassar's paste** is applied and kept covered by dressing.

Anthralin sometimes irritates the skin, stains the surrounding skin and clothings and often stains the hair to a purple to green colour. There is practically **no systemic toxicity.**

Lesions of psoriasis clear by this treatment in about 2 to 4 weeks time.

2. Tar

There are various tar and tar products available for the treatment of psoriasis e.g. coal tar, wood tar, liquor carbonis detergens. Tar contains a variety of compounds, most of which are not well defined. Very little is known how tars act in skin. But it is safe even after long use. It is used in 2 to 5% strength.

In Goeckerman regimen, crude coal tar is applied to the psoriatic skin for variable periods followed by exposure to sub-erythema dose of UVA radiation. It is thought that beneficial effect occurs due to photosensitizing capacity of tar. Instead of crude coal tar, other products as dithranol, liquor carbonis detergens or other cosmetically acceptable finer tars in gel bases are being now used.

Tar is often used with 2-4% salicylic acid, 5-10% liquor carbonis detergens, 5-10% ammoniated mercury for more beneficial results.

3. Topical corticosteroids

There is divergence of opinion as to the use of topical steroids. Some suggest that it should not be used because patient becomes dependent on it, relapses are more frequent and atrophy, striae, telangiectasia occur in long-term use. However, it is **widely used** and often along with 3-6% salicylic acid and/or 5-10% liquor carbonis detergens. **Occlusive dressing under polythene** enhances the effect of steroid. There is a wide choice of bases e.g. lotion, cream, ointment or gel. Similarly, there are various topical steroids with different potency.

In one pole there is 1% **hydrocortisone**, the least potent and in other extreme is **clobetasol propionate** 0.5%, the most potent. Tachyphylaxis or loss of effectiveness does occur with topical steroid. Hence changing of the brand is often necessary.

4. Miscellaneous local agents

i. 6% oil of cade + 2% precipitated sulphur + 2% salicylic acid in emulsifying ointment to apply t.i.d is helpful in scalp psoriasis.

ii. 6% salicylic acid + 60% propylene glycol + 20% ethyl alcohol in gel (keralyt gel[R]) to apply during night along with steroid cream during day.

iii. 3% salicylic acid + 3% sulphur + 4% cetyl alcohol coal tar distillate in cream base, to apply t.i.d.

iv. 5% tar distillate + 5% ammoniated mercury + 2% methanamine sulphosalicylate as unguentum to apply t.i.d.

v. Topical therapy with 0.1% methoxalen in oil or petrolatum and sun-exposure have cured some recalcitrant patches.

B. Systemic agents

1· Systemic steroids–It is used with **great caution** for despite transient relief of symptoms, the disease sometimes becomes more severe culminating in **acute pustular psoriasis.** Dose is at the range of 40 to 60 mg prednisolone.

2. Methotrexate (MTX)—It **inhibits DNA synthesis** by competing as a substrate for dihydrofolate reductase and is thought to **act primarily on the rapidly dividing epidermal cell** within psoriatic lesions. It also **inhibits** the **hyperactive functions of neutrophils** in psoriatic lesions. Various dosage and routes of administration are as follow.

i. Oral 5 mg every 12 hourly 3 doses over 36 hours per week.

ii. 0.2% to 0.4 mg/kg body weight I.M. or I.V., every 7 to 14 days interval.

It is **contraindicated** in liver dysfunction, pregnancy, anemia leucopenia, thrombocytopenia, excessive alcohol consumption and active infectious disease.

It is indicated when standard topical antipsoriatic therapy totally fails.

3. **Hydroxyurea**—Also inhibits DNA synthesis. It is used in MTX failure cases. Oral dose is 500-1000 mg b.i.d for 4-12 weeks.

4. **Photochemotherapy (PUVA)**—The systemic psoralens and UVA is called PUVA therapy. Its **effectiveness is confirmed**. Treatment consists of oral ingestion of 8 methoxypsoralen or **trimethoxypsoralen** 0.6 to 0.8 mg per kg of body weight and exposure of varying doses of UVA, 2 hours after. Dose of UVA is to produce just the erythema. Sittings of treatment are given 2-4 times per week. In majority of cases, 10 to 20 treatments are needed to clear the disease. In India, instead of UVA, solar exposure has been tried with unequivocal results. Psoralens form photoadducts with DNA in presence of UVA and these probably reduce the increased epidermal turnover of psoriasis.

5. **Oral Retinoids—Etretinate** 0.5-1 mg/kg of body weight per day has been recently used, especially in pustular psoriasis. Beneficial effect continues as long as therapy is continued. Relapses occur soon after stoppage. In this respect, it is inferior to anthralin, MTX and PUVA in which remissions are comparatively of long duration. Retinoids can be used to reduce the number of PUVA therapy.

6. **Benoxaprofen**—600 mg per day for 4 to 6 weeks improves psoriasis in majority of patients. It inhibits selectively 5-lypoxygenase cytoplasmic enzyme that catalyses the biosynthesis of leucotrines. But toxicity is so severe that it has been withdrawn from the market.

C. Miscellaneous agents and methods

1. Dialysis

(1) Hemodialysis (2) Peritoneal dialysis (3) Hemofiltration (4) Plasmapharesis.

Varied responses concluded that it may be effectively combined with other known antipsoriatic remedies in treating severe cases.

2. Climatotherapy

Sun-exposure of 4 to 6 hours daily with intervals of bathing in the sea, topical emollient, rest and relaxation for a period of 4 weeks have been successful in Dead sea, Swiss Alps and North sea islands.

3. Intralesional steroid

Injection of 2.5 mg of triamcinolone per c.c. intralesionally, weekly or fortnightly, can clear resistant patches. It can be injected under the nail bed for nail psoriasis.

4. **a.** Application of 20% urea in hydrolytic base followed by topical corticosteroid occulsive therapy can be of help in treating nail psoriasis.

b. 1% **5-fluouracil solution** applied twice daily to nail margins for 3-6 months helps clearing nail psoriasis.

5. Various **shampoos** and applications containing cetavlon[R] concetrate, tar, sulphur, salicylic acid, selenium sulphide, resorcinol and steroids have been used with success in scalp psoriasis.

6. Combined therapies

a. PUVA-UVA **b.** MTX-PUVA **c.** MTX-UVA

Advocates of these therapies believe that the combination reduces the total toxicity.

7. For **psoriatic arthritis**

Varieties of pharmacologic agents have been used.

a. **Aspirin** 600 mg t.i.d.

b. **Indomethacin** 75 to 100 mg per day.

c. **Ibuprofen** 2400 mg per day.

d. **Naproxen** 500-750 mg per day.

e. **Other agents are** fenoprofen, tolmetin, sulindac, zomepirac. These are gastric irritants.

f. **Hydroxychloroquin** has been found beneficial in psoriatic arthritis without aggravating skin lesions.

g. Gold in gradually increasing doses.

h. **6-mercaptopurine** is also effective.

i. **MTX**

j. **Zinc sulphate** 220 mg t.i.d.

k. **Colchicine** 0.02 mg/kg/day has been used.

8. **Where infection is a precipitating factor**

a. **Erythromycin** 250 mg q.i.d × 15 days or ampicillin 250 mg q.i.d × 10 days are often prescribed for bacterial infections.

b. **Ketoconazole** 200 mg daily for fungal infection.

c. **Metronidazole** 200-400 mg t.i.d to eradicate occult infection as prostatitis, vaginitis or cystitis.

d. **Long term antibiotic therapy** in cases with sinusitis, bronchitis and diverticulitis.

9. Atarax is used to reduce itching.

10. Tranquilisers to allay anxiety.

11. Niacinamide 100 mg t.i.d.

12. Cholesteramine 4 g q.i.d.

13. Bromocriptine 2.5 mg q.i.d.

14. Rifampicin with penicillin and erythromycin has also been used.

Main topical and systemic preparations used in management of psoriasis. (MackIE, Rona M : 1986)

	Preparation	Advantages	Disadvantages
Topical therapy	Dithranol based	Safe	Some staining and irritation common.
	Tar	Safe	Messy and cosmetically relatively unacceptable.
	Salicylic acid	Useful, particularly for the scalps, and hyperkeratotic palm and soles	Salicylism, if high concentration dose is used on large areas of the body.

	Preparation	Advantages	Disadvantages
	Topical Steroids	Clean and cosmetically acceptable.	Can cause severe side effects. To be used with caution.
	Ultraviolet light		Unknown future
	UVA-natural sunlight wavelengths	Cosmetically acceptable.	Risk of malignancy. Improvement in psoriatic lesions tends to be associated with some redness
Systemic therapy	Photo-chemo therapy (Psoralens + UVA=PUVA)	Cosmetically very acceptable.	Not suitable for potentially pregnant women. Regular treatment at PUVA centre needed. Unknown future, risk of malignancy.
	Cytotoxic drugs (Methotrexate, azathioprine, hydroxyurea)	Rapidity	Teratogenecity. Liver and marrow toxicity.
	Retinoid group of drugs. Etretinate (Tigason[R]) or 12-cis-retinoic acid (Ro-accutane[R])	Effective in 50% of chronic plaque psoriasis. Very effective in 80% of pustular psoriasis of palms and soles	Teratogenecity. Raised serum lipids. Cheilitis. Bony changes.

DISCUSSION

Diagnosis of psoriasis may be made by finding plaques with silvery scales, Auspitz sign, Koebner's phenomenon, nail changes, lesions of the scalp, arthropathy and biopsy. Morphological patterns may be of various types e.g. annular, circinate, follicular, geographic, guttate, gyrate, inverse, nummular, pustular and serpiginous. Exacerbating factors of psoriasis are excessive intake of alcohol, excessive weight gain, emotional disturbances, infection, trauma to the skin, excessive dryness of skin and drugs like lithium, beta-blockers, chloroquin and potassium iodide.

Tarsalicylic acid is the sheet anchor of treatment in the average case of psoriasis vulgaris. Quicker symptomatic relief might be obtained with local application of steriod. Tar ointment should gradually be introduced. In itching, atarax or doxepin might help a lot. If infection is suspected, proper antibiotic or chemotherapeutic agents should be prescribed. In highly anxious patients, tranquiliser may have good effect.

In recalcitrant local patches, steroid occulssive therapy (or intralesionally) is helpful.

MTX is still the **drug of choice** in patients where topical therapy has failed. Internal steroids should better be avoided.

Retinoids probably help pustular psoriasis.

Aspirin, nonsteroidal analgesics, colchicine and gold are used with partial success in psoriatic arthropathy.

Psoriasis can be managed but as yet cannot be cured.

PYODERMA

It is a generic term for any bacterial infection of skin associated with erythema, a purulent exudate and crusting.

A. **Fundamentals of cutaneous microbiology**

1. Skin of normal people is very resistant to invasion by most bacteria. This resistance is caused by the following.

a. **Acid mantle** of the skin containing free fatty acids which are bacteriostatic or bactericidal.

b. Process of keratinization and regular falling of keratin eliminate bacteria.

c. Intactness of the skin acts as barrier for invasion of bacteria into the skin.

d. **Immunological function** of skin, which depends on Langerhan's cells and cell mediated immunity.

e. Normal bacterial flora of skin offer resistance to other bacteria. They act by competitive antagonism or bacterial interference. **Resident cutaneous microflora of human skin consist of :**

i. **Micrococcaceae–Staphylococci** : epidermidis, saprophyticus. **Micrococci** : luteus, varians, sarcina.

ii. **Aerobic diphtheroids** : Corynebacterium, Brevibacterium.

iii. **Anerobic diphtheroids** : Propionibacterium : acnes, granulosum, avidum.

iv. **Lipophilic yeast** : Pityrosporum ovale and orbiculare and perhaps candida parapsilosis and other yeasts.

v. **Gram-negative organisms** : Klebsiella, Enterobactor, Proteus, Acinetobactor, Mima, Herellea, Pseudomonus (rarely) and E. Coli.

Almost all organism may survive temporarily on the cutanaeous surface under appropriate conditions. A complete enumeration of transient organisms would include essentially all the micro-organisms found in the environment of man.

Staphylococcus aureus is not a member of the resident flora except occasionally in the nose and perineum. Gram-negative organisms are sometimes recovered on repeated cultures from the axilla and toe web space.

Factors affecting normal micro-flora of skin

a. Different **climatic conditions**—e.g. humidity and sweating.

b. Body **hygiene**—scrubbing, disinfectants.

c. Skin **diseases**—new and divergent microflora is characteristic of dermatitic skin.

d. Organisms of nasopharynx and G.I. tract.

e. Macerated or traumatised skin.

f. Hypogammaglobinemia and agammaglobinemia severely alter the normal bacterial flora.

g. Normal general defence mechanism of the body plays a great role in fighting with the invading pathogens ; **cell mediated immunity** plays a vital role.

2. The microbes are aggregated into microcolonies which can be visualised by electron microscopy. These colonies are most predominant at the infundibulum of hair follicles.

3. Finding of polymorphonuclear leucocytes engulfing bacteria yields direct evidence of defence operation against pathogenic invasion. Leucocytes are usually absent in lesions in which the pathogenic organisms are simply colonists.

4. It is impossible to sterilise the skin completely.

5. There is normally an electrostatic repulsion between the skin's surface and its bacteria both having negative charge.

6. Patients having compromised immune system produce difficulties in keeping the skin surface free from any potential pathogen since in this situation normal resident flora may become dangerously pathogenic.

7. Normal flora is relatively stable but its composition and population vary regionally. In general, the density of organisms is higher in body-folds and in areas with many sebaceous glands. In wet areas 10^6 organisms per square centimeter may be present.

8. The use of topical antibacterial agents in deodorants and cosmetics inhibits the growth of gram-positive organisms and encourages the proliferation of potentially pathogenic gram-negative organisms and yeasts.

9. The usual surgical preparation that traumatises the skin by shaving and scrubbing and is followed by the application of an occlusive dressing is more likely to encourage the growth of pathogens than gentle washing with soap and water of intact skin.

10. In some people, pathogenic bacteria remains permanently at carrier sites e.g. nostril, external ear, behind the ears, axillae, naval regions, groins, genitalia, perianal region, natal cleft and webs of fingers and toes. From these sites organisms may get entry into sites of damaged skin giving rise to disease. Nasal carrier state is about 50%.

11. Normal skin defence depends upon the following.

a. Dry mechanical barrier from which the contaminating organisms are constantly being removed by desquamation.

b. Acid pH of skin (acid mantle).

c. Unsaturated fatty acids of skin, especially oleic acid. Growth of Str. pyogenes is inhibited by 1 in 40 oleic acid.

Following pyodermas would be described in short :

1. Impetigo (described already in page 189).
2. Ecthyma.
3. Staphylococcal scalded skin syndrome (SSSS)
4. Superficial pustular folliculitis.
5. Chronic pustular folliculitis.
6. Gram-negative folliculitis. 7. Erysepalus/Erysepaloid
8. Furunculosis. 9. Cellulitis.
10. Bacterial paronychia.

Pyoderma 2

STAPHYLOCOCCAL SCALDED SKIN SYNDROME (SSSS)

This is a rather new and well-recognised entity.

DIAGNOSIS

1. It is characterised by **erythema** followed by the development of **bullae** and extensive **loss of skin** in sheets.

2. The epidermal split occurs just beneath the stratum corneum and is the result of release of an exfoliative toxin by group II phase type 71, 3c or 55 S. aureus. The toxin is epidermolytic.

3. In SSSS patients, there is usually a colonization of S. aureus at mucosal surface and the absorption and subsequent dissemination of the toxin produce wide-spread symmetrical, superficial separation of the skin. Hence the **early bulla** of SSSS is **sterile.**

4. SSSS, most often, affects **children** below 8 years of age. It very often starts with low grade **fever, malaise, conjunctivitis** and **rhinitis.** In some cases, these symptoms may be absent. Often a markedly tender, scarlatiniform erythema around the mouth, eyes, body orifices and at the neck and flexural surfaces begins abruptly. Within 24 to 48 hours, there occur flaccid bullae which evolve into wide-spread epidermal separation. A **'potato-chip scaling'** is seen as the process heals in 5-7 days.

5. Histology and bacteriological diagnosis

a. Epidermal separation just beneath the stratum corneum.

b. Fluid from blister in culture is sterile.

c. Culture may be positive from the nose, throat, vagina and rectum where colonization of S. aureus is present.

TREATMENT

CLOXACILLIN NAFCILLIN	CEPHALOSPORIN ERYTHROMYCIN

1. SSSS resolves completely, with or without treatment, with little morbidity within 2 weeks.

2. **Antibiotic therapy**

a. **Penicillinase-resistant penicillin** is the drug of choice e.g. dicloxacillin to prevent spread of the disease to children.

Dose 50 mg/kg/day for 10 days orally. Nafcillin 50 mg per kg. I.V. for 7 days is an alternative.

b. **Cephalosporin**

c. **Erythromycin**

3. Use of steroid is controversial and most physicians are against its use.

4. **Supportive therapy**

a. **Soaks** or **baths** with Burow's solution or saline.

b. **Oral hygiene** is important. Diphenhydramine elixir or viscous lidocaine lessens oral discomfort. Only bland foods are tolerated.

c. In extreme cases, proper **fluid** and **electrolyte balance** are necessary.

DISCUSSION

SSSS is usually self-limited, and significant morbidity is uncommon. However, to prevent spread amongst other children, proper antibiotic therapy is needed. Severe cases need ancillary treatment for oral and occular hygiene, fluid and electrolyte balance and maintenance of nutrition. Recurrence is unusual as vigorous antibody response to the toxin confers protection. Ritter's disease is identical with SSSS. It should be differentiated with toxic epidermal necrolysis or Lyell's syndrome which occurs in adults often due to injury by a drug.

Pyoderma 3

ECTHYMA

It is a **chronic pyogenic infection** of the skin characterised by **deep ulcerated lesions** which are **crusted.**

DIAGNOSIS

1. Etiological factors

a. Causative organisms are same as that of impetigo, but chances of developing glomerulonephritis are more than in impetigo.

b. Age—Children and young adults.

c. Sites—Any site ; but legs and buttocks have special predilection.

d. Hygiene—The role of cleanliness and hygiene as predisposing factors are still controversial.

e. Nutrition—Status of general health also has not been proved to have any definite effect. But some believe that debilitated condition predisposes it.

f. Vectors of organisms—As ecthyma very often develops after insect bites, the mosquitos and other insects have been believed to be the vectors.

g. Other family members are frequently affected.

h. Trauma often predispose it.

2. Clinical features

The lesions may be **single** or **multiple** and begin as **transient vesicopustules** surrounded by an **erythematous** halo. These quickly ulcerate and become covered by thick **crust** or **eschar** and are surrounded by a few mm of indurted erythema. When the crust is removed, a **saucer-shaped ulcer** is seen having a rare base and elevated edges. Sometimes crust may be very firm and tightly adherent. Healing takes place in few weeks and scars develop. Local adenopathy may be present. Lymphadenopathy and low grade fever are early signs of ecthyma even in minor lesions.

3. **Histology**

a. Loss of epidermis

b. Pronounced infiltration with polymorphs and formotion of abscesses in dermis, especially around pilosebaceous follicles.

4. **Bacteriological diagnosis** : Culture shows in most cases β-hemolytic streptococci and/or S. aureus.

TREATMENT

SYSTEMIC ANTIBIOTICS	CLEANSING

1. **Cleansing** by

a. Soap and water. b. Antiseptic solution.

2. **Antibiotic ointments** to be applied as described in impetigo. Silver sulphadiazine and povidone iodine often help.

3. **Internal antibiotics** should always be administered.

a. **Penicillin** b. **Cloxacillin.**

c. **Erythromycin** etc. in normal dose for 2 weeks.

DISCUSSION

Ecthyma is an ulcerative form of pyoderma caused primarily by group A β-hemolytic streptococci but S. aureus very often invades secondarily. The ulcerations are most frequent on the legs of children. Although the lesions are ultimately self-healing, treatment with systemic antibiotics helps in prompt healing and eliminates the reservoir of infection from the community. This is specially important as nephritis-producing streptococcus is very often the etiologic organism.

Pyoderma 4

SUPERFICIAL PUSTULAR FOLLICULITIS
(Bockhart's impetigo)

It is a superficial infection of hair follicles and sebaceous glands by staphylococcus aureus.

DIAGNOSIS

1. Predisposing factors

a. Friction and trauma.

b. Irritating agents e.g. insect bites.

c. Hydration of keratin by increased moisture e.g. in case of occlusive dressing under polytheue and in hot and humid environment.

d. General debilitating disease.

e. Exposure to oils, grease and waxes.

2. Etiologic agent—Coagulase positive staphylococcus aureus.

3. Clinical features

Superficial pustular lesions occur in hair follicles, more often on the arms and legs. Pustules are flaccid and rupture easily or very often excoriated, followed by crusting. Anterior portion of thigh, posterior calf and extensor aspect of forearm are more often involved. In children, scalp is a common site. Perifolliculitis is often present. Lesions continue to erupt for several weeks and spread to near by follicles. Spontaneous healing may occur.

4. Histology shows

a. Non-specific follicular and perifollicular inflammatory reaction.

b. Superficial abscess formation.

5. Rarely, deeper form folliculitis, secondary cellulitis and ecthymatous lesions may result from infection.

TREATMENT

FUCIDIN   POVIDONE-IODINE   ANTIBIOTICS

1. Cleansing with soap and detergent, preferably containing hexachlorophene. Prophylactic use of the antibacterial cleanser prevent recurrences.

2. **Local applications**

   a. **Antibiotic** ointments e.g. neosporin®, terramycin®.

   b. **Fucidin®** ointment. c. **Piodine®** ointment.

   d. Silver sulphadiazine cream.

3. Systemic antibiotic is seldom necessary. Cloxacillin and erythromycin are very effective in severe and chronic cases.

DISCUSSION

In superficial pustular folliculitis, fragile pustules at the follicular orifices are seen. Perifolliculitis is more often present. Avoidance of predisposing factors, cleansing with antiseptic soap and application of antibiotic ointment can cure the condition in a week or two.

Pyoderma 5

CHRONIC PUSTULAR FOLLICULITIS (CPF)

It is a persistent infection of hair follicles by coagulase positive staphylococcus aureus.

DIAGNOSIS

1. Predisposing factors

a. Frictional trauma. **b.** Traction of hair.

c. Maceration of skin e.g. occlussive dressing.

d. Exposure to chemicals, oil and topical corticosteroid.

e. Nasal cavity is often the reservoir of infection.

f. Shaving with infected razors causes the disease at the beard area.

g. Low general resistance of the body.

2. Etiologic agents

a. Coagulase positive staphylococcus aureus.

b. Rarely, the streptococcus, proteus, pseudomonas and coliform organisms have been found.

3. Clinical features

a. Sites involved are

i. Beard area (Sycosis barbae). **ii.** Front of shin. **iii.** Thighs. **iv.** Buttocks. **v.** Hair follicles of eyelids. **vi.** Axilla and **vii.** Pubis.

b. The lesions are inflammatory papules and pustules involving hair follicles. Their **characteristics** are

i. They begin with erythema, burning and itching.

ii. By two days, they form pinhead-size pustules pierced by hairs. Later, after the destruction of the follicular aparatus, hairs may fall out leaving minute pitter scars.

iii. Due to inflammation of the hair follicles, hairs become loose and can be readily epilated.

iv. Pustules may be mildly painful.

v. There may be peripustular inflammatory erythema.

vi. They may conglomerate to form granular masses but even then, separate lesions are visible at the periphery.

vii. Lymphadenopathy is generally absent.

4. **Pathology**

a. It is essentially a pyogenic folliculitis and perifolliculitis.

b. Deeper parts of the follicles are involved with inflammatory changes.

c. There is edema and vascular dilatation in and around the follicles.

d. Cellular infiltrations are present and consist of

i. Polymorphs **ii.** Plasma cells **iii.** Histiocytes.

e. The follicles become minute abscesses, and pus escapes through the follicular orifices.

TREATMENT

ERYTHROMYCIN	BENZOYL PEROXIDE
LINCOMYCIN	FUCIDIN
DAPSONE	ELECTROLYSIS

1. **Compress**— **a.** Hot compresses with **Vleminckx's solution**. **b.** With **Condy's solution**. **c.** Burrow's solution.

2. **Topical therapy**

a. Antibiotic ointments—Gentamycin, Neosporin[R], Terramycin[R], Chloromycetin.

b. Antiseptic ointments— **i.** Fucidin, **ii.** Povidone iodine, **iii.** Iodohydroxyquinoline, **iv.** Benzoyl peroxide, **v.** Silver sulphadiazine.

c. Antiseptic lotions

i. Silver nitrate **ii.** Antibiotic lotions.

All these are to be applied 2 to 3 times daily for adequate length of time.

3. **Epilation** of hairs and/or destruction of hair follicles by **electrodesiccation** are/is replaced by fibrosis and cure(s) the nagging condition.

4. **Internal antibiotics/chemotherapeutic agents**

All drugs give temporary relief. Recurrence is the rule. **Erythromycin, cloxacillin, lincomycin** are favoured by many. They should be administered repeatedly and for prolonged period. There should be change of drugs to kill the highly resistant S. aureus. **Dapsone** has shown good results. Weekly courses of effective antibiotic for 6-12 months often help to have permanent cure.

5. **Increasing immunity against S. aureus.**

This has been tried with unpredictable results by

i. Regular administration of **levamisole** 150 mg weekly for few months.

ii. Injection of human **gamma-globulin.**

iii. Injection of **non-specific antigens** e.g. milk, omnadin[R] and sterodin[R] containing various non-specific antigenic substances.

DISCUSSION

CPF is one of the most recalcitrant skin diseases characterised by chronic pustular eruptions at hair follicles of beard area, shin, buttock, thighs, scalp, pubic area and eyelid margins. Intensive local and internal therapies are needed to get relief which is often temporary. Recurrence is almost the rule. However, it has been observed in some patients that the disease dies down automatically after total destruction of hair follicles. Electrodesiccation of hair follicles is a curative procedure. Potent local and internal antibiotics, administered repeatedly at regular intervals, sometimes cure the condition. Non-specific immunogens and staphylococcal toxoids show inconsistent results.

Pyoderma 6

GRAM-NEGATIVE FOLLICULITIS

It is a type of superficial folliculitis caused by gram-negative organisms.

DIAGNOSIS

1. Causative organisms

a. Enterobactor or Kbebsiella, **b.** Pseudomonas and **c.** Proteus.

2. Predisposing factors

a. Long term antibiotic therapy, especially in acne vulgaris.

b. Too frequent use of hot tubs or saunas.

c. Indulging in macerating activities.

3. Clinical features

a. Follicular pustules grouped about the nose in case of acne patients treated with long term antibiotics (4% of cases).

b. Superficial pustules at injured and macerated areas.

TREATMENT

AMPICILLIN

Bacterial sensitivity tests and proper antibiotic therapy are necessary. Usually they respond to **ampicillin** 1g daily in divided dose for 10 days. Long term tetracycline therapy for acne vulgaris should be temporarily stopped.

Topical application of **benzoyl peroxide** has been found to be useful in some cases.

DISCUSSION

Although rare, its appearance should be noticed and prompt treatment initiated.

Pyoderma 7

ERYSEPALUS

It is an acute cellulitis of the skin and subcutaneous tissue caused by group A β-hemolytic streptococci.

DIAGNOSIS

1. Predisposing factors

a. It occurs most frequently in the very young, the aged and the debilitated persons.

b. Carriers of the organism.

c. Persons with lymphedema.

d. Chronic ulcer of the skin.

e. Patients having abrasions, scratches, fissures, lacerations, puncture wounds, operative wounds and pustules. Any skin break seems significant.

f. Organisms may enter through small pox vaccinations, chicken pox, herpes zoster, herpes simplex and umbilical wound in new borns.

2. Clinical features

a. Cutaneous manifestations

i. The lesion : It begins as a small, bright or fiery red, irregular, raised, distinctly circumscribed plaque. It spreads peripherally for several days at a rate of about 2 to 10 cm per day. While the usual size is 10-15 cm, very large lesions may also be seen.

ii. Number of lesions : Usually single.

iii. There is usually no central clearing.

iv. It is hot, tender, bright rosy, shiny, indurated and blanches with pressure.

v. Sharply demarcated advancing edge causes the sensation of 'meeting a wall'.

vi. Vesicles and bullae may be seen in severe cases.

vii. Local gangrene may be observed.

viii. Subcutaneous painful induration without any erythema may be seen.

ix. Pain is characteristic but there may also be itching and burning.

x. Sites : Face, scalp, hands, feet, legs and genitalia are the usual sites. It may however occur anywhere. Cheek, in front of ear, is the most favourite site. Such lesion may cross the bridge of the nose to cause butterfly lesion.

xi. Grotesque edema is seen if periorbital area and scalp are involved.

xii. Desquamation is common during convalescence.

xiii. In scalp there may be permanent hair loss.

b. Systemic manifestations are

1. High temperature (103-105°F) 2. Shaking chills 3. Malaise 4. Prostration 5. Headache 6. Delirium 7. Back pain 8. Constitutional symptoms of severe toxicity, tachycardia, toxic look etc.

3. Pathology

It is the same as that of diffuse phlegmonous cellulitis **characterised** by

i. Prickle cells are swollen and show cloudy vacuolation. **ii.** Edema of dermis may cause subepidermal bullae. **iii.** Plenty of polymorphs scattered at the subcutaneous tissue. **iv.** Streptococci are present at the interstitium and lymphatics. **v.** Micro-abscesses are present but frank suppuration does not occur. **vi.** Chronic lesion leads to fibrosis and elephantiasis.

4. Laboratory findings

a. Leucocytosis to the level of 20,000/mm^3.

b. Polymorphs 80 to 95%.

c. Culture of aspirated material, blood or from swab taken out of pharynx shows growth of group A β-hemolytic streptococci.

d. If nephritis is accompanied, there are albuminuria, hematuria and blood cell casts.

e. High E.S.R.

5. Complications

a. Bacteremia can give rise to shock, acute bacterial endocarditis and metastatic abscesses.

b. In repeated attacks there may be browny induration and unremitting lymphedema.

i. At the lip—macrocheilia.

ii. At the legs—verrucose elephantiasis.

c. Acute glomerulonephritis.

TREATMENT

PENICILLIN	ERYTHROMYCIN

1. **Rest,** immobilization and elevation of the affected part.

2. **Cool wet dressing** allay inflammation and helps healing the bullae.

3. **Antibiotics**

a. Injection of crystalline penicillin 10 lac units I.M. b.i.d or t.i.d for 10 days is the drug of choice.

b. Other broad spectrum antibiotics in adequate doses e.g. Erythromycin, Lincomycin, Clindamycin, Cephalexin, Methicillin, Nafcillin, Oxacillin, Cephalothin, Cefazolin.

4. Injection of streptococcus toxin in desensitizing doses in chronic and repeated attacks.

5. Symptomatic treatment e.g. for pain and fever, aspirin or modern anti-inflammatory drugs may be advised.

DISCUSSION

Erysepalas is an acute infection of the skin and subcutaneous tissue by Group A β-hemolytic streptococcus. It is characterised by edematous, spreading, circumscribed, hot, erythematous area with or without vesicle or bulla formation. Pain, malaise, chills and fever are the frequent complaints. Leucocytosis and high E.S.R are found to be present. Penicillin is the treatment. Erythromycin is a good alternative.

Erysepaloid

It is usually a benign infection caused by Erysipelothrix rhusiopathiae, commonly seen in fishermen and meat handlers, characterised by edema and redness of the skin, more often of a finger or the back of the hand which gradually extend over a period of several days. Lesion tends to clear at the centre and is less well-demarcted than erysepalas. Systemic reactions are rare. Penicillin is promptly curative. Broad spectrum antibiotics are also effective.

Pyoderma 8

FURUNCULOSIS

A furuncle is an acute, localised, perifollicular, staphylococcal abscess of the skin and subcutaneous tissue. It has a tendency to undergo central necrosis and suppuration. Furunculosis refers to multiple or recurrent lesions.

DIAGNOSIS

1. **Etiological factors** are

a. Occurs at all ages but common in 5 to 15 years.

b. **Predisposing factors** are

(1) Acne vulgaris. (2) Seborrhea with oily skin. (3) Common in athelets. (4) Contact with oil and grease. (5) Severe malnourishment. (6) Alcoholism. (7) Diabetes mellitus. (8) Severe anemia. (9) Leucopenia. (10) Hypogammaglobinaemia. (11) Chronic diseases. (12) Allergic diathesis. (13) Poor personal hygiene. (14) Immunodeficient states. (15) Hairy areas and ingrowth of hair. (16) Obstruction of sebaceous glands. (17) Scratching and friction e.g. in scabies, pressure of belts. (18) Chemical irritation e.g. by oils and depilating agent. (19) Hyperhidrosis. (20) Colonization of staphylococcus aureus at anterior nares and other carrier sites. (21) Obesity. (22) Systemic steroid therapy.

c. **Season :** More in summer.

d. **Causative organism**

(1) Coagulase positive staphylococcus aureus, group I, phase types 29, 52, 80.

(2) Strains lysed by bacteriophages 80 and 81 are very important.

(3) More than 1 million virulent staphylococci are required to produce a furuncle.

(4) Presence of foreign body (e.g. suture material) increases the susceptibility to infection.

(5) Other occasional organisms are

(a) Streptococci (b) Coliform organisms (c) Coagulase negative S. epidermidis.

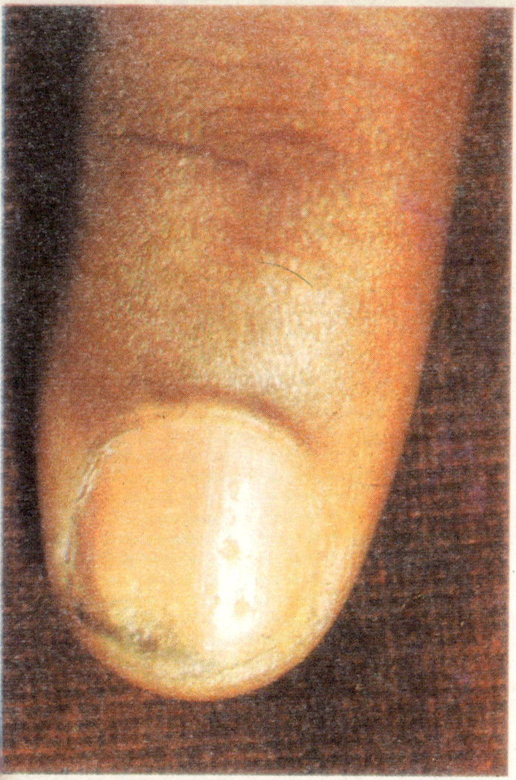

Fig. P-10. **Psoriasis Of Nails** showing typical pittings.

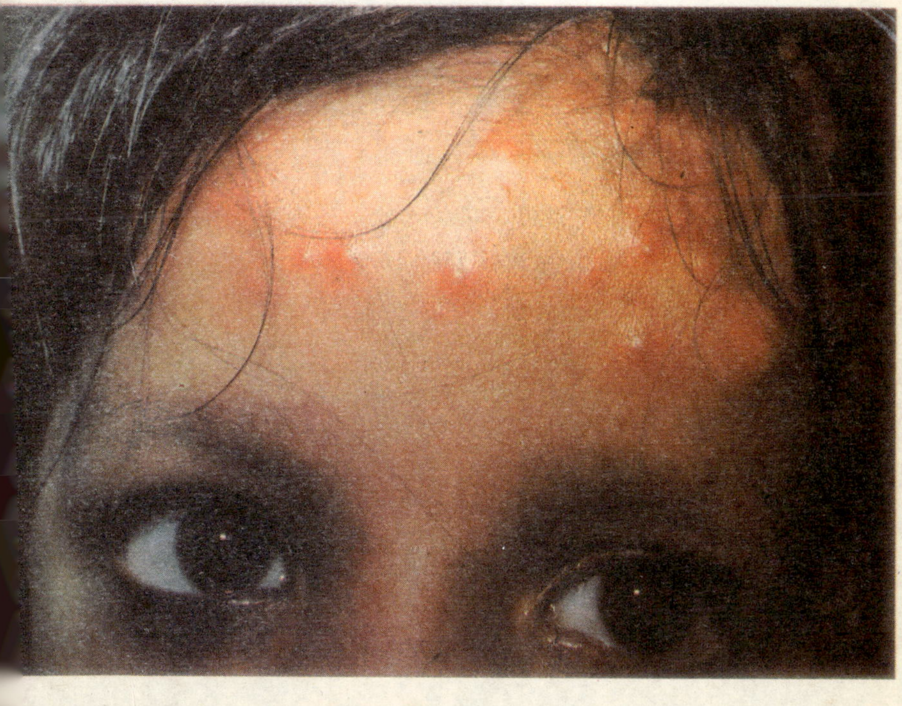

-11. **Furunculosis** of the forehead.

2. Clinical features

a. Sites are face, neck, back, buttocks, thighs, perineum, breasts, axilla and external ear.

b. Number of lesions : One, several or plenty.

c. Repeatitive crops of eruptions are common.

d. The lesion is **characterised** by the following features.

(1) It begins as a minute, painful induration of the skin and subcutaneous tissue in the region of a hair follicle.

(2) There may be itching and constant pain which may be very severe.

(3) Size of the lesion may be 1 to 5 cm.

(4) Skin is elevated, indurated, tender, shiny and bright red.

(5) In 2 to 4 days furuncle matures, becomes boggy and fluctuant and may develop a yellow and creamy-white head as suppuration and central necrosis occur within.

(6) Spontaneous rupture soon occurs to release thick, creamy, odourless, yellow pus tinged with blood and the pain subsides.

(7) Healing occurs in the next few days by granulation. Subcutaneous cysts may develop during healing.

(8) Some may be very tough and stringy, having tenacious core of central necrosis. These are very refractory to treatment.

(9) At thick skin areas (e.g. at the back), furuncles coalesce and extend subcutaneously to poduce a carbuncle with extensive multilocular inter-connected abscess.

(10) A sty is a furuncle involving a sebaceous gland of the eyelid margin.

e. Systemic effects

i. Fever (101° F to 102°F) may occur in severe cases.

ii. Malaise, and **iii.** Regional adenopathy

3. Pathology

a. Microscopically, a typical localized, walled off abscess is seen containing

(1) Polymorphs (2) Fibrin (3) Necrotic material (4) Plasma cells and foreign body giant cells in very chronic lesions.

b. **Fibrosis** occurs during the healing.

c. **Laboratory diagnosis**

i. **Gram stain** of pus shows clusters of gram-positive cocci with polymorphs.

ii. **Culture** shows S. aureus.

4. **Complications**

a. Bacteremia following manipulation may cause osteomyelitis, pyarthrosis, abscesses in different organs and endocarditis.

b. Septic thrombophlebitis which in turn may produce pulmonary emboli or multiple lung abscess.

c. Cavernous venous thrombosis may occur if the face is involved.

TREATMENT

CLOXACILLIN	TOLMETIN SODIUM
ERYTHROMYCIN	TOPICAL ANTIBIOTIC
RIFAMPICIN	

1. Avoidance of predisposing factors ; to help natural healing the following are advised.

a. Rest.

b. Protection from trauma and heat.

c. Elevation of the affected part.

d. In patients of hypo-gammaglobinaemia, injection of homologous IgG or pooled gammaglobulin.

e. Incision is contraindicated as it favours systemic extension.

f. Trauma (squeezing) and hot compress are better to be avoided.

g. Fluctuated lesions should be drained and anti-bacterial ointments should be applied to surrounding area.

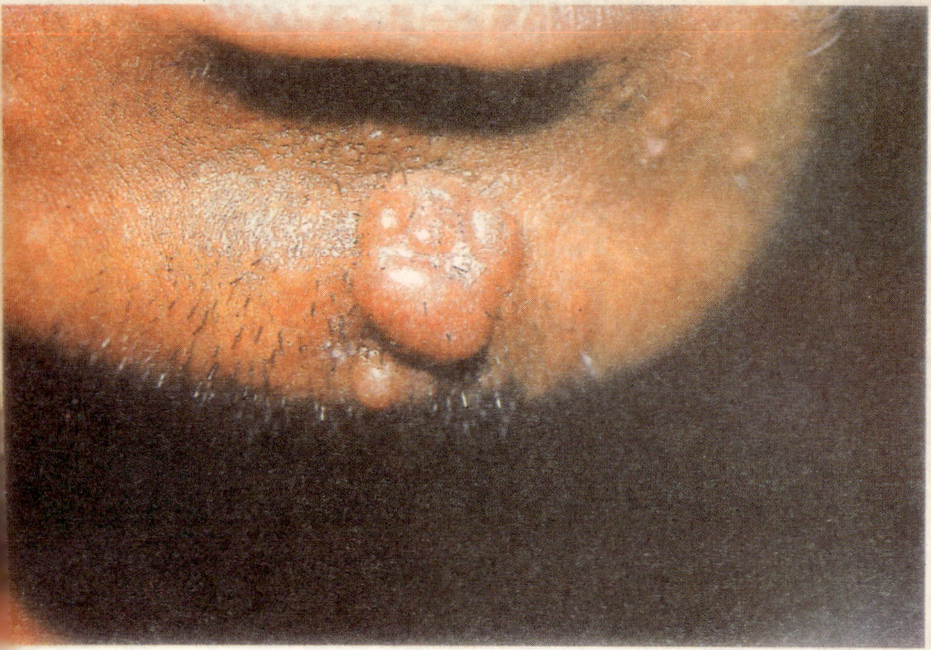

Fig. P-12. **PKDL** showing waxy papules of chin.

Fig. P-13. **Papular Urticaria** showing papules and vesicles on the shins of a child.

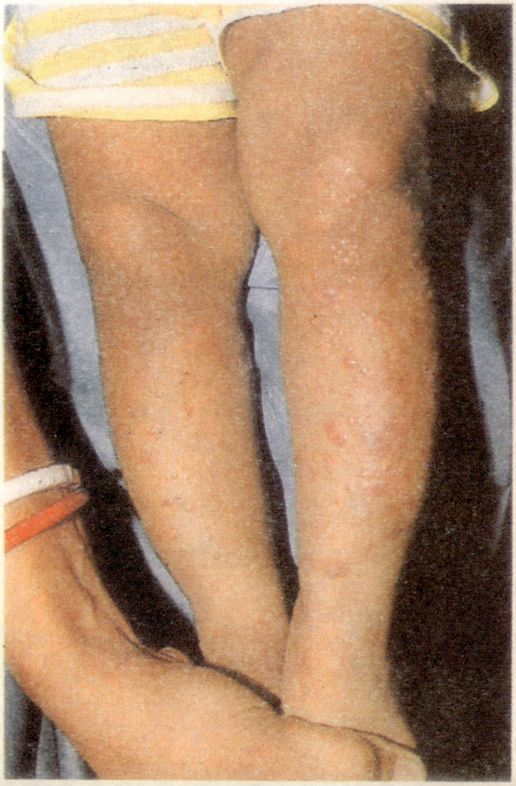

2. Local treatment

a. Regular application of low sensitizing antibiotic ointment on the furuncles along with carrier sites.

b. In some semi-ripe furuncle, hot compress hastens maturation. However, excessive compress should be avoided as it causes maceration and leads to the development of new lesions.

c. An alcoholic aluminium chloride solution may be very useful in controlling repeated attacks.

3. Internal treatment

a. Antibiotics

Organisms are often penicillin resistant.

i. Semi-synthetic penicillinase-resistant penicillin e.g. cloxacillin, dicloxacillin, nafcillin or cephalexin ; 2 g per day given 1 hour before or 2 hours after meals in divided doses for 10-14 days.

ii. Other parenteral antibiotics : Methicillin, oxacillin, cephalothin, cefazolin, kanamycin and vancomycin (all in normal dose).

iii. Miscellaneous antibiotics : Erythromycin, lincomycin, clindamycin, novobiocin and chloromycetin may also be given singly or in combination in normal dose.

b. Miscellaneous agents

1. Gamma-globulin. 2. Toxoids. 3. Vaccines.

4. Bacteriophage preparation.

5. Levamisole : 2.5 mg/kg for 3 days per week can sometime restore chemotaxis. These agents however have controversial use.

6. In multiple recurrences, intranasal inoculation of 10^8 to 10^9 of staphylococcus aureus 502 A (a non-pathogenic organism) has been successful in clearing the disease for about 6 months.

7. Vitamin C stimulates phagocytic bacterial killing.

8. Zinc sulphate orally might in some cases prevent recurrences.

9. Rifampicin for prolonged period can stop recurrence by helping neutrophil chemotaxis.

10. Tolmetin sodium 400 mg t.i.d, a non-steroidal anti-inflammatory agent, may be helpful.

DISCUSSION

Furuncles are basically boils involving hair follicles characterised by extremely painful inflammatory lesions caused by coagulase positive staphylococcus aureus.

Adequate importance should be attached to predisposing factors. Judicious use of internal antibiotics are the mainstay of treatment. Culture and antibiotic sensitivity tests often help in deciding the proper antibiotic.

In recurrent cases, local use of antibiotic ointments at carrier sites, especially at the nose, is beneficial. Immuno-deficiency states may be corrected and immuno-potentiation should be tried.

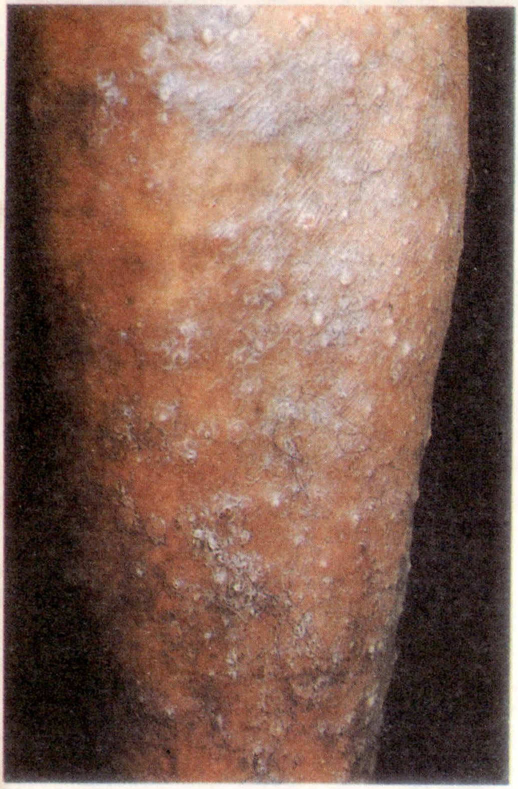

Fig. P-14. **CPF**
showing chronic follicular pustules pustules of shin

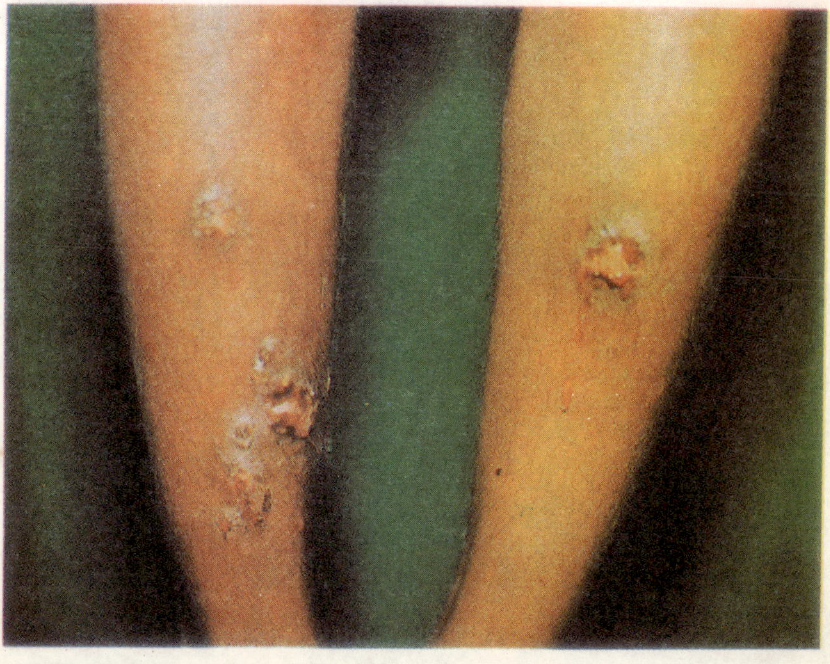

Fig. P-15. **Ecthyma** showing chronic deep crusted ulcerated lesions.

Pyoderma – 9

CELLULITIS

It is a generic term for diffuse suppurative deep infection involving both the dermis and the subcutaneous tissue.

DIAGNOSIS

1. **Etiological factors** are the following.

a. **Predisposing states** are

i. **Trauma** in the skin for the entry of the infective organisms or existing wounds.

ii. Lymphatic stasis. **iii.** Immuno-deficiency states.

iv. Complication of infected eczema. **v.** Erysepalus.

b. **Causative organisms** are

i. Streptococcus pyogenes : most frequent. **ii.** Staphylococci, **iii.** both i and ii. **iv.** Miscellaneous organisms e.g. Pneumococci, H. influenzae type b, Gonococcus.

2. **Clinical features** have the following characteristics.

a. Affected area is **deeply indurated**, **erythematous** and **tender**. Border may be prominent. **Edema, pitting** on pressure may also be observed.

b. Sometimes the central part becomes nodular and surmounted by a vesicle that ruptures and discharge **pus** and necrotic material.

c. **Regional adenopathy** is prominent with occasional streaks of lymphangitis.

d. **Gangrene, metastatic abscesses** and grave **sepsis** may follow.

e. Sites affected are the face, scalp, legs and the dorsum of hands.

f. **High fever, malaise, weakness** and **chilly sensation** may be complained of.

3. **Laboratory findings**

Taking 0.5 ml of sterile saline in a syringe and inserting a 20 gauze needle into the part, aspiration should be done and the aspirated material should be cultured in suitable media.

TREATMENT

REST ANTIBIOTICS

The treatment is almost similar to that of erysepalus.

1. **Rest** in bed is important.

2. Cool, wet dressings are helpful.

3. Internal antibiotics as are discussed in erysepalus. Chloramphenicol is suggested as the drug of choice for facial cellulitis caused by H. influenzae type b.

DISCUSSION

Cellulitis is characterised by **highly inflammed, tender, indurated area** with **lymphadenopathy** and **lymphangitis. Fever** is very often a sequel of pre-existing infection and fresh injury. It is a dermatologic emergency and should promptly be treated with adequate dose of proper antibiotic for two weeks. Recurrent lesions of lower leg often indicate the presence of an interdigital athelet's foot infection with fissures as the port of entry for bacteria. This should be treated by regular application of imidazoles.

Pyoderma—10

BACTERIAL PARONYCHIA

Acute bacterial paronychia is generally caused by Streptococci after an injury of the nail fold. This may be due to improper manicuring and nail biting. Paronychial tissue is **acutely inflammed, tender** and **swollen.** Pustule may form and burst to discharge **pus,** the culture of which would show the organism. Treatment is to be done by prompt **internal antibiotic** therapy.

ROSACEA

It is a chronic inflammatory disorder, usually beginning in middle age or later, and is characterised by telangiectasia, erythema, papules and pustules that appear particularly in central areas of the face.

DIAGNOSIS

1. Etiology

The cause of rosacea is as yet unknown. However, there exist several hypotheses and are briefly mentioned below.

i. Alimentary

Indigestion, constipation, diarrhoea, gall bladder disease, achlorhydria, hypochlorhydria, gastritis have all been implicated as causes of rosacea. There is however no scientific foundation in support.

ii. Psychologic

Patients of rosacea are often found psychically depressed, 'retiring' and have neuroticism. These probably are the effects of rosacea rather than its causes.

iii. Infective

Pathogenic micro-organisms and Demodex folliculorum are considered to be the possible etiologic agents since tetracycline and metronidazole have good effects on patients of rosacea. It appears however that their role, if any, is only secondary since many having these organisms do not suffer from rosacea and their surface lipids are well within normal limits.

iv. Climatic

Exact role of climate in the development of rosacea is still not clear but the patients show an increase in symptoms and signs in sunlight, with cold winds and in hot atmosphere. There are increased amounts of solar elastotic change in the dermal connective tissue and dystrophic change in dermis. Climatic vicissitudes, along with vascular change, are considered responsible for such changes.

v. Immunologic

Immunoglobulins and complement components get deposited in dermo-epidermal junction in rosacea. Further, the inflammatory cell infiltrate in rosacea have some characteristics of hypersensitivity reactions. Anticollagen antibodies and antinuclear antibodies in lymphocyte elutes have been detected. These may be due to actinic damage to type IV collagen. Circulating antinuclear bodies of IgM class are present in some patients. There exists a positive association of rosacea with autoimmune disorders and there are signs of immunodeficiency. However, all these facts require stricter analysis to arrive at a conclusion.

There are certain other factors which are implicated as having roles in causation or aggravation of rosacea. These are

1. Diet induced flushing e.g. hot tea, coffee (but not caffeine) and alcohols 2. Emotional instability 3. Vasomotor instability 4. Menopause 5. Endocrine disturbances 6. Riboflavin deficiency 7. Stimulation of bradykinin release by adrenaline 8. Photosensitivity 9. Seborrhea 10. Association with migraine 11. Focal infection 12. Prolonged application of fluorinated corticosteriods 13. Numerous demodices in the inflammed pustule of rosacea (but not with pustules of acne vulgaris) 14. Genetic overtones.

2. Clinical features

The cardinal features of rosacea, in order of importance, are (a) Erythema (b) Telangiectasia (c) Papules (d) Swelling and (e) Pustules. The patient may complain of burning and stinging.

The **erythema** and **telangiectasia** are usually found in cheeks, nose, chin and forehead. But the whole face may also be involved.

The **papules** are rose-red in colour, usually of 1-3 mm in diameter, firm and not tender in contrast to acne vulgaris.

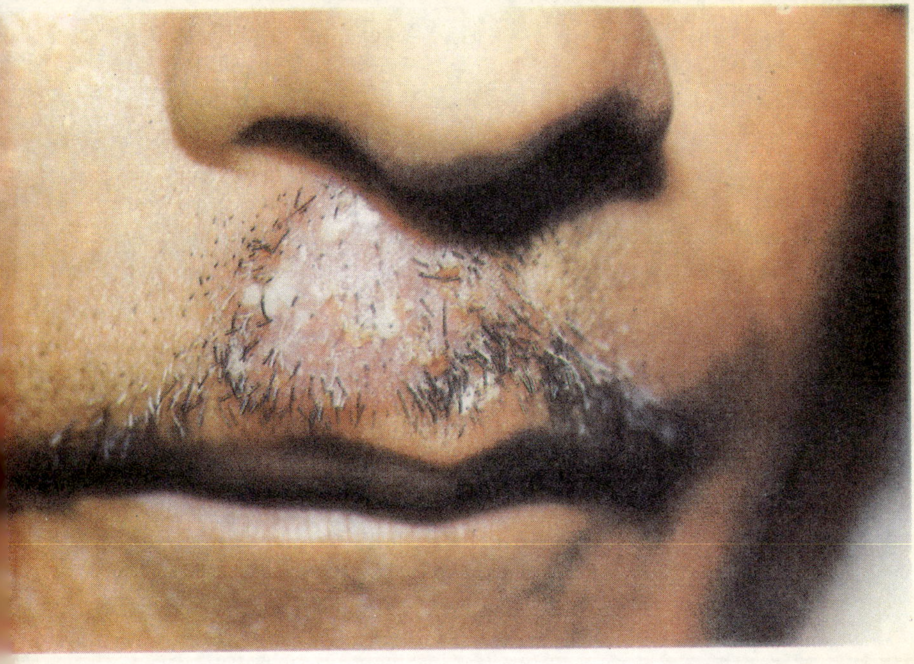

P-16. **CPF** at the upper lip showing chronic follicular pustules which have destroyed some of the hair
icles.

Fig. R-1 **Rosacea**
showing erythema, papules
and pustules of face.

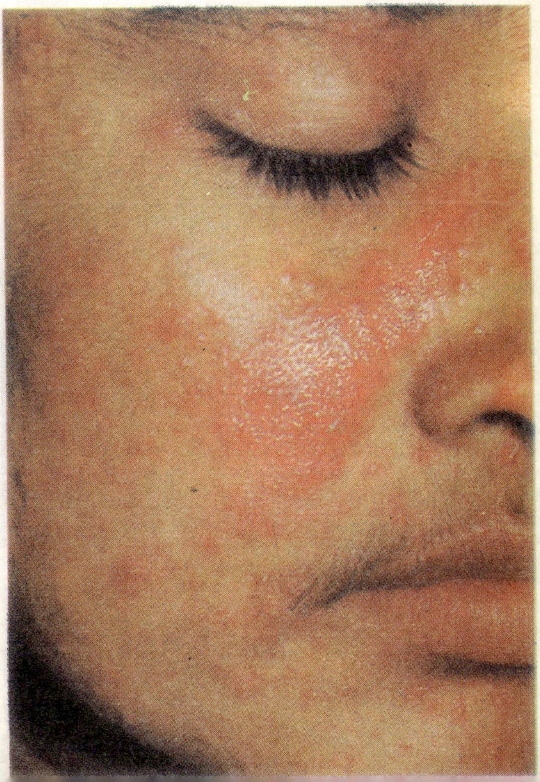

Besides the areas mentioned, they may be present in arms, chest and abdomen. **Papules do not show the presence of comedones.**

The **swelling** of rosacea due to edema may occur in association of acute episodes or there may be permanent swelling as rhinophyma.

Pustules are present, particularly around the nose, in about 20% patients.

All the above signs may not be present together and various permutations and combinations of them may occur.

3. Sites

i. Most common site is face ; usually symetrically involved and particularly marked on the prominences of cheeks, chin, forehead, eyebrows and nose. As mentioned earlier, the other sites are arms, neck, chest and back.

ii. A solitary site, e.g. one cheek or a portion of forehead, may also be involved in isolation. Bald area of scalp may as well be affected.

iii. Rare sites are wrists, legs and ears.

4. Clinical varieties

i. Erythematous–telangiectatic type.

ii. Papular type.

iii. Pustular type.

iv. Glandular hyperplastic type.

v. Pustulo-nodulo-cystic type simulating acne conglobata. There may be keliodal scarring.

vi. Combination of various types in the same patient.

vii. Menopausal type : onset having after menopause.

Age : 30-50 years.

Sex : Females are more affected (3 : 1), especially those having fair complexion ; but rhinophyma is present mostly in males (12 : 1).

5. Concomitant lesions

i. Occular–Blepharitis, chalazion, hordeolum, conjunctivitis, keratitis, episcleritis and iritis.

ii. Sebaceous hyperplasia—At nose, leading to rhinophyma characterised by bulbous and craggy swelling of nose. Severe seborrhea or seborrheic dermatitis may often be associated.

iii. Rosaceous lymphedema—Lymphedema may be present in periocular zones, forehead, cheeks and in one side of face, having firm feel and mild erythema.

iv. Perioral dermatitis

It is probably a distinctly separate entity affecting young women around the mouth having lesions similar to rosacea.

3. Histopathology

i. In erythematous telangiectatic type

A non-specific inflammatory infiltrate is seen in dermis around dilated capillaries.

ii. In pustular type

Aggregations of neutrophils are usually high in follicles and this may lead to total destruction of the follicles.

iii. In papular type

Papules show non-specific chronic inflammatory infiltrate. In 10% cases, there is foci of granulomatous infiltrate containing islands of epithelioid cells and a few giant cells surrounded by round cells simulating tuberculoid picture. Caseation is however often absent.

iv. In glandular hyperplastic type

Sebaceous glands are increased in size and number. Ducts are dilated and filled with keratinous material. Capillaries are also dilated and a chronic inflammatory infiltrate is present in the upper dermis.

TREATMENT

TETRACYCLINE	BENZOYL PEROXIDE
METRONIDAZOLE	SULPHUR
DAPSONE	ISOTRETINOIN

1. Control of precipitating factors

i. **Avoidance of flush** : Patients are to avoid hot food and atmosphere e.g. tea, coffee, sunlight, extreme heat and cold and emotional stress. Spices, condiments, hot showers or tub baths and saunas are to be eschewed.

ii. Avoidance of vasodilator and photosensitive drugs.

2. Topical therapy (Same as in acne vulgaris)

i. Topical tetracycline lotion : To be applied twice daily ; topical erythromycin is a good alternative.

ii. 5-10% Benzoyl peroxide lotion : Applications to be gradually tolerated ; may be continued as maintenance therapy even after withdrawal of tetracycline ; can be mixed with 5% precipitated sulphur.

iii. Metronidazole cream : Has been given trial with debatable results.

iv. Precipitated sulphur : 2-10% in lotion, cream, gel or ointment to apply twice daily or just nightly.

v. Lotio sulphuris alba : To apply twice daily.

vi. Topical salicylic acid : May help in rosacea through inhibiting prostaglandin synthesis.

vii. 0.05% desonite : Twice daily application with quinochlor compound on alternate days has been found to be useful.

viii. Danish ointment containing 5% beta-naphthol and 10% sublimated sulphur in equal parts of Peruvian balsum and petrolatum applied b.i.d. is often helpful.

3. Internal drugs

i. **Tetracycline**—To start with 250 mg q.i.d. between meals for about 2-6 weeks ; after improvement, maintenance dose as 250 mg daily or on alternate days. Oxytetracycline is also effective. Relapses are common (about 50%) after sudden withdrawal.

ii. Erythromycin and minocycline are less effective than tetracyline ; chloramphenicol has also been used.

iii. **Ampicillin** : 250 mg b.i.d. or t.i.d.

iv. **Metronidazole** : 200 mg t.i.d. for 3 weeks ; may be given even for 12 months.

v. Low dose clonidine, an alpha-adrenergic agonist, is effective in erythemato-telangiectatic rosacea, 0.05 mg b.i.d.

vi. **Isotretinoin** : 1-2 mg/kg given in 2 divided daily doses for 12-28 weeks.

vii. Indomethacin and aspirin can lessen flushing as prostaglandin inhibitors.

viii. **Dapsone** : 100 mg daily has been tried in tetracycline failure cases.

4. **Surgical procedures**

i. Light electrodesiccation with epilating needle for persistent telangiectasis.

ii. Ablation, plastic surgery or electrosurgery, carbon di-oxide slush, cryosurgery with liquid nitrogen, for rhinophyma.

5. **For eye complications** (in about 50% patients)

i. A topical ophthalmic steroid ointment.

ii. 10% sulphacetamide.

iii. Combination of sulpha and steroid.

iv. Ophthalmic consultation as and when necessary.

6. **In menopausal variety**—Hormonal replacement therapy e.g. estrogen.

7. **Tranquillisers in emotionally labile patients.**

8. **Chloroquin in patients** where sun aggravates rosacea.

DISCUSSION

Diagnosis of rosacea is not difficult. Erythema, telangiectasia, edema, papules and pustules are often present at centrofacial region. Acne vulgaris occurs in younger age group and there are comedones. Rarely, an overlap of rosacea and acne may also occur.

Treatment requires judicious use of local and internal drugs. However, it is a great therapeutic challenge, especially in patients who are topical steroid addict. We should convince that steroid can induce 'steroid rosacea'. This 'steroid-rosacea-steroid' cycle must be broken.

Oral tetracycline for prolonged period is the drug of choice. Concomitant local therapy with benzoyl peroxide or sulphur is definitely helpful. Precipitating factors should be seriously avoided.

Relapse and recalcitrance require proper reassurance. However, in the long run, most of the patients become free from the disease.

Rebound flare-up of erythema after withdrawal of steroid should be handled tactfully by a proper pursue of treatment.

Gentle centrifugal massage of face, regularly every day, for few minutes might help in lessening the erythema.

SCABIES

DIAGNOSIS

1. Scabies is caused by Sarcoptes scabiei var hominis. It is one of the commonest skin diseases of our country.

2. Salient features of the disease are (**a**) **nocturnal itching.** (**b**) **history of itching in the family members** or neighbourhood. (**c**) **pruritic papules, vesico-pustules** and **burrows,** especially at the sides of the **fingers, heels** and **palms.**

3. The disease is predominantly of **children** but adults are also often affected. In primary scabies, the incubation period is nearly a month. It is transmitted mostly from within the family or the neighbourhood.

4. The patient complains of itching of short duration. This aggravates while he removes dresses or goes to the warm bed. **Webs of fingers, sides of digits, ulnar border of hand, flexor surface of wrists, anterior axillary fold, female breast, abdomen** (particularly periumbilical), **genitalia, gluteal fold** are the usual sites of involvement. Palms, soles and face are comparatively less affected in adults but frequently in infants. Backs and scalp are usually not involved.

5. The most **significant** and **diagnostic lesion** of scabies is a **burrow.** A burrow is a 1 cm dark-coloured tunnel in the stratum corneum made by the adult gravid female. At the end of the tunnel often a minute vesicle is seen whence a living mite can be demonstrated.

6. Norwegian scabies is a special type of scabies occurring in (a) immuno-deficient patients, (b) senile dementia, (c) mentally retarded child (mongolism), (d) leprosy and syringomyelia due to the loss of sensation, (e) tuberculosis and (f) malignancy.

In Norwegian type, no part of the body is spared but **itching is minimal.** Sub-ungual, palmar and plantar hyperkeratosis or atypical psoriasiform lesions are seen. **Thousands of mites** are found where the average number of adult mites in normal scabies is only about 10-12.

7. The scabies mite and its products are mainly confined in stratum corneum. The pathological response produced by the mite is seen in epidermis, dermis and even in subcutaneous fat. The papulo-vesicular lesions of scabies may resemble histologically arthropod-bite reaction. Nodular scabies are histologically indistinguishable from lymphoma.

8. **Complications** of scabies are (a) secondary infection leading to impetigo, ecthyma, furunculosis and cellulitis (these may lead to systemic complications like pyelonephritis, internal abscesses, pyogenic pneumonia and septicaemia), (b) secondary eczematisation (common in children), (c) persistent nodules of scabies even after the complete therapy, (d) acarophobia and (e) exfoliative dermatitis.

9. For **microscopical confirmation** of the disease, the blind end of a burrow can be superficially shaved with a No. 15 blade parallel to the surface of the skin and the material placed on a microscopic slide with a drop of mineral oil (KOH is not used). Diagnosis requires visualization of either the eight-legged mite or its eggs or faeces.

10. Life cycle of sarcoptes scabiei var hominis

Male mite measures about 0.2×0.15 mm and the female 0.4×0.3 mm. They have four pairs of short legs. The fertilized female excavates a sloping burrow into the stratum corneum, granular layer and malpighian layers, about 2 mm each day and lays eggs 2-3 per day totalling about 10-25. Then it dies in the burrow. After 3-4 days six-legged larva emerges from the egg. This larva makes shallow pockets in the skin of the original host or a new one. It undergoes three moults to become adult in about 10 days. It requires 14-17 days to attain adulthood from the egg. Male and female adult mites copulate in the pocket of skin and the pregnant female starts excavating a new burrow for laying eggs. The male soon dies and the cycle repeats.

11. Animal scabies

The physiological races of Sarcoptes scabiei can infest horse, cow, buffalo, dog, pig, camel, sheep and goat. Sarcoptes scabiei var canis infests dogs from which human contacts can develop scabies. The clinical features are similar to human scabies but **without burrows.**

TREATMENT

1-2% GAMMABENZENE HEXACHLORIDE	10% SULPHUR
25 % BENZOYL BENZOATE	ANTIBIOTICS
10 % CROTAMITON	ANTIHISTAMINICS

1. All members of the family as well as sexual contacts must be simultaneously treated.

2. **Common anti-scabetic drugs**

a. **Topical agents**

i. Crotamiton (10%) lotion or cream : Mild acariside but often useful in children.

ii. Benzoyl benzoate (25%) emulsion : A bit irritant and burning sensation is felt in genitalia.

iii. Gamma benzene hexachloride (1-2%) – Most favoured amongst the modern antiscabetics. Adverse effects are : (a) primary irritant dermatitis, (b) allergic contact dermatitis, (c) absorption in children causing CNS toxicity giving rise to seizures.

iv. Sulphur ointment (10%) : May cause primary irritation or secondary allergy and has a peculiar bad smell.

v. Tetraethylthiurium monosulphate (Tetmosol) 25% lotion to be diluted 1 : 4 in water or soap—a bit irritant.

vi. Mesulphan (Mitigal[R]) oil or ointment.

vii. Topical thiabendazole 10% lotion.

viii. 0.2% nitrofurazone ointment.

ix. 0.5% malathion liquid.

b. **Systemic drugs**

i. Thiabendazole, mebendazole and metronidazole have been tried orally having equivocal results.

ii. Methotrexate 2.5 mg tab daily for 6 days, 6 days gap, again for 6 days in severe scabies with psoriasiform scales.

3. **Methods of application**

The lotion (preferably during summer) or the ointment (preferably during winter) is to be thoroughly applied from neck to feet (even on sole) thinly after lunch and at bed time for three consecutive days. After an interval of 7 days, the application should be repeated as before for 3 more days. Family members, without any evidence of the disease, should apply only for the first three days.

4. After the course, mild itchyness may persist. For this, however, application of antiscabetic should **not** be **continued.** This is due to allergic sensitivity of the body due to the mite. Continued application may give rise to dermatitis venenata. Bland applications of lotio calamine and oral antihistaminics are sufficient.

5. **Antibiotics** systemically may be needed in order to combat **secondary infection.**

6. **Oral antihistaminics** may be prescribed from the very beginning to control itching and this may prevent secondary infection from scratching.

7. **Secondary eczematisation** should properly be treated as and when noticed. If required, **topical steroid** may be applied. Caution against overuse of steroid is necessary, for it may cause exacerbation of scabies.

8. Nodules persisting after complete antiscabetic treatment are difficult to treat. Remedy lies in application of steroid cream or **tar gel** (night application) for 2-3 weeks or intralesional **injection of corticosteroid**. In recalcitrant cases, benign neglect is the best policy.

DISCUSSION

Diagnosis of scabies is made by : (1) itching, particularly at night, (2) same itching complaint in other family members, (3) papules, vesicles and pustules in preferred sites, (4) the detection of a burrow and (5) demonstration of mite, larva, nymph, egg or stool.

Doctors must be very serious right from the beginning in treating scabies for the rate of failures are quite high.

In uncomplicated scabies, that is, having only itching and a few scattered papules, application of 2% gamma benzene hexachloride lotion or ointment from neck to foot after lunch (otherwise, reapplication is necessary because of washing the drug during meals) and bed time for 3 consecutive days with a week's gap and repeat application for further 3 days cures most of the cases. During the gap of 7 days, 10% crotamiton can be similarly applied to reinforce the treatment. Antihistaminics may be added.

In cases where secondary bacterial infection has occurred giving rise to impetigo, furuncles and cellulitis appropriate antibiotic, preferably erythromycin (because of infection by staphylococcus pyogenes), should be administered for about 7 to 10 days. Topical treatment could be started at the earliest opportunity, say 2-3 days after, when local application would not cause any maceration and/or pain.

In patients having eczema, full anti-eczematous treatment, local application of steroid lotion or cream, antibiotics and antihistaminics should be instituted immediately. Thereafter, in earliest opportunity, antiscabetic treatment should start.

In certain cases, anti-infective, anti-eczematous and anti-scabetic treatment may have to be started simultaneously for unless mites are killed, allergy due to these would not cease, and unless allergy subsides, itching with concomitant secondary bacterial infection would not stop.

Average treatment of persistent papules of scabies is a continued local application of steroid creams with proper reassurance. Failing, intralesional steroids may be needed. Acarophobia should be treated by psychotrophic drugs along with, if necessary, psychotherapy.

In relapsed cases, topical antiscabetic agent should be changed and detailed direction should be given regarding compulsory and thorough treatment of all family members. Babies should be treated from neck up, as well as neck down, since head is not a mite-free site in children.

SEBORRHEIC DERMATITIS

DIAGNOSIS

1. It is a common, usually **chronic, superficial, inflammatory dermatosis** showing a predilection for areas of **increased sebaceous gland activity** and is classified as an endogenous eczema.

2. **Age and sex :** It is seen between the ages of 2 weeks to 12 months of age and occurs again after puberty. Males are affected more commonly than females at all ages.

3. **Etiology :** It is not exactly known. Following factors are considered to have some role.

a. Familial : No definite pattern of inheritance has yet been determined.

b. Infection

i. Pityrosporum ovale seems to be more numerous in scalps with seborrheic dermatitis.

ii. Staphylococcus aureus may be found more easily in patients with seborrheic dermatitis.

iii. Reduced number of propionibacterium acne is seen in patients with seborrheic dermatitis.

c. Emotional stress may also exacerbate seborrheic dermatits.

d. Diet : i. High fat in-take **ii.** Increased sugar consumption. **iii.** A deficiency of B-vitamins such as B_{12} or Biotin. These may contribute in precipitating seborrheic dermatitis.

e. Androgenic hormones : It may be relevant due to following reasons.

i. Seborrheic dermatitis is seen during infancy (influence of maternal hormone).

ii. More common in male **iii.** Seborrheic dermatitis is absent is eunachs.

iv. It decreases frequently during pregnancy. This hormonal influence may be due to endogenous hormone levels or an end-organ sensitivity stimuli.

f. It may be an inflammatory hypersensitivity reaction to epidermal or bacterial antigens.

g. Climate and atmosphere have some role.

4. There are several **clinical variants** of seborrheic dermatitis.

A. Seborrheic dermatitis of infancy

i. Cradle cap : It has the following **characteristics** : (a) Scalp is covered by erythematous, adherent, waxy, scaling. (b) It begins during the third or fourth week of life. (c) It may represent a vestigial vernix caseosa or more likely to be due to influence of maternal hormones. (d) It spontaneously clears by 8 to 12 months of age.

ii. Body lesions : Well-circumscribed, yellow-red patches covered with a greasy scale is found in the following regions : (a) Flexural areas (b) Diaper areas and (c) Trunk.

iii. Leiner's disease : It is a severe form of dermatitis in infants and is divided into two forms—non-familial and familial.

a. Non-familial : It is **characterized** by the following : (1) It is a generalized form of seborrheic dermatitis showing greasy type of scaling. (2) It is seen commonly among girls and breast-fed babies of both sexes. (3) Severe diarrhoea may be present with resultant failure to thrive. (4) Recurrent infections are common due often to gram negative organisms.

b. Familial : It is due to deficiency of C 5. The inheritance pattern is not known.

B. Seborrheic dermatitis of adults : It may begin as a non-inflammatory dry, flaky desquamation or, it may progress to a pruritic inflammatory dermatitis with erythema, greasy scaling, crusts, pustules and even papulo-vesicles. Following are the several forms of adult seborrheic dermatitis.

i. Seborrheic dermatitis of scalp

(a) Pityriasis sicca—dandruff without inflammation.

(b) Inflammatory—including extension to non-hairy adjacent areas such as post-auricular area and the forehead where it is called **'corona seborrheica'**.

ii. **Seborrheic dermatitis** of face is **characterised** by

(a) Pityriasis oleosa—The seborrheic diathesis : oily skin of face.

(b) Eyebrows—Scaly dermatitis.

(c) Marginal blepharitis and occasional conjunctivitis.

(d) Nasolabial fold—Scaly dermatitis.

(e) Beard involvement—Dermatitis of varying severity ; follicular involvement is common (folliculitis).

iii. **Otitis externa** : Seborrheic dermatitis is probably the most common cause. It is characterised by itchy scaly dermatitis.

TREATMENT

LOCAL STEROID WITH OR WITHOUT ANTIBIOTICS	
ANTIBIOTICS	SHAMPOO
ANTIHISTAMINICS	KETOCONAZOLE

Following preparations are judiciously used.

A. Local

1. **Shampoo containing** (a) Cetrimide 1% (b) Tar 5-10% (c) Salicylic acid 2-5% (d) Resorcinol 1-4% (e) Zinc pyrithione 1-2% (f) Selenium sulphide 2-5%.

2. **Corticosteroids** topically (a) Lotions with or without antibiotics. (b) Creams with or without antibiotics and chemicals e.g. iodohydroxyquinoline 3%, cetrimide 1%, chlorhexidine 1%, ketoconazole 2%. (c) Steroid ophthalmic ointment or lotion with or without antibacterial agents in seborrheic blepharitis.

3. **Miscellaneous**

(a) Keratolytics e.g. salicylic acid 2-5%, urea 10%.

(b) Anti-seborrheic agents e.g. sulphur, cetrimide, vioform, chlorhexidine, resorcinol, sodium sulphacetamide.

B. Internal

1. Antibiotics 2. Antihistaminics 3. Vitamin B_{12} 4. Vitamin B_6 5. Vitamin B-complex. 6. Ketoconazole.

DISCUSSION

It is an acute, subacute or chronic inflammatory disease of scalp and body, where sebaceous glands are overactive, characterised by redness, greasy scaling, crusting and exudation. Mild itching may be present. Rarely, it may progress to exfoliative dermatitis.

It usually responds quickly to mild corticosteroid cream such as hydrocortisone applied 2-3 times daily. If severe, it may require potent corticosteroid such as beclomethasone dipropionate 0.025% to 0.5% cream, ointment or lotion. Among the other topical therapies, low strength tar cream or gel 1-5% or iodochlorhydroxyquin 1-3%, either alone or in combination with a mild corticosteroid, are helpful. Systemic therapies are required occasionally and consist of antibiotic, antihistamines and vitamin B-complex. Recently, 2% cream of ketoconazole locally has been tried with good results. Internal ketoconzole is also helpful in severe cases.

Patient should avoid the atmosphere that increases dermatitis and the treatment should be prompt and persistent.

SEXUAL INADEQUACY

Normal sexual response

There are several phases which are described here in brief.

1. Phase of excitement

It starts with psychological stimulation (fantasy or the presence of a love object), physiologic stimulation (stroking or kissing) or a combination of the two. The excitement phase is characterised by the following :

i. Penile erection in the man.

ii. Vaginal lubrication in woman.

iii. The nipples of both sexes become erect.

iv. The clitoris becomes hard and turgid.

v. Labia minora becomes thicker due to the venous engorgement.

The parasympathetic component of the pelvic splanchnic nerves (S2, S3 and S4) stimulate the blood vessels of the area to dilate causing the penis to become erect.

This phase may last several minutes to several hours.

2. Phase of plateau

With continued stimulation

i. Testes increase in size by about 50% and elevate.

ii. The outer third of vagina shows a characteristic constriction called 'orgasmic platform'.

iii. The clitoris elevates and retracts behind the symphysis pubis and becomes, to some extent, inaccessible.

iv. Traction of the labia minora and prepuce occurs and there is intraprepucial movement of clitoral shaft.

v. Breast size increases by about 25%.

vi. Due to continuous engorgement of penis and vagina there occur colour changes which are particularly visible in labia minora that becomes bright red.

vii. Voluntary contraction of large muscle groups occurs.

viii. Heartbeat and respiration increase.

ix. B. P. rises.

This phase stays for 30 seconds to several minutes.

3. Phase of orgasm

It is characterised by the following features.

I. In man : Ejaculatory inevitability becomes the prime sense and there is forceful emission of semen associated with four to five rhythmic spasms of the prostate, seminal vesicles, vas deferens and urethra.

II. In woman : Orgasm is characterised by 3 to 15 involuntary contractions of the lower third of the vagina and strong sustained contraction of the uterus, flowing from the fundus downward to the cervix.

III. In both man and woman : There occur involuntary contractions of the internal and external anal sphincters ; voluntary and involuntary movements of large muscle groups ; facial grimacing ; carpopedal spasm, rise of B. P. ; increase of heart beat rate and slight clouding of consciousness.

Orgasm lasts for about 3 to 15 seconds.

IV. Physiology through hypogastric plexus : Sympathetic nervous system innervates the urethral crest, the muscles of the epididymis, vas deferens, seminal visicles and prostate. At the height of stimulation, ejaculation of seminal fluid occurs from these glands and ducts into the urethra. The passage of semen into the urethra causes a sensation of impending climax called 'ejaculatory inevitability' and once prostate starts contracting ejaculation is inevitable. The semen is propelled through the penis by urethral contractions. One ejaculate contains about 2.5 ml of semen that contains about 120 million sperm cells.

4. Phase of resolution

It consists of the disgorgement of blood of genitalia (detumescence) that brings the body back to resting state. If orgasm occurs, the resolution becomes quite rapid ; but if it is unsatisfactory, resolution may take even 2 to 6 hours accompanied with irritability and discomfort. A subjective sense of well-being is felt by resolution through orgasm.

5. **Refractory period**

Man becomes refractory to further stimulation after orgasm for several minutes to hours. But the refractory period does not exist in woman who can be repeatedly stimulated and is capable of multiple and successive orgasms.

Physiologic process of sex act involves increasing levels of vasocongestion and myotonia called **tumescence** and subsequent release of vascular activity and muscle tone (**detumescence**) after orgasm. The orgasm is identified as the highest pleasurable sensation.

Sexual dysfunction and disorders

Sexual response is in fact a psycho-physiologic experience. Arousal is caused by psychological and physical stimuli, a level of tension is experienced both emotionally and physiologically and with orgasm there is subjective perception of a peak of physical reaction and release.

Physiology of human sexual response has three basic components : (1) psychosexual development, (2) psychological attitudes towards sexuality and (3) attitudes towards one's sexual partner. Any abnormal deviation in these three can cause sexual disorder.

There is a wide range of sexual disorders and only the important and frequent ones would be discussed here in short (**Reference** : Synopsis of Psychiatry by H. I. Kaplan and B. J. Sadock, 5th Ed., Williams and Wilkins, London, 1988).

Major sexual dysfunctions and sexual disorders may be categorised as under.

1. Disorders of sexual desire.
2. Disorders of sexual arousal.
3. Disorders in orgasm.
4. Sexual pain disorders.
5. Non-specific sexual dysfunction.
6. Miscellaneous sexual disorders.

Sexual dysfunctions may be due to biological problems (biogenic), intrapsychic or interpersonal conflicts (psychogenic) or a combination of these factors. Normal sexual function can be severely affected by any kind of stress, emotional disorders or even due to lack of knowledge in normal sexual physiology. It can arise from the very beginning of sex life or after a period of normal functioning. It may also be generalised or situational, that is, limited to a specific partner or in a certain situation. Loss of function may be total or partial. A patient may suffer from several types of dysfunction at the same time.

Disorders of sexual desire

It is quite common. Women are more affected than men. Variety of etiological factors are associated with this problem. However, disorders of desire can be mainly sub-divided into : (1) **hypoactive sexual desire** due to deficiency or absence of sexual fantasies and desire of sexual activity and (2) **sexual aversion disorders**, characterised by an aversion or avoidance of sexual contact with a sexual partner. Probably, the former condition is more common. Certain facts are known about sexual desire disorder and are summarised below.

1. **Desire problem may arise** out of unconscious fears about normal sex, homosexual impulse, unresolved oedipal conflicts, fear of vagina with the belief that phalus would be castrated (Freudian concept of 'vagina dentata'); due to chronic stress, anxiety or depression ; due to drugs that depress the central nervous system, decreased testosterone production, prolonged abstinence from sex, major illness or surgery, mental complex of body image e.g. after mastectomy, ileostomy, hysterectomy and prostatectomy ; an expression of hostility or due to deteriorating mental relationship.

2. **Social factors** of men can influence sexual desire e.g. recent immigration, religion, employment of their wives or lack thereof.

3. Women may be influenced by perceptions about dominance, decision making, affection and the threat of the husband of leaving home.

4. **Lack of privacy** is an important reason.

5. **Marital discord** is of course the most important factor.

6. The final diagnosis is only made when the lack of desire is a source of distress of the patient.

Disorder of sexual arousal

A. In Male

It is characterised by recurrent and persistent partial or complete failure to attain or maintain an erection until the completion of sex act. It is thus called **impotence.** It is of two types : (1) **primary**—when the man has never been able to obtain an erection sufficient for vaginal insertion, (2) **secondary**—when the man has successfully achieved vaginal penetration at sometime of his sexual life but unable to do so later in life. There is another form which is called **selective impotence** where the patient is able to have coitus in certain circumstances but not in others e.g. may be very potent with a prostitute but becomes impotent with wife.

Primary impotence is a rare disorder (about 1%) but secondary impotence is very common (about 50% of sexual disorders). The incidence of impotence increases with age. The etiology of impotence may be organic, psychological or both. About 90% of cases is due to psychological causes. Organic causes can be classified as (Kaplan, H. I. and Sadock, B. J., 1988) :

1. **Infectious and parasitic diseases** : Elephantiasis, mumps.
2. **Cardiovascular diseases :** Atherosclerosis, aortic aneurysm, Leriche syndrome, Cardiac failure.
3. **Renal and urological disorders** : Peyronie's disease, chronic renal failure, hydrocele, varicocele.
4. **Hepatic disorder** : Cirrhosis (usually associated with alcoholism).
5. **Pulmonary disorder** : Respiratory failure.
6. **Genetic diseases** : Klinefelter's syndrome, congenital penile vascular or structural abnormalities.

7. **Nutritional disorders** : Malnutrition and vitamin deficiencies.

8. **Endocrine disorders** : Diabetes mellitus, dysfunction of the pituitary adrenal testis axes, acromegaly, Addison's disease, chromophobe adenoma, adrenal neoplasia, myxedema, hyperthyroidism.

9. **Neurological disorders** : Multiple sclerosis, transverse myelitis, Parkinson's disease, temporal lobe epilepsy, traumatic or neoplastic spinal cord disease, central nervous system tumors, amyotropic lateral sclerosis, peripheral neuropathies, general paresis, tabes dorsalis.

10. **Pharmacologic contributants** : Alcohol, heroin, methadone, morphine, cocaine, amphetamines, barbiturates, psychotropic drugs, antihypertensive drugs, estrogens, antiandrogens (further details given later).

11. **Piosoning** : Lead, herbicides.

12. **Surgical procedures** : Perineal prostatectomy, abdominal perineal colon resection, sympathectomy, aortoiliac surgery, radical cystectomy, retroperitoneal lymphadenectomy.

13. **Miscellaneous** : Radiation therapy, pelvic fracture, any severe systemic disease or debilitating condition.

Removal of testes does not always lead to impotence. Erection may still occur. A reflex arc, fired when the inner thigh is stimulated, presses through the sacral cord erectile center and accounts for the phenomenon.

Psychological causes of impotence are many, diverse and intricate. Important ones are

1. Lack of feelings or affection towards the woman.

2. Punitive super-ego. 3. Inability to trust.

4. Sense of being undesirable as a partner.

5. Inhibition due to fear, anxiety and anger or due to moral prohibition.

6. Lack of proper communication to the partner.

Impotence is non-organic if the man has

(1) spontaneous erections at times (2) morning erections (3) good erection during masturbation (4) erection with extramarital partner.

Further investigations can be made as

1. monitoring of nocturnal penile tumescence (erections that occur during sleep) which is normally associated with rapid eye movement ; monitoring of tumescence can be done with a strain gauze around penis. 2. measuring blood pressure in the penis with a penile plethysmograph or an ultrasound (Doppler) flow meter. These can assess blood flow in the internal pudendal artery. 3. measuring pudendal nerve latency time. 4. glucose tolerance tests. 5. plasma hormone assays. 6. liver function tests. 7. thyroid function tests : determinations of prolactin, FH, FSH. 8. cystometric examinations. 9. penile arteriography. 10. infusion cavernosography, and 11. radioactive xenon penography.

These investigations are costly and are done only when a patient seems to be a candidate for vascular reconstructive surgery. Expert interpretation is however necessary.

B. In female

Sexual arousal disorder in female is generally underestimated. Those who have excitement phase dysfunction often have orgasm problems as well. Maintenance of a proper level of sexual excitement even in happily married couples is quite often a problem (about 33%).

The usual causes are

(1) dyspareunia (2) lack of desire (3) hormonal level. Many women are particularly desirous of sex before the onset of menses ; others have greatest desire during ovulation or immediately following menses.

As already mentioned, drugs have a predominant role in male sexual dysfunction. The following chart is due to Kaplan and Sadock, 1988.

Pharmacologic agents implicated in male sexual dysfunction

Drugs	Impairs erection	Impairs ejaculation
Psychiatric drugs		
Heterocyclic antidepressants		
Imipramine (Tofranil®)	+	+
Protriptyline	+	+
Desmethylimipramine	+	+
Clomipramine	+	+
Amitriptyline	+	+
Trazadone	−	−
Monoamianase oxidase inhibitors		
Tranylcypromine	+	?
Mebanazine	+	+
Phenylzine (Nardil®)	+	+
Pargyline	−	+
Isocarboxazid	−	+
Other mood-active drugs		
Lithium	+	?
Amphetamines	+	+
Major tranquillisers		
Fluphenazine	+	?
Thioridazine (Melleril®)	+	+
Chlorprothixene	−	+
Mesoridazine	−	+
Perphenazine	−	+
Trifluoperazine (Stelazine®)	−	+
Butaperazine	−	+
Reserpine (Serpasil®)	+	+
Haloperidol	−	+
Minor tranquillisers		
Chlordiazepoxide (Librium®)	−	+

Drugs	Impairs erection	Impairs ejaculation
Antihypertensive drugs		
Clonidine	+	?
Debrisoquin	–	+
Methyldopa (Aldomet[R])	+	+
Spironolxactone (Aldactone[R])	+	–
Hydrochlorthiazide	+	–
Arramethidine	+	+
Commonly abused drugs		
Alcohol	+	+
Barbiturates	+	+
Cannabis	+	–
Cocaine	+	+
Heroin	+	+
Methadone	+	–
Morphine	+	+
Miscellaneous drugs		
Antiparkinsonians	+	+
Clofibrate (Atromid S[R])	+	–
Digoxin	+	–
Glutethemide	+	+
Indomethacin	+	–
Phentolamine	–	+
Propranolol (Inderal[R])	+	–

Compared to men, women appear to be less vulnerable to pharmacologically induced sexual dysfunction. Oral contraceptives are reported to lessen libido in some women and phenelzine (Nardil[R]) impairs the orgasmic response in some females. Both increase and decrease in libido have been reported with psychoactive agents. When the drug is discontinued, dysfunction generally disappears.

The incidence of erectile dysfunction associated with the use of tricyclic antidepressants is low. Impairment of sexual function is not common with the use of major tranquillisers. Priapism may occasionally occur due to trazadone and major tranquillisers. Monoamine oxidase inhibitors can impair the orgasmic response in women. Benzodiazepines may decrease libido, but in some patients the diminution of anxiety caused by these drugs may enhance sexual function.

Disorders in orgasm

A. In male

Inhibited male orgasm is often due to retarded ejaculation. A man is said to suffer from *primary retarded ejaculation* if he has never been able to ejaculate during coitus. It is called *secondary* if it develops after previous normal functioning. In retrograde ejaculation, semen passes backward into the bladder having always an organic cause e.g. after genito-urinary surgery or may be due to anticholinergic side effects of phenothiazines. There may be in some cases absence of subjective sense of pleasure even though ejaculation is normal. This is called **orgasmic anhedonia**.

The incidence of inhibited orgasm is much less than premature ejaculation or impotence (about 5%). A man may get orgasm by masturbation but may fail to reach orgasm in the vagina.

Important causes are : (1) physiologic, (2) genito-urinary surgery e.g. prostatectomy, (3) Parkinson's disease, (4) lumbar or sacral sections of the spinal cord, (5) antihypertensive drugs—guanethidine monosulphate, methyl dopa and phenothiazines, (6) severe psychopathology can produce primary inhibited male orgasm. The man often comes from puritanic background ; he perceives sex as sinful and genitals dirty. They usually have difficulty in closeness beyond the area of sexual relations. (7) interpersonal difficulties in relationship with partner e.g. loss of sexual attraction to the partner ; fear of pregnancy, demands by the partner for greater sexual commitment ; unexpressed hostility towards the woman, (8) obsessive compulsive disorders.

B. **In female** (Anorgasmia)

Women may be unable to get orgasm in coitus or by masturbation. Some females are able to experience orgasm during noncoital clitoral stimulation but unable to experience it during the coitus. Probably, it represents a psychological inhibition. Major depression may often be the cause of it. Orgasm reached at coitus gives a special sense of satisfaction ; may be due to intimate closeness of partners or be even due to better physiological experience. Many women experience orgasm during coitus by vaginal stimulation along with manual clitoral stimulation. Some women only perceive orgasm by noncoital clitoral stimulation but not during coitus. They probably suffer from anorgasmia. However, many believe that exclusively clitoral orgasm is a normal behaviour· variation.

In primary nonorgasmic dysfunction, woman has never experienced orgasm by any kind of stimulation and in secondary cases the woman has previously experienced at least one orgasm either by stimulation during masturbation or during sleep while dreaming. Primary anorgasmia is more common among unmarried woman. After 35 years of age, there is increased orgasmic potential due to less psychologic inhibition, greater sexual experience or both.

Secondary orgasmic dysfunction is quite common ($\simeq$30%).

Etiological factors are many. Important ones are : (1) fear of impregnation, (2) rejection by the sex partner, (3) damage to the vagina, (4) hostility towards male partner, (5) feeling of guilt regarding sexual impulse and (6) cultural and social restrictions.

Non-orgasmic women may show frustration and may complain of (1) itching, (2) lower abdominal pain, (3) vaginal discharge and (4) increased tension, irritability and fatigue.

female, vaginal tear often causes pain. Compulsive masturbation may cause physical injury leading to pain. In autoerotic asphyxiation, masturbation is done while hanging by the neck to increase pleasure through mild hypoxia. This is probably a masochistic practice and schizophrenia or major mood disorders may be associated with it.

Miscellaneous sexual disorders

There are many sexual disorders which cannot be correctly classified. Some of these are :

1. **Post-coital dysphoria** : At the resolution phase, people generally feel a sense of well-being with muscular and psychological relaxation ; some might of course show dysphoria i.e. exaggerated feeling of depression and urest at this stage. They become tense, anxious, irritable and may show psychomotor agitation. They dislike their partners and become verbally and physically abusive. Sex with prostitutes, adulterous sex and the fear of AIDS may be at the root of psychological factor.

2. **Problems in couple** : This is a dual dysfunction e.g. one might prefer morning sex while the liking of other is at night. Unequal frequencies of desire is quite common.

3. **Unconsummated marriage** : Though married, a couple may not have coitus. Intact hymen may be the first sign in female. Often the husband is concerned with his manliness and wife may feel put upon, abused and mutilated. Causes are many e.g. (1) lack of sex education (2) sexual prohibitions by parents or society (3) neurotic problem of oedipal nature (4) mental and physical immaturity (5) overdependance on the primary families (6) problems in sexual identification (7) religious orthodoxy causing the sex as sin or uncleanliness (8) women might have a false belief of having no vaginal opening or they may think that their vagina is too small or soft or confuse vagina with rectum (9) men may have a false belief of disortions of vagina (10) female may think that the penis is too big or too small or a weapon.

In most cases the problem is due to the lack of proper sexual eductaion.

4. **Body image problems** : Self-imposed standards of masculinity or femininity is the cause of this sexual disorder. They might prefer sex in total darkness. Dysmorphophia i.e. morbid fear of deformity is also not uncommon.

5. **Don Juanism** : It is often called *satyriasis* meaning excessive and often uncontrollable sexual drive in men. They need many sexual encounters. Probably this is due to desire of masking the deep feeling of inferiority. Some might have unconscious homosexual impulses which they try to deny by compulsive sexual contacts with women. One peculiar aspect is that after having the sex, most Don Juans are no longer interested in the women.

6. **Nymphomania** : This is excessive desire for coitus in women. The causes are not definitely known. Anorgasmia or other sexual disorders may be the etiological factor. Often there is intense fear for the loss of love and the woman tries to attempt to satisfy dependency rather than gratify the sexual impulse through her actions.

7. **Homosexuality**

It is quite common, especially among the males. Some believe that it is physiological.

A. **Etiology**

a. **Psychological** : There are several theories. Arrest of psychosexual development ; castration fear for the male ; fears for maternal engulfment in the preoedipal phase of psychosexual development ; strong fixation on the mother ; lack of effective fathering ; inhibition of masculine development by the mother ; fixation or regression of narcissistic stage of development ; losing competition with brother and sisters ; in female, there might be lack of resolution of penis envy in association with unresolved oedipus conflicts ; homosexual females have generally reported to have close and intimate fathers as compared to heterosexual females.

bodily pleasures without actual intercourse i.e. they are taught various techniques of foreplay having a role in actual intercourse and orgasm. These exercises are called *sensate focus exercises*. During the exercises, if one of the partners becomes highly sexually excited, the other is encouraged to bring him or her by manual means. Expression of mutual needs is thus known and satisfied. Genital stimulation is often accompanied by general body stimulation. The couples are instructed about various positions of intercourse and varieties of stimulating techniques. Gradually the couple learn to communicate—verbally, bodily and sexually. This leads to mutual sex satisfaction. However, dual-sex therapy works only when there is no gross psychopathology.

2. Specific techniques and exercises

Various methods are adopted in this regard. These are :

i. In vaginismus, woman is advised to dilate her vaginal opening by fingers or with dilators.

ii. In premature ejaculation, squeeze technique is followed. In it, on proper stimulation of the penis when there is the sensation of impending ejaculation, the woman partner forcefully squeezes the coronal ridge of the glans which diminishes the erection and thus prevents ejaculation. This procedure is repeated until the period of ejaculation is prolonged to the extent that female partner is satisfied and the male gets the confidence. A variation of this method is to stop copulatory activity just before the level of impending ejaculation and restart after a proper lapse of time. This is repeated three to four times and at last the ejaculation is allowed. This is called the 'stop and start' technique.

iii. If a male shows inhibited desire or excitement, he is advised to masturbate to demonstrate that full erection and ejaculation are possible. He is made to understand that sex is a normal physiological function.

iv. In cases of primary anorgasmia, the female is directed to masturbate and, if necessary, a vibrator can be used to stimulate the sensate focus leading to orgasm. Shaft of the clitoris is the masturbatory site and orgasm is dependent on adequate clitoral stimulation. *G-spot* is an area on the anterial wall of the vagina which is said to be a good site for sexual excitation. Ejaculatory phenomenon during orgasm in women has yet to be satisfactorily demonstrated.

v. Retarded ejaculation is managed at first by extra-vaginal ejaculations. Thereafter, the man is instructed to stimulate himself to the level of near-ejaculation and then enter the vagina.

3. Hypnotherapy

The essential features of hypnotherapy are as follow :

1. Hypnosis enables the patient to gain control of the symptom which lowers self-esteem. 2. It helps to regain disrupting psychological homeostasis. 3. First, cooperation of the patient is achieved by several non-hypnotic sessions. 4. Hypnosis helps in alteration of the attitude towards sex. 5. Often, hypnotherapy is added to basic individual pychotherapy.

However, this is a highly specialised field and proper expertise is needed in order to explain the trance experienced by the patient.

4. Behaviour therapy

It is based on the belief that sexual dysfunction is a mal-adaptive behaviour. Phobias and anxiety are removed by gradual systematic desensitization. Patients are gradually exposed to mild to severe anxiety prone situations. Medication hypnosis and special training in deep muscle relaxation are helpful additional measures. A cooperative partner is of course necessary to get good results. Patients are allowed to express sexual needs openly and without fear.

5. Group therapy

In it, groups for the treatment of sexual disorders are organised in various ways : 1. Members having same sexual problem e.g. premature ejaculation. 2. Members having different problems but are of the same sex. 3. Heterogeneous group with different sexual problems. 4. Groups containing sexually dysfunctional married couples.

Intra-psychic and interpersonal problems are discussed freely. Group provides a strong support system for a patient who feels ashamed, is anxious or guilty about a particular sex problem. It is an useful forum to dispel the sexual myths, correct misconceptions and provide accurate scientific information about anatomy, physiology and varieties of sex. Group therapy may be used as an adjunct to other forms of therapy. Behavioural approach is often a method adopted to treat a particular dysfunction.

6. Analytically oriented sex therapy

Integrated psychodynamic and psycho-analytically oriented psychotherapy is one of the most effective treatment modalities. Psycho-analytic therapy can be of much help to the patient if the various mental abnormlities e.g. relevant dreams, fear of punishment, aggressive feelings, difficulty in trusting the partner, fear of intimacy, oedepal feelings, fear of genital mutilation etc., are properly explained. A good knowledge of psychiatry is essential to conduct the treatment.

7. Biological treatment methods

Some important ones are mentioned here : 1. Intravenous injection of methohexital sodium has been used in desensitization therapy. 2. In tense patient, the anxiolytic agents have been used. 3. Tricyclic antidepressants have been used in phobias about sex and premature ejaculation and in depressive illness. 4. Testosterone has been used in male patients to increase libido where the level is low. 5. Penile prosthesis has been used in erectile dysfunction of organic origin. 6. Revascularization of the penis has been tried in erectile dysfunction of vascular origin. 7. Endarterectomy may be beneficial if aortoiliac occlusive disease is responsible for erectile dysfunction. 8. Hymenectomy in dyspareunia. 9. Vaginoplasty is done to increase vaginal sensation. 10. Release of clitoral adhesions helps women with inhibited excitement. 11. Injections of papaverine into the corporal bodies of the penis have been found to produce erection for several hours.

It is important to know that there are no known approdisiacs. They might have benefit only through power of suggestion.

DISCUSSION

Normal sexual behaviour and attitudes vary greatly in different cultures. Once the masturbation was regarded as a perversion. It is now taken as normal and harmless. However if it creates guilt in the mind, it can produce considerable distress and may damage the capacity for several performance. Guilt and shame occur in fetishistic fantasies. Autoerotic fatalities occur due to asphyxia resulting from hanging.

A good number of people (about 5%) are preferentially homosexual and in America it is no longer considered as an abnormality. Frequent sexual activity with many partners indicates diminished capacity for the pair-bonding. In India, premarital and extramarital sex are not encouraged but in many countries the premarital coitus is accepted as normal. Illegitimate children are very likely to develop psychiatric problems.

There is a great role of fetal androgens in preparing the brain for later sexual activity. Perental attitude towards sex is highly important. A forbidding atmosphere endangers guilt and shame and inhibits the capacity for enjoying sex. Children exposed to hostility, rejection and cruelty are liable to sexual maladjustment.

Proper sexual functioning in men and women depends on : state of desire, effective vasoconstrictive arousal i.e. erection in male and lubrication in female and orgasm. In male, orgasm is mediated by the contractions of the prostate, seminal vesicles and urethra and in female probably by the contraction of the muscles of the outer one-third of the vagina. However, most likely orgasm involves wider areas in both sexes e.g. generalised muscular tension, perineal contractions and involuntary pelvic thrusting. Orgasm is followed by the phase of resolution, a sense of general relaxation, well-being and muscular relaxation. This normal sexual response is mediated by a delicate balance between the sympathetic and the parasympathetic nervous systems. Vasocongestion is largely mediated by parasympathetic outflow and orgasm is predominantly sympathetic. Ejaculation is entirely sympathetic. There are also cortical, neural, hormonal and vascular influences. Hence, alpha and beta-adrenergic blocking agents have great influences on emission, ejaculation and perineal muscle contraction.

Inhibitions in the response cycle of sex can occur at one or more of sexual response phases. There may be disturbances in subjective dimensions of desire, arousal and pleasure and also in the objective performance, vasocongestion and orgasm. These disturbances may be primary or secondary, generalised or limited to certain situations or with certain partners and total or partial. Due to associated anxiety, guilt, shame and frustration, somatic symptoms may develop.

Etiological factors are varied which in short are : (1) poor communication between partners (2) anger directed towards partner (3) fear of partner's genitals, close intimacy, dependency or pregnancy (4) feeling of guilt (5) severe depression (6) anxiety of marital discord (7) stressful life situations (8) ageing (9) ignorance about sexual norms (10) fear of failure (11) demand for performance (12) excessive wish to please the partner (13) avoidance of sex (14) traumatic experience in childhood (rape) (15) feeling of inadequecy (16) antagonistic religious training e.g. excessive modesty, puritanical aversion and (17) physical factors. Besides, there are many other factors which might have definite role in sexual inadequacy.

As a result of these factors, there may be in male inhibited sexual desire and excitement, inhibition of orgasmic control, anorgasmia, sexual anhedonia (erection and ejaculation with no pleasure) and in female there may be frigidity, lack fo orgasm, dyspareunia and vaginismus.

Results of treatment are to some extent unpredictable and vary enormously. Severer the pyschopathology, longer is the duration of treatment and more adverse is the outcome. Lack of desire, impulse disorders, unresolved homosexual conflicts and phobic sex problems are very difficult to treat. Behavioural approaches with regular practice of assigned exercises often give rather good results. The flexibility of attitude is definitely positive prognostic factor. The younger couples generally have better prognosis. Dual-sex therapy has yielded better results. Training in behavioural-sexual skills, systematic desensitization, directive marital counselling, traditional psychodynamic approaches and group therapy are all modern methods which should be utilised with proper judgement in order to help these unfortunate people suffering from sexual inadequacy.

Treatment of individuals should also be borne in mind.

This area of medical science probably demands far more attention from physicians than what has been hither to given.

2. **Ketoconazole :** 200 mg tab. once or twice daily after meals until cure and therafter for 1-2 weeks more.

3. **Amphotericin B :** Dose is about 700 mg I.V., given only in disseminated cases ; highly toxic drug.

4. **Oral 5-fluocytosine, 8 g/day ; with conjoint amphotericin B,** 50 mg I.V., daily for 3 weeks ; highly toxic.

5. **Miscellaneous drugs or agents :** Zinc, iron, cimetidine, local heat, cotrimoxazole, miconazole and transfer factor have been tried with occasional benefit in refractory cases.

DISCUSSION

Sporotrichosis is a global chronic fungal infection. After trauma, organisms from soil, plants or decaying wood enter the skin of hand, forearm or foot.

The lymphocutaneous form is common (75%). It begins with a firm non-tender subcutaneous nodule. Later, within weeks many such nodules develop along the lymphatics which may turn into abscesses and even burst to form chancriform chronic ulcers. **Regional lymphnodes are not affected and general health remains normal.** Rare varieties show acneiform, plaque type and warty lesions or gummatous ulcerations. Disseminated sporotrichosis shows multiple firm subcutaneous nodules scattered all over the body. Lesions may as well develop in bones, joints and muscles.

Most of the patients are cured by **potassium iodide** orally. Ketoconazole is almost equally effective. **Amphotericin B** is rarely needed.

Except in disseminated type, **prognosis is generally good** in all cases of lymphocutaneons sporotrichosis.

SYPHILIS

DIAGNOSIS

1. It is defined as a **chronic infectious** disease caused by Treponema pallidum and characterized by **florid manifestations** at sometime and a period of latency at other times.

2. The disease is **systemic** from the very beginning.

3. Treponema pallidum has the following **characteristics.**

a. It is a tiny **spiral-shaped** organism.

b. 5 to 20 μm or more in length and 0.25 μm in breadth.

c. The number of coils are 5 to 20 ; the amplitude is about 1 μm.

d. It has different types of motility e.g. rotation, undulation, compression, expansion and angulation ; most characteristic is the angulation.

e. It has tapering ends and the body is entwined with a bundle of 3 to 4 fibrils that maintains its shape.

f. It cannot survive in heat. Drying kills it and soap damages it. Use of strong disinfectants by the physicians is therefore not necessary.

j. T. pallidum dies within 3 days in blood under normal refrigeration.

4. Syphilis may be divided into

a. Congenital and **b.** Acquired.

5. Acquired syphilis may be of the following types.

a. **Early** : 1. Primary 2. Secondary 3. Early latent

b. **Late** : 1. Late latent 2. Tertiary 3. Cardiovascular 4. Neurosyphilis

Some authorities classify the cardiovascular syphilis and the neurosyphilis as quarternary syphilis.

6. Histopathology

In all stages of syphilis, the basic changes are the same. They are as follow.

a. Cellular infiltration : There will be perivascular infiltration of lymphocytes and plasma cells. This infiltration will be responsible for

i. Induration at the base of primary lesion

ii. Papule iii. Rubbery enlargement of lymphnodes

b. Endarteritis : It will result in occlusion of the blood supply and is responsible for

i. Ulceration of primary lesion

ii. Mucosal ulceration

iii. Scaling of long-lasting papules

iv. Necrosis and ulceration in gummatous syphilis

v. Some of the tissue damage in cardiovascular and neurosyphilis

7. The **course** of untreated syphilis (after Wilkox, 1982) is shown diagrammatically in page 385.

8. Early acquired syphilis

a. Incubation period : 9-90 days.

b. Clinical features

i. History of exposure is present.

ii. The primary lesion, which is also called *primary chancre*, has the following characteristics.

a. It begins as a dull red macule which soon becomes papular and ulcerates.

b. It is painless non-tender rounded.

c. It has got a well-defined margin.

d. It has an indurated rubbery base.

e. It exudes more serum than blood after trauma.

f. The base of the ulcer may be dull red or may be covered with a yellowish slough.

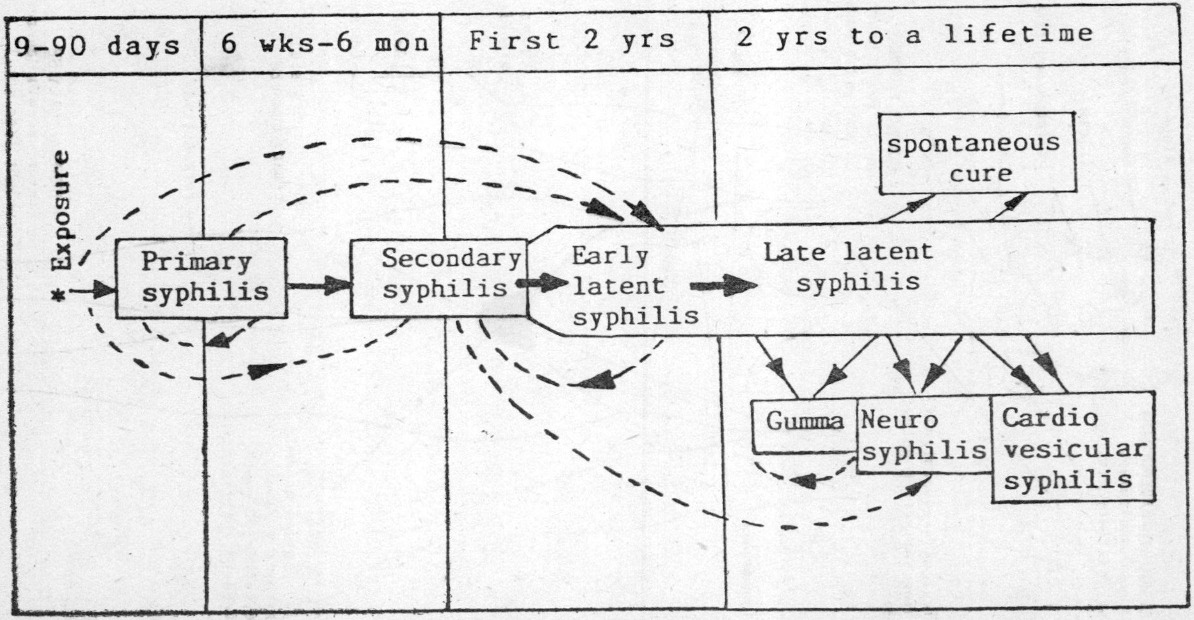

Fig. 3 The course of untreated syphilis (Willcox RR and Willcox Jr : venereology, 1982)

CORRECTION : Read 'Cardio vascular syphilis' in place of 'Cardio vesicular syphilis'.

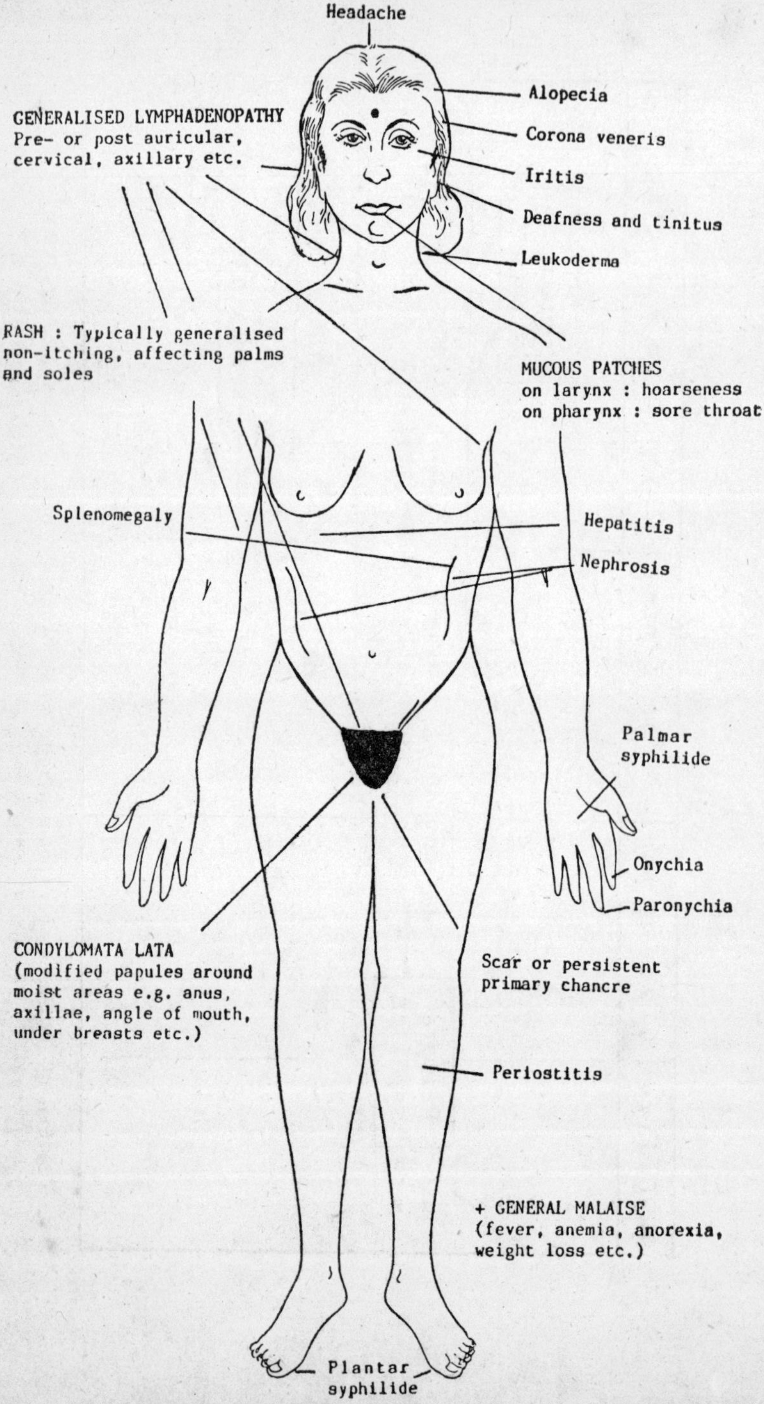

Fig.4 Manifestation of Secondary syphilis (Willcox RR and Jr : venereology, 1982)

g. The ulcer usually occurs on penis and vulva but it may occur on anus or rectum in homosexuals. It may occur on lips or breasts in case of oro-genital sex.

iii. The regional lymphnodes may be involved and have the following characteristics.

(a) Painless (b) Non-tender (c) Rubbery in consistency (d) Discrete (e) Only moderately enlarged.

9. Laboratory investigations

i. Identification of Treponema pallidum by the dark ground microscopy.

ii. If the patient has been applying antiseptics and if it is important to establish the diagnosis as soon as possible, lymphnode puncture may be undertaken. The fluid obtained is examined by the dark-ground method.

iii. Blood should always be taken for serological tests e.g. VDRL (Venereal Disease Reasearch Laboratory) test and TPHA (Treponema Pallidum Hemaglutation Assay)

10. Secondary acquired syphilis

The disease is obviously systemic in the secondary stage. Often there are prodromal features like headache, general aches and pains, malaise and low-grade fever. These features may be present for 1-3 weeks before the characteristic signs develop. The **characteristic signs** are

a. Papulosquamous lesions

i. They are present more on the sides of abdomen, proximal parts of the limbs, flexor surfaces of the limbs and most characteristically the palms and soles.

ii. These lesions are usually asymptomatic.

iii. They are symmetric in distribution. (See figure in page 386).

b. Condylomata lata

In the warm moist regions of the body, which favour the growth of T. pallidum, the papulosquamous lesions become large and are called *condylomata lata*. These are present on perianal region, vulva, axillae, under pendulous breasts, on the lateral aspects of scrotum and between folds.

c. There may be patchy alopecia called the **moth-eaten alopecia.**

d. The cutaneous lesions may heal by depigmented areas. These areas may be noticeable on the skin of the back of the neck, a condition known as **collar of venus.**

e. The lymphnodes are enlarged mainly in the cervical, axillary, supracondylar and inguinal regions and these nodes are only moderately enlarged, discrete, rubbery and non-tender.

f. Mucosal ulcers affect the mucosae of the genitals, mouth, pharynx and larynx. They may coalesce to form the so-called **snail-track ulcers.** Laryngeal involvement leads to hoarseness of voice.

g. In about 10% cases, there will be involvements of viscera, bones, eyes and central nervous system and present with hepatosplenomegaly, osteoperiostitis, choroidoretinitis and low-grade meningitis respectively.

h. Investigations

i. Demonstration of Treponema pallidum from moist lesions by dark-ground microscopy.

ii. Serological tests e.g., VDRL, TPHA, TPI, FTA, FTA-ABS (TPI=Treponema Pallidum Immobilization test, FTA=Fluorescent Treponemal Antibody test, AFT-ABS= Fluorescent Treponemal Antibody Absorption test).

11. Tertiary syphilis

a. If not diagnosed or treated earlier, a patient may develop, after the primary stage, tertiary syphilis within 3-10 years or more.

b. The **characteristic lesion** of this stage is gumma which is usually localised and may be single or multiple. It involves skin, mucosa, subcutaneous and submucosal tissues, bones, occasionally joints and ligaments.

c. The **diagnosis** rests on history, clinical findings, results of serological tests, radiographs and biopsy, if necessary.

12. Cardiovascular syphilis

a. It may appear after a latent period of 10-20 years or more in about 10% of untreated syphilitic patients.

b. Men are affected more than women.

c. The patients usually have ascending aortitis which cannot be detected clinically in uncomplicated cases. It may be complicated by

i. Coronory ostial stenosis leading to symptoms of coronary insufficiency.

ii. Aneurysm presenting in various ways according to sites involved.

iii. Aortic regurgitation which is often asymptomatic.

13. Neurosyphilis

a. It may appear after a latent period of 10-30 years or more in about 10% of untreated syphilitic patients.

b. Men are affected more than women.

c. It may be asymptomatic and may be present as meningovascular syphilis or parenchymatous syphilis.

d. Parenchymatous syphilis is called *general paralysis of insane* when it affects brain and *tabes dorsalis* when it affects spinal cord.

14. Congenital syphilis

a. Syphilis can be transmitted from the mother to the fetus via the placenta after 12-16 weeks of pregnancy. The possibility of transmission usually remains high in the first 2-4 years.

b. If the syphilitic mother is not treated, the following may be the consequences.

i. Still-born baby.

ii. The child may not get infection.

iii. Miscarriage—usually after 13-16 weeks of pregnancy.

iv. The child may get signs of early congenital syphilis.

v. The child may get signs of late congenital syphilis.

c. The placenta is bulky, heavy, pale and greasy.

d. **Clinical features of early congenital syphilis**

i. Maculopapular, bullous and polymorphic rashes over the body, around mouth, anogenital regions, palms and soles. The lesions around mouth heals with radiating scars called *rhagades.*

ii. Nasal discharge and obstructed breathing are often the first sign. It is also called *snuffles* and is due to syphilitic rhinitis. Moist papules and condylomata lata are found around anus, mouth or umbilicus.

iii. Marasmus, *senile facies*, cafe-au-lait colour, anemia, failure to thrive or reduced birth weight, intercurrent infection are the general features of congenital syphilis.

iv. There will be generalised lymphadenitis.

v. Among the bone lesions—osteochondritis, Parrots' pseudoparalysis, osteitis, periostitis and dactylitis are rather common.

vi. There may be syphilitic cirrhosis with hepatomegaly and ascitis. Splenomagaly and pneumonia alba may also be the presenting sign. Nephritis is rare.

vii. Asymptomatic neurosyphilis, syphilitic meningitis, hydrocephalus and convulsion are the presenting features of central nervous system affection.

viii. The eyes may be affected and may result in iritis and choroido-retinitis.

ix. **Investigations**

(a) Identification of Treponema pallidum by dark ground microscopy in material from the skin, mucosa and umbilical scrappings.

(b) Serological tests e.g. VDRL and TPHA will become positive by the time visible signs of syphilis appear (usually 6 weeks).

(c) X-ray examinations of long bones may reveal the following signs.

1. **Epiphysitis** i.e. jagged 'saw-toothed' appearance at the junction of the distal metaphysis and epiphysis in the temporary zone of calcification.

2. **Periostitis** will manifest in x-ray as double line on the surface of cortex.

3. **Osteitis** manifests as osteolytic lesion on the medial side of upper end of tibia and is called **Wimberger's sign.**

e. Clinical features of late congenital syphilis

i. Radiating scars called *rhagades* around mouth result from healing of infantile mucocutaneous lesions.

ii. Prominent facial bones, facial asymmetry and the depression of nasal bridge result from defective development of nasal bones and maxilla.

iii. Notched incisors called *Hutchinson's teeth* and *Moon's mulberry molars* having rounded cusps.

iv. Interstitial keratitis, iritis and choroiditis.

v. Eight nerve deafness. **vi.** Syphilitic aortitis.

vii. Gumma of nasal septum with perforation and the collapse of the bridge of nose.

viii. *Sabre tibia* marked with anterior convexity.

ix. *Clutton's joints* showing hydroarthosis of the knees.

x. Meningovascular syphilis, juvenile paresis with mental deterioration, juvenile tabes dorsalis, taboparesis.

TREATMENT

PENICILLIN	TETRACYCLINE
ERYTHROMYCIN	DOXYCYCLINE

1. Early syphilis i.e. primary, secondary and early latent.

a. Benzathine penicillin 2.4 mega-units deep intramuscularly in a single sitting.

b. Aqueous procaine penicillin G intramuscularly—the total dose is 6 mega-units and it should be given daily for 10 days after dividing the total dose.

2. Late latent

a. Benzathine pencillin 7.2 mega-units deep intramuscularly in 3 divided doses once weekly.

b. Aqueous procaine penicillin G intramuscularly—the total dose in 9 mega-units and should be given daily for 15 days after dividing the total dose.

3. Cardiovascular syphilis and neurosyphilis

Aqueous procaine penicillin G intramuscularly—the total dose is 12 mega-units and should be given once daily for 20 days after dividing the total dose.

4. Early congenital syphilis

a. Aqueous procaine pencillin 50,000 units per kg of body weight intramuscularly daily for 10 to 15 days.

b. Benzyl penicillin 50,000 units per kg of body weight intramuscularly daily for 10 days.

5. Late congenital syphilis

Aqueous procaine penicillin or benzyl penicillin 50,000 units per kg of body weight intramuscularly daily for 15 to 20 days or more.

6. Patients who are hypersensitive to penicillin

a. Tetracycline : (contra-indicated in children under 8 years of age) 500 mg, orally, q. i. d. for 15 days. It is to be taken in empty stomach.

b. Erythromycin : 500 mg, orally, q. i. d. for 15 days. It can be given to pregnant woman but it cannot cross the placental barrier. Hence the baby should be treated with penicillin at birth.

c. Doxycyline : 100 mg, b.i.d for 30 days.

d. Minocyline : 100 mg, b.i.d for 2 weeks.

7. Jarish-Herxheimer reaction

The patient with early infectious syphilis is most vulnerable to have this reaction. It is **characterised by** transient fever, flu-like symptoms of malaise, chills, headaches and myalgia. Usually, it appears within hours after treatment and subsides within 24 hours. Most reactions can be managed by **bed rest** and **aspirin.**

8. Penicillin anaphylaxis

It may occur immediately or be delayed up to 30 minutes or longer. It is **characterised by** urticaria, generalised itching, wheezing, dyspnea, itching of the eyes, nausea and vomiting, laryngeal edema, bronchospasm and cardiovascular collapse.

Treatment of choice of all manifestations of anaphylaxis is **epinephrine.**

DISCUSSION

Syphilis is a chronic infectious disease caused by Treponema pallidum. It is systemic from the very beginning. After exposure, the organisms are rapidly carried to the regional lymphnodes.

After an incubation period of 9-90 days, primary chancre develops at the site of entry. Painless enlargement of regional lymphnodes follows primary chancre which is also painless, non-tender and usually single.

Secondary syphilis appears usually after 1-6 months. History of exposure, remnant scar over genitals or continuation of the primary chancre, generalised maculo-papular and papulo-squamous lesions, generalised lymphadenitis and the mucocutaneous lesions are characteristics of this stage. In this stage, patients always exhibit positive serum reactions.

A period of latency comes within weeks or months, if the secondary stage remains untreated. Treponema pallidum lie dormant in the lymphnodes without any physical sign. In about 25% patients, secondary relapses may occur during the following 2-4 years. The patients will have cutaneous and mucocutaneous lesions.

Of latent syphilis, about 30% cases are spontaneously cured while in another 30% the latency persists throughout life.

In about 40% cases of untreated syphilis, late syphilis follows. This stage is characterised by gumma in about one third of cases. In the rest two-third of patients, cardiovascular and neurosyphilis may develop.

Treatment is by penicillin, either benzathine penicillin or aqueous procaine penicillin G. In patients who are hypersensitive to penicillin, either tetracycline or erythromycin is given. In children under 8 years of age, tetracycline is contra-indicated.

Treatment failures may occur with any of the recommended schedules. Hence follow up cardiolipin tests at 3, 6 and 12 months are mandatory. It is more important in patients treated with antibiotics other than penicillin. The possibility of re-infection should be kept in mind if patients with early syphilis need be treated a second time.

SYSTEMIC LUPUS ERYTHEMATOSUS (SLE)

DIAGNOSIS

1. **Criteria** for the diagnosis of systemic lupus erythematosus (American Rheumatism Association 1982 revision) are as follow :

i. Malar rash **ii.** Discoid lupus erythematosus lesions **iii.** Photosensitivity–by history or by observation **iv.** Oral ulcers—usually painless observed by physician **v.** Arthritis—non-erosive, involving two or more joints **vi.** Serositis, pleuritis or pericarditis **vii.** Renal disorder—proteinuria (500 mg/day) or cellular casts **viii.** Central nervous system disorder–seizures or psychosis (absence of known cause), **ix.** Hematologic disorder–hemolytic anemia, leukopenia ($< 4{,}000/mm^3$), lymphopenia ($< 1{,}400/mm^3$) or thrombocytopenia ($< 100{,}000/mm^3$) **x.** Immunologic disorder – LE cells, abnormal titer of anti-native DNA and anti-Sm, false positive VDRL **xi.** Antinuclear antibody.

If **four** or **more criteria** are present serially or simultaneously during any period of observation, the patient is said to have systemic lupus erythematosus.

2. **Sex ratio** (female : male) is 8 : 1.

3. In 4-5% cases, family history of SLE may be found. Family history of DLE, rheumatoid arthritis, rheumatic fever, polyarteritis nodosa, dermatomyosites or poikiloderma atrophicans vasculare may also be present.

4. **Precipitating factors**

i. Drugs : hydralazine, diphenyl hydantoin, procainamide, co-trimoxazole, griseofulvin, INH, methyldopa, oral contraceptive, PAS, penicillin, penicillamine, and streptomycin.

ii. Ultraviolet light (Sun) exposure. **iii.** Bacterial infection. **iv.** Physical and/or mental stress. **v.** Trauma.

5. **Symptoms**

i. Fever **ii.** Joint pain and/or swelling **iii.** Skin lesion **iv.** Loss of weight **v.** Anorexia **vi.** Malaise **vii.** Raynaud's

i. Eye changes

i. Blurring of disc margin **ii.** Central exudate **iii.** Venous congestion **iv.** Retinal cytoid bodies **v.** Superficial retinal hemorrhage.

j. Mascular changes

i. Calcinosis within muscles **ii.** Myopathy **iii.** Rupture of extensor tendons.

k. Bone changes : Avascular bone necrosis.

l. Lymphoreticular system

i. Lymphadenopathy in 50% cases **ii.** Splenomegaly.

m. Miscellaneous

i. Calcinosis **ii.** Swelling of parotid, submaxillary and lacrimal glands **iii.** Features of classical Sjogren's syndrome.

7. Laboratory diagnosis

i. Hemolytic anemia and raised ESR **ii.** Leukopenia **iii.** Thrombocytopenia **iv.** LE cell phenomenon (83%) **v.** Antinuclear antibody (87%) **vi.** Antinative DNA antibody is highly indicative **vii.** Anti-single stranded DNA (ss DNA) antibody **viii.** anti-RO (SSA) antibody **ix.** Anti-Sm antibody.

x. Anti-riboneucleoprotein (RNP) antibody.

Chances of finding a ANA varies in different autoimmune disorders e.g. SLE (95%), Rheumatoid arthritis (25%), Juvenile rheumatoid arthritis (20%,) Sjogren's syndrome (50%), Scleroderma (60%), Dermatomyositis or polymyositis (less than 10%), Polyarthritis nodosa (less than 10%) and Myasthenia gravis (40%).

xi. Anti-histone antibody—associated with drug induced lupus erythematosus.

xii. Urine (in renal involvement)—cellular cast, protinuria

xiii. Immunofluorescence—deposits of immunoglobulins and complements c_3, c_4 and clq at the dermo-epidermal junction.

TREATMENT

PREDNISOLONE	CHLORUMBUCIL
CYCLOPHOSPHAMIDE	AZATHIOPRINE

1. Bed rest.

2. Undue **exposure in the sun** should be avoided.

3. **Mental stress,** physical over-exertion and secondary infection are to be avoided.

4. **Anemia** must be corrected.

5. **Dapsone** is helpful in urticarial lesions.

6. **Diuretics** are indicated in nephrotic syndrome and cardiac failure.

7. Anticonvulsants are to be given for epilepsy.

8. **Chlorpromazine** can be given as sedative for psychosis.

9. **Aspirin** is useful in patients particularly with joint manifestation. **Indomethacin** may also be tried.

10. **Corticosteroids** are required in acute cases in adequate dosage. **Prednisolone**, 60-120 mg per day is the **steroid of choice** initially. Once the condition comes under control, the dose may be reduced gradually until a maintenance dose of about 5-15 mg per day is reached. Prolonged high dosage of corticosteroid for example, 60 mg of prednisolone daily for 6 months, is said to improve the renal lesions more than small suppressive doses.

11. The administration of **chloroquine** or **hydroxychloroquine** may allow the dose of steroids to be reduced but antimalarials are less useful than in DLE and for long term therapy may be dangerous.

12. Immunosuppressive drugs have been used for patients not respondiug to corticosteroids, but their value remains unproved.

a. **Azathioprine** is often added to reduce the high dose of prednisolone in the treatment of mild to moderate renal disease. Dose : 100 mg per day.

SYSTEMIC SCLEROSIS

It is a generalised disease of connective tissue involving mainly the skin, the gastro-intestinal tract, the lungs, the heart and the kidneys.

DIAGNOSIS

From clinical point of view, systemic sclerosis represents a spectrum of different disease entities. They range from localised scleroderma, passing through acrosclerosis, to the ill-defined group of overlap syndromes such as mixed connective tissue disease. Here the main features of classical systemic sclerosis only would be discussed in brief.

1. Epidemiology

a. Compared to other connective tissue diseases, systemic sclerosis is relatively rare.

b. Female to male ratio is 3 : 1.

c. It is seen more in coloured people.

d. Average entry age is 30 to 39 years ; only 10% patients develop the disease before the age of 20.

e. Systemic sclerosis affecting families, including cases in siblings, parents and child and second degree relatives, is rare.

f. HLA antigens which have been found to be associated with diffuse scleroderma are A_1, B_8 DR_5 and DR_3 ; and also in CREST syndrome (having calcinosis, Raynaud's disease, esophageal dysmotility, sclerodactyly and telangiectasia) DR_1, DR_5 and anticentromere antibodies are often present.

g. A strong genetic background is suspected among polyvinyl chloride workers developing scleroderma-like disease.

h. Chromosomal instability has been suggested and a certain genotype may have a predisposition for the development of systemic sclerosis.

2. Classification

a. Taking 'scleroderma' as a broad term it may be classified as

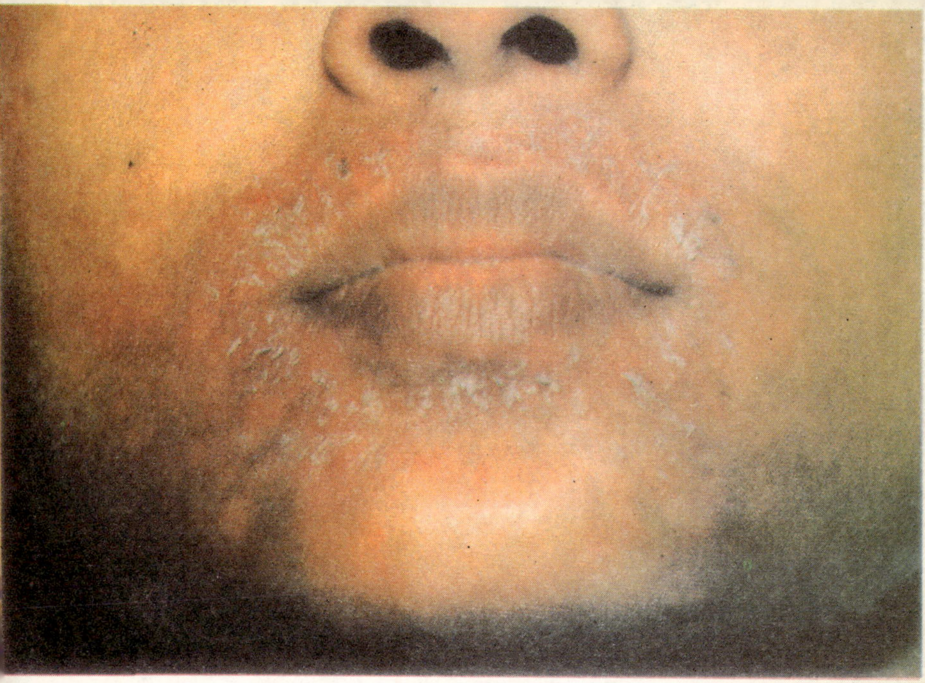

Fig. S-1. **Perioral Dermatitis.**

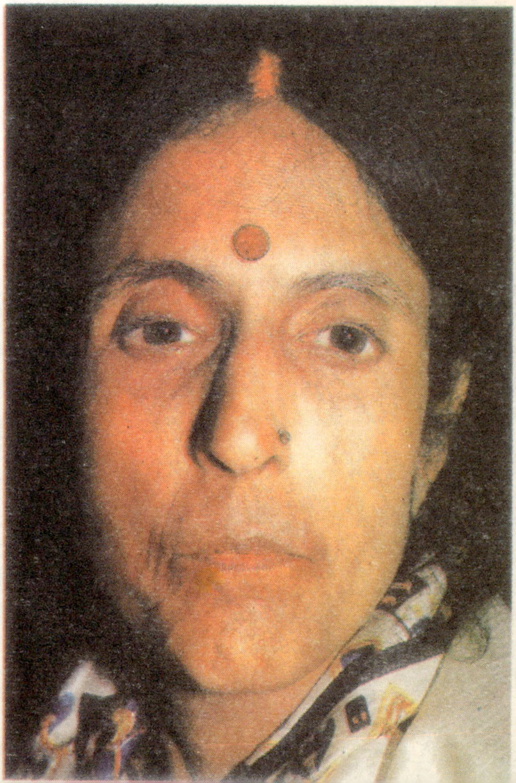

Fig. S-2. **Systemic Sclerosis** showing typical facies having beaked nose and furrowing around the lips.

i. **Systemic** : 1. Acrosclerosis 2. Acroscleroderma with ascending sclerosis 3. Diffuse scleroderma.

ii. **Localised.** iii. **Overlap** syndromes

b. Other diseases having some features of scleroderma are

i. Morphea **ii.** Scleredema of Buschke **iii.** Mixed connective tissue disease **iv.** Shulmans syndrome and **v.** Shoulder-hand syndrome.

vi. Pseudoscleroderma : 1. Porphyria cutanea tarda. 2. Polyvinylchloride disease. 3. Toxic Oil syndrome. 4. Scleromyxedema. 5. Werner's syndrome.

c. **Criteria of Scleroderma**

i. **Major** criterion : Proximal scleroderma.

ii. **Minor** criteria : 1. Sclerodactyly. 2. Pulmonary fibrosis. 3. Digital pitting scars.

d. **Miscellaneous classification**

i. By **Jablonska** : 1. Acroscleroderma 2. Diffuse scleroderma 3. Thibierge-Weissenbach syndrome 4. CREST syndrome 5. Visceral scleroderma without any cutaneous involvement.

ii. By **Winkelmann** : 1. Vascular scleroderma 2. Inflammatory scleroderma.

iii. By **Barnett** : Type I, II and III according to early stage skin involvement.

iv. By **Rodnan** et al : 1. CREST synrdome 2. Diffuse scleroderma 3. Overlap syndrome.

v. By **Giordano** et al :

1. Sclerosis sine scleroderma 2. Sclerodactyly 3. Acrosclerosis strictu sensu 4. Intermediate syndrome 5. Acute diffuse scleroderma.

None of the classifications however is entirely satisfactory. This is therefore a very heterogenous disease with a large variation in clinical manifestations among the patients.

3. Clinical features

A. Cutaneous manifestations

a. Raynaud's syndrome is usually an early symptom.

b. Early edematous phase : Skin is thickened, edematous and often shows a slight erythema indicating inflammation. It starts at acral areas and first involves the fingers and the hands, later the face and often the frenulum of the tongue. The fingers and hands appear swollen with nonpitting edema, becoming tumid and cannot be fully extended.

c. Next, sclerosis develops causing hardening of the skin followed by ulcerations, telangiectasis and atrophy. By the surrouning fibrosis there are loss of hairs and other appendages causing **anhidrosis.**

d. Later there may be painful ulcers developing around the fingertips, in areas underlying calcinosis and over the knuckles. Secondary infection may lead to gangrene. There might be osseous resorption with severe articular deformities or even complete dissolution of terminal phalanges.

Involvement of feet may be similar but it is less frequent.

Sclerosis of face results in **typical facies.** There are beaked nose, radial furrowing around the lips and constricted opening of the mouth.

Telangiectasia may develop at face, trunk and periungual areas. CREST syndrome (Calcinosis cutis, Raynaud's phenomenon, Esophageal involvement, Sclerodactyle and Telangiectasia) may also develop.

In some patients sclerosis remains confined to acral areas for several years. In others, it may gradually involve arms, upper part of legs, trunk and may be the whole body. Rarely, sclerosis might start at the trunk first and then quickly spreads to the periphery. These patients suffer from severe internal manifestations and have poor prognosis.

e. Pigmentary changes : Along with sclerotic changes, marked changes in pigmentation may develop either with

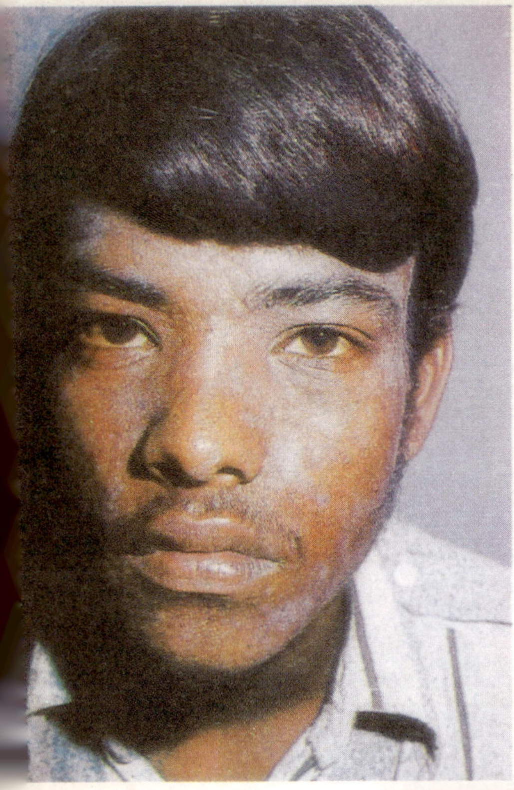

Fig. S-3. **Seborrheic Dermatitis** showing inflammatory dermatitis with scaling.

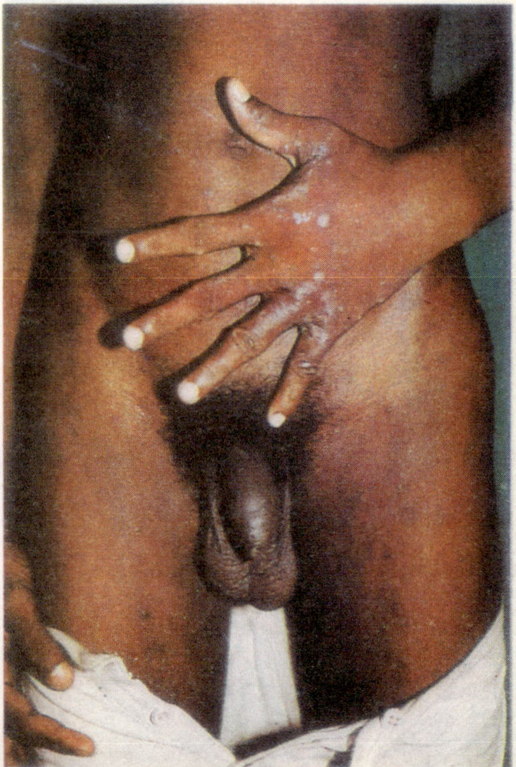

Fig. S-4. **Scabies** showing puritic papules and vesico-pustules at the webs of fingers and genitalia.

mottled or diffuse hyperpigmentation that resembles Addison's disease or with focal hypopigmentation due probably to post inflammatory changes. There may be guttate hypomelanosis.

f. Histopathology

i. Early stage

a. Mild cellular infiltrates consisting of lymphocytes, monocytes and histiocytes are present mainly in the vicinity of small blood vessels and at the interface between the dermis and the subcutaneous tissue.

b. Deposition of hyalinised collagen in reticular dermis around blood vessels.

c. There may be edema in the upper dermis.

ii. Late stage

a. The infiltrates gradually reduce in number or disappear completely.

b. Sclerotic, homogeneous or hyalinised bundles of collagen extend from reticular dermis into the subcutaneous tissue. They are thickened, closely packed and stain more eosinophilic. Eccrine glands are atrophic, as they are entrapped by these collagen fibres and seen higher up in dermis due to the deposition of collagen in subcutaneous fat.

c. Dermal vessels show thickening and hyalinisation of vessel walls.

B. Involvement of other organs

a. Esophagus and gastrointestinal tract

i. There are hypomotiltty of esophagus, peptic esophagitis and later on fibrotic stricture. These can be diagnosed by radiography and highly sensitive scintigraphic procedures.

ii. Hypomotility may affect lower part of gastrointestinal tract leading to chronic constipation. Decreased anorectal motility may lead to rectal prolapse.

iii. Megacolon, transverse and sigmoid colonic volvulus, stenosis and diverticular ulcerations may be present.

iv. Small bowel stagnation may lead to an altered bacterial growth causing malabsorption syndrome.

v. Multiple telangiectasis in the upper part of the gastrointestinal tract can cause severe bleeding.

b. Liver and pancreas

i. Altered liver functions are secondary to right ventricular heart disease.

ii. Nodular regenerative hyperplasia.

iii. Idiopathic portal hypertension.

iv. Primary billiary cirrhosis.

v. Involvement of pancreas is relatively rare.

c. Heart

In 80% of patients heart has been found to be involved at autopsy. Clinically, however, the affection is often overlooked. Improved techniques of myocardial perfusion scintigraphy, ventriculography and echocardiography can detect early myocardial abnormality which are

i. Myocardial fibrosis **ii.** Pericarditis **iii.** Contraction band necrosis **iv.** Conduction system fibrosis **v.** Intramural coronary artery lesions and **vi.** Vascular disease.

They usually indicate poor prognosis and can result in congestive heart failure, myocardial infarction and sudden death. Symptons may be chest pain, dyspnea, syncope and angina pectoris. They are probably caused by either endothelial damage of small coronary arteries or myocardial fibrosis.

d. Lungs

Functional tests, x-rays, scintigraphy and the bronchoalveolar lavage have thrown new lights on lung pathology. Generally, they are as follow :

i. Reduced respiratory volume and impaired diffusion capacity are due to restrictive changes.

ii. Obstructive changes involving both large and small airways may be present.

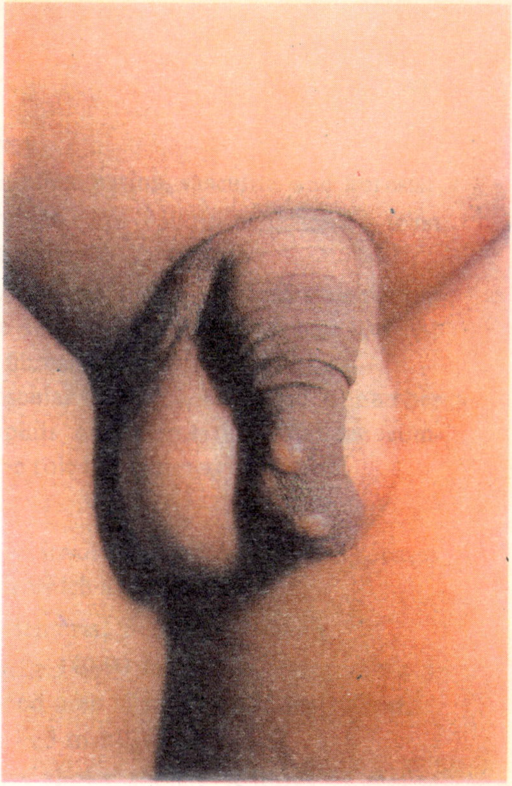

Fig. S-5. **Scabies** showing persistent nodules of the genitalia.

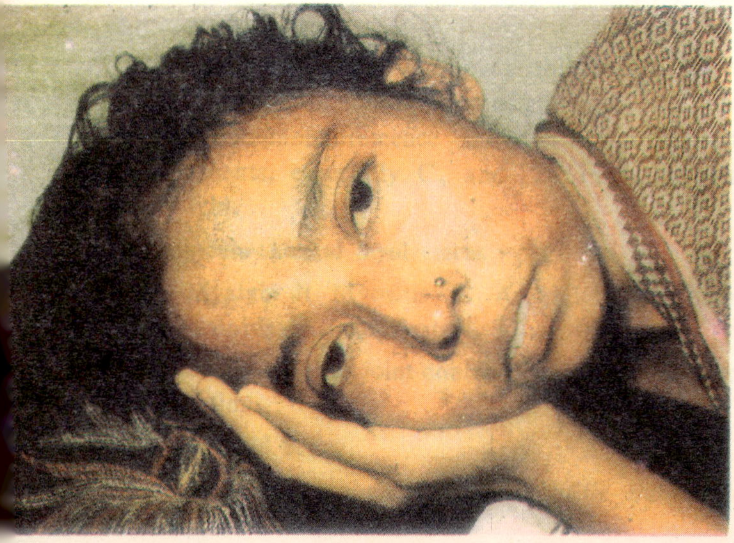

S-6. **SLE** showing pigmentation of face. Patient is pale and looks sick.

i. Pain and inflammation in joints of fingers, wrists, knees and ankles. There may be synovial effusion.

ii. Contractures due to surrounding sclerotic changes.

iii. Non-erosive hand deformity.

iv. X-rays show resorption of the tufts of the terminal phalanges, juxta-articular osteoporosis, peri-articular bone erosion and joint space narrowing. Osteolysis can also occur at feet, ribs and mandible.

v. There may be coexistence of true rheumatoid arthritis and scleroderma.

vi. Peri-articular subcutaneous calcification can occur around the iliac crest, spine protuberances, knees and elbows and may be complicated by painful ulcerations and superficial deposits.

vii. Fibrotic changes in juxta-articular tendons of the forearms, legs, fingers and neck may cause audible friction rubs.

viii. Fibrosis of tendons can cause peripheral entrapment neuropathy and carpal tunnel syndrome.

E. Sjogren's syndrome and polymyositis

i. In 5% cases Sjogren's syndrome may be present.

ii. Polymyositis with muscle wasting and weakness frequently involving proximal muscles e.g. pectoral girdle, the forearm flexors and small muscles of the hands has been reported.

iii. Myositic changes are evident by elevation of serum creatine, creatinuria and electromyographic changes e.g. (1) decrease of amplitude and duration of single potentials (2) concomitant increase of polyphasic potentials.

4. Laboratory investigations

A. Autoantibodies

a. By indirect immunofluorescence, using tissue culture cells such as human laryngeal tumour cells (HEp-2) as sub-

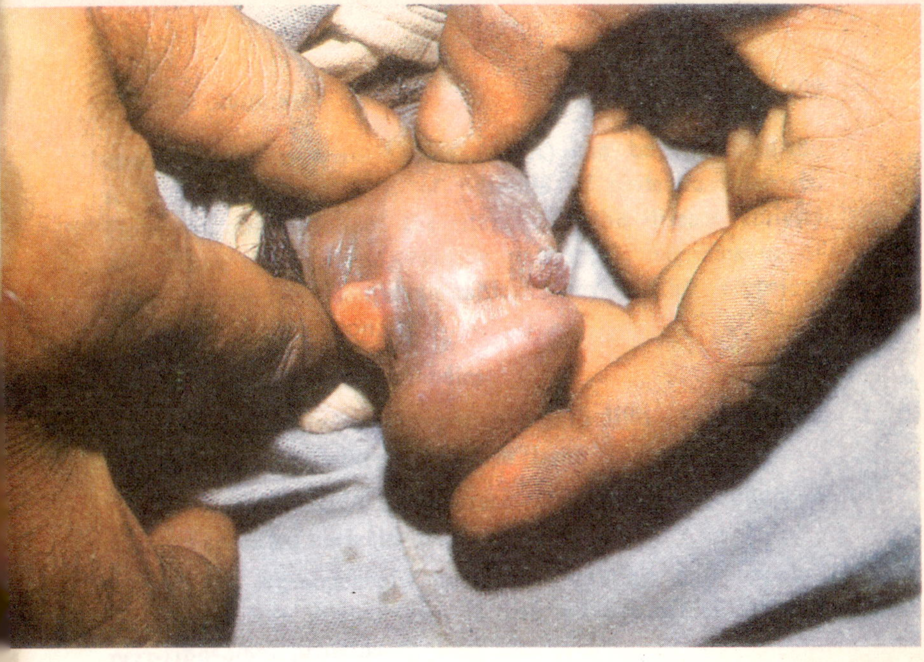

Fig. S-7. **Syphilis** showing primary chancre. It is a non-tender, rounded, indurated, well-defined ulcer. A lesion of condyloma accuminatum is also seen.

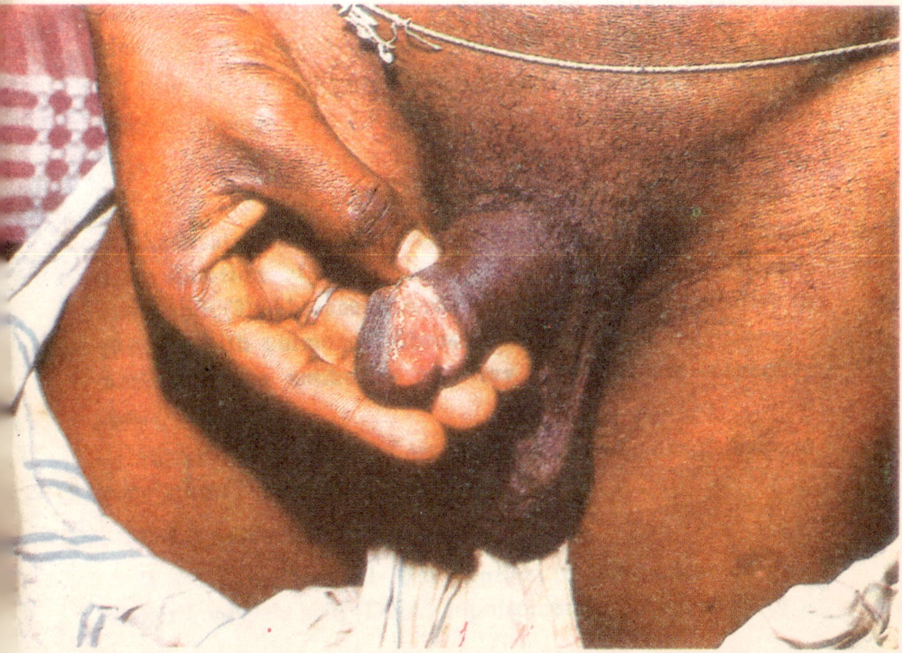

S-8. **Syphilis** showing a big primary chancre. There is a painless, non-tender, well-defined ulcer.

bably functioning in the control of chromosomal supercoiling during the cell cycle. By immunodiffusion, antibodies to scl-70 can be detected in about 20-30% of sera from patients with scleroderma. Scl-70 antibodies are highly specific for systemic scleroderma and rarely found in polymyositis or Raynaud's syndrome. They are more present in diffuse scleroderma ; about 60%. Presence of both scl-70 antibodies and anticentromere antibodies in one patient is extremely rare. Scl-70 positive sera may contain other antinuclear and antinucleolar antibodies.

5. Pathogenesis

It is still poorly understood. We only know that final result is the development of fibrosis in the involved tissue. Several factors are probably involved.

A. Role of vessel wall

a. Gaps between endothelial cells are seen in capillaries of the scleroderma skin. The endothelial cells show granular degenerations of the nucleus and there are multiple vacuoles.

b. There is reduplication of the basal lamina of the capillaries followed by disruption of the endothelial cells and obstruction of the vessel lumina.

c. Constitutents of the protein components to the basement membrane outlying the vessels are probably altered. The main constitutents are : (1) type IV collagen (2) laminin (3) nidogen entactin and (4) heparin sulphate proteoglycan. Probably the metabolism of these proteins are altered in scleroderma. Autoantibodies directed against type IV collagen have been found.

d. An endothelial cell cytotoxic activity has been detected in serum of scleroderma patients.

e. Damage of endothelial cells often leads to platelet aggregation and there is enhanced platelet adhesion to collagen. Platelets have large number of active mediators which can modulate functions of fibroblasts. Hence the endothe-

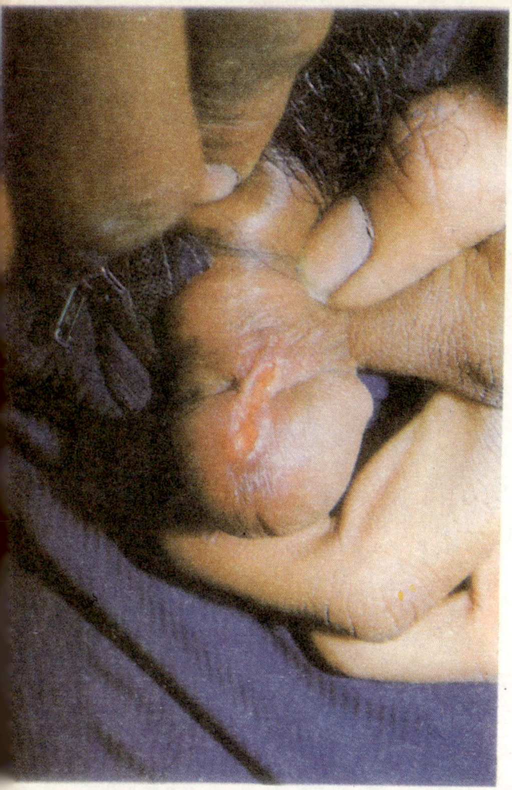

Fig. S-9. **Syphilis** showing kissing primary chancre.

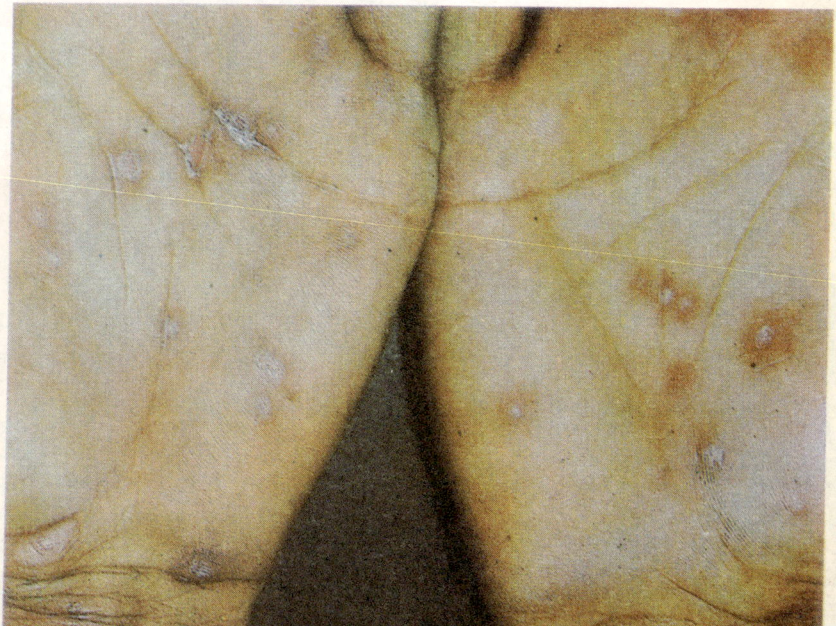

Fig. S-10. **Secondary syphilis** showing papulo-squamous lesions of palms.

lial cell damage probably represents a key event in the development of the fibrotic reaction.

f. Mononuclear cells come out of the damaged vessel. The breakdown products of type IV collagen can activate circulating cells to liberate highly potent mediators which can easily diffuse through defective basement membrane into the surrounding tissue inducing fibroblastic activity.

B. Role of immune system

a. Presence of lymphohistiocytic infiltration around the blood vessels.

b. Presence of autoantibodies against the cellular and nuclear antigens.

c. Presence of lymphopenia mainly affecting the T-cell population. An elevated ratio of T4/T8 lymphocytes has been found in scleroderma. T 8 cells are reduced in number.

d. There is increased B-cell activity due probably to augmented T-helper cell function. T-supressor cells are normal.

e. Interleukin I present in activated mononuclear cell supernatants has the potentiality to modulate fibroblast metabolism.

It appears that a complex mechanism is working behind the scene having different stimulatory and inhibitory substances in controlling the immunologic activity.

C. Role of connective tissue metabolism

a. Certain growth factors have effect on distinct fibroblast subpopulations.

b. There is a chemotactic activity leading to invasion of fibroblasts into the injured tissue.

c. There is specific activation of collagen synthesis.

As a whole, there is activation of connective tissue metabolism in scleroderma.

d. Fibroblasts are not homogeneous ; they rather represent a broad class of mesenchymal cells with distinct features.

Tendon fibroblasts differ from skin fibroblasts. In scleroderma, distinct populations of fibroblasts that differ in their collagen biosynthesis can be obtained. A particular clone of fibroblasts may be preferentially stimulated to produce a high amount of collagen in scleroderma.

e. Fibroblast chemotactic factors

Accumulation of fibroblasts in sclerosis probably plays a great role in fibrotic processes. Growth promoting factors of fibroblasts are : (1) fibronectin (2) collagen fragments (3) collagens (4) platelet derived growth factor and (5) eicosanoids. Further activation of complement system leads to the generation of C5a fragment which also attracts fibroblasts. Various cells that produce growth promoting factors accumulate in scleroderma and might initiate a distinct population of fibroblasts to overactivity.

f. Role of extracellular matrix

The most important feature in scleroderma is the excessive deposition of connective tissue, mainly collagen, in the affected organs. Connective tissue is composed of (1) collagen, (2) fibronectin, (3) proteoglycans and other substances. Chemical analysis of proteoglycans of sclerodermatous skin reveals divergent results. There are increases in dermatan sulphate and chodroitin sulphate. There is a high local accumulation of proteoglycans in the interfibrillar matrix around the irregularly arranged collagen fibrils. There is enhanced biosynthesis of collagen I and III in scleroderma. Proline hydroxylase activity is also increased. There is also an increase of circulating type III collagen propeptides and the level of aminopropeptides correlates well with the fibrotic activity.

Procollagen is synthesized and secreted by fibroblasts. The enzymatically controlled cleavage of the aminoterminal procollagen peptide occurs in the extracellular space. Free aminoterminal peptides are then taken up by the cells and can act as feed back inhibitors. Probably there is some defect in this feedback control of collagen biosynthesis in the sclerodermatous process.

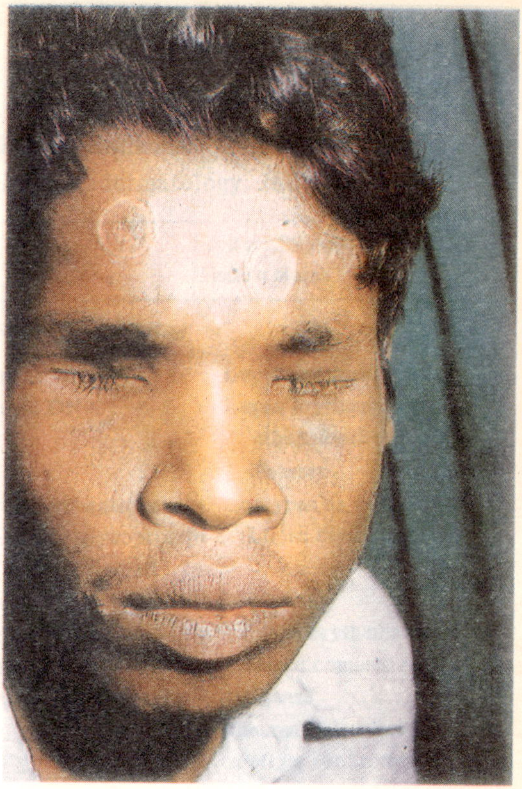

Fig. S-11. **Secondary Syphilis** showing annular lesions at the forehead.

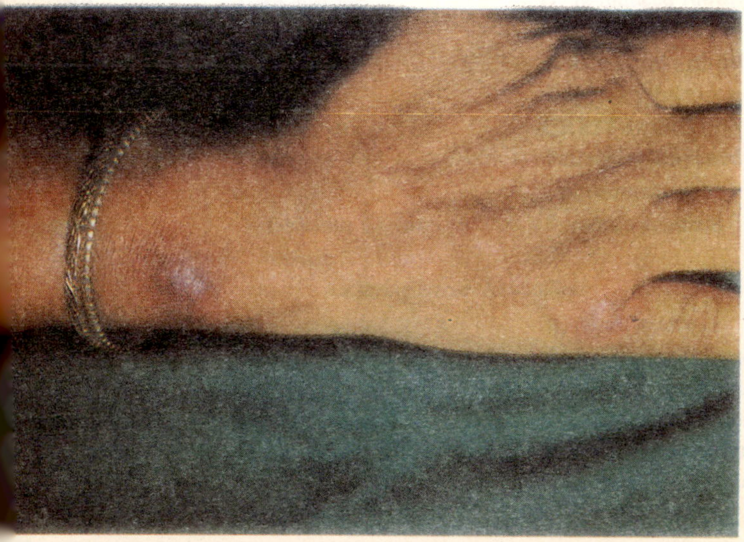

S-12. **Sporotrichosis** showing non-tender nodules of cutaneous lymphatic variety.

TREATMENT

NITROGLYCERINE OINTMENT	D-PENICILLAMINE
EMOLLIENTS	DILANTIN
NIFEDIPINE	KETANSERIN
CAPTOPRIL	PRAZOSIN
AZATHIOPRINE	ESTRIOL
STANOZOLOL	PHYSIOTHERAPY

1. General treatment

As specific treatment for systemic selerosis is yet to be available, all efforts should be made to improve the quality of life of the sufferers. These can be achieved by the following general measures.

a. Regular scientific physical therapy by qualified physiotherapists.

b. Positive nutritional support should be arranged in patients with gastrointestinal involvement.

c. Avoidance of cold climates.

d. Avoidance of cutaneous trauma. If minute trauma causes ulceration, application of nitroglycerine ointment or silver sulphadiazine is good.

e. Avoidance of nicotine and ergot alkaloids which might cause vasospasm.

f. Warm paraffin baths for hands.

2. Vasoactive agents

These include (1) Fibrinolytic enzymes (2) Plasma expanders (3) Prostacyclin (4) Calcium channel blockers (nifedipine) (5) Angiotensin-converting enzyme inhibitor (captopril) (6) Serotonin receptor blocker (ketanserin). Some of these are detailed below.

a. Nifedipine : 20 mg t.i.d. has positive effect proved by double blind control studies. Dose varies according to the severity. Prazosin (Minipress) 4 mg t.i.d is a good alternative.

b. Captopril is effective in patients with renal involvement. It is an enzyme inhibitor that reduces formation of the vasoconstrictor angiotensin.

c. Ketanserin is used in Raynaud's phenomenon.

d. Drugs which reduce platelet adhesiveness might be helpful in some patients.

e. **Tolazoline** : 30 to 60 mg/day.

3. Anti-inflammatory agents or immunosuppressive agents

Inflammation is often a major part in sclerosis. Hence anti-inflammatory agents are often used in the treatment. These are (1) corticosteroids (2) azathioprine, 100 to 200 mg daily for 1-5 months (3) cyclophosphamide (4) cyclosporine (5) plasmapharesis (6) chlorambucil 0.1 mg/kg/day for one to five months.

These are mainly used in patients with myositis, serositis or arthritis and interstitial lung disease. However, survival rate could not be improved by these agents.

Role of steroid is highly controversial. It often improves the well being of the patient but probably in long term therapy the damage outweighs the benefits.

4. Nonsteroidal antiphlogistic substances

Indomethacin : 50-75 mg/day for 1-6 months.

5. Antifibrolytic agents

Drugs which can inhibit biosynthesis of collagen are ideal but only a few potent drugs are at our disposal. These are (1) Cyclofenil (2) Proline analogs (3) Prolyl hydroxylase inhibitor (4) Procollagen peptides (5) γ-Interferon and (6) D-Penicillamine.

D-Penicillamine (cuprimine 1 g/day) in low dose for long term has been effective in reducing cutaneous involvement. It probably inhibits the cross-linkages within the collagen molecule.

Colchicine 1 mg daily for 6 months is used since this is considered to inhibit secretion of collagen.

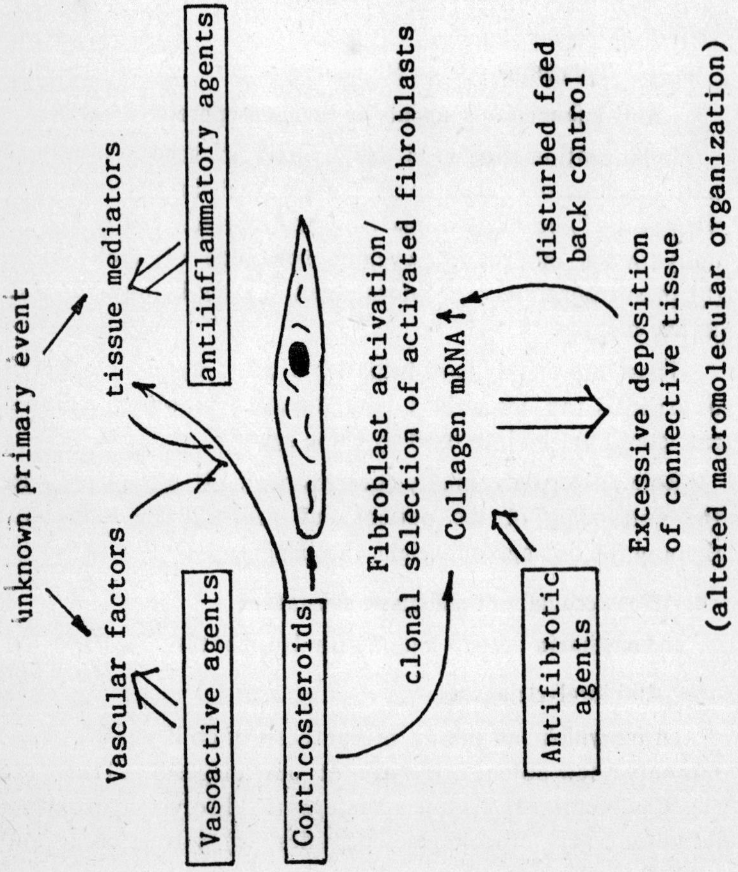

Fig. 5. Pathogenesis of scleroderma and hypothetic steps for interfering with therapeutic agents

Factor XIII inhibits collagen synthesis and improves the sclerosis.

6. Miscellaneous agents

i. Procaine penicillin.

ii. Procaine, 2% solution 4 c.c I. M. 2-3 times or even I.V. weekly for 10-12 weeks.

iii. Vitamin E, 300 mg PO or I.M. for 8-10 weeks to be repeated every 2 to 3 months.

iv. Piascledine, 50 mg daily for 6 months.

v. Di-sodium EDTA 2.5 to 3 g in 500 ml 5% dextrose, slow I.V. drip over 4 to 6 hours daily for 15 days up to 50 g. Supplementary treatment with pyridoxine 50 mg/per day and nicotinamide 200 mg/day.

vi. Epsilon-aminocaproic acid 1 to 4 g daily orally for 25 months.

vii. Low molecular weight dextran, 400 ml I.V. to a total dose of 10,000 ml.

viii. Beta-aminopropionitril 1 to 3 g daily for 6 weeks.

ix. Madecassol, 30 to 60 mg daily for several months or 2% I.M. every other day for several months.

x. Hyaluronidase, 1500 units I.V. three times weekly for five months to a total dose of 90,000 units.

xi. Para-aminobenozoic acid 12 g per day for several months.

xii. Norlestrin, 15 mg daily from days 16 to 19 of cycle to a total of 110 g in 18 months. A dose of 10-15 mg weekly may be given to men.

xiii. Relaxin, 20 mg I.M. daily for several weeks.

xiv. Chloroquin, 500 mg daily for 2 weeks, then 250 mg daily for 10 months.

xv. Phenoxybenzamine, 30-60 mg daily.

xvi. Phentolamine, 5 mg I.M. or I. V. daily or 40 mg PO b.i.d or t.i.d.

xvii. Reserpine.
xviii. Alphamethyldopa.
xix. Nicotinic acid.

} In usual dosage for specific symptoms.

xx. Griseofulvin, 500 mg daily.

xxi. Tetracycline, 250 mg q.i.d. to reduce overgrowth of bacteria in aperistaltic intestines.

xxii. Reserpine intra-arterially to dilate blood vessels.

xxiii. Topical DMSO, 46% aqueous solution; immersion of affected areas for 30 minutes q.i.d can heal ulcers.

xxiv. Prazosin hydrochloride, 1 mg t.i.d for 2 months can reduce vasospasm.

xxv. Estriol, 10 mg subcutaneously once a week for 10 months.

xxvi. Prostaglandin E_1, 6 to 10 mg/kg/min/I.V. in saline or 5% dextrose for 72 hours.

xxvii. Stanozolol, 5 mg b.i.d for 3 months.

xxviii. Ketaserin, 20 mg t.i.d for 1 week; then 40 mg t.i.d for 3 weeks.

xxix. Betablockers in ischemic heart disease.

xxx. Diphenylhydantoin, 100 mg q. i. d. for several months.

All the above mentioned drugs have been tried by various workers with equivocal results.

DIAGNOSIS

Systemic sclerosis is a generalised disorder causing fibrosis of the skin and internal organs. It is a heterogeneous disease but there is no general agreement as to its classification. Most common variety, seen in India, is acrosclerosis. Various types of autoantibodies help in classification and point to some extent to prognosis.

Pathogenesis is not well understood. However, vascular alteration e.g. defect in endothelial cell and the vessel wall are of prime importance. Chemomediators, released from platelets and mononuclear cells, deposit around the blood vessels. They activate proliferation of fibroblasts and induce connective tissue synthesis. The cleavage of the amino-peptides is altered resulting in the alteration of normal feedback control of collagen synthesis.

Management of systemic sclerosis is extremely difficult. Drugs available can only treat specific symptoms. Reversal of pathology is hardly possible. Early diagnosis is essential so that vasoactive therapy can be started early. Prednisolone and azathioprine are often used but probably cannot alter the ultimate prognosis. D-Penicillamine might be beneficial to some patients. Nifedipine is widely used in India but other vasodilators have hardly any persistent effect.

One in five patients will not survive for a period of more than five years.

TINEA VERSICOLOR (TV)

It is a superficial fungal disorder of the skin prevalent mostly in the tropics.

DIAGNOSIS

1. It is caused by Pityrosporum orbiculare.

2. Prevalence of TV may be as high as 50% in certain regions and in some ethnic groups. In India, it is frequently seen during **summer.**

3. It is mostly found in **young adults** of both sexes. However, children are not exempt from the disease. In old age it becomes rare, but records of cases affecting infants and persons older than 65 years also exist.

4. Organism is often a normal flora of the skin and the disease is caused when there is an excessive growth. Certain persons are particularly susceptible to develop the disease that depends on the physiology of the skin in respect of lipids and sebaceous activity. It is often found to be associated with cushing's syndrome.

5. **Predisposing factors** are

a. Moist hot weather. **b.** Obesity.

c. Diabetes mellitus and often endocrinopathies having high plasma cortisol.

d. Malnutrition and serious underlying disease.

e. Familial predisposition.

f. Poor personal hygiene. **g.** Pregnancy.

6. **Clinical features** are characterised by the following.

a. The lesions are perifollicular with fine scales and change in normal colour. These may merge to form scaly patches. The scales may not be obvious but scratching the lesions would show fine scaling. In India, the lesions are mostly hypopigmented. But brownish, blackish, blackish brown, pink and yellowish brown lesions are not uncommon.

b. **Sites** involved are mainly **trunk, face** and **neck.** But arms, forearms, dorsum of hands and thighs are also commonly affected. Medial sides of thighs are specially involved in children due probably to direct transfer of organisms during embracing infected adults by these parts. Palms and soles are not affected. Sebaceous sternal triangle is a very common site.

c. **Satellite lesions** and perifollicular involvement around big patches are important **clinical characteristics.** Papular lesions containing heaped up dormant scales are not uncommon. Rarely, the lesions may be acneiform.

d. Generally the lesions are **asymmetrically distributed** but wide-spread conglomerate lesions are often seen.

e. The mildly hypopigmented lesions become clinically more obvious just after a prolonged bath.

f. The lesions **fluoresce** by Wood's light. The colour may be coppery orange or bluish white.

g. Generally, TV is symptomless but there may be varying degree of itching.

7. Laboratory diagnosis

a. 15% KOH preparation of scales show bunches of short mycelia and groups of spores.

b. **Culture** is positive in Sabouraud's agar or Wort agar covered with sterile olive oil or with addition of Tween 80.

c. The **ink blue stain** shows the organisms in scales which are stable in KOH solution.

d. Using strippings of the stratum corneum with adhesive slides or scotch tape and stained with **methylene blue** would show the organism in most cases.

8. Pathophysiology

a. The hypopigmentation is caused by a product of fungus—**azaleic acid** which interferes with melanin-synthesis and probably the transfer of melanin from melanosomes to melanocyte. Azaleic acid is also directly cytotoxic to melanocytes.

b. A tyrosinase inhibitor has been isolated from the culture ; hence melanogenesis is hampered to form altered melanoids whose colours vary from yellow to brown and their combinations produce varied colours.

c. **Histology** : **i.** Shows hyphae and yeast like cells in the superficial stratum corneum which might have para-keratotic cells.

ii. There may be mild inflammatory changes.

iii. In follicular lesions, fungus may be found to penetrate quite some distance into the infundibulum of the hair follicle.

d. **Course** of TV is **persistent** and **recurrent.** However, spontaneous remission may occur.

TREATMENT

SELSUN	IMIDAZOLE	KETOCONAZOLE

1. Avoidance of precipitating factors.

2. Application of 1 to 2.5% **selenium sulphide** lotion according to tolerance, 1-8 hours daily, on alternate days or weekly. Cadmium sulphide is equally effective.

3. 1% Tolnaftate solution is costly but moderately effective if applied 2-3 times daily.

4. Chlotrimazole, miconazole, econazole and **ketoconazole** are well tolerated and effective. To be applied twice daily.

5. 20% to 25% solution of sodium thiosulphate applied twice daily for 3-8 weeks is often curative.

6. Keratolytic creams, ointments and lotions containing 3-6% salicylic acid and sulphur.

7. Resorcinol in lotion 1-3% is helpful.

8. Retinoic acid cream applied twice daily for 2 to 4 weeks is often curative.

9. Application of lotio sulphuris alba twice daily for 4 weeks to 4 months.

10. Application of zinc pyrithione 1% shampoo is found effective.

11. **Ketoconazole** 200 mg tab daily for 15 days followed by one tab each day on the first three days of every month.

12. Application of 50% propylene glycol in water twice daily for 15 days.

13. Application of 5% benzoyl peroxide lotion or gel nightly for one month.

14. Application of 1% ciclopirox cream twice a day for two weeks.

15. Once the infection is cleared, topical corticosteroids may aid in hastening the correction of dyschromic changes.

DISCUSSION

Tinea versicolor is a chronic, asymptomatic, superficial fungal infection caused by Pityrosporum orbiculare which is a normal skin resident. It occurs due to change in host resistance or because of certain strains that are capable of transforming into more aggressive form.

The lesions vary in colour from white to pink to brown but are usually hypopigmented, desquamating, round and perifollicular. Coalescing macular patches are found primarily on the trunk, face and neck. Wood's light examination and KOH preparation help in diagnosis, It should be differentiated from pre-vitiligo, pityriasis alba, seborrheic dermatitis, secondary syphilis and pityriasis rosea.

All therapeutic agents are good but are to be used for adequate length of time—even several weeks after the apparent cure. **Selenium sulphide** is by far the best drug. The pigmentary changes resolve slowly over a period of few months.

In spite of adequate therapy, the relapses are common. Monthly to half-yearly application of drugs could prevent relapse. Ketoconazole 200 mg tab daily for first three days each month prevents relapse. It does not however respond to griseofulvin.

process, tubercle or tuberculoid structures have a tendency to develop. But unexplainable variations are often faced by immunologists and histologists, let alone the clinicians. Thus a tuberculous histology is not to be identified with the diagnosis of tuberculosis. The histological signature of the tubercle bacillus may be a case of forgery. Typical features are more often of a definite nature. But variations invite confusion with diseases such as sarcoidosis, tuberculoid leprosy, leishmaniasis, blastomycosis and chromoblastomycosis, tertiary syphilis, rosacea, panniculitis and hypersensitivity to zirconinm, beryllium, dyes of tattoos, silk and nylon sutures, paraffin, silica particle of surgical gloves, starch powder and disintegration of hair structure. Thus, histologic diagnosis of tuberculosis always carries a risk. Bacteriological diagnosis, where also the failure rates are not insignificant, has therefore been given more importance. But bacterial culture and guineapig inoculation require a prolonged period for getting the results and are also not fool-proof. Atypical mycobacteria causing lesions of similar clinical picture have only added to newer problems.

It is observed that mycobacterium tuberculosis contains some 30 distinct antigenic substances, but none of them is definitely associated with virulence or protection. The human and bovine types cause identical skin manifestations. It is found that inner glycolipid layer (murein) of mycobacterial tuberculosis is covalently bound to a glycolipid, consisting of an arabinogalactone, esterlinked to an outer layer of long chain (C60-C90) lipid (mycolic acid). Crude fragments of this cell wall, known as Wax-Dand, can mimic many of the adjuvant, immunostimulatory and antitumour effects of the whole organism. These effects also modify the immune response of the host to the antigens of the organism itself. The outer layer of the cell wall contains polyanions which are able to block the fusion of macrophages, lysosomes with phagosomes and two glycolipids (sulphatide and cord factors) which are toxic for mitochondria.

The role of glycolipid fraction of M. tuberculosis is also debatable. If the tubercle bacilli survive phagocytosis by macrophages, there is the aggregation of mononuclear cells, epithelioid cells and typical giant cells, which are all formed in response to the lipid fraction of the organism.

In general, glycolipid fractions will reproduce the granuloma formation but not the caseation. The protein components of the cell wall and of the cell sap induce the T-lymphocyte dependent responses which mediate immunity and hypersensitivity. The role of an antibody is uncertain. It will not by itself confer immunity, but by coating the organism with complement it may assist fusion of lysosomes with phagosomes in macrophages. The cell mediated immune (CMI) response may effectively limit the primary focus. If it does not and the disease progresses, a spectrum of clinical and histopathological states may arise broadly analogous to Ridley-Jopling classification of Leprosy. Thus at the re-active pole of the spectrum, the correlates of CMI are positive (delayed hypersensitivity to protein containing extract *in vivo* and leucocyte migration test and lymphocyte transformation test *in vitro*) and organisms are scarce in the lesions. But at the anergic extreme the correlates of CMI tend to become negative and the antibody levels are high, with more complex, often disseminated, disease. Organisms are more numerous because they are less efficiently eliminated. In the anergic form, the tissue damage is mainly due to the toxicity of the organisms but in the negative form in which organisms are scarce, the damage is secondary to T-lymphocyte mediated exudative necrotic responses. Most patients fall nearer to the reactive extreme, the anergic type being commonest in the very old or young or immunologically deprived.

Recent histochemical and electron microscopic studies have revealed some fascinating facts. The so-called lymphocytes seen in the tuberculoid structures are really monocytes having a high content of lyosomal enzymes. They are derived from bone marrow and are carried to the sites of granuloma through the blood stream. Monocytes develop into macrophages which in turn give rise to epithelioid cells. Conglomerated epithelioid cells make Langerhans type of giant cell.

Macrophages phagocytise the tubercle bacilli through the formation of membrane-linked phagosomes. By way of interaction with primary lysosomes, containing hydrolytic enzymes such as acid phosphatase, the phagosomes develop into digestive vacuoles or secondary lysosomes. The reactive immunologic process then mainly depends on whether the macrophages, prior to disintegration, are able to kill all or nearly all the tubercle bacilli within them or if they first disintegrate and then release many viable bacilli. In the latter case, however, the bacilli are phagocytosed by a new series of macrophages so that their bactericidal ability may increase. Disintegrating macrophages form areas of necrosis. But the macrophages, capable of digesting the bacilli within them, assume the appearance of epithelioid cells. In many situations more macrophages enter the area than what are needed to engulf the organisms. The macrophages that never ingested bacilli may also thus develop into epithelioid cells.

As macrophages mature into epithelioid cells and lose their ability to divide, they show a greater tendency to fuse into multinucleated giant cells. T-lymphocytes, often specifically sensitized to M. tuberculosis, stimulate formation of macrophages from monocytes. These T-lymphocytes are responsible for delayed hypersensitivity reaction. In Mantaux test, when PPD tuberculin is injected into the skin there is at first an influx of relatively few antibody carrying lymphocytes resulting in antigen-antibody reaction. This would not only lead to tissue destruction but would also remove, along with macrophages, the local damage produced by the antigen-antibody reaction. The predominantly perivascular accumulation of monocytes produces the positive tuberculin reaction within 24 to 48 hours.

The immunologic mechanisms mediated by circulating immunoglobulins are impaired in patients with hypogammaglobulinemia. They show no reduction in their capacity to produce hypersensitivity to tuberculin, and in addition, handle tuberculosis well.

The relationship between hypersensitivity and immunity in tuberculosis is not well-understood. They do not always correspond to each other. Unfortunately, little is known about the antigens involved in the development of immunity and no immune reaction can as yet be reliably correlated with resistance. However, immunity does develop at the same time as hypersensitivity and may be that both represent different aspects of a single cellular mechanism involving mononuclear cells but elicited by different antigens.

C. Diagnosis of various cutaneous tuberculosis

1. Primary tuberculosis

a. Tuberculous chancre

i. Clinical features

(1) It usually occurs in children but may also develop in adults, not infected previously or not having a natural or artificial immunity to tubercle bacilli.

(2) The cutaneous lesion consists of a crusted chancre, with prominent regional lymphadenopathy which may suppurate to form sinus.

ii. Histopathology

Caseation is marked. This indicates that immunological potency of the patient against tuberculosis has not as yet been developed.

b. Miliary cutaneous tuberulosis

i. Clinical features

(1) It usually occurs in children and in infants after the hematogenous dissemination of tubercle bacilli from the pulmonary focus.

(2) It may be acute or more commonly chronic, depending upon the development of immunity of the individual against tubercle bacilli from established lesions.

(3) The cutaneous lesions consist of macules, papules, vesicles, pustules on erythematous base and occasionally hemorrhagic lesions develop in crops.

ii. Histopathology : In the acute stages, the histologic changes are non-specific. One finds necrosis, extravasation of red blood corpuscles and non-specific inflammatory infiltrates which sometimes form small abscesses. In a later stage, tubercles may be observed. A marked caseation in histology indicates a lack of immunity.

2. Secondary tuberculosis

A. Lupus vulgaris (LV)

i. Clinical features

1. It is the commonest of all post-primary tuberculosis of the skin.

2. It is most prevalent in exposed parts of the body. In the Western countries, involvement of face is maximum (50%), ranking next are the nose, cheek, lower limb and buttocks (30%), trunk and upper limb (10%). But in India, the distribution pattern of lesions is quite different. Cases show lesions on thighs, buttocks, legs, hands, neck, nose and axilla in the order of frequency.

3. Multiple lesions in LV have also been reported often by hematogenous dissemination, particularly following an attack of measles.

4. **Morphologically,** the lesions vary enormously e.g. apple-jelly nodules, ulcers, hypertrophic, verrucous, sclerotic, edematous, erythematous and elephantiatic. These are due to difference in local tissue response to the infection but atypical forms having special characters are also not uncommon, e.g.

a. Plaque form : Extension occurs with little or no central scarring and little infiltration. Scaling may cause psoriasis-like lesions, particularly on legs. The usual colour may be replaced by erythema. Large plaques may cover wide areas of the body. The margin is thickened and

g. T-1. **Tinea Versicolor** showing brownish patches on trunk.

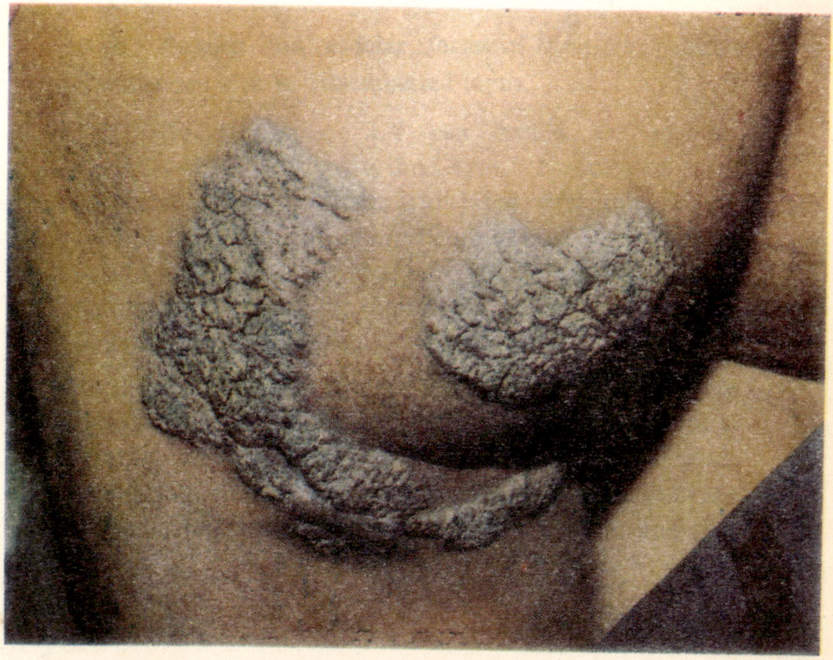

Fig. T-2. **Lupus Vulgaris** showing warty lesions with central scarring.

ii. Histopathology : LV occurs in persons with a high degree of immunity and it is **characterised** histologically by less evidence of caseation, a good amount of epithelioid cell response and almost always by absence of tubercle bacilli. In fact, the histological features are as widely variable as the clinical forms. Any feature may be absent or modified and it may sometimes be difficult to recognise the etiology as tuberculous from the histology.

B. Tuberculosis verrucosa cutis (TVC)

i. Clinical features

It occurs in a person with a high degree of immunity and when the organism is also supposedly of high virulence. The lesion is usually warty and granulomatous in appearance. Exposed parts are mostly affected. The mode of infection is usually exogenous and a lesion develops at the site of inoculation. Multiple lesions of TVC are frequent in India.

ii. Histology

There is a tuberculoid structure with a moderate amount of caseation, and though tubercle bacilli are not commonly found, they are more numerous than in LV. There is gross epidermal hypertrophy giving rise to a verrucous appearance. Often there is striking pseudo-ephitheliomatous hyperplasia and intense mixed infiltrate may only show sparse tuberculous foci. At times, the histopathology of TVC may show only non-specific dermal infiltrate.

C. Scrofuloderma

i. Clinical features

It represents a direct or a lymphatic extension to the skin of any underlying tuberculous focus that may be present in a lymphnode or in the lungs, in about 90% cases. The lesions are **characterised** by painless bluish-red swellings that break subsequently into multiple discharging sinuses with oval or linear ulcers. Due to both progression and regression (healing) of the disease, often there is formation of hypertrophic scars and cicatrical bands.

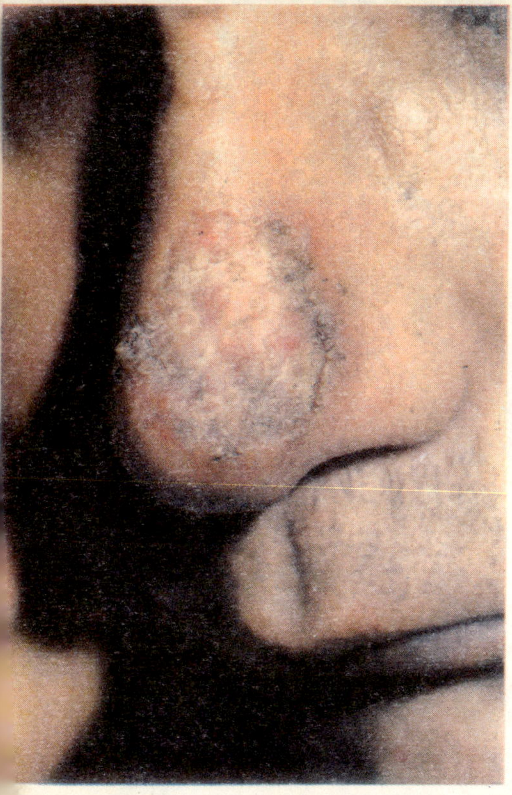

Fig. T-3. **Lupus Vulgaris** showing chronic ulcerative lesion at the nose.

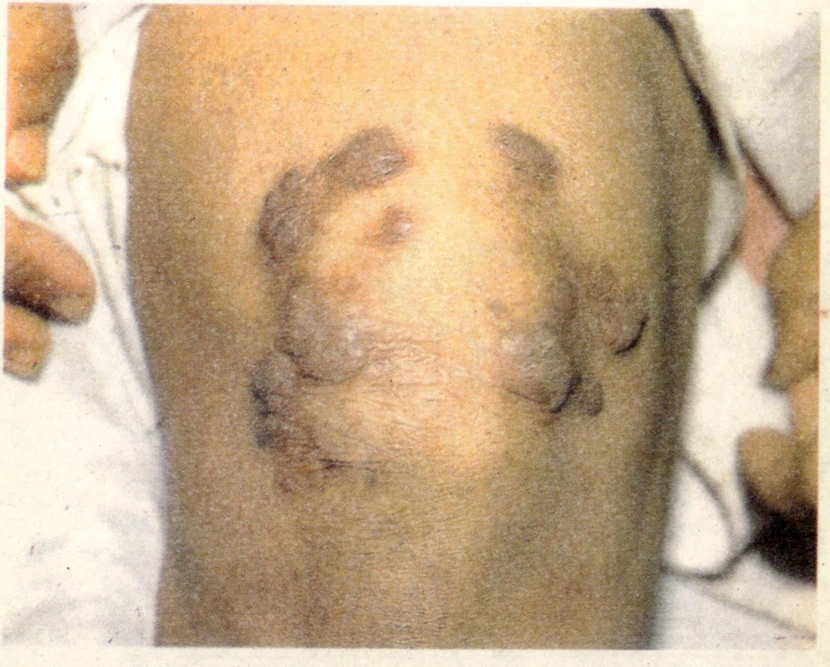

Fig. T-4. **Lupus Vulgaris** showing tumourlike lesions at the knee.

ii. **Histology**

The disease is *characterised* histologically by marked caseation necrosis with epithelioid reaction and the presence of sufficient number of tubercle bacilli.

D. Tuberculosis cutis orificialis

i. **Clinical features** : This type of tuberculosis occurs at mucocutaneous areas, usually in young adults with virulent internal tuberculosis. It represents a complete anergy to tuberculosis. The lesions are shallow ulcers with a granulating base.

ii. **Histology** : It is characterised by non-specific inflammatory infiltrate with a considerable number of tubercle bacilli and pronounced necrosis.

3. Tuberculids

It is a highly controversial subject and it includes four dermatoses : 1. Erythema induratum 2. Papulonecrotic tuberculid (PNT) 3. Lichen scrofulosorum and 4. Lupus miliaris disseminatus faciei.

A critical analysis of the facts available reveals that actually the pathogenesis and causes of tuberculids are poorly understood and probably the whole concept is hypothetical. Regarding histogenesis of tuberculids, opinions are highly divergent. The widely accepted view is the hematogenous dissemination of tubercle bacilli from an active body lesion. The arguments in favour of the definite existence of various tuberculids are mainly : (a) Tuberculoid structure is seen in histologic examination (b) Occasional improvement of lesions by antituberculous drugs and (c) Tuberculin skin test is usually strongly positive.

Facts contradicting these arguments are : (a) In most cases of tuberculids active focus of the patients cannot be traced. (b) Tuberculids fail to fulfil the Koch's postulates. (c) Many tuberculids do not show any improvement with anti-Koch's treatment e.g. LMDF and Lichen scrofulosorum. (d) In some cases of PNT and LMDF, there is spontaneous involution. (e) Antistreptolysin titre is increased in 95% of cases of PNT and (f) Some tuberculids respond to corticosteroid therapy.

To explain the above contradictions regarding the genesis, two hypotheses have been put forward. They are :

The skin is hyperergic to tubercle bacilli. If it holds true, then the focus from which the dissemination takes place should also be in a hyperergic state and should thus show clinically noticeable acute necrotizing inflammation. This however is not found in tuberculids.

The other hypothesis states that the skin may show tuberculous reaction due to the presence of decreased immunological resistance to tubercle bacilli in the absence of flaring of the original focus. But immunologically, this also cannot be explained. If the skin shows hypersensitivity to tubercle bacilli, the original focus must show reactivation. Thus the immunologic explanation for tuberculids is yet to be widely accepted.

Probably it is not unwise to regard : (1) LMDF as papular type of rosacea, (2) Erythema induratum as vasculitis of subcutaneous arteries and veins with subsequent fat necrosis and tuberculoid histological reaction. (3) Papulo-necrotic tuberculid also histologically shows features of vasculitis such as inflammatory infiltrate and thickening of walls of the vessels. (4) Lichen scrofulosorum shows epithelioid tubercles without caseation and mimics papular sarcoidosis or papular granuloma annulare.

4. A. Tuberculosis due to BCG vaccination

Although BCG vaccination affords protection against tuberculosis, the following specific lesions may rarely develop.

a. LV may develop at or in the vicinity of vaccination site after 6 months to 3 years.

b. Individuals previously sensitive to tuberculin may show development of Koch's phenomenon. Necrosis, ulceration and lymphadenopathy do occur.

Fig. T-5. **Lupus Vulgaris** showing chronic ulcerative lesion at the face with apple jelly nodules at the periphery.

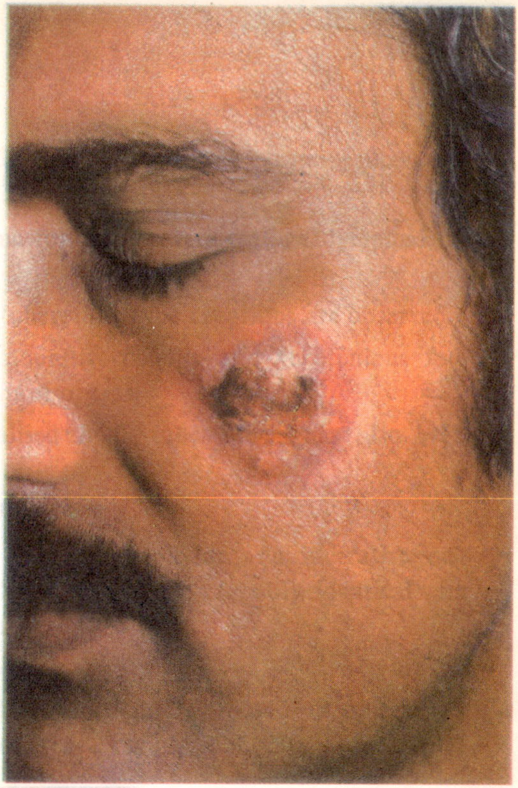

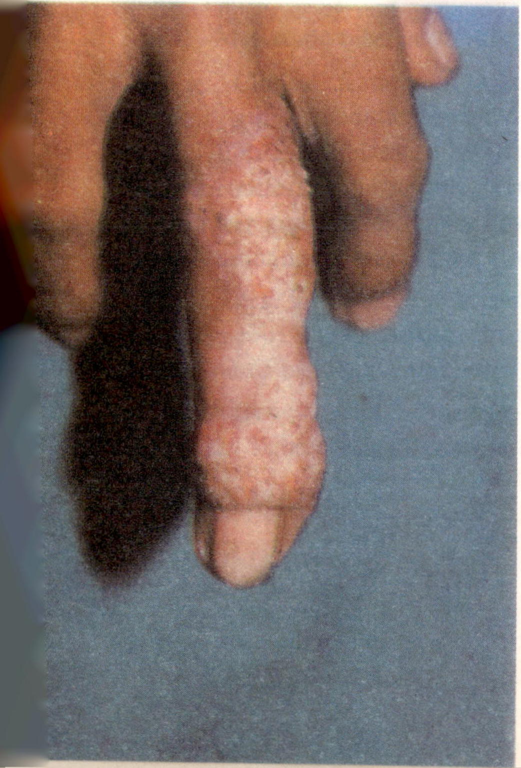

Fig. T-6. **Tuberculosis Verrucosa Cutis** of finger showing warty and granulomatous lesions.

The first line anti-tuberculous drugs are described below.

1. Isoniazid (INH)

a. **Dose** : 300 mg daily orally or I.M. or 15 mg/kg orally or I.M., twice a week.

b. Most common **side effects** are : 1. Hypersensitivity, 2. Peripheral neuritis, and 3. Hepatitis.

c. **Tests** for side effects : 1. SGOT 2. SGPT

d. **Drug interactions** : Synergistic with phenytoin and antagonistic to disulfiram.

e. **Pharmacology** : 1. Bactericidal to both the extra-cellular and intracellular organisms 2. Pyridoxin, 10 mg orally as prophylaxis for neuritis ; 100 mg for treatment.

2. Rifampicin

a. **Dose** : 600 mg orally daily in empty stomach.

b. Most common **side effects** : 1. Hepatitis, 2. Febrile reaction, and rarely 3. Purpura.

c. **Tests** for side effects : 1. SGOT 2. SGPT

d. **Drug interactions** : 1. Rifampicin inhibits the effects of oral contraceptives, quinidine, corticosteroids, coumarin anticoagulants, methadone, digoxin and oral hypoglycemics 2. PAS may interfere with the absorption of rifampicin.

e. **Pharmacology** : 1. Bactericidal to all populations of organisms. 2. Orange colouration of urine and body fluids. 3. Discolouration of contact lenses.

3. Streptomycin

a. **Dose** : 0.75 g to 1 g I.M. daily or 25-30 mg/kg I.M., bi-weekly.

b. Most common **side effects** : 1. Eighth nerve damage 2. Nephrotoxicty.

c. **Tests** for side effects : 1. Audiograms 2. Blood urea nitrogen and creatinine.

d. **Drug interactions** : Neuromuscular blocking agents may be potentiated and may cause prolonged paralysis.

e. **Pharmacology** : 1. Bactericidal to extracellular organisms. 2. To be used cautiously in old age and patients with renal disease.

4. Pyrazinamide

a. **Dose** : 2 g orally daily or 50-70 mg/kg bi-weekly.

b. Most common **side effects** are : 1. Hyperuricemia 2. Hepatotoxicity.

c. **Tests** for side effects : 1. Uric acid, 2. SGOT, and 3. SGPT.

d. **Pharmacology** : 1. Bactericidal to intracellular organisms. 2. Combination with aminoglycoside is bactericidal.

5. Ethambutol

a. **Dose** : 15-25 mg/kg orally daily or 50 mg/kg bi-weekly.

b. Most common **side effects** are : 1. Optic neuritis. 2. Drug rash.

c. **Tests** for side effects : 1. Red green colour. 2. Tests for visual acuity.

d. **Pharmacology** : 1. Bacteriostatic to both intracellular and extracellular organism. 2. Mainly used to inhibit development of resistant mutants. 3. Should be used with caution in renal disease or when ophthalmologic test is not feasible.

6. Standard regimens

a. **INH + rifampicin** for 9 months.

b. **INH + rifampicin + pyrizinamide** for first 2 months ; thereafter withdrawal of pyrizinamide ; total duration of treatment is 6 months.

c. In INH resistant cases (very rare) :

Rifampicin + ethambutol + pyrizinamide for first 2 months ; then without pyrizinamide for total 12 months.

7. **Alternative drugs**

a. **Para-amino-salicylic acid** (PAS) : 8-12 g orally daily.

b. **Ansamycin** : 0.15-0.3 g daily + **clofazimine** 0.1 mg/kg daily orally.

c. **Capreomycin** (A substitute for streptomycin) : 0.5-1.5 g daily intramuscularly.

d. **Cycloserin** : 0.5-1.0 g daily orally, either alone or with **isoniazid.**

e. **Ethionamide** : 0.5-1.0 g daily orally.

f. **Viomycin** : 2 g I.M. every 3 days.

Always a combination of 2 or 3 drugs should be prescribed.

There is now a wide choice of autituberculous drugs and, according to the patient's tolerance and the extent of the disease, a combination therapy for 9 to 12 months can cure most of the patients.

DISCUSSION

Tuberculosis of the skin manifests itself in extremely diverse manner. Starting from papule and passing through ulcer, scarring, various forms of granulomatous lesions, discharging sinuses, it can show ugly disfiguration. Unless secondary infection is there, lymphadenopathy is generally not found. Accompanying tuberculosis of other organs is not common. Presence of apple-jelly nodules in coloured Indian skin is difficult to demonstrate. Existence of tuberculids is still debatable. Long standing indolent granuloma should always be suspected as tuberculosis in our country. Lupus vulgaris is by far the commonest form.

Diagnosis is based on histopathology. But the variations are wide. Non-specific mononuclear infiltrate, epithelioid cells, Langerhan's giant cells and caseation may indicate tuberculosis but are not pathognomonic. A good correlation of histopathological findings with clinical features is very helpful. Bacteriological diagnosis is difficult.

Highly potent antituberculous drugs are available now. Two or three drug regimen may be followed. Rifampicin, isonex and ethambutol are highly effective drugs. Treatment should be continued at least for 2 more months even after clinical cure that usually takes 9 to 12 months. Resistant cases are rarely met with. Pyrizinamide in the three drug regimen is helpful in such cases.

Long-standing untreated lupus vulgaris may rarely develop into squamous cell carcinoma.

URTICARIA

Urticaria is a common dermatosis in which transient pruritic wheals of variable size occur on the skin.

DIAGNOSIS

1. The main symptom of urticaria is itching which might be moderate or extremely severe. There may be occasional burning.

2. The lesions are **characterised** by the following.

a. **Pea-sized red papules** or **plaques** to large circinate patterns with red borders. There may be **central white** clearing. The lesion can cover an entire side of a trunk or a thigh. There is always palpable elevated edge.

b. These wheals last for few minutes to hours and then subside only to reappear elsewhere. A skin area is refractory to further wheal formation for some 24 hours after an urticarial lesion subsides.

c. The lesions have a tendency to occur on **points of pressure** from clothing, belts, shoulder straps or girdles.

d. Simple diffuse swelling may be seen in the lips, mucous membranes, periorbital area or the eye lids. If buccal mucous membrane and tongue are affected, there is chance of development of **laryngeal edema** which is an emergency situation. If gastrointestinal mucosa is involved there may be **cramps, nausea** and **vomiting.**

e. **Vesicles** and **bullae** are seen in severe cases along with hemorrhagic effusions.

f. Typical lesions **blanch** completely, if pressed with the finger tip.

g. Lesions tend to flare up in the evening.

h. Non-specific vasodilation tends to worsen the attack e.g. hot bath, hot foods, alcohol, electric blankets etc.

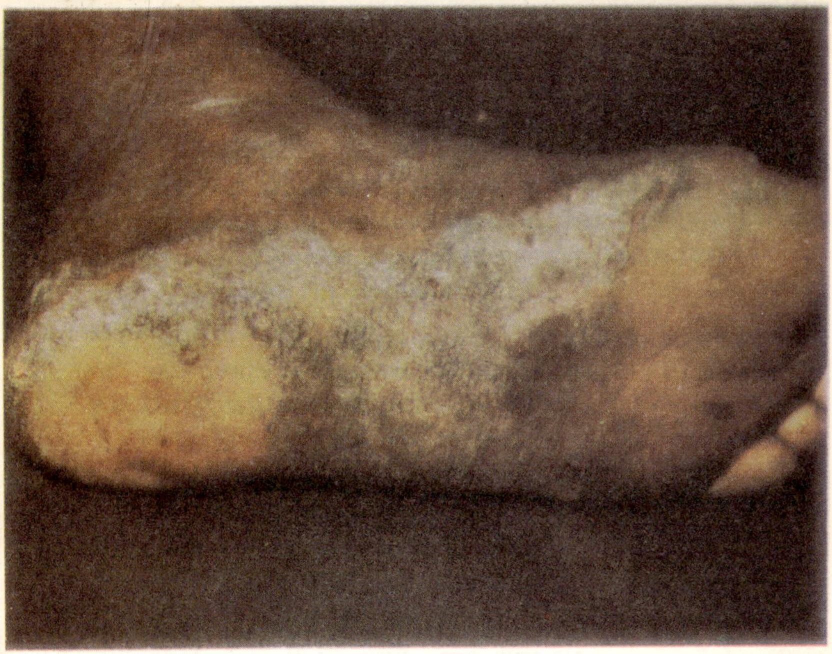

Fig. T-7. **Tuberculosis Verrucosa Cutis** of sole showing wide-spread warty lesions.

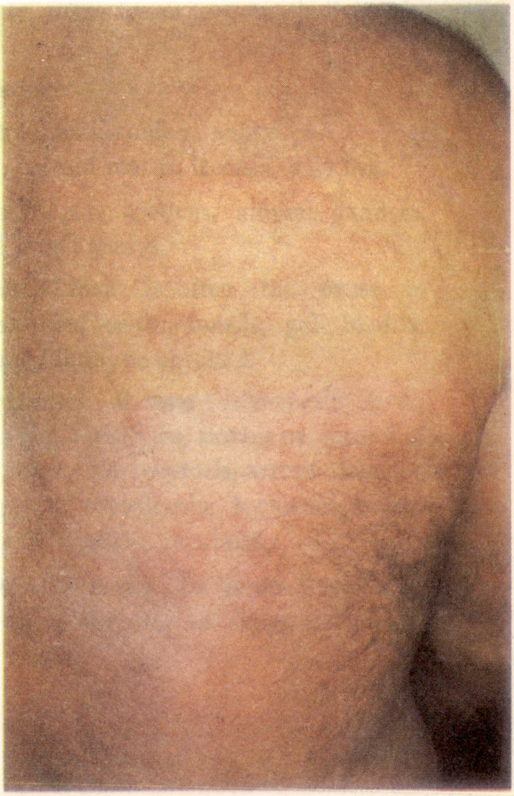

Fig. U-1. **Urticaria** showing erythematous evanescent wheals at the back.

i. **Neural** : Nervous stress, worries and fatigue.

4. **Clinical classification**

a. i. **Acute immediate allergic type**—Appears within minutes ; contactants, foods and drugs are often responsible.

ii. **Acute delayed urticaria**—Appears hours after the exposure to the causative factor ; generally wide-spread ; foods, inhalants and drugs are the causes.

iii. **Chronic urticaria**—More persistent ; less severe, less extensive, involves small areas only, continues for months or years, causative agents could rarely be detected.

b. i. **Cold contact urticaria**—Occurs within seconds or minutes of exposure to cold e.g. with cold air, cold glass, metal, ice ; extremely pruritic.

ii. **Heat contact urticaria**—Occurs usually at temperatures above 39°C, within seconds or minutes of contact.

iii. **Solar urticaria**—It occurs in some persons with a specific wavelength of light.

iv. **Cholinergic urticaria**—The lesions are less than 1 cm ; exercise, cutaneous flushing and external heat are often the causes.

v. **Aquagenic urticaria**—Lesions are mostly follicular and occur due to contact with water of varying temperatures.

vi. **Angioedema** has a tendency to extend deeper into subcutaneous fat. There is more edema and less inflammatory cells. Affects areas of loose areolar tissue.

c. i. **Immunologic**—In most cases of acute urticaria, type I hypersensitivity state is triggered by polyvalent antigen bridging the two specific IgE molecules that are attached to mast cells.

ii. **Non-immunologic**—In this type, histamine release is due to direct injury to mast cells e.g. morphine, codeine, lobster, caryfish, lower animals, bacterial toxins and the physical agents.

5. **Pathophysiology**—It is highly complex. Some of the important and pertinent facts are given below.

a. Histamine, the main chemical mediator of urticaria, is produced and stored in the granules of the mast cells. Once depleted, it requires 24 hours or more to replenish the stores. Antigen-antibody union involving IgE releases histamine from mast cells and basophils.

b. Kinins, prostaglandins and slow-reacting substances of anaphylaxis (SRS-A) can produce urticarial wheals.

c. Complement may induce histamine release.

d. Without the help of IgE, histamine liberation may occur e.g. with venoms, toxins, jellyfish, proteolytic enzymes, serums, tween 20, compound amine 48/80, morphine, codeine, aspirin, polymixin, quinine and curare.

e. Cyclic AMP may act as regulator of the immunopharmacology of histamine release depending on intracellular temperature, energy and calcium.

f. In chronic urticaria, there is a possibility of qualitative abnormality of basophil-bound IgE.

g. Localised dermographism can be produced by transferring serum of urticaria patients by intracutaneous injection to normal individuals. Anti-IgE serum eliminated this response proving the role of IgE.

h. Emotion can act as a precipitant of chronic urticarial lesions.

i. Histamine dilates the dermal blood vessels and serum leaks out causing edema and itching.

6. **Histology**

a. Epidermis—Normal.

b. Dermal edema, dilated small blood vessels and the lymphatics.

c. Sparse perivascular infiltrate of eosinophils, lymphocytes, neutrophils, or mast cells.

d. Endothelial swelling and pyknosis.

7. Investigations

a. Detailed history of foods, drugs, inhalants, contactants and environmental factors.

b. A thorough physical examination. A search for purulent foci is particularly essential.

c. WBC count, ESR, urine and stool examinations, x-ray chest.

d. ASO titer, rheumatoid factor, liver function test, LE cell test, x-rays of teeth and sinuses, estimation of serum, proteins, cryoglobulins, cold agglutinins, VDRL.

e. Challege testing with suspecting agents.

f. Prick test with various allergens.

g. Patch test with various allergens.

TREATMENT

ANTIHISTAMINES	H2-BLOCKERS
EPHEDRINE	DAPSONE
EPINEPHRINE	CHLOROQUIN
DOXEPIN	CHROMOLIN SODIUM

Treatment modality varies according to the acuteness of the patient. Etiological factors should always be avoided.

1. Acute immediate allergic urticaria with laryngopharyngeal edema.

i. Injection of epinephrine 1 : 1000, 0.5 to 1 c.c. subcutaneously slowly in 10 to 20 minutes.

ii. Ephedrine 25 mg b.i.d or t.i.d.

iii. I.M. or I.V. antihistamines.

iv. I.M. or I.V. glucocorticoids have slower effect.

2. Acute and chronic urticaria

Antihistamines are the mainstay of treatment. Choice of a particular drug is mostly intuitive being dictated by the physician's own experience.

i. Diphenhydramine hydrochloride

ii. Tripelennamine iii. Chloropheneramine maleate

iv. Cyclizine v. Promethazine hydrochloride.

vi. Hydroxyzine (most favoured drug), cyproheptadine (often effective).

vii. Tranquillizers viii. H2 blockers : Cimetidine and ranitidine.

ix. Doxepin is highly effective having strong antihistaminic effect.

x. Combination of various antihistaminics.

3. Ancillary miscellaneous measures

i. Starch or oatmeal bath : 1 cup in half bath tub of lukewarm water. Bath for 15 minutes.

ii. Application of 1% camphor in alcohol, topical steroids (costly), a mixture of methol, phenol and camphor each 0.5%.

iii. Bacterial vaccine : 0.05 ml S.C. increased by 0.05 ml, twice or once in a week up to 1 c.c. iv. Deworming.

v. Diethylcarbamazine citrate : 100 mg t.i.d for 6 weeks.

vi. Histamine in gradually increasing doses for desensitization.

vii. Calcium : orally, I.M. or I.V. is said to have lessening vascular permeability effect.

viii. Random trial of anti-infective agents.

ix. Metronidazole : 400 mg t.i.d for 5 days followed by ketoconazole 200 mg daily for 2 weeks and then erythromycin 250 mg q.i.d for 2 weeks.

x. Thiabendazole : 25/kg b.i.d for 3 days.

xi. Vaginal clotrimazole has been used.

xii. Dapsone might help in some cases.

xiii. Terbutaline 1.25 mg t.i.d for 2 months.

xiv. Chloroquin helps in curing solar urticaria.

xv. Methoxalen helps tolerating the sun.

xvi. Beta-blocker propanalol : 20 mg t.i.d helps in adrenergic urticaria.

xvii. Danazole : 600 mg daily, gradually reducing to 200 mg daily, often cures hereditary angioedema.

xviii. Theophylline, cromolyn sodium and doxantrazole stabilize mast cells.

xix. In some cases, vaccines made by the known allergens can cure urticaria by gradual desensitization.

DISCUSSION

Over 50% of cases of chronic urticaria are not amenable to diagnosis as to their cause. Often therefore they are called 'idiopathic'. Each urticaria patient comes with the challenging question : why is this ? It is assumed that the majority of agents causing urticaria act via IgE attached to mast cells and basophils. The reaction leads to liberation of histamine and other mediators resulting in vasodilatation and increased capillary permeability. Urticaria occurs when the lesions are superficial and angioedema involves subcutaneous tissue. Certain cases result from type III IgE reactions while others are not immunologically mediated.

Most of the acute cases of urticaria are related to foods, drugs, inhalants or infections. Even the most chronic case will spontaneously subside within 2-5 years. Cold and solar urticaria patients may experience extensive whealing, hypotension, angioedema, wheezing, asthma and syncope on having severe exposure.

In acute cases, antihistamines to the point of suppression for about two weeks would help in automatic antigen degradation and subsequent elimination ; patient would then remain free of symptoms.

For chronic urticaria, a serious steady search for the etiological factor should be made. In this pursuit, a total co-operation of the patient is essential.

Besides routine therapy with antihistaminics, epinephrine, ephedrine, H2 blockers, betablockers, doxepin and many other drugs are empirically used with claims of success. These drugs include ketoconazol, mycostatin, antibiotics, metronidazol, theophylline, indomethacin, cromolyn, terbutaline, di-ethylcarbamazine, chloroquin, methoxalen, doxantrazole, thiabendazole, griseofulvin, dapsone and sulpha-pyridine. This long list of drugs only indicates our inability to pinpoint the etiology.

Until the exact biomechanism of urticaria is clearly known, we are somewhat perplexed and only personal experience and effort would count most in treating this challenging disease.

Indiscriminate use of internal steroid does more **harm** than **good** to the patient.

VERRUCA OR WARTS

Warts are infection of the skin and contiguous mucous membranes by specific members of the Papova virus group —Human Papilloma Viruses (HPV).

1. **Incubation period** : Viruses infect epidermal cells by direct inoculation with infected material. Incubation period after experimental inoculation ranges from 1-20 months, average being 4 months. Incubation period in genital warts is 3-8 months, occasionally shorter.

2. **Predisposing factors** : Susceptibility to infection with the wart virus and the rate of growth depend on immune responses. Incidence of warts is high in immunosuppressed transplant patients. It is also increased in patients with Hodgkin's disease and to a less extent in patients with malignant lymphomas and chronic lymphatic leukemia. Immune defect, common to these conditions, is depression of cell-mediated response.

3. **Age, sex and regional incidence** : Warts occur throughout the world. Though the comparative figures are lacking, there are striking variations in regional incidences. It is less common in tropics. A limited survey suggests that the incidence may be considerably lower in New Zeland than in Europe.

Age and sex incidence vary according to different types of warts. Common warts are unusual in infancy and early childhood. Incidence increases during the schooling years, peak incidence being at 12-16. It then declines sharply to the age of 20, and gradually thereafter. **Plantar warts** are rare below the school age, become increasingly common after 5 or 6. After the age of 25, plantar warts are relatively uncommon but no age is immune. In early childhood, **both sexes** are **equally affected** but from the age of 6 onward, plantar warts are more common in girls. **Plane warts** are seen in young children of both sexes, occasionally in young women but is unusual in boys after puberty. Genital warts, common in both sexes, occur at any age including infancy.

4. Mode of transmission : Warts are transmitted by direct or mediate contact. Virus can be autoinoculated from hand to foot and vice-versa. Community bathing and changing facilities are associated with an increased incidence of plantar warts. It may also be transmitted by contaminated objects. Trauma and nail biting are important factors favouring successful inoculation of the virus. Hyperhidrosis, flat foot, other plantar deformities, and unsuitable foot wear greatly increase the incidence of plantar warts. Trauma of shaving causes dissemination of filiform or digitate warts of the beard area.

5. Immunology : Numerous and persistent warts should cause suspicion for an underlying disease impairing the cell mediated response. The role of the humoral antibodies is uncertain. Complement fixing antibodies were demonstrated in the sera of 20% of patients with warts. The cure of warts is associated with complement fixing IgG antibodies. In patients with IgM and/or low titres of IgG, the warts tend to persist. The appearance of IgG antibodies may cause the disappearance of the warts.

6. Virology : The wart virus or human papilloma virus (HPV) is a DNA virus belonging to the papova group. There are several types of human papilloma viruses, each with a distinct DNA genome and type-specific antigen. Several serotypes can thus be recognized. They are HPT-1, 2, 3, 4, 5, 6 to 18. The details are given under classification.

In electron microscopic (EM) study, no difference has been noted in the appearance among the virus particles. Only the quantity varies in different types, being sparse in HPV 2 and HPV 6 and profuse in HPV 5. Frequently, no virus particles can be found in verruca vulgaris on EM examination. Virus particles are spherical bodies, diameter being 50 nm, each particle consisting of an electron dense nucleoid surrounded by a less dense capsid. Wart virus replicates in the nucleus. It does not grow in tissue cultures and is not pathogenic for any animal.

7. **Classification :** Three classifications exist (Lever, 1983).

A. **Traditional classification :** Based on clinical appearance and location.

i. **Verruca vulgaris** or the common wart including filiform wart.

ii. **Deep hyperkeratotic palmo-plantar wart.**

iii. **Superficial mosaic type palmo-plantar wart.**

iv. **Verruca plana.** v. **Condyloma accuminata.**

vi. **Epidermo-dysplasia verruciformis.**

B. **Histologic classification**

i. Inclusion warts : Seen in deep hyperkeratotic palmo-plantar warts.

ii. Papillomatous warts with foci of vacuolization and parakeratosis : Seen in common warts, superficial mosaic type of palmo-plantar warts and in condyloma acuminata.

iii. Warts with diffuse vacuolization in the upper epidermis : Seen in some cases of epidermo-dysplasia verruciformis.

iv. Warts with dysplastic vacuolization : Seen in some cases of epidermo-dysplasia verruciformis.

C. **Classification based on serotyping**

For this, please see the table in page 451.

8. **Clinical features**

A. **Verruca vulgaris (V. vulgaris ; Common warts)**—These are circumscribed, firm, **elevated papules with verrucous hyperkeratotic surface** occurring singly or in groups, the diameter varying from 1 mm to 1 cm ; occur anywhere on the skin ; common sites are dorsal aspects of the fingers and hands. **Koebner-isomorphic phenomenon** is a feature. Usually these are symptomless but may be tender on palmar aspects of the fingers. Warts on the eye lids may cause conjunctivitis or keratitis. Two-third of warts disappear spontaneously within 2 years. Rarely, development of squamous cell carcinoma may occur. **Verruca filiformis or filiform warts**—a variant of

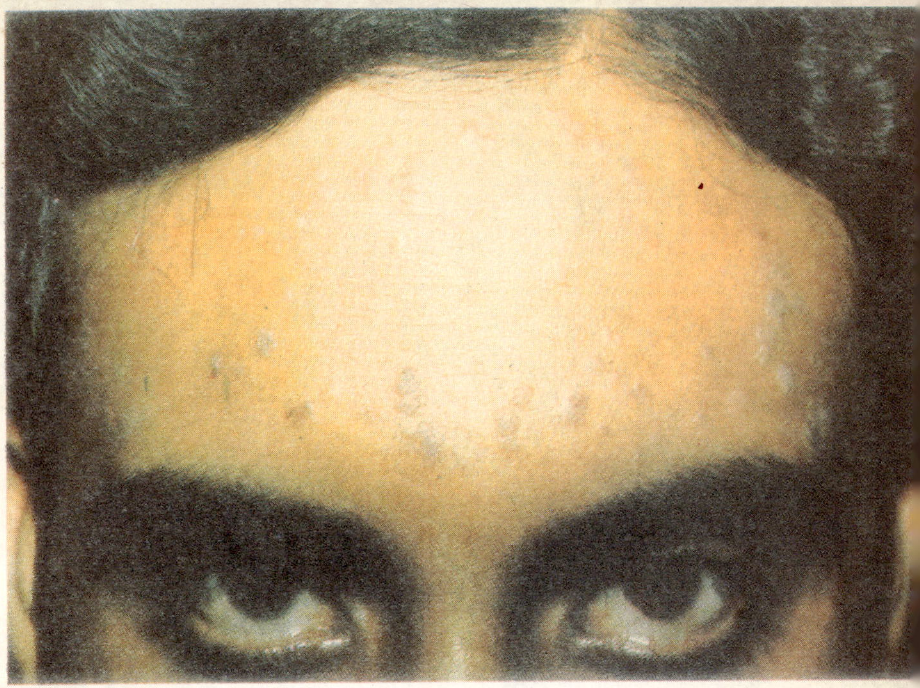

Fig. V-1. **Verruca Plana** at the forehead.

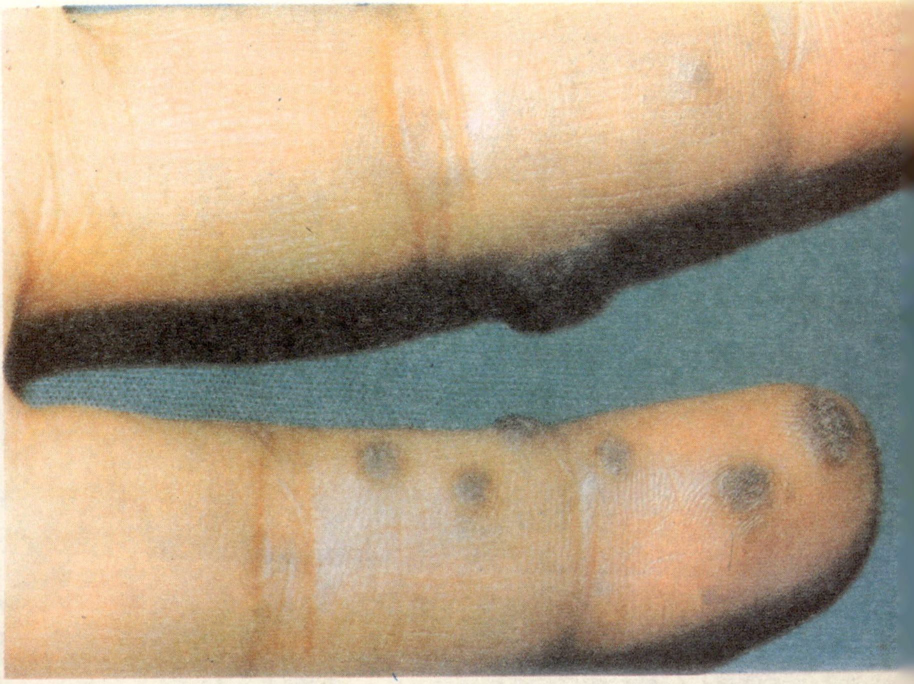

Fig. V-2. **Verruca Vulgaris** of the fingers.

Predominant virus	Types of lesions
1. HPV 1	Plantar warts
2. HPV 2	Verruca vulgaris
3. HPV 3	Verruca plana
4. HPV 4	Plantar wart and verruca vulgaris
5. HPV 5	Epidermodysplasia verruciformis
6. HPV 6	Genital warts
7. HPV 7	Meat handler warts.
8. HPV 8	Epidermodysplasia verruciformis
9. HPV 9	Epidermodysplasia verruciformis
10. HPV 10	Verruca plana
11. HPV 11	Genital warts, flat warts of the cervix, laryngeal papillomas
12. HPV 12	Epidermodysplasia verruciformis
13. HPV 13	Focal epithelial hyperplasia (Heck).
14. HPV 14 & 15	Epidermodysplasia verruciformis, flat wart like lesions, red plaques
15. HPV 16	Flat warts of cervix, carcinoma of cervix
16. HPV 18	Flat warts of cervix, carcinoma of cervix

Types 5, 8, 11, 12, 16 and 18 above are associated with malignancy.

verruca vulgaris shows thread like horny projections arising from a horny base, seen mostly on the face and scalp. **Verruca digitata** is a thicker form of filiform variety occurring often at the neck. It has a broader stalk.

B. Verruca-plana (V. plana, Plane warts) : These are smooth, round or polygonal, flat or slightly elevated, skin coloured or greyish yellow or pigmented papules ; size varying from 1-5 mm and number varying from 2-3 to even many hundreds. Sites of predeliction are **face** and **backs of the hands** and **shins**. Koebner isomorphic phenomenon is more marked and linear arrangement in a scratch mark is a characteristic feature. It may disappear suddenly after few weeks or months or may persist for years.

C. Plantar warts : The lesion first appears as a small sago-grain papule, soon becoming sharply defined and rounded with a rough keratotic surface, surrounded by a collar of thickened horn. Most warts are beneath pressure points–heel or metatarsal heads. But it can occur anywhere at the sole. Deep palmo-plantar warts are usually covered with thick callus. When it is removed with a scalpel, wart proper becomes visible as a soft, granular, white or brownish tissue. Pain is a common but variable symptom and often absent in conglomerated **mosaic warts**. Duration is variable ; regression occurs sooner in children and is delayed in case of hyperhidrosis or orthopedic defects. Average duration is less than a year. Plantar warts may change into carcinoma. Mosaic warts tend to be persistent.

D. Epidermo-dysplasia verruciformis : There are two variants of epidermo-dysplasia verruciformis ; one is caused by HPV 3 and another by HPV 5. Lesions caused by HPV 3 are indistinguishable from V. plana. Both have a familial tendency. Individual lesions are flat, warty papules, 2-6 mm in diameter. Most favoured sites are **face** and **neck, trunk** and **extremeties**, but may be generalised over the entire body surface. It appears first in childhood but no age is immune. It is persistent and remains unchanged for decades. Malignant change (squamous epithelioma) may occur often on exposed skin suggesting the role of actinic radiation.

E. **Genital-warts** (**Condyloma accuminata**) : It consists of soft verrucous papules of the anogenital region which may coalesce into cauliflower like masses. It can occur at any age including infancy. Both the sexes are involved. It is commomly transmitted by sexual contact, incubation period varying between 3-8 months.

Duration varies from few weeks to many months. Reversal of the condition that provokes their rapid development e.g. trichomonal infection and pregnancy may accelerate cure. Malignant degeneration can occur in rare instances.

9. **Histopathology**

A. **Verruca vulgaris** : There is acanthosis, hyperkeratosis and papillomatosis ; rete ridges are elongated. Three main **characteristic** features are

a. **Foci of vacuolated cells in the upper stratum malpighii and granular layer**. Vacuolated cells possess small, round, deeply basophilic nuclei, pale staining cytoplasm surrounded by a narrow clear halo. These cells contain few or no keratohyalin granules even when they are located in the granular layer.

b. **Vertical tyres of parakeratotic cells** ; nuclei being larger and more deeply basophilic and rounded as opposed to ordinary parakeratotic cells.

c. **Foci of clumped keratohyalin granules**

Involution of V. vulgaris is associated with a mononuclear cell infiltration, exocytosis and also degenerative epidermal changes.

B. **Palmo-plantar warts** : Resembles V. vulgaris ; stratum corneum is much thicker and shows extensive parakeratosis. It is characterised by the presence of **keratohyalin** which differs from normal keratohyalin by being eosinophilic. The cytoplasm of the cells in uppper stratum malpighii contains numerous eosinophilic granules which enlarge and coalesce to form inclusion bodies. Intranuclear eosinophilic inclusion bodies are also seen in the upper stratum malpighii which is round and about the size of nucleolus. An actual granular layer does not exist.

C. **V. plana** : It shows hyperkeratosis and acanthosis but no papillomatosis, slight elongation of rete ridges and there is no area of parakeratosis. In the upper stratum malpighii and the granular layer, there is diffuse vacuolization of cells. Granular layer is uniformly thickened and stratum corneum has a pronounced basket-weave appearance resulting from the vacuolization of horny cells. Dermis appears to be normal.

D. **Epidermo-dysplasia verruciformis** : Epidermal changes are uneven. Affected cells are swollen and irregularly shaped. Cytoplasm stains pale blue and may have foamy appearance. Some nuclei appear pyknotic and others appear large, round and empty due to marginal distribution of chromatin. All these give the swollen cell a dysplastic appearance.

E. **Condyloma accuminata** : There is slight hyperkeratosis ; parakeratosis is present in lesion of mucosa ; acanthosis, papillomatosis, thickening and elongation of the rete ridges occur. A picture of pseudo-epitheliomatous hyperplasia may result. Considerable number of mitotic figures may be present. Malignancy may be ruled out by the retention of polarity of epithelial cells and a sharp border between epithelial proliferation and dermis. The epithelial cells show distinct perinuclear vacuolization. Dermis appears edematous and shows dilated capillaries and a moderately dense chronic inflammatory infiltrate.

TREATMENT

LIQUID NITROGEN	FORMALDEHYDE
DUOFILM^{R}	CANTHARIDIN
CURETTAGE	BLEOMYCIN
PODOPHYLLUM	CONTACT SENSITIZATION
LASER BEAM	

A. **General considerations** : Two points must be considered in the treatment of warts.

i. Not all warts need treatment. If a wart is not multiplying and causing no problem, therapy can be avoided. All that is needed then is reassurance. About 30% lesions may recur after successful treatment.

ii. Wart is a bengin condition and whatever therapy is undertaken, there should be minimal scarring both from the consideration of skin and psychological point of view.

B. **Specific**

i. **Verruca vulgaris** : a. **Freezing with liquid nitrogen** either with a cotton tipped applicator or hand held spray machines. Freezing should be done until the warts remain white for 15 seconds for small warts and 30 seconds for larger warts. Blister appears within 12-48 hours depending on the depth of freezing. No special care of the blister other than keeping the area clean is necessary. Topical antibiotics may be used.

b. **Electrodesiccation and curettage** : This treatment is successful, specially in case of single warts. After infiltrating the area with local anesthetic, the wart is electrodesiccated until it appears friable and surface turns slightly brown.

c. **Chemical treatment** : Application of varying acids is a popular method e.g. **duofilm**^{R} which is a combination of 16.7% salicylic acid, 16.7% lactic acid in flexible collodion. Hyperkeratotic lesions should be pared before treatment and medication is applied after soaking the affected area in warm water for 5 minutes. Acids such as **dichloro-acetic acid** or **trichloro-acetic acid** are available but have only limited value and are slow to work. Daily use of **buffered glutaraldehyde** solution or formaldehyde solution may be advocated. **Cantharidin** is a blistering agent best used for periungual warts.

d. **Intralesional injection of bleomycin sulphate** : It is best used for resistant type and large number of warts. 15 mg of bleomycin is added to 15 ml of isotonic saline to make a dilution of 1 mg/ml. Solution must be kept in a refrigerator. Small warts less than 5 mm in diameter require 0.2 ml and larger lesions up to 0.8 ml. In periungual or plantar warts up to 2 ml can be injected at a single site.

e. **Di-nitro-chlor-benzene (DNCB)** : It is another recent therapy for resistant warts. At first, a sensitizing dose is applied. Sensitization may occur with an eczematous response. If sensitization does not at all occur, a larger dose is applied 2-3 weeks later. Then several weeks after the sensitizing dose, a 0.1% solution of DNCB in acetone is painted on the warts with an applicator. The area must be kept dry for 24 hours. Inflammatory response occurs in 1-2 days. Re-application at daily or weekly intervals is needed to keep the area slightly inflammed. Potential risk of this therapy is auto-sensitization with generalized eczematous response or localized blistering response.

f. **Water-soluble vitamin A** : 100,000 units taken 3 times daily in combination with cimetidine 300 mg t.i.d is an impressive therapy for adult patients with numerous recalcitrant warts. This therapy should not be used longer than 6 weeks. It alters the host keratinocytes and thereby helps dislodge the unwelcome virus.

ii. **V. Plana** : a. **Tretinoin (Retino A[R])**—Applied to the lesions and surrounding skin several times daily ; therapy should be started at first once daily.

b. **5% Topical 5-fluorouracil cream**—Applied once or twice daily ; can be combined with tretinoin.

c. **Electrodesiccation** or **liquid nitrogen therapy** : It is quite effective.

iii. **Condyloma accuminata**

a. **Podophyllum** : It is a standard treatment for moist surface warts. A 25% solution in benzoin is applied weekly to warts in non-pregnant patients only. Not more than 1-2 cm of skin should be treated in one time. Usually

1-3 treatments are sufficicnt. It is essential to paint the warts with a minimal extension to the surrounding skin. Most patients tolerate an initial application time of 4-8 hours. Next week, it is applied for 6-12 hours again if tolerated. Sexual relations are restricted during the treatment.

b. Topical liquid nitrogen : It is satisfactory in anal and/or genital area. It is quite painful ; white frost should persist for about 15-30 seconds in average condylomata.

c. Electrodesiccation and curettage : For massive or recalcitrant lesions.

d. Topical 5-fluorouracil solution : Starting with a low dose and increasing the quantity according to the patient's tolerance.

iv. Filiform warts : Patient should be informed of their spread while shaving and be convinced about the use of a disposable shaving razor or blade.

a. The most practical treatment is local infiltration at the base of each lesion with lidocaine, followed by light cautery or **electrodesiccation and curettage.**

b. Liquid nitrogen therapy is acceptable in lesions with a relatively broad stalk.

c. Topical application of tretinoin twice daily for several weeks to months.

v. Plantar warts

a. Topical application of 40% salicylic acid plasters and secured in place with adhesive tapes for 24 hours and re-applied after daily baths.

b. Blunt dissection.

c. Liquid nitrogen therapy.

d. Electrodesiccation is frequently scarring and is not the first choice.

e. Other topical remedies include duofilm[R], bleomycin injection and formaldehyde.

vi. Epidermo-dysplasia verruciformis

Treatment is extremely unsatisfactory.

All procedures advised for warts may be attempted but failures are rather frequent.

G. Miscellaneous agents and procedures

Many new agents and procedures have been tried and they are briefly mentioned below.

a. **Oral zinc :** Zinc sulphate, 220 mg t.i.d. probably enhances the cell-mediated immunity in immuno-compromised patients.

b. **Colchicine :** 0.02 mg/kg/day.

c. **Photochemotherapy :** PUVA, light and dyes.

d. **Gammaglobulin :** 16.5% 2 ml, I.M. weekly.

e. **B.C.G. vaccine :** Small pox vaccine weekly intra-dermally, 10 such ; or once inside the lesion.

f. **Interferon :** 10 I.U. alpha 2 interferon contained in 0.2 ml, intralesionally, thrice weekly for three weeks.

g. **60% salicylic acid** in petrolatum, weekly application with curetting off dead tissue, especially in plantar warts.

h. **Soaking of sole in 3% aqueous formalin** for 10 minutes each night for 3-6 weeks in plantar warts ; similarly with 2% glutaraldehyde solution.

i. **2% sulphur gel application** twice daily in verruca plana.

j. **Vitamin A acid, 2% in petrolatum,** applied daily under occlusive dressing for 2-10 weeks.

k. **Diluted liquid ammonia** applied every 4 to 10 days for 10 minutes for 5 weeks.

l. Occlusive dressing with inner side of **banana skin.**

m. Nightly application of **tuberculin jelly.**

n. **Acyclovir ointment, 2.5%** under occlusion.

o. **45 °C warm water** bath daily for 15 minutes.

p. **Levamisole,** 50 mg tab for 3 consecutive days in a week.

q. **Retinoid 1 mg/kg** of body weight for 10 days.

r. **Hypnotherapy.**

s. Application of an equal amount of **phenol** and **nitric acid.**

t. **Carbon di-oxide laser** can destroy warts. 81% cure rate has been claimed.

u. **5% benzoyl peroxide** alternating with **0.05% retinoic acid.**

v. **Application of ultrasound** ; cure rate is 35%.

The results of the above mentioned drugs or procedures vary widely. Controlled trials were not performed in most instances. However, many claim their beneficial effects.

DISCUSSION

Verrucae or warts are common, contagious epithelial tumours caused at least by 35 different types of human papilloma virus (HPV). Children are the common victims. It is rare in the elderly. Warts have been classified according to the size, shape and location. The course is often erratic. Lesions may be multiple, few or even single. They may spread by autoinoculation. A complete regression, even without treatment, may occur after several months but some may recur at the same or different sites and some may persist for years.

Serologic or cell mediated immunity is probably important. As the wart viral particles are only seen in the granular layer and above, some believe that they have little chance to get deep to serve as good antigens. But patients of epidermodysplasia verruciformis do suffer from immunosuppression. Spontaneous cure is due probably to immune mechanism.

Treatment of wart is an individual art. Numerous therapeutic modalities only indicate that our knowledge about wart is inexact and partial. Each modality has its advocates, but the treatment of wart may frequently be a frustrating dermatologic challenge. Over-zealous treatment may cause local burns, erosion, ulcers, scars, keloids, ectropion and permanent nail dystropy. Treatment of choice depends on the type, number and location of lesions. Cryotherapy with liquid nitrogen is most favoured. Single wart can be treated cautiously by electrodesiccation. Application of 40% salicylic acid, 50-100% trichloroacetic acid, 0.7% cantharidin in flexible collodion and 0.05% retinoic acid are quite popular. Oral isotretinoin is needed in epidermodysplasia verruciformis. Alpha interferon intralesionally or I.M. is effective. Application of modern laser therapy (although costly) shows a great promise.

If one can patiently await spontaneous resolution (excepting in few cases), the maximum gain could be achieved.

Giant condyloma accuminatum, often called the **Busche-Lowenstein tumour** is probably caused by a virulent strain of HPV. Though clinically it simulates malignancy, histologically it is always benign.

VITILIGO

It is an acquired idiopathic hypopigmentation of the skin. About 1% of people suffer from it.

DIAGNOSIS

1. Clinical features

A. The lesions

a. A typical vitiligo lesion is a white macule, several mm to several cm in diameter, round to oval in shape with little vague or distinct margin. The skin is otherwise normal.

b. There might be narrow or wide ring of tan or intermediate colour referred to as **trichrome vitiligo**—trichrome means normal coloured skin, intermediate tan and pure white. If this is surrounded by a ring of more pigmented skin, it is called **quadrichrome vitiligo**.

c. Rarely, a vitiligo patch may have a raised erythematous pruritic border. Then it is known as **inflammatory vitiligo**.

d. Hairs with the lesion may be depigmented called **leucotricia** in 9-45% of cases.

B. Extent

It is extremely variable : one to hundred or more. The size is also quite variable.

Progressive enlargement of existing macule and development of new macules constitute the natural course but the rate may be slow or rapidly progressive. There may be a total or near total depigmentation. Hypopigmented macules generally have a convex border.

C. The distribution

a. Areas chracteristically involved are the extensor bony surfaces e.g. skin overlying digits, knees and elbows ; perioroficial areas e.g. around eyes, nose, mouth and rectum ; genitalia may be involved, with or without other parts.

b. Segmental–dermatomal, multidermatomal or quasi-dermatomal areas crossing the midline.

c. Lip-tip syndrome consists of vitiligo at the lips and distant part of digits.

d. Symmetrical vitiligo shows a mirror-image type of lesions.

e. At traumatised areas, vitiligo may show Koebner phenomenon developing at lacerated or burnt areas. Often, vitiligo is seen at the waist of band areas of women wearing sarees very tightly, at the shoulder strap areas or at the collar area where frequent rubbing by clothes do occur.

f. Mucosal vitiligo shows affliction of the lips, gingiva, genitalia and nipples.

g. Palms and soles are often the main sites involved in some patients.

D. Clinical varieties and classification (Fitzpatrick, 1987).

a. Localised

i. **Focal**—One or more macules in a single area but not segmental.

ii. **Segmental**—One or more macules in a dermatomal or quasidermatomal distribution. Sometimes vitiligo looks like zosteriform.

b. Generalised

i. **Acrofacial**—Face and distal parts of extremities.

ii. **Vulgaris**—Scattered macules in symmetrical or asymmetrical areas.

iii. **Universal**—Total or near total body involvement.

c. **Mixed**—Segmental plus vulgaris or acrofacial.

2. Course of vitiligo

It is unpredictable. But, in most cases, the natural course is one of slow progression with periods of stability or rapid progression. Total body involvement has been found to develop from few days to weeks.

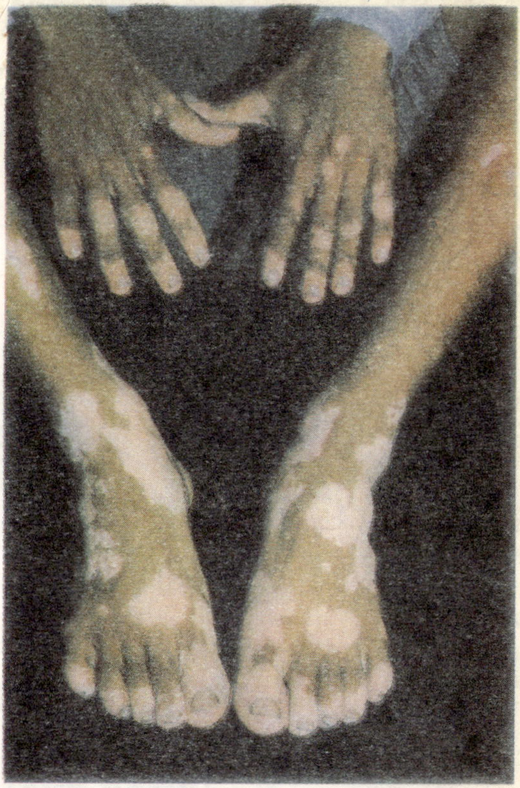

Fig. V-3. **Vitiligo** showing acroteric bilateral symmetrical lesions.

Fig. V-4. **Vitiligo** segmental variety showing dermatomal distribution.

Spontaneous repigmentation often occurs. It might occur in two ways : 1. arising as marginal pigmentation or 2. more commonly, as perifollicular pigmentation gradually coalescing.

Depigmentation of scalp hairs may run along with vitiligo. The prognosis in these patients should be guarded.

3. Associated abnormalities with vitiligo

a. Iris and rentinal pigmentary abnormalities.

b. Iritis and chrioretinitis **c.** Deafness.

d. Graves disease **e.** Hypo or hyperthyroidism and thyroiditis.

f. Diabetes mellitus **g.** Addison's desease.

h. Pernicious anemia **i.** Achlorhydria

j. Defective vitamin B_{12} absorption

k. Gonadal dysfunction **l.** Halo nevi

m. Alopecia areata **n.** Malignant melanomal

o. Psoriasis **p.** Canitis.

All these associations have been noted but as yet no pathologic correlation could in most cases be established.

4. Histology and histochemistry

a. Melanin and melanocytes in basal layer are decreased or absent. Dopaoxidase stain is very helpful to reveal these changes.

b. Perivascular mononuclear infiltrate in early lesions, especially at the active margin.

c. Vacuolatd keratinocytes are often present.

d. Pigment incontinence may be seen at the border.

e. Number of indeterminate cells is increased, but in later stage decreased.

f. Number of Langerhans cells is unchanged.

g. Absence of tyrosinase in vitiligo skin but plasma tyrosinase level is normal.

5. Etiolglocal factors

Since the exact etiology is not known, several hypotheses have been put forward and are briefly mentioned below.

A. Immune hypothesis

a. It suggests an aberration of immune surveilance which results in melanocyte destruction, dysfunction or both.

b. Primary autoimmunization with the formation of autoantibodies against an antigen of the melanocytic system so that melanocyte toxicity or inhibition of melanin formation results.

c. There may be primary injury to melanocytes with the release of antigenic substance and the subsequent autoimmunization.

d. Presence of lympocytes.

e. Occurrence with halo-nevi.

f. Frequent association of autoimmune disorders.

g. Cytotoxic circulating autoantibodies against normal melanocytes have been demonstrated.

h. Cytotoxic peripheral lymphocytes have been found.

All these favour the immune hypothesis.

B. Neural hypothesis

It is said that neurochemical mediator destroys melanocytes or inhibits melanin production. Some clinical as well as laboratory observations support this hypothesis e.g.

a. Segmental vitiligo.

b. Vitiligo in neurologically compromised skin.

c. Vitiligo sparing paralysed skin.

d. Vitiligo occurring after viral encephalitis.

e. Vitiligo occurring following peripheral nerve injury.

f. Association with multiple sclerosis with Horner's syndrome.

g. Development of vitiligo after psychic stress or its incidence among psychiatric patients.

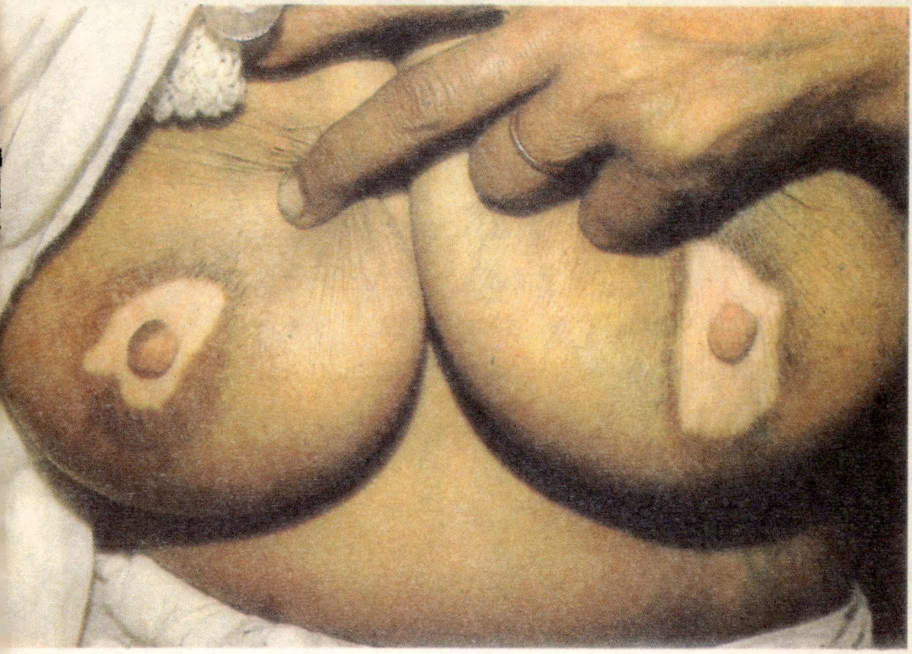

V-5. **Vitiligo** around the nipples with hyperpigmented border.

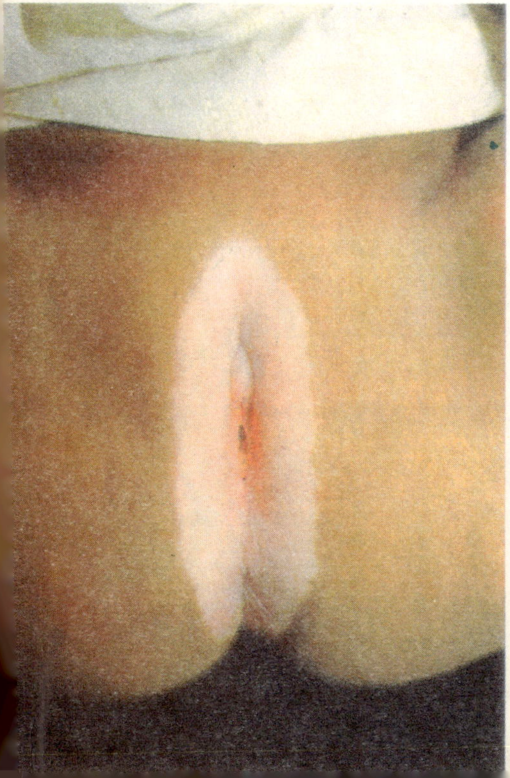

Fig. V-6. **Vitiligo** of the vulva.

h. Neuron-melanoncyte interface.

i. Neuronalchanges in vitiligo.

C. Self-destruction hypothesis

It proposes that an intermediate or metabolite in melanin synthesis causes the melanocyte destruction. Many phenolic compounds can induce depigmentation. Tyrosine, dopa and tryptophan have selective toxicity towards melanocytic cells.

D. Composite hypothesis

None of the previous theories alone can explain development of vitiligo entirely satisfactorily. Absence of mononuclear cells in many patients goes against immune hypothesis. After denervation, vitiligo does not develop and there is no exact evidence for neural control of melanocytes in human.

Most reasonable explanation which has been put forward is that the destruction of melanocytes perhaps occur due to unchecked self-destruction mechanism or through the damage of melanocytes by a toxic mediator which releases an antigenic substance toxic to melanocytes. Once the antigen-antibody reaction starts, the presence of further lymphocytes is unnecessary. A special 'set' is probably necessary between the nerve end plate and adjacent melanocytes for the triggering of destructive mechanism.

E. Hereditary theory

In about 30% vitiligo patients there is a history of vitiligo in another member of the family. Vitiligo has been seen in three generations. It has been reported in monozygotic twins. Inheritance is considered to be autosomal dominant with variable expression and incomplete penetrance. But probably multifactorial inheritance is at play. HLA-DR 4 in blacks, B-13 in Moroccean Jews and BW-35 in Yemenite Jews with vitiligo have been reported.

6. Miscellaneous etilogical factors

a. General incidence is 1 to 2% ; figure varies from 0.14 to 8.8%.

b. No race–whites, orientals and blacks–is spared.

c. Distribution is world wide, particularly in India, Egypt, Japan, Malayasia, Russia, Western Europe, Mexico and the United States.

d. Male to female ratio is 1 : 1.

TREATMENT

PSORALENS (Local and internal)	CHLOROQUIN	STEROID (Local and internal)

As the disease affects the patient mostly psychically, physicians should try to alleviate the mental tension as far as practicable with tender care. Treatment modalities are many and the patient might have a choice. It is better to discuss all the details with the patients before embarking on any particular schedule.

1. Cover up or **camouflage**

a. Opaque sun-screen formulations.

b. Make ups—Potassium permanganate solution, eye brow pencil, drawing ink, kajal, calamine.

c. Dyes—Vitadye. Dye-o-Derm are solutions which are resistant to wash off.

d. A reasonable cosmetic result with topical artificial tanning creams containing dihydroxyacetone.

2. For isolated small macule

Application of 2.5% hydrocortisone cream b.i.d or topical psoralens (starting with very low concentrations) and artificial UVA radiation in tolerable dose after 1-2 hours e.g. 0.15% 8-methoxy-psoralen solution.

3. For wider patches

PUVA therapy i.e. oral psoralens and UVA is said to yield the best result. But certain criteria have been laid down by Fitzpatrick et al (1987) in this regard. They are

a. Age should be over 10 years.

b. Not allowed in pregnancy and lactating period.

c. Involvement not limited to mucosal or distal digital areas (unresponsive areas).

d. No history of photosensitivity.

e. Able to commit 100 to 300 treatments.

Programme of PUVA treatment (Fitzpatrick et al, 1987)

a. Begin with 0.6 mg/kg of Trimethyl psoralen (TMP).

b. If no response in 25 treatments, increase to 0.9 mg per kg of TMP.

c. If no response in another 15-25 treatments, switch over to 0.3 mg/kg of 8-methoxypsoralen (8-MOP).

d. If still no response in 25 treatments, increase to 0.6 mg/kg of 8-MOP.

e. If no response in 15-25 treatments, combine 0.3 mg per kg plus 0.6 mg/kg TMP.

f. If no response in 15-25 treatments, discontinue the treatment as a failure.

Repigmentation is usually preceded by marked darkening of the normal skin enhancing the contrast.

Good response is evident by appearance of hair follicular pigmentation which gradually enlarges to cover the area.

Phototoxic response appear in 48 to 72 hours ; hence twice weekly treatment has been advocated.

TMP has less risk of acute phototoxicity, and it can be used safely with the sun as a UVA source.

Problems associated with oral psoralen therapy

These are (Fitzpatrick et al, 1987) as under.

a. Acute

1. Subjective complaints of nausea, gastrointestinal upset or itching. 2. Phototoxicity of vitiligo skin. 3. Darkening of normal skin. 4. PMLE-like eruptions. 5. Possibility of Koebnerization. 6. Idiosyncratic reactions.

b. Chronic

1. Chronic UV degenerative changes. 2. Enhanced risk of non-melanoma skin cancer. 3. Small hypomelanotic confetti macules. 4. Puva lentigines. 5. Possible premature cataract production in unprotected eyes. 6. Treatment failures or reversal of repigmented macules. 7. Develoyment of new macules. 8. Idiosyncratic reactions.

Nausea and gastrointestinal upsets are less common with TMP than with 8-MOP.

Once the total repigmentatio n is achieved, no further treatment is necessary as there is no evidence to suggest that maintenance therapy is beneficial.

4. Depigmentation of solitary or **few islands** of normal skin in case of total vitiligo.

a. Twice daily application of 20% monobenzyl ether of hydroquinone cream is helpfu l by about 3-4 months period. Total period should be 12 month s. Burning and eczematisation often occur when it is better to put a stop to the treatment temporarily.

b. Oral β-carotene 30-120 mg q.i.d would help further.

5. Miscellaneous therapy

1. Copper chloride orally, 1-3 mg in capsule or in mixture or in the form of intravenous injection 200 micrograms twice in a week.

2. Chemical tattooing with flesh-coloured dyes such as conway.

3. Indigenous drugs e.g. Liv 52[R], Geriforte[R] and Placentrex[R].

4. Vitamin B_{12} and liver extract injections.

5. Internal steroid with or without immunosuppresive agents.

6. Plastic surgery.

7. Chloroquin.

DISCUSSION

Vitiligo is a serious cosmetic disorder. In our society, it creates tremendous psychic stress because of social unacceptibility. Most people think that it is a 100% genetic disorder. As about 1% people suffer from vitiligo in our country and as it carries considerable social stigma the dermatologists should do their best to help the patient.

Results of treatment however are far from satisfactary. In our country, centres for PUVA therapy are few. Oral psoralens followed, two hours after, by an exposure to sun is advocated in most of the patients. Dose of psoralen should be gradually increased. Similarly the period of sun-exposure is also to be increased gradually. Erythema developing after the sun-exposure should ideally persist for 24 hours. Alternate day therapy probably yields better results. Any irritation e.g. itching, vesicle formation, thickening of the skin should make the stoppage of treatment immediately.

Application of local psoralen should start after a few weeks' treatment with internal psoralen therapy. This increases the tolerance. Many proprietory drugs are available. One should start applying these with much dilution, say 1 in 50, 30, 20 or 10, according to the skin texture. Higher strength and more sun-exposure can give rise to severe blistering which might cause further damage to the existing melanocytes.

Local and internal steroid sometimes give good result but side effects of prolonged use limit their usefulness. Chloroquin has wide use.

There is often normal healing of vitiligo even without any treatment. Further, patient might show improvement in some patches, deterioration in others or even development of new patches with a particular regimen of treatment.

Empirical treatment with the liver extract, vitamin B_{12}, indigenous drugs have not yet been evaluated properly.

Prognosis of the disease is unfortunately not predictable.

DERMATOPHARMACOLOGY

Drugs used in dermatology can be broadly divided into

I. **Local** (Topical, epicutaneous, intradermal)

II. **Systemic** (Oral, subcutaneous, intramuscular and intravenous)

A wide range of drugs come under the domain of dermatopharmacology. Many of the topically used substances may give rise to allergic reactions or even primary irritant dermatitis. Certain drugs are being used over many many years though their pharmacology is poorly understood. Such traditional drugs are dithranol, icthammol, resorcinol, sulphur, wood tar, coal tar etc. Recently, psoralens and tretinoin have been used locally. Calamine, starch, talc, titanium dioxide and zinc oxide are old drugs having protective function. New agents having antimicrobial activity are being used quite frequently. Use of pigmentogenic agents e.g. dihydroxyacetone, methoxsalen and trioxsalen are of recent development. Similarly, depigmentogenic drugs e.g. hydroquinone, mequinol and monobenzone have come in the field rather recently.

Topical agents are used mainly to : 1. Cleanse, debride and protect the skin, 2. Destroy causative organisms e.g. virus, bacteria, fungi or protozoa, 3. Relieve symptoms such as pruritus, burning, pain etc. and 4. Reduce inflammation and promote healing.

It is difficult to classify topical agents because : 1. The same agent is used in different conditions, 2. The mode of action in all drugs is not scientifically known, results being obtained empirically, 3. It is not always possible to decipher the chemical structure and establish correlation with pharmacodynamics and 4. The number of drugs are too many.

However, an attempt has been made here to classify the topically used drugs and highlight the pharmacodynamics of commonly used accepted drugs.

Classification

Topically used drugs can be broadly classifed as

I. Topical drugs **according to vehicles** used e.g. soaks, lotions, creams, ointments etc.

II. Topical drugs **according to mode of action** (Functional classification) e.g. antiseptics, antibacterials, antifungals etc.

III. **Miscellaneous** e.g. coal tar, dithranol, retinoic acids etc. etc.

Selection of the route of administration

The major determinant of topical preparations in the skin is the ability of the agent to penetrate cutaneous tissue, particularly the epidermis. Drug concentration declines from the skin surface to subcutis after topical application ; the reverse is true for systemic administration. This should be considered in selecting the route (whether topical or systemic) of administration while treating pathologic processes that may involve the epidermis, papillary dermis, the lower dermis or the subcutis.

Percutaneous absorption

It is a passive diffusion process, stratum corneum being the major barrier to the percutaneous absorption of topically applied drugs. They penetrate the stratum corneum transcellularly i.e. they pass through multiple lipophilic structures (interstitial space and cell membrane) and hydrophilic structures (intracellular components) within the stratum corneum.

Most of the drugs reaching the dermis is re-absorbed by blood and lymph vessels. Lipophilicity of a drug influences the liberation from the vehicle, diffusion pathway and resistance against penetration. Percutaneous absorption occurs in a series of steps or processes.

1. Molecules of a drug must adsorb to the surface of the epidermis.
2. They must reach the viable epidermis.
3. Molecules must diffuse through stratum corneum.

4. They must move through the viable epidermis into the upper dermis where they penetrate the vascular compartments and are transferred through the circulation to other areas ; the remaining process generally occurs quite rapidly.

Factors favouring percutaneous absorption

1. **Partition coefficient**—It is the distribution of a solute between two different phases. Drugs having large partition coefficient, i.e. loosely held by its vehicle, penetrate readily into thc stratum corneum.

2. **Hydration of stratum corneum** increases the drug permeability.

3. **Binding** of chemicals **to the skin** is necessary for absorption.

4. **Vehicles** used affect the permeability of drug by altering the physical state of the skin e.g. hydration of stratum corneum, skin temperature etc. The different vehicles have either positive or negetive effect on stratum corneum hydration depending on their composition. Vehicles increasing hydration are ointments, emulsions etc. which act by their occlusive effect and by adding water to the tissue.

Diffusion constant is directly proportional to temperature. A rise in skin temperature increasses drug diffusion.

5. **Frequency** and **amount** of drug applied to the skin.

6. Thickness of stratum corneum is inversely proportional to percutaneous absorption. Percutaneous absorption is increased in premature, damaged and scrotal skin.

7. Degree of hairiness, and body region e.g. flexures increase percutaneous absorption.

Factors retarding percutaneous absorption

1. Drugs with **small partition coefficient** i.e. drugs held tightly, tend to remain in its vehicle rather than penetrating the skin.

2. **Low ambient temperature.**

3. **Intact and thick stratum corneum.** 4. **Old age.**
5. **Vasoconstrictive disorders** of skin.
6. **Extensor aspects** of the body.

I. Topical drugs according to vehicles, **role of vehicles, their advantages and disadvantages**

There are several methods of applysng topical medicine according to different conditions of the skin. These are soaks, baths, lotions, solutions, emulsions, powders, pastes etc.

They act as adsorbents, anti-infectives, anti-inflammatory, **astringents** (**drying agents that precipitate protein and shrink and contract the skin**), cleansing agents, emollients (skin softeners) and keratolytics (agents that soften, loosen and facilitate exfoliation of the squamous cells of the epidermis).

Vehicle is the base or carrier for topical medication. Many ingredients are used in different vehicles although most are pharmacologically inert and some of which may be allergenic. Toleration and absorption of a drug depend to a great extent on the properties of the vehicles. Hence a **drug action depends greatly upon vehicles.**

All topical preparations consist of a permutation and combination of three things—Liquids, greases and powders.

Liquids : Wet dressings (soaks), baths, tinctures.

Liquid + Powder : Shake lotion.

Liquid + Greases : Creams, ointments etc.

Grease + Powder : Greasy paste.

Powders + Liquids + Greases : Cooling pastes.

Greases consist of true fats, mineral greases and poly-ethylenglycol or their derivatives.

Oils are fluid fats containing triglycerides of oleic acid or other fatty acids. Lanolin and its derivatives are highly effective wetting and suspending agents and powerful emulsifiers, solubilizers and spreading agents. Among the solid fats, cetyl alcohol, steryl alcohol and lanette wax are used for preparing oil in water (O/W) emulsions. **Paraffins** are the products of distillation of petroleum and form the base of most greasy ointments. **Orabase consists of sodium carboxymethyl cellulose, pectin and gelatin in a liquid paraffin polythene base.** They are adhesive paste for moist areas e.g. buccal mucosa, tongue etc.

A. Soaks

They are cooling and drying agents used in acute exudative phase of dermatitis. Examples are : **1.** Water **2.** Normal Saline **3.** Condy's solution—1 : 4000 to 1 : 10,000 potassium-permanganate. **4.** Burow's solution—1 : 20 aluminium sub-acetate. **5.** Silver nitrate solution, 0.5 to 2% in distilled water. **6.** Acetic acid solution, 2-4 table spoonful of white vinegar in a pint of water.

The above solutions are soaked in gauze and are applied on lesional areas for 10-15 minutes, 3-4 times daily. Alternatively, if possible, the part can be immersed into the solution for 10-15 minutes.

Soaks are used in two ways. **1. Open wet dressing** and **2. Closed wet dressing,** the latter being used under plastic occlusion. It causes maceration and hence is not desirable.

Soaks cause vasoconstriction, diminish vasodilatation and thus lessen local blood flow in inflammed area. They cleanse skin exudate and crusts and help in debridement and drainage of infected area.

B. Baths

In India, most patients cannot afford the tub bath which requires 80-100 litres of water along with the drug. They are less cooling and less drying than soaks. Diseases requiring baths are exfoliative dermatitis, generalised psoriasis etc.

Several types of baths are in use. They are : 1. Water bath 2. Saline bath 3. Tar bath : 1 to 2 oz per tub 4. Epsom salt bath : 50 g in a tub 5. Potassium permanganate : Twenty five 5 grain tablets in a tub.

6. Oat meal bath: Half to 1 cup in a tub. 7. Oil bath: Half to 1 oz oil per tub; cocoanut oil, olive oil etc.

C. **Lotions**

Lotions are suspensions of various types of powders in water with suspending agents. These powders are calamine (**zinc carbonate, coloured with ferric oxide**), kaolin, starch zinc oxide, titanium dioxide, magnesium carbonate, zinc sterate and talc. Glycerine 10-15% is often added in lotions. Concentration of powder varies between 10-40%. Lotions are used in acute non-weeping dermatoses.

They are soothing agents and when water evaporates, the residual powder protects the skin. Lotions are contraindicated in lesions which are very oozing since they would form cakes over the lesion and are likely to retain the debris. However, after proper cleansing of the lesions with soaks, lotions having less concentration of powders can be used for the first few days in comparatively less oozing lesions.

Compositions of some important lotions are given below.

1. **Calamine lotion** (B.P.)

Calamine	15 g
Zinc oxide	0.5 g
Sodium citrate	500 mg
Bentonite	3 g
Liquid phenol	0.5 ml
Glycerine	5 ml
Water to	100 ml

2. **Shamberg's lotion**

Menthol	0.25%
Phenol	1%
Peanut oil	45%
Calcium hydroxide solution	45%
Zinc oxide powder	8%

3. **Lotio sulphuris alba**

Zinc sulphate	4%
Sulphuretted potash	4%
Distilled water	92%

4. **Basic-Shake lotion**

Zinc oxide	14 c.c
Talc	15 c.c
Glycerine	10 c.c
Water ad	100 c.c

D. **Liniments**

They are lotions to which oil has been added in order to reduce excessive drying. Important examples of liniments are given.

1. Liniment calamine

Calamine	5 g
Wool fat	1 g
Oleic acid	0.5 ml
Arachis oil	50 ml
Calcium hydroxide solution ad	100 ml

2. Modified liniment calamine

Calamine	5 g
Wool fat	5 g
Zinc stearate	2 g
Oleic acid	1 ml
Light liquid paraffin	45 ml
Calcium hydroxide solution ad	100 ml

E. Emulsions

Various emulsions are used in skin diseases. They can be subdivided into **creams, gels** and **ointments.**

a. Creams : They are emulsions having a discontinuous oil phase in a continous water phase and is termed *oil in water* (O/W). Creams, when applied, completely vanish from the skin and can be easily washed off with water. Numerous creams are now available in the market.

b. Gels : They are transparent emulsions which liquify in contact with warm skin. If they dry up, a non-occlusive film is formed.

c. Ointments : These are emulsions having a discontinuous water phase in a continuous oil phase and is termed *water in oil* (W/O). They are difficult to wash off from the skin and is insoluble in water. They act as occlusive agents and reduce water loss from the skin. If they are applied after hydrating the skin, the absorbed water is sealed into the stratum corneum and thus helps in the hydration of skin. Medicinal agents are better absorbed in skin thro' ointments.

There has been a spectacular improvement in chemical technology in preparing creams, gels and ointments. The situation is such that there is hardly any well-defined border between creams and ointments.

Some of the vehicles used for emulsions may also have medicinal effect e.g. white petrolatum, being an inhibitor of cyclo-oxygenase formation, decreases the level of prostaglandins in skin and thereby promotes healing of certain conditions (e. g. thermal burns) associated with increased prostaglandin synthesis.

F. Powders

They are fine particles and act as cooling and drying agents for the skin by increasing the available surface area for evaporation. They decrease friction between intertriginous areas and lessen maceration. Plenty of proprietory powders are available in the market. Talcum powder is widely used. Antifungal powders are useful in preventing intertrigo.

Some proprietory preperations are given below.

1. **Mycoderm^R**

Salicylic acid 3%
Boric acid 19.4%
Camphor 0.52%
Menthol 0.08%
Starch 31%
Talcum as base

2. **Daktarin^R, Zole^R**

Miconazole nitrate 2%

3. **Nebasulf^R**

Neomycin sulphate 5 mg
Bacitracin 250 units
Sulphacetamide 60 mg

4. **Candid^R, Statum^R**

Clotrimazole USP 1% w/w
Talcum powder base q.s.

5. **Zinoderm^R**

Zinc undecyclinate	I.P	2.0%
Zinc oxide	I.P.	2.0%
Salicylic acid	I.P.	2.0%
Camphor	I.P.	2.0%
Purified talc	I.P.	q.s.

G. Pastes

These are combinations of powders and hydrophilic ointments. Powder content is rather high : 20-30%. But they are difficult to apply and also to remove. They do not interfere with perspiration and hence cannot keep moisture in the skin. They act as a protective layer for it is difficult to scratch the skin through them. Important examples are

1. **Lasser's paste (zinc oxide paste)**

Zinc oride	25 g
Starch	25 g
White petrolatum ad	100 g

With this paste dithranol is often used in case of psoriatic patients.

2. **Unna paste**

Zinc oxide	15 g
Gelatin	15 g
Glycerine	35 ml
Water ad	100 ml

3. Burow's paste

Burow's solution	17 ml
Hydrophilic oint	35 g
Zinc oxide paste ad	100 g

H. Oils

Various oils are in use in dermatology. They soften the skin and remove the crusts. Olive oil, sesame oil, peanut oil and castor oil are often used. Keratolytics are also often mixed with oils. Oil of cade is used with keratolytics in treating psoriasis.

I. Soaps

Soaps are agents to emulsify fats with water. They can be classified into : **1. Regular soap** having alkaline pH **2. Neutral soap 3. Superfatted soap** and **4. Medicated soaps** containing various chemicals of medicinal value e.g. tetmosal soap[R], sulphur soap, soaps containing chlorhexidine and povidone iodine.

Neutral soaps are least irritating to the skin. Superfatted soaps are indicated in dry skin.

Some important properties and uses of common dermatological bases are given in the chart (Crossland's **Medicine to-day**, April-June, 1988, p 14) in p. 479.

II. Topical drugs according to mode of action

1. Antibacterials

i. Sulphonamides and sulphur : Topical use of sulphonamides is contraindicated as they are potent sensitisers. Sulphur, in contact with living tissue, forms hydrogen sulphide and pentathionic acid, both having germicidal and fungicidal properties. Sulphur has also a local stimulating and keratolytic action on the skin.

ii. Aminoglycosidic antibiotics : These are isolated from various species of streptomyces. Gentamycin is produced from species of micromonospora. These are all glycosides with various sugars linked to an aglycone. They interfere

Surface and Disease	Base	Effect	Examples/Notes
Dry and scaly : Psoriasis, dry eczema, ichthyosis	Ointment	Occlusive Emollient	Soft white or soft yellow paraffin Emulsifying ointmennt Synthetic bases Lanolin (may sensitise)
Moist or dry : Eczema in various stages	Cream	Cooling, Emollient and moist-urising	Oily cream Aqueous cream Cetomacrogol cream Synthetic bases (preservative may sensitise)
Acutely inflammed, wet and oozing : Weeping eczema, Bullous diseases	Lotions	Drying, soothing and cooling	Saline solution Calamine lotion Aluminium acetate solution Potassium permanganate solution
Lichenified : Eczema and Psoriasis	Pastes	Protective, prevent spreading of active ingredient	Zinc compound paste Lasser's paste Coal tar paste Impregnated bandage protects eczema from scratching Dithranol paste in psoriasis

Surface and Disease	Base	Effect	Examples/Notes
Flexures, especially if sore and moist : Intertrigo, Flexural eczema, Psoriasis, Candidiasis	Dusting powders	Lessen friction and are drying	Talc dusting powder. Zinc, starch and talc can be used as a vehicle for antifungal drugs.
Flexures : Intertrigo, Candidiasis, Ulcers	Paints	Drying	Castellani's magenta paint (better than powders for very moist areas).

with synthesis of protein by attaching to ribosomal surface and permitting an *mRNA* molecule to couple with an incorrect *tRNA*. This causes faulty protein synthesis and leads to a further failure of metabolic function within bacterial cell.

Kanamycin, neomycin and gentamycin can be applied topically. After absorption, drugs are widely distributed in body fluids and tissues and are rapidly excreted through urine. **Dermatologic indication** : The topical use of neomycin is restricted, for it increases the incidence of contact dermatitis. Gentamycin, when used topically, is effective against gram-negative organisms in concentration of 0.1%. Some proprietary preparations are : Gentamycin, Genticyn[R] sulphate cream, Supragent[R], Neosporin[R] containing polymyxin B sulph 5000 u/g, neomycin sulph 3,400 u/g, Zinc bacitracin 400 u per g.

iii. Pyrithione : Used as fungicide and bactericide and also as antiseborrheic agent in 2% concentration.

iv. Tetracyclines : Effectively used in acne and perioral dermatitis (e.g. Terramycin[R], Oxytetracycline).

v. Erythromycin : Suppresses the anerobic Propionibacteria acne within the sebaceous follicle and improves acne with topical administration e.g. Acnicin[R].

vi. **Lincomycin** and **Clindamycin** : Used primarily as topical agents in the management of acne vulgaris (e.g. Dalacin T[R], Cleocin T[R]). Pitted keratolysis responds to topically applied clindamycin.

vii. **Polymyxin B** : Acts against gram-negative bacteria (e.g. Neosporin[R] in combination with bacitracin and neomycin).

viii. **Bacitracin** : Acts against gram-positive organisms, available as topical preparations.

ix. **Fusidic acid** : It is a steroidal antibiotic, marketed as 2% sodium salts (Fucidin Leo[R]) and in combination with β-methasone (Fucibet[R]). They act by inhibiting bacterial protein synthesis. It is inhibitory to staphylococci, corynebacteria and clostridia but inactive against coliform bacteria.

x. **Nitrofurazone** : It is a yellowish and odourless crystalline powder. It has an antibacterial action against a number of gram-negative and gram-positive bacteria. It is used in superficial wounds, burns, ulcers etc. The major drawback of its topical application is the high rate of sensitisation and generalised allergic skin reactions. It is found to be carcinogenic in rats. Proprietory prepartion is Furacin[R] (0.2% Nitrofurazone oint).

2. Antiseptics

i. **Iodine** : It is one of the most potent antiseptics. Iodophors are aqueous complexes of iodine and is a solubilizing agent or carrier which libertes free iodine in solution. They are less bactericidal and less irritating to the skin than elemental forms of iodine. Iodophors are active against gram-postive and gram-negative organisms and do not require repeated application for optimal antibacterial effect. Examples include Betadine[R], Piodine[R] etc.

ii. **Organic mercurials** : Was used in the past; but because of their irritating properties and potential toxicity, their use is no longer desirable.

iii. Alcohol : 70% ethanol or isopropyl alcohol has slight antimicrobial properties but is rather drying to skin.

iv. Hexachlorophene : Has antibacterial effects primarily against gram-positive organisms. Its effect is cumulative when applied repeatedly over several days. It may occasionally cause CNS toxicity in infants in case of generalised application e.g. bathing.

v. Chlorhexidine : It is active against gram-positive and gram-negative bacteria and has also cumulative antibacterial effect.

3. Antifungal

i. Nystatin : It is available in a variety of dosage and forms, including drops, suspension, powder, cream and ointment, for topical use to skin and mucous membranes.

Each preparation contains 1000,000 units of active drug per g or per ml. It is used for treatment of local candidiasis of the skin. Although rare, it may also cause allergic contact dermatitis. Examples are : Kenacomb^{R} (in combination with triamcinolone acetonide, neomycin and gramicidin), Mycostatin^{R} ointment.

ii. Amphotericin B : Available in a concentration of 3% in the form of lotion, cream and ointment. It can be used as an alternative to nystatin in the treatment of candidal infections of the skin. Side effects include yellow-orange discoloration of the skin. Examples are Talsutin^{R} vaginal tablet (in combination with tetracyclin 100 mg and amphotericin B 50 mg).

iii. Imidazoles : These agents are applied topically for the treatment of candidiasis, tinea infections, pityriasis versicolor and can be used in vaginal candidiasis. Commercial preparations have clotrimazole, miconazole, econazole etc.

Clotrimazole is available as 1% cream or solution e.g. Imidil^{R}, Lotril^{R}, Canesten^{R}, Statum^{R} etc. It is also available as 100 mg vaginal foaming tablets. Miconazole nitrate is available as 2% cream/lotion for skin e.g. Daktarin^{R}, Zole^{R},

Gynodaktarin[R] as 2% cream for vagina. Econazole is also available as 1% cream e.g. Econazole[R], Vaginal tabs, Ecoderm[R] (in combination with Cinchocaine hydrochloride).

All these agents may cause allergic contact dermatitis.

iv. **Gentian violet** : It is hexamethyl pararosaniline hydrochloride mixed with other methyl pararosanilines. It is used in concentration of 0.5-2% ; side effects include staining of the skin with a deep purple colour.

v. **Castellani's paint** : It is also known as magenta paint or carbol fuchsin topical solution. Composition is 0.3% basic fuchsin + 4.5% phenol + 10% resorcinol + 5% ethanol + 10% acetone.

It is used in tinea pedis and tinea cruris. Side effects include staining of the skin and occasional allergic sensitisation.

vi. **Whitfield's ointment** : It contains a mixture of benzoic acid 6% and salicylic acid 3% and is used for dermatophyte infection.

vii. **Tolnaftate** : It is a thiocarbamate derivative ; effective against dermatophytes and pityrosporum orbiculare but has no effect against candida. Available in 1% concentration as an aerosol (powder + solution), solution, gel, cream and powder. Some proprietory preparations are Tolnaderm ointment[R], Tinaderm lotion[R], Tinavate cream[R]. Side effect is allergic contact dermatitis.

viii. **Haloprogin** : It is a halogenated phenolic ether having a broad spectrum of antimycotic activity including dermatophytes, candida and pityrosporum orbiculare.

It is available as 1% solution or cream. Side effects are irritation, pruritus and occasional vesicle formation.

ix. **8-hydroxyquinoline** : These include iodoquinol (di-iodo-hydroxyquin) and clioquinol (iodochlorhydroxyquin). Available as 3-4% cream or ointment, alone or in combination with hydrocortisone e.g. Dermoquinol[R], Vioform[R], Millicorten vioform[R]. Side-effects are yellow staining of clothing and allergic contact sensitisation.

4. Antiviral

i. Acyclovir : It is an acyclic purine nucleoside analogue and is effective in the treatment of herpes virus infection. It inhibits herpes virus DNA polymerase. Topical acyclovir reduces the local signs and symptoms in primary genital herpes infection within 3 to 4 days. Topical application of acyclovir is often associated with transient burning. This is due to the base, polyethylene glycol. It is available as 5% acyclovir cream (Herpex^{R}, Herperax^{R}, Cyclovir^{R} cream).

ii. Idoxuridine (IDU) : It is an iodinated pyrimidine used in the treatment of herpes simplex infection. It is available as 0.1% ophthalmic solution (Ridinox^{R}) in distilled water. A 0.5% ophthalmic ointment in a petrolatum base is also available. An allergic sensitisation has been reported by idoxuridine.

iii. Phosfonoacetic acid (PFA) : Phosfonoacetic acid and its analogue phosfonoformate have antiviral properties against HSV 1 and HSV 2. They inhibit HSV DNA-polymerase. A 3% ointment of PFA is used.

iv. Adenine arabinoside (vidarabine) : It is a purine nucleoside interfering with the early steps of viral DNA synthesis of herpes simplex, zoster-varicella and vaccinia viruses. It is applied three times daily into the conjunctival sac for herpes simplex keratitis.

5. Antiperspirants

i. Inorganic salts : Aluminium chloride, aluminium chlorhydroxide complex and aluminium sulfocarbonate are antiperspirants. Action is caused by the alteration of epidermal duct to permit large amount of sweats to invade the surrounding tissue but not reach the skin surface. Side effects are irritation and staining of clothes.

ii. Formaldehyde : It is used in treating hyperhydrosis of the hands and feet. Glutaraldehyde 5% or 10% solution has been suggested as a substitute. It appears to function by producing a plug at or near the skin surface and thus occluding the eccrine ostium and preventing the flow of perspiration.

Side effects include irritation.

iii. **Anticholinergics** : Local application of atropine and scopolamine acts as antiperspirant. Derivatives have also resulted in anhidrosis. It blocks the CNS stimulation of both eccrine and apocrine glands and prevents secretion.

6. Sun screeing agents

These agents block UV light and prevent acute and chronic sun-mediated skin changes.

i. **Para aminobenzoic acid (PABA)** absorbs UV light between 280-320 nm.

ii. **Benzophene compounds** absorb ultraviolet radiation from 250-400 nm.

iii. **Red veterinary petrolatum** blocks UV upto 340 nm.

iv. **Titanium dioxide,** bentonite and zinc oxide powders physically block the sunlight.

v. **Salicylates** and **cinnamates** can also protect the skin from the bad effects of sunlight.

7. Pigmentogenic agents

Two psoralens, **methoxsalen** and **trioxsalen,** are pigmenting and photoprotective agents. Methoxsalen is obtained from fruit (Ammi-majus) ; trioxsalen is a synthetic compound. It increases melanin pigmentation of the skin under stimulation of sunlight (Long UV, 290-380 nm). Topical use may cause erythema, severe edema, blistering and pain. It is mainly used in vitiligo, photodermatoses and psoriasis e.g. Melanocyl[R] ointment, solution ; Psorlin[R] ointment and solution ; Meladinine[R] ointment and solution ; Tripsoren[R] solution.

8. Depigmentogenic agents

i. **Hydroquinone** : 2-4% hydroquinone is moderately effective in the treatment of melasma. Treatment must be continued for months or years to get the effective results.

Rapid result can be obtained with addition of salicylic acid 2-3%, tretinoin 0.1% and/or topical steroids. Some proprietory preparations are Melalite[R] and Depig[R].

ii. **Monobenzone** : It is a monobenzyl ether of hydroquinone. It prevents the formation of melanin pigments in the skin without destruction of melanocytes. It often causes skin irritation and eczematous sensitisation. Excessive depigmentation may occur beyond the areas of treatment.

9. **Scabicidal and pediculocidal agents**

i. **Benzyl benzoate** : It is an effective parasiticide used in the form of 25% emulsion with triethanolamine and oleic acid. Single treatment is usually effective against pediculosis and scabies. Example is Ascabiol[R].

ii. **Carbaryl** : It is a contact insecticide acting as an easily reversible cholinesterase inhibitor. Concentrates of carbaryl cause skin irritation and systemic poisoining.

iii. **Chlorphenothane (Dicophane, DDT)** : It is a chlorinated diphenylethane derivative, insoluble in water and stable in light and air. It is both contact and stomach poison for insects. It is effective against lice but not mites. It can be applied to the skin in 5-10% concentration in an inert base e.g. talc.

iv. **Gamma benzene hexachloride** (GBH) : It is very effective parasiticide, available in the form of lotion and ointment containing 1-2% active ingredient. It is effectively used in pediculosis and scabies. Examples are Scabiped[R] Gab[R], Gamaderm[R], Pediscab[R] etc.

v. **Crotamiton** (N-ethylcroton-O-toluidide) : It is an acaricidal preparation used effectively in the treatment of scabies. It is also an antipruritic agent and local application gives relief from itching of pruritus ani, pruritus vulvae and scroti, senile pruritus associated with various dermatoses. It occasionally causes transient erythema and sense of warmth. Its use is contraindicated in acute exudative or vesicular dermatitis or in the eyes. It is available as 10% lotion or cream e.g. Crotorax[R], Crotorax HC[R].

vi. **Malathion** : It is effective in prevention and treatment of pediculosis.

vii. **Pyrethrin** : It is a rapid acting compound derived from chrysanthemum plants and is used in the treatment of pediculosis. It should not be used more than twice a day. It is as effective as GBH in the treatment of pediculosis capitis and pubic pediculosis.

9. Hair growth promoter

Minoxidil (Mintop[R], Gromane[R], Hebald[R], Multigain[R]) : It is a newly introduced drug proved effective mainly for male pattern baldness and also for alopecia areata and totalis.

The exact mechanism of action of minoxidil in promoting hair-growth is not completely known. However, it may act through various mechanisms such as

1. It enhances micro-circulation around hair follicles through its vasodilatory effect and accelerate hair growth.

2. It directly stimulates the resting hair follicle cells (telogen) to enter into active proliferative phase, anagen.

3. It alters the effect of androgens on the genetically predetermined hair follicles. It also acts by affecting the androgen metabolism in the scalp and inhibiting the capacity of the androgens to affect the hair follicles.

It is poorly absorbed from intact skin after topical application. About 95% of the systemically absorbed minoxidil from topical doses is eliminated within 4 days. Metabolism of minoxidil absorbed after topical application is yet to be fully explained. When administered orally, approximately 90% of the drug is metabolised by conjugation with glucoronic acid. Metabolites are excreted principally in urine and the renal clearence is dependant upon glomerular filtration rate. It does not cross the blood-brain barrier. It requires application twice daily for at least 4 months before any new hair growth is noticed. Dose should not exceed 2 ml/day.

Side-effects : Local irritation including erythema, flushing, dry skin, burning sensation, itching and rash. Dermatitis and hypertrichosis may also occur. It may also cause allergic reactions, dizziness, headache, tingling sensation, weakness, edema, eye irritation, otitis externa or visual disturbance. Other systemic side-effects after topical application include tachycardia, edema, angina or potentiation of orthostatic hypotension.

It is contraindicated in hypersensitivity, pregnant and nursing mothers.

III. Miscellaneous agents used in dermatology

1. **Anthralin (Dithranol)** : It is a semisynthetic substance prepared by oxidation and sulphonation of anthracene. Chrysarobin is a naturally occurring mixture obtained from the wood of Andira araroba. Anthralin is closely related to pure substance. It exists normally in the form of a dihydroxyanthrone which is extremely irritating to tissue because of the presence of strongly reducing methylene group. It takes oxygen from the skin and causes a burning sensation. **It prevents the oxygen uptake by cells and slows down the growth rate of rapidly proliferating cells.** It also interacts with mitochondrial DNA with psoriatic epidermis resulting in the formation of respiratory deficient mitochondria. It is used in psoriasis and is irritating to skin and stains skin and clothing. Examples are Derobin^R (dithranol 1.15%, salicylic acid 1.15%), Derobin HC^R (dithranol 1.15%, salicylic acid 1.15% and hydrocortisone 0.5%).

2. **Allantoin** : It stimulates tissue formation and hastens wound healing. It has keratin dispersing activity and is used in psoriasis.

3. **Cade oil** : It is obtained from destructive distillation of wood of Juniperus oxycedrus. It is used as an ointment and shampoo in the treatment of psoriasis and eczema.

4. **Cadmium** : Cadmium sulphide has been used in the control of seborrheic dermatitis and dandruff, usually as a

shampoo containing 1% cadmium sulphide suspended in a detergent base. It is also effective in pityriasis versicolor.

5. **Calamine** : As already mentioned, it is zinc carbonate coloured with ferric oxide. It is a pink or reddish-brown powder, colour depending on the amount of ferric oxide present. It is insoluble in water and has mild astringent and antipruritic action.

6. **Cantharidin** : It is a mitochondrial poison leading to changes in cell membrane, epidermal cell dyshesion, acantholysis and blister formation. It is used in treating warts and other benign cutaneous lesions.

7. **Caustics** : They are used either alone for hemostasis or in combination with electrosurgery for superficial treatment of some hyperplastic cutaneous lesions e.g. warts, keratoses, xanthelasma, basal cell carcinoma etc. and are also used in cosmetic therapy for ageing, e.g. in wrinkled facial skin.

A. **Mono- di and trichloroacetic acids** : They are strongly corrosive and act by precipitation and coagulation of skin proteins. A 35-50% trichloroacetic acid is the most useful preparation for xanthelasma palpebrarum, flat warts and condyloma accuminata. They may be used in granuloma telangiectaticum in combination with electro- or cryosurgery.

B. **Silver nitrate** : Concentration stronger than 5% is used for its caustic action. A 5-10% solution may be applied to fissures or excessive granulation tissue and corns.

8. **Collodion** : It is a solution of pyroxylin in a mixture of alcohol 1 volume and solvent ether 3 volumes diluted with the same mixed solvent to a kinematic viscosity. Salicylic acid and lactic acid are often used in this vehicle.

9. **Dihydroxyacetone** : When applied to the skin, it causes slow development of a brown coloration due to reaction with the amino acid of the skin. Coloration disappears within 8-14 days on stopping the application. It may be used in vitiligo.

10. **Fluorouracil** : It is a pyrimidine antagonist acting by interfering with DNA synthesis by innibiting thymidylate synthetase activity. It is used topically in the treatment of multiple actinic keratoses, superficial basal cell carcinoma, Bowen's disease and some types of warts.

11. **Hydroxyquinoline** : Hydroxyquinoline sulphate possesses antibacterial, antifungal and deodorant properties. Iodochlorhydroxyquin (Vioform[R]) contains 40% iodine ; used alone or in combination with steroids in the treatment of eczema, impetigo, dermatophytosis, yeast and trichomonal infections. It may cause contact allergy and stain skin, hair and clothing with yellow colour.

12. **Podophyllum resin** : Active ingredient is podophyllotoxin obtained from Podophyllum emodi (in India) or Podophyllum peltatum (North America). It is used in the treatment of condyloma accuminata and other genital warts.

Its mode of action is not exactly known. It probably acts by inducing arrest of mitosis in metaphase and causes epithelial cell death. Vacuolation, nuclear degeneration and also swelling are seen in podophyllin-treated cell.

Side-effects include chemosis and conjunctivitis when it comes in contact with eye. Peripheral neuropathy and intrauterine fetal death have been reported. It is applied as a 25% suspension in compound tincture of benzoin or in alcohol.

13. **Phenol** : Rarely used as an antiseptic because of its low acidity and high toxicity. It is used as an antipruritic in lotions and ointments in a concentration of 0.1-1%.

14. **Propylene glycol** : A 2% isotonic solution is used as a vehicle in dermatologic preparations. When applied to skin under polythene occlusion, it hydrates the skin and causes desquamation of scales. It is used effectively in patients with X-linked ichthyosis, ichthyosis vulgaris and other abnormalities of keratinization with hyperkeratosis, scaling and dryness.

15. **Resorcinol** : It is a phenol derivative having bactericidal and fungicidal property. It is irritating and sensitising to the skin. A 1-2% solution has been used in seborrhea, acne and psoriasis.

16. **Retinoic acids** (Tretinoin, vitamin A acid, trans-retinoic acid): These are used mainly in the treatment of acne. Also used in senile comedones, pseudofolliculitis, palmoplantar hyperkeratosis, Darier's disease, early actinic keratosis, melasma, acanthosis nigricans and warts. They act by inhibiting the synthesis of tonofilaments and thereby decreasing the attachments between keratinized cells. They also stimulate epidermal mitosis and enhance desquamation. Toxicity includes irritation, erythema and scaling, temporary hyper- or hypopigmentation, increased risk of phototoxicity. Examples are Eudyna®, Retino A®.

17. **Salicylic acid** : It is keratolytic (>6%) and also keratoplastic at concentrations between 3-6% i.e. causes softening of the horny layers and shedding of scales.

It acts by solubilization of intercellular cement and enhances the shedding of corneocytes by decreasing intercellular cohesion. It is used in the treatment of superficial fungal infection (Whitfield's oint in combination with benzoic acid), acne, psoriasis, seborrheic dermatitis and other scaling dermatoses. It has got synergistic keratolytic effect with sulphur. It is used in combination with equal parts of lactic acid in flexible collodion (Duofilm®) in the treatment of warts.

18. **Selenium** : Used in the form of sulphide compounds in the treatment of seborrheic dermatitis of scalp and pityriasis versicolor. Its mode of action is unknown. Example is selsun shampoo®.

19. **Sulphur** : It is used in combination with other agents in the treatment of acne, rosacea, ringworm, psoriasis, scabies, seborrheic dermatitis etc. It inhibits the growth of micro-organisms, particularly fungi and parasites.

20. **Silver sulphadiazine** : Used in the prevention and treatment of wound sepsis and in patients with 2nd and 3rd

degree burn. It is bactericidal against many gram-positive and gram-negative bacteria. Recently, it is being used in herpes zoster.

21. Tar compounds : Tar is a product of destructive distillation of organic substances obtained from various sources. There are different types e.g. (1) **Wood tars** including oil of cade, beech, birch and pine. (2) **Bituminous tars** including ichthyol and ammonium ichthyosulphonate which is a distillation product of fossilized fish. (3) **Coal tars** are by-products of destructive distillation of bituminous coal **containing more than 10,000 different compounds**, particularly enriched with polyaromatic hydrocarbons.

It contains 2-8% **light oil** (benzene, toluene, xylene), 2-10% **middle oil** (phenols, cresols, naphthaline) ; 8-10% **heavy oil** (naphthaline and derivatives) ; 16-20% **anthracene oil** and about 50% pitch. Coal tars are brownish black and slighly soluble in water and have photosensitising property. Because of numerous phenolic derivatives, it has antiseptic property. Effectively used in treating psoriasis in Goeckerman regimen.

Side-effects include phototoxic response known as **tar smarts**—a burning and stinging reaction in the skin occurring during exposure to sunlight or large doses of UVA. Folliculitis of hair bearing or intertriginous areas may also occur. Repeated exposures to tars for many years are said to be carcinogenic.

Coal tar solution (Liquor Picis Carbonis) : It is prepared by extracting coal tar with alcohol and polysorbate (Tween 80) —an emulsifying agent. 100 ml of solution is equivalent to 20 g of coal tar. It is extensively used in treating psoriasis.

Ichthammol : It is obtained by the destructive distillation of certain bituminous schists. It is a black viscous liquid containing ammonium salts and organically combined sulphur. It has got bacteriostatic effect and is used in chronic skin diseases including psoriasis.

22. Urea : It has got a hydrating effect on stratum corneum and is used in the treatment of dry skin. It has got also antipruritic effect. Urea compounds disrupt the normal hydrogen bonds of epidermal protein and thus help to remove adherant scales. It has also antibacterial activity and is used in wounds and skin infection in the form of lotion, cream and ointment. Examples are : Urea 10[R], Urea 20[R], Cotaryl[R], Dericream[R] etc.

23. Topical steroids

Topical corticosteroids are the most widely used preparations in dermatological practice. Hence they are discussed separately in details. They are marketed in various concentrations, vehicles and in combination with other agents e.g. antimicrobial agents, antifungal agents etc.

General principles of topical steroid therapy : When prescribing a topical steroid, the following three points should be considered.

A. Vehicle selection

i. **Gels, solutions** and **lotions**—used in acute dermatitis and hairy areas.

ii. **Creams** and **ointments**—used in subacute and chronic dermatitis and glabrous skin.

B. Drug selection : More potent agents should be used first and then tapered to less potent ones.

C. Amount to be prescribed

i. 1-8 g per 9% of the body surface.

ii. 20-30 g to cover the entire body in a single application.

Mechanism of action of corticosteroids may be discussed in the following steps.

i. penetration of the stratum corneum.

ii. passage across the cell membranes.

iii. binding to specific cytoplasmic receptors.

iv. translocation of the complex to the nucleus.

v. interaction with high-affinity binding sites via the process of *mRNA* transcription resulting in the formation of new proteins.

Classification of topical corticosteroids

Potency	Name	Strength	Proprietary name
A. Very potent	i. Clobetasol	0.05%	Exel, Tenovate
	ii. Halcinonide	0.01%	Cortilate, Cortilate N
	iii. Beclomethasone dipropionate	0.05%	Diproform, Diprogenta, Diprolene
	iv. Diflucortalone valerate	0.03%	
	v. Fluocinolone acetonide	0.02%	Flucort
B. Potent	i. Betamethasone dipropionate	0.025% -0.05%	Diprovate, Gentalene Diprolene
	ii. Betamethasone valerate	0.1%	Betnovate, Fucibet, Walacort
	iii. Difluocortalone valerate	0.1%	
	iv. Fluocinolone acetonide	0.025%	Flucort
	v. Fluocinonide	0.05%	
C. Moderately potent	i. Desonide	0.5%	
	ii. Triamcinolone acetonide	0.1%	Kenacomb, Kenacort
	iii. Hydrocortisone butyrate	0.1%	Ledercort
D. Mildly potent	i. Clobetasone butyrate	0.05%	
	ii. Fluocortolone hexonate	0.1%	
	iii. Fluocortolone	0.25%	Ultralan
	iv. Fluocortolone hexonate	0.25%	
E. Weakly potent	i. Hydrocortisone	0.1-2.5%	Wycort
	ii. Methylprednisolone	0.025%	(Acetate)

On application of topical corticosteroids to the skin, the first change is the **vasoconstriction followed by reduction of inflammation.** Vasoconstriction may be due to the alteration of catecholamine and histamine effects on the peripheral blood vessels.

Side effects of topical corticosteroids

These can be divided into : **1. Systemic side effects** and **2. Local side effects** and are discussed below.

1. Systemic side effects

i. Edema due to sodium retention.

ii. Hyperglycemia, glycosuria, hypertension, Cushing's syndrome with striae, buffalo hump, moon face and hirsutism.

iii. Hypokalemia and induction of peptic ulceration.

iv. Occurrence of osteoporosis and the growth retardation in children with topical corticosteroid therapy are still controversial.

2. Local side effects

i. Masking of clinical features of primary diseases e.g. tinea incognito, scabies etc.

ii. Atrophic changes accompanied by erythema, telangiectasia and thinning of skin. Formation of papules and pustules is often seen. Perioral dermatitis may occur. Striae in flexural areas are permanent.

iii. Gluteal granulomas related to the use of fluorinated corticosteroids in the napkin area.

iv. Leucoderma following fluorandrenolone tape.

v. Pustular psoriasis—a complication of withdrawal of steroid therapy.

vi. Sensitisation to topical corticosteroids is extremely rare and due in most cases to vehicle used.

SYSTEMIC THERAPY

Histamine and Histamine antagonists (antihistamines)

1. Physiological antagonists : In anaphylaxis and in angioedema, massive release of histamine is counteracted by **adrenaline** and related amines. Adrenaline injection[R] (0.5 to 1 ml) is given subcutaneously or intramuscularly.

2. Competitive antagonists (Antihistamines)

Nearly all antihistamines resemble histamine in having the group CH_2–CH_2–N=. They antagonize most of the pharmacological effects of histamine and block H_1 receptors on the blood vessels and the smooth muscles. They also have anticholinergic, antiadrenaline and antiserotonin effects.

Histamine : (3-aminoethylimidazole) is present in almost all mammalian tissues, in certain insect venoms and bacteria. Histamine is formed by decarboxylation of amino acid histidine. **Histamine is synthesized and stored in tissue mast cells and circulating basophils** in the blood. These cells store histamine in secretory granules. Other sites of histamine synthesis include epidermal cells, enterochromaffin-like cells in gastric mucosa, CNS cells and regenerating tissue. Major effects of histamine on human tissue include

a. Localized erythema due to direct vasodilatation.

b. Erythematous flare due to the histamine-induced axon reflex.

c. A wheal which is secondary to increased capillary permeability.

d. Contraction of extravascular smooth muscle mediated through H_1 and relaxation through H_2 receptors.

e. Activation of H_2 receptors releases histamine from non-mast cell stores in the gastro-intestinal tract and is a potent stimulator of gastric secretion. Secretion of histamine can be regulated by increasing the intracellular cyclic AMP. Drugs having this effect are epinephrine and theophylline.

Histamine may regulate its own release by a negative feed back mechanism involving H_2 receptors. It is available in the market as histamine[R] — 1 ml ampule containing 2.5 mg of it per ml. Its dermatological use lies in distinguishing hypopigmented patches of leprosy from the other type of hypopigmented patches.

Mode of action of antihistamines

The mode of action of H_1 and H_2 antagonists involves a competitive and reversible binding of drug to receptor site.

H_1 antihistamines inhibit the power of histamine to contract smooth muscles including respiratory tree, G.I.T and vusculature. They also inhibit itch and flare and increased permeability of venules ; have sedative and excitatory effects on CNS and anticholinergic effect on muscarinic receptors.

H_2 antagonists are capable of inhibiting histamine-induced gastric acid secretion.

There may be more than one type of H_2 receptors in skin. H_2 antihistamines are widely used in dermatologic practice for sympotmatic relief of allergic disorders. Antihistamines can be divided into several groups and choice must be made by considering the side effects and cost. In case of combination use, they should be selected from different categories. Use of H_2 antagonists in treating urticaria is based on the fact that there are both H_1 and H_2 receptors for histamine in the skin.

Classification of H_1 antagonists

A. Alkylamines

1. **Chlorpheniramine** tablets, elixir and injections e.g. Zeet[R], Zeet SR[R], Piriton[R], Cepiam TR[R].

2. **Brompheniramine** tablets and elixir. Widely used drugs and cause little sedation.

B. Phenothiazines

1. **Promethazine hydrochloride** tablets (Phenergan[R]), elixir and injections.

2. **Trimeprazine tartrate** tablets (Vallergan[R], 10 mg), elixir 7.5 mg in 15 ml ; vallergan forte elixir[R] 30 mg/5 ml.

It is less potent but has strong sedative effect.

C. **Ethylene-diamines**

1. **Mepyramine**[R] tablets (50 mg and 100 mg) ; elixir (25 mg/5 ml) and **Anthisan**[R]-injection (50 mg in 2 ml).

Not particularly potent, causes little sedation and gastro-intestinal side-effects.

D. **Ethanolamines**

1. **Diphenhydramine** capsules (Benadryl[R]), 25 and 50 mg. Potent and has strong sedative action.

2. **Dimenhydrinate** tablets (Dramamine[R]), 50 mg.

E. **Piperazines**

1. **Chlorcyclizine** 2. **Cyclizine** & 3. **Meclizine** (Histantin[R], Margine[R], Ancolaxin[R]) : They have prolonged action and are primarily used to combat motion sickness. They are terato-genic and should be avoided in pregnancy.

F. **Miscellaneous groups**

1. **Hydroxyzine pamoate** (Atarax[R], Vistaril[R]) ; 25 mg and **hydrozyzine hydrochloride** ; 10 and 25 mg.

They have antihistamine and antiserotonin activity.

2. **Cromoglycate** is a synthetic drug inhibiting the release of histamine and slow reacting substance from mast cells. Proprietory name is Ifiral[R]—inhaler, eyedrop and nasal spray.

3. **Doxepin** (Doxetar[R], Sinepix[R], Spectra[R])—a heterocyclic variant of tricyclic antidepressant amitriptyline—is a highly effective H_1 antihistamine.

4. **Astemizole** (Stemiz[R], Alerzole[R], Astelong[R])—a potent H_1 histamine receptor antagonist with a long duration of action permitting once daily application ; anticholinergic effect and central depression is much less.

5. **Clemastine fumarate** (Tavist[R], 1 mg per tab) : Has superior skin retention effect ; effective in urticaria ; long acting (12 hours) ; less central depression effect.

H_2 antagonist—Cimetidine, oral tablets 150-300 mg, liquid 60 mg/ml, Parenteral injection 150 mg/ml ; Ranitidine hydrochloride (Rantac[R], Histac[R], Ultac[R] etc.), oral tablets 150-300 mg.

Used in chronic urticaria in combination with an H_1 blocker, and in systemic mastocytosis.

Side effects of antihistamines

A. H_1 antihistamine

1. **Common** : Sedation, dizziness, tinnitus, fatigue, dryness of mouth, palpitation.

2. CNS : Insomnia, blurred vision, nervousness, hallucinations, ataxia, athetosis, convulsion, coma, respiratory arrest.

3. **Urinary** : Hesitancy and retention.

4. **Blood** : Leucopenia, agranulocytosis and hemolytic anemia.

5. **Skin** : Allergic and photocontact dermatitis.

B. H_2 antagonist

Nausea, diarrhoea, muscle pain, slurred speech, hallucinations, confusion, coma, gynecomastia, galactorrhea, dermatitis, inhibition of hepatic microsomal enzymes.

Antibiotics

Almost all antibiotics are used in dermatology. They are substances produced by one organism which are toxic to other organisms. Antibiotics may be bactericidal or bacteriostatic depending on the nature of infecting organism and the drug concentration achieved. In clinical use, antibiotics can be divided into **narrow spectrum** and the **broad spectrum** acting against both the gram-positive and the gram-negative organisms.

Modes of action of antibiotics can be divided as

a. Interfering with bacterial cell synthesis e.g. Penicillin and cephalosporin.

b. Affecting the cell membrane permeability e.g. Polymyxins, nystatin and amphotericin.

c. Inhibiting protein biosynthesis e.g. Tetracyclines, aminoglycosides, lincomycin and chloramphenicol.

d. Those which affect the nucleic acid metabolism e.g. Rifamycins.

1. Penicillins

It consists of three parts—thiazolidine ring, beta-lactum ring and a side chain ; beta-lactum ring is responsible for antibacterial properties of penicillin. Penicillinase, an enzyme produced by certain bacteria, cleaves this ring and yields penicilloic acid, a substance with little or no antibacterial activity. Semi-synthetic penicillins are produced by treating penicillin with the enzyme amidase, and they modify the susceptibility of the beta-lactum ring to cleavage by bacterial penicillinase.

Mode of action—Either affecting cell wall integrity or by interfering with bacterial protein synthesis.

Metabolism—Poorly absorbed from GIT as the drug is inactivated at acid pH in the stomach. Penicillin V is more stable at acid pH, thus enhancing its gastrointestinal absorption. Plasma level of penicillin V is 2-5 times higher than penicillin G. After oral administration, peak plasma concentration is achieved after 30-60 minutes. After intramuscular or subcutaneous injection, peak plasma concentration is reached in 15-30 minutes.

Probenecid inhibits the renal tubular secretion of penicillin, a major route of excretion of these drugs from the body. Penicillins are widely distributed in the body except CSF. They are little metabolized and rapidly eliminated by kidney. Ampicillin, amoxicillin, semi-synthetic penicillins such as oxacillin, cloxacillin, dicloxacillin are all acid stable and well absorbed orally.

Types

1. **Benzyl penicillin** (Penicillin G) : 150 mg/ml injection, Dose—300 mg (0.5 mega-units), four times daily up to 1.8 g, 3 mega units/day.

2. **Phenoxymethylpenicillin** : Verpen[R], Crystapen V[R], Penivoral[R], Fenocin[R] (Penicillin V), 125-250 mg tab ; Dose—250 to 500 mg 6 hourly orally.

3. **Flucloxacillin** (Floxapen[R]) : 250 mg capsules ; Dose—250-500 mg 6 hourly. It is resistant to staphylococcal penicillinase and is therefore effective against penicillin resistant staphylococcus aureus.

4. **Methicillin** (Celbenin[R] 1 g vial) : Active against penicillin resistant staphylococcal infections.

5. **Ampicillin** (Synthocillin[R], Ampilin[R]) : 250-500 mg capsules ; 100, 250 and 500 mg injections.

6. **Amoxicillin** (Mox[R], Amoxycillin[R], Amlin[R], Basimox[R], Alox[R], Ranoxyl[R]) : 250 mg capsules.

Dermatological use—Used in infections caused by staphylococcus aureus, streptococcus pyogenes, streptococcus pneumoniae, treponema pallidum, Neisseria gonorrhoeae, N. meningitidis, Actinomycetes, Bacillus anthracis.

Side-effects—Hypersensitivity reactions e.g. maculopapular eruption, urticaria, angioedema, fever, bronchospasm, vasculitis, serum sickness, exfoliative dermatitis, Stevens-Johnson syndrome, anaphylaxis, FDR, TEN, neutropenia, interstitial nephritis. **Penicillins** and **ampicillin may trigger pemphigus vulgaris.**

2. **Aminoglycosides**

This group includes streptomycin, kanamycin, neomycin, gentamycin and tobramycin. They are chiefly used against gram-negative infections.

Structure—They consist of at lesast two aminosugars joined in glycosidic linkages to hexose. This hexose is either streptidine e.g. in streptomycin or 2-deoxystreptamine in other aminoglycosides.

Mode of action—They are all bactericidal and act by inhibiting bacterial protein synthesis and altering translation of genetic code on the bacterial 30s ribosome.

Structure—It is a dichloro-acetic acid derivative containing a nitrobenzene side chain. It is stable and water soluble.

Mode of action : Inhibits the bacterial protein synthesis through its binding to 50s ribosome.

Metabolism : Readily absorbed after oral administration with peak plasma levels occurring within 1-2 hours ; can reach CSF ; its metabolites are excreted through the kidney and the active drug by glomerular filtration.

Dermatological use : Rickettsial infections, Brucellosis, and Lymphogranuloma venereum.

Side effects : Nausea, vomiting, diarrhoea, pancytopenia, aplastic anemia, superinfections with other organisms, transient hearing impairment following large doses ; inhibited absorption of oral contraceptives in some patients.

5. **Erythromycin** (Emycin[R], Erythrocin[R], Althrocin[R], EES 400[R]) : Derived from streptomyces erythreus.

Structure : Multi-membered lactone ring with one or more deoxy sugars. There are five chemical forms of the drug namely, **i.** Base parent compound **ii.** Propionyl **iii.** Estolate **iv.** Stearate and **v.** Ethyl succinate esters.

All erythromycins are soluble in organic solvents e.g. acetone, alcohol but are insoluble in water.

Mode of action : Binds to 50s ribosome and thereby inhibits bacterial protein synthesis.

Metabolism : Best absorbed from first part of small intestine. It is acid-sensitive and is thus generally made enteric coated. This drug reaches most extracellular fluid except brain and CSF. Excretion occurs primarily through the bile after concentration in the liver.

Dermatological use : Acne vulgaris, various types of pyoderma e.g. impetigo, ecthyma, folliculitis, furunculosis and cellulitis secondary to staphylococci and/or streptococci ; erythrasma due to Corynebacterium minutissimum and sexually transmitted diseases including syphilis and gonorrhoea.

Side effects : Occasional gastro-intestinal irritation, hypersensitivity reactions e.g. urticaria, fever, eosinophilia and rash. A major toxic effect of estolate esters is cholestatic hepatitis.

6. **Cephalosporins** (Sporidex®, Primspor®, Felopen®, Cefalex®, Sepexin®) : Derived from a fungus isolated from sea. It is a steroid compound related chemically to helvoic and fusidic acid.

Structure : Basic nucleus is 7-amino-cephalosporanic acid, resistant to penicillinase. Derivatives include cephalothin, cephalexin, cephaloridine and ceflaclor.

Mode of action : Cephalosporins, like the penicillins, contain a beta-lactum ring and inhibit cell wall synthesis.

Metabolism : Oral absorption is variable. Drugs can cross the placenta and reach the CSF. They are excreted in the urine by tubular secretion and glomerular filtration. Excretion is prolonged by concomitant treatment with probenecid.

Dermatological use : Various forms of pyoderma caused by staphylococci and streptococci including impetigo, cellulitis, carbuncles, furuncles, folliculitis etc.

Side effects : Hypersensitivity including maculo-papular rash, urticaria, fever, bronchospasm, cutaneous vusculitis, serum sickness, even anaphylaxis ; cross sensitivity is common with penicillin, granulocytopenia, thrombocytopenia ; in high doses renal tubular necrosis.

7. **Lincomycin and clindamycin** (Lincocin®, Dalacin®, Cleocin®) : Lincomycin and its derivative clindamycin act against gram-positive cocci including some penicillin-resistant staphylococci. They are active against bacteriodes infections and penetrate well into bone.

Side effects : Diarrhoea and pseudomebranous colitis.

8. **Polymyxins** : Polymyxin B and Polymyxin E are very toxic and are not absorbed from GIT. They are occasionally used against gram-negative bacteria.

9. **Cefotaxime sodium** (Omnatax[R], Oritaxim 500[R] Inj): Contains 0.5-1 g cefotaxime and 2.09 m mol of sodium/g; a good drug for gonorrhoea and pyoderma; a variant of cephalosporin.

Side effects – Skin rash, eosinophilia, drug fever, anaphylaxis, transient leucopenia, diarrhoea, transient rise of SGOT and SGPT, pseudomembranous colitis, positivity of direct Coom's test and false-positive urinary glucose with non-enzymatic methods.

Antimycobacterial drugs

1. **Rifampicin**

Structure: It belongs to rifamycins, complex unacryocyclic antibiotic produced by Streptococcus medditeranei.

Plenty of rifampicins are available in the market.

Mode of action: It inhibits the beta-subunit of DNA dependant RNA polymerase of mycobacteria; well absorbed after oral administration; peak plasma levels occurring in 2-4 hrs; distributed in all body-tissues including CSF; less than 30% of the drug is excreted in the urine.

Indications: Infections caused by M. tuberculosis, M. leprae, M. kansasii, M. scrofulaceum, M. marinum and M. intercellulare. Available as 150, 300, 450 and 600 mg capsules.

Side effects: Rash, nausea, vomiting, fever, pruritus, urticaria, eosinophilia, stomatitis, hemolysis, hematuria, renal insufficiency, anemia, hepatitis with jaundice, hepatorenal syndrome; decreases the effectiveness of oral contraceptives, gastrointestinal irritation, fatigue, headache and weakness. It also inhibits the delayed hypersensitivity responses. **Flu-like syndrome sometimes occur during pulse therapy in Hanseniasis.**

2. **Ethambutol** (Emutol 400[R], EBL 200[R], Eclobutol[R], Albutol[R])

Structure: The d-isomer of ethylene-di-imino-di-1-butanol dihydrochloride.

Mode of action : Is not known.

Metabolism : Well absorbed after oral administration ; peak plasma concentration is reached within 2-4 hours ; stored in erythrocytes and excreted via kidney by glomerular filtration and tubular secretion.

Effective against M. tuberculosis and M. kansasii.

Side effects : Optic neuritis, loss of green colour vision, diminished visual acuity, hypersensitivity reactions e.g. rash, fever, pruritus, joint pain, headache, confusion, anaphylaxis and anemia.

3. **Clofazimine** (Hansepran^R, Eklof^R) : It is a phenazine congener and inhibits template function of DNA by binding to it ; also has anti-inflammatory effects and hence can prevent erythema nodosum leprosum ; well absorbed after oral administration ; stored in tissues allowing intermittent dosing (twice weekly) for the treatment of leprosy ; used in patients infected with Microbacterium leprae that have developed resistance to sulphones ; available as 50 mg and 100 mg capsules.

Side effects are red discoloration of the skin, acquired ichthyosis, eosinophilic enteritis and hemorrhage in gastro-intestinal tract.

4. **Isoniazid** (Isonex^R, Isoniazid^R) : It is a derivative of nicotinamide ; mechanism of action is unknown ; can inhibit the synthesis of mycolic acids which are major constituents of the cell walls of tubercle bacilli ; absorbed rapidly after oral administration ; peak plasma level occurring 1-2 hours after ingestion of the drug ; diffuses into all body fluids and cells including CSF ; more than 80% of the administered dose is excreted in urine within 24 hours ; available in tablets 100-300 mg and as a syrup 10 mg/c.c ; usual daily dose is 5 mg/kg ; M. kansasii is susceptible to isoniazid.

Side effects : Lichenoid rash, fever, jaundice, peripheral neuropathy, seizures, optic neuritis and atrophy, ataxia, encephalopathy and personality change.

5. **Pyrazinamide** (Pyrazil[R], Coxamide[R], P-Zide[R], Pyride[R] Mitizide[R]) : A synthetic pyrazine derivative of nicotinamide ; mechanism of action is unknown ; well absorbed after oral administration ; distributed widely in the body fluids and tissues ; excreted primarily through the kidney by glomerular filtration ; a second line of drug in treating tuberculosis. Available as 500 mg tablets.

Side effects : Side effects include arthralgia, anorexia, nausea, vomiting, dysuria, malaise, fever, hepatic injury and death due to hepatic necrosis.

6. **Aminosalicylic acid** (PAS[R]) : It increases the oxygen consumption of tubercle bacilli and inhibits their growth in vitro. It is a structural analogue of P-aminobenzoic acid which results in an inhibitory effect on folate synthesis ; well absorbed after oral administration ; peak plasma concentration occurs 1.5-2 hours after ingestion ; distributed in all body fluids except CSF ; rapidly excreted in urine ; usually used in combination with other antitubercular drugs ; available as capsules in various doses.

Causes gastro-intestinal upset and also hypersensitivity reactions.

7. **Ethionamide** : Ethyl derivative of thio-isonicotinamide ; mechanism of action is unknown ; absorbed orally ; distributed widely and excreted in the urine ; used in combination with other agents. Amongst atypical mycobacteria, photochromogens are susceptible.

Side effects include rash, stomatitis, gynecomastia, acne, alopecia, arthralgia, hepatitis—particularly in patients with diabetes mellitus.

Sulphonamides, Sulphones and sulphapyridines

Sulphonamides

Sulphonamides are derivatives of para-amino-benzene sulphonamide ; several thousands are known but few are of clinical significance ; they act as competitive antagonists and prevent bacteria from utilising para-amino-benzoic acid

(PABA). Sulphonamide-sensitive bacteria require PABA for the synthesis of folic acid.

They are bacteriostatic and inhibited by pus. Oral absorption is good in most cases. Distributed through all body tissues, metabolized in the liver and excreted by the kidney.

Crystalluria is a serious risk and high fluid intake should be maintained.

Dermatological use : They are used in nocardiosis and toxoplasmosis combined with pyrimethamine. Sulphapyridine is used as an alternative to Dapsone in DH and in atypical mycobacterial infection, acne vulgaris, chronic pustular folliculitis, furunculosis, cellulitis etc.

Preparations

1. Sulphadimidine 500 mg tablets ; Dose : initially 3 g followed by 6 g in divided doses.

2. Sulphapyridine 500 mg tablets ; Dose : 0.5-1.5 g daily as an alternative to dapsone.

3. Cotrimoxazole (Septran^R^, Bactrim^R^, Nicotrim^R^) tablets contain sulphamethoxazole 400 mg and trimethoprim 80 mg. Dose : two tabs twice daily ; two components of this drug act on successive stage of folate metabolism of bacteria ; there is a bactericidal action against a wide range of gram-positive and gram-negative organisms.

Sulphonamides should not be used in patients with folate deficiency and in pregnancy, though the effect on the fetus is still not definitely known.

Side effects : Sulphonamides are potentially toxic drugs ; can cause crystalluria, blood dyscrasia, fever, serum sickness and skin manifestations including erythema nodosum, erythema multiforme and Steven-Johnson syndrome.

Sulphones

Structure : Sulphones and sulphonamides are structurally similar, the major difference being that DDS (Di-amino diphenyl-sulphones) link sulphur to two carbon atoms whereas sulphonamides are linked to one carbon and one nitrogen atom.

Mechanism of action

1. **Bacteriostatic action**

i. Inhibits the incorporation of P-aminobenzoic acid and thereby kills those bacteria dependant on endogenously synthesized folic acid.

ii. Interaction with tissue & bacterial polysaccharides.

2. **Anti-inflammatory action**

i. Suppresses arthus reaction and also experimental arthritis.

ii. Suppresses polymorphonuclear leucocyte chemotaxis to potassium iodide patch test.

iii. Suppresses the lymphocyte response to phytohemagglutinin.

iv. May interfere with activation of alternative complement pathway.

v. Prevents chondrolysis in rabbit ear treated with high dose vitamin A, perhaps by intefering with release or effect of lysosomal enzymes.

vi. It interferes with the formation of iodine from sodium iodide and since iodine is important in killing cells or micro-organisms by myeloperoxidase or hydrogen peroxide (both products of polymorphs), depletion of tissue iodine would be expected to have some anti-inflammatory effects.

Metabolism and excretion : About 85% of ingested dapsone is absorbed ; peak serum concentration occurs within 2-6 hours ; distributed to all body tissues including skin, liver, kidney and erythrocytes ; metabolised in the liver ; 80-90% of dapsone is excreted as glucoronide via the kidneys and 10% is excreted in bile.

Administration of probenecid is found to prolong the half-life of dapsone by interfering with its renal excretion. **Rifampicin,** on the other hand, **appears to decrease the half life of dapsone.**

Preparations (Dapsone[R], Novophone[R], DDS[R]) : 10, 25, 50 and 100 mg tablets.

Dermatological and other uses (From Clinical Pharmacology of Skin Disease, Bickers. R.D. et al, 1984) :

I. Infections

i. Leprosy, tuberculosis **ii.** Malaria and malaria prophylaxis **iii.** Bacteria (Acne vulgaris) **iv.** Fungus (Actinomycotic mycetoma)

II. Bullous diseases

i. Dermatitis herpetiformis **ii.** Pemphigus **iii.** Bullous pemphigoid **iv.** Herpes gestationis **v.** Hailey-Hailey disease **vi.** Epidermolysis bullosa acquisita.

III. Epidermal inflammatory diseases

i. Subcorneal pustular dermatosis **ii.** Pustular psoriasis **iii.** Acrodermatitis continua of Hallopeau.

IV. Dermal/adnexal inflammatory diseases

i. Granuloma faciale **ii.** Erythema elevatum diutinum **iii.** Vasculitis **iv.** Cystic acne **v.** Hidradenitis suppurativa **vi.** Dissecting cellulitis of the scalp **vii.** Alopecia mucinosa **viii.** Relapsing polychondritis **ix.** Sweets' syndrome (acute febrile neutrophilic dermatosis) **x.** DLE.

V. Subcutaneous, ulcerative and systemic inflammatory diseases

i. Vasculitis **ii.** Pyoderma gangrenosum **ii.** Weber-Christian panniculitis.

Side effects of sulphones

Common side effects : Nausea, vomiting, fatigue, dizziness, weakness, nervousness, shortness of breath, headache.

Less common side effects : Hemolysis, methemoglobinemia, agranulocytosis, skin rash, hepatotoxcity, neuropathy, psychosis, hypersensitivity reactions, nephrotoxicity.

Antifungal agents

1. Griseofulvin : Initially isolated from Penicillium griseofulvin in 1939 ; a colourless remarkably thermostable antibiotic of neutral pH ; insoluble in water.

Mechanism of action : Inhibits the mitosis of fungal cells causing disruption of the mitotic spindle by interacting with polymerised microtubules.

The drug is fungistatic for major dermatophytes e.g. Trichophyton, microsporum and epidermophyton. But it has no inhibitory effect on other fungi, yeast, bacteria, actinomycetes or nocardia.

Metabolism : Considerable absorption does not occur after oral administration because of its low water solubility. Factors influencing absorption are the particle size, dietary intake, formulation, dissolution rate and dosage regimen.

Reduction of particle size enhances the gastrointestinal absorption of the drug. Fat intake, solubilizing the drug in polyethylene glycol and a divided dose regimen (4 × daily), enhances the absorption. Major site of absoprtion is the duodenum. It is distributed in most tissues including skin and the drug has a higher affinity for diseased skin than normal. It is metabolized by the hepatic microsomal mono-oxygenase enzyme system. Treatment with griseofulvin decreases the anticoagulant activity of warfarin sodium in some patients. Griseofulvin is excreted in urine with trace amounts of unmetabolized drug present in the feces.

Preparations

a. Tablet of 125, 250 and 500 mg.
b. Capsules of 125 and 250 mg.
c. Oral suspension of 125 mg/5 ml.
d. Micronised tablets of 250 and 500 mg.
e. Ultramicronised tablets of 125, 165, 250 and 330 mg.

Proprietory drugs : Idifulvin^R, Fulcin^R, Fluvin forte^R, Walavin FP^R, Grisovin FP^R, Gris OD^R etc.

Dermatological use : Effective against dermatophytes that cause superficial infection of the skin, hair and nails.

Dose : For children 10 mg/kg ; for adult 500-1000 mg/day.

Duration : 4 weeks in localised infection of glabrous skin or scalp ; 4-12 weeks in palms and soles ; 4-6 months in onychomycosis of finger nails ; 6-18 months in onychomycosis of toe-nails.

Other uses : Angina, gout, herpes simplex, herpes zoster, leprosy (ENL), lichen planus, Raynaud's phenomenon and scleroderma.

Side effects : Headache, nervousness, blurred vision, fatigue, GI upset, diarrhoea, xerostomia, transient leucopenia, neutropenia, monocytosis, proteinuria, skin rashes e.g. morbilliform rash, urticaria and photosensitivity reaction ; can induce hepatic porphyria.

2. Nystatin (Mycostatin[B] suspension, tablets and vaginal tablets) : It is derived from Streptomyces noursei and is a member of polyene antibiotics. It is a tetraene containing a hydrophilic region of hydroxylated hydrocarbons and a lipophilic segment containing multiple conjugated double bonds. It is insoluble in water.

Mechanism of action : The drug binds to sterol (Ergosterol) in the cell wall leading to the formation of pores or channels resulting in increased permeability of the membrane and leakage of small molecules, particularly sodium and potassium.

Metabolism : No absorption occurs after oral administration and the entire amount can be found in the feces.

Preparations, doses and uses : Tablets containng 500,000 u and a flavoured suspension of 10,000 u/ml ; the adult dose for oral, esophageal and intestinal candidiasis is 500,000 to 10,00,000 u 3-4 times a day ; for the children the dose is 100,000 u 3-4 times a day.

Side effects : May cause nausea, vomiting and diarrhoea.

3. Amphotericin B : Derived from Streptomyces nodosus, another member of polyene antibiotics ; insoluble in water and is very unstable.

Mechanism of action : Identical with that of nystatin. In addition to its antifungal action, it has effects on immune system being capable of stimulating the number of antibody producing cells in the spleen and lymphnodes of many mouse-strains.

Metabolism : No absorption occurs from GI tract ; usually administerd intravenously with 5% glucose solution, and by gradually increasing the daily dose up to approximately 0.5-1 mg/kg ; a plasma concentration of 0.2-2 mg/ml can be achieved.

It is slowly excreted unchanged in the urine.

Side effects : Nausea, vomiting, fever, chill, anaphylaxis, thrombocytopenia, convulsions, impaired renal function e.g. azotemia—reversible on stoppage of therapy. Renal tubular acidosis and hypokalemia may also occur.

4. **Imidazoles** : Imidazole derivatives include **i.** Clotrimazole **ii.** Miconazole **iii.** Econazole and **iv.** Ketoconazole.

Ketoconazole is the only available imidazole for oral administration.

Mechanism of action : **i.** At low concentration, it is fungistatic and directly inhibits the synthesis of ergosterol, an important constituent of fungal membrane. **ii.** There is accumulation of methylated derivatives such as lanosterol, the precursor of ergosterol leading to changes in membrane permeability and retardation of growth of susceptible micr-obes. **iii.** At higher concentrations, imidazoles can directly inhibit triglyceride and fatty acid synthesis. **iv.** Can block cytochrome C peroxidase activity leading to higher levels of hydrogen peroxide which has substantial toxic effects.

Metabolism : Miconazole has been used parenterally for the treatment of systemic fungal infections. After a dose of 600-1000 mg of miconazole (I.V.) peak plasma level of 7.5 mg/ml is achieved. The drug is metabolized in the liver, excreted primarily in the feces and therefore not contra-indicated in renal failure.

Ketoconazole : A single oral dose of 200 mg tablet produces peak plasma concentrations of 3 - 4.5 mg/ml in 1-2 hours after administrtion ; it should be administered just after a meal for better absorption and to produce higher plasma levels. It is also metabolized in the liver ; urinary excretion is small and hence not contrain dicated in renal impairment.

Preparations, dose and uses—Ketoconazole 200 mg tablet ; single daily dose (Phytoral[R], Keto-zole[R], Nizral[R], Fungicide[R]).

This is effective against mucocutaneous candidiasis ; deep mycoses e. g. coccidioido-mycosis, paracoccidioido-mycosis, histoplasmosis and chromomycosis. Therapy should be continued for 2-6 months in a dose of 200 mg once or twice daily. It is also found effective against trichopyton infections, pityriasis versicolor, both oral and vaginal candidiasis, and onychomycosis.

Clotrimazole is not administered parenterally because of its toxic effects.

Miconazole has been used intravenously in chronic mucocutaneous candidiasis. Initial dose is 30-60 mg/kg 8-hourly in hospitalized patients followed by 10-20 mg/kg weekly in out-door patients.

Side effects : Parenterally administered, imidazoles can cause anaphylaxis, tachycardia and other cardiac arrythmias, fevers, chills, nausea, vomiting and phlebitis. Hematologic changes include leucopenia and thrombocytopenia. Ketoconazole may cause nausea and vomiting. Major drawback is the hepatocellular damage.

5. **Flucytosine** : A synthetic, orally administered, antifungal agent. It is a 5-flurocytosine, a fluorinated pyrimidine. It causes inhibition of RNA and DNA synthesis. Absorption is good after oral administration. It is widely distributed in the body. Plasma half-life is 4 hours and peak plasma concentration is 70-80 mg/ml in 1-2 hours after oral administration of 37.5 mg/kg. It is excreted in urine unmetabolized. Available as 250-500 mg capsule. Dose is 50-150 mg/kg/day given orally in divided doses. It is effective against candida, cryptococcus and aspergillus. Side effects include nausea,

vomiting, diarrhoea, intestinal perforation, mild hepatocellular dysfunction and transient bone marrow depression.

6. **Iodide** : Used in the treatment of cutaneous lymphatic form of sporotrichosis. It has no inhibitorry effect against the fungus in vitro. It enhances leucocyte chemotaxis ; proteolytic, phagocytic and bactericidal action of polymorphonuclear leucoytes. It gets readily absorbed after an oral administration and is mainly excreted through urine. In adults, the dose is started with 1.5 to 3 ml (5-10 drops) of saturated solution diluted in water or milk and increased up to 9-12 ml ; if tolerated, it is continued for 6-8 weeks even after visible regression of lesions. This drug is also used for the treatment of erythema nodosum, nodular vasculitis, and subacute nodular migratory panniculitis.

Side effects include increased lacrimation, metallic taste, nausea, vomiting, swollen salivary glands, halogen acne, and goitre in chronic administration. It flares up pustular psoriasis and erythema multiforme.

Antimalarials

Antimalarial drugs of dermatological importance include quinacrine, chloroquine and hydroxychloroquine. Quinacrine is a substituted acridine whereas chloroquine, hydroxychloroquine and amodiaquine are all substituted 4-aminoquinolines. Chloroquine (Resochin[R], Lariago[R], Melubrin[R]) is widely used in dermatological practice.

Mechanism of action : These have additional pharmacologic effects other than antimalarial e.g.

i. **Anti-inflammatory effects** : They are capable of stabilizing lysosomal membranes and thereby inhibit the release of enzymes from organelles, a normal accompaniment to inflammation. Chloroquine can inhibit neutrophil and eosinophil chemotaxis, prostaglandin biosynthesis and smooth muscle contraction evoked by histamine.

ii. **Immunosuppressive actions** : They have either little or no inhibitory effect on antibody responses to antigenic stimulation.

iii. **DNA repair** : They can inhibit DNA synthesis and interfere with the formation of thymine dimers in DNA, irradiated with ultraviolet radiation. Excision repair of induced dimers is also inhibited.

iv. **Pigment binding :** Antimalarials, except quinacrine, become concentrated in pigmented tissues as a result of the formation of drug-melanin complex.

v. **Sun screen effect** : Antimalarials can also block the penetration of ultraviolet radiation into the skin.

vi. **Effects on hepatic porphyrin metabolism** : Chloroquine and hydroxychloroquine are capable of binding to porphyrins in the hepatocytes and enhances the water solubility of the complex resulting in increased urinary excretion. Thus intermittent administration (twice weekly) of lower doses can cause remission of the disease without any acute hepatotoxicity.

Metabolism : Absorbed considerably and completely from the gastro-intestinal tract after an oral administration. It accumulates in various tissues including skin. About 70% of the administered drug is excreted unchanged.

Dermatological uses : **1**. Lupus erythematosus **2**. Rheumatoid arthritis **3**. Scleroderma–inflammatory stages of morphea **4**. Sarcoidosis–cutaneous and extracutaneous manifestations **5**. Porphyria cutanea tarda **6**. Polymorphous light eruption **7**. Solar urticaria **8**. Other diseases e.g. disseminated granuloma annulare. Miescher's granuloma, cutaneous cryptococcosis, leishmaniasis, epidermolysis bullosa, acrodermatitis chronica atrophicans, lymphocytic infiltrate of Jesner.

Side effects : Nausea, vomiting, pruritus, sweating and headaches ; eye mainfestations include blurred vision, diplopia, keratopathy, retinopathy ; optic atrophy, pigmentary degeneration of macula and arteriolar narrowing ; skin manifestations include discoloration of skin to lemon yellow colour, blue gray pigmentation of the hard palate, face, nails and pretibial regions due to deposition of a combination of melanin and hemosiderin ; lichenoid eruption, exfoliative erythroderma, aggravation of psoriasis ; reversible agranulocytosis, aplastic anemia, toxic psychosis, neuromyopathy with progressive proximal muscle weakness and degeneration of muscle fibres.

Cytotoxic and immunosuppressive agents

Medications used for the management of neoplasia have been used in dermatology in hyperproliferative and autoimmune processes e.g. Psoriasis, Mycosis fungoides, Lupus erythematosus, Dermatomyositis and various cutaneous malignancies. These agents can alter the synthesis of various macromolecules including DNA, RNA and protein. Many cytotoxic agents act at specific phases of the cell cycle and therefore affect only dividing cells.

Reproductive cell cycle is defined as the period between the completion of one mitosis in a cell to the completion of the subsequent mitosis in a daughter cell. The cell cycle has been arbitrarily divided into four phases.

G_1-Presynthetic phase : Period of time from the completion of mitosis to the beginning of chromosomal replication ; during the terminal portion of this the cell is preparing for DNA synthesis.

S-Period of DNA synthesis.

G_2-Post-synthetic phase : Onset of the cellular division to the end of chromosomal replication.

M–Period of mitosis.

G_0 – An additional **non-proliferative phase** or **interphase** defines those cells not currently in cycle.

Cytotoxic drugs can be divided into four groups.

I. Alkylating agents

a. Nitrogen mustards : Cyclophosphamide, chlorambucil, melphelan.

b. Ethylenimine derivatives : Triethylenemelamine.

c. Alkyl sulphonates : Busulphan.

d. Nitrosoureas : Lomustine, carmustine, streptozotocin.

e. Triazenes : Dacarbazine.

II. Antimetabolites

a. Folic acid antagonists–Methotrexate.

b. Pyrimidine analogues–Azarabine, cytarabine and fluorouracil.

c. Purine analogues—Mercaptopurine, azathioprine, mycophenolic acid.

III. Natural products

a. Alkaloids–Vinblastine, Vincristine, Colchicine.

b. Antibiotics—Bleomycin, Actinomycin D.

c. Enzymes–L-asparaginase.

IV. **Miscellaneons agents** : Hydroxyurea, Procarbazine and radioactive isotopes.

Here the drugs used in dermatological practice only will be discussed in brief.

1. **Cyclophosphamide** (Endoxan®, Cycloxan®) : It is a synthetic mechlorethamine with substitution of cyclic phosphamide for the nitrogen methyl group.

Pharmacological action : It interferes with DNA cross-linkage. It is a potent immunosuppressant, affecting both humoral and cellular immunity.

Metabolism : May be administered orally and intravenously, distributed to all body tissues, plasma half-life achieved within 1 hour after oral administration. Drugs such as barbiturates, when used concomitantly, can influence the effectiveness and toxicity of cyclophosphamide.

Preparations and clinical use : Available as 25 and 50 mg tablets and 100, 200 and 500 mg vials. Oral dose is 1-3 mg/kg per day in 2-3 divided doses. It is *effectively used* in

i. SLE ii. Pemphigus vulgaris iii. Polyarteritis nodosa iv. Systemic necrotizing vasculitis v. Pyoderma gangrenosum vi. Wegener's granulomatosis ; used in *combination therapy* in

i. Mycosis fungoides **ii.** Metastatic carcinoid tumour **iii.** Letterer-Siwe disease **iv.** Kaposi's sarcoma.

Side effects and toxicity : Nausea, vomiting, mucosal irritation, anagen effluvium causing alopecia, lymphopenia, leucopenia and thrombocytopenia, sterile hemorrhagic cystitis, azoospermia, anovulation, teratogenicity and increased incidence of bladder cancer.

2. **Chlorambucil** (Leukeran[R]) : It is an aromatic derivative of mechlorethamine. It is a synthetic nitrogen mustard with phenyl butyric acid substitution for the nitrogen methyl group of mechlorethamine.

Pharmacological action : Acts by exerting its alkylating action on DNA. It is an effective immuno-suppressant, affecting both humoral and cell mediated immunity. Cytotoxicity is increased with concomitant administration of barbiturates.

Metabolism : Readily absorbed after oral administration. Serum half-life is less than 12 hours.

Preparations and clinical use : Available as 2 mg tablet for the oral administration. Dose is 0.1-0.2 mg/kg per day in a single or 2 divided doses.

It is **used** in **i.** Mycosis fungoides **ii.** Sezary syndrome **iii.** Bechet's syndrome **iv** SLE **v.** Wegener's granulomatosis **vi.** Scleroderma.

Side effects and toxicity : Lymphopenia, leucopenia, thrombocytopenia, alopecia and gastro-intestinal disturbance.

3. **Dacarbazine** : It is an imidazole derivative.

Pharmacological action : Probably inhibits the synthesis of RNA and protein and to a lesser extent DNA.

Metabolism : After intravenous administration, the drug leaves the plasma compartment within 5 hours, excreted in the urine by tubular secretion.

Preparations and clinical use : Available as 100 mg and 200 mg vials. Dose is 3.5 mg/kg/day intravenously for 10 days, repeated every 28 days ; used in the treatment of malignant melanoma.

4. **Methotrexate** (Neotrexate®, Biotrexate®)

Pharmacological action : Competitive inhibitor of the enzyme dihydrofolate reductase and inhibits the formation of tetrahydrofolic acid. It blocks DNA and RNA synthesis by inhibiting purine production.

Metabolism : Rapidly absorbed after oral administration, the peak blood concentration is reached within 1 hour of ingestion ; distributed in most body tissues but penetrates blood-brain barrier poorly. Pharmacologic and toxic effects of the drug may be enhanced by concomitant use of sulfonamides, salicylates, barbiturates, diphenyl-hydantoin and oral contraceptives. It is excreted intact in urine.

Preparation and dermatological use : Available as 2.5 mg tablet and 20, 50 and 100 mg sterile injectible solution. It is used in psoriasis and other cellular hyperproliferative disorder e.g. in Pityriasis rubra pilaris, Norwegian scabies, Mucha-Habermann disease, oral florid papillomatosis, epidermolytic hyperkeratosis, all forms of pemphigus, bullous pemphigoid, dermatomyositis, polymyositis, mycosis fungoides, Wegener's granulomatosis, Midline-granuloma, steroid-resistant sarcoidosis, metastatic carcinoid tumour and Reiter's syndrome.

Side effects and toxicity : Nausea, vomiting, fever, chills, mucosal ulceration, leucopenia, thrombocytopenia, pancytopenia, acute hepatitis, chronic fibrosis and cirrhosis of liver. It is an abortificient and teratogenic drug.

5. **Azathioprine** (Imuran®) : It is formed by attachment of an imidazole group to the sulphur atom at the 6 position of mercaptopurine.

Pharmacological action : Azathioprine can inhibit both DNA and RNA synthesis. It has immunosuppressive and anti-inflammatory effects—suppresses both humoral and cell mediated immunity. It is converted in the body to mercaptopurine—an inhibitor of purine synthesis.

Preparation and clinical use : Available as 50 mg tablets and 100 mg vials. The dose is 1-3 mg/kg per day in 2-3 divided doses.

Dermatological use : Psoriatic arthropathy, pemphigus vulgaris, bullous pemphigoid, dermatomysitis, SLE, Wegener's granuloma and Pityriasis rubra pilaris.

Side effects and toxicity : Nausea, vomiting, oral ulceration ; bone marrow depression producing leucopenia, anemia, thrombocytopenia and pancytopenia ; reversible cholestatic jaundice, pancreatitis.

6. **Colchicine** : It is an alkaloid derived from the plant colchicum autumnale and is a 3-ringed compound known as acetyl-trimethyl-colchicinic acid.

Pharmacologic action : Arrests mitosis in metaphase by interacting with microtubules.

Metabolism : Rapidly absorbed after oral administration, excreted predominantly in the feces and 10-20% in urine.

Preparation and clinical use : Available as 0.5 mg and 0.6 mg tablet and sterile solution of 0.5 mg/ml. It is used in acute attacks of gouts, Bechet's syndrome and necrotizing vasculitis.

Side effects and toxicity : Nausea, vomiting, diarrhoea, abdominal pain, transient leucopenia followed by basophilic leucocytosis ; chronic toxicity include agranulocytosis, aplastic anemia, myopathy and alopecia.

7. **Bleomycin** : It consists of a mixture of copper chelating glycopeptides.

Pharmacological action : Chain scission and the fragmentation of DNA molecule.

Metabolism : Poorly absorbed after an oral administration ; administered intravenously or intramuscularly.

Preparations and clinical use : Available as 15 Units ampules to be reconstituted in saline, 5% dextrose or sterile water. Dose is 0.2-0.5 U/kg/week, until 300-400 U ; used in the treatment of mycosis fungoides, Kaposi's sarcoma, keratoacanthoma, squamous cell carcinoma and verruca vulgaris.

Side effects and toxicity : It has got no immunosuppressive action. Cutaneous toxicity includes erythema, scaling, ulceration, alopecia, reticular hyperpigmentation, striae and petechae, sclerodermoid changes of fingers and hands. The most serious complication is pulmonary toxic reaction manifested by cough and dyspnoea.

Antiviral agents

1. **Acylovir** (Acycloguanosine ; Cyclovir[R], Herpex[R], Herperax[R]) : It is an analogue of deoxyguanosine with replacement of deoxyribose component by hydroxymethoxymethyl substituent on the purine ring.

Pharmacological action : It inhibits the viral DNA polymerase resulting in a preferential chain termination of the viral DNA.

Little is known about the metabolism of acyclovir. It is eliminated unmetabolized through kidney by tubular secretion and glomerular filtration.

Preparations and clinical use : It is available in intravenous, oral and topically administered form ; used in herpes simplex virus infection ; also effective in immunosuppressed patient with cytomegalovirus pneumonia, disseminated zoster and peroneal herpes simplex infection.

Side effect and toxicity : Renal dysfunction after rapid intravenous administration, lethargy, tremor.

2. **Vidarabine** (Adenosine arabinoside ; ARA-A[R]) : It is a pruine nucleoside analogue with activity against HSV 1, HSV 2, VZV and EBV.

Pharmacological action : Inhibits DNA synthesis.

Topical and parenteral preparations are available ; dose is 100 mg/kg per day given intravenously.

Side effects and toxicity : Anemia, leucopenia and thrombocytopenia ; neurotoxic side effects include tremor, alteration in mentation, coma, seizures, unusual pain syndrome in the extremities.

3. Cytarabine (Cytosine arabinoside, ARA-C[R]) : It is a 2 β-OH analogue of deoxycytidine with substitution of arabinose for the ribose moiety.

Pharmacological action : Inhibits DNA formation ; it is a potent immunosuppressant affecting both cellular and humoral immunity.

Metabolism : Poorly absorbed after an oral administration ; given I.V. by rapid injection or slow perfusion.

Preparation and clinical use : Available in 100 mg and 500 mg vials ; used in the treatment of disseminated herpes simplex, herpes zoster and the cytomegalic inclusion virus infection.

Side effects and toxicity : Nausea, vomiting, diarrhoea, mucosal ulceration, thrombophlebitis, leucopenia, thrombocytopenia, teratogenicity.

4. Idoxuridine : Synthetic nucleoside, effective against DNA virus—primarily herpes group ; topical idoxuridine is effective in the treatment of HSV keratitis ; local toxicity occur in the form of inflammation, pruritus and allergic manifestations.

5. Interferons : Studies with human leucocyte demonstrated interferon to be effective in prophylaxis of experimentally induced rhinovirus infections in humans and in the treatment of varicella zoster infections in immunosuppressed patients.

Antihelminthics and antiprotozoal drugs

A great majority of drugs come under this domain. The drugs used in dermatological practice are :

1. Thiabendazole (Litozon[R], Mentezol[R]) : It is a substituted benzimidazole compound and is a potent antihelminthic ; active against a wide range of gastrointestinal nematodes. It is larvicidal at a concentration of 10 mg/ml. Gastrointestinal side effects and hyper-sensitivity may occur.

2. Mebendazole (Mebex[R], Sandin[R], Idibend[R]) : It is an effective antihelminthic, analogue of thiabendazole, non-toxic and useful in treating multiple infestations.

3. **Diethylcarbamazine** (Hetrazan®, Banocide®) : Piperazine derivative ; drug of choice in the treatment of all forms of filariasis. Side effects include headache, joint pain, nausea and vomiting.

4. **Piperazine** (Antepar®) : It is an effective alternative to treatment for thread worms. Single dose of 4 g is effective.

5. **Metronidazole** (Flagyl®, Aristogyl®, Aldezole®) : It is a nitroimidazole compound. It is trichomonacidal and is effective against amebiasis and lambliasis. Recently, it is proved to be bactericidal for many anerobic bacteria including bacteriodes ; side effects include nausea, vomiting, tiredness, neutropenia, peripheral neuropathy.

6. **Sodium stibogluconate** (Abanate®) : It is a pentavalent antimony compound and is leishmanicidal ; effective against oriental sore but hardly with any value in mucocutaneous leishmaniasis.

7. **Pentamidine** : It is a diamidine ; second line of drug for leishmaniasis and is also effective in early trypanosomiasis. It may cause disturbed glucose metabolism and hypotension when given intravenously.

8. **Emetine** : Alkaloid with direct lethal action on entameba histolytica ; used in cutaneous amebiasis.

Analgesics & non-steroidal anti-inflammatory (NSAI) drugs

The prototypical non-steroidal anti-inflammatory drug is **aspirin** (Aspirin®, Mejoral®, Pyralgin®). It remains the chief and most widely used analgesic, antipyretic and anti-inflammatory agent. It can be given in divided doses up to a dose of 5 g daily. Administration of adequate dosage may be complicated by gastric irritation and chornic gastro-intestinal blood loss causing anemia.

Besides aspirin, there are several other non-steroidal anti-inflammatory drugs which include ibuprofen, fenoprofen, indomethacin, naproxen and piroxicum. These drugs are capable of blocking the activity of enzyme cyclo-oxygenase and thereby inhibit the production of prostaglandins, prostacyclins and thromboxanes. They have analgesic anti-inflammatory and antipyretic property. These agents have a wide spectrum of toxicity e.g. gastric irritation, azotemia, platelet dysfunction, exacerbation of allergic rhinitis and asthma. None of these agents have been shown to be more effective than aspirin.

Anticholinergics

Systemic anticholinergics such as propantheline can be used as an antiperspirant. Glycopyridate is also a typical anticholinergic. Anticholinergics, both topical and systemic, block the central nervous system stimulation of both eccrine and apocrine glands thus preventing secretion. However, the dose required to minimize sweating will frequently produce undesirable side effects. Propantheline (Probanthine®) 15 mg 4 times a day will sometime prove helpful.

Chelating agents

Chelation is the action of certain substances in forming complexes (heterocyclic rings) with metal ions and binding them in order to render them inactive. Chelating agents form complexes with a number of heavy metals. They are occasionally used in dermatology.

1. **Dimercaprol** : Used in the treatment of poisoning by arsenicals, mercurials, gold salts, bismuth, chromium and nickel.

2. **D-penicillamine** : It is a degradation product of penicillin and chelates copper, mercury, zinc and lead. It is used in Wilson's disese, lead poisoning, cystinuria and rheumatoid arthritis. It can also induce SLE-like syndrome and the Pemphigus-like bullous eruption.

Steroid hormones

Basic structure : Steroids contain as their basic structure a cyclopentanoperhydrophenanthrene nucleus consisting of three 6-carbon hexane rings and a single 5-carbon pentane ring ; carbon atoms are numbered in a sequence beginning with ring A.

Nomenclature of steroids

Adrenal steroids contain either 19 or 21 carbon atoms. C_{19} steroids have methyl groups at positions C-18 and C-19. C_{19} steroids that have a ketone group at C-17 are termed 17-ketosteroids. C_{19} steroids have predominant androgenic activity.

C_{21} steroids have a 2-carbon side chain (C-20, C-21) attached at position 17 and methyl groups at C-18 and C-19. They have either the glucocorticoid or the minerelocorticoid properties.

Bisoynthesis of adrenal steroids

Steroid is synthesised from cholesterol from the diet and from endogenous synthesis via acetate. Separate zones of adrenal cortex synthesize specific hormones. The outer zone (zona glomerulosa) is mainly involved in aldosterone biosynthesis and the inner zone (zona fasciculata and reticularis) is the site for the cortisol and androgen biosynthesis (glucocorticoids).

Androgens : Androgens are responsible for the development of secondary sexual characteristics in male and enlargement of clitoris, deepening of the voice and hirsutism in female. Testosterone is the most potent androgen, produced mainly by the testes and some by adrenal cortex and ovary. Many derivatives of testosterone have been synthesized e.g. anabolic steroids which dissociate the anabolic and body building effects. In dermatological practice, they are used in conditions where there is excessive nitrogen loss e.g. exfoliative dermatitis and pemphigus group. They are also used to prevent osteoporosis in wasting diseases e.g. dermatomysitis. Androgens are sebotrophic.

Antiandrogens : Cyproterone acetate is a potent antiandrogen and also possesses progestational activity. If administered orally, it reduces the sebum excretion rate and is also of value in female balding.

Estrogens : It is responsible for the development of genitalia in female, development of female breast, increase in size of uterus. Excess estrogens are anti-androgenic and cause secondary atrophy of the testes in males. For severe scarring acne, when all antibiotics have proved unsuccessful, estrogen in the form of contraceptive pill can be considered. It should not be given in males because of the danger of impotency, gynecomastia and testicular atrophy. It can also be used in Fox-Fordyce disease and hidradenitis suppurativa. Estrogen preparations are contraindicated in obstructive jaundice, thrombo-embolism, carcinoma of breast, herpes gestationis or porphyria cutanea tarda.

Some estrogenic preparations are :

i. Ethinylestradiol tablets 1, 10, 20, 50 mg.

ii. Stilbesterol tablets 1, 5, 25, 100 and 500 mg.

Progestogens : It is a natural hormone and its release from corpus luteum leads to the development of endometrium (secretory) and modifies the vaginal epithelium in pregnancy and prepares the breast for lactation.

Adrenocortical steroids (Corticosteroids)

Natural adrenocortical steroids are classified as glucocorticoids, minerelocorticoids or androgenic corticoids according to their predominant physiological activity. The glucocorticoids (cortisone) influence carbohydrate metabolism by means of an anti-insulin effect, induce protein catabolism and are anti-inflammatory. Minerelocorticoids such as deoxycorticosterone and aldosterone control electrolyte balance and have sodium retaining and potassium excreting properties.

Glucocorticoids are secreted by the zona fasciculata of the adrenal cortex from the cholesterol which is produced in the adrenal gland from acetate by a series of enzymatic reactions requiring the presence of coenzyme A and a number of intermediates.

Pharmacological action

i. **Anti-inflammatory effect :** Inhibit the release of lysosomal enzymes and certain T-lymphocyte functions. They may cause redistribution of the circulating cells, high doses causing decrease in circulating monocytes, lymphocytes and eosinophils and increase in the number of circulating polymorphs ; can also inhibit antibody production by B-lymphocytes ; inhibit macrophage function and depress their bactericidal and fungicidal activity in vitro.

ii. **Immunosuppressive effects** : Can suppress both the immediate (antibody mediated) and delayed (cell mediated) forms of hypersensitivity.

iii. **DNA synthesis** : Topically applied corticosteroids can inhibit epidermal mitosis and DNA synthesis.

iv. **Vasoconstriction** : Topically applied corticosteroids have vasoconstrictor effect on the skin.

Metabolism : All forms of glucocorticoids are suitable for oral administration. Once absorbed or injected into the body, the drugs undergo metabolism in the liver and also in fibroblasts and other cells. Principal metabolic reaction involves the following steps.

1. Reduction of double bond at C-4, followed be reduction of ketone at C-3.

2. Oxidation of C-11 betahydroxyl to a ketone group (hydrocortisone to cortisone).

3. Reduction of the C-20 ketone to an alcohol, followed by removal of the side chain at C-17. This side chain and the C-20 ketone are essential for anti-inflammatory activity ; increased activity can be acquired by preventing these reactions. This is done by adding a group at C-16, usually either a methyl group (dexamethasone, betamethasone) or a hydroxyl group (triamcinolone, fluocinolone).

Metabolism followed by conjugation with a water soluble group such as glucoronide is required for rapid removal from the body.

Clinical use : Because of the profound inhibitory effect on immunologic and inflammatory responses (**morbidistatic effect**), systemic corticosteroids are widely used in dermatological practice for the management of a variety of acute and chronic conditions.

Orally administerd corticosteroids are generally used in three major ways : **single daily dose, divided daily dose** and **alternate day dose. Dose of corticosteroids varies greatly with the condition being treated.**

Indications

A. Absolute indications

i. Acute and severe reactions running a well defined course e.g. erythema multiforme exudativum, acute urticaria of known cause, severe drug eruptions, acute contact sensitivity.

ii. Acute allergic or anaphylactic reactions causing danger to life e.g. anaphylactic shock, multiple bee or wasp stings, poisonous bites.

iii. Immunological disorders e.g. systemic lupus erythematosus, active dermatomyositis and pyoderma gangrenosum.

iv. Generalised vascular disorders of immunological pathogenesis e.g. polyarteritis nodosa, temporal arteritis, Wegener's granulomatosis, thrombocytopenic purpura, allergic vasculitis involving vital organs.

v. Chronic disorders, otherwise fatal or disabling e.g. pemphigus, pemphigoid, mucous membrane pemphigoid, exfoliative dermatitis.

vi. Epidermolysis bullosa in childhood and persistent aphthosis accompanied by great pain.

vii. Sarcoidosis.

B. Relative indications

i. Lichen planus **ii.** Erythema multiforme **iii.** Reticuloses **iv.** Severe eczema v. Reiter's disease **vi.** Sjogren's syndrome **vii.** Occasionally, acne & hidradenitis suppurativa.

C. Contraindications

i. Pityriasis rosea **ii.** Erythema nodosum **iii.** Chronic urticaria **iv.** Lichen simplex **v.** Prurigo **vi.** Alopecia areata **vii.** Psoriasis excepting acute generalized pustular psoriasis, acute psoriatic erythroderma, fulminating psoriatic arthritis, disabling palmo-plantar pustular psoriasis.

Side effects

a. **Dermatologic** : Atrophy, striae, telangiectasia, acne, folliculitis, rosacea, purpura, pseudoscarring.

b. **Infections** : Increased susceptibility to bacterial, mycobacterial and deep fungal infection.

c. **Hematologic** : Neutrophilic granulocytosis, monocytopenia, lymphocytopenia, eosinopenia.

d. **Musculoskeletal** : Osteoporosis, aseptic necrosis of femoral head, myopathy with muscle wasting.

e. **Metabolic** : Obesity, growth retardation, hyperglycemia, hypertriglyceridemia, pancreatitis, sodium retention, potassium loss, altered fat distribution in the form of cushi goid appearance.

f. **Ophthalmologic and psychologic** : Posterior subcapsular cataract, open angle glaucoma, psychosis.

Photochemotherapy

Photochemotherapy requires a light source and the use of photosensitising drugs or chemicals e.g. psoralens – furocoumarin compounds derived from a number of plants, crude coal tar, porphyrins and derivatives.

The term PUVA (**P**soralens + **U**ltra **V**iolet **A**) describes a form of treatment embracing psoralens and exposure of the patient to a source of ultraviolet light of 320-400 nm. The psoralens are : 8 methoxypsoralen (8 MOP), methoxsalen, 4, 5, 8 trimethoxypsoralen (Trisoralen, TMP).

Pharmacological action of psoralens : Psoralens are pharmacologically inert until they are exposed to UVA ; maximum effectivness is at 360 nm, when they become cytotoxic, cause lethal sensitisation to bacteria and viruses, mutagenesis and enzyme inactivation. It is carcinogenic in albino mice. In addition to its ability to inhibit DNA synthesis, psoralen photochemo-therapy is a potent stimulator of melanin pigmentation. PUVA therapy also reduces the capacity of skin to have delayed hypersensitivity reponses to potent contact sensitizers e.g. DNCB.

Sources of UVA : Sun is a potent source of UVA energy. Now-a-days high intensity fluorescent tubes are manufactured with an emission spectrum of 310-390 nm (peak is 355-365 nm). Dose is assessed in terms of joules/cm^2 received by the patient in a unit of time.

Dosage and details of treatment : 8 MOP is given orally as 10 mg tablets in a dose of 0.6 mg/kg, 2 hours before irradiation. There should be an interval of 48 hours between treatments to prevent cumulative phototoxicity. Initial dose of light depends on the skin colour of the patient, varying between 1.0 to 2.0 joules/cm_2 increasing by 0.5-1.0 joules/cm^2 every 2-3 treatments. Dark sun glasses should be worn for at least 8 hours after ingestion of the tablets to protect the eyes from natural or other artificial UVA sources. Topical application of 0.15% methoxsalen in isopropyl alcohol is a substitute for oral therapy with very few long term risks and is suitable for palmo-plantar psoriasis, pustulosis and acrodermatitis.

Clinical uses : **1.** Vitiligo **2.** Psoriasis **3.** Mycosis fungoides **4.** Atopic dermatitis **5.** Alopecia areata **6.** Dyshidrotic eczema **7.** Polymorphous light eruption.

Side effects : Painful erythema, blistering, nausea, pruritus, headache, fatigue, drowsiness, pigmentary abnormalities, premature aging, actinic keratoses, Bowen's disease, cataract formation.

Occasionally PUVA therapy produces a Koebner response with development of a subacute eruptive papular psoriasis at the treated sites. Bullous pemphigoid may occur with tar and short wave UV light. No proved case of skin malignancy has been reported even after long term photochemotherapy.

Contraindications : Childhood, pregnancy and patients with known light sensitivity.

Oral retinoids

Retinoids may generally be divided into two major categories **1.** Naturally occuring and **2.** Synthetic compounds.

Naturally occuring retinoids include **i.** Vitamin A, alchol and its derivatives retinoic acid, retinyl esters and retinaldehyde and **ii.** Carotenoids. All vitamin A compounds are fat-soluble containing three major portion—**a.** cyclic ring **b.** a polyene chain and **c.** a polar terminal group.

The carotenoids (β-carotene) are provitamin A compounds found in many yellow orange vegetables e.g. carrots. They are physiologically inactive in their natural state but are metabolized to form vitamin A.

Pharmacological action : They can influence cell division, lysosomal membrane stability, cell membrane integrity, prostaglandin synthesis, RNA synthesis, protein synthesis and post-translational glycosylation of proteins, e.g.

1. Interaction with cytoplasmic proteins.

2. Effects on cell nucleus.

3. Effects on cell membranes—Membrane integrity may be influenced by retinoids. In high doses, they cause lysosomal membrane labilization.

4. Effects on gap junction—Gap junction proliferation has been noted to occur after retinoid therapy.

5. Effects on keratinizing epithelium—It has antikeratinizing effect.

6. Effects on vision—It is concerned with the formation of visual pigments.

7. Effects on reproduction—It can cause defective reproduction e.g. increased fetal loss, azoospermia, defective bone growth, endocrine dysfunction and central nervous system abnormalities.

8. Effects on immunologic function—It can enhance humoral antibody formation to a variety of antigens ; augment human lymphocyte responses to mitogens ; stimulate cell mediated cytotoxicity by inducing killer T-cells ; enhance skin graft rejection.

9. Effects on fibroblasts—Can inhibit the production of collagenase and gelatinase.

DERMATOSURGERY

A. Electrodesiccation

Indications

Multiple small growths like papilloma, verruca, seborrheic keratoses, actinic keratoses.

Pre-operative care—Nil

Procedure

Each lesion is touched with the electrodesiccating needle until it is completely transformed into a charred crust.

Post-operative care

The crusts are allowed to shed spontaneously in 10 to 14 days. Dryness of the skin should be maintained until spontaneous shedding of scars.

Advantages : 1. Rapid method 2. Scarring is minimum.

Disadvantages : Painful, if local anesthesia is avoided; multiple injections of local anesthesia are also similarly painful.

B. Electrodesiccation and Curettage

Indications

1. Warts. 2. Kerato-acanthoma. 3. Seborrheic and actinic keratoses. 4. Small epitheliomas.

Pre-operative care

1. Local anesthesia. 2. Antiseptic measures.

Procedure

1. By hooking the curet along the distal side of the tumor, a strong pulling action is given. The growth is thus removed.

2. As hemostasis, trichloracetic acid is applied.

3. The acid, after controlling the bleeding, is washed with alcohol. The alcohol is dried with cotton.

4. The base is electrodesiccated to produce an eschar.

Post-operative care

1. The wound is kept dry.

2. Bandaging is unnecessary, unless bleeding occurs.

3. The patient is kept under observation for 10 to 14 days, until spontaneous shedding of the crust occurs.

Advantages : **1.** Simple proce dure. **2.** Scarring is minimum

Disadvantage : Slow healing.

C. Electrocoagulatiou

Electrocoagulation is ideally performed with a dipolar current. For practical purpose, most dermatosurgeons use the monopolar desiccating needle.

Indications : **1.** Small angi omas. **2.** Telangiectasia.

Pre-operative preparations

1. Antiseptic preparation. **2.** Local anesthesia.

Procedure

1. The active needle is inserted into the vascular channel or tumor.

2. The current is made on with the foot or hand switch.

3. This is continued till the blanching and crusting of the lesion is produced.

Post-operative care

1. Dryness should be maintained.

2. Bandaging is avoided.

3. The crust is shed in 10-14 days.

Advantage : A simple procedure.

Disadvantage : Scarring by too much burning.

D. Cryosurgery

Indications : **1.** Verruca. **2.** Seborrheic and actinic keratoses. **3.** Bowen's disease. **4.** Leukoplakia. **5.** Basal cell epithelioma. **6.** Hemangioma. **7.** Keratoacanthoma. **8.** Keloids. **9.** Dermatofibromas.

transposition scalp flaps. 4. 'Juri' Flap (controversial).

Pre-operative care

1. Motivation of the patient.

2. Determination of the etiology of alopecia.

3. Medical history.

a. bleeding diathesis b. cardiovascular disorder c. diabetes d. hypertension e. Glaucoma f. Allergies etc.

4. Drug history.

5. Following laboratory tests are advisable.

a. Hemogram b. Urine analysis c. Prothrombin time d. Platelet count e. Partial thromboplastin time f. Bleeding time.

Technical precautions

1. Aseptic measures.

2. Punches should be sharp.

Procedure

1. A hairline should be drawn, after noting the patient's physiognomy, by an ordinary cosmetic eyebrow pencil.

2. Pre-operative medication, diazepam 10 mg, is administered 30 minutes prior to surgery.

3. The donor and recepient areas are sponged with alcohol and anesthetised with 0.5% lignocaine and 1 : 200,000 epinephrine.

4. The hair in the donor site is trimmed to 0.3 or 0.6 cm in length, assuring that the angle and the direction of the hair growth are visible to the surgeon.

5. After the local anesthesia, the injection of 10 to 30 ml of saline solution in the prepared donor area produces a bulging effect, resulting in increased tissue stability.

6. Donor grafts are extracted in rows leaving 4 mm between spaces. This prevents excessive trauma to the area and permits future extractions of grafts from the same area.

Since the hair in the donor sites grows vertically, the adjacent hair will provide excellent coverage when worn at a suitable length and the scars will not be easily discernible.

7. For donor graft extractions, the punch instrument should be held at the same angle as the hairs emerge. Penetration into the subcutaneous fat should be to a depth of approximately 5 mm. Efficient sponging and firm manual pressure will restrict bleeding to a minmum. The grafts are extracted by gently grasping the margin of the graft with Adson forceps and lifting it so that the bulb is visible before excising with specially designed scissors.

8. The grafts are placed in petri dish containing a saline solution until they are cleaned, trimmed and graded. Thereafter they are implanted into the recipient area. A continuous modified vertical mattress suture with 3.0 prolone is advisable for closure of the donor area.

9. In extraction of the plug from balding recipient site, a slightly forward and curving angle of the punch space will assure the natural hair growth pattern when donor grafts are inserted. Plugs from the recipient area are normally discarded.

10. The number of grafts implanted at any one session varies with the motivation of the patient and the experience of the surgeon. The average number of grafts implanted at one session are from 60 to 80 ; the maximum should be approximately 180.

11. On completion of the transplantation, non-adherent covering is to be applied. An elastic bandage, wrapped turban-wise, with proper amount of pressure to enhance hemostasis, assures that grafts are even and smooth with the scalp. Removal of the bandage after 24 to 48 hours is recommenned.

12. A mild sedative is recommended.

13. The patient is cautioned not to bend forward, overexert or drive a car any considerable distance immediately after the surgery.

Complications : **1.** Infection : herpes simplex, bacterial. **2.** Pigmentary changes. **3.** Scarring. **4.** Bleeding. **5.** Eczematoid eruption.

Results : Most patients get 50 to 75% improvement.

Evaluation : It is an imperfect and often crude modality but it is the best available for post-acne scarring.

b. Removal of tattoos

Indication

1. Professional, amateur or accidental tattooing. Results are better in fresh tattoos and in professional ones.

Equipments : Same as before.

Contraindications : Same as before.

Technique : The area is planed, after the anesthesia, superficially with whirling brush. It should be carried only to the papillary area. Bleeding should be minimum. The abraded area is dressed daily with petrolatum gauge.

Results : Sometimes the tattoo is removed completely. However, in most cases, the design is decreased, but islands of pigment remain.

Complications : Same as before.

c. Mini-planning

This mini-abrasion machines have certain advantages over the standard equipment. For instance :

1. They rotate much faster.

2. They are easier to control.

3. They are more convenient in treating a single or few localised lesions such as seborrheic keratoses.

BIBLIOGRAPHY AND GENERAL REFERENCE

A

1. Abramobits W : Clinics in Dermatology—Cosmetic Dermatology, Vol 6, No 3, July-Sept, 1988.

2. Adams RM : Occupational Skin Disease, Grune & Stratton, New York, 1983.

3. Anderson JR : Muir's Text Book of Pathology, Ed 12, ELBS, London, 1985.

4. Arndt KA : Common Dermatologic Disease—Diagnosis and Therapy, Ed 4, Little Brown and Company, Boston, 1989.

5. Arya OP, Osoba AO and Bennett FJ : Tropical Venereology, Churchill Livingstone, Edinburgh, 1980.

B

6. Behl PN : Practice of Dermatology, Ed 6, CBS Publishers and Distributors, Delhi, 1987.

7. Bellanti JA : Immunology III, Saunders International Edition, WB Saunders Company, Philadelphia, 1985.

8. Benett RG : Fundamentals of cutaneous surgery, CV Mosby Company, St Louis, 1988.

9. Bhutani LK : Colour Atlas of Sexually Transmitted Diseases, Interprint, New Delhi, 1986.

10. Bickers DR, Hazen PG and Lynch WS : Clinical Pharmacology of Skin Disease, Churchill-Livingstone, New York, 1984.

11. Braunwald E, Isselbacher KJ, Petersdorf RG, Wilson JD, Martin JB and Fauci AS : Harrison's Principles of Internal Medicine, Ed 11, McGraw Hill Book Company, New York, 1987.

12. Brown AFT : Accident and Emergency Diagnosis and Management, Heinemann Medical Books, London, 1987.

8. Berkow R : The Emerck Manual, Ed 15, Merck Sharp and Dohme Research Laboratories, USA, 1987.

13. Bryceson A and Pfaltzgruff RE : Leprosy, Ed 2, Churchill Livingstone, New York 1979.

C

14. Callen JP, Dahl MV, Golitz LE, Schachner LA and Stegman SJ : Advances in Dermatology, Vol 4, Year Book Medical Publishers, Inc, Chicago, 1989.

15. Callen JP, Stawiski MA and Vorhees JJ : Manual of Dermatology, Year Book Medical Publishers, Inc, Chicago, 1980.

16. Catterall RD : Short Text Book of Venereology, Ed 2, ELBS, 1978.

17. Chatterjee KD : Human Parasites and Parasitic Diseases, Pub-Author, Calcutta, 1952.

D

18. Dahl MV : Clinical Immunodermatology, Ed 2, Year Book Medical Publishers, Inc, Chicago, 1988.

19. Demis DJ : Clinical Dermatology, Vol I-IV, Ed 12, Harper & Row, Philadelphia, 1985.

20. Dharmendra : Leprosy, Vol I, Kothari Medical Publishing House, Bombay, 1978 and Vol II, Samant and Company, Bombay, 1985.

21. Dobson RL and Abele DC : The Practice of Dermatology, Harper and Row Publishers, Philadelphia, 1985.

22. Domonkos AN, Arnold HL Jr and Odom RB : Andrews' Diseases of the Skin, Ed 7, WB Saunders Company, Philadelphia, 1982.

23. Dutta AK : Vitiligo—Neural and Immunologic Linkages, Indira Publications, Calcutta, 1988.

E

24. Emond RTD and Rowland HAK : Infectious Diseases, Wolfe Medical Publications Ltd, London, 1987.

25. Epstein E : Controversies in Dermatology, WB Saunders Co., Philadelphia, 1984.

26. Epstein E : Regional Dermatology : A System of Diagnosis, Ed 2, Grune & Stratton, Inc, 1984.

F

27. Fandeyev L : Skin and Venereal Diseases, MIR Publishers, Moscow, 1968.

28. Felman YM : Sexually Transmitted Diseases, Churchill-Livingstone, Inc, New York, 1986.

29. Ferrandiz C : Clinical Atlas of Dermatology, Year Book Medical Publishers, Inc, Chicago, 1987.

30. Fitzpatrick TB, Eisen AZ, Wolff K, Freedberg IM and Austen KF : Dermatology in General Medicine, Ed 3, McGraw Hill Book Company, New York, 1987.

31. Fleischmajer R : Progress in Diseases of the Skin, Vol. 1 and 2, Grune & Stratton, Inc, New York, 1981 and 1984.

32. Flowers FP and Krusinski PA : Dermatology in Ambulatory & Emergency Medicine, Year Book Medical Publishers, Inc, Chicago, 1984.

33. Frazier CA : Annual Review of Allergy, Toppan Company (S) Pvt Ltd, Singapore, 1977.

34. Fry L and Cornell MNP : Dermatology, PG Publishing Pvt Ltd, Singapore, 1985.

35. Fudenberg HH and Graber CD : Microbiology and Immunology, Toppan Company (S) Pvt Ltd, Singapore, 1977.

G

36. Ganong WF : Review of Medical Physiology, Ed 13, Lange Medical Book, London, 1987.

37. Gilman AJ, Goodman LS, Rall TW and Murad F : Goodman and Gilman's The Pharmacological Basis of Therapeutics, Ed 7, Macmillan Publishing Company, New York, 1985.

38. Goldman HH : Review of General Psychiatry, Ed 2, Prentice Hall International (UK) Ltd, London, 1988.

39. Goolamali SK : Dermatology Revision, Churchill-Livingstone, Edinburgh, 1984.

40. Gupta AB, Haldar B and Mukherjee S : Selected Topics of Dermatophysics, Calcutta Skin Institute Publications, Calcutta, 1989.

H

41. Haldar B : 1200 MCQ on Dermatology, Venereology and Leprology, Calcutta Skin Institute Publications, Calcutta, 1984.

42. Harber LC and Bickers DR : Photosensitivity diseases, WB Saunders Co., Philadelphia, 1981.

43. Harper J : Hand Book of Paediatric Dermatology, Butterworths, London, 1985.

44. Harris JRW : Recent Advances in Sexually Transmitted Diseases, Churchill-Livingstone, London, 1981.

45. Hastings RC and Convit J : Leprosy, Churchill-Livingstone, Edinburgh, 1985.

46. Hawkins R : Treatment and Prognosis—Medicine, William Heinemann Medical Books, London, 1986.

47. Hollingworth P : Mainstream Medicine—Rheumatology, Heinemann Medical Books, London, 1988.

48. Holmes KK, Mardh PA, Sparling PF and Wiesner PJ : Sexually Transmitted Diseases, McGraw Hill Book Company, New York, 1984.

49. Hurwitz S : Clinical Pediatric Dermatology, WB Saunders Co., Philadelphia, 1981.

50. Hurwitz S : The Skin and Systemic Disease in Children, Year Book Medical Publishers, Inc, Chicago, 1985.

I

51. Ingram JT : Clinical Dermatology, J & A Churchill Ltd, London, 1969.

J

52. Jacobs PH and Anhalt TS : Hand Book of Skin Clues of Sytemic Diseases, Lea and Febiger, Philadelphia, 1987.

53. Jaju BP : Doctors Drug Reference, Joypee Brothers, New Delhi, 1988.

54. Jalali VP : A Clinical Atlas of Oral Diseases, Vol 2, Journal of the Indian Dental Association, 1985-86.

55. Jawetz E, Melnick JL and Adelberg EA : Review of Medical Microbiology, Ed 17, Lange Medical Publications, California, 1987.

56. Jopling EH : Hand Book of Leprosy, ELBS, 1985.

K

57. Kaplan HI and Sadock BJ : Synopsis of Psychiatry—Behavioral Science-Clinical Psychiatry, Ed 5, Williams and Wilkins, Baltimore, 1988.

58. Kempe CH, Silver HK, O'Brien D and Fulginiti VA : Current Pediatric Diagnosis and Treatment, Ed 9, Appleton & Lange, Norwalk, 1987.

59. Kirby JD : Roxburgh's Common Skin Diseases, Ed 15, HK Lewis & Co. Ltd, London, 1986.

60. Korting GW : Diseases of the Skin in Children and Adolescence, Ed 3, WB Saunders Co., Philadelphia, 1979.

61. Korting GW : Geriatric Dermatology, WB Saunders Co., Philadelphia, 1980.

62. Korting GW : Practical Dermatology of the Genital Region, WB Saunders Company, Philadelphia, 1981.

63. Korting GW and Denk R : Differential Diagnosis in Dermatology, WB Saunders Company, Philadelphia, 1976.

64. Kreig T and Meurer M : Systemic Scleroderma, J Am Dermatol 18, 457-81, 1988.

L

65. Landow RK : Hand Book of Dermatologic Treatment, Jones Medical Publications, California, 1983.

66. Launey WEde and Land WA : Principles & Practice of Dermatology, Ed 2, Butterworths, Sydney, 1984.

67. Laurence DR and Bennett PN : Clinical Pharmacology, ELBS, 1987.

68. Lebwohl M : Difficult Diagnosis in Dermatology, Churchill-Livingstone, New York, 1988.

69. Leiblum SR and Pervin LA : Principles and Practice of Sex Therapy, Tavistock Publications, London, 1980.

70. Levene GM and Calnan CD : Colour Atlas of Dermatology, Wolfe Medical Books, London, 1974.

71. Levene GM and Goolamali SK : Diagnostic Picture Tests in Dermatology, Wolfe Medical Publications Ltd, London, 1986.

72. Lever WF and Lever GS : Histopathology of the Skin, Ed 6, JB Lippincott Company, Philadelphia, 1983.

73. Lience E : Clinical Atlas of Rheumatology, Year Book Medical Publishers, Inc, Chicago, 1987.

74. Lookingbill DP and Marks JG : Principles of Dermatology, WB Saunders Company, Philadelphia, 1986.

75. Lynch PJ : Dermatology for the house officers, Williams & Wilkins, London, 1982.

M

76. Mackie RM : Clinical dermatology, Ed 2, Oxford University Press, Oxford, 1986.

77. Maddin S : Current Dermatologic Therapy, WB Saunders Company, Philadelphia, 1982.

78. Maibach HI : Occupational and Industrial Dermatology, Ed 2, Year Book Medical Publishers, Inc, Chicago, 1987.

79. Maitra AK and Haldar B : Tuberculosis of Skin with Special Reference to Immunological Aspect, The Indian Practitioner, 34 : 2, p 55-67, 1981.

80. Marks R : Practical Problems in Dermatology, PG Publishing Pvt Ltd, Singapore, 1984.

81. Marshall J : Diseases of the Skin, E & S Livingstone Ltd, London, 1960.

82. McCarthy PL and Shklar G : Diseases of the oral Mucosa, Ed 2, Lea & Febiger, Philadelphia, 1980.

83. McCormac WM : Diagnosis and Treatment of Sexually Tramsnitted Diseases, John Wright PSG Inc, Boston, 1983.

84. McLeod J, Edwards C and Bouchier I : Davidson's Principles and Practice of Medicine, Ed 15, ELBS, 1987.

85. Mehregan AH : Pinkus' Guide to Histopathology, Ed 4, Appleton-Century-Crofts, Norwalk, 1986.

86. Melnick JL, Adelberg EA and Jawetz E : Review of Medical Microbiology, Ed 7, Prentice-Hall International, Inc, 1987.

87. Monk BE, Graham Brown RAC and Sarkany I : Skin Disorders in the Elderly, Blackwell Scientific Publications, Oxford, 1988.

88. Montague DK : Disorders of Male Sexual Functions, Year Book Medical Publishers, Inc, Chicago, 1988.

89. Moschella SL and Hurley HJ : Dermatology, Ed 2, WB Saunders Company, Philadelphia, 1985.

90. Mygaind N : Essential Allergy, Blackwell Scientific Publications, Oxford, 1986.

N

91. Nasemann T, Sauerbrey W and Burdorf WHC : Fundamentals of Dermatology, Springer-Verlag, New York, 1983.

92. Nikol Thin R : Lecture Notes on Sexually Transmitted Diseases, Blackwell Scientific Publications, Oxford, 1983.

93. Noble WC : Microbial Skin Disease : Its Epidemiology, Edward Arnold, 1983.

94. Noojin RO : Dermatology—A practitioners guide, Toppan Company (S) Pvt Ltd, Singapore, 1977.

O

95. Orland MJ and Saltman RJ : Manual of Medical Therapeutics, Ed 25, Little Brown and Company, Boston, 1986.

P

96. Pasricha JS : Contact Dermatitis in India, Ed 2, Government of India, 1988.

126. Vickers CFH : Modern Management of Common Skin Diseases, Churchill-Livingstone, Edinburgh, 1986.

127. Vivier A du : Atlas of Clinical Dermatology, Churchill-Livingstone, London, 1986.

W

128. Wallin J, Thin RNT and Emamuli A : Epidemiology, Etiology & Treatment of Non-Gonococcal Urethritis, Proceedings of the International Symposium, Rome, 1980.

129. Way LW : Current Surgical Diagnosis and Treatment, Ed 8, A Lange Medical Book, London, 1988.

130. Weigand DA and Olson RL : Dermatology—Continuing Education Review, Medical Examination Publishing Company Inc, New York, 1974.

131. Weston WL : Practical Pediatric Dermatology, Little Brown and Co., Boston, 1979.

132. WHO Scientific group : Technical report series 660—Non-Gonococcal Urethritis and other selected sexually trasmitted diseases of public health importance, Geneva, 1981.

133. Willcox RR and Willcox Jr : Venereology, Maruzen Asian Edition, Singapore National Printers Pvt Ltd, 1982.

134. Wisdom A : A colour Atlas of Venereology, Wolfe Books, London, 1973.

135. Wolff K and Winkelmann RK : Vasculitis, LLyod-Luke (Medical Books) Ltd, London, 1980.

INDEX